Nationalism and Ethnic

International Security Readers

Strategy and Nuclear Deterrence (1984)

Military Strategy and the Origins of the First World War (1985)

Conventional Forces and American Defense Policy (1986)

The Star Wars Controversy (1986)

Naval Strategy and National Security (1988)

Military Strategy and the Origins of the First World War,
revised and expanded edition (1991)

—published by Princeton University Press

Soviet Military Policy (1989)

Conventional Forces and American Defense Policy, revised edition (1989)

Nuclear Diplomacy and Crisis Management (1990)

The Cold War and After: Prospects for Peace (1991)

America's Strategy in a Changing World (1992)

The Cold War and After: Prospects for Peace, expanded edition (1993)

Global Dangers: Changing Dimensions of International Security (1995)

The Perils of Anarchy: Contemporary Realism and International Security (1995)

Debating the Democratic Peace (1996)

East Asian Security (1996)

Nationalism and Ethnic Conflct (1997)

—published by The MIT Press

Nationalism and Ethnic Conflict

EDITED BY

Michael E. Brown
Owen R. Coté, Jr.
Sean M. Lynn-Jones
and Steven E. Miller

THE MIT PRESS
CAMBRIDGE, MASSACHUSETTS
LONDON, ENGLAND

The contents of this book were first published in *International Security* (ISSN 0162-2889), a publication of The MIT Press under the sponsorship of the Center for Science and International Affairs at Harvard University. Copyright in each of the following articles is owned jointly by the President and Fellows of Harvard College and of the Massachusetts Institute of Technology.

Stephen Van Evera, "Hypotheses on Nationalism and War," 18:4 (Spring 1994); Jack Snyder and Karen Ballentine, "Nationalism and the Marketplace of Ideas," 21:2 (Fall 1996); David Lake and Donald Rothchild, "Containing Fear: The Origins and Management of Ethnic Conflict," 21:2 (Fall 1996); V.P. Gagnon, "Ethnic Nationalism and International Conflict: The Case of Serbia," 19:3 (Winter 1994/95); Stuart Kaufman, "Spiraling to Ethnic War: Elites, Masses, and Moscow in Moldova's Civil War," 21:2 (Fall 1996); Šumit Ganguly, "Explaining the Kashmir Insurgency: Political Mobilization and Institutional Decay," 21:2 (Fall 1996); Chaim Kaufmann, "Possible and Impossible Solutions to Ethnic Civil Wars," 20:4 (Spring 1996); Gil Loescher and Alan Dowty, "Refugee Flows as Grounds for International Action," 21:1 (Summer 1996); Barry Posen, "Military Responses to Refugee Disasters," 21:1 (Summer 1996); Jeffrey Herbst, "Responding to State Failure in Africa," 21:3 (Winter 1996/97); Herbert Howe, "Lessons of Liberia: ECOMOG and Regional Peacekeeping," 21:3 (Winter 1996/97).

Selection and preface, copyright © 1996–97 by the President and Fellows of Harvard College and of the Massachusetts Institute of Technology.

Library of Congress Cataloging-in-Publication Data
Brown, Michael E. (Michael Edward), 1954-
  Nationalism and Ethnic Conflct / edited by Michael E. Brown, Owen R. Coté, Jr., Sean M. Lynn-Jones, and Steven E. Miller.
    p. cm.
  An international security reader
  Includes bibliographical references.
  ISBN 0-262-52224-1
  1. Nationalism. 2. Ethnic relations. 3. Ethnic relations—Political aspects. 4. World politics—1985–1995. 5. War. 6. Refugees. I. Brown, Michael E. (Michael Edward), 1954–. II. Coté, Owen R., Jr. III. Lynn-Jones, Sean M. IV. Miller, Steven E. V. Series.
  JC311.N315 1997
  320.54—dc21   52337
                                                          CIP

Contents

The Contributors

MICHAEL E. BROWN is Managing Editor of *International Security* and Associate Director of the International Security Program at the Center for Science and International Affairs, Harvard University.

OWEN R. COTÉ, JR. is Editor of *International Security* and Assistant Director of the International Security Program at the Center for Science and International Affairs, Harvard University.

SEAN M. LYNN-JONES is Editor of *International Security* and Research Associate at the Center for Science and International Affairs, Harvard University.

STEVEN E. MILLER is Editor-in-Chief of *International Security* and Director of the International Security Program at the Center for Science and International Affairs, Harvard University.

STEPHEN VAN EVERA is Associate Professor of Political Science at the Massachusetts Institute of Technology.

JACK SNYDER is Professor of Political Science and Director of the Institute of War and Peace Studies, Columbia University.

KAREN BALLENTINE is a Ph.D. candidate in political science at Columbia University and a Research Fellow at the Center for Science and International Affairs, Harvard University.

DAVID LAKE is Professor of Political Science at the University of California, San Diego, and Research Director for International Relations at the Institute of Global Conflict and Cooperation.

DONALD ROTHCHILD is Professor of Political Science at the University of California, Davis.

V.P. GAGNON, JR. is Assistant Professor of Politics at Ithaca College in Ithaca, New York.

STUART KAUFMAN is Assistant Professor of Political Science a the University of Kentucky.

ŠUMIT GANGULY is a Professor of Political Science at Hunter College of The City University of New York.

CHANTAL DE JONGE OUDRAAT was, from 1981–94, a Senior Research Associate at the United Nations Institute for Disarmament Research (UNIDIR) in Geneva, where she was founder and editor of *The UNIDIR Newsletter.* She is currently a Research Affiliate at the Center for Science and International Affairs, Harvard University.

CHAIM KAUFMANN is Assistant Professor of International Relations at Lehigh University.

ALAN DOWTY is Professor of International Relations at the University of Notre Dame and a Fellow at the Kroc Institute for International Peace Studies. He is the author of *Closed Borders: The Contemporary Assault on Freedom of Movement* (Yale University Press, 1993).

GIL LOESCHER is Professor of International Relations at the University of Notre Dame and a Fellow at the Kroc Institute for International Peace Studies. He is the author of *Beyond Charity: International Cooperation and the Global Refugee Crises* (Oxford University Press, 1993).

BARRY POSEN is Professor of Political Science at the Massachusetts Institute of Technology and a member of its Defense and Arms Control Studies Program. He is the author of *Inadvertent Escalation* (Cornell University Press, 1991) and *The Sources of Military Doctrine* (Cornell University Press, 1984).

JEFFREY HERBST is Associate Professor of Politics and International Affairs at the Woodrow Wilson School, Princeton University.

HERBERT HOWE is Research Professor of African Politics at Georgetown University's School of Foreign Service.

Acknowledgments

The editors gratefully acknowledge the assistance that has made this book possible. A deep debt is owed to all those at the Center for Science and International Affairs (CSIA), Harvard University, who have played an editorial role at *International Security*. We are grateful for support from the Carnegie Corporation of New York. Special thanks go to Kristen Cashin, Meara E. Keegan, Teresa Lawson and Karen Motley at CSIA as well as Katy Stenhouse at the MIT Press for their invaluable help in preparing this volume for publication.

Preface | *Michael E. Brown*

Nationalistic and ethnic conflicts are important for five main reasons. First, they are widespread. Most of the approximately thirty-five armed conflicts that rage around the world today have nationalistic or ethnic dimensions.[1] Second, nationalistic and ethnic conflicts usually cause tremendous amounts of suffering because they often involve direct, deliberate attacks on civilian populations. The numbers of people displaced or killed in such conflicts are frequently counted in tens and hundreds of thousands, and sometimes even in millions. Third, nationalist and ethnic conflicts almost always involve neighboring states, thereby undermining regional security. Fourth, these conflicts often engage the interests of distant international powers and the attention of regional and international organizations. Fifth, policymakers at the national level and in regional and international organizations are currently in the process of reassessing their efforts to deal with such conflicts.

Contrary to what one might think, nationalistic and ethnic conflicts are not rare, isolated problems. They are very high on the list of contemporary international security concerns. Scholars who care about war and peace issues should care about the causes and consequences of nationalistic and ethnic conflicts. Policymakers who have responsibilities for national and international security should care deeply about these problems as well.

This volume seeks to advance our understanding of nationalism and the causes of nationalistic and ethnic conflicts, as well as international options for dealing with the problems generated by these conflicts. The first part of this volume focuses on nationalism and the causes of nationalistic and ethnic conflicts. The second part examines international options with respect to these problems.

Part I begins with an overview of the scholarly literature on the causes of internal conflicts, developing four main arguments along the way. First, I contend that the literature on internal conflict has focused on the underlying factors or permissive conditions that make some places and some situations more predisposed to violence than others. Four sets of factors have been singled out in this regard: structural factors; political factors; economic/social factors; and cultural/perceptual factors. Second, the scholarly literature is weak when it comes to analyzing the catalytic factors or proximate causes of internal conflicts. I argue that internal conflicts can be triggered in four different ways:

---

1. See Michael E. Brown, "Introduction," in Brown, ed., *The International Dimensions of Internal Conflict* (Cambridge, Mass.: MIT Press, 1996), pp. 1–31.

by internal, mass-level factors (bad domestic problems); by external, mass-level factors (bad neighborhoods); by external, elite-level factors (bad neighbors); and by internal, elite-level factors (bad leaders). Third, the scholarly literature pays insufficient attention to the role played by domestic elites in transforming potentially violent situations into deadly confrontations. Many internal conflicts are triggered by the actions of domestic elites, and these actions therefore merit special attention. Here, too, we need to distinguish between different kinds of conflicts: ideological conflicts, criminal assaults on state sovereignty, and raw power struggles. Fourth and more generally, it is important to recognize that there are many different types of internal conflict, each caused by different things. The challenge for scholars is to identify these different types of conflicts and the different sets of factors that bring them about. The search for a single factor or set of factors that explains everything is comparable to the search for the Holy Grail—noble, but futile.

In the next essay in this volume, Stephen Van Evera notes that while it is often taken for granted that nationalism causes war, this causal connection has not been examined carefully. He takes this task on by developing a set of twenty-one hypotheses about nationalism and the onset of war, focusing on the structural, political, and perceptual factors that make war more likely. To illustrate these hypotheses, he assesses the risks that nationalism now poses in Europe, concluding that it constitutes very little danger in Western Europe but poses large dangers in the East, especially in the former Soviet Union.

The following essay is by Jack Snyder and Karen Ballentine, who agree with the conventional wisdom that propaganda and political manipulation of the media often play a central role in causing nationalistic and ethnic conflict. However, they take issue with the antidote usually prescribed. They maintain that promoting unconditional freedom in public debates in democratizing countries often makes the problem worse. In fact, sudden liberalizations of press freedoms are often associated with violent outbursts of nationalism. They argue that increased debate in the political marketplace leads to better outcomes only when there are mechanisms in place to correct market imperfections. They test their arguments by reviewing ethnic conflicts in the former Yugoslavia and Rwanda, and conclude with suggestions for improving the quality of public debate in emerging democracies.

Next, an explanation of the origins of ethnic conflict based on a rational choice approach is developed by David Lake and Donald Rothchild. They argue that intense ethnic conflict is most often caused by collective fears of the future, which in turn are driven by group fears about their safety, security dilemmas, information failures, and the polarizing actions of ethnic activists and political opportunists. Within-group and between-group strategic interactions produce conditions that can explode in violent conflict. The authors conclude with lessons for the effective management of ethnic conflict.

In a detailed examination of Serbian behavior and the origins of the war in the former Yugoslavia, V.P. Gagnon, Jr. asserts that the conflict was not caused by ancient ethnic hatreds or by security concerns. Rather, it was driven by domestic politics, and, in particular, by the competition for power between and among Serbian leaders. The war, which was characterized domestically as a struggle for survival against external ethnic enemies, had its origins in the struggle for domestic political power. Ethnic conflict was provoked by members of the ruling Serbian communist party who were most threatened by prospective changes to the domestic order. War, they hoped, would deflect demands for radical change and allow them to reposition themselves and survive politically.

Stuart Kaufman argues that three factors—hostile masses, belligerent leaders, and inter-ethnic security dilemmas—combine to create ethnic spirals that can lead to violent conflict. When belligerent leaders stoke mass hostility, hostile masses support belligerent leaders, and both together threaten other groups, security dilemmas are created which in turn encourage even more mass hostility and belligerence on the part of elites. He observes that there are two main paths to war: a mass-led pattern, which begins with mass hostility; and an elite-led pattern, which begins with belligerent leaders. He also observes that foreign powers can play an important role in the onset of ethnic wars. He develops these arguments by examining different aspects of the civil war in Moldova in 1991–92.

Šumit Ganguly analyzes the causes of the ethno-religious insurgency that developed in Kashmir in 1989. He argues that the Kashmir insurgency demonstrates the dangers of political mobilization against a backdrop of institutional decay. The failure of governments to accommodate rising political demands within an institutional context can culminate in violence. These dangers are especially acute in multiethnic societies when discontented and politicized ethnic minorities encounter few institutional channels for expressing their discontent. He contends that attempts to fend off such demands through coercive means can only contribute to the process of deinstitutionalization, which has high risks and costs for states. In the long run, states have little choice but to develop institutional capacities for accommodating rising demands for political participation.

All of the contributions to Part I of this volume make implicit or explicit recommendations for preventing and dampening nationalistic and ethnic conflicts: analyses of the causes of conflicts naturally suggest ways of keeping conflicts from breaking out in the first place, or from escalating if they do break out. In Part II of this volume we turn more directly to options for international action with respect to these problems.

Chantal de Jonge Oudraat and I begin Part II with an overview of options for international action. We begin with an examination of the ten main policy instruments at the disposal of international actors. Seven are cooperative measures that depend in important ways on the consent of local parties: humanitarian assistance; fact-finding; mediation; confidence-building measures; traditional peacekeeping operations; multifunctional peacekeeping operations; and military and economic technical assistance. Three instruments are fundamentally coercive: arms embargoes and economic sanctions; judicial enforcement measures; and military force. We then turn to the three main tasks international actors face: conflict prevention; conflict management; and conflict resolution. Our aim is to identify the conditions under which different kinds of international actions are most likely to succeed. This provides a foundation for the development of some policy recommendations.

Chaim Kaufmann then analyzes the nature of ethnic wars in order to determine what remedies are feasible. He argues that in ethnic wars, ethnic identifications become so hardened that rebuilding states becomes impossible. Intermingled populations polarized by violence face intractable security dilemmas, he argues; violence can be stopped only if these intermingled populations are physically separated. He contends that, to save lives threatened by genocide, the international community must abandon attempts to restore war-torn multiethnic states. Instead, it must facilitate and protect population movements to create genuine—and comparatively safe—ethnic and national homelands. The author assesses the November 1995 Dayton accord on Bosnia on these grounds.

In the following essay, Alan Dowty and Gil Loescher argue that states often have security interests, quite apart from humanitarian concerns, that justify intervention in the internal affairs of other states from which refugees are fleeing. Traditional notions of security and sovereignty are beginning to give way, they argue, to a growing international awareness, grounded in principles of international law and Chapter VII of the United Nations Charter, that governments cannot afford to ignore the brutalities of civil and communal conflicts and human rights abuses that uproot entire communities.

There have been many recent calls for military intervention by the international community to remedy conditions that are causing people to flee their homes. This leads Barry Posen to ask what kinds of military actions, with what military goals, can accomplish this. The author examines how, and how effectively, potential military instruments such as punitive bombing, truce enforcement, and the establishment of safe zones or safe havens might be applied to specific situations that cause people to flee. He argues that the preponderance of U.S. military power and the greatly increased capabilities of air power demonstrated in Operation Desert Storm contribute to misplaced optimism about the usefulness of military power with respect to refugee problems. He contends that it will often be politically and militarily difficult to use military power effectively in such cases. Humanitarian intervention, he warns, will often prove to be less gentle than it sounds.

Our final two chapters take us to Africa. Jeffrey Herbst notes that failed and failing states in Africa have caused millions of people to suffer, and that international responses to these crises have usually revolved around efforts to resurrect the states in question. He argues that the current fixation on maintaining existing political units should be abandoned, and that other responses to state failure should be developed even if this means making significant changes in international legal and diplomatic practices. He goes on to develop some alternative strategies for dealing with state failure in Africa and elsewhere.

Many policy analysts and policymakers have suggested that regional security organizations should play a much more active role in peacekeeping and peace enforcement operations. Herbert Howe assesses the case for regional peacekeeping by taking a close look at the experience of the military intervention in Liberia's civil war undertaken by the Economic Community of West African States (ECOWAS) Cease-fire Monitoring Group, known as ECOMOG. He draws some sobering lessons about the strengths and weaknesses of regional efforts in this area.

The contributions to this volume represent neither the first nor the final word on this tremendously important subject. However, the editors of this volume hope that the analyses contained herein make some useful contributions to our understanding of the causes of nationalistic and ethnic conflicts, and what the international community can do about them.

Nationalism and Ethnic Conflict

Part I:
The Sources of Nationalism and Ethnic Conflict

The Causes of Internal Conflict

Michael E. Brown

An Overview

$\mathbf{M}$any policymakers and journalists believe that the causes of internal conflicts are simple and straightforward.[1] The driving forces behind these violent conflicts, it is said, are the "ancient hatreds" that many ethnic and religious groups have for each other. In Eastern Europe, the former Soviet Union, and elsewhere, these deep-seated animosities were held in check for years by authoritarian rule. The collapse of authoritarian rule, it is argued, has taken the "lid" off these ancient rivalries, allowing long-suppressed grievances to come to the surface and escalate into armed conflict. U.S. President George Bush, for example, maintained that the war in Bosnia between Serbs, Croats, and Muslims grew out of "age-old animosities."[2] His successor, Bill Clinton, argued that the end of the Cold War "lifted the lid from a cauldron of long-simmering hatreds. Now, the entire global terrain is bloody with such conflicts."[3] Writing about the Balkans, the American political commentator Richard Cohen declared that "Bosnia is a formidable, scary place of high mountains, brutish people, and tribal grievances rooted in history and myth born of boozy nights by the fire. It's the place where World War I began and where the wars of Europe persist, an ember of hate still glowing for reasons that defy reason itself."[4]

Serious scholars reject this explanation of internal conflict.[5] This simple but widely held view cannot explain why violent conflicts have broken out in some places, but not others, and it cannot explain why some disputes are more violent and harder to resolve than others. It is undeniably true that Serbs, Croats, and Bosnian Muslims have many historical grievances against each other, and that these grievances have played a role in the Balkan conflicts that have raged since 1991. But it is also true that other groups—Czechs and Slovaks, Ukrainians and Russians, French-speaking and English-speaking Ca-

1. This chapter is based on Michael E. Brown, "Introduction" and "The Causes and Regional Dimensions of Internal Conflict," in Brown, ed., *The International Dimensions of Internal Conflict* (Cambridge, Mass.: MIT Press, 1996), pp. 1–31, 571–601.
2. Bush is quoted in Jack Snyder, "Nationalism and the Crisis of the Post-Soviet State," in Michael E. Brown, ed., *Ethnic Conflict and International Security* (Princeton, N.J.: Princeton University Press, 1993), pp. 79–101 at p. 79.
3. Clinton is quoted in Ann Devroy, "President Cautions Congress on 'Simplistic Ideas' in Foreign Policy," *Washington Post*, May 26, 1994.
4. Richard Cohen, "Send in the Troops," *Washington Post*, November 28, 1995.
5. See, for example, Snyder, "Nationalism and the Crisis of the Post-Soviet State"; Barry Posen, "The Security Dilemma and Ethnic Conflict," in Brown, *Ethnic Conflict and International Security*, pp. 103–124; Susanne Hoeber Rudolph and Lloyd I. Rudolph, "Modern Hate," *New Republic*, March 22, 1993, pp. 24–29.

nadians, the Flemish and the Walloons—have historical grievances of various kinds that have *not* led to violent conflict in the 1990s. This single-factor explanation, in short, cannot account for significant variation in the incidence and intensity of internal and ethnic conflict.

In this chapter, I will provide an overview of the scholarly literature on the causes of internal conflict, developing four main arguments along the way. First, the literature on internal conflict has focused on the underlying factors or permissive conditions that make some places and some situations more predisposed to violence than others. Four sets of factors have been singled out in this regard: structural factors; political factors; economic/social factors; and cultural/perceptual factors. Second, the scholarly literature is weak when it comes to analyzing the catalytic factors or proximate causes of internal conflicts. I contend that internal conflicts can be triggered in four different ways: by internal, mass-level factors (bad domestic problems); by external, mass-level factors (bad neighborhoods); by external, elite-level factors (bad neighbors); and by internal, elite-level factors (bad leaders). Third, the scholarly literature pays insufficient attention to the role played by domestic elites in transforming potentially violent situations into deadly confrontations. Many internal conflicts are triggered by the actions of domestic elites, and these actions therefore merit special attention. Here, too, we need to distinguish between different kinds of conflicts: ideological conflicts, criminal assaults on state sovereignty, and raw power struggles. Fourth and more generally, it is important to recognize that there are many different types of internal conflict, each caused by different things. The challenge for scholars is to identify these different types of conflicts and the different sets of factors that bring them about. The search for a single factor or set of factors that explains everything is comparable to the search for the Holy Grail—noble, but futile.

The first section of this chapter will analyze the scholarly literature on the underlying causes of internal conflict. The second section will examine the proximate causes of internal conflict and develop a framework for analyzing different sets of proximate causes. The third section will focus on the roles played by domestic elites in different types of internal conflicts. I conclude with some observations about the policy implications of this analysis, and with some thoughts on the implications of this analysis for the study of internal conflict.

The Underlying Causes of Internal Conflict

The scholarly literature on internal conflict has tended to focus on the under-lying factors or permissive conditions that make some places and some situ-

Table 1. Underlying Causes of Internal Conflict	
Structural Factors	*Economic/Social Factors*
Weak states	Economic problems
Intra-state security concerns	Discriminatory economic systems
Ethnic geography	Economic development and modernization
Political Factors	*Cultural/Perceptual Factors*
Discriminatory political institutions	Patterns of cultural discrimination
Exclusionary national ideologies	Problematic group histories
Inter-group politics	
Elite politics	

ations more prone to violence than others. More specifically, scholars have identified four main clusters of factors that make some places more predisposed to violence than others: structural factors; political factors; economic/ social factors; and cultural/perceptual factors. (See Table 1.)

STRUCTURAL FACTORS
Three main structural factors have drawn scholarly attention: weak states; intra-state security concerns; and ethnic geography.

Weak state structures are the starting point for many analyses of internal conflict.[6] Some states are born weak. Many of the states that were carved out of colonial empires in Africa and Southeast Asia, for example, were artificial constructs. They lacked political legitimacy, politically sensible borders, and political institutions capable of exercising meaningful control over the territory placed under their nominal supervision. The same can be said of many of the states created out of the rubble of the Soviet Union and Yugoslavia. The vast majority of these new entities came into existence with only the most rudimentary political institutions in place.

In many parts of the world, Africa perhaps most notably, states have become weaker over time. In some cases, external developments such as reductions in foreign aid from major powers and international financial institutions and drops in commodity prices played key roles in bringing about institutional decline. In others, states have been weakened by internal problems such as endemic corruption, administrative incompetence, and an inability to promote

---

6. See I. William Zartman, "Introduction: Posing the Problem of State Collapse," in Zartman, ed., *Collapsed States: The Disintegration and Restoration of Legitimate Authority* (Boulder, Colo.: Lynne Rienner Publishers, 1995), pp. 1–11; Gerald B. Helman and Steven R. Ratner, "Saving Failed States," *Foreign Policy*, No. 89 (Winter 1992–93), pp. 3–20.

economic development. Many countries have suffered from several of these problems.

When state structures weaken, violent conflict often follows. Power struggles between and among politicians and would-be leaders intensify. Regional leaders become increasingly independent and, should they consolidate control over military assets, become virtual warlords. Ethnic groups which had been oppressed by the center are more able to assert themselves politically, perhaps in the form of developing more administrative autonomy or their own states. Ethnic groups which had been protected by the center or which had exercised power through the state find themselves more vulnerable. Criminal organizations become more powerful and pervasive, as we have seen in the Caucasus, Afghanistan, and elsewhere. Borders are controlled less effectively. Cross-border movements of militia, arms, drugs, smuggled goods, refugees, and migrants therefore increase. Massive humanitarian problems, such as famines and epidemics, can develop. Widespread human rights violations often take place. The state in question might ultimately fragment or simply cease to exist as a political entity.

When states are weak, individual groups within these states feel compelled to provide for their own defense; they have to worry about whether other groups pose security threats. This is the second structural factor that has drawn attention in the scholarly literature.[7] If the state in question is very weak or if it is expected to become weaker with time, the incentives for groups to make independent military preparations grow. The problem is that, in taking steps to defend themselves, groups often threaten the security of others. This can lead neighboring groups to take steps that will diminish the security of the first group: this is the security dilemma. These problems are especially acute when empires or multiethnic states collapse and ethnic groups suddenly have to provide for their own security. One group's rush to deploy defensive forces will appear threatening to other groups. Moreover, the kinds of forces most commonly deployed—militia and infantry equipped with light arms—have inherent offensive capabilities even if they are mobilized for defensive purposes; this inevitably intensifies the security concerns of neighboring groups.

The third structural factor that has received attention is ethnic geography.[8] More specifically, states with ethnic minorities are more prone to conflict than

---

7. See Posen, "The Security Dilemma and Ethnic Conflict." See also Milton J. Esman, *Ethnic Politics* (Ithaca, N.Y.: Cornell University Press, 1994), pp. 244–245.
8. See Stephen Van Evera, "Hypotheses on Nationalism and War," in this volume; Posen, "The Security Dilemma and Ethnic Conflict."

others, and certain kinds of ethnic demographics are more problematic than others. Some states are ethnically homogeneous, and therefore face few problems on this score. However, of the more than 180 states in existence today, fewer than 20 are ethnically homogeneous in the sense that ethnic minorities account for less than 5 percent of the population.[9] Some of these states, such as Japan and Sweden, have had a uniform ethnic composition for some time. Others—contemporary Poland, Hungary, the Czech Republic—have few minorities today because of the population transfers and the genocide that took place during World War II, and the way borders were drawn after the war. One of the reasons why Poland, Hungary, and the Czech Republic are relatively stable today is their lack of contentious minorities. It is important to note, however, that ethnic homogeneity is no guarantee of internal harmony: Somalia is the most ethnically homogeneous state in sub-Saharan Africa, yet it has been riven by clan warfare and a competition for power between and among local warlords.

In some states with ethnic minorities, ethnic groups are intermingled; in others, minorities tend to live in separate provinces or regions of the country. Countries with different kinds of ethnic geography are likely to experience different kinds of internal problems.[10] Countries with highly intermingled populations are less likely to face secessionist demands because ethnic groups are not distributed in ways that lend themselves to partition. However, if secessionist demands develop in countries with inter-mingled populations, ethnic groups will seek to establish control over specific tracts of territory. Direct attacks on civilians, intense guerilla warfare, ethnic cleansing, and genocide may result. Countries with groups distributed along regional lines are more likely to face secessionist demands, but warfare, if it develops, will generally be more conventional in character.

Most states, particularly those carved out of former empires, have complex ethnic demographics and face serious ethnic problems of one kind or another. In Africa, for example, arbitrary borders have divided some ethnic groups and left them in two or more countries. Most African countries contain large numbers of ethnic groups, some of which are historic enemies.[11] Many of the

---

9. See David Welsh, "Domestic Politics and Ethnic Conflict," in Brown, *Ethnic Conflict and International Security*, pp. 43–60 at p. 45.
10. See Alicia Levine, "Political Accommodation and the Prevention of Secessionist Violence," in Brown, *International Dimensions of Internal Conflict*, chap. 9.
11. See Stephen John Stedman, "Conflict and Conciliation in Sub-Saharan Africa," in Brown, *The International Dimensions of Internal Conflict*, chap. 7.

states of the former Soviet Union inherited borders that were deliberately designed to maximize ethnic complications and cripple the political effectiveness of local leaders with respect to what used to be the center.[12]

POLITICAL FACTORS

Four main political factors have attracted attention in the scholarly literature on internal conflict: discriminatory political institutions; exclusionary national ideologies; inter-group politics; and elite politics.

First, many argue that the prospects for conflict in a country depend to a significant degree on the type and fairness of its political system. Closed, authoritarian systems are likely to generate considerable resentment over time, especially if the interests of some ethnic groups are served while others are trampled. Even in more democratic settings, resentment can build if some groups are inadequately represented in government, the courts, the military, the police, political parties, and other state and political institutions. The legitimacy of the system as a whole can, over time, fall into question. Internal conflict is especially likely if oppression and violence are commonly employed by the state or if a political transition is under way. The latter can take many forms, including democratization, which can be destabilizing in the short run even if it promises stability in the long run.[13]

Second, it is said that much depends on the nature of the prevailing national ideology in the country in question. In some places, nationalism and citizenship are based on ethnic distinctions, rather than the idea that everyone who lives in a country is entitled to the same rights and privileges. Although the existence of civic conceptions of nationalism is no guarantee of stability—civic nationalism prevails in Indonesia—conflict is more likely when ethnic conceptions of nationalism predominate. Under what conditions are these two conceptions of nationalism likely to emerge? According to Jack Snyder,

civic nationalism normally appears in well institutionalized democracies. Ethnic nationalism, in contrast, appears spontaneously when an institutional vacuum occurs. By its nature, nationalism based on equal and universal citizenship rights within a territory depends on a supporting framework of laws to guar-

---

12. See Matthew Evangelista, "Historical Legacies and the Politics of Intervention in the Former Soviet Union," in Brown, *The International Dimensions of Internal Conflict*, chap. 3.
13. See, for example, Ted Robert Gurr and Barbara Harff, *Ethnic Conflict and World Politics* (Boulder, Colo.: Westview Press, 1994), chap. 5; Arend Lijphart, *Democracy in Plural Societies* (New Haven, Conn.: Yale University Press, 1977); Edward D. Mansfield and Jack Snyder, "Democratization and the Danger of War," *International Security*, Vol. 20, No. 1 (Summer 1995), pp. 5–38.

antee those rights, as well as effective institutions to allow citizens to give voice to their views. Ethnic nationalism, in contrast, depends not on institutions, but on culture. Therefore, ethnic nationalism is the default option: it predominates when institutions collapse, when existing institutions are not fulfilling people's basic needs, and when satisfactory alternative structures are not readily available.[14]

It is not surprising, therefore, that there are strong currents of ethnic nationalism in parts of the Balkans, East-Central Europe, and the former Soviet Union, where state structures and political institutions have diminished capacities, and in those parts of the developing world where state structures and political institutions are weak.

It is important to keep in mind that exclusionary national ideologies do not have be based on ethnicity. Religious fundamentalists committed to establishing theocratic states divide societies into two groups: those who subscribe to a theologically derived political, economic, and social order; and those who do not.

Third, many scholars argue that the prospects for violence in a country depend to a significant degree on the dynamics of domestic, inter-group politics.[15] The prospects for violence are great, it is said, if groups—whether they are based on political, ideological, religious, or ethnic affinities—have ambitious objectives, strong senses of identity, and confrontational strategies. Conflict is especially likely if objectives are incompatible, groups are strong and determined, action is feasible, success is possible, and if inter-group comparisons lead to competition, anxiety, and fears of being dominated. The emergence of new groups and changes in the inter-group balance of power can be particularly destabilizing.

Fourth, some scholars have emphasized elite politics and, more specifically, the tactics employed by desperate and opportunistic politicians in times of political and economic turmoil. According to this line of thinking, ethnic

---

14. Snyder, "Nationalism and the Crisis of the Post-Soviet State," p. 86. See also William Pfaff, "Revive Secular Citizenship Above 'Ethnic' Nationality," *International Herald Tribune*, July 20, 1993.
15. See Joseph Rothschild, *Ethnopolitics: A Conceptual Framework* (New York: Columbia University Press, 1981); Donald L. Horowitz, *Ethnic Groups in Conflict* (Berkeley: University of California Press, 1985); Charles Tilly, *From Mobilization to Revolution* (Reading, Mass.: Addison-Wesley, 1978); Charles Tilly, "Does Modernization Breed Revolution?" *Comparative Politics*, Vol. 5, No. 3 (April 1973), pp. 425–447; Lewis Coser, *The Functions of Social Conflict* (Glencoe, Ill.: Free Press, 1956); Gurr and Harff, *Ethnic Conflict and World Politics;* Van Evera, "Hypotheses on Nationalism and War." For an overview, see Saul Newman, "Does Modernization Breed Ethnic Conflict?" *World Politics*, Vol. 43, No. 3 (April 1991), pp. 451–478; Jack A. Goldstone, "Theories of Revolution: The Third Generation," *World Politics*, Vol. 32, No. 3 (April 1980), pp. 425–453.

conflict is often provoked by elites in times of political and economic turmoil in order to fend off domestic challengers. Ethnic bashing and scapegoating are tools of the trade, and the mass media are employed in partisan and propagandistic ways that further aggravate inter-ethnic tensions. The actions of Slobodan Milošević in Serbia and Franjo Tudjman in Croatia stand out as cases in point.[16]

ECONOMIC/SOCIAL FACTORS

Three broad economic and social factors have been identified as potential sources of internal conflict: economic problems; discriminatory economic systems; and the trials and tribulations of economic development and modernization.

First, most countries experience economic problems of one kind or another sooner or later, and these problems can contribute to intra-state tensions. In the industrialized world, problems can emerge even if a country's economy is growing—if it is not growing as fast as it once was, or fast enough to keep pace with societal demands. In Eastern Europe, the former Soviet Union, parts of Africa, and elsewhere, transitions from centrally-planned to market-based economic systems have created a host of economic problems, ranging from historically high levels of unemployment to rampant inflation. Many countries in what we would like to think of as the developing world seem to be in a semi-permanent state of economic shambles. Others are in an economic free-fall. Unemployment, inflation, and resource competitions, especially for land, contribute to societal frustrations and tensions, and can provide the breeding ground for conflict. Economic reforms do not always help and can contribute to the problem in the short term, especially if economic shocks are severe and state subsidies for staples, services, and social welfare are cut. In short, economic slowdowns, stagnation, deterioration, and collapse can be deeply destabilizing.[17]

---

16. See V.P. Gagnon, Jr., "Ethnic Nationalism and International Conflict: The Case of Serbia," in this volume; Human Rights Watch, *Playing the "Communal Card": Communal Violence and Human Rights* (New York: Human Rights Watch, 1995); Warren Zimmermann, "The Last Ambassador: A Memoir of the Collapse of Yugoslavia," *Foreign Affairs*, Vol. 74, No. 2 (March–April 1995), pp. 2–20.
17. For a general discussion and several case studies, see S.W.R. de A. Samarasinghe and Reed Coughlan, eds., *Economic Dimensions of Ethnic Conflict* (London: Pinter Publishers, 1991). For a detailed discussion of the economic roots of the wars in the former Yugoslavia, see Susan L. Woodward, *Balkan Tragedy: Chaos and Dissolution After the Cold War* (Washington: The Brookings Institution, 1995), especially chap. 3. For a discussion of the economic sources of turmoil in South Asia, see Sandy Gordon, "Resources and Instability in South Asia," *Survival*, Vol. 35, No. 2 (Summer 1993), pp. 66–87.

Second, discriminatory economic systems, whether they discriminate on a class basis or an ethnic basis, can generate feelings of resentment and levels of frustration prone to the generation of violence.[18] Unequal economic opportunities, unequal access to resources such as land and capital, and vast differences in standards of living are all signs of economic systems that disadvantaged members of society will see as unfair and perhaps illegitimate. This has certainly been the case in Sri Lanka, for example, where Tamils have been discriminated against in recent decades by the Sinhalese majority. Economic development is not necessarily the solution. Indeed, it can aggravate the situation: economic growth always benefits some individuals, groups, and regions more than others, and those who are on top to begin with are likely to be in a better position to take advantage of new economic opportunities than the downtrodden. Even if a country's overall economic picture is improving, growing inequities and gaps can aggravate intra-state tensions.

Third, many scholars have pointed to economic development and modernization as taproots of instability and internal conflict.[19] The process of economic development, the advent of industrialization, and the introduction of new technologies, it is said, bring about a wide variety of profound social changes: migration and urbanization disrupt existing family and social systems and undermine traditional political institutions; better education, higher literacy rates, and improved access to growing mass media raise awareness of where different people stand in society. At a minimum, this places strains on existing social and political systems.[20] It also raises economic and political expectations, and can lead to mounting frustration when these expectations are not met. This

---

18. For an overview of Marx on this question, see James B. Rule, *Theories of Civil Violence* (Berkeley: University of California Press, 1988), chapter 2; A.S. Cohan, *Theories of Revolution* (New York: Wiley, 1975), chaps. 4–5. For a discussion of how this applies to the developing world in particular, see Gordon, "Resources and Instability in South Asia."

19. See Samuel P. Huntington, *Political Order in Changing Societies* (New Haven, Conn.: Yale University Press, 1968); Samuel P. Huntington, "Civil Violence and the Process of Development," in *Civil Violence and the International System*, Adelphi Paper No. 83 (London: International Institute for Strategic Studies, 1971), pp. 1–15; Ted Robert Gurr, *Why Men Rebel* (Princeton, N.J.: Princeton University Press, 1970); Walker Conner, "Nation-Building or Nation-Destroying?" *World Politics*, Vol. 24, No. 3 (April 1972), pp. 319–355; Walker Conner, *Ethnonationalism: The Quest for Understanding* (Princeton, N.J.: Princeton University Press, 1994). For an overview of this literature, see Newman, "Does Modernization Breed Ethnic Conflict?" For critiques of this approach, see Rod Aya, "Theories of Revolution Reconsidered: Contrasting Models of Collective Violence," *Theory and Society*, Vol. 8, No. 1 (July 1979), pp. 1–38; Tilly, "Does Modernization Breed Revolution?"

20. See Chalmers Johnson, *Revolutionary Change* (Boston: Little, Brown, 1966); Mark Hagopian, *The Phenomenon of Revolution* (New York: Dodd, Mead, 1974). For an overview, see Cohan, *Theories of Revolution*, chap. 6; Goldstone, "Theories of Revolution," pp. 425–434.

can be particularly problematic in the political realm, because demands for political participation usually outpace the ability of the system to respond. According to Samuel Huntington, "The result is instability and disorder. The primary problem . . . is the lag in the development of political institutions behind social and economic change."[21]

CULTURAL/PERCEPTUAL FACTORS

Two cultural and perceptual factors have been identified in the scholarly literature as sources of internal conflict. The first is cultural discrimination against minorities. Problems include inequitable educational opportunities, legal and political constraints on the use and teaching of minority languages, and constraints on religious freedom. In extreme cases, draconian efforts to assimilate minority populations combined with programs to bring large numbers of other ethnic groups into minority areas constitute a form of cultural genocide. Aggressive forms of these policies were implemented by Josef Stalin in the Soviet Union in the 1930s and 1940s, particularly in the Caucasus. Similar policies have been pursued by China in Tibet since the 1950s. Somewhat less vicious forms of assimilationist policies have been pursued in Bulgaria with respect to ethnic Turks, in Slovakia with respect to ethnic Hungarians, and in Thailand with respect to members of northern and western hill tribes, for example.[22]

The second factor that falls under this broad heading has to do with group histories and group perceptions of themselves and others.[23] It is certainly true that many groups have legitimate grievances against others for crimes of one kind or another committed at some point in the distant or recent past. Some "ancient hatreds" have legitimate historical bases. However, it is also true that groups tend to whitewash and glorify their own histories, and they often demonize their neighbors, rivals, and adversaries. Explaining away the Hutu slaughter of 800,000–1,000,000 Tutsi in Rwanda in 1994, one Hutu who had

---

21. Huntington, *Political Order in Changing Societies*, p. 5.
22. Many argue that formal, minority rights safeguards are the solution. See, for example, Jonathan Eyal, "Eastern Europe: What About the Minorities?" *World Today*, Vol. 45, No. 12 (December 1989), pp. 205–208; Wiktor Osiatynski, "Needed Now: Bills of Rights," *Time*, December 24, 1990; L. Michael Hager, "To Get More Peace, Try More Justice," *International Herald Tribune*, July 30, 1992; Stephen S. Rosenfeld, "Serbs Are the Problem, Minority Rights the Solution," *International Herald Tribune*, September 26–27, 1992.
23. See Van Evera, "Hypotheses on Nationalism and War"; Posen, "The Security Dilemma and Ethnic Conflict," p. 107; Snyder, "Nationalism and the Crisis of the Post-Soviet State," pp. 92–93; Donald Rothchild and Alexander J. Groth, "Pathological Dimensions of Domestic and International Ethnicity," *Political Science Quarterly*, Vol. 110, No. 1 (Spring 1995), pp. 69–82.

been training for the priesthood insisted, "It wasn't genocide. It was self-defense."[24] Stories that are passed down from generation to generation by word of mouth become part of a group's lore. They often become distorted and exaggerated with time, and are treated as received wisdom by group members.

These ethnic mythologies are particularly problematic if rival groups have mirror images of each other, which is often the case. Serbs, for example, see themselves as heroic defenders of Europe and Croats as fascist, genocidal thugs. Croats see themselves as valiant victims of Serbian hegemonic aggression. When two groups in close proximity have mutually exclusive, incendiary perceptions of each other, the slightest provocation on either side confirms deeply held beliefs and provides the justification for a retaliatory response. Under conditions such as these, conflict is hard to avoid and even harder to limit once started.

The Proximate Causes of Internal Conflict

The existing literature on internal conflict does a commendable job of surveying the underlying factors or permissive conditions that make some situations particularly prone to violence, but it is weak when it comes to identifying the catalytic factors—the triggers or proximate causes—of internal conflicts. As James Rule put it in his review of the literature on civil violence, "We know a lot of things that are true about civil violence, but we do not know when they are going to be true."[25] The result is that we know a lot less about the causes of internal conflict than one would guess from looking at the size of the literature on the subject.

However, the existing literature gives us a running start at developing a framework for analyzing the proximate causes of internal conflict because it provides us with a well-rounded set of factors that predispose some places to violence. If we assume that each of these twelve underlying factors can play a more catalytic role if rapid changes take place in the area in question, then we also have a list of twelve possible proximate causes of internal conflict.

In brief, states are especially prone to violence if state structures are collapsing due to external developments (such as sharp reductions in international financial assistance, sharp declines in commodity prices), internal problems (new, incompetent leaders or rampant corruption), or some combination of the

---

24. This Hutu apologist is quoted in "You're Saying We Did It?" *Economist*, June 3, 1995, p. 38.
25. Rule, *Theories of Civil Violence*, p. 265.

above. Under these circumstances, states are increasingly unable to cope with societal demands.[26] When state structures weaken or when new states are created out of the rubble of a larger entity, groups have a heightened sense of potential security problems. They are more likely to take measures to protect themselves which, in turn, are more likely to generate fears in other groups. In situations such as these, security dilemmas are especially intense and arms races are especially likely. Changing military balances—or fears about possible adverse developments—make arms racing and conflict escalation difficult to control.[27] Demographic changes brought about by birth rate differentials, migration, urbanization, or sudden influxes of refugees can aggravate ethnic problems and further complicate the picture by changing the domestic balance of power.

Political transitions brought about by the collapse of authoritarian rule, democratization, or political reforms also make states particularly prone to violence.[28] The emergence and rise of exclusionary national ideologies, such as ethnic nationalism and religious fundamentalism, can be destabilizing as well. The emergence of dehumanizing ideologies, which literally deny the humanity of other ethnic groups, is particularly dangerous because it is often the precursor to genocidal slaughter.[29] The rise of new groups or changes in the intergroup balance of power can intensify inter-group competition and anxieties, making political systems more volatile.[30] The emergence of power struggles between and among elites can be particularly problematic, because desperate and opportunistic politicians are particularly prone to employing divisive ethnic and nationalistic appeals.

Potentially catalytic economic and social problems include mounting economic problems, intensifying resource competitions, growing economic inequities and gaps, and fast-paced development and modernization processes.[31] Industrialized countries, countries attempting to make the transition from centrally-planned to market-driven systems, and developing countries gener-

---

26. See Zartman, "Introduction: Posing the Problem of State Collapse," pp. 1–11.
27. See Posen, "The Security Dilemma and Ethnic Conflict."
28. See Mansfield and Snyder, "Democratization and the Danger of War," pp. 5–38.
29. On ethnic nationalism, see Snyder, "Nationalism and the Crisis of the Post-Soviet State." On dehumanizing ideologies, see Helen Fein, "Explanations of Genocide," *Current Sociology*, Vol. 38, No. 1 (Spring 1990), pp. 32–50; Leo Kuper, *Genocide: Its Political Use in the Twentieth Century* (New Haven, Conn.: Yale University Press, 1981), chap. 3.
30. See Rothschild, *Ethnopolitics*; Tilly, *From Mobilization to Revolution*; Horowitz, *Ethnic Groups in Conflict*; Gurr and Harff, *Ethnic Conflict and World Politics*; Van Evera, "Hypotheses on Nationalism and War."
31. See, for example, Gordon, "Resources and Instability in South Asia."

Table 2. The Proximate Causes of Internal Conflict.

	Internally-driven	Externally-driven
Elite-triggered	Bad Leaders	Bad Neighbors
Mass-triggered	Bad Domestic Problems	Bad Neighborhoods

ally have to contend with different kinds of problems, but they are all susceptible to economically and socially induced turmoil.

Finally, states are especially prone to violence if discrimination against minorities intensifies, or if politicians begin to blame some ethnic groups for whatever political and economic problems their country may be experiencing. Ethnic bashing and scapegoating are often precursors to violence.

Creating lists of possible underlying and proximate causes of internal conflict is a useful starting point for analyzing these issues, but it does not take us far enough. For starters, this list of twelve possible proximate causes does not distinguish sharply between elite-level and mass-level factors. It is incomplete, moreover, because it does not take into account the catalytic role that neighboring states and developments in neighboring states can play in triggering violence.

I argue that internal conflicts can be categorized according to: (1) whether they are triggered by elite-level or mass-level factors;[32] and (2) whether they are triggered by internal or external developments. There are, therefore, four main types of internal conflicts, and they can be depicted in a two-by-two matrix. (See Table 2.) Put another way, internal conflicts can, in theory, be triggered by any one of four sets of proximate causes.

First, conflicts can be triggered by internal, mass-level phenomena, such as rapid economic development and modernization or patterns of political and economic discrimination. To put it more prosaically, they can be caused by "bad domestic problems." The conflicts in Punjab and Sri Lanka are examples, the former being galvanized by rapid modernization and migration and the latter by long-standing patterns of political, economic, and cultural discrimination.[33]

---

32. The utility of the distinction between elite-level and mass-level factors has been noted by others. See Renée de Nevers, *The Soviet Union and Eastern Europe: The End of an Era*, Adelphi Paper No. 249 (London: International Institute for Strategic Studies, 1990), pp. 27–29; Stuart J. Kaufman, "An 'International' Theory of Inter-Ethnic War," *Review of International Studies*, Vol. 22, No. 2 (April 1996), pp. 149–171.
33. See Sumit Ganguly, "Internal Conflict in South and Southwest Asia," in Brown, *The International Dimensions of Internal Conflict*," chap. 4.

Another example is the conflict over Nagorno-Karabakh, which was triggered by problematic ethnic geography and patterns of discrimination highlighted by the break-up of the Soviet Union.

The proximate causes of a second set of conflicts are mass-level but external in character: swarms of refugees or fighters crashing across borders, bringing turmoil and violence with them, or radicalized politics sweeping throughout regions. These are conflicts caused by the "contagion," "diffusion," and "spill-over" effects to which many policymakers, analysts, and scholars give much credence.[34] One could say that such conflicts are caused by "bad neighbor-hoods." The expulsion of radical Palestinians from Jordan in 1970 led many militants to resettle in Lebanon, where Muslim-Christian tensions were already mounting. This, one could argue, was the spark that ignited the civil war in Lebanon in 1975.

The proximate causes of a third set of conflicts are external but elite-level in character: they are the results of discrete, deliberate decisions by governments to trigger conflicts in nearby states for political, economic, or ideological pur-poses of their own. This only works, one must note, when the permissive conditions for conflict already exist in the target country; outsiders are gener-ally unable to foment trouble in stable, just societies. Such conflicts, one could say, are caused by "bad neighbors." Examples include the Soviet Union's meddling in and subsequent 1979 invasion of Afghanistan, which has yet to emerge from chaos, and Russian meddling in Georgia and Moldova in the 1990s.[35] Another example is Rhodesia's establishment of RENAMO in 1976 to undermine the new government in Mozambique.[36]

The proximate causes of the fourth and final type of internal conflict are internal and elite-level in character. Variations include: power struggles involv-ing civilian (Georgia) or military (Nigeria) leaders; ideological contests over how a country's political, economic, social, and religious affairs should be organized (Algeria, Peru); and criminal assaults on the state (Colombia). To put

---

34. See, for example, John A. Vasquez, "Factors Related to the Contagion and Diffusion of Inter-national Violence," in Manus I. Midlarsky, ed., *The Internationalization of Communal Strife*, (London: Routledge, 1992), pp. 149–172; Ted Robert Gurr, *Minorities at Risk: A Global View of Ethnopolitical Conflicts* (Washington: U.S. Institute of Peace Press, 1993), pp. 132–135. For an excellent overview of this literature, see Stuart Hill and Donald Rothchild, "The Contagion of Political Conflict in Africa and the World," *Journal of Conflict Resolution*, Vol. 30, No. 4 (December 1986), pp. 716–735.
35. On Afghanistan, see Ganguly, "Internal Conflict in South and Southwest Asia." On Moldova and Georgia, see Evangelista, "Historical Legacies and the Politics of Intervention in the Former Soviet Union."
36. I thank Stephen Stedman for this observation.

it in simple terms, conflicts such as these are triggered and driven by "bad leaders."

The Importance of Domestic Elites

The scholarly literature on the causes of internal conflict is strong in its examination of structural, political, economic, social, and cultural forces that operate at a mass level—indeed, it clearly favors mass-level explanations of the causes of internal conflict—but it is weak in its understanding of the roles played by elites and leaders in instigating violence. The latter has received comparatively little attention. The result is "no-fault" history that leaves out the pernicious effects of influential individuals, which is an important set of factors in the overall equation.

Although mass-level factors are clearly important underlying conditions that make some places more predisposed to violence than others, and although neighboring states routinely meddle in the internal affairs of others, the decisions and actions of domestic elites often determine whether political disputes veer toward war or peace. Leaving elite decisions and actions out of the equation, as many social scientists do, is analytically misguided. It also has important policy implications: under-appreciating the import of elite decisions and actions hinders conflict prevention efforts and fails to place blame where blame is due.

The proximate causes of many internal conflicts are the decisions and actions of domestic elites, but these conflicts are not all driven by the same domestic forces. There are three main variations: ideological struggles, which are driven by the ideological convictions of various individuals; criminal assaults on state sovereignty, which are driven primarily by the economic motivations of drug traffickers; and power struggles between and among competing elites, which are driven by personal, political motivations. Admittedly, these compartments are not water-tight.[37] It is nonetheless important to make these distinctions, however rough they might be: there are several, distinct motivational forces at work here—several identifiable proximate causes of internal violence. It is important to have an appreciation of the multifaceted nature of the problem,

---

37. Some conflicts have mutated over time and have more than one distinguishing characteristic. Most power struggles are characterized by those involved in politically convenient ethnic or ideological terms. Many of these conflicts have powerful ethnic dimensions. These problems make analysis difficult, but not impossible.

particularly if one is interested in enhancing international efforts to prevent, manage, and resolve internal conflicts.

IDEOLOGICAL CONFLICTS

First, some internally-driven, elite-triggered conflicts are ideological struggles over the organization of political, economic, and social affairs in a country. Some ideological struggles are defined in economic or class terms; others are fundamentalist religious crusades guided by theological frameworks. Ideological struggles over how political, economic, and social affairs should be organized have not gone away with the end of the Cold War, but they have tended to take on new forms. Class-based movements with Marxist agendas have faded from the scene in many parts of the world, including Southeast Asia, the Middle East, Africa, and Latin America, although some rebels in Colombia and Peru have remained largely true to form. Some rebel movements, have mutated and taken on the political agendas of indigenous peoples and ethnic minorities. In many places—Afghanistan, Algeria, Egypt, India, Iran, Sudan—conflicts have formed around new secularist-fundamentalist fault lines. These ethnic and fundamentalist movements draw on many of the same sources that impelled class-based movements in the Cold War era—patterns of political, economic, and cultural discrimination, and widespread dissatisfaction with the pace and equitability of economic development—but they are channeled in different directions. In other words, many of the underlying causes of these conflicts are the same, but their proximate causes have changed.

CRIMINAL ASSAULTS ON STATE SOVEREIGNTY

Second, some internally-driven, elite-triggered conflicts are in effect criminal assaults on state sovereignty. In several countries in Asia and Latin America, in particular, drug cartels have accumulated enough power to challenge state control over large tracts of territory. This is certainly true, for example, in Afghanistan, Brazil, Burma, Mexico, Tajikistan, and Venezuela. In Colombia, most notably, state sovereignty has been directly challenged by drug barons and their criminal organizations.[38] This problem shows no sign of abating. A related problem is that, with the end of the Cold War and reductions in financial support from Moscow and Washington, many ethnic groups and

---

38. For a detailed discussion of drug-related problems in Latin America, see Marc Chernick, "Peacemaking and Violence in Latin America," in Brown, *The International Dimensions of Internal Conflict*, chap. 8.

political movements turned to drug trafficking to finance their activities. This is true, for example, of various groups in Colombia and Peru.[39] In addition to its other pernicious effects, drug trafficking complicates the nature of the conflicts in question and therefore makes conflict management and resolution more difficult.

POWER STRUGGLES

Third, some conflicts are in essence power struggles between and among competing elites. Of the three types of internally-driven, elite-triggered conflicts outlined here, raw power struggles are clearly the most common. Some are sustained government campaigns to repress ethnic minorities and democratic activists. This would seem to be a fair characterization of the conflicts in Burma, Cambodia, Guatemala, Indonesia, Iraq, and Turkey, for example. Government repression is a prominent feature of other conflicts as well, but power struggles are particularly intense and the "ethnic card" is played very aggressively. Examples abound: Angola, Bosnia, Burundi, Croatia, Kenya, Liberia, the Philippines, Russia/Chechnya, Rwanda, Somalia, and Tajikistan.

One type of power struggle is particularly prominent and particularly pernicious: it accounts for the slaughter in the former Yugoslavia and Rwanda, and has played a role in the conflicts in Azerbaijan, Burundi, Cameroon, Chechnya, Georgia, India, Kenya, Nigeria, Romania, Sri Lanka, Sudan, Togo, Zaire, and elsewhere.[40] The starting point is a lack of elite legitimacy, which sooner or later leads to elite vulnerability. Vulnerabilities can be brought about by weakening state structures, political transitions, pressures for political reform, and economic problems. Those who are in power are determined to fend off emerging political challengers and anxious to shift blame for whatever economic and political setbacks their countries may be experiencing. In cases where ideological justifications for staying in power have been overtaken by events, they need to devise new formulas for legitimizing their rule. Entrenched politicians and aspiring leaders alike have powerful incentives to play the "ethnic card," embracing ethnic identities and proclaiming themselves the champions of ethnic groups.[41]

This produces a shift in the terms of public discourse from civic nationalism to ethnic nationalism and to increasingly virulent forms of ethnic nationalism.

---

39. Ibid.
40. See Human Rights Watch, *Playing the "Communal Card."* See also Stedman, "Conflict and Conciliation in Sub-Saharan Africa."
41. See Human Rights Watch, *Playing the "Communal Card."*

Ethnic minorities are often singled out and blamed for the country's problems: ethnic scapegoating and ethnic bashing become the order of the day. When power struggles are fierce, politicians portray other ethnic groups in threatening terms, and inflate these threats to bolster group solidarity and their own political positions; perceived threats are extremely powerful unifying devices.[42] When leaders have control over the national media, these kinds of campaigns are particularly effective: a relentless drumbeat of ethnic propaganda can distort political discourse quickly and dramatically. Political campaigns such as these undermine stability and push countries towards violence by dividing and radicalizing groups along ethnic fault lines. In the former Yugoslavia, Serbian leader Slobodan Milošević and Croatian leader Franjo Tudjman rose to power by polarizing their societies even though Serbs and Croats had coexisted peacefully for decades.

WHY DO FOLLOWERS FOLLOW?

It is easy to understand why desperate and opportunistic politicians in the midst of power struggles would resort to nationalist and ethnic appeals. For many politicians, tearing their countries apart and causing thousands of people to be killed are small prices to pay for staying in or getting power. The more interesting question is: why do followers follow?[43] Given that politicians all over the world employ ethnic appeals of one kind or another, why do these appeals resonate in some places but not others? Why do large numbers of people follow the ethnic flag in some places at some times, but not others?

Two factors are particularly important in this regard: the existence of antagonistic group histories; and mounting economic problems. If groups have bad histories of each other and especially if they see themselves as victims of other, aggressive communities, ethnic bashing and inflated threats seem plausible. If economic problems such as unemployment and inflation are mounting and resource competitions are intensifying, ethnic scapegoating is more likely to resonate and more people are likely to accept a radical change in a country's political course, including armed confrontation. In short, the emergence of elite competitions might be the proximate causes of conflicts in places such as the former Yugoslavia and Rwanda, but hostilities escalate only because of the existence of other underlying problems or permissive conditions—problematic group histories and economic problems.

---

42. See Esman, *Ethnic Politics*, p. 244.
43. See Horowitz, *Ethnic Groups in Conflict*, p. 140.

It appears that all three factors—intensifying elite competitions, problematic group histories, and economic problems—must be present for this kind of conflict to explode. Russians and Ukrainians, for example, have had to contend with collapsing economies and standards of living, and many Ukrainians do not have benign historical images of Russians. However, Ukrainian politicians have by and large refrained from making the kinds of nationalistic appeals that have caused trouble elsewhere. They undoubtedly recognize that provoking a Russian-Ukrainian confrontation would not bode well for Ukraine or for their own positions as leaders of an independent state. Some Russian politicians have been far less responsible in this regard, but their nationalistic appeals have not yet taken over the Russian national debate. Whether or not nationalistic and pseudo-nationalistic politicians remain confined to the margins of the Russian political debate is certainly one of the keys to its future and to the stability of a large part of the world.

A few parts of the world have experienced economic turmoil and power struggles, but have been blessed with homogeneous populations and few internal ethnic problems. Finland, for example, has experienced a sharp economic decline since the late 1980s, but has not experienced inter-ethnic strife because minorities are few and small and because inter-group relations are relatively harmonious. Similarly, Poland has gone through a complete political and economic transformation since 1989, but it has few minorities and few inter-group problems: nationalistic appeals have no audience. Poland's hotly contested 1995 presidential election was consequently fought along ideological lines.

Other parts of the world have deeply troubled ethnic histories and leaders who have not hesitated to do whatever was necessary to get and keep power, but they have been spared massive bloodlettings because of their comparatively rosy economic pictures. For example, Malaysia and Thailand experienced considerable turmoil during the Cold War but are quite stable today because of the economic boom that has swept most of the region. Indonesia has had to contend with simmering conflicts in East Timor, Irian Jaya, and Aceh, but these conflicts have not escalated dramatically, nor has the country as a whole splintered into dozens or hundreds of ethnic fragments as it might have.[44] Much of this can be traced to a track record of sustained economic growth, which gives groups, even relatively disadvantaged groups, incentives to avoid

---

44. See Trevor Findlay, "Turning the Corner in Southeast Asia," in Brown, *The International Dimensions of Internal Conflict*, chap. 5.

conflict and destruction of a system that is bringing more and more economic benefits to more and more people.

One can also point to East-Central Europe, which has experienced more than its share of turmoil in the past and which is not blessed with leaders steeped in the principles of Jeffersonian democracy, but which has nonetheless avoided the carnage that has consumed the former Yugoslavia a few hundred miles to the south. East-Central Europe has been comparatively peaceful, even though every country in the region has been going through a political transition of the most profound sort; elites have been jockeying for position ever since 1989. If one had to point to one reason for East-Central Europe's stability, one would point to its comparatively good economic performance and prospects. The fact that the states of this region have a good chance of joining the European Union at some point in the not-too-distant future gives people powerful incentives to ignore nationalistic appeals and not rock the boat. This point is driven home with even greater force when one looks at differences within the region: nationalistic appeals have been less successful in Hungary, which has an ethnic diaspora but one of the region's strongest economies and one of the region's best chances of joining the European Union quickly, than in Romania, which has struggled economically.

Economic developments have also marked important turning points in the Middle East and Africa. The Middle East experienced considerable domestic turmoil in the 1950s and 1960s, when weak states were unable to meet societal demands, but less instability in some places in the 1970s and 1980s, when high oil prices and high levels of foreign aid from the United States and the Soviet Union gave governments more largesse to spread around. Potential opposition forces were pacified and, in essence, bought off. The fact that oil prices and foreign assistance levels have declined sharply in the 1990s does not bode well for the region's future.[45]

Much of sub-Saharan Africa has experienced similar problems for similar reasons. Many governments in West, Central, and East Africa were able to hold their heads above water in the 1970s and 1980s, even though they were riddled with ethnic problems and run by corrupt, incompetent leaders, because they received substantial amounts of financial support from two external sources: the superpowers and Western Europe; and international financial institutions

---

45. See Rachel Bronson, "Cycles of Conflict in the Middle East and North Africa," in Brown, *The International Dimensions of Internal Conflict,* chap. 6.

such as the International Monetary Fund (IMF) and the World Bank. In the late 1980s, however, two things happened: the Cold War ended, and international financial institutions changed their ways of thinking about how financial assistance would be handed out. Direct aid from Washington and Moscow dried up, and most aid from Western Europe was redirected to Central and Eastern Europe. In addition, international financial institutions threatened to withhold aid unless governments overhauled their corrupt political systems and ineffective economic systems. This placed many leaders in Africa between a rock and a hard place: if they overhauled their patronage systems they would lose the support of their domestic constituencies and subsequently lose power; if they told the IMF and the World Bank that they would not implement political and economic reforms, they would not get financial assistance from abroad, their governments and economies would collapse, and they would lose power anyway. Many leaders in West, Central, and East Africa failed to resolve this dilemma, and consequently threw their countries into turmoil in the late 1980s and early 1990s.[46] Nigeria, which had substantial oil reserves, suffered similar financial setbacks when oil prices dropped and its government mismanaged the country's oil income. Although parts of Africa, particularly southern Africa, have stabilized since the end of the Cold War, much of the continent has moved in the other direction.

This points to how precarious Russia's position is. Russia is a country with a deeply xenophobic world view; it is comprised of dozens of ethnic groups, many of whom have spent centuries despising each other; with the break-up of the Soviet Union, many Russians now live as minorities in other, contiguous states; and the Russian economy has been in a free-fall since the mid-1980s. The fact that rabid nationalistic appeals have not yet taken over Russia's political debate is a minor miracle, attributable in large part to Boris Yeltsin's reluctance to go down this path and his willingness to use force to squelch his opposition. However, there are good reasons for fearing that more formidable nationalists will enter the picture, leaders not burdened with Vladimir Zhirinovsky's self-defeating tendencies. Given Russia's continuing economic crisis and its deeply troubled ethnic picture, the emergence of powerful nationalistic politicians could be the spark that ignites a highly combustible mixture. The key to defusing this situation—and a lever over which outside powers have at least some control—is turning Russia's economy around.

---

46. See Stedman, "Conflict and Conciliation in Sub-Saharan Africa."

Policy Implications

My discussion of the causes of internal conflict has three main policy implications. First, conflict prevention efforts should be guided by a two-track strategy. One track should be a series of long-term efforts aimed at the underlying conditions that make violent conflicts more likely. Particular attention should be paid to economic problems, distorted group histories, and patterns of political, economic, and cultural discrimination. A second track should focus on the proximate causes of internal conflict, the catalytic factors that turn potentially violent situations into deadly confrontations.

Second, conflict prevention efforts need to take into account the fact that internal conflicts can be triggered by any one of four sets of proximate causes: internal, mass-level forces; external, mass-level forces; external, elite-level forces; and internal, elite-level forces. Different kinds of conflict prevention efforts will be needed in each case. No single set of preventive actions will suffice.

Third, conflict prevention efforts should focus very aggressively on the decisions and actions of domestic elites, who are often responsible for sparking internal conflicts. Ambitious individuals will always aspire to power; the challenge is to keep power struggles from exploding into civil wars. Those interested in conflict prevention need to think systematically about ways of neutralizing the ethnic bashing, ethnic scapegoating, hate mongering, and propagandizing that are often the precursors to violence.

One of the implications of this analysis is that distant powers and the international community in general are not as helpless as the conventional wisdom would have us believe. Internal conflicts are often triggered by the decisions and actions of domestic elites, not mass unrest or some uncontrollable form of domestic or regional mass hysteria. Bad leaders and bad behavior are discrete problems that can be identified and targeted for action. These decisions and acts are not necessarily immune to international pressure: they mark moments when distant international powers can try to use their leverage and influence the course of events.

Implications for the Study of Internal Conflict

The main message of this chapter is that there are several distinct types of internal conflict. As a result, no single factor or set of factors can explain everything. The problem with "ancient hatreds" theorizing is not that historical grievances are irrelevant but that a single factor is said to be responsible for a wide range of developments. Replacing this single-factor explanation with another—based on economic problems, for example—would not solve this problem. The starting point for advancing our understanding of the causes of internal conflict is identifying different types of conflicts and the different sets of causal factors that are decisive in different settings.

It should go without saying that the framework outlined above does not constitute the final word on this tremendously complex subject. First, the distinctions between and among different kinds of underlying and proximate causes need to be sharpened if we are to refine our classification of conflicts according to their causes. Second, it is entirely possible that other types of conflicts driven by different combinations of factors will be identified as more work is done in this area. Finally, one of the keys to advancing knowledge in this area will be the production of detailed case studies carefully focused on the proximate causes of internal conflicts—more specifically, on the precise moments when political disputes become violent confrontations. Most case histories lack a sharp analytic focus, and the theoretical literature on this subject, as noted above, tends to focus on the permissive conditions of internal conflicts, not the proximate causes of violence. In short, much more work needs to be done.

Hypotheses on Nationalism and War

Stephen Van Evera

$\mathbf{S}$cholars have written widely on the causes of nationalism[1] but said little about its effects, especially its effects on international politics. Most strikingly, the impact of nationalism on the risk of war has barely been explored. Most authors take the war-causing character of nationalism for granted, assuming it without proof or explanation.[2] Factors that govern the size of the dangers posed by nationalism are neglected. What types of nationalism are most likely to cause war? What background conditions catalyze or dampen this causal process? These ques-

Stephen Van Evera teaches in the political science department at the Massachusetts Institute of Technology.

Thanks to Robert Art, Don Blackmer, David Laitin, John Mearsheimer, Barry Posen, Jack Snyder, and Stephen Walt for sharing their thoughts on nationalism and their comments on this paper. A version of this article will appear in 1994 in a Council on Foreign Relations volume edited by Charles Kupchan.

1. A survey is Anthony D. Smith, *Theories of Nationalism*, 2nd ed. (New York: Harper & Row, 1983). Prominent recent works include: Ernest Gellner, *Nations and Nationalism* (Ithaca: Cornell University Press, 1983); Anthony D. Smith, *The Ethnic Origins of Nations* (Oxford: Basil Blackwell, 1986); E.J. Hobsbawm, *Nations and Nationalism Since 1780* (New York: Cambridge University Press, 1990); Benedict Anderson, *Imagined Communities: Reflections on the Origin and Spread of Nationalism*, rev. ed. (London: Verso, 1991); Liah Greenfeld, *Nationalism: Five Roads to Modernity* (Cambridge: Harvard University Press, 1992); and Barry R. Posen, "Nationalism, the Mass Army, and Military Power," *International Security*, Vol. 18, No. 2 (Fall 1993), pp. 80–124. However, the nationalism literature leaves ample room for more work on nationalism's causes: much of it fails to frame hypotheses clearly and much does not systematically test hypotheses against empirical evidence; hence the literature leaves many questions unresolved.

2. Thus Anthony Smith notes that "the prevailing image of nationalism in the West today is mainly negative," and Boyd Shafer states his "belief that nationalism, especially when carried to extremes, leads to war and destruction." Smith, *Theories of Nationalism*, p. 8; Boyd C. Shafer, *Faces of Nationalism* (New York: Harcourt Brace Jovanovich, 1972), p. xiii. Yet the entry under "Nationalism and War" in Louis Snyder's 435-page *Encyclopedia of Nationalism* fills only two pages, and its bibliography lists no works focused on the topic. Louis L. Snyder, *Encyclopedia of Nationalism* (New York: Paragon, 1990), pp. 248–250. Exceptions exist: a few scholars have held a less purely critical view of nationalism, arguing that it has the potential for both good and evil. See, for example, Carlton J.H. Hayes, *Essays on Nationalism* (New York: Macmillan, 1926), pp. 245–275; Hayes's views are summarized in Snyder, *Encyclopedia of Nationalism*, pp. 132–133. And the impact of nationalism on the risk of war is now receiving more attention: see especially Jack Snyder, "Nationalism and the Crisis of the Post-Soviet State," *Survival*, Vol. 35, No. 1 (Spring 1993), pp. 5–26; and Barry R. Posen, "The Security Dilemma and Ethnic Conflict," *Survival*, Vol. 35, No. 1 (Spring 1993), pp. 27–47. The Snyder and Posen pieces are also published in Michael E. Brown, ed., *Ethnic Conflict and International Security* (Princeton: Princeton University Press, 1993).

International Security, Vol. 18, No. 4 (Spring 1994), pp. 5–39
© 1994 by the President and Fellows of Harvard College and the Massachusetts Institute of Technology.

tions are largely undiscussed, hence the causal nexus between nationalism and war presents an important unsolved riddle.

This article explores that nexus. I define nationalism as a political movement having two characteristics: (1) individual members give their primary loyalty to their own ethnic or national community;[3] this loyalty supersedes their loyalty to other groups, e.g., those based on common kinship or political ideology; and (2) these ethnic or national communities desire their own independent state.[4] I leave the origins of nationalism unexplored, instead focusing on its effects on the risk of war. Seven questions are addressed: Does nationalism cause war? If so, what types of nationalism are most likely to cause war? How and why do they cause war? What causes these war-causing nationalisms? Under what conditions are they most dangerous? How, if at all, can the war-causing attributes of nationalism be suppressed

---

3. My usage of "ethnic community" follows Anthony Smith, who suggests that an ethnic community has six characteristics: a common name, a myth of common ancestry, shared memories, a common culture, a link with a historic territory or homeland (which it may or may not currently occupy), and a measure of common solidarity. See Smith, *Ethnic Origins of Nations*, pp. 22–30. Summarizing Smith nicely is Michael E. Brown, "Causes and Implications of Ethnic Conflict," in Brown, ed., *Ethnic Conflict and International Security*, pp. 3–26 at 4–5.
Smith's second criteria (myth of common ancestry) would exclude immigrant societies of diverse origin that have developed the other five characteristics of ethnic community, such as the immigrant peoples of the United States, Cuba, Argentina, Chile, and Brazil. The common usage of "nation" and "nationalism" includes these groups as nations that can have a nationalism, e.g., "American nationalism," "Argentine nationalism," "Chilean nationalism." I define nationalism as a movement of a "national community" as well as an "ethnic community" in order to include these nationalisms. My usage of "national" follows the *Dictionary of the Social Sciences*, which defines "nation" as "the largest society of people united by a common culture and consciousness," and which "occupies a common territory." Julius Gould and William L. Kolb, eds., *A Dictionary of the Social Sciences* (New York: Free Press of Glencoe, 1964), p. 451.
4. The academic literature defines nationalism in an annoyingly wide range of ways. My definition follows no other exactly, but it amalgamates the more prominent definitions: each of these include at least one element of my definition, that prime loyalty is owed to one's ethnic/ culture group, and/or that the group to which prime loyalty is given should have its own state. My usage most closely follows Rupert Emerson and Richard Cottam, who define nationalism (in Cottam's words) as "a belief on the part of a large group of people that they comprise a community, a nation, that is entitled to independent statehood, and a willingness of this group to grant their community a primary and terminal loyalty"; quoted in Shafer, *Faces of Nationalism*, p. 4. Similar is Hans Kohn, whose nationalists give "supreme loyalty" to their own nationality, and who see "the nation-state as the ideal form of political organization." Ibid. Also similar are E.J. Hobsbawm and Ernest Gellner, who define nationalism as "primarily a principle which holds that the political and national unit should be congruent." Hobsbawm, *Nations and Nationalism since 1780*, p. 9, quoting and adopting Gellner's definition. However, their definition, by describing nationalism as an idea holding that states and nationalities should be coterminous, omits the many nationalisms that would claim their own state while also denying the statehood aspirations of other nationalities, and also omits more modest nationalisms that are content to allow a diaspora beyond their state borders.

or neutralized? How large are the risks to peace posed by nationalism in today's Europe, and how can these risks be minimized? In answer I offer unproven hypotheses that I leave untested for now. Our stock of hypotheses on the consequences of nationalism is meager, hence our first order of business should be to expand it. This can set the stage for empirical inquiry by others.[5]

Causes of war or peace can be classified as proximate (causes that directly affect the odds of war) or remote (causes of these proximate causes, or background conditions required for their activation.) I explore proximate causes first, then turn to remote causes. Specifically, the next section of this article identifies varieties of nationalism that are most likely to cause war (including both civil and inter-state war). The section that follows it identifies the causes of these dangerous varieties of nationalism and the conditions that govern the size of the dangers they produce. Twenty-one hypotheses are proposed in all—nine main hypotheses and twelve sub-hypotheses. Some focus on the impact of the environment that surrounds nationalist movements; this environment can incline the movement toward peaceful or toward warlike behavior. Others focus on the impact of the movement's internal character, especially its ideology and vision of history; this, too, can incline the movement toward peace or war. These hypotheses are highlighted because they are deductively sound, survive plausibility probes, and in some cases generate policy prescriptions. They are summarized in Table 1.[6] Viewed together, they suggest that the effects of nationalism are highly varied: some types of nationalism are far more dangerous than other types, all types of nationalism are more dangerous under some conditions than under others, and nationalism can even dampen the risk of war under some conditions.

If accepted, these hypotheses provide a checklist for assessing the dangers posed by a given nationalist movement or by the spread of nationalism in a given region. To illustrate, I use them in the concluding section to assess the risks that nationalism now poses in Europe, because Europe is a region in flux whose future is much debated. This exercise suggests that nationalism

---

5. A similar exercise whose example influenced my design is Robert Jervis, "Hypotheses on Misperception," *World Politics*, Vol. 20, No. 3 (April 1968), pp. 454–479; reprinted in Robert J. Art and Robert Jervis, ed., *International Politics: Anarchy, Force, Political Economy, and Decision Making*, 2nd ed. (Glenview, Ill.: Scott, Foresman, 1985), pp. 510–526.

6. The text of this article identifies factors that govern the size of the risk posed by nationalism, and explains the proposed causal relationship. Table 1 restates these factors and explanations as hypotheses.

Table 1.   Hypotheses on Nationalism and War: Summary.

I. IMMEDIATE CAUSES
  1. The greater the proportion of state-seeking nationalities that are stateless, the greater the risk of war.
  2. The more that nationalities pursue the recovery of national diasporas, and the more they pursue annexationist strategies of recovery, the greater the risk of war.
  3. The more hegemonistic the goals that nationalities pursue toward one another, the greater the risk of war.
  4. The more severely nationalities oppress minorities living in their states, the greater the risk of war.

II. CAUSES OF THE IMMEDIATE CAUSES AND CONDITIONS REQUIRED FOR THEIR OPERATION

Structural Factors:
  1. Stateless nationalisms pose a greater risk of war if they have the strength to plausibly reach for freedom, and the central state has the will to resist their attempt.
  2. The more densely nationalities are intermingled, the greater the risk of war.
      a. The risks posed by intermingling are larger the more local (house-by-house) rather than regional (province-by-province) the pattern of intermingling.
      b. The risks posed by intermingling are larger if the rescue of diasporas by homelands is difficult but possible; smaller if rescue is either impossible or easy.
  3. The greater the defensibility and legitimacy of borders, and the greater the correspondence between these political borders and communal boundaries, the smaller the risk of war.
      a. The less secure and defensible the borders of emerging nation-states, the greater the risk of war.
      b. The greater the international legitimacy of the borders of emerging nation-states, the smaller the risk of war.
      c. The more closely the boundaries of emerging nation-states follow ethnic boundaries, the smaller the risk of war.

---

poses very little danger of war in Western Europe, but poses large dangers in the East, especially in the former Soviet Union. Current Western European nationalisms are benign, and the conditions required for a return to the malignant nationalisms of 1870–1945 are almost wholly absent. In contrast, many Eastern nationalisms have many (though not all) of the attributes that

---

Table 1, cont.

Political/Environmental Factors:

4. The greater the past crimes committed by nationalities toward one another, the greater the risk of war.
   a. The better these crimes are remembered by the victims, the greater the risk of war.
   b. The more that responsibility for past crimes can be attached to groups still on the scene, the greater the risk of war.
   c. The less contrition and repentance shown by the guilty groups, the greater the risk of war.
   d. The greater the coincidence of power and victimhood, the greater the risk of war.
5. The more severely nationalities oppress minorities now living in their states, the greater the risk of war. (This restates Hypothesis No. I.4; I list it twice because it operates as both a direct and a remote cause of war.)

Perceptual Factors:

6. The more divergent are the beliefs of nationalities about their mutual history and their current conduct and character, the greater the risk of war.
   a. The less legitimate the governments or leaders of nationalist movements, the greater their propensity to purvey mythical nationalist beliefs, hence the greater the risk of war.
   b. The more the state must demand of its citizens, the greater its propensity to purvey mythical nationalist beliefs, hence the greater the risk of war.
   c. If economic conditions deteriorate, publics become more receptive to scapegoat myths, hence such myths are more widely believed, hence war is more likely.
   d. If independent evaluative institutions are weak or incompetent, myths will more often prevail, hence war is more likely.

I argue make nationalism dangerous; hence the risk of large-scale violence stemming from the now-rising tide of Eastern nationalism is substantial.

What prescriptions follow? The character and consequences of nationalism are not written in stone. The Western powers have some capacity to influence the character and consequences of Eastern nationalist movements, and should try to channel it in benign directions. Most importantly, the Western powers should promote full respect for minority rights, democracy, and official respect for historical truth; if Eastern nationalisms adopt these programs, the risks they pose will sharply diminish.

Varieties of Nationalism: Which Cause War?

Four primary attributes of a nationalist movement determine whether it has a large or small potential to produce violence. These are: (1) The movement's political status: is statehood attained or unattained? (2) The movement's stance toward its national diaspora (if it has one): if the movement has a national state, but some members of the nation are dispersed or entrapped beyond the state's borders, does the nation accept continued separation from this diaspora, or does it seek to incorporate the diaspora in the national state? And if it seeks the diaspora's incorporation, will it accomplish this by immigration or by territorial expansion? (3) The movement's stance toward other nations: does it respect or deny other nationalities' right to national independence? (4) The movement's treatment of its own minorities: are these minorities respected or abused?

IS NATIONAL STATEHOOD ATTAINED OR UNATTAINED?
Nationalist movements without states raise greater risks of war because their accommodation requires greater and more disruptive change. Their struggle for national freedom can produce wars of secession, which in turn can widen to become international wars. Their freedom struggle can also injure the interests of other groups, displacing populations whose new grievances sow the seeds of future conflict, as Zionism's displacement of the Palestinian Arabs in 1948 sowed the seeds of later Arab-Israeli wars. Finally, the appearance of new states creates a new, less mature regional international system that lacks "rules of the game" defining the rights and obligations of its members toward one another, and norms of international conduct; these rights, obligations, and norms can take years to define, raising the risk of crises and collisions in the meantime.

The international system tolerates change poorly, but the accommodation of new nationalist movements requires it.[7] Thus the first measure of the risks

---

7. The dichotomy between stateless and state-possessing nationalist movements is analogous to the dichotomy in international relations between "satisfied" and "dissatisfied" powers; the latter disturb the peace in their effort to gain satisfaction, while the former cause less trouble.

to the peace of a region posed by nationalism is found in the proportion of its nationalist movements that remain unfulfilled in statehood, a factor expressed in the nation-to-state ratio. Are the supply of and demand for states in equilibrium or disequilibrium? Peace in a region is more likely the more closely a supply/demand equilibrium is approached.[8] Modern nationalism disrupted peace over the past two centuries partly because so many of the world's current nationalist movements were stateless at the outset, requiring vast change to accommodate their emergence. Nationalism still threatens peace because its full accommodation would require vast additional change: the number of states in the world has more than tripled since World War II (up from the 50 signers of the UN Charter in 1945, to 180-odd states today), but many nationalities remain stateless; the world has some 6000 language groups,[9] many of which have dormant or manifest aspirations for statehood.

In Western Europe the transition of nations to statehood is largely behind us: that region's remaining stateless nationalities are relatively few and weak. In Eastern Europe and the former Soviet Union, the problem is more serious because the transition to statehood, while largely fulfilled, is still incomplete. The bulk of these stateless nationalities are found in the former Soviet Union; 15 of the 104 nationalities in the former USSR have attained states, but the other 89 have not; these stateless nationalities total 25.6 million people, comprising 10 percent of the former USSR's total population.[10] Most of these nationalities are not potential candidates for statehood (e.g., the Jews) but

---

8. Wars can result from having too many states, as well as too few. If states are too many, wars of national unification will result, as they did in Germany and Italy in the nineteenth century, and as they might someday in the Arab world. In Europe, however, the problem everywhere is an excess of demand for states over the supply.

9. Alan Thein Durning, *Guardians of the Land: Indigenous Peoples and the Health of the Earth,* Worldwatch Paper No. 112 (Washington, D.C.: Worldwatch Institute, December 1992), p. 9. Durning reports that measured by spoken languages the world has 6000 cultures. Of these some 4000–5000 are indigenous, and comprise some 10 percent of the world's population. See also Michael Krauss, "The Language Extinction Catastrophe Just Ahead: Should Linguists Care?" paper presented at the 15th International Congress of Linguists, Quebec City, Quebec, Canada, August 10, 1992. For another estimate see Gunnar P. Nielsson, "States and 'Nation-Groups': A Global Taxonomy," in Edward A. Tiryakian and Ronald Rogowski, eds., *New Nationalisms of the Developed West* (Boston: Allen and Unwin, 1985), pp. 27–56. He identifies a global total of 589 ethnic groups, most of which are stateless (p. 33). He also found that only 41 of 161 states surveyed were ethnically homogeneous (in which one ethnic group comprises over 95 percent of the state's population); see ibid., Table 2.1, pp. 30–31.

10. These figures are for 1979, and are calculated from John L. Scherer, ed., *USSR Facts and Figures Annual,* Vol. 5 (Gulf Breeze, Fla.: Academic International Press, 1981), pp. 51–52. Of these stateless groups the ten largest are the Tatar (6.3 million), German (1.9 million), Jewish (1.8 million), Chuvash (1.8 million), Dagestan (1.7 million), Bashkir (1.4 million), Mordvin (1.2 million), Polish (1.2 million), Chechen (.8 million), and Udmurt (.7 million).

some might be (e.g., the Tatars, Chechen, Ingush, and Ossetians), and their reach for statehood could sow future friction.

ATTITUDE TOWARD THE NATIONAL DIASPORA: IS PARTIAL OR TOTAL NATIONAL UNITY PURSUED? ARE IMMIGRATIONIST OR EXPANSIONIST TACTICS USED?
Does the nationalist ideology posit that all or only a part of the national ethnic community must be incorporated in the national state? And if the whole nationality must be incorporated, will this be accomplished by immigration (bringing the diaspora to the state) or by territorial expansion (bringing the state to the diaspora)?

These questions suggest a distinction among three types of nationalism: "diaspora-accepting," "immigrationist," and "diaspora-annexing." Some nationalisms (the diaspora-accepting variety) are content with partial union (e.g., Chinese nationalism);[11] such nationalisms are less troublesome because they make fewer territorial demands on their neighbors. Some nationalisms (the immigrationist type) seek to incorporate their diasporas in the national state, but are content to pursue union by seeking immigration of the diaspora (current German nationalism and Zionist Jewish nationalism.) Such immigrationist nationalisms are also easy to accommodate. Finally, some nationalisms seek to incorporate their diasporas by means of territorial expansion (pre-1914 Pan-Germanism and current Pan-Serbianism are examples.) Such diaspora-annexing nationalisms are the most dangerous of the three, since their goals and tactics produce the greatest territorial conflict with others. Thus one scenario for war in the former Soviet Union lies in the possible appearance of a Pan-Russian nationalism that would seek to reincorporate by force the vast Russian diaspora now living in the non-Russian republics. This diaspora includes some 24 million Russians, or 17 percent of all Russians.[12] The future hinges heavily on whether Russian nationalism accepts separation from this diaspora (or seeks to ingather it by immigration), or instead forcibly seeks to annex it.[13]

---

11. The Chinese state has historically left the overseas Chinese to their own political devices. John E. Wills, "Maritime Asia, 1500–1800: The Interactive Emergence of European Domination," *American Historical Review,* Vol. 98, No. 1 (February 1993), pp. 83–105, at p. 87.
12. Calculated from Scherer, *USSR Facts and Figures Annual,* pp. 49–51.
13. Russia's extensive military meddling in the affairs of the other former Soviet republics during 1992–94 and the political rise of Vladimir Zhirinovsky in 1993 warns that a new Russian expansionism is already emerging. On this military meddling see Thomas Goltz, "Letter From Eurasia: The Hidden Russian Hand," *Foreign Policy,* No. 92 (Fall 1993), pp. 92–116.

ATTITUDE TOWARD OTHER INDEPENDENT NATIONALITIES:
TOLERANT OR HEGEMONISTIC?

Does the ideology of the nationalism incorporate respect for the freedom of other nationalities, or does it assume a right or duty to rule them? In other words, is the national ideology symmetrical (all nationalities deserve states) or asymmetrical (only our nationality deserves statehood; others should be denied it)?

Hegemonistic, or asymmetrical, nationalism is both the rarest and the most dangerous variety of nationalism. Interwar Nazi nationalism in Germany, fascist nationalism in Mussolini's Italy, and militarist nationalism in imperial Japan illustrate such hegemonistic nationalism; the wars they caused illustrate its results.[14] No European nationalism today displays such hegemonism, but the vast trouble that it caused in the past advises alertness to its possible reappearance in Europe or elsewhere.

THE DEGREE OF NATIONAL RESPECT FOR MINORITY RIGHTS: HIGH OR LOW?

Is the nationalism minority-respecting, or minority-oppressing? A minority-respecting nationalism grants equal rights to other nationalities lying within the boundaries of its claimed state; it may even grant their right to secede and establish their own state. A minority-oppressing nationalism denies such rights to these other nationalities, subjugating them instead. Many of the nationalisms of immigrant nations (American, Anglo-Canadian) have been relatively minority-respecting (in the Canadian case this includes a tacit right to secession, which the Quebecois may soon exercise.) Non-immigrant nationalisms often display far less tolerance for their minorities: prominent current examples include Iraq's and Turkey's oppression of their Kurdish minorities, Bulgaria's oppression of its Turks, China's cruelties in Tibet, Croatia's intolerance toward its Serb minority, and Serbian oppression of its

---

14. On twentieth-century German nationalism, see Louis L. Snyder, *German Nationalism: The Tragedy of a People*, 2nd ed. (Port Washington, New York: Kennikat Press, 1969); Louis L. Snyder, *From Bismarck to Hitler: The Background of Modern German Nationalism* (Williamsport: Bayard Press, 1935); and Hans Kohn, *The Mind of Germany: The Education of a Nation* (New York: Harper and Row, 1960). On official ideas and perceptions in fascist Italy see Denis Mack Smith, *Mussolini's Roman Empire* (Harmondsworth, U.K.: Penguin, 1977). On domestic currents in imperial Japan see Saburo Ienaga, *The Pacific War, 1931–1945* (New York: Pantheon, 1978); and Ienaga, "The Glorification of War in Japanese Education," *International Security*, Vol. 18, No. 3 (Winter 1993/94), pp. 113–133. Nationalism is not, of course, the only possible source of claims against neighbors. These can also arise from non-nationalist expansionist political ideologies (communism), from hegemonistic religious ideas (the crusading Christianity of the middle ages), from safety concerns arising from the security dilemma, from economic greed, and so forth.

Slavic Moslem and Albanian minorities. Nazi German nationalism was an extreme case of a minority-oppressing nationalism.

The first three attributes—is statehood attained? attitude toward diaspora? attitude toward other independent nationalities?—define the scope of a nationalist movement's claims against others; conversely, the fourth attribute—policy toward minorities?—helps determine the scope of others' claims against the movement. The larger these others' goals become, the more they will collide with the movement's goals, raising the risk of war. Minority-oppressing nationalism can cause war in two ways: (1) by provoking violent secessions by its captive nations; or (2) by spurring the homelands of these captive nations to move forcefully to free their oppressed co-nationals[15] (as Croatian threats against the Serb minority in Croatia helped spawn the Serb attack on Croatia in 1991).[16] Minority-oppressing nationalism is most dangerous if the oppressed minorities have nearby friends who have the capacity to protect the oppressed nation by force. (The Serbo-Croat war exploded partly because Croatia's Serbs had such a friend in Serbia). The attitude of many nationalisms in Eastern Europe and the former Soviet Union toward their minorities remains undefined, and the future hinges on whether they evolve toward minority respect or oppression.

These four attributes can be used to create a nationalism "danger-scale," expressing the level of danger posed by a given nationalism, or by the spread of nationalism in a given region. If all four attributes are benign, the nationalism poses little danger of war, and may even bolster peace. Specifically, a nationalism is benign if it has achieved statehood; has limited unity goals (i.e., accepts the existence of any unincorporated diaspora) or adopts an immigrationist strategy for ingathering its diaspora; posits no claim to rule other nationalities living beyond its national territory; and respects the rights of minorities found in this territory. Multiplied, such nationalisms may even dampen the risk of war, by making conquest more difficult: where these nationalisms are prevalent, conquest is harder because nation-states are

---

15. Thus the second and fourth attributes are related: if some states oppress their minorities (the fourth attribute) this affects other states' propensity to pursue diaspora recovery (the second attribute).

16. On the war's origins, including the important role of Croatia's pre-war threats against its Serb minority, see Misha Glenny, "The Massacre of Yugoslavia," *New York Review of Books,* January 30, 1992, pp. 30–35, at 30–31; and Misha Glenny, *The Fall of Yugoslavia: The Third Balkan War* (London: Penguin, 1992), pp. 12–14, 123. An account stressing international aspects of the war's origins is Morton H. Halperin and David J. Scheffer with Patricia L. Small, *Self-Determination in the New World Order* (Washington, D.C.: Carnegie Endowment, 1992), pp. 32–38.

among the most difficult type of state to conquer (since nationalism provides an inspirational liberation doctrine that can be used to mobilize strong popular resistance to conquest).[17] As a result strong states will be deterred from reaching for regional or global hegemony, and will also be less fearful that others might achieve it; hence all states will compete less fiercely with one another.[18] In contrast, a nationalism is bound to collide with others if all four attributes are malign: If the nationalism has no state, the risk of civil war arising from its struggle for national independence is increased; this also raises the risk of inter-state war, since civil war can widen to engulf nearby states. If, after achieving statehood, the nationalism seeks to incorporate a diaspora by force, oppresses minorities found in its claimed national territory, and seeks hegemony over nationalities lying beyond that territory, violence between the nationalism and its neighbors is inevitable.

Causes and Conditions for War-Causing Nationalism

What factors determine whether these four variables will have benign or malignant values? What conditions are required for malignant values to have malignant effects? The deciding factors and conditions are grouped below into three broad families: structural (those arising from the geographic and demographic arrangement of a nation's people); political-environmental (those arising from the past or present conduct of a people's neighbors); and perceptual (those arising from the nationalist movement's self-image and its

---

17. On the greater peacefulness of a defense-dominant world, see Robert Jervis, "Cooperation Under the Security Dilemma," *World Politics,* Vol. 30, No. 2 (January 1978), pp. 167–214.

18. Thus the evident power of nationalism helped dampen Soviet-American competition during the Cold War, by persuading some in the West that nationalism imposed a natural limit on Soviet expansion. These observers argued that the Western powers need not actively check Soviet expansionism at every point because local nationalism could defeat it alone, nor move actively to roll back Soviet gains, because these gains would eventually be rolled back by indigenous nationalism, and in the meantime nationalist resistance would bleed Soviet power. For example, George Kennan took a calm approach to containment partly because he believed that resistant local nationalism would check Soviet expansion in the short run, and would rend the Soviet empire in the long run. See John Lewis Gaddis, *Strategies of Containment: A Critical Appraisal of Postwar American National Security Policy* (New York: Oxford University Press, 1982), pp. 42–48. Other arguments for Cold War restraint that rested in part on the power of nationalism included Arthur M. Schlesinger, *The Bitter Heritage: Vietnam and American Democracy 1941–1968,* rev. ed. (Greenwich: Fawcett, 1968), pp. 78–80; Jerome Slater, "Dominos in Central America: Will They Fall? Does It Matter?" *International Security,* Vol. 12, No. 2 (Fall 1987), pp. 105–134, at 113; and Stephen M. Walt, "The Case for Finite Containment," *International Security,* Vol. 14, No. 1 (Summer 1989), pp. 3–49, at 26–27. Had nationalism been weaker, these arguments would have lost force, leaving a stronger case for more aggressive American policies.

images of others, including its images of both sides' past and present conduct and character).

STRUCTURAL FACTORS: THE GEOGRAPHIC, DEMOGRAPHIC,
AND MILITARY SETTING

The size of the risks posed by nationalism is influenced by the balance of power and of will between stateless nationalisms and the central states that hold them captive; by the degree and pattern of regional ethnic intermingling; by the defensibility and legitimacy of the borders of new national states; and by the correspondence of these borders with ethnic boundaries.

THE DOMESTIC BALANCE OF POWER AND OF WILL. Unattained nationalisms are more troublesome under two conditions: (1) the movement has the strength to reach plausibly for statehood; and (2) the central state has the will to resist this attempt.

Stateless nationalisms whose statehood is unattainable will lie dormant, their emergence deterred by the power of the central state.[19] Nationalism becomes manifest and can produce war when the power-balance between the central state and the captive nationalism shifts to allow the possibility of successful secession. Thus two safe conditions exist: where national statehood is already attained; and where it is not attained, but clearly cannot be. The danger zone lies between, in cases where statehood has not been attained yet is attainable or appears to be.[20] In this zone we find wars of nationalist secession.[21] Such conflicts can, in turn, grow into international wars: examples include the 1912–14 Balkan secessionist struggles that triggered World War I, and the 1991–92 Serbo-Croatian conflict.

---

19. If nationalism is unattainable it may not even appear: the captive nation will submerge the nationalist thought. This is similar to the realist argument that imperialism is a function of capability: states imperialize simply when and where they can. Likewise, and conversely, nationalism is in part simply a function of capability: it emerges where it can.

20. We can scale up this logic from single states to regions by asking: do nations have states in proportion to their power? That is, does the state-to-nation ratio correspond with the state-to-nation power ratio? Or do nations have fewer states than their power justifies? If the former is the case, peace is more likely. But if nations have fewer states than their power would allow, trouble results in the form of wars of secession.

21. Overall, then, three variables matter: (1) the supply of states; (2) the demand for states; (3) the capacity of submerged nations to acquire states. Peace is stronger if supply and demand are in equilibrium; or if supply and capacity are in equilibrium. In one case, nationalism is satisfied; in the other, it is dissatisfied but impotent. Dangers arise if both supply and demand, and supply and capacity, are not in equilibrium. We then have submerged nationalisms that both desire and can assert the demand for statehood.

The Third World nationalisms of the twentieth century erupted partly because the spread of small arms and literacy shifted the balance of power in favor of these nationalisms, and against their imperial captors. Nationalism emerged because it could. Likewise, nationalism exploded in the former Soviet Union in the late 1980s partly because Soviet central power had waned.

War is inevitable if central states have the will to resist emerging nationalist/ secessionist movements, but these movements can win freedom without violence if that will is missing. Many sub-Saharan African states gained freedom in the 1960s without violence because the European colonial powers lost their imperial will. Likewise, the emergence of non-Russian nationalisms in the former Soviet Union was accompanied by (and encouraged by) the loss of imperial will in Moscow; this loss of will at the center allowed the non-Russians to escape the Soviet empire without waging wars of secession. French decolonization was far more violent, spawning large wars in Vietnam and Algeria, because the French metropole retained its will even after nationalism gained momentum in the French empire.

The will of the central state is largely governed by its domestic politics, but is also determined partly by demographic facts. Specifically, central governments can allow secession more easily if secession would leave a homogeneous rump central state, since permitting secession then sets a less damaging precedent. Thus the Czechs could accept Slovak independence without fear of setting a precedent that would trigger another secession, since there is no potential secessionist group in the rump Czech Republic. Likewise, the United States could grant independence to the Philippines fairly easily in 1946 because the United States had few other colonies, and none of these were large or valuable, hence Philippine independence set no dangerous precedents. Conversely, the Austro-Hungarian empire strongly resisted secessions before 1914 because the empire contained many potential secessionists who might be encouraged if any secession were allowed.

THE DEMOGRAPHIC ARRANGEMENT OF NATIONAL POPULATIONS: ARE THEY INTERMINGLED OR HOMOGENEOUS? Are nationality populations densely intermingled? If they are, does this create large or small national diasporas? Intermingling raises the risk of communal conflict during the struggle for national freedom, as groups that would be trapped as minorities in a new national state oppose its reach for freedom. Dispersion and intermingling will also trap some co-ethnics outside the boundaries of their nation-states; this raises the danger that new nation-states will pursue diaspora-recovering expansionism after they gain statehood, and the possibility that their abuse of minorities will trigger attack from outside.[22]

These dangers are reduced if national populations are compact and homogenous—diasporas and minorities then occur only if political boundaries fail to follow ethnic boundaries. They are intensified if the nationality is dispersed abroad, and intermingled with others at home. The Czechs, for example, can pursue nationalism with little risk to the peace of their neighborhood, because they have no diaspora abroad, and few minorities at home. They need not limit their goals or learn to accommodate minorities. The 1947 partition of India was a far bloodier process than the 1992 Czech-Slovak divorce partly because Hindus and Moslems were far more intermingled than Czechs and Slovaks. The partition of Yugoslavia has been especially violent partly because nationalities in former Yugoslavia are more densely intermingled than any others in Eastern or Western Europe outside the former Soviet Union.[23]

Overall, nationalism poses greater dangers in Eastern than Western Europe because the peoples of Eastern Europe are more densely intermingled. A survey of Eastern Europe reveals roughly a dozen minority group pockets that may seek independence or be claimed by other countries.[24] The ethno-

---

22. The scope and structure of intermingling governs the acuteness of what might be called the "inter-ethnic security dilemma": this dilemma is posed where one group cannot achieve physical security without diminishing the physical security of other groups. It is analogous to the interstate security dilemma of international relations, except that the clashing units are ethnic or culture groups, not states.

23. Moreover, Yugoslavia's one easy secession—that of Slovenia—was easy because the Slovene population was not intermingled with others. An excellent ethnographic map of the former Yugoslavia that details its intermingling is Central Intelligence Agency, "Peoples of Yugoslavia: Distribution by Opstina, 1981 Census," Map No. 505956 9-83 (543994). A useful though less detailed ethnographic map covering all of Eastern Europe including former Yugoslavia is Central Intelligence Agency, "Ethnic Majorities and Minorities," in Central Intelligence Agency, *Atlas of Eastern Europe* (Washington, D.C.: U.S. Government Printing Office [U.S. GPO], August 1990), p. 6. A good ethnographic map of the former USSR is National Geographic Society, "Peoples of the Soviet Union," supplement to *National Geographic*, Vol. 149, No. 2 (February 1976), p. 144A; back issues of *National Geographic* containing this map are available from the National Geographic Society, Washington, D.C.

24. These include Hungarians in Romania, Slovakia, and Serbia; Poles in Lithuania, Belarus, Ukraine, and the Czech Republic; Germans in Poland and the Czech Republic; Turks in Bulgaria; Greeks in Albania; Albanians in Serbia and Macedonia; Croats in Bosnia-Herzegovina; and Serbs in Croatia and Bosnia-Herzegovina. Summaries include F. Stephen Larrabee, "Long Memories and Short Fuses: Change and Instability in the Balkans," *International Security*, Vol. 15, No. 3 (Winter 1990/91), pp. 58–91; Istvan Deak, "Uncovering Eastern Europe's Dark History," *Orbis*, Vol. 34, No. 1 (Winter 1989), pp. 51–65; Barry James, "Central Europe Tinderboxes: Old Border Disputes," *International Herald Tribune*, January 1, 1990, p. 5; and the CIA map cited above, "Ethnic Majorities and Minorities, 1990."

graphic structure of the former Soviet Union is even more ominous; an ethnographic map of the former USSR reveals massively intermingled nationalities, scattered in scores of isolated pockets, a mosaic far more tangled and complex than any found elsewhere in Europe except the former Yugoslavia.[25]

Two aspects of intermingling determine the size of the dangers it poses: the scope of intermingling, and the pattern of intermingling. All intermingling causes trouble, but some patterns of intermingling cause more trouble than others.

Groups can be intermingled on a regional scale (regions are heterogeneous, small communities are homogeneous) or local scale (even small communities are heterogeneous, as in Sarajevo.) Regional intermingling is more easily managed, because inter-group relations can be negotiated by elites. In contrast, elites can lose control of events when intermingling extends to the local level: conflict can flare against the wishes of elites when unofficial killers seize the agenda by sparking a spiral of private violence. Local intermingling can also produce conflict-dampening personal friendships and inter-ethnic marriages, but the Bosnian conflict shows the limits of this tempering effect. Overall, local intermingling is more dangerous.

The most dangerous pattern of regional intermingling is one that leaves elements of one or both groups insecurely at the mercy of the other, but also allows for the possibility of forcible rescue—either by self-rescue (secession) or external rescue (intervention by an already-free homeland).

If rescue is impossible, then the goal of secession or reunion with a homeland will be abandoned. Israel cannot rescue Soviet Jewry, except by immigration, and Ukraine cannot rescue the Ukrainian diaspora in Russia; hence neither considers forceful rescue. This lowers the risk of war.

If rescue is easy, it may not be attempted, since the threat of rescue is enough to deter abuse of the diaspora. Russia could fairly easily rescue the Russian minority in the Baltics and perhaps elsewhere on the Russian periphery, because much of the Russian diaspora lies clustered near the Russian

---

25. See the maps cited in note 23 above. Overall, 16 percent of the titular peoples of the 15 successor states of the former Soviet Union, totalling 39 million people, live outside their home states ("titular peoples": the peoples after whom republics are named, e.g., Armenians, Kazakhs, Russians, etc.). Calculated from Scherer, *USSR Facts and Figures Annual*, pp. 49–51. And, as noted above, another 10 percent of the former Soviet population (26 million people) are members of the 89 smaller nationalities without titular home republics ("titular home republic": a republic named after the nationality).

border, and Russia holds military superiority over its neighbors. These power realities may deter Russia's neighbors from abusing their Russian minorities, leaving Russia more room to take a relaxed attitude.[26]

It is in-between situations—those where rescue is possible, but only under optimal conditions—that are most dangerous. This situation will tempt potential rescuers to jump through any windows of opportunity that arise. Forceful rescue is then driven by both fear and opportunity—fear that later the abuse of diasporas cannot be deterred by threatening to rescue them (since the difficulty of rescue will rob that threat of credibility), and by the opportunity to rescue the diaspora now by force.[27] Thus Serbia would have probably been unable to rescue the Serb diaspora in normal times: Serbia is too weak, and the Serbian diasporas in Croatia and Bosnia are too distant from Serbia. But rescue was feasible if Serbia made the attempt at a moment of peak Serbian military advantage. Such a moment emerged in 1990, after Serbia consolidated the weaponry of the Yugoslav army under its control, but before the Croatian and Bosnian states could organize strong militaries.[28] In contrast, such a moment may never emerge for Russia, because it can always rescue large parts of its diaspora should the need ever arise, leaving less need to seize an early opportunity.

These in-between situations are most troublesome when the diaspora is separated from the homeland by lands inhabited by others: wars of rescue then cause larger injury. In such cases rescue requires cutting a secure corridor through these lands; this, in turn, requires the forcible expulsion of the resident population, with its attendant horrors and cruelties. In 1991 the Serbian diaspora in Croatia and Bosnia was cut off from the Serb homeland by walls of Moslem-inhabited territory,[29] and the vast Serbian cruelties against the Bosnian Moslems during 1992–93 grew mainly from Serbia's effort to punch corridors through these walls in order to attach these diasporas to Serbia proper. In contrast, more of Russia's diaspora is contiguous to Russia, hence a Russian war of rescue would do relatively less harm to others innocently in the way (though it would still do plenty of harm.)

---

26. Making this argument is Posen, "The Security Dilemma and Ethnic Conflict," pp. 32–35.
27. See Posen, "The Security Dilemma and Ethnic Conflict," pp. 32–38.
28. The intensification of fighting between Armenia and Azerbaijan in 1991–92 had similar origins: Armenia moved to free Nagorno-Karabakh at a moment that Armenia's power relative to Azerbaijan's was at its peak.
29. See Central Intelligence Agency, "Peoples of Yugoslavia."

BORDERS: DEFENSIBILITY, LEGITIMACY, AND BORDER/ETHNIC CORRESPON-
DENCE. The risks to peace posed by a nationalism's emergence are governed
partly by the defensibility and international legitimacy of the nation's borders, and by the degree of correspondence between these political borders
and ethnic boundaries.

The satisfaction of national demands for statehood extends international
anarchy by creating more states: hence nationalism's effects are governed
partly by the character of the extended anarchy that it creates. Some anarchies
are relatively peaceful, others more violent. The acuteness of the security
dilemma is a key factor governing the answer. Anarchy is a precondition for
international war, hence extending anarchy may expand the risk of war, but
this is not always the case: the fragmentation of states can deepen peace if
it leaves the world with states that are more difficult to conquer, hence are
more secure, than the older states from which they were carved. The character of boundaries helps decide the issue: if the new borders are indefen-
sible, the net impact of the creation of new national states will be warlike; if
borders are highly defensible, the net impact may be peaceful.[30]

Defensible boundaries reduce the risk of war because they leave new states
less anxious to expand for security reasons, while also deterring others from
attacking them. The nations of Western Europe can be more peaceful than
those of the East because they are endowed with more defensible borders:
the French, Spanish, British, Italian, and Scandinavian nations have natural
defenses formed by the Alps and the Pyrenees, and by the waters of the
English Channel, the Baltic, and the North Sea. Icelandic nationalism is
especially unproblematic because geography makes Iceland unusually secure,
and almost incapable of attack. In contrast, the nationalities living on the
exposed plains of Eastern Europe and western Asia contend with a harsher
geography: with few natural barriers to invasion, they are more vulnerable
to attack, hence are more tempted to attack others in preemptive defense.[31]
They are therefore more likely to disturb the status quo, or to be victims of
other disturbers.

The international legitimacy of a new nation's borders helps determine the
level of danger raised when it gains independence: if borders lack interna-

---

30. The new states may also be more defensible than their parent states because they can call
upon nationalism as a mobilizing defensive force, as their multi-ethnic parent states could not.
31. Likewise, Germany has produced the most troublesome Western nationalism partly because
German borders are relatively exposed.

tional legitimacy or are unsettled altogether, demands for border changes will arise, providing new occasions for conflict. The successor states of the former Soviet Union find themselves with borders drawn by Stalin or other Bolshevik rulers; these have correspondingly small legitimacy. Israel's post-1948 boundaries at first lacked international legitimacy because they had no historical basis, having arisen simply from truce lines expressing the military outcome of the 1948 war. In contrast, the borders of the recently-freed states of Eastern Europe have greater legitimacy because they have firmer grounding in history, and some were the product of earlier international negotiation and agreement.

Borders may bisect nationalities, or may follow national demographic divides. Nation-bisecting borders are more troublesome, because they have the same effect as demographic intermingling: they entrap parts of nationalities within the boundaries of states dominated by other ethnic groups, giving rise to expansionism by the truncated nation. Thus Hungary's borders bisect (and truncate) the Hungarian nation, giving rise to a (now dormant but still surviving) Hungarian revanchism against Slovakia, Serbia, and Rumania.[32] The Russian/Ukrainian border bisects both nationalities, creating the potential for movements to adjust borders in both countries.

The borders of new states can arise in two main ways: from violent military struggle (e.g., Israel) or as a result of cession of sovereignty to existing administrative units whose boundaries were previously defined by the parent multiethnic state (e.g., former Soviet Union). War-born borders often have the advantage of following ethnic lines, because the cruelties of war often cause ethnic cleansing, and offensives lose strength at ethnic boundaries; inherited administrative borders (e.g., the boundaries of Azerbaijan, which entrap the Armenians of Nagorno-Karabakh) more often plant the charge of future conflict by dividing nations and creating diasporas. The peaceful dissolution of the former Soviet Union was thus a mixed blessing: its successor states emerged without violence, but with borders that captured unhappy diasporas behind them.

---

32. On latent Hungarian revanchism see, for example, Judith Ingram, "Boys Impatient for 'Great Hungary' to Take Wing," *New York Times*, January 15, 1993, p. A4. On its official manifestations see Stephen Engelberg with Judith Ingram, "Now Hungary Adds Its Voice to the Ethnic Tumult," *New York Times*, January 25, 1993, p. A3.

POLITICAL/ENVIRONMENTAL FACTORS: HOW HAVE NEIGHBORS BEHAVED?
HOW DO THEY NOW BEHAVE?

The conduct of nationalities and nation-states mirrors their neighbors' past and present conduct.

PAST CONDUCT: WERE GREAT CRIMES COMMITTED? The degree of harmony or conflict between intermingled nationalities depends partly on the size of the crimes committed by each against the other in the past; the greater these past crimes, the greater the current conflict. Memories of its neighbors' cruelties will magnify an emerging nation's impulse to ingather its diaspora, converting the nation from a diaspora-accepting to a diaspora-annexing attitude. Thus the vast Croatian mass-murders of Serbs during the 1940s were the taproot that fed violent pan-Serbianism after 1990: Serbs vowed "never again," and argued that they must incorporate the Serbian diaspora in Croatia to save it from new pogroms.[33] Past suffering can also spur nations to oppress old tormentors who now live among them as minorities, sparking conflict with these minorities' home countries. Thus the past horrors inflicted on the Baltic peoples by Stalinism fuels their discrimination against their Russian minorities today;[34] this discrimination, in turn, feeds anti-Baltic feeling in Russia. In contrast, non-victim nations are less aggressive toward both neighbors and minorities. Czech nationalism is benign partly because the Czechs have escaped real victimhood; Quebec nationalism is mild for the same reason.

Mass murder, land theft, and population expulsions are the crimes that matter most. Past exterminations foster diaspora-recovering ideologies that are justified by self-protection logic. Past land theft fosters territorial definitions of nationhood (e.g., the Israeli Likud's concept of "the Land of Israel," a place including once-Jewish lands that Likud argues were wrongfully taken by others) and claims to land that excludes the rights of peoples now on that land (the Likud rejects equal rights for the Palestinian inhabitants of these

---

33. See Bette Denich, "Unbury the Victims: Nationalist Revivals of Genocide in Yugoslavia," Paper presented at the American Anthropological Association Annual Meeting, Chicago, Illinois, November 1991.

34. On the Baltic states' policies see Steven Erlanger, "Baltic Identity: Russians Wonder If They Belong: New Citizenship Rules May in Effect Expel the Ex-'Occupiers'," *New York Times*, November 22, 1992, p. 1. This Baltic anti-Russian discrimination reflects the great cruelties inflicted on the Baltic peoples by Stalin's government: during the years 1940–49 some 36 percent of the indigenous population of Latvia, 33 percent of the indigenous population of Estonia, and 32 percent of the indigenous population of Lithuania were killed, deported, or driven into exile. Dag Sebastian Ahlander, "Help Baltics Deal with Russian Minority," *New York Times* (letter to the editor), December 6, 1992, p. E18.

once-Jewish lands; Serbs likewise reject equal rights for Albanian Kosovars who Serbs claim wrongfully took Serb land.) Past expulsions and dispersions feed diaspora-intolerance: if others created the diaspora, it is argued, then others should pay the price for restoring the diaspora to the nation by making territorial concessions.

The scope of the dangers posed by past crimes is a function, in part, of whether these crimes are remembered, and whether victims can attach responsibility for crimes to groups that are still present. Crimes that have faded in the victims' memories have a less corrosive effect on intergroup relations; thus mayhem that occurred before written records poses fewer problems than more recent crimes that are better-recorded.[35]

Crimes committed by groups still on the scene pose more problems than crimes committed by vanished groups. This, in turn, is a matter of interpretation: who committed the crime in question? Can inherited blame be attached to any present group? Thus the Ukrainians can assess responsibility for Stalin's vast murders of Ukrainians in several ways.[36] Were they committed by a crazed Georgian? This interpretation is benign: it points the finger at a single man who is long gone from the scene. Were they committed by that now-vanished tribe, the Bolsheviks? This interpretation is also benign: those responsible have miraculously disappeared, leaving no target for violence. Or, more ominously, were these the crimes of the Russian empire and the Russian people? This interpretation would guarantee bitter Russian-Ukrainian conflict, because the crimes in question were so enormous, and many of the "criminals" live in Ukraine,[37] making ready targets for hatred, and setting the stage for a Russian-Ukrainian conflict-spiral. Such a spiral is more likely because Russians would not accept the blame assigned them: they count themselves among the victims, not the perpetrators, of Bolshe-

---

35. For example, native Americans can coexist, albeit uneasily, with European immigrants partly because the enormous horrors that the Europeans inflicted on the natives have faded into the mists of history. On these horrors see David E. Stannard, *American Holocaust: Columbus and the Conquest of the New World* (New York: Oxford University Press, 1992). Stannard estimates that the native population of the Americas fell by roughly 95 percent—in absolute numbers by about 71–95 million people—after the European arrival in 1492 (p. 268). If so, this was the greatest human-caused human death in world history.

36. On these murders see Robert Conquest, *The Harvest of Sorrow: Soviet Collectivization and the Terror-Famine* (New York: Oxford University Press, 1986). Stalin's other crimes are covered in Robert Conquest, *The Great Terror: A Reassessment* (New York: Oxford University Press, 1990).

37. Ukraine contains 10.5 million Russians, 21 percent of its total population. Calculated from Scherer, *USSR Facts and Figures Annual*, p. 49.

vism's crimes, and they would view others' demands that they accept blame as a malicious outrage.

The danger posed by past crimes also depends on the criminal group's later behavior: has it apologized or otherwise shown contrition? Or has it shown contempt for its victims' suffering? Nazi Germany's crimes were among the greatest in human history, but Germany has re-established civil relations with its former victims by acknowledging its crimes and showing contrition, e.g., by postwar German leaders' public apologies and symbolic acts of repentance. Conversely, Turkey has denied the great crimes it committed against the Armenian people during World War I;[38] this display of contempt has sustained an Armenian hatred that is still expressed in occasional acts of violent anti-Turkish retribution.

A final significant factor lies in the degree of coincidence of power and victimhood. Are the groups with the greatest historic grievances also the groups with the greatest power today? Or is past victimhood confined to today's weaker groups? Things are more dangerous when power and aggrievement coincide, since this combination brings together both the motive and the capacity to make trouble; when power and aggrievement are separated, grievances have less effects. On this count the past crimes of the Russian and Bolshevik states leave a less dangerous legacy than the crimes committed in the former Yugoslavia during World War II, because the strongest group in the former Soviet Union (the Russians) is the least aggrieved; in contrast, in former Yugoslavia the strongest group (the Serbs) is the most aggrieved.

CURRENT CONDUCT: ARE MINORITY RIGHTS RESPECTED? As noted earlier, nations are less diaspora-accepting if others abuse the rights of that diaspora; such abuse magnifies the impulse to incorporate the territory of the diaspora by force. Thus Serbia's 1991 attack on Croatia was spurred partly by Croatian threats against the Serbian minority.[39] Likewise, Russia's attitude toward the

---

38. On Turkish denial of these murders see Roger W. Smith, "The Armenian Genocide: Memory, Politics, and the Future," in Richard G. Hovannisian, ed. *The Armenian Genocide: History, Politics, Ethics* (New York: St. Martin's, 1992), pp. 1–20; Vahakn N. Dadrian, "Ottoman Archives and Denial of the Armenian Genocide," in Hovannisian, *Armenian Genocide*, pp. 280–310; and Roger W. Smith, "Genocide and Denial: The Armenian Case and Its Implications," *Armenian Review*, Vol. 42 (Spring 1989), pp. 1–38. On the general disappearance of the Armenian people from Turkish historical writings, see Clive Foss, "The Turkish View of Armenian History: A Vanishing Nation," in Hovannisian, *Armenian Genocide*, pp. 250–279.
39. Glenny, "The Massacre of Yugoslavia," pp. 30–31; and Glenny, *The Fall of Yugoslavia*, pp. 12–14, 123.

Russian diaspora will be governed partly by the treatment of the Russian diaspora in their new homelands. Oppressive policies will provoke wider Russian aims.[40]

PERCEPTUAL FACTORS: NATIONALIST SELF-IMAGES AND IMAGES OF OTHERS

The effects of nationalism depend heavily on the beliefs of nationalist movements, especially their self-images and their images of their neighbors. Nations can co-exist most easily when these beliefs converge—when they share a common image of their mutual history, and of one another's current conduct and character. This can be achieved either by common convergence of images on something close to the "truth," or by convergence on the same distortion of the truth. Relations are worst if images diverge in self-justifying directions. This occurs if nations embrace self-justifying historical myths, or adopt distorted pictures of their own and others' current conduct and character that exaggerate the legitimacy of their own cause. Such myths and distortions can expand a nation's sense of its right and its need to oppress its minorities or conquer its diaspora. If carried to extreme such myths can also transform nationalism from symmetrical to asymmetrical—from a purely self-liberating enterprise into a hegemonistic enterprise.[41]

---

40. Even moderate Russian officials have voiced deep concern over the rights of Russian minorities in nearby states. See, for example, Sergei Stankevich, "Russia in Search of Itself," *The National Interest*, No. 28 (Summer 1992), pp. 47–51, at 49–51; and "Four Comments" in ibid. pp. 51–55, at 51–53. They have so far proposed solutions within the framework of international law and institutions: for example, Russian Foreign Minister Andrei Kozyrev suggested in 1992 that the UN establish a mechanism to protect the rights of Russians in non-Slavic former Soviet republics. Thomas Friedman, "Russian Appeals to U.N. to Safeguard Minorities," *New York Times*, September 23, 1992, p. A17. If the rights of these minorities remain otherwise unprotected, however, it seems likely that Russia will act on its own to protect them.

41. In the past I referred to such myth-poisoned nationalism as "hypernationalism." See Stephen Van Evera, "Primed for Peace," *International Security*, Vol. 15, No. 3 (Winter 1990/1991), pp. 7–57, at 47–48n ("Hypernationalism is artificially generated or magnified by chauvinist myths. Conflicts arising from hypernationalism thus derive from the beliefs of nations," not from their circumstances.) However, my usage is narrower than others: see, for example, John Mearsheimer, who defines hypernationalism as the belief that other nationalities are "both inferior and threatening," and as an "attitude of contempt and loathing" toward other nations; Mearsheimer suggests these beliefs can arise from false propaganda or from real experience. John Mearsheimer, "Back to the Future: Instability in Europe After the Cold War," *International Security*, Vol. 15, No. 1 (Summer 1990), pp. 5–56, at 21. Others use the term "hypernationalism" still more broadly to refer to any type of nationalism that spawns aggressive conduct and war. I avoid the term in this paper because it has acquired these several meanings. I regret adding to the confusion, and suggest we settle on a single usage—probably Mearsheimer's, since it has seniority.

Chauvinist mythmaking is a hallmark of nationalism, practiced by nearly all nationalist movements to some degree.[42] These myths are purveyed through the schools, especially in history teaching;[43] through literature; or by political elites. They come in three principal varieties: self-glorifying, self-whitewashing, and other-maligning. Self-glorifying myths incorporate claims of special virtue and competence, and false claims of past beneficence toward others.[44] Self-whitewashing myths incorporate false denial of past wrong-doing against others.[45] Both types of myths can lead a nation to claim a right

---

42. Indeed, the intellectual history of Western nationalisms is largely a record of false claims of special self-virtue and of overwrought blaming of others. See examples in Shafer, *Faces of Nationalism*, pp. 313–342. However, myth is not an essential ingredient of nationalism: nationalism can also rest on a group solidarity based on truth, and the effects of nationalism are largely governed by the degree of truthfulness of the beliefs that a given nationalism adopts; as truthfulness diminishes, the risks posed by the nationalism increase.

43. As Ernst Renan has said, "Getting its history wrong is part of being a nation." Quoted in Hobsbawm, *Nations and Nationalism since 1780*, p. 12.

44. World War I–era European nationalists provide abundant examples of such self-glorification. General Friedrich Bernhardi, the German army's main propagandist, proclaimed in 1912 that the Germans are "the greatest civilized people known to history," and have "always been the standard-bearers of free thought" and "free from prejudice." Friedrich von Bernhardi, *Germany and the Next War*, trans. Allen H. Powles (New York: Longmans, Green, 1914, first published in Germany in 1912), pp. 14, 72. In 1915 German economist Werner Sombart declared that the Germans were "the chosen people of this century," and that this chosenness explained others' hostility: "Now we understand why other people hate us. They do not understand us but they fear our tremendous spiritual superiority." Kohn, *Mind of Germany*, p. 300–301. Richard Dehmel, a German writer, proclaimed in 1914: "We Germans *are* more humane than the other nations; we *do have* better blood and breeding, more soul, more heart, and more imagination." Klaus Schröter, "Chauvinism and its Tradition: German Writers and the Outbreak of the First World War," *Germanic Review*, Vol. 43, No. 2 (March 1968), pp. 120–135, at 126, emphasis in original. In Britain Thomas Macaulay wrote that the British were "the greatest and most highly civilized people that ever the world saw" and were "the acknowledged leaders of the human race in the causes of political improvement." Paul M. Kennedy, "The Decline of Nationalistic History in the West, 1900–1970," *Journal of Contemporary History*, Vol. 8, No. 1 (January, 1973), pp. 77–100, at 81. In the United States Senator Albert Beveridge proclaimed in 1899 that "God . . . has made us the master organizers of the world. . . . He has made us adept in government that we may administer government among savage and senile peoples. . . . He has marked the American people as His chosen nation . . ." Albert K. Weinberg, *Manifest Destiny: A Study of Nationalist Expansionism in American History* (Chicago: Quadrangle, 1963), p. 308. The Soviet government continued this tradition after 1918: the standard Soviet school history text of 1948 claimed that Russian scientists invented the telegraph, steam engine, electric lamp, and the airplane. E.H. Dance, *History the Betrayer: A Study in Bias* (Westport: Greenwood, 1960), pp. 67–68.

45. Innocence can be asserted by denying a barbarous action, or by reinterpreting the action to put a benign "spin" on it. Post-1919 German textbooks illustrate whitewash-by-denial: Weimar German textbooks denied German responsibility for World War I, falsely claiming that "there was no wish for war in Berlin" in 1914, and that "today every informed person . . . knows that Germany is absolutely innocent with regard to the outbreak of the war, and that Russia, France, and England wanted the war and unleashed it." Dance, *History the Betrayer*, p. 62. Nazi-era texts likewise claimed that "England willed the war" in 1914 after having "set Japan on Russia" in 1904. Dance, *History the Betrayer*, p. 57. Whitewash-by-spin is also common. When Nazi forces

to rule others ("we are especially virtuous, so our expansion benefits those we conquer"). They also lead a nation to view others' complaints against them as expressions of ungrateful malice: ("we have never harmed them; they slander us by claiming otherwise"). This can produce conflict-spirals,[46] as the nation responds to others' legitimate complaints with hostility, in expectation that the claimant knows its claims are illegitimate and will back down if challenged. The targets of this hostility, in turn, will take it as further evidence of the nation's inherent cruelty and injustice. Self-glorifying myth, if it contains claims of cultural superiority, can also feed false faith in one's capacity to defeat and subdue others, causing expansionist wars of optimistic miscalculation.

Other-maligning myth can incorporate claims of others' cultural inferiority, false blame of others for past crimes and tragedies, and false claims that others now harbor malign intentions against the nation.[47] Such myths sup-

---

overran Norway and Denmark in 1940 the Nazi party newspaper announced the invasion, but its headline proclaimed "GERMANY SAVES SCANDINAVIA!" William L. Shirer, *The Rise and Fall of the Third Reich: A History of Nazi Germany* (New York: Simon and Schuster, 1960), p. 698n. Similarly, after Soviet forces invaded Afghanistan in 1979 Leonid Brezhnev admitted the action but told the Soviet public: "There has been no Soviet 'intervention' or 'aggression' at all." Rather, Soviet forces were sent to Afghanistan "at its government's request," to defend Afghan "national independence, freedom and honor." L.I. Brezhnev, "Interview for Pravda, January 13, 1980," from *SShA: Ekonomika, Politika, Ideologiya*, No. 2 (February 1980), trans. Joint Publication Research Service, in *U.S.S.R. Report*, No. 75485 (April 14, 1980), p. 3. Japanese imperialists of the 1930s and 1940s claimed Japan was saving China from the "death grip" of the Comintern, and liberating Asia from the Western imperialism. Robert J.C. Butow, *Tojo and the Coming of the War* (Stanford: Stanford University Press, 1969), p. 134; Ienaga, *Pacific War*, pp. 153–154. Earlier a French textbook proclaimed the philanthropy of the French North African empire—"France is kind and generous to the peoples she has conquered." Dance, *History the Betrayer*, p. 44.

46. Thus German whitewashing of German responsibility for World War I helped fuel German hostility toward Europe during the interwar years, and laid the basis for popular German support for Nazi foreign policy. On the post-1918 German "innocence" campaign see Holger H. Herwig, "Clio Deceived: Patriotic Self-Censorship in Germany After the Great War," *International Security*, Vol. 12, No. 2 (Fall 1987), pp. 5–44. A good account of Germany's actual pre-1914 conduct is Imanuel Geiss, *German Foreign Policy, 1871–1914* (Boston: Routledge & Kegan Paul, 1976).

47. For example, Wilhelmine and Nazi German nationalists often asserted others' inherent inferiority. Kaiser Wilhelm II declared in 1913: "the Slavs were not born to rule but to serve, this they must be taught." Fritz Fischer, *War of Illusions: German Policies from 1911 to 1914*, trans. Marian Jackson (New York: W.W. Norton, 1975), p. 222. Historian Heinrich von Treitschke thought the English suffered from "cowardice and sensuality," and the French from "besotted-ness," while an earlier German textbook declared France was "a fermenting mass of rottenness." Snyder, *From Bismarck to Hitler*, p. 35; Antoine Guilland, *Modern Germany and Her Historians* (Westport: Greenwood Press, n.d., reprint of 1915 ed.), pp. 304, 154, quoting an 1876 text by A. Hummel. Writer Richard Dehmel described an England with "only practical talents but not 'culture'." Schröter, "Chauvinism and its Tradition," p. 125. Later, Hitler thought Russia was "ripe for dissolution" because it was ruled by the Jews, who were "a ferment of decomposition." Jeremy Noakes and Geoffrey Pridham, eds., *Naziism 1919–1945: A History in Documents and*

port arguments for the rightness and necessity of denying equal rights to minorities living in the national territory, and for subjugating peoples further afield. These minorities and distant peoples will appear to pose a danger if they are left unsuppressed; moreover, their suppression is morally justified by their (imagined) misconduct, past and planned.

Self-whitewashing myths are probably the most common of these three varieties.[48] The dangers they pose are proportional to the gravity of the crimes they whitewash. If small crimes are denied, their denial is disrespect that victims can choose to overlook. The denial may even spring from simple ignorance; if so, it conveys little insult. If great crimes are denied, however, their denial conveys contempt for the victims' very humanity. The denial cannot be ascribed to unintended ignorance; if truly great crimes are forgotten, the forgetting is willful, hence it conveys greater insult. And being willful, the denial implies a dismissal of the crime's wrongness, which in turn suggests an ominous willingness to repeat it. As a result, the denial of great crimes provokes greater hostility from the victims than the denial of minor crimes.[49] Thus Croatian historians and politicians who whitewashed the Croatian Ustashi's vast murders of Serbs during World War II were

---

Eyewitness Accounts, Vol. 2 (New York: Schocken, 1988), pp. 615–616. He likewise viewed the United States, in Gerhard Weinberg's paraphrase, as a "mongrel society, in which the scum naturally floated to the top," that "could not possibly construct a sound economy." Gerhard L. Weinberg, "Hitler's Image of the United States," *American Historical Review*, Vol. 69, No. 4 (July 1964), pp. 1006–1021, at 1010.

Wilhelmine German nationalists also falsely accused others of malign intentions. Pan-German nationalists wove what Hermann Kantorowicz later termed a "fairy tale of encirclement" that posited a British-French-Russian plot to destroy Germany. See Geiss, *German Foreign Policy*, pp. 121–127. Imperial Japanese nationalists likewise saw a mythical anti-Japanese "ABCD encirclement" by America, Britain, China, and the Dutch, with the USSR and Germany sometimes thrown in as co-conspirators. See Butow, *Tojo and the Coming of the War*, chapter 8, pp. 188–227. During the Korean War Chinese writers demonized the United States as a "paradise of gangsters, swindlers, rascals, special agents, fascist germs, speculators, debauchers and all the dregs of mankind." President Truman and General Douglas MacArthur became "mad dogs," "blood-stained bandits," "murderers," "rapists," and "savages." At the same time General MacArthur warned that China "has become aggressively imperialistic, with a lust for expansion." John G. Stoessinger, *Nations in Darkness: China, Russia, and America*, 5th ed. (New York: McGraw-Hill, 1990), pp. 50–51.

For an example of falsely blaming others for past tragedies see notes 45 and 46 on the German post-1918 innocence campaign: in making this claim of innocence Germans also blamed others for starting the war.

48. Conversely, other-denigration is less common than both self-whitewashing and self-glorification, but is often implicit in self-glorification (others suffer in comparison to the virtuous self-image: if one's own group is spotlessly virtuous, others look worse by comparison).

49. Moreover, the victims' charges will anger the criminal nation, since it believes itself innocent, hence it views the victims' charges as malicious slander.

playing with especially powerful dynamite:[50] the crimes they denied were enormous, hence their denial had serious ramifications, feeding Serb hostility that led to the Serbo-Croatian war of 1991–92. Likewise, the question of historical responsibility for Stalin's crimes in the former Soviet Union is especially explosive because the crimes in question are so vast.

Why are myths purveyed? They emanate largely from nationalist political elites, for whom they serve important political functions. Some of these functions also serve the nation as a whole, while others serve only the narrow interests of the elite. Self-glorifying myths encourage citizens to contribute to the national community—to pay taxes, join the army, and fight for the nation's defense. These purposes are hard to fault, although the myths purveyed to achieve them may nevertheless have pernicious side-effects. Myths also bolster the authority and political power of incumbent elites: self-glorifying and self-whitewashing myths allow elites to shine in the reflected luster of their predecessors' imagined achievements and the imagined glory of the national institutions they control; other-maligning myths bolster the authority of elites by supporting claims that the nation faces external threats, thus deflecting popular hostility away from national elites and toward outsiders. Myths that serve only these purposes injure intercommunal relations without providing countervailing benefits to the general community.

Although mythmaking is ubiquitous among nationalisms, the scope and character of mythmaking varies widely across nations. Myths flourish most when elites need them most, when opposition to myths is weakest, and when publics are most myth-receptive. Four principal factors govern the level of infection by nationalist myth:

THE LEGITIMACY OF THE REGIME (or, if the national movement remains stateless, the legitimacy of the movement's leaders). As just noted, nationalist myths can help politically frail elites to bolster their grip on power. The temptation for elites to engage in mythmaking is therefore inversely propor-

---

50. After Germany and Italy conquered Yugoslavia in 1941 they established a puppet state, the Independent State of Croatia, under the leadership of the Croatian Ustashi, a nationalist Croat extremist-terrorist organization headed by Ante Pavelic. Without prompting from the Nazis the Ustashi then launched a mass murder campaign against other ethnic groups, killing by one estimate 500,000–700,000 Serbs, 50,000 Jews, and 20,000 Gypsies. Alex N. Dragnich, *Serbs and Croats: The Struggle for Yugoslavia* (New York: Harcourt Brace, 1992), pp. 96, 101–103. Dragnich reports that even the Germans were reportedly horrified by the nature and extent of the killings, and German officials protested to Pavelic (p. 103). On these murders see also Aleksa Djilas, *The Contested Country* (Cambridge: Harvard University Press, 1991), pp. 120–127; he endorses a smaller estimate by Bogoljub Kočović of 234,000 Serbs murdered (p. 126). Noting Croatian denials of the Ustashi's mass murders is Denich, "Unbury the Victims," pp. 5–6.

tional to their political legitimacy: the less legitimate their rule, the greater their incentive to make myths.

A regime's legitimacy is in turn a function of its representativeness, its competence and efficiency, and the scope of the tasks that face it. Unrepresentative regimes will face challenge from under-represented groups, and will sow myths to build the support needed to defeat this challenge.[51] This motive helped fuel the extreme nationalism that swept Europe in the late nineteenth century: oligarchic regimes used chauvinist myths, often spread through the schools, to deflect demands from below for a wider sharing of political and economic power.[52] Corrupt regimes or regimes that lack competence due to underinstitutionalization will likewise deploy chauvinist myths to divert challenges from publics and elites. This is a common motive for mythmaking in the Third World. Finally, regimes that face overwhelming tasks—e.g., economic or social collapse, perhaps caused by exogenous factors—will be tempted to use myths to divert popular impatience with their inability to improve conditions. Thus the Great Depression fueled nationalist mythmaking in some industrial states during the 1930s.[53]

These factors correlate closely with the ebb and flow of nationalist mythmaking through history. Nationalist mythmaking reached high tide in Europe when Europe's regimes had little legitimacy, during 1848–1914. It then fell dramatically as these regimes democratized and their societies became less stratified, which greatly lessened popular challenge to elites.[54]

THE SCOPE OF THE DEMANDS POSED BY THE STATE ON ITS CITIZENRY. The more the regime asks of its citizens, the harder it must work to persuade its

---

51. Such mythmaking has two targets: the public at large, and state instruments of coercion, which may need special motivation to carry out their tasks.

52. Regime illegitimacy provides the largest motive for elite mythmaking when the state cannot rule by pure force: mythmaking is then the elite's only means to preserve its rule. The proximate cause of mythmaking can therefore sometimes be found in the decline of the state monopoly of force, not the decline of elite legitimacy. This was the case in Europe in the nineteenth century: nationalist mythmaking rose with the rise of mass armies and popular literacy, which diminished the capacity of the state to govern by pure coercion. Elites were therefore forced to resort to persuasion, hence to mythmaking. (Mass literacy in this context proved a double-edged sword for newly-literate publics. Literacy enabled mass political mobilization by spreading social knowledge and ideas; this led to popular empowerment, but literacy also made publics easier to control from above, by enabling elites to purvey elite-justifying myths through the written word; this limited or reduced popular power.)

53. Making a similar argument, although casting it in somewhat different terms, is Snyder, "Nationalism and the Crisis of the Post-Soviet State," pp. 14–16.

54. On the decline of nationalistic history in Europe since the world wars see Kennedy, "Decline of Nationalistic History in the West."

citizens to fulfill these demands; this increases its temptation to deploy nationalist myths for purposes of social mobilization. Regimes at war often use myths to motivate sacrifice by their citizens and to justify their cruelties against others.[55] These myths can live on after the war to poison external relations in later years. Mass revolutionary movements often infuse their movements with mythical propaganda for the same reason; these myths survive after the revolution is won.[56] Regimes that are forced by external threats to sustain large peacetime military efforts are likewise driven to use myths to sustain popular support. This is especially true if they rely on mass armies for their defense.[57] Finally, totalitarian regimes place large demands on their citizens, and use correspondingly large doses of myth to induce their acquiescence.

DOMESTIC ECONOMIC CRISIS. In societies suffering economic collapse, myth-making can take scapegoating form—the collapse is falsely blamed on domestic or international malefactors. Here the mythmaking grows from increased receptivity of the audience: publics are more willing to believe that others are responsible when they are actually suffering pain; when that pain is new and surprising, they search for the hand of malevolent human agents. Germany in the 1930s is the standard example.[58]

THE STRENGTH AND COMPETENCE OF INDEPENDENT EVALUATIVE INSTITUTIONS. Societies that lack free-speech traditions, a strong free press, and free universities are more vulnerable to mythmaking because they lack "truth squads" to counter the nationalist mythmakers. Independent historians can provide an antidote to official historical mythmaking; an independent press is an antidote to official mythmaking about current events. Their absence is a permissive condition for nationalist mythmaking.[59] Wilhelmine Germany

---

55. See, for example, Omer Bartov, *Hitler's Army: Soldiers, Nazis, and the War in the Third Reich* (New York: Oxford University Press, 1991), pp. 106–178, describing the myths purveyed by the Nazi regime to motivate its troops on the Eastern Front.
56. Advancing this argument is Stephen M. Walt, "Revolution and War," *World Politics*, Vol. 44, No. 3 (April 1992), pp. 321–368, at 336–340.
57. For this argument see Posen, "Nationalism, the Mass Army, and Military Power."
58. This hypothesis is widely accepted but has not been systematically tested; more empirical research exploring the relationship between economic downturns and scapegoating would be valuable.
59. The existence of a free press and free universities does not guarantee that myths will be scrutinized; these institutions also require a truth-squad ethos—a sense that mythbusting is among their professional missions. This ethos is often missing among university faculties, who frequently pursue research agendas that have little relevance to the worries of the real world. A discussion that remains valuable is Robert S. Lynd, *Knowledge For What? The Place of Social Science in American Culture* (Princeton: Princeton University Press, 1939). A recent discussion is

illustrates: the German academic community failed to counter the official myths of the era, and often helped purvey them.[60]

Several conclusions follow from this discussion. Democratic regimes are less prone to mythmaking, because such regimes are usually more legitimate and are free-speech tolerant; hence they can develop evaluative institutions to weed out nationalist myth. Absolutist dictatorships that possess a massive military superiority over their citizens are also less prone to mythmaking, because they can survive without it. The most dangerous regimes are those that depend on some measure of popular consent, but are narrowly governed by unrepresentative elites. Things are still worse if these governments are poorly institutionalized, are incompetent or corrupt for other reasons, or face overwhelming problems that exceed their governing capacities. Regimes that emerged from a violent struggle, or enjoy only precarious security, are also more likely to retain a struggle-born chauvinist belief-system.

Conclusion: Predictions and Prescriptions

What predictions follow? These hypotheses can be used to generate forecasts; applied to Europe, they predict that nationalism will pose little risk to peace in Western Europe, but large risks in Eastern Europe.

Most of the nationalisms of the West are satisfied, having already gained states. Western diasporas are few and small, reflecting the relative homogeneity of Western national demography, and Western minorities are relatively well-treated. The historic grievances of Western nationalities against one another are also small—many of the West's inter-ethnic horrors have faded from memory, and the perpetrators of the greatest recent horror—the Germans—have accepted responsibility for it and reconciled with their victims. The regimes of the West are highly legitimate, militarily secure, and economically stable; hence chauvinist mythmaking by their elites is correspondingly

---

Russell Jacoby, *The Last Intellectuals: American Culture in the Age of Academe* (New York: Basic Books, 1987), pp. 112–237. On this problem in political science see Hans J. Morgenthau, "The Purpose of Political Science," in James C. Charlesworth, ed., *A Design for Political Science: Scope, Objectives, and Methods* (Philadelphia: American Academy of Political and Social Science, 1966), pp. 63–79, at 69–74. German academics also cooperated with official German myth-making after World War I; see Herwig, "Clio Deceived."

60. A good survey of German historiography of this era is Snyder, *German Nationalism*, chapter 6 (pp. 123–152). An older survey is Guilland, *Modern Germany and Her Historians*. Also relevant are John A. Moses, *The Politics of Illusion: The Fischer Controversy in German Historiography* (London: George Prior, 1975), chapter 1 (pp. 7–26); and Snyder, *From Bismarck to Hitler*, chapter 3 (pp. 25–35).

rare. The West European nationalisms that caused the greatest recent troubles, those of Germany and Italy, are now clearly benign, and the conditions for a return to aggressive nationalism are absent in both countries. Outsiders sometimes fear that outbreaks of anti-immigrant extremism in Germany signal the return of German fascism, but the forces of tolerance and decency are overwhelmingly dominant in Germany, and the robust health of German democracy and of German academic and press institutions ensures they will remain dominant. As a result nationalism should cause very little trouble in Western Europe.

In the East the number of stateless nationalisms is larger, raising greater risk that future conflicts will arise from wars of liberation. The collapse of Soviet power shifted the balance of power toward these nationalisms, by replacing the Soviet state with weaker successor states. This shift has produced secessionist wars in Georgia and Moldova, and such wars could multiply. The tangled pattern of ethnic intermingling across the East creates large diasporas. Eastern societies have little tradition of respect for minority rights, raising the likelihood that these diasporas will face abuse; this in turn may spur their homelands to try to incorporate them by force. The borders of many emerging Eastern nations lack natural defensive barriers, leaving the state exposed to attack; some borders also lack legitimacy, and correspond poorly with ethnic boundaries. Some new Eastern regimes, especially those in the former Soviet Union, lack legitimacy and are under-institutionalized, raising the risk that they will resort to chauvinist mythmaking to maintain their political viability. This risk is heightened by the regional economic crisis caused by the transition from command to market economies. Evaluative institutions (free universities and a free press) remain weak in the East, raising the risk that myths will go unchallenged. The Soviet regime committed vast crimes against its subject peoples; this legacy will embitter relations among these peoples if they cannot agree on who deserves the blame.[61]

---

61. The emerging nations of the former USSR now stand knee-deep in the blood of Stalin's victims, and in the economic ruin that Bolshevism left behind. If every nation blames only others for these disasters, civil relations among them will be impossible: each will hope to someday settle accounts. Civil relations depend, then, on a convergence toward a common history of the Bolshevik disaster. Things would be best if all converged on a version that blamed the Bolsheviks—who, having vanished, can be blamed painlessly. (Bolshevism would then usefully serve as a hate-soaker—its final, and among its few positive, functions in Soviet history.) Absent that, things would be better if the successor nations agree on how to allocate blame among themselves.

The Eastern picture is not all bleak. The main preconditions for democracy—high levels of literacy, some degree of industrial development, and the absence of a landed oligarchy—exist across most of the East. As a result the long-term prospects for democracy are bright. Moreover, the East's economic crisis is temporary: the conditions for prosperous industrial economies (a trained workforce and adequate natural resources) do exist, so the crisis should ease once the market transition is completed. These relatively favorable long-term prospects for democracy and prosperity dampen the risk that chauvinist mythmaking will get out of hand.[62] The fact that the new Eastern states managed to gain freedom without violent struggles also left them with fewer malignant beliefs, by allowing them to forgo infusing their societies with chauvinist war propaganda. The power and ethnographic structures of the East, while dangerous, are less explosive than those of Yugoslavia: historic grievances and military power coincide less tightly—there is no other Eastern equivalent of Serbia, having both military superiority and large historical grievances; and ethnographic patterns create less imperative for a diaspora-rescue operation by the state most likely to attempt such a rescue, Russia.

---

62. However, in the East's heterogeneous interethnic setting democracy is a mixed blessing: if it takes a strict majoritarian form it can produce majority tyranny and the oppression of minorities, as it has in the past in Northern Ireland and the American Deep South. To produce civil peace in a multi-ethnic setting, democracy must adopt non-majoritarian principles of power-sharing, like those of Swiss democracy. On this question see Arend Lijphart, "Consociational Democracy," *World Politics*, Vol. 21, No. 2 (January 1969), pp. 107–125; Arend Lijphart, *Democracy in Plural Societies: A Comparative Exploration* (New Haven: Yale University Press, 1977); Arend Lijphart, *Democracies: Patterns of Majoritarian and Consensus Government in Twenty-One Countries* (New Haven: Yale University Press, 1984); Arend Lijphart, "The Power-Sharing Approach," in Joseph V. Montville, ed., *Conflict and Peacemaking in Multiethnic Societies* (Lexington, Mass.: Lexington Books, 1990), pp. 491–509; Kenneth D. McRae, "Theories of Power-Sharing and Conflict Management," in Montville, *Conflict and Peacemaking*, pp. 93–106; Jurg Steiner, "Power-Sharing: Another Swiss 'Export Product'?" in Montville, *Conflict and Peacemaking*, pp. 107–114; Hans Daalder, "The Consociational Democracy Theme," *World Politics*, Vol. 26, No. 4 (July 1974), pp. 604–621; Kenneth D. McRae, ed., *Consociational Democracy: Political Accommodation in Segmented Societies* (Toronto: McClelland and Stewart, 1974); and Vernon Van Dyke, "Human Rights and the Rights of Groups," *American Journal of Political Science*, Vol. 18, No. 4 (November, 1974), pp. 725–741, at 730–740. See also James Madison, "The Same Subject Continued . . ." (Federalist No. 10), *The Federalist Papers*, intro. by Clinton Rossiter (New York: New American Library, 1961), pp. 77–84, which addresses the danger of majority tyranny and remedies for it; Madison discusses the risks that arise when "a majority is included in a faction" (p. 80) and the dangers of tyranny by "the superior force of an interested and overbearing majority" (p. 77). Also relevant is Robert M. Axelrod, *Conflict of Interest: A Theory of Divergent Goals with Applications to Politics* (Chicago: Markham, 1970), whose theory of winning coalition membership explains why majoritarian rules distribute power unequally in deeply divided societies.

All in all, however, conditions in Eastern Europe are more bad than good; hence nationalism will probably produce a substantial amount of violence in the East over the next several decades.[63]

What policy prescriptions follow? The Western powers should move to dampen the risks that nationalism poses in the East, by moving to channel manipulable aspects of Eastern nationalism in benign directions. Some aspects of Eastern nationalist movements are immutable (e.g., their degree of intermingling, or the history of crimes between them). Others, however, can be decided by the movements themselves (e.g., their attitude toward minorities, their vision of history, and their willingness to reach final border settlements with others); these can be influenced by the West if the movements are susceptible to Western pressure or persuasion. The Western powers should use their substantial economic leverage to bring such pressure to bear.

Specifically, the Western powers should condition their economic relations with the new Eastern states on these states' conformity with a code of peaceful conduct that proscribes policies that make nationalism dangerous. The code should have six elements: (1) renunciation of the threat or use of force; (2) robust guarantees for the rights of national minorities, to include, under some stringent conditions, a legal right to secession;[64] (3) commitment

---

63. Nationalism is also likely to produce substantial violence in the Third World, largely because a high nation-to-state ratio still prevails there; hence many secessionist movements and wars of secession are likely in the decades ahead. A discussion of the policy issues raised by this circumstance is Halperin, Scheffer, and Small, *Self-Determination in the New World Order*; for a global survey of current self-determination movements see ibid., pp. 123–160.

64. Minority rights should be defined broadly, to include fair minority representation in the legislative, executive, and judicial branches of the central government. The definition of minority rights used in most international human rights agreements is more restrictive: it omits the right to share power in the national government, and includes only the right to political autonomy and the preservation of minority language, culture, and religion. See Edward Lawson, *Encyclopedia of Human Rights* (New York: Taylor & Francis, 1991), p. 1070; on the neglect of minority rights by Western political thinkers, see Vernon Van Dyke, "The Individual, the State, and Ethnic Communities in Political Theory," *World Politics*, Vol. 29, No. 3 (April 1977), pp. 343–369.

When should minority rights be defined to include the right to secession and national independence? Universal recognition of this right would require massive redrawing of boundaries in the East, and would raise the question of Western recognition of scores of now-unrecognized independence movements worldwide. One solution is to recognize the right to secede in instances where the central government is unwilling to fully grant other minority rights, but to decline to recognize the right to secede if all other minority rights are fully recognized and robustly protected. In essence, the West would hold its possible recognition of a right to secede in reserve, to encourage governments to recognize other minority rights. A discussion of the right to secession is Vernon Van Dyke, "Collective Entities and Moral Rights: Problems in Liberal-Democratic Thought," *Journal of Politics*, Vol. 44, No. 1 (February 1982), pp. 21–40, at 36–37. Also relevant is Halperin, Scheffer, and Small, *Self-Determination in the New World Order*.

to the honest teaching of history in the schools,[65] and to refrain from the propagation of chauvinist or other hate propaganda; (4) willingness to adopt a democratic form of government, and to accept related institutions—specifically, free speech and a free press;[66] (5) adoption of market economic policies, and disavowal of protectionist or other beggar-thy-neighbor economic policies toward other Eastern states; and (6) acceptance of current national borders, or agreement to settle contested borders promptly though peaceful means. This list rests on the premise that "peaceful conduct" requires that nationalist movements renounce the use of force against others (element 1), and also agree to refrain from policies that the hypotheses presented here warn against (elements 2–6).

Hypothesis I.4 (see Table 1) warns that the risk of war rises when nationalist movements oppress their minorities; hence the code requires respect for minority rights (element 2). Hypothesis II.6 warns that divergent beliefs about mutual history and current conduct and character raise the risk of war; hence the code asks for historical honesty and curbs on official hate propaganda (element 3). Hypothesis II.6.a warns that illegitimate governments have a greater propensity to mythmake, and hypothesis II.6.d warns that chauvinist myths prevail more often if independent evaluative institutions are weak; hence the code asks that movements adopt democracy (to bolster legitimacy) and respect free speech and free press rights (to bolster evaluation) (element 4). Hypothesis II.6.c warns that economic collapse promotes chauvinist mythmaking; hence the code asks movements to adopt market reforms, on grounds that prosperity requires marketization (element 5). Hypothesis II.3.b warns that the risk of war rises if the borders of emerging nation states lack legitimacy; hence the code asks movements to legitimize their borders through formal non-violent settlement (element 6).[67]

---

65. States should not be asked to accept externally-imposed versions of history in their texts, since no society can arbitrarily claim to know the "truth" better than others. But states could be asked to commit to international dialogue on history, on the theory that free debate will cause views to converge. Specifically, they could be asked to accept the obligation to subject their school curricula to foreign criticism, perhaps in the context of textbook exchanges, and to allow domestic publication of foreign criticisms of their curricula. Schemes of this sort have a long history in Western Europe, where they had a substantial impact after 1945. See Dance, *History the Betrayer*, pp. 127–128, 132, 135–150. This West European experience could serve as a template for an Eastern program.

66. These democratic governments should adopt consociational power-sharing rules, not majoritarian rules; otherwise ethnic minorities will be denied equal political power (see footnote 62.)

67. Such a code could be applied more widely, and serve as the basis for an international regime

The Western powers should enforce this code by pursuing a common economic policy toward the states of the East: observance of the code should be the price for full membership in the Western economy, while non-observance should bring exclusion and economic sanctions.[68] This policy should be married to an economic aid package to assist marketization, also conditioned on code observance.

The Bush and Clinton administrations have adopted elements of this policy, but omitted key aspects. In September 1991, then–Secretary of State James Baker outlined five principles that incorporate most of the six elements in the code of conduct outlined above (only element 3—honest treatment of history—was unmentioned), and he indicated that American policy toward the new Eastern states would be conditioned on their acceptance of these principles.[69] During the spring and summer of 1992 the administration also proposed a substantial economic aid package (the Freedom Support Act) and guided it through Congress.

However, Baker's principles later faded from view. Strangely, the Bush administration failed to clearly condition release of its aid package on Eastern compliance with these principles. It also failed to forge a common agreement among the Western powers to condition their economic relations with the Eastern states on these principles. The principles themselves were not elaborated; most importantly, the minority rights that the Eastern states must protect were not detailed, leaving these states free to adopt a watered-down definition. The Bush administration also recognized several new Eastern governments (e.g., Azerbaijan's) that gave Baker's principles only lip service while violating them in practice.[70] The Clinton administration has largely

---

on nationalist comportment; a nationalist movement's entitlement to international support would correspond to its acceptance and observance of the code.

68. The Western powers should also offer to help the Eastern powers devise specific policies to implement these principles, and offer active assistance with peacemaking if conflicts nevertheless emerge. Specifically, Western governments and institutions should offer to share Western ideas and experience on the building of democratic institutions; the development of political and legal institutions that protect and empower minorities; the development of market economic institutions; and the best means to control nationalism in education. (On this last point an account is Dance, *History the Betrayer*, pp. 126–150.) Finally, if serious conflicts nevertheless emerge, the West should offer active mediation, as the United States has between Israelis and Arabs.

69. For Baker's principles see "Baker's Remarks: Policy on Soviets," *New York Times*, September 5, 1991, p. A12. Baker reiterated these principles in December 1991; see "Baker Sees Opportunities and Risks as Soviet Republics Grope for Stability," *New York Times*, December 13, 1991, p. A24. Reporting Baker's conditioning of American recognition of the new Eastern governments on their acceptance of these standards is Michael Wines, "Ex-Soviet Leader Is Lauded By Bush," *New York Times*, December 26, 1991, p. 1.

70. See "Winking at Aggression in Baku" (editorial), *New York Times*, February 14, 1992, p. A28.

followed in Bush's footsteps: it continued Bush's aid program, but omitted clear political conditions.[71]

There is still time for such a policy, but the clock is running out. A policy resting on economic sticks and carrots will be too weak to end major violence once it begins; hence the West should therefore move to avert trouble while it still lies on the horizon.

---

71. In April 1993 the Clinton administration forged agreement among the Group of Seven (G7) states (Britain, France, Germany, Italy, Canada, Japan, and the United States) on a $28 billion aid package for the former Soviet Union, and Congress approved a substantial aid package in September 1993. See Serge Schmemann, "Yeltsin Leaves Talks With Firm Support and More Aid," *New York Times*, April 5, 1993, p. 1; David E. Sanger, "7 Nations Pledge $28 Billion Fund To Assist Russia," *New York Times*, April 16, 1993, p. 1; Steven Greenhouse, "I.M.F. Unveils Plan for Soviet Lands," *New York Times*, April 21, 1993, p. A16; and Steven A. Holmes, "House Approves Bill Including 2.5 Billion in Aid for Russians," *New York Times*, September 24, 1993, p. A6. The aid was conditioned on Eastern moves toward marketization, but political conditions were omitted. President Clinton did declare that "we support respect for ethnic minorities," and "we stand with Russian democracy" as he announced the American aid pledge. Schmemann, "Yeltsin Leaves Talks." However, press accounts do not mention explicit political conditions.

Nationalism and the Marketplace of Ideas

Jack Snyder and Karen Ballentine

The conventional wisdom among human rights activists holds that a great deal of the ethnic conflict in the world today is caused by propagandistic manipulations of public opinion. Human Rights Watch, for example, points the finger at unscrupulous governments who try to save their own skins by "playing the communal card." As antidotes, such groups prescribe democratization, wide-open debate in civil society, and greater freedom of the press.[1] Scholars likewise argue that a major stimulus to belligerent nationalism is the state's manipulation of mass media and mass education to infuse the nation with a sense of in-group patriotism and out-group rivalry.[2] They, too, prescribe greater freedom of speech.[3]

We agree that media manipulation often plays a central role in promoting nationalist and ethnic conflict, but we argue that promoting unconditional

Jack Snyder is Professor of Political Science and Director of the Institute of War and Peace Studies, Columbia University. Karen Ballentine is a Ph.D. candidate in political science at Columbia University and in 1996–97 will be a Research Fellow at the Center for Science in International Affairs, Harvard University.

We thank Fiona Adamson, Laura Belin, Mark Blyth, V.P. Gagnon, Šumit Ganguly, Robert Jervis, Arvid Lukauskas, Edward Mansfield, Anthony Marx, Helen Milner, Alexander Motyl, Anne Nelson, Bruce Pannier, Laura Pitter, Ronald Rogowski, Aaron Seeskin, Robert Shapiro, Kevin Smead, Stephen Van Evera, Robin Varghese, and Leslie Vinjamuri for helpful comments or other assistance, and the Harry Frank Guggenheim Foundation, the Institute for the Study of World Politics, and the Pew Charitable Trusts for financial support.

1. Human Rights Watch, *Playing the "Communal Card"* (New York: Human Rights Watch, April 1995), reprinted as *Slaughter among Neighbors: The Political Origins of Communal Violence* (New Haven, Conn.: Yale University Press, 1995); Human Rights Watch, "'Hate Speech' and Freedom of Expression," *Free Expression Project*, Vol. 4, No. 3 (March 1992); see also Leonard Sussman, *Press Freedom 1996: The Journalist as Pariah* (New York: Freedom House, 1996); Article 19, the International Centre Against Censorship, *Guidelines for Election Broadcasting in Transitional Democracies* (London: Article 19, August 1994).
2. Eric Hobsbawm, "Mass Producing Traditions," in Hobsbawm and Terence Ranger, eds., *The Invention of Tradition* (Cambridge, U.K.: Cambridge University Press, 1983), pp. 263–307; Eric Hobsbawm, *Nations and Nationalism since 1780* (Cambridge, U.K.: Cambridge University Press, 1990), pp. 80–100, 141–142; Stephen Van Evera, "Hypotheses on Nationalism and War," *International Security*, Vol. 18, No. 4 (Spring 1994), pp. 26–33; Paul Kennedy, "The Decline of Nationalistic History in the West, 1900–1970," *Journal of Contemporary History*, Vol. 8, No. 1 (January 1973), pp. 77–100. V.P. Gagnon, Jr., "Ethnic Conflict as Demobilizer: The Case of Serbia," Institute for European Studies Working Paper No. 96.1 (Cornell University, May 1996), argues that propaganda does not mobilize popular nationalism, but rather that ethnic conflict and media control demobilizes opposition to the regime.
3. Van Evera, "Hypotheses," p. 37; V.P. Gagnon, Jr., "Ethnic Nationalism and International Conflict: The Case of Serbia," *International Security*, Vol. 19, No. 3 (Winter 1994/95), pp. 130–166, at 165.

International Security, Vol. 21, No. 2 (Fall 1996), pp. 5–40
© 1996 by the President and Fellows of Harvard College and the Massachusetts Institute of Technology.

freedom of public debate in newly democratizing societies is, in many circumstances, likely to make the problem worse. Historically and today, from the French Revolution to Rwanda, sudden liberalizations of press freedom have been associated with bloody outbursts of popular nationalism. The most dangerous situation is precisely when the government's press monopoly begins to break down.[4] During incipient democratization, when civil society is burgeoning but democratic institutions are not fully entrenched, the state and other elites are forced to engage in public debate in order to compete for mass allies in the struggle for power.[5] Under those circumstances, governments and their opponents often have the motive and the opportunity to play the nationalist card.

When this occurs, unconditional freedom of speech is a dubious remedy. Just as economic competition produces socially beneficial results only in a well-institutionalized marketplace, where monopolies and false advertising are counteracted, so too increased debate in the political marketplace leads to better outcomes only when there are mechanisms to correct market imperfections.[6] Many newly democratizing states lack institutions to break up governmental and non-governmental information monopolies, to professionalize journalism, and to create common public forums where diverse ideas engage each other under conditions in which erroneous arguments will be challenged. In the

---

4. Van Evera, "Hypotheses," p. 33. Human Rights Watch, *Playing the "Communal Card,"* p. viii, points this out, but disregards it when drawing conclusions. According to Freedom House's ratings, civil liberties, which include freedom of speech, improved in Yugoslavia, Rwanda, and Burundi shortly before the recent outbreaks of massive ethnic violence there. Raymond Gastil and R. Bruce McColm, eds., *Freedom in the World* (New York: Freedom House, 1988–93), pp. 411–412 (1988), 272–274 (1989–90), 104–105, 313–315 (1990–91), and 153–155, 429–431 (1992–93).

5. Van Evera, "Hypotheses," p. 33. In mature democracies, government policy is made by officials chosen through free and fair elections on the basis of wide suffrage; the actions of officials are constrained by constitutional provisions and commitments to civil liberties; and government candidates sometimes lose elections, and leave office when they do. We define states as democratizing if they have recently adopted some of these democratic characteristics, even if they retain important non-democratic features. See Edward D. Mansfield and Jack Snyder, "Democratization and the Danger of War," *International Security*, Vol. 20, No. 1 (Summer 1995), pp. 8–10. On the gap between institutions and participation, see Samuel Huntington, *Political Order in Changing Societies* (New Haven, Conn.: Yale University Press, 1968).

6. R.H. Coase, "The Market for Goods and the Market for Ideas," *American Economic Review*, Vol. 64, No. 2 (May 1974), pp. 384–391, argues that imperfect markets for ideas are in no less need of regulation than imperfect markets for goods. On the benefits of gag rules in ethnically or religiously divided societies undergoing democratization, see Stephen Holmes, *Passions and Constraint: On the Theory of Liberal Democracy* (Chicago: University of Chicago, 1995), chapter 7, esp. pp. 206–213.

absence of these institutions, an increase in the freedom of speech can create an opening for nationalist mythmakers to hijack public discourse.

In developing these arguments, we first define nationalist mythmaking and explain the scope of our claims. Second, we present our concept of the marketplace of ideas and offer hypotheses about conditions that facilitate nationalist mythmaking, illustrating these propositions with examples from that classic hotbed of nationalist mythmaking, the Weimar Republic, and from other recent and historical cases. Third, we test our argument against two hard cases, ethnic conflict in the former Yugoslavia and in Rwanda, both dramatic clashes that seem superficially to fit the conventional view that a government media monopoly is the problem, and unfettered speech the antidote. Fourth, we explore cases with comparatively moderate outcomes to determine the conditions under which democratization does not produce intense nationalist mythmaking. We conclude with suggestions for better institutionalizing public debate in new democracies.

Nationalist Mythmaking

Conventional wisdom is right in focusing on inflammatory propaganda as a cause of nationalism and ethnic conflicts. The archetype for this notion is the stem-winding oratory of Adolf Hitler, with its renowned pied-piper effect on malleable audiences.[7] Likewise, the world's first instance of aggressive nationalism, the Wars of the French Revolution, was sparked by an outpouring of warlike commentary in France's newly free press, which swept the demagogic journalist Jacques Pierre Brissot into power.[8] Recent reincarnations of this phenomenon, stressed in analyses by non-governmental organizations (NGOs) and by scholars, include the Hutu "hate radio" stations that encouraged genocide against Rwanda's Tutsi minority, as well as President Slobodan Milošević's

---

7. The impact of Hitler's oratory before his rise to power was mainly in motivating supporters who were already predisposed toward his outlook. Few people heard him on the radio until after he had been elected chancellor. Ian Kershaw, "Ideology, Propaganda, and the Rise of the Nazi Party," in Peter Stachura, ed., *The Nazi Machtergreifung* (London: Allen & Unwin, 1983), pp. 162–181; Thomas Childers, "The Social Language of Politics in Germany: The Sociology of Political Discourse in the Weimar Republic," *American Historical Review,* Vol. 95, No. 2 (April 1990), pp. 331–358.

8. T.C.W. Blanning, *The Origins of the French Revolutionary Wars* (London: Longman, 1986), p. 113; Jeremy Popkin, *Revolutionary News: The Press in France, 1789–1799* (Durham, N.C.: Duke University Press, 1990), p. 41.

use of the television monopoly to foster an embattled, surly mentality among Serbs.[9]

Conventional wisdom is one-sided, however, when it blames nationalist demagogy primarily on governmental media monopolies and consequently prescribes unfettered free speech as the remedy. A 1995 report by Human Rights Watch, for example, concluded that in ten of the hottest contemporary ethnic conflicts, manipulative governments had "played the communal card" as a way to forestall declining popularity or to pursue strategies of divide-and-rule. "Dictatorship offers the ideal condition for playing the 'communal card'," because "official control of information makes public opinion highly manipulable."[10] Yet almost all of the countries studied in the report—India, Israel, South Africa, Romania, Sri Lanka, the former Yugoslavia, Lebanon, Russia, Armenia, and Azerbaijan—had recently held openly contested elections where powerful opposition groups were more nationalist than the government.[11] In addition, Human Rights Watch argued that, because "conditions for polarization along communal lines are less propitious in a society where public debate is encouraged," where past human rights abuses are vigorously prosecuted, and where there is "free participation in a broad range of voluntary and public associations," the cure is "vigorous civic debate" in a "well developed civil society."[12] But in fact, the Hindu fundamentalist Bharatiya Janata Party, the Armenian Karabakh Committee, and most of the instigators of ethnic conflict in the Human Rights Watch cases *are* "civil society," that is, voluntary organizations not created by the state. The Weimar Republic had record numbers of newspapers per capita, choral societies, and grassroots nationalist organiza-

---

9. Rakiya Omaar and Alex de Waal, Africa Rights, *Rwanda: Death, Despair and Defiance* (London: Africa Rights, September 1994, exp. ed., 1995, all page references to 1994 ed.); Mark Thompson, Article 19, *Forging War: The Media in Serbia, Croatia and Bosnia-Herzegovina* (London: Article 19, May 1994).

10. Human Rights Watch, *Playing the "Communal Card,"* pp. viii, xiv.

11. Thus, the Indian Congress government was outflanked by the nationalist Bharatiya Janata Party, the Israeli Labor government by Likud, South Africa's De Klerk government by irreconcilable Afrikaners, Romania's Iliescu government by the anti-Hungarian nationalist party, the Sri Lankan government by grassroots Buddhist organizations, Serbia's Slobodan Milošević by Vojislav Seselj, the Syrian-backed Lebanese government by leaders of the various communal groups, Russian President Boris Yeltsin by Vladimir Zhirinovsky, the moderate Armenian government of Levon Ter-Petrosian by the nationalist Dashnaks, and the inert Azerbaijani government of Ayaz Mutalibov by the ethno-populist Abulfez Elchibey. Human Rights Watch's own study often acknowledges this phenomenon, but blames the government for weakly resisting these pressures. *Playing the "Communal Card,"* p. 28.

12. Human Rights Watch, *Playing the "Communal Card,"* xiv, xvii. For a more nuanced NGO view, see Bruce Allyn and Steven Wilkinson, *Guidelines for Journalists Covering Ethnic Conflict* (Cambridge, Mass.: Conflict Management Working Paper, January 1994).

tions, all indicators of a vigorous civil society; likewise, the nationalistic Jacobin Clubs of the French Revolution were spontaneous emanations of civil society.[13]

Conventional analyses fail to emphasize that a "well developed" civil society is not simply a matter of many clamoring voices, but also the set of institutions and social norms that make pluralism a civil process of persuasion and reconciling of differences.[14] No matter how well-intentioned and knowledgeable, non-governmental organizations promoting human rights tend to understate the tension between their ideal of an open society and the difficulty of establishing its preconditions in newly democratizing societies. As a consequence, their remedies may sometimes fuel nationalist mythmaking rather than dampen it. It is understandable that such groups are reluctant to explore the trade-offs entailed in promoting free speech, since there is undoubtedly a risk that qualifications to the argument for free speech can be exploited by dictators who wish to snuff out freedom of expression entirely. Nonetheless, because the risks of uncritical advocacy of unconditional free speech can be very high, these trade-offs must be analyzed forthrightly.

DEFINING NATIONALISM AND MYTHS

Nationalism, according to the most widely accepted definition, is the doctrine that the state and the nation should be congruent. Nationalism holds that legitimate rule is based on the sovereignty of a culturally or historically distinctive people in a polity that expresses and protects those distinctive characteristics.[15] We examine under this definition both the state-seeking activity of ethnic groups in multi-ethnic states and also the rivalries of established and more ethnically homogeneous nation-states, insofar as their leaders seek to legitimate their power and appeal for popular support for their policies by claiming to fulfill the historical mission or cultural identity of the nation.[16]

---

13. Pierre Birnbaum, *States and Collective Action* (Cambridge, U.K.: Cambridge University Press, 1988), pp. 39–40; Peter Fritzsche, *Rehearsals for Fascism: Populism and Political Mobilization in Weimar Germany* (New York: Oxford University Press, 1990), p. 75. Robert Putnam, *Making Democracy Work* (Princeton, N.J.: Princeton University Press, 1993), fails to address the Weimar case.

14. Larry Diamond, "Rethinking Civil Society: Toward Democratic Consolidation," *Journal of Democracy*, Vol. 5, No. 3 (September 1994), pp. 5–6; Steven Fish, "Russia's Fourth Transition," *Journal of Democracy*, Vol. 5, No. 3 (September 1994), pp. 31–33.

15. Ernest Gellner, *Nations and Nationalism* (Ithaca, N.Y.: Cornell University Press, 1983), chap. 1.

16. Although narrower definitions are in principle preferable, we adopt a broader definition that includes both state-seeking ethnic nationalism and nationalism in comparatively homogeneous, established states, on the grounds that our theory illuminates a dynamic that occurs equally in both types of case. On the relative merits of broad versus narrow definitions of nationalism, see Alexander Motyl, "The Modernity of Nationalism," *Journal of International Affairs*, Vol. 45, No. 2 (Winter 1992), pp. 307–324.

"Myths," for our purposes, are assertions that would lose credibility if their claim to a basis in fact or logic were exposed to rigorous, disinterested public evaluation. [17] The assertion that the Holocaust never happened is an example of a myth, in this sense. Nationalist mythmaking, then, is the attempt to use dubious arguments to mobilize support for nationalist doctrines or to discredit opponents. For some scholars, nationalist mythmaking is understood exclusively in this sense of promoting demonstrable falsehoods: in Ernest Renan's words, "getting its history wrong is part of being a nation."[18] Other scholars of nationalism, however, conceive of myth in the sense of *mythomoteur*, that is, as a story about the origins, special character, and destiny of the "nation."[19] The values embodied in such mythomoteurs are not subject to falsification, no matter how astutely they are scrutinized. Assertions like "it is good to be Ruritanian" or "Ruritanians deserve their own state" cannot be falsified, not because they are irrational, but because they are normative claims which exist independently of objective standards of argumentation. Nationalist mythomoteurs can, on occasion, lead to conflict: for example, when both Ruritanians and Megalomanians identify the same territory as "our historic homeland," and each claims to "deserve" exclusive, sovereign control over it. Because of the non-falsifiability of national mythomoteurs, even a well-constituted marketplace of ideas cannot provide iron-clad restraints against this kind of mythology. A well-constituted marketplace can, however, effectively mitigate the propagation of falsifiable nationalist myths. This capacity is of no small consequence since, typically, nationalist conflict is not the spontaneous emanation of vague mythomoteurs but the product of deliberate elite efforts to mobilize latent solidarities behind a particular political program, which falsifiable myths are used to justify. Thus, some of the justifications offered for why Ruritanians deserve to rule a territory (e.g., "we ruled it six centuries ago") or why they should preventively attack the Megalomanians (e.g., "they were able to kill ten million of us during the last war, because we let our guard down") entail empirical claims or causal inferences that are subject to objective scrutiny and perhaps verification or refutation.

---

17. Similarly, John Zaller, *The Nature and Origins of Mass Opinion* (Cambridge, U.K.: Cambridge University Press, 1992), p. 313, defines "elite domination" of opinion as "a situation in which elites induce citizens to hold opinions that they would not hold if aware of the best available information and analysis."
18. Quoted in Hobsbawm, *Nations and Nationalism*, p. 12.
19. Anthony D. Smith, *The Ethnic Origins of Nations* (Oxford, U.K.: Blackwell, 1986), pp. 15, 24; John Armstrong, *Nations before Nationalism* (Chapel Hill: University of North Carolina Press, 1982).

We do not contend that all nationalist ideas are myths, let alone falsifiable ones. Nor do we argue that nationalists are uniquely prone to political myth-making, nor that nationalism and nationalist conflict stem only from mythmaking. Besides myths, scholars have identified many factors that plausibly contribute to nationalism or nationalist conflict: the rise of the modern state, economic change, political repression, socio-economic inequality, security threats, and so forth. Our focus on mythmaking is not intended to compete with these approaches, but to complement them. We argue that these factors work their effects on nationalism through the process of persuasion and myth-making in the marketplace of ideas. As many scholars have stressed, whatever background factors may contribute to nationalism, nationalist agitation and propaganda are always necessary conditions to the development of a mass nationalist movement.[20]

Though nationalism and nationalist myths are not the only cause of conflict between nations, we do argue that a tendency to breed conflict is inherent in typical nationalist myths, because they overemphasize the cultural and histori-cal distinctiveness of the national group, exaggerate the threat posed to the nation by other groups, ignore the degree to which the nation's own actions provoked such threats, and play down the costs of seeking national goals through militant means.[21] Nationalist mobilization against alleged threats from other national groups, whether within the state or abroad, heightens the risk of conflict by stereotyping opponents as irremediably hostile, yet inferior and vulnerable to vigilant preventive attack.[22] Whether such myths can be success-fully sold depends in large measure on the structure of the marketplace of ideas in which they are advanced.

Imperfect Markets and Nationalist Mythmaking

Liberal conventional wisdom, steeped in John Stuart Mill's argument that truth is most likely to emerge from no-holds-barred debate, optimistically expects

20. Miroslav Hroch, *Social Preconditions of National Revival in Europe* (Cambridge, U.K.: Cambridge University Press, 1985), pp. 11–13; Elie Kedourie, *Nationalism* (London: Hutchinson, 1960).
21. However, where democratic norms are intimately bound to national self-conceptions, nation-alism may in fact support peaceful democracy by promoting loyalty to civic institutions. See Victor Zaslavsky, "Nationalism and Democratic Transition in Postcommunist Societies," *Daedalus*, Vol. 12, No. 2 (Spring 1992), pp. 97–122; Rogers Brubaker, *Citizenship and Nationhood in France and Germany* (Cambridge, Mass.: Harvard University Press, 1992), chaps. 2 and 5.
22. Van Evera, "Hypotheses," pp. 26–33; Jack Snyder, *Myths of Empire* (Ithaca, N.Y.: Cornell Uni-versity Press, 1991), pp. 5–6.

the invisible hand of free competition to check the mythmaking of nationalist demagogues. Under conditions of "perfect competition" in the political marketplace, it may indeed be true that, on balance, unfettered debate tends to discredit ill-founded myths by revealing their factual inaccuracies, their logical contradictions, or the hidden costs of acting on their implications.[23] That is probably one reason why mature democracies never fight wars against each other.[24] However, when waning authoritarian power is newly challenged by the forces of mass politics, competition in the marketplace of ideas is likely to be highly imperfect, and opportunities for nationalist mythmaking abound.

In the political marketplace, governmental and non-governmental elites advance arguments about the benefits of policies and commit themselves to these policies in order to gain political support.[25] Consumers in the marketplace decide whom to support based in part on the persuasiveness of the arguments of elite entrepreneurs and on the credibility of the elites' commitments to implement desired policies. Middlemen in the marketplace (journalists and policy experts) and market institutions (the media, analytical institutions, and the laws regulating them) convey political entrepreneurs' commitments and arguments to consumers in ways that provide varying degrees of information about their credibility and accuracy. The better institutionalized the market, the better it scrutinizes arguments and forces ideas to confront each other in common forums, and therefore the better the information the market provides. The media that comprise the marketplace include not only instruments of mass communication like television and newspapers, but also local networks of face-to-face persuasion, as well as elite publications and discourse that generate ideas for mass dissemination.[26]

---

23. We define perfect competition in the marketplace of ideas, which exists only as an ideal type, as a situation of no monopolies of information or media access, low barriers to entry, full exposure of all consumers to the full range of ideas, the confrontation of ideas in common forums, and public scrutiny of factual and causal claims by knowledgeable experts. On the benefits of a free market of ideas, see John Stuart Mill, *On Liberty* (Cambridge, U.K.: Cambridge University Press, 1989), part 2. Mill himself argued only that unconstrained debate was a guarantee that superior ideas would not be permanently suppressed; even he did not contend that the invisible hand of competition would automatically lead to the victory of the best idea, let alone of truth.

24. Stephen Van Evera, "Primed For Peace: Europe after the Cold War," *International Security,* Vol. 15, No. 3 (Winter 1990/91), p. 27.

25. Gary Becker, "A Theory of Competition among Pressure Groups for Political Influence," *Quarterly Journal of Economics,* Vol. 98, No. 3 (August 1983), pp. 371–400.

26. Our conception of the free marketplace of ideas includes features commonly ascribed to "civil society" and Jürgen Habermas's notion of "the public sphere." Like civil society, of which it is part, the free marketplace requires a legally sanctioned societal capacity for voluntary and autonomous organization. Like the "public sphere," a well-functioning marketplace is characterized by a public

Thus, the commodities exchanged in the market are consumers' political support and suppliers' policy commitments. The role that ideas play in the "marketplace of ideas" is not that of goods, but that of advertisements for political support.[27] Ideas put forward in the marketplace convey purported information about values and interests, and also about facts and causal inferences from facts. Thus, the supplier uses advertising to convince the consumer to want what the supplier has to offer: for example, to believe that the fulfillment of the nation's destiny is rightful and valuable, and that the consumer's personal interests and values will be served by it. The supplier also tries to convince the consumer that the offered policies will produce the advertised benefits with a high probability at a low cost, and that alternative policies will lead to worse results. To accomplish this, the suppliers' advertising includes claims about, for example, the nature of the nation's opponents, the likelihood of cooperation with other national groups, the history of past interactions with them, and the prospects of success from nationalist mobilization or armed conflict.[28]

Our conception of the marketplace of ideas is based on the description of economic markets provided by standard economic analysis. The structure of the market consists of the degree of concentration of supply, the degree of segmentation of demand, and the strength of institutions regulating market interactions, including those that provide information or regulate advertising. Imperfect competition occurs when there are few sellers because of large scale economies and high barriers to entry, and when products are differentiated for sale to segmented markets. Market segmentation may occur as a result of consumers' distinctive tastes for differentiated products, the artificial inculcation of differentiated preferences through targeted advertising, transportation costs or other advantages in distribution and marketing to a particular set of consumers, or political barriers to exchange between market segments. Under these conditions, sellers tend to engage either in competitive advertising, col-

---

debate in which rational arguments are more decisive than appeals to tradition or the status of actors. However, whereas both civil society and the public sphere are typically conceived as exclusively non-state realms of activity, the marketplace of ideas embraces both state and non-state actors, focusing on their discursive and institutional interaction. Craig Calhoun, "Civil Society and The Public Sphere," *Public Culture*, Vol. 5, No. 2 (Winter 1993), pp. 267–280; Jürgen Habermas, *The Structural Transformation of the Public Sphere* (Cambridge, Mass.: MIT Press, 1989).

27. Becker, "A Theory of Competition," p. 392.

28. Ideas may also serve as signals of commitment, staking suppliers' reputation on their promise to deliver on a policy pledge. For example, nationalists may choose to enhance their credibility with their supporters through extremist rhetoric that burns bridges to alternative constituencies.

lusion to divide up market share, or a combination of the two.[29] Rivalry is more likely when barriers to entry are falling, or in a "young industry," where "sellers may not have learned what to expect of rivals" and "may be scrambling to secure an established place in the industry, in the process inadvertently starting a price war."[30] To achieve socially beneficial outcomes under imperfect competition, regulation is needed to break up trusts, prohibit collusion, and insure truth in advertising.

The marketplace of ideas in newly democratizing states often mirrors that of a young, poorly regulated industry, where barriers to entry are falling, competition is imperfect, and oligopolistic elites exploit partial media monopolies in intense competition to win mass support in a segmented market. This kind of imperfectly competitive market may yield the worst of both worlds: elites are driven to compete for the mobilization of mass support, but by targeting niche markets, they can avoid debating in a common forum where ideas are publicly held up to rigorous scrutiny by competitors and expert evaluators. In these circumstances, nationalism may help elites to gain support in an ethnic market niche and also to maintain high barriers to entry by diverting demands for civic participation into mobilization for national goals. Thus, market conditions in newly democratizing states often create both the incentive for nationalist advertising and the conditions for its success, as we explain below.

PARTIAL MONOPOLIES OF SUPPLY

What human rights advocates fear most is a complete governmental monopoly over the press. In this situation, the government can propagate any nationalist myth without having to face countervailing arguments. While we agree that perfect monopoly is hardly desirable, we argue that it is not the only—and perhaps not the most—dangerous condition for nationalist mythmaking. Conditions of perfect monopoly make the audience skeptical. In communist and

---

29. Paul Samuelson, *Economics*, 15th ed. (New York: McGraw-Hill, 1995), chaps. 9–10, esp. p. 152; Edwin Mansfield, *Microeconomics*, 4th ed. (New York: Norton, 1982), chaps. 11–12, esp. pp. 323, 344–346, 353–355; James W. Friedman, *Oligopoly Theory* (Cambridge, U.K.: Cambridge University Press, 1983), pp. 138–145; Robert Kuenne, *The Economics of Oligopolistic Competition* (Oxford, U.K.: Blackwell, 1992), pp. 469–476.

30. Richard Leftwich and Ross Eckert, *The Price System and Resource Allocation*, 9th ed. (Chicago: Dryden, 1985), p. 407. The same uncertainty that fuels rivalrous behavior in a "young industry" typically characterizes periods of democratization and, in the absence of shared norms or effective enforcement mechanisms, often produces the same results. See Adam Przeworski, *Democracy and the Market* (Cambridge, U.K.: Cambridge University Press, 1991).

other authoritarian states, for example, people tend to discount propaganda precisely because they know that it comes from a monopolistic source, and typically turn to informal networks and stratagems for reading between the lines of official discourse.[31] Moreover, perfect monopolists often lack a motive to mobilize their population's nationalism. Facing no active opposition and ruling without popular consent, they face little need to compete for the mantle of popular legitimacy by whipping up mass enthusiasms. Indeed, unleashing mass nationalism would only hinder their goal of depoliticizing domestic politics and would introduce needless complications into their management of foreign relations.[32] For this reason, dictatorships play the nationalist card only under two conditions: when their ability to monopolize power and discourse is slipping, like that of the Argentine junta on the eve of the Falklands War, or when their ascent to power, and hence their legitimacy, have been based on the use of popular nationalism to prevail in an initially pluralistic setting, such as Bonaparte after the French Revolution, Hitler after the Weimar Republic, or the Japanese military regime after the collapse of the Taisho democracy of the 1920s.[33]

Especially prone to nationalist mythmaking are situations of partial monopoly over supply in the marketplace of ideas, which often occur during the earliest stages of democratization. In such conditions of intra-elite competition, governments and other elite interests often enjoy residual market power as the legacy of authoritarian monopoly control: the state or economic elites of the threatened ruling circles may still control key components of the mass media or have the resources to shape its content. Nationalist militaries may invoke their monopoly of specialized expertise to exaggerate foreign threats; the government may tendentiously regulate broadcast media in what it calls "the public interest"; private economic lobbies may buy journalists, supposedly

---

31. Ellen Mickiewicz, *Split Signals: Television and Politics in The Soviet Union* (New York: Oxford University Press, 1988); Allyn and Wilkinson, *Guidelines for Journalists*, pp. 17–18; Ithiel de Sola Pool, "Communication in Totalitarian Societies," in Ithiel de Sola Pool, Wilbur Schramm, et al., *Handbook of Communication* (Chicago: Rand McNally, 1973), pp. 462–511.
32. Stanislav Andreski, "On the Peaceful Disposition of Military Dictatorships," *Journal of Strategic Studies*, Vol. 3, No. 3 (December 1980), pp. 3–10.
33. Robert B. Holtman, *Napoleonic Propaganda* (Baton Rouge: Louisiana State University Press, 1950); Richard Smethurst, *A Social Basis for Prewar Japanese Militarism* (Berkeley: University of California Press, 1974); on the role of the Japanese press in promoting nationalism and empire, see John A. Lent, ed., *Newspapers in Asia* (Hong Kong: Heineman Asia, 1982), pp. 103, 106–108; on the nationalist rhetoric of the increasingly free Argentine press on the eve of the Falklands War, see Richard Ned Lebow, "Miscalculation in the South Atlantic," in Robert Jervis et al., *Psychology and Deterrence* (Baltimore, Md.: Johns Hopkins University Press, 1985), pp. 98–99.

neutral experts, and media access. For example, Alfred Hugenberg, the chairman of the board of directors of Krupp Steel during World War I and the chairman of the German National People's Party during the Weimar Republic, established the Telegraph Union wire service, which gave him control over half of Germany's press.[34] By providing loans, reduced-rate newsprint, and accounting services to inflation-ridden papers, Hugenberg achieved substantial control over many papers while maintaining their facades of independence. Though even small cities often had multiple newspapers, Hugenberg's service fed them all the same nationalist-slanted copy.

As a democratizing political system opens up, old elites and rising counter-elites must compete for the support of new entrants into the marketplace through popular appeals, including appeals to the purported common interests of elites and mass groups in pursuing nationalistic aims against out-groups. In many instances, including the case of Serbian President Slobodan Milošević, these elites evince little interest in nationalism until rising pressure for mass political participation gives them an incentive to do so.[35] This strategy worked extremely well, for example, for the Kaiser-appointed governments of Bismarckian and Wilhelmine Germany, which faced the dilemma of winning budgetary approval from a Reichstag elected by universal suffrage. Five times between the founding of the Reich and 1914 the government chose to fight elections on what it styled as "national" issues—the Kulturkampf against the Catholics in 1874, the campaign of 1878 tarring socialists as anti-national, the campaigns to support bills to strengthen the army in 1887 and in 1893, and the "Hottentot election" on German colonial policy in 1907. Each time elections were fought on "national" grounds, voter turnout increased and more rightist candidates were elected, in part because conservative candidates got more votes overall and in part because coalitions of right-wing parties were more cohesive. Hidden financing of nationalist movements and publications by the Navy and by industrial interests, combined with prosecutions of opposition voices under a restrictive press law, played an essential part in this strategy.[36]

---

34. Modris Eksteins, *The Limits of Reason: The German Democratic Press and the Collapse of Weimar Democracy* (London: Oxford University Press, 1975).

35. Laura Silber and Allan Little, *Yugoslavia: Death of a Nation* (New York: TV Books, 1996), pp. 38–39.

36. Brett Fairbairn, "Interpreting Wilhelmine Elections: National Issues, Fairness Issues, and Electoral Mobilization," in Larry Eugene Jones and James Retallack, eds., *Elections, Mass Politics, and Social Change in Modern Germany* (Cambridge, U.K.: Cambridge University Press, 1992), pp. 20–23; Robert J. Goldstein, *Political Repression in Nineteenth Century Europe* (London: Croom Helm, 1983),

Rising counter-elites also tend to play the nationalist card; indeed, they often make the initial move in a spiral of nationalist outbidding. From the French revolution to contemporary Armenia, Azerbaijan, Georgia, and Croatia, it has often been elites from outside the ruling circles who pushed nationalist issues to the fore of the public debate, asserting a right to rule on the grounds that old elites were lax in pursuing the national or ethnic interest. In principle, populist counter-elites in conditions of incipient democratization can opt for any of several ideological stances *vis-à-vis* the old authoritarian regime. They can pursue a liberal strategy, criticizing the old elites' denial of individual civic rights; a socialist line, criticizing class domination; an ethnic line, criticizing the old elite for favoring a particular cultural group; or a more inclusive nationalist line, arguing that the narrow, venal old elite was ignoring the broader national interest. Nationalism is often attractive to rising counter-elites in part for the same reason that old ruling elites adopt it: unlike liberalism or socialism, nationalism allows the aspiring elite to make claims in the name of the masses without necessarily committing itself to a policy of sharing power and wealth with the masses once it has seized control of the state. Other incentives may depend more on context: e.g., which ideologies are discredited by association with the hated *ancien régime*, whether cultural differences are already salient and thus available to be politicized as ethnonationalism, and whether the rising counter-elite has some particular comparative advantage as the standard bearer for a distinctive national culture, as might be the case with literary or religious elites.[37] Also important, however, is whether the structure of demand in the marketplace of ideas is highly segmented, and thus permissive for nationalist mythmaking.

SEGMENTATION OF DEMAND

A well-constituted marketplace of ideas depends not only on the expression of diverse views by different groups in society, but also on individuals' exposure to diverse ideas. A highly segmented marketplace has the former, but not the latter. In a segmented marketplace of ideas, individuals in one market segment

---

p. 39; Dirk Stegmann, "Between Economic Interests and Radical Nationalism," in Larry Eugene Jones and James Retallack, eds., *Between Reform, Reaction, and Resistance: Studies in the History of German Conservatism from 1789 to 1945* (Providence, R.I.: Berg, 1993), pp. 173, 183; Geoff Eley, *Reshaping the German Right* (New Haven, Conn.: Yale University Press, 1980), pp. 140–147.

37. On the latter point, see Karen Barkey, "Consequences of Empire," in Karen Barkey and Mark von Hagen, eds., *After Empire: Multi-Ethnic Societies and Nation-Building* (Boulder, Colo.: Westview, forthcoming 1997). On the contending discourses of class and nation, see Ronald Suny, *The Revenge of the Past* (Stanford, Calif.: Stanford University Press, 1993).

lack exposure to ideas expressed in other segments, or exposure is filtered through sources that distort those ideas.

Demand in the marketplace of ideas is likely to be segmented in newly democratizing states. A common sphere of democratic discourse depends on the development of unifying institutions, such as state-wide non-partisan media, which take time to construct. In many cases, the authoritarian states or colonial powers that were the democratizing states' predecessors leave a legacy of divisive institutions and ideas that were elements in a strategy of divide-and-rule. In other cases, democracy and freedom of expression are newly thrust upon traditional societies whose political horizons have historically been local and communal.[38] Even in democratizing post-communist states with a legacy of hypercentralization, the media's financial vulnerability often leaves it vulnerable to capture by partisan segments, thus spoiling it as a neutral forum for debate.[39]

Narrow market segments magnify the effects of oligopolistic control over supply, because they are more susceptible to domination by a single, myth-purveying supplier. Unlike true monopolists, oligopolists *are* forced to compete, but they often do so by increasing sales to consumers in segments of the market that they can monopolize, rather than in market segments where they face strong competitors. When this happens, there is no common marketplace of ideas, in which contending discourses and evidence confront each other directly on an even playing field. Instead, the existence of parallel monopoly discourses creates the illusion of market pluralism and free choice of ideas and, by vitiating skepticism, makes oligopolistic propaganda more effective than under pure monopoly.[40] Thus, the more segmented the market, the more the effects of partial monopolies of supply are magnified, and the more feasible is mythmaking.

Nationalist groups in the newly democratic Weimar Republic, including those backed by heavy industrial cartels, competed for mass electoral support against labor parties and liberals not so much by preaching to the constituencies of their opponents as by exploiting partial propaganda monopolies to mobilize their own. Hugenberg had only 50 percent of the overall Weimar

38. Gérard Prunier, *The Rwanda Crisis: History of a Genocide* (New York: Columbia University Press, 1995), p. 140.
39. On market segmentation in the Russian case, see Laura Belin, "Russia: Wrestling Political and Financial Repression," ibid., pp. 59–63; Victor Davidoff, "Regional Press Fights Political Control," ibid., p. 65; Laurie Wilson, "Communication and Russia: Evolving Media in a Changing Society," *Social Science Journal*, Vol. 32, No. 1 (January 1995), p. 113.
40. For related arguments, see Edward S. Herman and Noam Chomsky, *Manufacturing Consent* (New York: Pantheon, 1988).

media market, but he enjoyed a virtual monopoly over the flow of news to papers in Germany's small cities and towns, the locations that later voted most heavily for Hitler.[41] Exploiting Hugenberg's priming of middle class opinion, Hitler's successes came not from winning over liberal, socialist, or undecided opinion in open debate, but by cornering the nationalist market segment through skillful penetration of grassroots voluntary organizations, such as veterans groups and beer-drinking societies.[42] Since Hitler attained a dominant position in the Reichstag with only one-third of the vote, and used this as a platform for an unconstitutional seizure of the media and other state powers, monopolizing one segment of the market was enough to be decisive in a splintered polity.[43]

Segmented markets of ideas in democratizing states are conducive to nationalism for several reasons. The most fundamental reason is that elites have an incentive to promote nationalist populism as a substitute for true democratization. Segmented markets allow elite oligopolists to carve out a market niche where their nationalist ideas are not held up to systematic scrutiny. This is true even if the segmental divisions do not follow linguistic, ethnic, or communal lines. The nationalist market niches in Weimar Germany and in contemporary Russia, for example, reflect segmental cleavages *within* the majority ethnic group, such as those between urban and rural groups, between large cities and small towns, between soldiers or veterans and civilians, between economic strata, or between age groups. In these cases, mobilization of support by nationalists and by nationalistic Russian communists relied more heavily on face-to-face ward-heeling, handbills, and pamphlets targeted to specialized constituencies than on open media debate aimed at a broader range of society.[44]

---

41. Eksteins, *Limits of Reason*, pp. 80–81; Thomas Childers, *The Nazi Voter* (Chapel Hill: University of North Carolina Press, 1983), pp. 157–159.
42. Richard Bessel, "The Formation and Dissolution of a German National Electorate," in Larry Eugene Jones and James Retallack, eds., *Elections, Mass Politics, and Social Change in Modern Germany* (Cambridge, U.K.: Cambridge University Press, 1992), pp. 404, 412–413; Peter Fritzsche, "Weimar Populism and National Socialism in Local Perspective," in Jones and Retallack, *Elections*, pp. 301–304; Wolfgang Mommsen, "Government without Parties," in Jones and Retallack, *Between Reform, Reaction, and Resistance*, pp. 359, 372.
43. E.J. Feuchtwanger, *From Weimar to Hitler* (London: Macmillan, 1993), pp. 298, 313–314. On the negative effects of unmodified proportional representation systems like Weimar's in fragmented polities, see Donald Horowitz, *A Democratic South Africa? Constitutional Engineering in a Divided Society* (Berkeley: University of California Press, 1991), pp. 166–176.
44. Childers, "The Social Language of Politics in Germany," pp. 331–358; Laura Belin, "Ultranationalist Parties Follow Disparate Paths," *Transition*, Vol. 1, No. 1 (June 23, 1995), pp. 8–12; Jerry F. Hough, Evelyn Davidheiser, and Susan Goodrich Lehmann, *The 1966 Russian Presidential Election* (Washington: Brookings, 1996), esp. pp. 2–13, 45–46, 69–70.

Market segmentation in newly democratizing states sometimes follows communal or linguistic lines. Language differences and exclusive face-to-face social networks may channel the dissemination of ideas along ethnic lines. These ethnic segments rarely start out with a highly developed sense of national political identity or nationalist political goals. On the contrary, ethnicity typically becomes politicized as nationalism only after the emergence of mass political discourse. Still less do ethnic market segments start out with consumer preferences for militant, xenophobic nationalism, based on "ancient hatreds." An ethnically differentiated market segment may, however, share a set of common experiences and a common, parochial discourse, which mythmakers can exploit.[45]

Propaganda is most effective when it taps into the audience's predispositions or when it can link a new idea to attitudes that the audience already holds.[46] Thus, Milošević's success in mobilizing Serbian ethnic sentiment was due not only to his monopoly over Belgrade television but also to the historical legacy of ethnic conflict and the tense situation between Albanians and Serbs in Kosovo, which left his Serbian audience primed to accept his divisive and uncontested message. In this situation, there was positive feedback between supply and demand, in that segmented public opinion was ripe for nationalist appeals, which in turn increased nationalism and deepened the segmentation of the market.

Even those scholars who tout the rationality of public opinion attach two crucial qualifications, one on the supply side and one on the demand side: the public responds rationally to events within the limits of the information and analysis that it receives, and given its predispositions.[47] John Zaller, for example, shows that American voters rely for their opinions on perceived experts whom they believe share their own values.[48] In this view, experts do not tell

45. Susanne Hoeber Rudolph and Lloyd Rudolph, "Modern Hate," *New Republic*, Vol. 208, No. 12 (March 22, 1993), pp. 24–29; Milton Esman, *Ethnic Politics* (Ithaca, N.Y.: Cornell University Press, 1994), pp. 28–31.
46. Paul Keckemeti, "Propaganda," in Pool, *Handbook of Communication*, pp. 844–870; Donald Kinder and David Sears, "Public Opinion and Political Action," in Gardner Lindzey and Elliot Aronson, eds., *Handbook of Social Psychology*, Vol. 3 (New York: Random House, 1985), pp. 659–741; Robert Jervis, *Perception and Misperception in International Politics* (Princeton, N.J.: Princeton University Press, 1976).
47. Benjamin Page and Robert Shapiro, *The Rational Public* (Chicago: University of Chicago, 1992). Consumers' level of education—and presumably their sophistication about propaganda—seems to have mixed effects. Page and Shapiro, pp. 178, 203–205, 313–330.
48. John Zaller, *The Nature and Origins of Mass Opinion* (Cambridge, U.K.: Cambridge University Press, 1992).

people what to care about, but they do shape people's estimates of the costs and feasibility of various means for pursuing the ends that they value. Consequently, demand reflects not only the preferences of consumers but also the extent to which consumers with similar predispositions are isolated in separate market segments, each dominated by a single supplier.

Often the ethnic or communal segmentation of the market is not a spontaneous reflection of language or traditional social organization, but rather the modern artifact of elite strategies of divide and rule. For example, European colonial rulers—whether Stalin in Central Asia or Belgians in Rwanda—often highlighted or even created ethnic cleavages in order to split local populations and insure the dependence of native functionaries. Even in the heart of Europe, Bismarck and his successors concocted the segmentation of the German marketplace of ideas through their nationalistic agenda-setting and electoral propaganda, which divided the middle classes from socialists and Catholics, who were stigmatized as "enemies of the Reich." The belligerent tone of the bourgeois press, pressure groups and associations like the Navy League and Colonial Society, and political parties were all shaped by the nationalist themes around which elections were fought. Militarist ideas promoted in these campaigns and fostered by the middle-class, Protestant, patriotic organizations they spawned—including the notions of a need for *Lebensraum*, victimization by the encircling great powers, the superiority of German culture, and the spiritual benefits of war—became standard fare in right-wing thinking. In this way, electoral tactics erected high walls between segments of German society, which continued to shape political discourse and electoral strategies down through the Weimar period.[49]

Sometimes elites segment the marketplace in a way that inadvertently loads the dice in favor of nationalist ideas. Tito's decentralizing reforms of the 1960s, which were intended in part to assuage and defuse ethno-nationalism, put Yugoslavia's media in the hands of regional leaderships, which in the 1980s fell into the hands of nationalists like Milošević. This federalization of power left pan-Yugoslav reformers like Ante Marković with no instrument for transcending the Serb and Croat nationalists' media monopoly over their respective ethnic niche markets.

---

49. Stegmann, "Between Economic Interests and Radical Nationalism," in Jones and Retallack, *Between Reform,* p. 170; Fairbairn, "Interpreting Wilhelmine Elections," in Jones and Retallack, *Elections,* pp. 22–23.

While governmental elites in democratizing states are segmenting the emerging marketplace of ideas, counter-elites and consumers are rarely passive. Often, elite manipulations produce unintended consequences, and nationalist mobilization spins out of control. In Wilhelmine Germany, for example, the strategy of popular nationalism became less and less manageable for the "iron and rye" coalition of heavy industrialists and landed aristocrats. Numerically, the working class grew faster than other constituencies, shrinking the base from which the government could mobilize a majority. Moreover, the conservative elites' mass allies increasingly tried to use nationalist issues to push the old elites aside. After Germany's supposed humiliation by France in the Moroccan Crisis of 1911, mass nationalist groups and middle-class military officers claimed that the old elites running the German state lacked the dynamism to meet the looming challenge from Germany's enemies. To stay ahead of this tide of popular criticism, even the Junker aristocrats leading the Conservative party felt compelled to slam the weak policy of the Bethmann Hollweg government.[50] The elites had unleashed a power that they were unable to control.

Segmentation of demand, in short, may be shaped by a number of factors: the pre-existing preferences or experiences of groups sharing a common outlook; differentiated preferences induced by targeted advertising; division of media markets by language or region; or divisions imposed by political boundaries, as in federal systems. Such factors may be overridden, however, if political discourse is channeled into a wider framework by strong catchall parties or non-partisan media institutions.

MEDIA INSTITUTIONS AND NORMS

Where markets are imperfect, increased freedom of speech will tend to exacerbate nationalist mythmaking unless institutions and norms correct the flaws in the market. A well-institutionalized marketplace of ideas requires anti-trust and equal time regulations guaranteeing media access, the training of journalists in the verification of sources and the separation of fact from opinion, and the development of expert evaluative institutions whose prestige depends on maintaining a reputation for objectivity. Without such regulatory institutions, free speech by itself will not guarantee that a range of voices is effectively heard, that competing arguments are forced to confront each other on the

---

50. Eley, *Reshaping the German Right*, chap. 11; James Retallack, "The Road to Philippi: The Conservative Party and Bethmann Hollweg's 'Politics of the Diagonal,' 1909–1914," in Jones and Retallack, *Between Reform*, pp. 286–287.

merits, that participants in debate are held accountable for the accuracy of their statements, that factual claims are scrutinized, that experts' credentials are verified, that hidden sources of bias are exposed, or that violators of the norms of fair debate are held up to public censure.[51]

Regulation entails some risk of abuse, the severity of which depends in part on how it is carried out. In centralized forms of regulation, a state official or governmental body decides who has access to the media and what are the ground rules for its use. In contrast, decentralized regulation is achieved through routines of professional behavior in institutions such as the professional media, universities, think tanks, and legislative oversight bodies. Both forms of regulation may be useful antidotes to market imperfections, and both may be used in combination. Decentralized regulation is generally preferable, since centralized regulation creates the risk that the state will exploit its regulatory power to establish its own media monopoly. However, where decentralized institutions are weak or lack the required professional norms, centralized regulation, especially if it is subject to democratic control or held accountable to international standards, may be preferable to an imperfect, unregulated marketplace.

Similarly, the regulation of the content of speech, such as the banning of hate speech, is more subject to abuse than the establishment of norms of debate, which set standards for how people are expected to argue their cases. The latter would include the professional journalist's norm of distinguishing facts from opinion, the scholar's norm of citing sources of alleged facts, and the League of Women Voters' norm of expecting candidates to debate issues in a common forum in front of a panel of disinterested expert questioners. Establishing strong norms of debate is generally preferable to regulating the content of speech, but when norms are weak, content regulation may also be needed. Like centralized regulation, content limits should be accountable to democratic oversight or international standards.

Regulation is not a panacea. Indeed, skeptics doubt how well media institutions structure public debate even in the most mature democracies. Nevertheless, there is substantial evidence that effective evaluative institutions do have an impact on public views. Studies show that, apart from the influence of a

---

51. For various approaches to regulating speech and media, see Judith Lichtenberg, ed., *Democracy and the Mass Media* (Cambridge, U.K.: Cambridge University Press, 1990), esp. pp. 52, 127–128, 144–145, 186–201.

popular president, American public opinion is swayed most strongly by the media testimony of experts who are perceived to be credible and unbiased.[52]

If the marketplace of ideas is imperfect even in mature democracies, its flaws are still more grave in new democracies. An integrated public sphere, in which each idea confronts every other idea on its merits, does not get created overnight. Without the functional equivalents of institutions like the *New York Times*, the MacNeil-Lehrer News Hour, the Brookings Institution, and the Congressional Budget Office, discussion may be open, but an exchange and evaluation of contending views before a common audience may not occur. In many newly democratizing societies, press laws are biased and capriciously enforced.[53] The middlemen of the marketplace of ideas—journalists, public intellectuals, and public-interest watchdogs—tend to perform poorly in the initial stages of the expansion of press freedom. Instead of digging out the truth and blowing the whistle on fallacious arguments, journalists in emerging markets are often beholden to a particular party or interest group, make little attempt to distinguish between fact and opinion, and lack training in the standards of journalistic professionalism.[54] While Thomas Jefferson said that if forced to choose, he would rather have a free press than a democratic government, in assessing the actual state of the press in young America, he remarked that "a suppression of the press could not more completely deprive the nation of its benefits, than is done by its abandoned prostitution to falsehood. Nothing can now be believed which is seen in a newspaper. Truth itself becomes suspicious by being put into that polluted vehicle."[55]

Even if a new democracy has a responsible elite press, its ability to impose a coherent structure on discourse may not penetrate to the grassroots level. Weimar's liberal, Jewish-owned, mass circulation newspapers were objective and even erudite, but their ideas failed to penetrate beyond Berlin or Hamburg. Even in those urban centers, workers read the liberal press only for the sports, feature stories, and movie listings, ignoring the political views of the "class enemy." Today, India's elite English-language press has a laudable system of self-regulation and responsible coverage of communal conflict, but the populist

---

52. Page and Shapiro, *The Rational Public*, pp. 339–354; for a skeptical view, see Robert Entman, *Democracy without Citizens* (New York: Oxford University Press, 1989).
53. See the periodic country studies by Article 19 and Freedom House.
54. Phillip Knightly, *The First Casualty* (New York: Harcourt, Brace, Jovanovich, 1975), pp. 21–25; Michael Schudson, *Discovering the News: A Social History* (New York: Basic, 1978); Belin, "Russia: Wrestling Political and Financial Repression," pp. 59–63; Lent, *Newspapers in Asia*, pp. 176, 211.
55. Letter to John Norvell, June 14, 1807, in Merrill D. Peterson, ed., *The Portable Thomas Jefferson* (New York: Viking, 1975), p. 505.

vernacular press remains immune to these high standards. In newly democratizing states, the penetration of ideas to the grassroots often requires face-to-face contacts. In India, at least before Indira Gandhi's time, this was accomplished by the moderate, secularist political machine of the Congress Party. In contrast, at the dawn of Sri Lankan democracy in the 1950s, only Sinhalese Buddhist priests, who fiercely opposed toleration of the Tamil Hindu minority, had networks for persuading voters at the crucial village level.[56]

MARKET FORCES THAT PROMOTE NATIONALIST MYTHMAKING
In summary, under conditions of incipient democratization, the increased openness of public debate often fosters nationalist mythmaking and ethnic conflict because opportunistic governmental and non-governmental elites exploit partial monopolies of supply, segmented demand, and the weakness of regulatory institutions in the marketplace of ideas. We argue that the greater these market imperfections (that is, the greater the rivalry between oligopolistic elites, the greater the consumer segmentation, and the more dependent and partisan are media institutions), then the greater the likelihood for nationalist mythmaking to dominate public discourse, and the greater the likelihood for mythmaking to promote conflict. Conversely, the more perfect the marketplace and the more integrated the public sphere, the less effective is nationalist mythmaking. These hypotheses are probabilistic, not invariant relationships or sufficient causes. This article does not present a systematic test of all these propositions. As a first step towards evaluating them, however, we examine two hard cases, Yugoslavia and Rwanda, which are often invoked on behalf of the conventional wisdom that governments are largely responsible for nationalist mythmaking and that unconditional free speech is the best antidote.

Monopolizing Market Segments in the Former Yugoslavia

On the surface, the story of the media in the Yugoslav conflict may seem to fit the Human Rights Watch analysis quite well. Government officials in the republics of Serbia and Croatia used their near-monopoly control of the news media to fuel their publics' ethnic prejudices, mobilizing a popular nationalist constituency to support their rule while discrediting more liberal opponents. However, the media monopoly merely gave elites in the republics the tools to

---

56. James Manor, "The Failure of Political Integration in Sri Lanka (Ceylon)," *Journal of Commonwealth and Comparative Politics*, Vol. 17, No. 1 (March 1979), pp. 21–44, esp. 21–23.

sell nationalist myths. The motive and the opportunity were created by the Serbian elite's fear of democratization, by the plausibility of these myths to consumers in a segmented market, and by the unevenness of journalistic standards. Under these highly imperfect market conditions, the weakening of the central Yugoslav state created a potential opening for increased political pluralism, which threatened the oligarchs who ruled the federal republics and also created an opportunity for political entrepreneurs—including politicians, journalists, and intellectuals—to exploit their media market power in the competition for mass support. Tito's dispersion of control over television to the republics in the 1960s and 1970s, under the theory that a federalist devolution of power would dampen underlying ethnic tensions, turned out to have been a grave mistake. By 1989, when Yugoslav Prime Minister Ante Marković finally embarked on the creation of an all-Yugoslav television network, it was already too little, too late. This suggests that NGOs' standard prescription of reducing centralized state media power needs strong qualifications.

In 1987, Slobodan Milošević, head of the Serbian Central Committee of the League of Communists, mounted a systematic campaign using his control over the Serbian state television monopoly to convince the Serbian people that Serbs residing in Kosovo province, the historic cradle of Serbdom, were suffering discrimination, repression, and rape at the hands of the Albanian majority there. He chose the television correspondent who would report to Belgrade from Pristina, the capital of Kosovo, and personally phoned the station almost daily to tell the editors what stories to highlight.[57] After Milošević's April 1987 speech in Kosovo, Belgrade TV showed the local Albanian police clubbing the Serbian crowd, and Milošević saying "From now on, no one has the right to beat you," but it left out the pictures of the crowd stoning the police.[58] Exploiting the wave of chauvinist sentiment touched off by this media campaign, Milošević used the Kosovo issue as a pretext to purge anti-Milošević journalists, charging them with issuing "one-sided and untrue reports," and to consolidate conservative domination in party circles in Belgrade. Thus, nationalist media manipulation was the centerpiece of Milošević's successful strategy for defeating liberal reformers in the scramble for both mass and elite support as power devolved from the center in the post-Tito period. Milošević never

---

57. Thompson, *Forging War,* p. 20; Zdenka Milivojević, "The Media in Serbia from 1985 to 1994," in Dušan Janjić, ed., *Serbia Between the Past and the Future* (Belgrade: Institute of Social Sciences, 1995), pp. 168–169.
58. Velko Vujacic, "Serbian Nationalism, Slobodan Milosevic and the Origins of the Yugoslav War," *The Harriman Review,* Vol. 8, No. 4 (December 1995), p. 29; Thompson, *Forging War,* p. 20.

achieved an absolute monopoly over the Serb media, but he controlled its commanding heights, the state television station and Belgrade's three major daily newspapers. An independent TV station and the semi-independent *Borba* newspaper were prevented by low wattage and limited newsprint from reaching beyond the Belgrade suburbs into Milošević's stronghold in rural Serbia.[59]

Because of Yugoslavia's decentralized federal structure, republican television stations were totally independent of the central government, but were monopolized by the republican Communist parties. The Yugoslav media, like most other aspects of Yugoslav life, had become by the 1980s "an alliance of regional oligarchies."[60] Republican television stations would not even show Prime Minister Marković's speeches. To combat this, Marković established an all-Yugoslav network, Yutel, in 1989. However, the central government's financial limitations, themselves a consequence of Yugoslavia's federal structure, left Yutel dependent on army surplus equipment and the sufferance of local broadcasters. After only four months on the air, Croatia pulled the plug on Yutel over a sensitive story on Slavonia, and most other republics followed suit. As the *coup de grace*, Serbian nationalist thugs trashed Yutel's Belgrade office.[61] Thus, the ability of republican government leaders to manipulate the mass media reflected the collapse of the multi-national Yugoslav state.

However, the ethnic segmentation of the media market cannot be blamed entirely on republican governments. Journalists and scholars also played the ethnic card, in some cases well before Milošević. Many Serbian intellectuals were obsessed with the Albanian threat in Kosovo even before Milošević began his media campaign on the issue. In 1986, for example, a large number of prominent members of the Serbian Academy of Sciences published a memorandum on the "genocide" being perpetrated against Serbs in Kosovo. This document was condemned by the Serbian Central Committee and the mainstream Belgrade press, still operating under traditional Yugoslav norms of comity between ethnic groups, though Milošević urged them to keep the condemnation secret. Some of these nationalist intellectuals and a portion of

59. Gagnon, "Ethnic Nationalism and International Conflict: The Case of Serbia"; Susan Woodward, *Balkan Tragedy* (Washington, D.C.: Brookings, 1995), pp. 99, 230–232, 293; Branka Magaš, *The Destruction of Yugoslavia* (London: Verso, 1993), pp. 3–76; Thompson, *Forging War*, p. 56, 65–66, 114–116, 124.

60. Thompson, *Forging War*, pp. 6–7, 16.

61. Thompson, *Forging War*, pp. 38–43; Woodward, *Balkan Tragedy*, p. 230. In Croatia, only 600,000 people out of ten million get their news from media not controlled by the government, according to a survey conducted by Miklos Biro, "Is Anybody Out There?" *War Report*, No. 39 (February/March 1996), p. 17.

the Serbian journalistic community may have been acting partly out of sincere concerns. But in the view of some analysts, these intellectuals saw the Kosovo issue as a vehicle for breaking down communist limitations on intellectual freedom and for press "liberalization."[62] This reflected the necessity for all Yugoslav elites to reposition themselves on a new foundation of ideological legitimacy in the context of the waning of centralized communist authority. In this setting, the professional journalistic community split, some choosing the nationalist route and energetically aiding the Milošević takeover, some resisting it and ultimately being forced out.[63] Mark Thompson of the journalism NGO Article 19, though generally a strong partisan of Yugoslavia's independent journalists, describes the Milošević takeover in the fall of 1987 as "a collusion among Serbia's Communist politicians, its bureaucracy, its intellectual class, and its news media."[64]

Thus, organized forces in "civil society," no less than in government, saw the benefits of the strategy of monopolizing media control within a market niche. They were sometimes even willing to conspire explicitly with the ethnic archfoe to accomplish it. For example, after Serb, Croat, and Muslim nationalist parties emerged as the winners of Bosnia's 1991 elections, the three nationalist foes tried to collude to divide up among them the assets of Bosnia's integrated, civic television service, and to exclude the moderate parties of their respective ethnic groups.[65]

The success of media propaganda depended both on monopoly of supply and also on the nature of demand, including the plausibility of the message in light of consumers' predispositions. Some propaganda campaigns were strikingly successful. For example, the Serbs enjoyed a six-month period of television monopoly in northern Bosnia, which they used to prime their population for the 1992 campaign of "ethnic cleansing" by repeatedly charging that Muslims were plotting to establish an Islamic fundamentalist state. Later, Serbs guarding prison camps accused their Muslim captives of precisely the charges that had been reiterated on the news. Similarly, as a result of Serb propaganda, 38 percent of Belgrade residents in a July 1992 poll thought that it was the Muslim-Croat forces who had recently been shelling the Bosnian capital of

62. Milivojević, "The Media in Serbia," p. 164; Thompson, *Forging War*, p. 54; Silber and Little, *Yugoslavia*, p. 33; see also Magaš, *Destruction*, pp. 49–76.
63. Gagnon, "Ethnic Nationalism and International Conflict: The Case of Serbia," pp. 145–152; Vujacic, "Serbian Nationalism," p. 30; Thompson, *Forging War*, pp. 23–24, 52–53.
64. Thompson, *Forging War*, p. 55.
65. Thompson, *Forging War*, pp. 221–224; Woodward, *Balkan Tragedy*, p. 230.

Sarajevo, versus only 20 percent who knew it had been the Serbs.[66] However, viewers refused to swallow every lie whole. When the popular nationalist Vuk Drašković mounted a mass anti-war rally in March 1991, the government-controlled media's attempts to portray him as in league with the Croats and Albanians fizzled as too implausible. The following year, only 8 percent of Serbian respondents thought that state television kept them "well informed," versus 43 percent for the independent media.[67]

Thus, the impact of the supply of nationalist propaganda must be assessed in light of the demand for it. As Mark Thompson put it: "People's bedrock attitudes toward the wars in Croatia and Bosnia are not created by the state media; rather, the media play variations upon those attitudes, which derive from other sources (national history, family background, education, oral culture). Media did not inject their audiences with anti-Muslim prejudice or exploitable fear of Croatian nationalism. The prejudice and fear were widespread, latently at least; there was a predisposition to believe 'news' which elicited and exploited the prejudice; without the media, however, Serbia's leaders could not have obtained public consent and approval of its nationalist politics."[68]

The importance of underlying predispositions is demonstrated by comparing the propaganda strategies that Milošević tailored for the Serbs and those Tudjman adopted for the Croats. Belgrade television portrayed the Serbs as always on the defensive, the perennial victims of every battle. Dead Serbs were favored imagery. This was thought to strike the right chord in a people who glorify a defeat at the hands of the Turks half a millennium ago in the battle of Kosovo. In contrast, government propaganda directives told Croatian television to soft-pedal defeats, never show footage of destroyed Croat towns, and "always finish such reports with optimistic declarations and avowals."[69] The

---

66. Changes in media content were also used successfully to shift opinion in favor of peace. On April 9, 1993, 70 percent of Serbian respondents said they opposed the Vance-Owen peace plan, but on April 27, after a reversal of policy by the Serbian government and media, only 20 percent opposed it, and 39 percent were in favor. Thompson, *Forging War*, pp. 127–128, 209, 264.
67. Nonetheless, even the independent media found itself caught in the self-fulfilling prophecies generated by nationalist mythmaking. As Serbian journalist Stojan Cerovic said in May 1992, "Anybody who explains the truth can do so only at his own cost. Reality sounds like the blackest anti-Serbian propaganda, and anyone who describes it will frighten people and turn them against him." Thompson, *Forging War*, pp. 73–75, 127–129. For a dissenting view which stresses the limited success of appeals to Serbian nationalism, see Gagnon, "Ethnic Conflict as Demobilizer."
68. Thompson, *Forging War*, pp. 127–128.
69. Thompson, *Forging War*, pp. 105–111, 161.

government feared that Croats, lacking as firm a tradition of statehood as the Serbs had, might simply give up hope if they knew the odds they faced.

What was lacking in the Yugoslav case was not just free speech, but strong institutions to counteract market imperfections and to promote a professional, unbiased, pan-Yugoslav mass media. Standard antidotes to state power would have been of doubtful effectiveness in this case, even though it is true that media monopolies in the hands of republican governments caused most of the damage. Federalism, that standard remedy for constraining state exploitation of ethnic minorities, was in fact one of the main problems. Moreover, "consociational" power-sharing, which is often prescribed as a complement to federalism, was also troublesome. In the Bosnian media, for example, the practice of allotting equal time for each group's biases made the evening news a series of stories with different slants, while the true story of the Yugoslav army's role in the attacks on Sarajevo, for example, was suppressed as a violation of consociational comity.[70] Likewise, providing piecemeal subsidies to individual newspapers in the capital city, as the International Federation of Journalists did for *Borba,* failed to go to the heart of the problem, since the backbone of support for nationalism lay in the Serb countryside, where Milošević's media monopoly was uncontested. Finally, simply prescribing maximum freedom of speech would have been unavailing, given the inclinations and the capacity of various elite strata, both inside and outside the government, to exploit the population's predispositions to ethnic anxiety.

Rwandan Hate Radio

The 1994 mass murder of some 800,000 Tutsi and moderate Hutu organized by extremist Hutu in top circles of the Rwandan government is another case that may seem to fit the Human Rights Watch analysis perfectly. Officials of the authoritarian regime of President Juvénal Habyarimana, feeling their power endangered, used their monopoly control of mass media and university appointments to create a "finely tuned propaganda machine" that played on Hutu fears of the former Tutsi elite and purveyed false, inflammatory versions of the history of relations between the two groups. In April 1994, the Hutu official clique unleashed militias trained in the techniques of genocide. Independent journalists were a special target in the first wave of the killings. At the same time, Radio-Télévision Libre des Mille Collines, a pseudo-private station

---

70. Thompson, *Forging War,* pp. 225–225, 229–231.

established by Habyarimana's wife, spread the word that Tutsi rebels were about to rise up and kill Hutu, and consequently that all Hutu should join the militias in a campaign of preventive killing. Militias threatened to kill Hutu who did not participate in the genocide, so it is difficult to judge how much of the killing was triggered by the radio propaganda *per se*.[71] Nonetheless, all sources agree that the hate broadcasts played a significant role in the second phase of the killing, after the initial militia sweeps. Holly Burkhalter, the Washington director of Human Rights Watch, argued that jamming the hate radio was "the one action that, in retrospect, might have done the most to save Rwandan lives." The radios instead withdrew from the advancing Tutsi army into the safe haven of the French army zone, where they continued to broadcast.[72]

NGOs such as Human Rights Watch and Africa Rights, as well as many independent scholars, drew the lesson that the international community needs to encourage Rwanda and Burundi to democratize, to foster an independent press, and to bring the perpetrators of genocide to justice.[73] However, upon closer examination, their prescriptions are contradicted by their own highly persuasive analyses of the causes of the Rwandan genocide. After the genocide, NGOs continue to advocate precisely those measures that their analyses show to have triggered the killings: an increase in political pluralism, the prospect of trials of the guilty, and the promotion of anti-government media.[74]

In the late 1980s and early 1990s, falling coffee prices and economic disruptions caused by fighting with Uganda-based Tutsi rebels put the Habyarimana regime on the defensive. Under intense pressure from the domestic Hutu opposition and from international aid donors, the regime agreed under the 1993 Arusha Accords to a limited political opening, involving power-sharing with opposition groups, the legalization of numerous opposition political parties calling for democratic elections and, as an Africa Rights report puts it, "an explosion in the number of newspapers and journals" published by anti-

---

71. Quotation from Africa Rights, *Rwanda,* p. 35; also pp. vi, 37–38, 63–64, 69–72, 150; Human Rights Watch, *Playing the "Communal Card,"* pp. 7, 9.
72. Holly Burkhalter, "The Question of Genocide," *World Policy Journal,* Vol. 11, No. 4 (Winter 1994–95), pp. 44–54, esp. 51, 53.
73. Human Rights Watch, *Playing,* pp. 16–17; Africa Rights, *Rwanda,* p. 720; Reporters sans Frontières, *Rwanda: L'impasse? La liberté de las presse après le génocide, 4 juillet 1994–28 août 1995* (Paris: Reporters sans Frontières, 1995), pp. 48–50; Alison Des Forges, "The Rwandan Crisis," paper prepared for a conference on Sources of Conflict in Rwanda (Washington, D.C.: U.S. Department of State, October 17, 1994).
74. Compare Africa Rights, *Rwanda,* pp. 32–34 with 720; also compare Des Forges, "Rwandan Crisis," pp. 1 with 9.

government groups after the abandonment of the press monopoly in July 1990.[75] "A vibrant press had been born almost overnight," says Gérard Prunier, but its biased commentary was written "in terrible bad faith."[76] Hutu extremists attached to the regime continued to monopolize the radio, a key asset among a population that was 60 percent illiterate. After a Tutsi rebel attack on the capital in 1993 was parried only with the help of French troops, Habyarimana had had no alternative but to accept the Arusha agreement, which provided for Tutsi participation in government, a rebel military unit to provide security for Tutsi politicians in the capital, and the exclusion of Hutu extremists from the joint Hutu-Tutsi government. Moderate Hutu from southern Rwanda, where "Hutu" and "Tutsi" were racially almost indistinguishable, began to mobilize politically against Hutu extremists in the government clique and their northern Rwanda social base.[77]

As part of the settlement, an international commission named names of highly placed Hutu extremists who were complicit in small-scale killings of Tutsi. "Individuals named were promised an amnesty," says Africa Rights's Alex de Waal, "but knew that their actions were under scrutiny," and so distrusted these guarantees. Human rights groups were active in this period of internationally sponsored power-sharing and pluralization. "Rwanda had one of the most vigorous human-rights movements in Africa," says de Waal. "Six independent human rights organizations cooperated in exposing abuses by government and rebel forces."[78]

In this setting, the clique around Habyarimana had every reason to fear democratization and calls for justice from the international community. To forestall a fall from power and judicial accountability, these officials developed the plan for a mass genocide. "The extremists' aim," says Africa Rights, "was for the entire Hutu populace to participate in the killing. That way, the blood of genocide would stain everybody. There could be no going back for the Hutu population."[79] But there was a flaw in this plan. Habyarimana, heavily depend-

---

75. Africa Rights, *Rwanda*, p. 150.
76. Prunier, *The Rwanda Crisis*, chap. 4, "Slouching towards Democracy," esp. pp. 131–133, 157, on the low quality and extremism of these new entrants into public discourse.
77. Africa Rights, *Rwanda*, pp. 30–34, 44; Bruce D. Jones, "The Arusha Process," in Howard Adelman and Astri Suhrke, eds., *Early Warning and Conflict Management in Rwanda* (forthcoming); Alan J. Kuperman, "The Other Lesson of Rwanda: Mediators Sometimes Do More Damage Than Good," *SAIS Review*, Vol. 16, No. 1 (Winter–Spring 1996), pp. 221–240.
78. Alex de Waal, "The Genocidal State," *Times Literary Supplement*, July 1, 1994, pp. 3–4; see also Africa Rights, *Rwanda*, pp. 30–32.
79. Africa Rights, *Rwanda*, p. v; also pp. 568–596; Prunier, *The Rwanda Crisis*, p. 170; Jones, "Arusha."

ent on foreign aid to prop up his system of official patronage, balked at implementing a bloodbath that he knew would cut him off from foreign funds. The president's extremist allies in the military and security services had no such qualms. From January to March 1994, their unofficial journal *Kangura*, an example of the "flowering" of Rwandan media in the period of pluralism and incipient power-sharing, warned Habyarimana not to flinch from the destruction of the Tutsi and predicted with astonishing accuracy the details of his assassination:[80] Habyarimana was killed in April by his own presidential guard upon returning from a meeting at Dar Es Salaam where he made renewed concessions to international donors, the UN, and the Organization of African Unity. As de Waal aptly states, "Habyarimana was a victim of the international peace industry."[81]

Despite the clear evidence that NGO analysts themselves recite, they fail to acknowledge that the very solutions they continue to promote are the same as the steps that caused the killings. Human Rights Watch correctly notes that the "free and fair" election of Burundi's first Hutu president in October 1993 set the stage for the killing of some 50,000 Hutu and Tutsi. The Tutsi military, fearing that the elected government's power-sharing scheme would neutralize the army as a security guarantee for the Tutsi minority, launched a coup to protect its monopoly of force, touching off a series of reprisals. Yet Human Rights Watch urges democratic accountability and prosecution of the killers "to deter further slaughter," despite the fact that it was precisely the threat of such accountability that provoked the slaughter in Rwanda and Burundi in the first place.[82]

Both the Rwanda and Burundi cases show that the ideals of democratic rights, uncompromising justice, and free speech must make pragmatic accommodations to recalcitrant reality. Recognizing this, *Reporters sans Frontières* warns that the "error committed in Rwanda, which consisted of applying the rule of 'laissez faire' in the name of the principle of liberty of the press, must not be repeated in Burundi." While working to reconstitute the private news media in both countries and to bring journalists implicated in the genocide campaign to justice, the French NGO acknowledges that the thirteen newspapers that it is helping in Rwanda are short on personnel, paper, and facilities; have a circulation under 1,000 each; cost a day's wage to buy one issue; and

---

80. Africa Rights, *Rwanda*, pp. 66–68.
81. De Waal, "The Genocidal State," p. 4; also Jones, "Arusha." On Habyarimana's death, see Prunier, *Rwanda Crisis*, pp. 213–229.
82. Human Rights Watch, *Playing*, pp. 16–17.

consist primarily of opinions, not news. Realistically skeptical about some of the journalists it supports, *Reporters sans Frontières* conditions aid on a pledge to forswear ethnic hate speech. In Burundi, *Reporters sans Frontières* notes the paradox that many journalists working under a new law on press freedom are calling for an ethnic dictatorship that would shut down non-official expression of views. Since the invisible hand of the marketplace of ideas is so unreliable in such circumstances, *Reporters sans Frontières* relies also on the visible hand of two international radio stations broadcasting into Rwanda and Burundi from Zaire.[83]

Conditions for Successful Liberalization of the Marketplace of Ideas

In numerous recent cases, such as South Africa, increases in press freedom and democratic participation in politics spawned no sanguinary outbursts of nationalism. Historically, Britain democratized and evolved a free press without developing German-style populist nationalism. These cases had better outcomes because their elites had weaker motivations to propound nationalist myths, because their markets were not as segmented, or because effective institutions of free debate were in place before the democratization of political participation. If elites believe that the expansion of free speech and democratic participation poses little threat to their interests, nationalism will be moderate. This pattern suggests that activists should target their efforts at patiently putting in place these preconditions of constructive public discourse, rather than clamoring for no-holds-barred press freedom across the board. Institutional foundations of free debate are achieved either by historical evolution or by conscious design, not instantaneously by the invisible hand of competition.

The paradigm-setting case for these conditions is Great Britain. England did fight an intense civil war in the seventeenth century shortly after a dramatic increase in the number of newspapers and the freedom of political expression in them.[84] However, by the dawn of the age of mass nationalism in the late eighteenth and early nineteenth centuries, Britain had already achieved a set of well-established norms of free speech among wide circles of the elite. The decisive move to end censorship in Britain came at the beginning of the

---

83. Reporters sans Frontières, *Rwanda*, pp. 6, 41–42; 52–53; Reporters sans Frontières, *Burundi, le Venin de la Haine: Étude sur les médias extrémistes*, 2d ed. (Paris: Reporters sans Frontières, July 1995), pp. 63, 68–69; quotation on p. 69.
84. Tim Harris, "Propaganda and Public Opinion in Seventeenth-Century England," in Jeremy Popkin, ed., *Media and Revolution* (Lexington: University Press of Kentucky, 1995), pp. 48–73.

eighteenth century, at a time when the political position of the Whig aristocracy was at its strongest and the proportion of the British population who could vote in parliamentary elections was actually declining. In that same era, Britain's integration of the Scottish and Welsh peoples into a centralized state before the era of mass democracy prevented ethnic segmentation of the market, at least in the core of the realm.[85] By the mid-nineteenth century, when the penny press and the expansion of the electoral franchise further widened the scope of political debate to include the middle class, existing journalistic institutions and norms of debate provided a structure to channel and regulate the exchange of ideas. Moreover, Britain's traditional ruling class shared many commercial interests with the rising middle class, and so had little reason to "play the nationalist card" to forestall democratic policies like the repeal of tariffs on imported food. In a limited way, some aristocratic demagogues, most notably Lord Palmerston on the eve of the Crimean War, succeeded in diverting public opinion away from political reform towards a foreign policy of nationalist expansion, but these adventures were moderate in scope. Though Britain conquered vast portions of the globe, it generally did so in a cost-conscious way: it appeased foes strategically, pulled back from overcommitments, and never placed its nationalism beyond the pale of rational discussion weighing the costs and benefits of imperial policies.[86]

Several contemporary success cases of relatively peaceful democratization and media liberalization share one or more of these characteristics of the British case: that is, guarantees of the interests of powerful elites, no ethnic segmentation of the market, or thorough institutionalization of the marketplace of ideas before democratization. Indeed, some of these moderate cases are former British colonies, which inherited along with the English language a tradition of professionalized journalism from the colonial period. One factor in the smooth South African transition, for example, was the well-established English-language opposition press, exemplified by the Rand *Daily Mail* and its successors, which for decades had been consistently more liberal than many of its readers.[87] The political opening in the 1990s permitted the English-language

---

85. Geoffrey Holmes and Daniel Szechi, *The Age of Oligarchy* (London: Longman, 1993), chap. 13, esp. pp. 194–195; Martin Daunton, *Progress and Poverty* (Oxford: Oxford University Press, 1995), p. 482; Linda Colley, *Britons* (New Haven, Conn.: Yale University Press, 1992), esp. pp. 25, 220.
86. Snyder, *Myths of Empire*, chap. 5; Paul Kennedy, *Strategy and Diplomacy* (London: Allen and Unwin, 1983), chaps. 1 and 8; for a more critical view, see Charles Kupchan, *The Vulnerability of Empire* (Ithaca, N.Y.: Cornell University Press, 1994), chap. 3.
87. Elaine Potter, *The Press as Opposition: The Political Role of South African Newspapers* (Totowa, N.J.: Rowman and Littlefield, 1975).

press to report more freely, and a new black press was funded by churches and through Danish and Norwegian subsidies. Television and especially print news, already staffed with a professional cadre, moved quickly toward international norms. This allowed the divisions between Afrikaner, English, and black media that had prevailed under apartheid to be overcome rapidly.[88] Moreover, Nelson Mandela's moderate rhetoric reassured whites about the consequences of free speech, as does their residual power to veto threatening developments.

India is another case in which a balanced marketplace of ideas was well institutionalized long before the transition to democratic politics, and in which the central ruling elite saw its interests as served by moderate, secular policies rather than divisive, ethno-communal ones. By the turn of the century, the English-language Indian press was already able to use the pressure of open public debate to constrain the non-elected British regime's policies.[89] By the time of independence, a number of highly professional, major urban newspapers had developed a voluntary press code for reporting on communal riots, which abjured inflammatory headlines, refrained from specifying casualty figures during the heat of the moment, scrupulously cited sources, and dug for accurate information on the causes of riots. These informal codes were institutionalized in the Press Council, modeled on its British forebear. The Council was given the same statutory powers to investigate violations as a civil court.[90] Smaller, partisan papers sometimes inflamed communal tensions, however, and during the 1947 riots a restrictive press ordinance with pre-publication censorship was temporarily adopted.[91] In provincial towns, publishers and journalists are highly dependent on the support of local business elites, and expedience often gets in the way of truth in reporting on communal tensions. The vernacular (i.e., non-English) press commonly circulates false reports, inflated death figures, and unevaluated statements by communal leaders. This gap between the restrained, professional, state-wide press and the inflammatory communal press has been growing over the past two decades, as a result

---

88. On the segmented market, see William Finnegan, *Dateline Soweto* (New York: Harper and Row, 1988), pp. 24–33, and Potter, *The Press as Opposition*, p. 164; on the transition, see Timothy Sisk, *Democratization in South Africa* (Princeton, N.J.: Princeton University Press, 1995).
89. S.N. Paul, *Public Opinion and British Rule* (New Delhi: Metropolitan, 1979).
90. R.C.S. Sarkar, *The Press in India* (New Delhi: S. Chand, 1984), pp. 190–193, 295–296; Allyn and Wilkinson, *Guidelines for Journalists*, appendix.
91. Moti Lal Bhargava, *Role of Press in the Freedom Movement* (New Delhi: Reliance, 1987), pp. 336, 341–342.

of economic change and the growth of literacy in provincial areas.[92] Social change, sharply rising newspaper readership, and the emergence of a local intelligentsia has played a central role in reigniting communal conflict in Kashmir, for example.[93]

In the heyday of the Congress Party's centralized, secular leadership, local Congress notables kept a short leash on the expression of communal prejudices. In the 1970s, however, Indira Gandhi sought to free herself from Congress's grassroots organizational structure through direct appeals not only to religious groups, but also to increasingly politicized lower-caste and lower-class segments of Indian society. As Human Rights Watch argues correctly, these segmental appeals touched off an increasing communalization of Indian politics.[94] However, the problem nowadays is hardly that the central, secular elites, including the elite media, are too demagogic, but that their power was weakened *vis-à-vis* nationalist challengers by the de-institutionalization of the Congress Party.

In other contemporary cases, the nationalist dogs are not barking because old elites have found a safe haven in the new regime. In many of the democratizing post-communist states of Eastern Europe, former apparatchiks have profited from the privatization of industry, attracted a mass constituency based on appeals to economic security rather than nationalism, and still rule many of these countries. Likewise, in Latin America, former military elites have been given "golden parachutes," and journalistic institutions were already well established as the result of earlier periods of democratization.[95]

Prescriptions for an Integrated Marketplace of Ideas

Democratization and free speech can be made compatible with ethnic harmony and the moderation of nationalist sentiment only under favorable conditions

---

92. S.B. Kolpe, "Caste and Communal Violence and the Role of the Press," pp. 342, 349, in Asghar Ali Engineer, ed., *Communal Riots in Post-Independence India* (Hyderabad: Sangam, 1984); and Asghar Ali Engineer, "The Causes of Communal Riots," ibid., pp. 36–38; Hamish McDonald, "Paper Tigers," *Far Eastern Economic Review*, Vol. 158, No. 40 (October 5, 1995), pp. 28–30; Zenab Banu, *Politics of Communalism* (Bombay: Popular Prakashan, 1989), p. 21.

93. Šumit Ganguly, *Between War and Peace: The Crisis in Kashmir* (Cambridge, U.K.: Cambridge University Press, forthcoming); Ganguly, "Explaining the Kashmir Insurgency: Political Mobilization and Institutional Decay," *International Security*, Vol. 21, No. 2 (Fall 1996), pp. 76–107.

94. Human Rights Watch, *Playing the "Communal Card,"* p. 21.

95. Article 19, *Guidelines for Election Broadcasting*, p. 5.

of supply, demand, and institutional regulation. If these conditions do not exist, they need to be created before, or at least along with, the unfettering of speech and political participation.

On the supply side, the international community may be needed to help break up information monopolies, especially in states with very weak journalistic traditions and a weak civil society. In Cambodia, for example, the UN's successful media and information program was designed, according to the UN commander, to "bypass the propaganda of the Cambodian factions" by directly disseminating information about the elections.[96] The breakup of monopoly power over politics and discourse must coincide, however, with measures to reduce elites' incentives for nationalist mythmaking or to eliminate their capacity to make trouble. As our cases show, it is reckless for the international community to threaten elites with across-the-board exposure and prosecution of past crimes, unless there exists the will and capability to render harmless the likely backlash from elites that are pushed to the wall. Otherwise, elites that are potentially threatened by democratization and the end of censorship should be guaranteed a soft landing in the emerging open society. Many Latin American and East European countries have done well by keeping prosecutions limited. In contrast, fine moral declarations without effective actions are the worst possible policy.

On the demand side, ethnically segmented markets should be counteracted by the promotion of civic-territorial conceptions of national identity, as in Ukraine. Inclusive national identities can be fostered through an integrative press, which expresses a variety of outlooks on the same pages. All too often, international aid goes to the opposition press in democratizing countries regardless of its journalistic quality, on the grounds that creating a pluralism of voices is the essential objective. In Romania, for example, the U.S. Agency for International Development has subsidized anti-government newspapers that fail to meet even the most minimal standards of accuracy in reporting.[97] Instead, aid should go to forums that present varied ideas, not a single line, in a setting that fosters effective interchange and factual accuracy. In post-1945 Germany, for example, American occupiers licensing newspapers showed a

---

96. Michael W. Doyle, *UN Peacekeeping in Cambodia: UNTAC's Civil Mandate* (Boulder, Colo.: Lynne Rienner, 1995), pp. 54–55. For other cases, see Dan Lindley, "Collective Security Organizations and Internal Conflict," in Michael E. Brown, ed., *The International Dimensions of Internal Conflict* (Cambridge, Mass.: MIT Press, 1996), pp. 562–567.
97. Thomas Carothers, *Assessing Democratic Assistance: The Case of Romania* (Washington, D.C.: Carnegie Endowment for International Peace, 1996), pp. 80–89.

strong preference for editorial teams whose members spanned diverse political orientations.[98] This approach extends Donald Horowitz's critique of Arend Lijphart's strategy of "consociational" representation of communal power blocs into the realm of public discourse. Whereas Lijphart's approach rewards politicians who mobilize support along ethnic lines, Horowitz advises electoral rules that reward vote-pooling, in order to promote cross-ethnic political alliances and to break down the communal segmentation of politics. Applying Horowitz's principles to the marketplace of ideas, we counsel idea-pooling through integrative public forums, to break down the intellectual boundaries between ethnically exclusive "imagined communities."[99]

For this reason, we urge NGOs and other aid donors to reconsider projects to provide ethnic minorities with their "own" media.[100] Instead, we suggest supporting media that strive to attract a politically and ethnically diverse audience, invite the expression of various viewpoints, and hold news stories to rigorous standards of objectivity. This can be done by expanding existing NGO programs to train journalists from newly democratizing countries, such as those of the International Press Institute in Vienna,[101] and by providing quality news organizations with equipment, subsidized newsprint, or other logistical support. Special efforts should be made to encompass the regional and local press in these efforts. In case after case—Weimar, Germany, India, Sri Lanka, and contemporary Russia—key vehicles of nationalist mythmaking have been face-to-face networks and rough-hewn periodicals. To provide an effective alternative to these, media projects should focus on the inclusion of local journalists in the activities of state-wide media associations, mid-career training sabbaticals for grassroots journalists, and financial subsidies to make a high quality local press independent and affordable.

Major efforts should be made to promote the institutionalization of effective norms of elite discourse, journalistic professionalism, and independent evaluative bodies *before* the full opening of mass political participation. Whenever

---

98. Richard L. Merritt, *Democracy Imposed: U.S. Occupation Policy and the German Public, 1945–1949* (New Haven, Conn.: Yale University Press, 1996), pp. 291–315, esp. 296, emphasizes the effectiveness of this strategy.
99. Horowitz, *A Democratic South Africa?* chaps. 4 and 5; Arend Lijphart, *Democracy in Plural Societies* (New Haven, Conn.: Yale University Press, 1977). On common media as a precondition for an integrated national consciousness, see Benedict Anderson, *Imagined Communities* (London: Verso, 1983).
100. Stephen Harold Riggins, *Ethnic Minority Media* (Newbury Park, Calif.: Sage, 1992).
101. Larry Diamond, *Promoting Democracy in the 1990s* (New York: Carnegie Corporation, Report to the Carnegie Commission on Preventing Deadly Conflict, December 1995), pp. 24–25.

possible, market imperfections should be counteracted by decentralized institutions, not centralized regulatory directives, and by the promotion of norms of fair debate, not by restrictions on the content of speech. In some cases, however, certain kinds of constraints on speech may be necessary in multiethnic societies while these institutions are being built. This may be ethically uncomfortable for Western liberals; moreover, it is politically difficult to design constraints on democracy and free speech that do not play into the hands of elites who want to squelch freedom entirely. When electoral polarization touched off communal riots in Malaysia in 1969, for example, Malay elites banned public discussion of ethnic issues and imposed a regime of ethnic coexistence that insured Malay political domination and economic prosperity for the Chinese business community. After a quarter-century of tight press controls, the uneasy communal peace still holds, but this interlude, which might have been used to prepare an institutional infrastructure for a more durable, democratic solution, has been squandered.[102]

Neither the ethnic strife unleashed by unchecked democratization in cases like Sri Lanka nor the temporary, repressive communal cease-fire in cases like Malaysia is desirable. One element of a better solution is for international donors to offer incentives to political and economic to elites to prepare the institutionalization of open discourse, while tolerating some limits on free expression, including limits on ethnic hate speech, in the short run. Another element is direct aid to professionalize those elements of the media that are attempting to create a integrated forum for responsible, accurate debate. But when these remedies are unavailing, those who value both unfettered speech and peace must, without illusions, assess the tradeoff between them.

---

102. Gordon P. Means, *Malaysian Politics: The Second Generation,* 2d ed. (Oxford: Oxford University Press, 1991), esp. pp. 137–138, 313–314, 418–422, 439; Karl von Vorys, *Democracy without Consensus: Communalism and Political Stability in Malaysia* (Princeton, N.J.: Princeton University Press, 1975), pp. 394–412.

Containing Fear

The Origins and Management of Ethnic Conflict

David A. Lake and Donald Rothchild

Since the end of the Cold War, a wave of ethnic conflict has swept across parts of Eastern Europe, the former Soviet Union, and Africa. Localities, states, and sometimes whole regions have been engulfed in convulsive fits of ethnic insecurity, violence, and genocide. Early optimism that the end of the Cold War might usher in a new world order has been quickly shattered. Before the threat of nuclear armageddon could fully fade, new threats of state meltdown and ethnic cleansing have rippled across the international community.

The most widely discussed explanations of ethnic conflict are, at best, incomplete and, at worst, simply wrong. Ethnic conflict is not caused directly by inter-group differences, "ancient hatreds" and centuries-old feuds, or the stresses of modern life within a global economy. Nor were ethnic passions, long bottled up by repressive communist regimes, simply uncorked by the end of the Cold War.

We argue instead that intense ethnic conflict is most often caused by collective fears of the future. As groups begin to fear for their safety, dangerous and difficult-to-resolve strategic dilemmas arise that contain within them the potential for tremendous violence. As information failures, problems of credible commitment, and the security dilemma take hold, groups become apprehensive, the state weakens, and conflict becomes more likely. Ethnic activists and political entrepreneurs, operating within groups, build upon these fears of insecurity and polarize society. Political memories and emotions also magnify these anxieties, driving groups further apart. Together, these between-group

David A. Lake is Professor of Political Science at the University of California, San Diego, and Research Director for International Relations at the Institute on Global Conflict and Cooperation. Donald Rothchild is Professor of Political Science at the University of California, Davis.

This is an abridged version of two chapters by the authors that will appear in David A. Lake and Donald Rothchild, eds., *Ethnic Fears and Global Engagement: The International Spread and Management of Ethnic Conflict* (forthcoming). This research was sponsored by the Institute on Global Conflict and Cooperation (IGCC) at the University of California and supported by a generous grant from the Pew Charitable Trusts. An earlier draft of this paper was discussed by IGCC's Working Group on the International Spread and Management of Ethnic Conflict. We are indebted to the members of the working group for many productive discussions over a two-year period. We would especially like to thank Miles Kahler, Arnold Kanter, Charles Kupchan, Charles William Maynes, Barnett Rubin, Timothy D. Sisk, Stephen John Stedman, and John Steinbruner for comments on an earlier draft of this paper.

International Security, Vol. 21, No. 2 (Fall 1996), pp. 41–75

and within-group strategic interactions produce a toxic brew of distrust and suspicion that can explode into murderous violence.

Managing ethnic conflicts, whether by local elites and governments or concerned members of the international community, is a continuing process with no end point or final resolution. It is also an imperfect process that, no matter how well-conducted, leaves some potential for violence in nearly all multi-ethnic polities. Ethnic conflict can be contained, but it cannot be entirely resolved. Effective management seeks to reassure minority groups of both their physical security and, because it is often a harbinger of future threats, their cultural security. Demonstrations of respect, power-sharing, elections engineered to produce the interdependence of groups, and the establishment of regional autonomy and federalism are important confidence-building measures that, by promoting the rights and positions of minority groups, mitigate the strategic dilemmas that produce violence.

International intervention may also be necessary and appropriate to protect minorities against their worst fears, but its effectiveness is limited. Noncoercive interventions can raise the costs of purely ethnic appeals and induce groups to abide by international norms. Coercive interventions can help bring warring parties to the bargaining table and enforce the resulting terms. Mediation can facilitate agreement and implementation. A key issue in all interventions, especially in instances of external coercion, is the credibility of the international commitment. External interventions that the warring parties fear will soon fade may be worse than no intervention at all. There is no practical alternative to active engagement by the international community over the long term.

This essay presents a framework for understanding the origins and management of ethnic conflict. Focusing on the central concept of ethnic fear, we attempt to provide a broad framework for comprehending, first, how the various causes of ethnic conflict fit together and potentially interact and, second, how policies can be crafted to address these causes. Moreover, while our approach is largely "rational choice" oriented, we also seek to examine how non-rational factors such as political myths and emotions interact with the strategic dilemmas we highlight. We recognize that many of the ideas presented here have already appeared in the burgeoning literature on ethnic conflict, and do not claim to be presenting an entirely novel approach, although we note some areas of disagreement with prevailing approaches.

Our analysis proceeds in two steps. The first section examines the inter-group and intra-group strategic dilemmas that produce ethnic violence. Building on this diagnosis, the second section discusses several ways of managing ethnic conflicts both before and after they become violent. We consider, first, confidence-building measures that can be undertaken by local elites and governments—or promoted by members of the international community—to quell real or potential violence and, second, external interventions led by concerned states and organizations. The concluding section highlights several policy initiatives that follow from our analysis.

Strategic Interactions and the Causes of Ethnic Conflict

Most ethnic groups, most of the time, pursue their interests peacefully through established political channels. But when ethnicity is linked with acute social uncertainty, a history of conflict, and fear of what the future might bring, it emerges as one of the major fault lines along which societies fracture.[1] Vesna Pešić, a professor at the University of Belgrade and a peace activist in the former Yugoslavia, says it well: ethnic conflict is caused by the "fear of the future, lived through the past."[2]

Collective fears of the future arise when states lose their ability to arbitrate between groups or provide credible guarantees of protection for groups. Under this condition, which Barry Posen refers to as "emerging anarchy," physical security becomes of paramount concern.[3] When central authority declines, groups become fearful for their survival. They invest in and prepare for violence, and thereby make actual violence possible. State weakness, whether it arises incrementally out of competition between groups or from extremists actively seeking to destroy ethnic peace, is a necessary precondition for violent ethnic conflict to erupt. State weakness helps to explain the explosion of ethnic violence that has followed the collapse of communist regimes in Eastern Europe and the former Soviet Union, and it has also led to violence in Liberia, Somalia, and other African states.

State weakness may not be obvious to the ethnic groups themselves or external observers. States that use force to repress groups, for instance, may appear strong, but their reliance on manifest coercion rather than legitimate

---

1. Kathleen Newland. "Ethnic Conflict and Refugees," in Michael E. Brown, ed., *Ethnic Conflict and International Security* (Princeton, N.J.: Princeton University Press, 1993), p. 161.
2. Vesna Pešić, Remarks to the Institute on Global Conflict and Cooperation (IGCC) Working Group on the International Spread and Management of Ethnic Conflict, October 1, 1994.
3. Barry R. Posen, "The Security Dilemma and Ethnic Conflict," in Brown, *Ethnic Conflict and International Security*, pp. 103–124. See also Jack Snyder, "Nationalism and the Crisis of the Post-Soviet State," in ibid., pp. 79–101.

authority more accurately implies weakness. More important, groups look beyond the present political equipoise to alternative futures when calculating their political strategies. If plausible futures are sufficiently threatening, groups may begin acting today as if the state were in fact weak, setting off processes, discussed below, that bring about the disintegration of the state. Thus, even though the state may appear strong today, concerns that it may not remain so tomorrow may be sufficient to ignite fears of physical insecurity and a cycle of ethnic violence. The forward-looking nature of the strategic dilemmas emphasized here makes the task of forecasting or anticipating ethnic conflicts especially difficult, both for the participants themselves and external actors who would seek to manage them effectively through preventive diplomacy.

Situations of emerging anarchy and violence arise out of the strategic interactions between and within groups. Between groups, three different strategic dilemmas can cause violence to erupt: information failures, problems of credible commitment, and incentives to use force preemptively (also known as the security dilemma). These dilemmas are the fundamental causes of ethnic conflict. Within groups, ethnic activists and political entrepreneurs may make blatant communal appeals and outbid moderate politicians, thereby mobilizing members, polarizing society, and magnifying the inter-group dilemmas. "Non-rational" factors such as emotions, historical memories, and myths can exacerbate the violent implications of these intra-group interactions. Together, these inter-group and intra-group interactions combine, as we explain in this section, to create a vicious cycle that threatens to pull multi-ethnic societies into violence.[4]

STRATEGIC INTERACTIONS BETWEEN GROUPS

Competition for resources typically lies at the heart of ethnic conflict. Property rights, jobs, scholarships, educational admissions, language rights, government contracts, and development allocations all confer benefits on individuals and groups. All such resources are scarce and, thus, objects of competition and occasionally struggle between individuals and, when organized, groups. In

---

4. In this article, we are concerned mostly with internal ethnic conflict. For a discussion of transnational ethnic conflict, and especially its international diffusion and escalation, see David A. Lake and Donald Rothchild, eds., *Ethnic Fears and Global Engagement: The International Spread and Management of Ethnic Conflict* (forthcoming).

societies where ethnicity is an important basis for identity, group competition often forms along ethnic lines.[5]

Politics matter because the state controls access to scarce resources. Individuals and groups that possess political power can often gain privileged access to these goods, and thus increase their welfare.[6] Because the state sets the terms of competition between groups, it becomes an object of group struggle. Accordingly, the pursuit of particularistic objectives often becomes embodied in competing visions of just, legitimate, and appropriate political orders.

In multi-ethnic societies, resource rivalries and the struggle to control state policy produce competing communal interests. In Nigeria, for example, each ethno-regional group looks to the state to favor it when distributing public resources, producing, as Claude Ake observes, an "overpoliticization" of social life which gravely weakens the state itself.[7] In Yugoslavia, Slovenians and Croatians resented the system of federal redistribution to the poorer regions of the country; their publics backed their leaders' expressions of indignation, ultimately fueling the demand for greater political autonomy.[8] When groups conclude that they can improve their welfare only at the expense of others, they become locked into competitions for scarce resources and state power.

Analytically, however, the existence of competing policy preferences is—by itself—not sufficient for violence to arise. Observers too often fail to recognize this important theoretical point and misattribute violence to competition over scarce resources. Violence, after all, is costly for all communal actors: people are killed; factories, farms, and whole cities are destroyed; resources that might have been invested in new economic growth are diverted instead to destructive ends. As violence, and preparing for violence, is always costly, there must exist in principle some potential bargain short of violence that leaves both sides in a dispute better off than settling their disagreements through the use of force; at the very least, the same *ex post* agreement could be reached without the use

5. This is, of course, not true as a universal rule. Although ethnic identities are often strong, groups can also form along class, religious, or other lines. The more politically salient ethnicity is, however, the more likely it is that groups will organize on this basis. This is an important way in which the between-group and within-group variables examined here interact.

6. Russell Hardin, *One for All: The Logic of Group Conflict* (Princeton, N.J.: Princeton University Press, 1995), pp. 34–37; and Milton J. Esman, *Ethnic Politics* (Ithaca, N.Y.: Cornell University Press, 1994), p. 216.

7. Claude Ake, *"Why Is Africa Not Developing?"* *West Africa*, No. 3538 (June 17, 1985), p. 1213.

8. Susan Woodward, *Balkan Tragedy: Chaos and Dissolution After the Cold War* (Washington, D.C.: Brookings, 1995), pp. 69–70.

of force, and the resources that would have been expended in violence divided somehow between the parties *ex ante*.[9] This holds irrespective of the breadth of the group demands or the extent of the antagonisms. The farther apart the policy preferences of the groups are, the greater the violence necessary for one group to assert its will over the other, and the greater the resources that can be saved by averting the resort to force.[10]

Despite appearances, then, competing policy preferences by themselves cannot explain the resort to violence. The divorce between the two halves of Czechoslovakia is a sterling example of two ethnic groups, in conflict over the distribution of resources within their federal state but anxious to avoid the costs of war, developing a mutually agreeable separation to avoid a potentially violent confrontation. For negotiations to fail to bridge the demands of opposing groups, at least one of three strategic dilemmas must exist. Each dilemma alone is sufficient to produce violent conflict. Nonetheless, they typically occur together as a dangerous syndrome of strategic problems.

INFORMATION FAILURES. Because violence is costly, groups can be expected to invest in acquiring knowledge about the preferences and capabilities of the opposing side and bargain hard, but eventually reach an agreement short of open conflict.[11] Groups might even be expected to reveal information about themselves to prevent violence from erupting. When individuals and groups possess private information and incentives to misrepresent that information, competing group interests can produce actual conflict. We refer to this as an information failure. When information failures occur, groups cannot acquire or share the information necessary to bridge the bargaining gap between themselves, making conflict possible despite its devastating effects.

Incentives to misrepresent private information exist in at least three common circumstances. In each, revealing true information undercuts the ability of the group to attain its interests. First, incentives to misrepresent occur when groups are bargaining over a set of issues and believe they can gain by bluffing. By

---

9. James Fearon, "Ethnic War as a Commitment Problem," unpublished manuscript, University of Chicago, 1993; and Fearon, "Rationalist Explanations for War," *International Organization*, Vol. 49, No. 3 (Summer 1995), pp. 379–414.

10. Moreover, a mutually preferred bargain must exist even if the resources available to groups are declining, because violence only further reduces the resource pool relative to possible agreements. For an empirical demonstration of this point, see Valerie Percival and Thomas Homer-Dixon, *Environmental Scarcity and Violent Conflict: The Case of Rwanda* (Washington, D.C.: American Association for the Advancement of Science, 1995).

11. The following two sub-sections draw heavily upon Fearon, "Ethnic War as a Commitment Problem," and "Rationalist Explanations for War," two of the best theoretical works on conflict between organized groups.

exaggerating their strengths, minimizing their weaknesses, and mis-stating their preferences, groups seek to achieve more favorable divisions of resources. Through such bluffs, however, they increase the risk that negotiations will fail and conflicts arise.[12]

Second, groups may be truly aggressive but do not want to be branded as such. They may seek to minimize internal opposition, or to insulate themselves from repercussions in the broader international community. Although typically only minimal sanctions are imposed by other states, most groups seek to avoid the label of an aggressor or violator of international norms and the political isolation that such a classification can carry.

Finally, in conflicts where the groups are simultaneously negotiating and preparing for ethnic war, any attempt to facilitate compromise by having each side explain how it plans to win on the battlefield will seriously compromise the likelihood that it will win should war occur. Thus, groups cannot reveal their strategies or derive accurate predictions of their likely success. Paradoxically, each party is bound by its own self-interest to withhold the information crucial to bringing about an agreement. Concerned that private information they provide on how they intend to protect themselves or attack others will redound to their disadvantage, groups may refrain from revealing the information necessary to forge a mutually satisfactory compromise.[13]

Information failures are possible whenever two or more ethnic groups compete within the political arena. Groups always possess private information and, as these three circumstances suggest, often possess incentives to misrepresent that information. Information failures are thus ubiquitous in ethnic relations. In multi-ethnic societies, states can often communicate and arbitrate successfully between groups and thereby help preclude and resolve information failures. Indeed, communication and arbitration can be understood as two of the primary functions of the state. When effective, states create incentives and a sense of security that allow groups to express their desires and articulate their political aspirations and strategies. Not only do ethnic leaders respond to sidepayments offered by state elites, but—in seeking to curry favor—they are more prepared to provide private information to a "third party" than they are

---

12. In game-theoretic terms, actors will choose to bluff depending upon 1) the beliefs each actor holds about the other's "type" (i.e., the actor is more likely to bluff if it believes the other is "weak" and the second actor believes the first is "strong") and 2) the relative benefits (payoff) and costs (signal) of successful bluffing, unsuccessful bluffing, and not bluffing (i.e., the higher the payoff from success and the smaller the cost of the signal, the more likely the actor is to bluff).
13. Fearon, "Rationalist Explanations for War," p. 400.

to an adversary.[14] As the state weakens, however, information failures become more acute and violence more likely. If one group believes that the other is withholding information, it too may begin to hold back crucial data or anticipate the failure of negotiations. Groups become suspicious of the intentions of others, and may begin to fear the worst. In this way, information failures and even the anticipation of such failures may drive groups to actions that undermine the ability of the state to maintain social peace. When this occurs, even previously effective states will begin to unravel. State capabilities, then, are at least partly affected by the magnitude of the information failure and the beliefs and behaviors of the groups themselves.

Information failures cut two ways. On the one hand, all policy differences can be bridged—at least in theory—if the alternative is a costly conflict. Even cultural symbols and practices central to a people's conception of itself as a distinct ethnic group may be negotiable if the known alternative is the outright destruction of the group. On the other hand, strategic incentives to misrepresent private information are a primary impediment to peaceful compromise, and these incentives may be present in a wide range of circumstances. Thus, careful mediation by third parties who can probe the true preferences of groups and communicate them to relevant others is important for creating and maintaining cooperative ethnic relations. States able to arbitrate between groups are normally the preferred instrument to this end, but sometimes they too fall victim to the information failures they are designed, in part, to prevent. When this occurs, mediation by outside parties may be required.

PROBLEMS OF CREDIBLE COMMITMENT. Ethnic conflicts also arise because groups cannot credibly commit themselves to uphold mutually beneficial agreements they might reach.[15] In other words, at least one group cannot effectively reassure the other that it will not renege on an agreement and exploit it at some future date. As exploitation can be very costly—up to and including the organized killing of one group by another—groups may prefer to absorb even high costs of war today to avoid being exploited tomorrow.

---

14. We recognize, of course, that the state is not always a neutral third party in domestic disputes, but this simply indicates that the state has already forfeited at least in part the ability to perform this function.
15. Fearon, "Ethnic War as a Commitment Problem"; and Fearon, "Rationalist Explanations for War"; Hardin, *One for All*, p. 143; and Barry R. Weingast, "Constructing Trust: The Political and Economic Roots of Ethnic and Regional Conflict," unpublished manuscript, Stanford University, 1995.

Stable ethnic relations can be understood as based upon a "contract" between groups.[16] Such contracts specify, among other things, the rights and responsibilities, political privileges, and access to resources of each group. These contracts may be formal constitutional agreements or simply informal understandings between elites. Whatever their form, ethnic contracts channel politics in peaceful directions.

Most importantly, ethnic contracts contain "safeguards" designed to render the agreement self-enforcing. They contain provisions or mechanisms to ensure that each side lives up to its commitments and feels secure that the other will do so as well. Typical safeguards include, first, power-sharing arrangements, electoral rules, or group vetoes that prevent one ethnic group from setting government policy unilaterally;[17] second, minority control over critical economic assets, as with the whites in South Africa or Chinese in Malaysia;[18] and third, as was found in Croatia before the breakup of Yugoslavia, maintenance of ethnic balance within the military or police forces to guarantee that one group will not be able to use overwhelming organized violence against the other.[19] These political checks and balances serve to stabilize group relations and ensure that no group can be exploited by the other. In Barry R. Weingast's words, "reciprocal trust can be induced by institutions."[20]

---

16. The term "ethnic contract" was, we believe, coined by Leonard Binder at the first meeting of the IGCC Working Group on the International Spread and Management of Ethnic Conflict, May 13–14, 1994. On relational contracting more generally, see Oliver Williamson, *The Economic Institutions of Capitalism: Firms, Markets, and Relational Contracting* (New York: Free Press, 1985); for an application to inter-state relations, see David A. Lake, "Anarchy, Hierarchy, and the Variety of International Relations," *International Organization*, Vol. 50, No. 1 (Winter 1996), pp. 1–33.

17. Arend Lijphart, *The Politics of Accommodation: Pluralism and Democracy in the Netherlands* (Berkeley: University of California Press, 1967); Donald L. Horowitz, *Ethnic Groups in Conflict* (Berkeley: University of California Press, 1985); Timothy D. Sisk, *Democratization in South Africa: The Elusive Social Contract* (Princeton, N.J.: Princeton University Press, 1995); and Weingast, "Constructing Trust."

18. Heribert Adam and Kogila Moodley, "South Africa: The Opening of the Apartheid Mind," in John McGarry and Brendan O'Leary, eds., *The Politics of Ethnic Conflict Regulation* (New York: Routledge, 1993), pp. 226–250.

19. Misha Glenny, *The Fall of Yugoslavia* (New York: Penguin Books, 1992); and Hardin, *One for All*, pp. 58 and 159.

20. Weingast, "Constructing Trust," p. 15. Aleksa Djilas, "Fear thy Neighbor: The Breakup of Yugoslavia," in Charles A. Kupchan, ed., *Nationalism and Nationalities in the New Europe* (Ithaca, N.Y.: Cornell University Press, 1995), p. 99, argues that the communist party served as the primary safeguard in Yugoslavia, largely through coercion and repression, and that the defeat of the party in the 1990 elections left a political vacuum. He faults the party for not developing "stable institutions" that could have regulated relations among the republics. In "Constructing Trust," on the other hand, Weingast credits Yugoslav President Josip Broz Tito for constructing a set of veto mechanisms institutionalizing trust among the groups.

The terms of the ethnic contract reflect the balance of political power between the groups and their beliefs about the intentions and likely behaviors of one another. Safeguards are crafted to respond to the specific circumstances of each set of groups. However, ethnic contracts can be undermined and problems of credible commitment created by changes in either the ethnic balance of power or the beliefs of groups about others. These changes and their implications are captured in two separate but related models, one by James Fearon that focuses on the balance of political power between groups and one by Weingast that emphasizes beliefs.[21]

The political power of groups is determined by demography, the resources available to each group, and their capacity to organize effectively.[22] More powerful groups have a larger say in setting the terms of the contract. However, for the less powerful group to agree voluntarily to enter and abide by the contract, its interests must also be addressed, including its concern that the more powerful group will try to exploit it and alter the terms of the contract at some future date. Indeed, it is the minority, fearful of future exploitation and violence, that ultimately determines the viability of any existing ethnic contract. When the balance of ethnic power remains stable—and is expected to remain stable—well-crafted contracts enable ethnic groups to avoid conflict despite their differing policy preferences.

However, the ethnic balance of power does evolve over time. As in Lebanon, disparities in population growth rates will eventually alter the balance between groups. Differing access to resources may increase prosperity for some groups and poverty for others, also shifting the ethnic balance. When multi-ethnic polities fragment, as in Yugoslavia and the former Soviet Union, the relevant political space alters rapidly and the various ethnic groups that once counted their numbers on a national scale must now calculate their kin in terms of the new, smaller territorial units, and may find themselves in a stronger or weaker position. It is apprehension over the consequences of any dissolution, for instance, that motivates Protestants in Northern Ireland to hold tenaciously onto union with the largely Protestant United Kingdom rather than merge with the predominantly Catholic state of Ireland. When such changes in the ethnic

---

21. Fearon, "Ethnic War as a Commitment Problem"; and Fearon, "Rationalist Explanations for War"; see also Fearon, "Commitment Problems and the Spread of Ethnic Conflict," in Lake and Rothchild, *Ethnic Fears and Global Engagement*. See Weingast, "Constructing Trust"; this model is also discussed in Robert H. Bates and Barry R. Weingast, "Rationality and Interpretation: The Politics of Transition," paper presented to the Annual Meeting of the American Political Science Association, Chicago, August 31–September 3, 1995.
22. Hardin, *One for All*, p. 56.

balance of power have not been anticipated, or if the safeguards are overly rigid and cannot be renegotiated easily, the ethnic contract will be at risk of collapse.

Problems of credible commitment arise, as Fearon shows, whenever the balance of ethnic power shifts.[23] As the influence of one side declines, previously enforceable ethnic contracts become unenforceable. The checks and balances that safeguard the agreement today become insufficient tomorrow. Even if the group that is growing stronger promises not to exploit the weaker group in the future, there is nothing to prevent it from breaking its promise when it actually is stronger. Recognizing this, the declining side may choose to fight today rather than accede to an ethnic contract that will become increasingly unenforceable as time progresses.

Independent of changes in the ethnic balance of power, Weingast demonstrates that if information is incomplete and there are costs to becoming a victim in the future, changes in the beliefs of one group about the intentions of another can play a large role in setting the parties on the road to violence.[24] If a group believes that there is even a small chance that it may become a target of a genocidal attack, it may choose conflict over compromise and the risk of future destruction. To provoke conflict, one group need not believe that the other really is aggressive, only fear that it might be. With incomplete information, even small changes in beliefs about the intentions of the other group can generate massive violence.

Information is costly to acquire and, as a result, there is always some uncertainty about the intentions of other groups. Groups compensate for their informational limitations by acting on the basis of prior beliefs about the likely preferences of others (as well as the costs of resorting to violence and other variables). These beliefs are formed through historical experience—the "past," in Pešić's words—and represent each group's best guess about the other's intentions. Groups then update these beliefs as new information becomes available to them. Nonetheless, information is always incomplete and groups are forever uncertain about each other's purposes. Conflict, then, always remains possible in ethnic interactions.

Problems of credible commitment in ethnic relations are universal. Concerned that the balance of power may tip against them or that the other may

---

23. Fearon, "Ethnic War as a Commitment Problem."
24. Weingast, "Constructing Trust"; and Bates and Weingast, "Rationality and Interpretation." The term "beliefs" is used here in its game-theoretic sense to refer to the conditional probability of an actor holding one set of preferences (intentions, in the text; payoffs from a game, more formally) rather than another. Actors form beliefs subjectively, largely on the basis of past interactions.

have hostile intentions, groups worry that agreements made today will not be honored tomorrow. Effective states can help to mitigate these problems of credible commitment by enforcing existing ethnic contracts. When the future risk of exploitation is high, however, current relations and the state itself can quickly unravel. Fearful of the future, weaker groups may resort to preemptive violence today to secure their position in times to come. When this happens, outside peacekeepers or peace enforcers with sufficient military capabilities and political will may be the only way to ensure ethnic peace.

THE SECURITY DILEMMA. Posen has recently extended the concept of the security dilemma, first developed in international relations, to the study of ethnic conflict. In the broadest sense of the concept, the security dilemma is understood to follow axiomatically from anarchy. Under anarchy, states are dependent upon self-help for their security and must therefore maintain and perhaps expand their military capabilities. This can threaten others, who react by maintaining and expanding their capabilities, creating a spiral of arms-racing and hostility. The dilemma follows from the inability of the two sides to observe each other's intentions directly; if each party knew the other was arming strictly for defensive purposes, the potential spiral would be cut short. But because states cannot know the intentions of others with certainty, in Posen's words, "what one does to enhance one's own security causes reactions that, in the end, can make one less secure."[25]

Understood in this broad way, however, the security dilemma more accurately rests on the information failures and problems of credible commitment just discussed. It is the inability both to know with certainty the intentions and abilities of others and to commit credibly not to arm for offensive purposes that drives the spiral. The unique analytic core of the security dilemma lies in situations where one or more disputing parties have incentives to resort to preemptive uses of force. We use the term here to refer to these specific incentives.[26] As Robert Jervis observes, incentives to preempt arise when offensive military technologies and strategies dominate more defensive postures, and thus the side that attacks first reaps a military advantage.[27] The offense is likely to dominate when there are significant military benefits from surprise

---

25. Posen, "The Security Dilemma and Ethnic Conflict," p. 104.
26. We recognize that some readers may prefer the broader use of the term "security dilemma." We believe that the distinctions between information failures, problems of credible commitment, and incentives to use force preemptively are useful and important, and we see no reason to use a less precise catchall term when more precise and analytically refined definitions are available.
27. Robert Jervis, "Cooperation Under the Security Dilemma," *World Politics*, Vol. 30, No. 2 (January 1978), pp. 167–213. See also George H. Quester, *Offense and Defense in the International System* (New York: John Wiley, 1977).

and mobility. Geography will also matter, because some kinds of terrain (such as mountainous areas) and settlement patterns (such as exclusive ethnic zones) are easier to defend than others.[28] When the offense dominates, even *status quo* groups (and states), it follows, may be tempted to launch preemptive strikes to avoid a possibly even worse fate.

When incentives to use force preemptively are strong, the security dilemma takes hold and works its pernicious effects. Fearful that the other might preempt, a group has an incentive to strike first and negotiate later. In ethnic relations, as in international relations, when there are significant advantages to preemption, a cycle of violence can seize previously peaceful groups even as they seek nothing more than their own safety. By the same logic, previously satisfied groups can be driven to become aggressors, destroying ethnic harmony in the search for group security.

STRATEGIC INTERACTIONS WITHIN GROUPS

As we have just shown, strategic interactions between groups create the unstable social foundations from which ethnic conflict arises. Information failures, problems of credible commitment, and the security dilemma demonstrate that even when groups mean well and calculate the costs and benefits of alternatives realistically, conflict can still erupt. Even in "the best of all possible worlds," these strategic dilemmas can produce violent conflict.

Under conditions of actual or potential state weakness, and as the strategic dilemmas described above begin to take hold, two catalysts—ethnic activists and political entrepreneurs—can produce rapid and profound polarization within a multi-ethnic society. Social polarization, in turn, magnifies the strategic dilemmas and potential for conflict described above. As we explain in this section, political memories, myths, and emotions also magnify the polarizing effects of activists and entrepreneurs, further accelerating the vicious cycle of ethnic fear and violence.

All individuals desire to belong to groups, but the strength of this desire differs.[29] In a model of "ethnic dissimilation," Timur Kuran demonstrates that ethnic activists—individuals with especially strong needs to identify with ethnic kin—can manipulate such desires to produce a process of social polarization that is rapid, apparently spontaneous, and essentially unpredictable.[30] By

---

28. Posen, "The Security Dilemma and Ethnic Conflict."
29. Horowitz, *Ethnic Groups in Conflict.*
30. Timur Kuran, "Ethnic Dissimilation and its Global Transmission," in Lake and Rothchild, *Ethnic Fears and Global Engagement.*

persuading others to increase their public ethnic activity in order to maintain standing within the group, Kuran argues, ethnic activists can drive individuals to represent falsely their true preferences. While they might prefer, for instance, not to associate exclusively with members of their own group, individuals are pressed by activists and the social pressures they spawn to alter their behavior in a more "ethnic" direction. In this way, Kuran finds, ethnic activists can cause previously integrated communities to separate along ethnic lines.

Political entrepreneurs—individuals who may not share the beliefs of extremists but who seek political office and power—may reflect the polarization of societies and, through their actions, propel this process further. Ethnicity often provides a key marker for self-aggrandizing politicians seeking to build constituencies for attaining or maintaining political power.[31] Politicians in the middle of the political spectrum or those who court ethnically heterogeneous constituencies are vulnerable, in turn, to political extremists seeking to draw electoral support from only a more ethnically homogeneous and possibly more militant constituency. When faced with the threat of such challenges, even centrist politicians can be driven to embrace a more "ethnic" position and defend communal interests more vigorously, a phenomenon often referred to as ethnic outbidding.[32] Political entrepreneurs can also reinforce processes of social polarization. Like activists, they can highlight and legitimate ethnic associations and affinities and raise the political saliency of ethnicity. In framing issues for the public, moreover, political entrepreneurs can exaggerate the hostility of others and magnify the likelihood of conflict—thereby distorting public debate and images of other groups and driving co-ethnics toward them for power and support. President Slobodan Milošević's control over the media in Serbia, for instance, allowed him to present a one-sided view of Croat violence toward Croatian Serbs.[33] In short, political entrepreneurs both reflect and stimulate ethnic fears for their own aggrandizement.

Many analysts mistakenly focus on social polarization and the role of ethnic activists and political entrepreneurs in fomenting violence as the primary if not sole cause of ethnic conflict. Empirically, it is important to note that social polarization by itself does not necessarily lead to violence; Belgium provides

---

31. Stephen M. Saideman, "Is Pandora's Box Half-Empty or Half-Full? The Limited Virulence of Secessionism and the Domestic Sources of Disintegration," in Lake and Rothchild, *Ethnic Fears and Global Engagement.*
32. Joseph Rothschild, *Ethnopolitics: A Conceptual Framework* (New York: Columbia University Press, 1981); and Horowitz, *Ethnic Groups in Conflict.*
33. Weingast, "Constructing Trust," p. 20.

a particularly salient example of a polarized society that manages to conduct politics on a peaceful if not necessarily always harmonious basis, partly because the state remains robust enough to prevent significant information failures, problems of credible commitment, and security dilemmas from arising. Ethnic extremists, in turn, are nearly always present, and they can be expected to become prominent whenever at least one of the strategic dilemmas above is initiated. Analytically, ethnic activists and political entrepreneurs are as much a product as a producer of ethnic fears and are dependent for their "success" upon the underlying strategic dilemmas. Nonetheless, they do play an important role in exacerbating ethnic tensions and propelling societies along the road to violence.

The polarization of society is also magnified by such "non-rational" factors as political memories and myths, on the one hand, and emotions, on the other. Political memories and myths can lead groups to form distorted images of others and see others as more hostile and aggressive than they really are. Such myths are often rooted in actual events, and probably could not be long sustained absent a historical basis. Yet, historical events can, over time, evolve into legends that justify the superiority of one group over another, stimulate desires for retribution, or sustain group hatreds. In Africa, following decolonization as well as in the contemporary period, political memories of past conflict have directly contributed to violent encounters, even instances of genocide.[34] In Eastern Europe, political memories and myths have both defined the groups themselves and stimulated acute fears of mutual exploitation. The Croats and Serbs, formerly citizens within the same state and now enemies, have both used history and religion to support a view of the other as a tight ethnic bloc determined on a destructive course and therefore deserving of pitiless retaliation.

Emotions may also cause individuals and groups to act in exaggerated or potentially "irrational" ways that magnify the chances of conflict. Many analysts point to a deep psychological—perhaps even physiological—need for humans to belong to a group.[35] In the process of drawing distinctions, however, individuals often overstate the goodness of their own group while simultaneously vilifying others. Where such emotional biases exist, groups are likely to interpret the demands of others as outrageous, while seeing their own as

---

34. René Lemarchand and David Martin, *Selective Genocide in Burundi*, No. 20 (London: Minority Rights Group, 1974).
35. Horowitz, *Ethnic Groups in Conflict*.

moderate and reasonable; to view the other as inherently untrustworthy, while believing themselves to be reliable; to insist upon adequate safeguards against the possible defection of the other, but interpreting the efforts of others to impose similar restrictions on them as a sign of "bad faith"; to believe that the other is withholding information or deceptive, while they are being open and honest; and so on.

The emotional power of ethnic attachments is typically increased by the unifying effects of what are perceived to be external threats. People who have little in common with others may unite when they feel threatened by external enemies. Thus, the shared identity of the Hutu in Burundi emerged only recently with the Tutsi repressions of 1972.[36] Similarly, in Chechnya, when very disparate interests felt threatened by Russian power, they overcame their differences and made common cause in the face of Russian intervention.

Together, strategic interactions between and within groups can produce environments of fear in which ethnic tensions and conflicts can grow. As Pešić recognizes, it is the future that threatens, but the future is interpreted through the past. While each strategic dilemma alone is sufficient to produce and explain the outbreak of ethnic conflict, they almost always occur simultaneously. Ethnic activists and political entrepreneurs can polarize societies, exacerbating these strategic dilemmas. The tendency toward polarization, in turn, is magnified by political memories and myths and emotions. Combined, these forces create a devastating brew of ethnic rivalry and potential violence.

The Management of Ethnic Conflict

Effective management of ethnic conflicts by local elites and governments and by external states and organizations must reassure minority groups of their physical and cultural safety. To foster stability and constructive ethnic relations, the rights and position of the minority must be secured. Confidence-building measures undertaken by local elites are the most effective instrument to this end, and we discuss these first. In light of group fears and individual ambitions, however, international intervention may be necessary and appropriate either to support local leaders in their confidence-building efforts or to enforce new, externally imposed ethnic contracts. Even so, confidence-building measures and international interventions are imperfect. Unlike other, more optimis-

---

36. Warren Weinstein, "Conflict and Confrontation in Central Africa: The Revolt in Burundi," *Africa Today*, Vol. 19, No. 4 (Fall 1972), p. 27.

tic observers, we see no permanent resolutions, only temporary "fixes." In the end, ethnic groups are left without reliable safety nets. There is no form of insurance sufficient to protect against the dilemmas that produce collective fears and violence. We can only hope to contain ethnic fears, not permanently eliminate them.

CONFIDENCE-BUILDING MEASURES

Confidence-building measures seek to reassure ethnic peoples about their future. To overcome minority fears, confidence-building measures must be appropriate to the needs of those who feel vulnerable to the majority-backed state. The challenge, as I. William Zartman observes, "is to keep the minority/ies from losing."[37] Such safeguards, if handled sensitively over the years, may be able to cope with the central problems of sharing private information and making credible commitments. There are four major trust-building mechanisms for helping ethnic minorities deal with perceived insecurity.

DEMONSTRATIONS OF RESPECT. The security of ethnic peoples is in no small way based on a reciprocity of respect. Unless each side views its opponent as honorable and having legitimate interests, relations are likely to be marred by a history of intended or unintended affronts that widen the social distance between groups and exacerbate fears among ethnic minorities that their children will be relegated indefinitely to second-class status.

Relations in Bosnia, worsened by polarization and increasingly hostile perceptions, have been further aggravated by the contempt Serbs have shown their Muslim adversaries. Describing themselves as the only people in former Yugoslavia "who have the talent, energy, experience, and tradition to form a state," they characterize their adversaries as representing "all that is base, undesirable, and naturally subordinate."[38] In the Sudan, southerners with strong memories of slavery and perceptions of low status bridle at any new evidence of disrespect. Thus, they viewed the Sudanese government's decision to apply Islamic (*Shari'a*) law to them as well as to the Muslims living in the country's north as a confirmation of their second-class status.[39] Their resentment boiled over in 1994, when the minister of state in the president's office, at the mediation talks

---

37. I. William Zartman, "Putting Humpty-Dumpty Together Again," in Lake and Rothchild, *Ethnic Fears and Global Engagement*.
38. Norman Cigar, *Genocide in Bosnia: The Policy of "Ethnic Cleansing"* (College Station: Texas A & M University Press, 1995), pp. 74–75.
39. Amnesty International, *"The Tears of Orphans": No Future Without Human Rights* (New York: Amnesty International, 1995), p. 57.

in Nairobi held by the Inter-Governmental Authority on Drought and Development (IGADD), allegedly treated both the southerners and the IGADD mediators with contempt when rejecting the southerners' call for self-determination and a secular state.[40]

The fears of ethnic minorities may often be overstated. Minorities in Eastern Europe are described as having "an exaggerated fear of the loss of identity," a legacy of distrust of majority authorities that causes them to make broad demands for legal guarantees. The majorities, fearful that this will start them down the slippery slope toward the breakup of their states, refuse to consent to these demands.[41] But to build confidence it is imperative that dominant state elites take minority ethnic resentments and anxieties into account. Those involved in the management of ethnic disputes can learn much from C.E. Osgood's Graduated and Reciprocated Initiatives in Tension Reduction (GRIT) strategy for easing conflict between the superpowers during the Cold War.[42] His suggested approach of repeated overtures without expectations of an immediate tit-for-tat response could stimulate full negotiations between equals. Unless past wrongs are redressed and the sting of disparagement is removed from current ethnic interactions, internal negotiations will remain clouded by an overhang of bitterness and suspicion; minority uncertainty regarding adversary intentions will then contribute to serious conflicts.

POWER-SHARING. Conflict management requires an effort by the state to build representative ruling coalitions. In conceding to ethnic minority leaders and activists a proportionate share of cabinet, civil service, military, and high party positions, the state voluntarily reaches out to include minority representatives in public affairs, thereby offering the group as a whole an important incentive for cooperation. In South Africa, for example, President Nelson Mandela agreed to include power-sharing provisions in the interim constitution in an effort to reconcile the economically dominant local white community as well as to build confidence among mostly white investors abroad. Significantly, this concession was withdrawn in 1996 with the enactment of a new majority rule constitution. National Party leader F.W. de Klerk was quick to describe the ending of multiparty participation in cabinet decision-making as a "mistake" that would cause a loss of confidence in the country.[43]

---

40. *Sudan Democratic Gazette*, No. 53 (October 1994), p. 3.
41. Larry L. Watts, "Ethnic Tensions: How the West Can Help," *World Policy Journal*, Vol. 12, No. 1 (Spring 1995), pp. 92–93.
42. C.E. Osgood, *An Alternative to War or Surrender* (Urbana: University of Illinois Press, 1962).
43. "SA Will Pay Price For New Constitution: FW," *ANC Daily News Briefing*, May 9, 1996, p. 9, as transmitted on gopher://gopher.anc.org.za:70/00/anc/newsbrief/1996/news0509.

Power-sharing can be informal (e.g., Kenya, 1960s) or formal (e.g., Nigeria, 1979), and can take place in authoritarian (e.g., Zambia, 1980s) or democratic (e.g., South Africa, mid-1990s) settings. In both Eastern Europe and Africa, there has been a mixed pattern of "hegemonic exchange" regimes: centrally controlled one- or no-party regimes that allow a limited amount of bargaining to take place between state, ethnic, and other elites. Under the authoritarian administrations of Josip Broz Tito in Yugoslavia or Félix Houphouët-Boigny in Côte d'Ivoire, nationality or ethnic representatives met with the president in cabinet sessions, where strong differences were sometimes aired by group spokespersons behind closed doors. The resulting power-sharing systems are quite diverse, yet they have in common a form of coordination in which a somewhat autonomous state and a number of less autonomous ethnic-based and other interests engage in a process of mutual accommodation in accordance with commonly accepted procedural norms, rules, or understandings.[44] These elite power-sharing arrangements are inevitably fragile and temporary because the communal pillars upon which they rest remain firmly in place and resist the integrative pulls that would lead to countrywide loyalties. Even so, while these arrangements last they provide some security for political and ethnic minorities.

With ethnic balances of power constantly evolving and information limited, these arrangements are necessarily transitional ones. If poorly negotiated and implemented, the incomplete ethnic contracts may eventually be rejected by the groups they are designed to protect. The number of people appointed to the cabinet or civil service, for example, is not in and of itself a guarantee of proportional group influence.[45] When not applied with great care, power-sharing arrangements can backfire. Ethnic elites must be prepared to interact with other elite representatives they find personally repugnant, something difficult to do under normal circumstances but especially so where the norms of collaborative politics are not in place. Where majority-dominated states remain unprepared to respond to legitimate minority demands for full participation in decision-making activities, power-sharing schemes are likely to unravel and become themselves a source of grave insecurity.

ELECTIONS. Although elections represent only a brief episode in a larger political process, they can have enormous influence on inter-group collabora-

---

44. Donald Rothchild, "Hegemonial Exchange: An Alternative Model for Managing Conflict in Middle Africa," in Dennis L. Thompson and Dov Ronen, eds., *Ethnicity, Politics, and Development* (Boulder, Colo.: Lynne Rienner, 1986), p. 72.
45. Robert B. Mattes, "Beyond 'Government and Opposition': An Independent South African Legislature," *Politikon*, Vol. 20, No. 2 (December 1993), p. 76.

tion and conflict. Where favorable circumstances prevail (i.e., an agreement on the rules of the political game, broad participation in the voting process, and a promising economic environment), elections can promote stability. In democratic regimes, where institutionalized uncertainty provides many players with an incentive to participate, the election process can legitimate the outcome.[46] All groups have a reason to organize and, through coalitions with other parties, they are given an opportunity to gain power in the future. This prospect of competing in accordance with the procedural norms of the system can be reassuring to minority interests; not only do they have a chance to advance their individual and collective interests, but they are encouraged by the majority's commitment to the electoral contract. The effect is to preempt conflict.

The implications of elections, however, can also be troubling in multi-ethnic settings. Even where minority groups are represented in the legislature, there is a real possibility that they will remain shut out of the decision-making process. Hence, unless election mechanisms can be linked with other types of political institutions such as multiparty coalitions, regional autonomy, or federalism, they may not be able to provide security against ethnic discrimination. Moreover, when political entrepreneurs seek to outbid their centrist rivals through militant appeals to their ethnic kinsmen, elections can prove very destabilizing, threatening minorities with the possibility of discrimination, exclusion, and even victimization.

Electoral systems have been organized in two main ways to promote inclusive coalitions. First, electoral rules can be set so that candidates are forced to appeal to more than one ethnic group. In an effort to give presidential candidates an incentive to appeal to a broad cross-section of communal groups, for example, both the 1979 and the 1995 (draft) constitutions in Nigeria provided variously that, if there are two candidates for election, a candidate would be deemed to be elected when that person secured a simple majority of the total number of votes cast as well as one-quarter of the votes cast in at least two-thirds of the states. In securing a majority of votes in this multi-ethnic society, moderate appeals, with their overarching themes, were expected to win out over parochial ones.

Second, electoral rules can also be crafted to ensure some minimal representation of all ethnic groups in the society. Those seeking to encourage minority representation in party lists and in ruling coalitions have looked favorably

46. Adam Przeworski, *Democracy and the Market* (Cambridge: Cambridge University Press, 1991), p. 26.

on systems of proportional representation (PR). For example, in structuring the elections for the Russian State Duma (the lower chamber of parliament) in 1993, legal drafters provided for a chamber of 450 members, half on the basis of single-member constituencies and half on the basis of PR. Constituencies also vary enormously in size. Such a system ensures the representation of smaller ethnic groups in the State Duma. Similarly, in South Africa, the African National Congress agreed, somewhat reluctantly, to use PR during the transition period to give racial and ethnic minorities a sense of security.[47] Although the PR system seemed cumbersome and failed to generate close links between a member of parliament and his or her constituents, ANC leaders nonetheless agreed to continue use of this mechanism for electing members to the National Assembly under the 1996 Constitution.

The way that state elites structure electoral arrangements is likely to prove critical in building confidence in minority circles. A broad-based electoral formula, like that of Nigeria, and proportional representation are two possible ways of encouraging minority ethnic participation and inclusion; yet they are likely to endure only as long as they retain support among key groups and state elites. If the majority shifts its concern away from the values of representativeness, a change in electoral rules can take place. Unless this change is handled fairly and with extreme sensitivity, it can be perceived by minority groups as inimical to their interests. As a consequence, considerable experience is required before minorities come to see electoral laws as reliable foundations for their security.

REGIONAL AUTONOMY AND FEDERALISM. Political and administrative decentralization can play a role in managing political conflict. By enabling local and regional authorities to wield a degree of autonomous power, elites at the political center can promote confidence among local leaders. Measures on decentralization, regional autonomy, and federalism featured in peace negotiations in Bosnia, Sri Lanka, Cyprus, Sudan, Angola, Mozambique, and South Africa. In each, they provided insurgent militias with an important incentive for responding positively to the government or third-party mediator's proposals for settling the conflict. The U.S.-brokered peace initiative in Bosnia achieved a key breakthrough in the September 1995 negotiations, for example, when the Bosnian government agreed to recognize an autonomous Bosnian Serb entity, called Republika Srpska. In exchange, Serbia and Croatia accepted

---

47. Timothy D. Sisk, "South Africa Seeks New Ground Rules," *Journal of Democracy*, Vol. 4, No. 1 (January 1993), p. 87.

the legal existence of Bosnia and Herzegovina with its present borders and endorsed the division of the country, 51 percent of the territory to the Bosnian government and Bosnian Croats, and 49 percent to the Bosnian Serbs. All three parties perceived control of Bosnia's territory to be critically important for their survival once peace came into effect.

In attempting to create a new balance between state and society, groups turn to decentralization as a means of placing institutional limitations on unbridled central authority. Politically marginalized groups have vivid memories of excessive state penetration and a continuing fear of majority domination. Decentralization and the authority these schemes allow local elites can, therefore, become confidence-building mechanisms that safeguard the place of minorities in the larger society. In Ethiopia, for example, President Meles Zenawi looks to a scheme of ethnic federalism as a means of reversing the repressive, hegemonic practices of previous governments that have led to internal wars.[48] The 1994 Constitution gives the nations making up Ethiopia wide powers, including an unconditional right of self-determination and secession.

Nevertheless, experiments with decentralized systems in India, Pakistan, Cyprus, Sri Lanka, Kenya, Uganda, South Africa, Sudan, and Ethiopia reveal serious practical difficulties in securing majority-backed state acceptance for these attempts to insulate minority interests from central authority. Determined to prevent the division of the state, public officials have taken firm action to avert a weakening of control. In extreme cases, they have revoked previous concessions. Thus, as Yugoslavia began to disintegrate in 1989, Milošević rescinded the autonomous provincial status within Serbia that Tito had given to largely Albanian-populated Kosovo. Sudan's President Gaafar el-Nimeiry, who had been the main advocate of political accommodation with the Southern Sudan Liberation Movement insurgents in 1972, backtracked on his commitments formalized in the Addis Ababa accords and in the late 1970s began to dismantle the federal compromise; to placate hard-line, Muslim elements within his government, Nimeiry intervened in southern regional elections, changed regional boundaries, redivided the southern region, applied *Shari'a* law to non-Muslims, and ultimately abrogated the agreement itself. In both Yugoslavia and Sudan, revocation of concessions on autonomy heightened tensions and led to new violence.

---

48. Cameron McWhirter and Gur Melamede, "Ethiopia: The Ethnicity Factor," *Africa Report,* Vol. 37, No. 5 (September/October, 1992) p. 33.

While regional autonomy and federalism have been used as safeguards, they have had, in some instances, unintended consequences that have actually increased conflict. Despite efforts to decentralize power in South Africa and Ethiopia, the fiscal dominance of the political center has tended to undercut the significance of regional authorities. Moreover, efforts to delineate boundaries have increased conflict between ethno-regional identity groups. In contemporary Russia, the arbitrary way in which internal boundaries divide ethnic peoples has been a major source of tension.[49] In Ethiopia, the regional boundaries set up by the government appear to favor Tigray and the Afars, at the expense of the formerly dominant Amhara and the Somali Isaks in the Awash Valleyland. Unless carefully crafted, decentralization schemes may worsen rather than improve inter-ethnic relations.

CONFIDENCE-BUILDING MEASURES EVALUATED. Confidence-building measures are potentially creative instruments by which states can reassure ethnic minorities. They indicate a sympathetic concern on the part of those in power to the fears and uncertainties of minorities. By acknowledging and showing respect for difference and by agreeing to share resources, state positions, and political power with exposed and vulnerable groups, these measures reduce the perceived risks of association and provide incentives for cooperation with other groups. They can also become the basis over time for a shared sense of common fate among diverse communities. States seeking ethnic accommodations have used confidence-building measures effectively in the past, and they will continue to do so in the future. The international community should encourage states at risk of significant ethnic conflict to make use of confidence-building measures.

However, such confidence-building measures represent conflict management, not conflict resolution. They can reduce some of the factors giving rise to ethnic fears, but they do not alter the basic dilemmas that cause these fears in the first place. The risks in ethnic encounters remain in place, even if papered over by concessions. Because there is always the possibility that groups will adopt more threatening forms of interaction, these confidence-building measures never eliminate the information failures, problems of credible commitment, and security dilemmas that are embedded in ethnic encounters. As Adam Przeworski astutely observes, "if sovereignty resides with the people, the

---

49. Gail W. Lapidus and Renée de Nevers, eds., *Nationalism, Ethnic Identity and Conflict Management in Russia Today* (Stanford, Calif.: Stanford University Center for International Security and Arms Control, 1995), p. 3.

people can decide to undermine all the guarantees reached by politicians around a negotiating table. Even the most institutionalized guarantees give at best a high degree of assurance, never certainty."[50]

EXTERNAL INTERVENTION

If states fail to restrain the incentives for violence rooted in the strategic interactions of groups, it is necessary to turn to the international environment and ask whether external intervention can safeguard minorities against their worst fears. For many observers, sovereignty is linked to responsibility: state elites are expected to guarantee minority rights and provide the means for establishing and maintaining regularized patterns of state-society and inter-ethnic relations. The state, with its monopoly of force, is often in a position, as one South African mediator described it in 1995, to "enforce stability" between local warring parties (in this case, in the East Rand townships in his country). But who will intercede if the state is unable or unwilling to secure the safety of its minority peoples? What forms will this intervention take? Which of the interventions, if any, are likely to have a significant impact on intra-state conflicts?

The principle of sovereignty has never been articulated or respected in the clear-cut manner often assumed by scholars of international relations. As Stephen D. Krasner and Daniel K. Froats demonstrate, states have a long history of intervention in the ethnic (and religious) affairs of others.[51] Many of the treaties settling European affairs in the aftermath of World War I contained provisions obligating states to protect the political and religious rights of minorities within their borders. More recently, the United Nations Charter affirmed an international commitment to basic human rights and fundamental freedoms. UN Secretary General Boutros Boutros-Ghali now believes that "the time of absolute and exclusive sovereignty has passed."[52]

Nonetheless, since 1945 there has been a strong insistence by many countries on the protection of national autonomy afforded by the juridical principle of sovereignty. This emphasis on internal autonomy has often been strongest where states themselves were weakest.[53] Yet today, ethnic conflicts and their

---

50. Przeworski, *Democracy and the Market*, p. 79.

51. Stephen D. Krasner and Daniel K. Froats, "The Westphalian Model and Minority-Rights Guarantees in Europe," in Lake and Rothchild, *Ethnic Fears and Global Engagement*. See also Krasner, "Compromising Westphalia," *International Security*, Vol. 20, No. 3 (Winter 1995/96), pp. 115–151.

52. Boutros Boutros-Ghali, *An Agenda for Peace* (New York: United Nations, 1992), p. 9.

53. Robert H. Jackson and Carl G. Rosberg. "Why Africa's Weak States Persist," *World Politics*, Vol. 35, No. 1 (October 1982), pp. 1–24.

possible spread have thrust issues of "humanitarian" intervention onto the policy agendas of the United States and many other countries. As Edmond Keller indicates, even in Africa, where the norm of juridical sovereignty has been strong, there is a new willingness on the part of state leaders to entertain limitations on the notion of sovereignty, but it remains an open question whether these leaders will be prepared to sanction international interventions directed against their own countries.[54]

External intervention takes three broad forms: noncoercive intervention, coercive intervention, and third-party mediation during both the negotiation and implementation stages. We look briefly at each of these forms, drawing conclusions in each case about their anticipated effects on intra-state conflicts.

NONCOERCIVE INTERVENTION. A sense of alarm over the violation of minority rights taking place in other countries has, at times, prompted outside states and multilateral organizations to protest infractions or exert pressure on the transgressors. Western governments, encouraged by their domestic publics to denounce breaches of human rights in Bosnia, Chechnya, Rwanda, and Sudan, have criticized these abuses through quiet, behind-the-scenes diplomacy and at public fora.

Assertions of international norms are important in raising the costs of unacceptable behavior, especially when their advocates offer an alternative set of interests around which defectors can mobilize and challenge the ensconced ethnic leaders.[55] States are also in a strong position to use inclusion in or exclusion from the international community to reward or punish regimes and ethnic leaders who deviate from internationally accepted norms. The promises of inclusion or the pains of exclusion can at times create strong incentives to behave in a more responsible fashion. Thus Milošević's desire to be accepted by Europeans and North Americans enabled Western diplomats to influence his behavior at the bargaining table, even causing him to make concessions on the emotionally charged issue of Bosnian government control over a unified Sarajevo. Similarly, conditions on membership in international organizations appear to be mitigating ethnic conflicts in Hungary and Romania, while Turkey's desire for acceptance in Europe may be limiting its actions against its Kurdish minority.

---

54. Edmond J. Keller, "Transnational Ethnic Conflict in Africa," in Lake and Rothchild, *Ethnic Fears and Global Engagement*.
55. V.P. Gagnon, Jr., "Ethnic Nationalism and International Conflict: The Case of Serbia," *International Security*, Vol. 19, No. 3 (Winter 1994/95), p. 139.

In South Africa, external protests and sanctions raised the costs of doing business, access to technology and raw materials, and travel. Sanctions physically punished the regime, something that became painfully evident in South Africa's loss of dominance in the air war over Angola, brought on in part by the air force's inability to secure spare parts. The symbolic impact of sanctions was also important because it represented a clear statement of sympathy for black hardship and moral disapproval of apartheid policies by the international community.[56] Above all, international condemnation challenged state and governmental legitimacy. While the costs of sanctions were discomforting and burdensome, they did not hurt the main body of the white constituency sufficiently to alter priorities, until de Klerk's remarkable change of heart on negotiating with the anti-apartheid opposition in the early 1990s.[57]

Given the extreme emotionalism over security issues that brings aggressive ethnic leaders to the fore in the first place, we are skeptical that external appeals, exhortations, and pressures will in and of themselves dissuade determined elites from their abusive courses. Bosnian Serb leader Radovan Karadžić, Bosnian Serb military commander Ratko Mladić, and their ilk remain sufficiently insulated from world pressures that what transpires at diplomatic meetings or in the global press may have little immediate impact on them or their militant followers.

Noncoercive interventions can be helpful in raising the costs of purely ethnic appeals and in structuring the incentives of group leaders prepared to accept international norms for the purposes of recognition, acceptance, and inclusion in the international community. Where conflicts are intense, however, exhortations and international warnings may not deter or end violence. The most that noncoercive intervention can do in such situations is to create a climate in which ethnic appeals and violence are perceived by all as illegitimate and, therefore, marginally less likely to be used.

COERCIVE INTERVENTION. The rise in ethnic conflict today creates new demands and opportunities for coercive intervention by outside states and international organizations.[58] External interventions have two primary effects. First, intervention can alter the internal balance of ethnic power and may lead groups

---

56. Harry R. Strack, *Sanctions: The Case of Rhodesia* (Syracuse, N.Y.: Syracuse University Press, 1978).
57. Sisk, *Democratization in South Africa.*
58. For discussions of the motivations of outside states to intervene in ethnic conflicts, see Michael E. Brown, "Causes and Implications of Ethnic Conflict," in Brown, ed., *Ethnic Conflict and International Security*, pp. 16–20, and Robert Cooper and Mats Berdal, "Outside Intervention in Ethnic Conflicts," in ibid., p. 197.

to moderate their demands. Except perhaps where the sides have reached a "hurting stalemate" and the purpose of the intervention is exclusively to separate the forces and keep the peace, interventions always have political implications.[59] Even in Somalia, where negotiations on establishing a transitional national council led to hopes for a settlement in 1993, the initial humanitarian mission eventually favored one claimant to power (Ali Mahdi Mohamed) over the other (Mohamed Farah Aideed), ultimately causing the politicization of the mission.[60] Typically favoring, by design or default, the weaker side in any internal conflict, external powers reduce the stronger side's chances for success. This, in turn, restrains the stronger party's demands. To the extent that such restraint takes hold, intervention can improve the prospects for agreement. However, the weaker side is likely to increase its demands and ask for more at the bargaining table as its prospects of failure decline and its chances for success improve.[61] For instance, once the NATO countries intervened decisively in September 1995 on behalf of the Bosnian government, and against the Bosnian Serb forces, the latter—pressured by Milošević—quickly moderated their demands and moved towards accepting the territorial partition they had earlier rejected.[62] At the same time, however, the Croats saw new opportunities on the battlefield and at the negotiating table, and the United States and its allies had to exert pressure on the Bosnian government and Croatia not to exploit their increased leverage. With both effects occurring simultaneously in any intervention, the "bargaining gap" between the parties may remain as wide as ever. Unless pressure is exerted on both sides to moderate their demands, intervention by itself will not necessarily enhance the prospects for agreement.

The second primary effect of intervention is to provide guarantees for new ethnic contracts between the warring parties, at least during an interim period. As discussed above, problems of credible commitment hinder the efforts of groups to resolve their differences peacefully. The primary attraction of external

59. On "hurting stalemates," see I. William Zartman, *Ripe for Resolution: Conflict and Intervention in Africa* (New York: Oxford University Press, 1985). On the inevitable political implications of intervention, see Caleb Carr, "The Consequences of Somalia," *World Policy Journal*, Vol. 10, No. 3 (Fall 1993), pp. 1–4.
60. John L. Hirsch and Robert B. Oakley, *Somalia and Operation Restore Hope: Reflections on Peacemaking and Peacekeeping* (Washington, D.C.: United States Institute of Peace Press, 1995).
61. Donald Wittman, "How a War Ends: A Rational Model Approach," *Journal of Conflict Resolution*, Vol. 23, No. 4 (December 1979), pp. 743–763.
62. Milošević's role in the October 1995 negotiations carried with it an implied threat: if the Bosnian Serbs refused to be more accommodating at the bargaining table, their Serb kinsmen across the border could further reduce their military support.

intervention is that an outside state can enforce an agreement, thereby providing the necessary credibility that is otherwise lacking. Indeed, when the future risk of exploitation is high, but the declining group is still strong enough to possess some chance of victory, outside enforcers may be the only way to ensure ethnic peace.[63] Thus, in Namibia in 1989, the third-party enforcer was in a position to raise the costs of breaking agreements by monitoring the implementation process, highlighting violations of the peace agreement, and focusing an international spotlight on any breaches that occurred.[64] The lack of any equally effective third-party enforcer in neighboring Angola following the signing of the Bicesse accords, and UNITA President Jonas Savimbi's poor showing in the first round of the 1992 elections, increased incentives to defect from the agreement and resume the civil war.

The promise of the post–Cold War world is that the great powers, freed from the shackles of superpower competition, can now intervene to mitigate ethnic conflicts by providing external guarantees of social order. If the warring parties themselves cannot make credible commitments to uphold their pacts, external powers can lead the groups to peaceful solutions by enforcing any agreement they might reach. The paradox of the post–Cold War world, however, is that absent the bipolar competition that drove them into the far reaches of the globe, the United States and other powers now lack the political will necessary to make a sustained commitment to this role.

The key issue in determining the success of any external guarantee is the commitment of the international community. In a way not sufficiently appreciated by current policy makers in Washington and elsewhere, external guarantees work only when the local parties to the conflict believe that the outside powers are resolved to enforce the ethnic contract in a fair manner into the indefinite future. The behavior of the external powers today is not the crucial factor. Rather, a more fundamental question is whether the warring parties or potential combatants believe the external powers will be there to protect them tomorrow, and in the days and years after that. Absent a belief in the fair-mindedness and stamina of the external powers, intervention in any form will fail to mitigate the conflict.

---

63. Stephen J. Stedman, *Peacemaking in Civil Wars: International Mediation in Zimbabwe, 1974–1980* (Boulder, Colo.: Lynne Rienner, 1991); and Barbara F. Walter, "The Resolution of Civil Wars: Why Negotiations Fail," unpublished paper, Columbia University, 1995.
64. Virginia P. Fortna, "Success and Failure in Southern Africa: Peacekeeping in Namibia and Angola," in Donald C.F. Daniel and Bradd C. Hayes, eds., *Beyond Traditional Peacekeeping* (New York: St. Martin's, 1995), pp. 282–299.

Unfortunately, even countries with strong interests in intervening often find themselves unable to offer credible external guarantees. Countries vitally affected by the fighting or the outcome either tend to be partisan or are perceived by the combatants as partisan, as was the case with France's intervention in Rwanda in 1994. One or both sides to the conflict, therefore, will doubt the willingness of the outside power to enforce the new ethnic contract in an evenhanded manner, and they will be less likely to reach an effective and enforceable agreement. However, when outside powers have interests in a stable outcome, rather than in the victory or loss of either side, they may be perceived by all as fair-minded facilitators. Britain's role in Zimbabwe in the 1970s is a positive example of an interested party able to work with a coalition of external mediators to push negotiations ahead to a successful outcome.

Countries with weak interests in the conflict, on the other hand, will tend to lack or will be perceived as lacking the political stamina to enforce any new ethnic contract into the future. The United States was unwilling to bear any substantial cost in human lives to guarantee the peace in Somalia, for instance. There are many reasons why states might possess only weak interests in guaranteeing a new ethnic conflict. Most important, political instability abroad is typically broad but shallow in its effects, producing incentives for states to seek to free ride on the efforts of others.[65] This is one plausible interpretation of the hesitancy of the United States in taking a leadership role in Bosnia. In this view, Presidents George Bush and Bill Clinton held back hoping that the Europeans would step forward and carry the financial and military burden; only when the Europeans proved unprepared to assume the costs did the United States take the lead.

Weak commitments produce ambiguous policies that may, in the end, exacerbate rather than resolve conflicts. Public commitments encourage the weaker party to believe that the external power supports it, thereby prompting the group to fight on and hold out for a better deal than its position on the battlefield warrants.[66] Ambiguity and vacillation, however, may simultaneously persuade the stronger party that the external power does not possess sufficient stamina, and that it too may improve its position by continuing to fight. This ambivalent commitment is the true tragedy of the current United States policy in the Balkans. One of the most important lessons from this

---

65. Mancur Olson, *The Logic of Collective Action* (Cambridge, Mass.: Harvard University Press, 1965).
66. Djilas, "Fear thy Neighbor: The Breakup of Yugoslavia," p. 102.

analysis is that if external powers are going to intervene in ethnic conflicts, either alone or in concert with others, they must do so in a way that is credible to the groups involved. An external guarantee that the parties expect will evaporate is no guarantee at all.

THIRD-PARTY MEDIATION. Given the limitations of confidence-building measures and external interventions, there are few alternatives to negotiations if both sides are to be brought into the solution. For a mutually satisfactory peace to take place, a two-step negotiating process is essential: first, among the key elements within each group, and then between the groups themselves. Operating rules must be hammered out in these talks regarding inclusive coalitions, proportionality in recruitment and allocations, autonomy, provisions on electoral competition, and so forth. The ensuing negotiations are likely to be protracted and difficult, largely because the various factions and groups lack a clear chain of command (making commitments difficult to produce) and because they understand fully that the terms they accept will cast a long shadow over their future. But if each of the parties concludes that its alternatives are limited, its present course unduly costly, and its stake in its rival's willingness to cooperate with an agreement significant, they may then begin to negotiate in good faith. External mediators can play an important role in facilitating negotiations by encouraging adversaries to open up channels of communication, to reconsider their alternatives, and to opt for peaceful, negotiated solutions. A mediator's ability to influence the strategies of the adversaries must not be overstated; nevertheless, the ability of a third party to make effective use of pressures and incentives can prove decisive, especially if the parties to the conflict have nowhere else to go.

In intense ethnic disputes, mediators can use a variety of noncoercive and coercive incentives to increase the information available to the adversaries, facilitate a change in their strategies, or find a way to save face. Noncoercive incentives extend benefits or rewards for compliance, while coercive incentives punish or threaten to punish a targeted actor to bring it into line with preferred types of political behavior. Provided that the demands of the two sides are negotiable and neither party can anticipate a military victory, mediators can make use of a package of carrots and sticks in the hopes that the targeted party (or parties) will accept a compromise and thus allow some degree of mutual cooperation to materialize.

Normally, noncoercive incentives will be preferred by third parties, because of their low cost and expected impact. Thus, mediators frequently make use of sidepayments to enlarge the pie and alter the payoff structure, thereby enhancing the benefits of making concessions (as occurred most dramatically in the Egyptian-Israeli negotiations at Camp David in 1978). Third parties can also influence the choices of ethnic minorities by guaranteeing them against possible future abuses at the hands of the majority after an agreement has been reached.

However, when ethnic conflicts grow in intensity and can no longer be resolved by means of rewards, it sometimes becomes necessary for the third party to force movement toward cooperation by means of threats or punishments. These coercive incentives become increasingly punitive as they move from pressure to economic sanctions to military intervention, as occurred at different stages in the Bosnian confrontation. In the contemporary period, only a coalition of mediators seems likely to have the political capacity to create the mix of noncoercive and coercive incentives necessary to overcome a stalemate and move the parties toward a negotiated settlement.

But the scope for third-party initiative at both the negotiation and implementation stages is highly circumscribed. Internal wars are particularly difficult to negotiate, largely because ethnic enmities tend to be so deep and the stakes so high. Data on negotiations indicate that settlements are difficult to achieve and at least as difficult to maintain, even where a third party is prepared to step between the adversaries. Roy Licklider, largely reconfirming earlier studies by Stephen Stedman and Paul Pillar, finds that only 14 out of 57 civil wars between 1945 and 1993 were settled through negotiations.[67] Even with its focus on opening channels of communication and facilitating the flow of information, third-party mediation cannot wholly eliminate potential information failures. The conflicting groups are bound by the same incentives not to reveal all of their private information, even to third parties. Moreover, problems of credible commitment loom large. Barbara Walter suggests that inter-state wars are easier to bring to a negotiated conclusion because the two parties remain on opposite sides of a border; in internal wars, the disputants must re-merge themselves into a single unit and, as a result, face more difficult problems of credible commitment.[68]

The difficulties normally associated with mediation are compounded by the obstacles to implementation. Several laboriously negotiated agreements have

---

67. Roy Licklider, "The Consequences of Negotiated Settlements in Civil Wars, 1945–1993," *American Political Science Review*, Vol. 89, No. 3 (September 1995), p. 684; Stedman, *Peacemaking in Civil Wars*, pp. 5–7; Paul R. Pillar, *Negotiating Peace: War Termination as a Bargaining Process* (Princeton, N.J.: Princeton University Press, 1993), p. 25.
68. Walter, "The Resolution of Civil Wars."

been signed only to fall apart at the implementation stage—for example, in Ethiopia and Eritrea (1962), Sudan (1982), Uganda (1985), Angola (1975, 1992), and Rwanda (1994). A large part of the responsibility for these failures lies with adversary parties and their inability to make credible and reliable commitments. Their distrust of one another's intentions was so deep that the peace agreement crumbled when ambiguity on security-related matters opened the way to renewed confrontation.

However, the failure of these agreements is also partly attributable to the unwillingness of the international community to provide mediators with the economic, logistical, police, and military support needed to oversee the processes of disarmament, integration of the armed forces, repatriation of refugees, and holding of general elections. In addition, the guarantees made to one or more rivals by foreign governments and multilateral organizations have come to lack credibility as local actors now expect the domestic publics of the third-party mediators to lose interest over time in far-off conflicts and retreat from commitments made at the high point of the struggle.

As internal wars reach a hurting stalemate and leaders on both sides perceive an "intolerable situation" with little expectation of military victory, fatigued parties may come to the table and bargain in earnest.[69] Despite the emotionalism and organizational imperatives surrounding civil wars, a number of them— including those in Cambodia, Nicaragua, Zimbabwe, Angola, Namibia, Mozambique, and possibly now Chechnya and Bosnia—have been or are close to being settled by means of negotiations. One must not anticipate too much from mediatory efforts, but a grim outlook is also not appropriate and could be self-fulfilling.

THE LIMITS OF INTERVENTION. External interventions, whether they are noncoercive, coercive, mediatory, or—as is common—a combination of the three, are not likely to solve the underlying strategic dilemmas that produce ethnic fear and violence. Information failures remain possible, despite the efforts of outside actors to facilitate communication and protect the parties from the potentially disastrous consequences of revealing private information. Enforcing ethnic contracts depends upon the credibility of the external parties, who often have far less at stake in the conflict than the warring groups themselves. External actors can seek to raise the costs of using force, in general, and preemptive uses of force, in particular, by punishing groups that strike first; such initiatives or the threat of such initiatives may have a moderating effect

---

69. Zartman, *Ripe for Resolution*, p. 232.

on the security dilemma. Through early action, they may also be able to shape military doctrines and force structures in groups beginning to prepare for self-defense. Nevertheless, once incentives to use force preemptively are in place, outsiders can do little to restrain the security dilemma. In the final analysis, conflict management requires an effort by the local parties to engage in efforts to work out acceptable rules of interaction. External intervention does not by itself create a desire among the parties to restore normal relations. This is not to say that international efforts to contain conflict are not important, only that containment by itself is not a solution.

Toward Practical Initiatives

Most of the time, most ethnic groups live side by side with one another comfortably and amicably. Even in cases where ethnic minorities might otherwise be at risk, states have promoted stable ethnic relations and made concessions on minority group inclusion, participation, autonomy, and access to resources. However, an awareness that regimes can always change their preferences and retract these concessions leaves minorities fearful of the future. Information failures, problems of credible commitment, and the security dilemma lurk in the background of all ethnically divided polities. Conflict always remains a possibility.

Where an element of local anarchy is present and the state is at least potentially weak, a spiral of negative encounters that leads to violence remains a very real possibility. Information failures occur as the state loses its ability to arbitrate between factions, and as groups hold back information and suspect others of doing the same. Problems of credible commitment arise as ethnic contracts collapse and groups come to fear that others will not uphold their promises. Incentives to preempt drive groups to fight first and seek the basis for compromise later. In situations of increasing state weakness, appeals by ethnic activists and political entrepreneurs may awaken long dormant "malignant nationalisms" and lead to escalating violence.[70] In multi-ethnic polities with past histories of conflict and distrust, the social fabric can be very weak and easily torn apart.

In their fear, political minorities, recognizing the state's limited capacity to ensure their physical and cultural safety, look outward to the international

---

70. Stephen Van Evera, "Hypotheses on Nationalism and War," *International Security*, Vol. 18, No. 4 (Winter 1994), p. 8.

community for protection. They hope the international community will restore a balance of power and hence make systematic, state-sanctioned ethnic killing too costly for the hard-line majority leadership to condone. The international response, however, has all too often been feeble and unconvincing.

In the end, and despite the limits on international interventions discussed above, there can be no substitute for greater global commitment and involvement. The international community has already been involved at nearly every stage of some confrontation around the globe. This is a hopeful sign. But so far, many of the international responses have been conducted separately, sporadically, and outside of any comprehensive strategy for achieving ethnic peace, thereby limiting their effectiveness. Recognizing the inherent limits on the ability of international interventions to solve the strategic dilemmas we have identified, as well as the limits of public support in outside states, we recommend three specific avenues of action.

MANAGE INFORMATION

Given the importance of private information and the beliefs that groups hold about the intentions of others, one of the most effective policy instruments in the hands of international actors today is to ensure that objective, unbiased, and balanced information is made widely available in states threatened with intense conflict. This will require a continuing but largely preventive effort. As conflict escalates, outside states and international organizations can consider jamming radios that make inflammatory appeals, as did Radio Télévision Libre des Mille Collines in Rwanda. After the crisis has eased, external actors can use a variety of means, such as radio, fax, and the internet, for sharing information with the warring parties to help verify compliance with new ethnic contracts.

ASSIST "FAILING" STATES

Growing state weakness is a symptom of the strategic dilemmas discussed above. As information failures occur, problems of credible commitment arise, and security dilemmas begin to take hold, groups either turn away from the state or attempt to seize it to further their own quest for security. A decrease in a state's capacity to arbitrate between groups and enforce ethnic contracts is a clear herald of violence. Preventing the breakdown of the state can, in turn, help mitigate the potential for violence. External actors should seek to ensure that confidence-building measures are in place and that elites live up to minimum standards of legal order and political and human rights. The support of the international community for the anti-apartheid struggle in South Africa is a prime example. Trade, financial aid, and other benefits from inclusion in the international community should be linked to the maintenance of minimum international standards of domestic order. In advance of crises, international bodies should also assemble data banks, early warning systems, advance plans for possible mediators, units for peacemaking and enforcement, and personnel to assist in the creation of unified armies. It will be necessary to provide a solid financial basis for such international actions, but the costs will be small compared to the long-run benefits of reduced conflict.

INVEST IN IMPLEMENTATION

Negotiating a peace agreement between warring ethnic groups is only half the job. Implementing the agreement is just as important, and can be more difficult and complex than the negotiations. None of the strategies of external involvement discussed above "solves" the problem of ethnic conflict. Even if external pressure brings the parties to the table and produces an agreement, the underlying strategic dilemmas remain in place. A stable peace can only arise as effective institutions of government are re-established, as the state once again begins to mediate effectively between distrustful ethnic groups, and as the parties slowly gain confidence in the safeguards contained within their new ethnic contracts. This necessarily involves an element of state-building and the possibility of forcible intervention to protect minorities. It is also a slow, incremental process that is likely to require years to bear fruit.

The United States and other countries, individually or collectively, should invest substantially in implementing peace agreements. The very fact that rival parties have consented to an agreement indicates they have jointly come to accept certain outcomes and understandings. At this stage, implementation becomes the decisive factor in the successful creation of internal order. Even when backed by a peacekeeping force, implementing a peace agreement involves a limited commitment on the part of an individual intervener or a coalition of interveners; they are committed to this agreement, not others, and need not fall prey to the inevitable pressures for "mission creep." Successful implementation offers potentially large returns. The alternative is renewed or, in some cases, unending conflict.

Ethnic Nationalism and International Conflict

The Case of Serbia

V.P. Gagnon, Jr.

Does ethnicity affect the international system? What are the causes of violent conflict along ethnic lines? Since the collapse of the Soviet Union and the outbreak of war in the Balkans, these questions have seized the attention of international relations scholars and policy makers.[1] In the former Yugoslavia, war conducted in the name of ethnic solidarity has destroyed the Yugoslav state, leveled entire cities, and resulted in hundreds of thousands of casualties and millions of refugees.[2] It has also brought NATO's first out-of-area actions, the largest United Nations peacekeeping operation in history, and the very real possibility of war spreading to other parts of the Balkans.

Is the Yugoslav case a look into the future of international relations? Are ethnically-mixed regions in the post–Cold War era inevitably the sites of violent conflict that will spill over into the international arena? If so, the only apparent solution would be the creation of ethnically pure states; yet the greatest threats to peace in this century have tended to come from those regions in which partitions along ethnic or religious lines have taken place.[3] This paradox is a

V.P. Gagnon, Jr., is an SSRC-MacArthur Foundation post-doctoral fellow in Peace and Security in a Changing World in the Peace Studies Program, Cornell University. In the current academic year, he is a visiting scholar at Zagreb University in Croatia and Belgrade University in Serbia.

An earlier version of this paper was presented at the September 1992 APSA meeting in Chicago. For helpful suggestions and criticisms, thanks to Dominique Caouette, Roger Petersen, Liz Wishnick, and Peter Katzenstein. Funding for revisions of this paper were provided by the Social Science Research Council–MacArthur Foundation Post-doctoral Fellowship in Peace and Security in a Changing World, and the Department of State Title VIII program in Russian and East European Studies, administered by the Hoover Institution, Stanford University.

1. See, for example, John Mearsheimer, "Back to the Future: Instability in Europe After the Cold War," *International Security*, Vol. 15, No. 1 (Summer 1990), pp. 5–56; Stephen Van Evera, "Hypotheses on Nationalism and War," *International Security*, Vol. 18, No. 4 (Spring 1994), pp. 5–39; Jack Snyder, "The New Nationalism," in Richard Rosecrance and Arthur A. Stein, eds., *The Domestic Bases of Grand Strategy* (Ithaca, N.Y.: Cornell University Press, 1993), pp. 179–200; Michael E. Brown, ed., *Ethnic Conflict and International Security* (Princeton, N.J.: Princeton University Press, 1993).
2. The best English-language sources on the Yugoslav wars include Lenard Cohen, *Broken Bonds: The Disintegration of Yugoslavia* (Boulder, Colo.: Westview, 1993); James Gow, *Legitimacy and the Military: The Yugoslav Crisis* (New York: St. Martin's Press, 1992); Rabia Ali and Lawrence Lifshutz, eds., *Why Bosnia? Writings on the Balkan War* (Stony Creek, Conn.: Pamphleteers Press, 1993).
3. Examples include Greece-Turkey (1922), Ireland (1921), the Sudetenland (1938), India-Pakistan (1947), South African apartheid (1948), Palestine (1948), and Cyprus (1974). John Mearsheimer and Robert Pape, "The Answer: A Partition Plan for Bosnia," *The New Republic*, June 14, 1993, pp. 22–28, argue for partition of Bosnia-Hercegovina as the best solution to the current conflict.

International Security, Winter 1994/95 (Vol. 19, No. 3), pp. 130–166
© 1995 by the President and Fellows of Harvard College and the Massachusetts Institute of Technology.

major challenge to international peace and stability, especially given the growing number of violent conflicts described and justified in terms of ethnicity, culture, and religion.

Despite the urgency of this issue, theories of international relations have until quite recently not addressed the question of ethnic nationalist conflict. The main challenge is conceptual: how to establish the causal link between ethnic nationalist sentiment and interstate violence.[4] Existing approaches tend to assume either that ethnic sentiment itself is the main cause of violent conflict, or that external security concerns lead national decision-makers to inflame such sentiment.[5] In this paper I argue that such violent conflict is caused not by ethnic sentiments, nor by external security concerns, but rather by the dynamics of within-group conflict.[6] The external conflict, although justified and described in terms of relations with other ethnic groups and taking place within that context, has its main goal within the state, among members of the same ethnicity.[7]

---

4. One of the shortcomings of the literature on ethnic and nationalist conflict is the lack of a precise conceptual definition. The term "nationalism" (or "hypernationalism") is commonly used, either implicitly or explicitly, to mean simultaneously (and confusingly) ethnic national sentiments or beliefs; political rhetoric that appeals to ethnic nationalist sentiment; and violent conflict that is described and justified in terms of ethnicity. To avoid this confusion, and to clarify the dependent variable (violent conflict, rather than ethnic sentiment) "ethnic nationalism" in this article refers to the rhetoric by which political actors describe, justify, and explain policies with reference to the interest of the "nation" defined in ethnic terms. It does not refer to sentiment or belief. This definition also makes clear that the root causes of a conflict that is described as ethnic may have little to do with ethnicity *per se*, and thereby points to the questions that must be answered to understand ethnic nationalist conflict: when do political elites resort to conflictual definitions of ethnic national interest? When and how do such definitions come to dominate the policies of the state? What are the goals of this conflictual behavior?

5. Examples of international relations works which look to ethnic sentiment as the key to understanding the link between nationalism and foreign policy include Alexis Heraclides, *The Self Determination of Minorities in International Politics* (Portland, Ore.: Cass, 1991); William Bloom, *Personal Identity, National Identity and International Relations* (London: Cambridge University Press, 1990). For those that look to external security concerns, see Mearsheimer, "Back to the Future"; and Barry Posen, "Nationalism, the Mass Army, and Military Power," *International Security*, Vol. 18, No. 2 (Fall 1993), pp. 80–124. The literature on ethnic conflict also tends to explain violent conflict as a response to external threats to or opportunities for the ethnic group *vis-à-vis* other groups. The most prominent such work is Donald Horowitz, *Ethnic Groups in Conflict* (Berkeley: University of California Press, 1985).

6. One work that explores the domestic roots of conflictual nationalist policy is Snyder, "The New Nationalism." For a review of earlier works that look at domestic sources of international conflict, see Jack Levy, "The Diversionary Theory of War: A Critique," in Manus I. Midlarsky, ed., *Handbook of War Studies* (Boston: Unwin Hyman, 1989), pp. 259–288.

7. This type of conflict is one example of the more general phenomenon of violent conflict in the international arena which is described and justified by national leaders in terms of ideas such as religion, class, and culture, as well as ethnicity. Given the extent to which international conflicts have been justified not in purely security terms but rather in such ideational terms, identifying the causal link between such ideas and violent conflicts carried out in their names is clearly of importance.

I argue that violent conflict along ethnic cleavages is provoked by elites in order to create a domestic political context where ethnicity is the only politically relevant identity. It thereby constructs the individual interest of the broader population in terms of the threat to the community defined in ethnic terms. Such a strategy is a response by ruling elites to shifts in the structure of domestic political and economic power: by constructing individual interest in terms of the threat to the group, endangered elites can fend off domestic challengers who seek to mobilize the population against the status quo, and can better position themselves to deal with future challenges.

The dominant realist approach in international relations tells us very little about violent conflict along ethnic lines, and cannot explain the Yugoslav case. Focusing on external security concerns, this approach argues that conflictual behavior in the name of ethnic nationalism is a response to external threats to the state (or to the ethnic group).[8] The general literature on ethnic conflict likewise uses the "ethnic group" as actor and looks to factors outside the group to explain intergroup conflict.[9] But in fact, the Serbian leadership from 1987 onward actively created rather than responded to threats to Serbs by purposefully provoking and fostering the outbreak of conflict along ethnic lines, especially in regions of Yugoslavia with histories of good inter-ethnic relations.[10]

Although the Serbian leadership itself has justified its policies in terms of an external security threat to Serbia and Serbs, over the past thirty years a significant part of the Serbian elite has advocated a very different strategy based on democratic pluralism, peaceful negotiation of political conflict, and modernization of the Serbian economy.[11] This strategy would probably have been

---

8. Mearsheimer, "Back to the Future"; Posen, "Nationalism, the Mass Army, and Military Power." For a realist approach that takes ethnic groups rather than states as actors, see Barry Posen, "The Security Dilemma and Ethnic Conflict," *Survival*, Vol. 35, No. 1 (Spring 1993), pp. 27–47.

9. Horowitz, *Ethnic Groups in Conflict*; and "Democracy in Divided Societies," *Journal of Democracy*, Vol. 4, No. 4 (October 1993), pp. 18–38.

10. In both Croatia and Bosnia, forces allied with Belgrade went to great lengths to destroy the long-standing harmony between Serbs and non-Serbs. Although the Croatian regime had resorted to nationalist rhetoric and actions worrisome to local Serbs, both sides were willing to negotiate over key issues until Belgrade began terrorizing moderate Serbs. This strategy was repeated in Bosnia. In Serbian-controlled regions of Croatia and Bosnia, the extremists in power have silenced and even killed dissenting Serbs. See *NIN*, November 8, 1991, p. 15; *Vreme*, November 4, 1991, pp. 12–15; Milorad Pupovac, head of the Zagreb-based moderate Serbian Democratic Forum, in *Vreme*, October 21, 1991, pp. 12–14; Peter Maass, "In Bosnia, 'Disloyal Serbs' Share Plight of Opposition," *Washington Post*, August 24, 1992, p. 1.

11. For example, Latinka Perović and Marko Nikezić, heads of the Serbian party in the late 1960s and early 1970s [see Perović's *Zatvaranje kruga: Ishod političkog rascepa u SKJ 1971/1972* (Sarajevo: Svjetlost, 1991); and Slavoljub Dukić, *Slom Srpskih Liberala* (Belgrade: Filip Višnjić, 1990)]. On the war in Croatia, nationalist opposition party leader Vuk Drašković from the summer of 1991

much more successful and much less costly than conflict in ensuring the interests of Serbs and Serbia, even if the goal had been an independent, enlarged Serbia.[12] It is difficult to argue that an objective security threat exists when even nationalistically-oriented elites in Serbia denounce the war and claim there was no need for it.

Another common explanation for violent conflicts along ethnic lines, particularly for the Yugoslav case, is that ancient ethnic hatreds have burst to the surface.[13] But this too is unsupported by the evidence: in fact, Yugoslavia never saw the kind of religious wars seen in Western and Central Europe, and Serbs and Croats never fought before this century;[14] intermarriage rates were quite

---

denounced the war in Croatia (*Vreme*, November 4, 1992, pp. 9–11; *Danas*, February 18, 1992). Drašković has also denounced the Bosnian war as harmful to Serbs (see his speech to "Congress of Serbian Intellectuals," May 1994); Milan Panić, first prime minister of the new Serbian-dominated Yugoslavia, also criticized the war ("Four Immediate Tasks," *Review of International Affairs*, no. 1005–6 (June 1-July 1, 1992), pp. 4–6.

12. Indeed, the policies of the Serbian leadership and its allies have alienated the 33 percent of the Serbian republic's population that is non-Serb, thus decreasing its internal security. The Croatian and Bosnian territories that have been gained in the process are among the poorest regions of the former Yugoslavia, with very low rates of education and income, and are for the most part strategically very difficult to defend, since they are connected with Serbian-contiguous lands only by a very thin corridor. The atrocities against and expulsions of most of the very large number of non-Serbs—who before the war made up about 55 percent of the population of the Croatian and Bosnian territories held by Serbian forces in mid-1994—have produced enormous antagonisms and created a situation in which a long-term strategy of low-level guerilla warfare is quite likely. Figures derived from the 1991 Population Census of Bosnia-Hercegovina, cited in Stjepko Golubić, Susan Campbell and Thomas Golubić, "How not to divide the indivisible," in *Why Bosnia*, pp. 230–231; and the 1991 census in Croatia, *Popis Stanovništva 1991* (Zagreb: Republićki zavod za statistiku, 1992).

13. See, for example, Robert Kaplan, "Ground Zero," *New Republic*, August 2, 1993, pp. 15–16, "A Reader's Guide to the Balkans," *New York Times Book Review*, April 18, 1994; "History's Cauldron," *Atlantic Monthly*, June 1991, pp. 92–104; and Robert Kaplan, *Balkan Ghosts: A Journey Through History* (New York: St. Martin's Press, 1993). See also Elizabeth Drew, "Letter from Washington," *New Yorker*, July 6, 1992, p. 70.

14. On the history of relations between Serbs and Croats in Croatia before this century, see, for example, Wolfgang Kessler, *Politik, Kultur und Gesellschaft in Kroatien und Slawonien in der ersten Hälfte des 19. Jahrhunderts* (Munich: R. Oldenbourg, 1981); Sergei A. Romanenko, "National Autonomy in Russia and Austro-Hungary," in *Nationalism and Empire* (New York: St. Martin's Press, 1992); Ivo Banac, *The National Question in Yugoslavia: Origins, History, Politics* (Ithaca, N.Y.: Cornell University Press, 1984), p. 410. On cooperation in the first Yugoslavia between Serb and Croat parties in Croatia against Belgrade, see Ljubo Boban, *Svetozar Pribićević u opoziciji (1928–1936)* (Zagreb: Institut za hrvatsku povijest, 1973); Drago Roksandić, *Srbi u Hrvatskoj od 15. stoljeća do naših dana* (Zagreb: Vjesnik, 1991). During World War II, the ruling Ustaša forces in the puppet Independent State of Croatia perpetrated massive atrocities against Serbs and others; they were a marginal party imposed by the Germans and Italians after the highly popular Croatian Peasant Party refused to collaborate. The Ustaša policy of genocide against Serbs, and its use of Muslims to carry out this policy in Bosnia, combined with its authoritarian repression of Croat and Muslim dissent, rapidly alienated most of the state's population. Fikreta Jelić-Butić, *Ustaše i Nezavisna Država Hrvatska* (Zagreb: Sveučilišna Naklada Liber, 1978). And while the Serbian nationalist Četnik

high in those ethnically-mixed regions that saw the worst violence;[15] and sociological polling as late as 1989–90 showed high levels of tolerance, especially in these mixed regions.[16] Although some tensions existed between nationalities and republics, and the forcible repression of overt national sentiment added to the perception on all sides that the existing economic and political system was unjust, the evidence indicates that, notwithstanding claims to the contrary by nationalist politicians and historians in Serbia and Croatia, "ethnic hatreds" are not the essential, primary cause of the Yugoslav conflict.

In the following sections I lay out an alternative theoretical framework and hypotheses about ethnic nationalist conflict that look to internal dynamics to explain external conflict. I then apply this to the specific case of Yugoslavia, concentrating on five episodes in which elites within the Serbian republic resorted to conflictual strategies described and justified in terms of the interest of the Serbian people.[17] In the conclusion I look at how this framework can illuminate other cases, and what it says about strategies for conflict resolution.

Domestic Power and International Conflict: A Theoretical Framework

This section lays out a framework and proposes some hypotheses about the link between ethnicity (and other ideas such as religion, culture, class) and international conflict. It is based on the following four premises: first, the domestic arena is of central concern for state decision-makers and ruling elites because it is the location of the bases of their power. Ruling elites will thus

---

forces perpetrated atrocities against Muslims in Bosnia, most Serbs in Croatia and Bosnia joined the multi-ethnic communist partisan forces rather than the purely nationalistic Četniks. Thus the image of "ethnic groups" in conflict even during World War II must be seen as part of an ideological construct in which "ethnic groups" are portrayed as actors by nationalist politicians and historians.

15. For example, throughout the 1980s, 29 percent of Serbs living in Croatia married Croat spouses. *Demografska statistika* (Belgrade: Savezni zavod za statistiku), 1979–1989 (annual), Table 5–3.

16. Randy Hodson, Garth Massey and Dusko Sekulic, "National Tolerance in the Former Yugoslavia," *Global Forum Series Occasional Papers*, No. 93-01.5 (Durham, N.C.: Center for International Studies, Duke University, December 1993).

17. This article represents part of a broader work that looks at the dynamics of ethnic nationalist conflicts in other Yugoslav republics as well. The Serbian case, however, merits the most attention because the actions of its leadership from the mid-1980s onward have driven the current conflict and created nationalist backlashes in other Yugoslav republics, and because the *de facto* alliance between the Serbian leadership and the Yugoslav Army has given Serbia a massive military and thus political advantage. The Croatian leadership since 1990 has carried out similarly conflictual policies in the name of Croatian ethnic nationalism; but these policies can only be understood within the context of the Serbian strategy.

focus on preserving these domestic bases of power. Second, persuasion is the most effective and least costly means of influence in domestic politics. One particularly effective means of persuasion is to appeal to the interest of politically relevant actors as members of a group. Third, within the domestic arena, appeals for support must be directed to material and nonmaterial values of the relevant target audiences—those actors whose support is necessary to gain and maintain power. Ideas such as ethnicity, religion, culture, and class therefore play a key role as instruments of power and influence, in particular because of their centrality to legitimacy and authority.

Finally, conflict over ideas and how they are framed is an essential characteristic of domestic politics, since the result determines the way political arguments can be made, how interests are defined, and the values by which political action must be justified. The challenge for elites is therefore to define the interest of the collective in a way that coincides with their own power interests. In other words, they must express their interests in the "language" of the collective interest.

These premises lead to the following hypotheses about the conditions under which national leaders will resort to conflictual policies described and justified in terms of threats to the ethnic nation.

First, if ruling elites face challenger elites who seek to mobilize the majority of the politically relevant population in a way that threatens the rulers' power or the political or economic structure on which their power is based, the ruling elites will be willing to respond by undertaking policies that are costly to society as a whole, even if the costs are imposed from outside. Behavior *vis-à-vis* the outside may thus have its main goal in the domestic arena. If the most effective way to achieve domestic goals involves provoking conflict with the outside, then, as long as the net benefit to the threatened elites is positive, they will be willing to undertake such a strategy.

Second, threatened elites will respond to domestic threats in a way that minimizes the danger to the bases of their domestic power. They must gain the support, or neutralize the opposition, of the majority. But if domestic legitimacy precludes the massive use of force against political opponents and depends on respecting certain political forms and "rules of the game," elites are circumscribed in how they can respond to domestic threats. One effective strategy in this context is to shift the focus of political debate away from issues where ruling elites are most threatened—for example, proposed changes in the structure of domestic economic or political power—toward other issues, defined in cultural or ethnic terms, that appeal to the interest of the majority in non-economic terms.[18] But ethnicity or culture in and of itself does not determine policies; the interest of the collective defined in ethnic terms can be defined in any number of ways.

Competing elites will thus focus on defining the collective interest by drawing selectively on traditions and mythologies and in effect constructing particular versions of that interest. The elite faction that succeeds in identifying itself with the interest of the collective, and in defining the collective interest in a way that maximizes its own ability to achieve its goals, wins an important victory. It has framed the terms of political discourse and debate, and thus the limits of legitimate policy, in a way that may delegitimize or make politically irrelevant the interests of challenger elites and prevent them from mobilizing the population on specific issues or along certain lines.

Third, in this competition over defining the group interest, images of and alleged threats from the outside world can play a key role in this domestic political strategy. A strategy relying on such threatening images can range from citing an alleged threat to provoking conflict in order to create the image of threat; conflict can range from political to military. Since political mobilization occurs most readily around grievances, in order to shift the political agenda, elites must find issues of grievance unrelated to those issues on which they are most threatened, and construct a political context in which those issues become the center of political debate. It is at this point that focus on the interest of the group *vis-à-vis* the outside world proves to be useful. If the grievance or threat is to the collective rather than to individuals, it creates an image of potentially very high costs imposed on the group regardless of the direct impact on individuals. It therefore defines the individual's interest in terms of a particular threat to the group. Moreover, if the threat or grievance is outside the direct experience of the majority of politically relevant actors, there is no way to verify whether the grievance is real, or indeed whether it is being addressed or not. Such a strategy also becomes in effect a self-fulfilling prophecy, as the reactions provoked by the conflictual policies are pointed to as proof of the original contention. Thus is created a grievance that, if violence is involved, is sure to continue for years.

The effect of creating an image of threat to the group is to place the interest of the group above the interest of individuals. This political strategy is crucial

---

18. On agenda setting as a power strategy, see P. Bachrach and M.S. Baratz, "The Two Faces of Power," *American Political Science Review*, Vol. 56, No. 4 (1962), pp. 947–952.

because, in the case of aggressive nationalism and images of threats to the ethnic nation, it creates a context where ethnicity is all that counts, and where other interests are no longer relevant. In addition, such an image of overwhelming threat to the group delegitimizes the dissent of those challengers who attempt to appeal to members of the relevant group as individuals or who appeal to identities other than the "legitimate" identity in a "legitimate" way, especially if dissenters can be portrayed as selfish and uninterested in the well-being of the group, and can therefore be branded as traitors.[19]

Thus, by using a strategy of agenda-setting to shift the focus of political attention toward the very pressing issue of threats to the group from the outside, and by actively provoking and creating such threats, threatened elites can maximize the domestic benefits while minimizing the costs imposed on their own supporters, and thus the danger to their own power bases.

Fourth, in this domestic political context, information and control over information play a vital role. Control or ownership of mass media, especially television, therefore bestows an enormous political advantage where the wider population is involved in politics, and is a key element in the success of such a strategy.

Fifth, elites will tend to define the relevant collective in ethnic terms when past political participation has been so defined; when such a definition is encouraged by international circumstances; and when these elites are seen as credible defenders of ethnic interests and concerns. Clearly, for grievances or threats to the group to be politically relevant, a majority of actors must be able to be identified as members of that group. That does not mean, however, that their main or primary identity must be to the group; in fact, people have multiple identities and such identities are highly contextual. The key is to make a particular identity, and a specific definition of that identity, the only relevant or legitimate one in political contexts. This identity will be closely related to the ideas of culture, ethnicity, and religion that the majority of the population values. Ideas such as ethnicity have an impact on the international arena precisely because they are so central to domestic power.

Since conflictual policies tend to take place along these previously politicized lines of identity, they also tend to create the impression of continuity between

---

19. This strategy is thus especially effective in discrediting those who appeal to liberal democratic ideology, which defines the collective interest of the citizenry as best ensured by ensuring the rights and well-being of the individual.

past conflicts and current ones, and indeed are specifically portrayed in this way. But there is nothing natural about ethnic interest that requires it to be defined in a conflictual way.

Sixth, the larger and more immediate the threat to the ruling elite, the more willing it is to take measures which, while preserving its position in the short term, may bring high costs in the longer term; in effect it discounts future costs. The intensity and thus costliness of a conflictual strategy depends on the degree of the threat to the old elites. These factors include, first, the time frame of the threat to power. While the conflictual policies may over the long run result in an untenable position and ultimately undermine their bases of political influence, elites' political behavior in a situation of immediate threat is motivated by that threat and by the concern for keeping the power in the short run, which at least leaves open the possibility of their survival in the long run. This also gives them time to fashion alternative strategies for dealing with change, including shifting the bases of their power.

Also, the strength of the challenger elites also affects the immediacy of the threat. If the challenger elites are successfully mobilizing the majority of the politically relevant population against the status quo, ruling elites will feel quite threatened and be willing to incur high costs to preserve their position. Threatened elites will also attempt to recruit other elites, at the local and regional as well as national levels, to prevent such a mobilization.

A further factor is the costs to the threatened elites of losing power; that is, the resources and fallback positions they have if change does take place. If they have everything to lose and nothing to gain, they will be much more likely to undertake conflictual policies costly to society as a whole than if they have resources that would allow them to remain involved in power to some degree.

For the conflictual strategy to include the use of military force, especially against other states, the status-quo coalition must include a dominant faction within the military.

Seventh, threatened elites may use marginal neo-fascist parties as part of their conflictual strategy in conditions where the wider population is included in the political system. Every country has small extremist groups whose mainstay is ethnic hatred and violence; their motivations may be political, personal, or psychological. But the very existence of this option is clearly not enough for it to come to dominate state policy. An advantage of giving neo-fascists media coverage and weapons is that by bringing extremists into the political realm, the right becomes the "center"; a statement that ten years earlier may have been unacceptably racist may be perceived after this kind of strategy as relatively moderate.[20] By making issues of ethnic nationalism the center of political discourse, this strategy also turns those who are archconservatives on economic issues into moderate centrists.

Eighth, internal costs of a conflictual strategy are closely monitored, since they must be outweighed by benefits. Of particular importance is the need to prevent popular mobilization against costs of the conflictual external strategy. While conflict remains in the realm of political rhetoric, it may have great support among the population, since it is basically costless. But if military conflict is involved, the costs to the general population rapidly start to mount.[21] Conflict will be undertaken with an eye toward minimizing the costs for those parts of the populations which are key for support, and will therefore tend to be provoked outside the borders of the elite's power base, with great efforts taken to prevent war from spilling over to the domestic territory. Thus, in the Soviet case anti-reform conservatives provoked violent ethnic conflict outside of Russia, in Moldova, Georgia, and the Baltics; in the Yugoslav case armed conflict has not taken place within Serbia itself, and the Croatian conservatives' conflictual strategy affected mainly central Bosnia, rather than Croatia.

Of course, if material conditions deteriorate enough and if the discrepancy between the interest of the collective group and the interest of the status quo power elite becomes great enough, challenger elites may successfully lead the wider population to revolt against the power structure. In this case members of the old elite may jump on the bandwagon of the new elites who lead such revolutionary revolts.

Finally, external costs are also key. Such a strategy is most likely when the potential international costs, in terms of how they would affect the status-quo elites' domestic power position, are minimal. But if the cost of external reaction were to threaten elements of the status-quo coalition, they might defect, since losses at the hands of domestic elites could be less than at the hands of external foes, especially if challenger elites were willing to offer a deal to the defectors. This strategy will thus be very sensitive to the kinds of costs it provokes from the outside.

---

20. See Anna Marie Smith, *New Right Discourse in Race and Sexuality: Britain 1968–1990* (New York: Cambridge University Press, 1994).

21. Despite the assumption that ethnic political mobilization inevitably pushes politics towards extremism (referred to as "ethnic outbidding" by Horowitz, *Ethnic Groups in Conflict*, p. 348), there is in fact little evidence of a natural inevitable progression from ethnic mobilization to violent ethnic conflict. See V.P. Gagnon, Jr., "Ethnic Conflict as a Political Demobilizer," forthcoming.

This type of conflictual policy thus comes to dominate some states or regions and not others, depending on the degree of threat to the existing power structure and the size of the coalition (at both national and regional levels) of those within the power elite threatened by change. If a challenge to the existing power structure takes place in such a way that most of the old elite perceives a way out, either by cooptation into the new system or by being permitted to retain some privileges and benefits, a coalition will probably not be strong enough to impose a costly conflictual strategy as state policy. It may nevertheless incite conflict and violence in the hopes of gaining wider support. Such conflict takes the form of violence along ethnic lines when the wider population is involved in political decision making, and when political participation in the past has been defined in ethnic terms.

The Case of Serbia

The violent conflict along ethnic lines in the former Yugoslavia was a purposeful and rational strategy planned by those most threatened by changes to the structure of economic and political power, changes being advocated in particular by reformists within the ruling Serbian communist party. A wide coalition—conservatives in the Serbian party leadership, local and regional party elites who would be most threatened by such changes, orthodox Marxist intellectuals, nationalist writers, and parts of the Yugoslav army—joined together to provoke conflict along ethnic lines. This conflict created a political context where individual interest was defined not in terms of economic well-being, but as the survival of the Serbian people. The conservatives' original goal was to recentralize Yugoslavia in order to crush reformist trends throughout the country, but especially in Serbia itself. By 1990, in a changed international context and with backlashes against their centralization strategy in other republics, the conservative coalition moved to destroy the Yugoslav state and create a new, Serbian-majority state. By provoking conflict along ethnic lines, this coalition deflected demands for radical change and allowed the ruling elite to reposition itself and survive in a way that would have been unthinkable in the old Yugoslavia, where only 39 percent of the population was Serb.

Serbian conservatives relied on the particular idea of ethnicity in their conflictual strategy because political participation and legitimation in this region historically was constructed in such terms. From the nineteenth century, the great powers used the standard of national (usually ethnically-defined) self-determination to decide whether a territory merited recognition as a sovereign state—a practice that continues today. Those elites who could make the best case for representing the interests of an ethnic group could increase their power *vis-à-vis* the domestic arena by being internationally recognized as the representative of their ethnic or national group.[22] In Eastern and Central Europe this factor reinforced the Ottoman, Romanov, and Habsburg empires' definitions of political participation in terms of religion in the first two cases and language in the latter, and the subsequent construction of politicized identities in the nineteenth century.[23] The Serbian national myth, molded in the struggle against the Ottoman Turks and in the expansion of the Serbian state in the nineteenth and early twentieth centuries, played a central role in Yugoslav politics between 1918 and 1941, and remained important for the communist partisans, who relied on popular support during World War II.[24] The ethnic national bases of the Yugoslav republics was the result of this wartime need for popular political support, and was maintained as more than a façade after the 1948 break with the Soviet Union again forced the communists to rely on some level of popular support. This emphasis on ethnicity was reinforced by a system of ethnic "keys" within each republic which determined the distribution of certain positions by ethnic identity according to the proportion of each group in the republic's population.[25] This political reification of ethnicity, along with the suppression of expressions of ethnic sentiment, combined to reinforce the historical construction of political identity in terms of ethnic identity, and made ethnic issues politically relevant when the political system opened up to include the wider population.

---

22. For example, arguments about carving up the Ottoman Empire's European territories were made in terms of "ethnic territories" despite the very ethnically intermixed nature of those territories.

23. On the Romanov Empire's construction of national identity, see John Slocum, "The Boundaries of National Identity: Religion, Language, and Nationality Politics in Late Imperial Russia," Ph.D. dissertation, University of Chicago, 1993; on the Ottomans, Kemal Karpat, "Millets and Nationality: The Roots of the Incongruity of Nation and State in the Post-Ottoman Era," in Benjamin Braude and Bernard Lewis, eds., *Christians and Jews in the Ottoman Empire: The Functioning of a Plural Society*, Vol. 1 (New York: Holmes & Meier, 1982), pp. 141–169; on Hungary, Benedict Anderson, *Imagined Communities* (London: Verso, 1991), pp. 101–109.

24. The relation to religious identity is a complex issue, and is related to the fact that in traditional Serbian national mythology, born in the fight against the Ottomans, the Muslim Turks are seen as the ultimate enemy. Although religion *per se* was minimally relevant to interpersonal relations in Yugoslavia before the most recent wars, as part of the Serbian national mythology it was drawn upon in a selective way to the political ends of demonizing Albanians and Slavic Muslims.

25. On the ways in which socialist regimes reinforced the relevance of ethnic identity, see Katherine Verdery, "Nationalism and National Sentiment in Post-socialist Romania," *Slavic Review*, Vol. 52, No. 2 (Summer 1993), pp. 179–203. A similar process was seen in India, where colonial powers, drawing on real or sometimes mythic differences, politicized cultural difference and played groups off against each other. Paul Brass, *Ethnicity and Nationalism: Theory and Comparison* (Sage: New Delhi, 1991).

In addition, the rhetoric of threats to the ethnic nation was available to Serbian conservatives in a way that it was not in other republics, in part because the Serbian party was one of the few that was ethnically homogeneous enough that such a strategy would not automatically alienate a significant portion of the party membership. The Serbian republic (even without its provinces) also had regional differences in economic development that were more extreme and significant than in any other republic. Thus because liberals were stronger, conservatives entrenched in some underdeveloped regions were also more threatened; however, they had a grassroots base upon which to rely for support. Serbia's conservatives were also well-placed to oppose change, given Serbia's importance in the Yugoslav federation and the frequent congruence of interests between Serbian conservatives and conservative elements in the Yugoslav army.

Five episodes are described below in which conservative forces, especially those in Serbia, were threatened with the radical restructuring of political and economic power. In order to test the hypotheses laid out above, each section looks at the threat to the conservatives and the status quo; their responses; and the effect of those responses.

1960S: THREATS TO THE STATUS QUO

In the early 1960s, in response to an increasingly dysfunctional economic system, reformists in the Yugoslav party leadership, with Tito's support, began a radical restructuring of the Yugoslav political and economic system. At the local level the 1965 reform was a direct attack on party bureaucrats in enterprises as well as those in local administrative positions,[26] and also involved a loosening of party control of society, including tolerance of more open expressions of national sentiment.[27]

---

26. Economic decisions were no longer to be made according to political criteria, and Tito himself openly dismissed "propaganda work," the mainstay of many party workers, stressing instead the need for technical knowledge and "detailed understanding" of economics and management. Tito, speech at fifth plenum of League of Communists of Yugoslavia Central Committee, *Borba*, October 6, 1966, p. 2. Economic reform was accompanied by political reform in the form of a radical restructuring of party relations at the local level, with the goal of undermining the position of conservative party bureaucrats by bringing rank-and-file party members into decision-making, and dismantling the institutional bases of bureaucratic power at the local level (including the local party cells and regional party organizations). Gagnon, "Ideology and Soviet-Yugoslav Relations, 1964–1969: Irrational foreign policy as a rational choice," Ph.D. dissertation, Columbia University, 1992, pp. 579–583; April Carter, *Democratic Reform in Yugoslavia: The Changing Role of the Party* (London: Frances Pinter, 1982).

27. See Savka Dabčević-Kučar, series of interviews in *Nedeljna Dalmacija*, January 14, 21, and 28, 1990.

At the macro-political level the reform radically decentralized the federation, and almost all decision-making was given to the republics. This allowed the top leadership to bypass the conservatives who dominated the central bureaucracy and to rely instead on the republic-level leaders and central committees, which were dominated by young technocratically-oriented reformists. Indeed, this decentralization was enthusiastically supported by all the party leaderships, including Serbia's. By the summer of 1971 there was also discussion of decentralizing the party itself, a topic which was to be addressed at a party meeting in November 1971.[28] If undertaken, the effect would have been to institutionalize reformism in each republic, remove all power from the conservatives who dominated the center, and remove even the possibility of a conservative comeback.

The conservatives were clearly threatened by the popularity of the young republic-level reformist leaderships within the central committees, as well as among the wider population. Indeed, the goal of the reforms had been in part to broaden the legitimacy of the communist party by building a base in that wider population; this meant, however, that conservatives were faced with leaders who could mobilize the population in support of irreversible radical changes in the structure of power.

RESPONSE TO THE THREATS. The conservatives at first tried to sabotage implementation of the reform. The result, however, was that in 1966 Tito purged conservatives from the leadership of the party, and the reform became even more radically threatening to conservatives. Some conservatives in the Serbian party then began publicly to argue that the reforms were harmful to the Serbian nation, and linked the reforms to the "historical enemies" of Serbia. These conservatives were expelled from the party in 1968; however, by 1971, as the party faced the possibility of radical decentralization, other conservatives in the Serbian party and army pointed in particular to the open expression of nationalist sentiment in Croatia, which included some extremist views. Conservatives blamed the Croatian leadership for revival of Croatian nationalism.[29]

---

28. Dušan Bilandžić, *Historija SFRJ* (Zagreb: Školska Knjiga, 1979), p. 427.
29. Although this period did see some extreme demands, including calls for a Croatian army, a seat for Croatia in the UN, and a division of Bosnia-Hercegovina, as well as some expression of chauvinistic Croatian nationalism, such demands were never made by the Croatian party leadership, which appealed instead in a positive sense to material well-being, freedom of expression, and cultural creativity. Pedro Ramet, *Nationalism and Federalism in Yugoslavia: 1963–1983* (Bloomington: Indiana University Press, 1984), pp. 104–143; Ante Ćuvalo, *The Croatian National Movement, 1966–1972* (New York: East European Monographs, 1990). Indeed, despite the official explanation, the Croatian party leaders never felt either party rule or socialism to be in danger. The then-leader of the Serbian party also subsequently admitted that the purges of the Croatian leadership had been a mistake. See Dabčević-Kučar, interviews in *Nedeljna Dalmacija*, January, 1990; Miko Tripalo, *Hrvatsko proljeće* (Zagreb: Globus, 1990); Perović, *Zatvaranje kruga*.

These conservatives allied with some conservatives in the Croatian and Bosnian parties, party workers and war veterans who had been forced into early retirement, members of the central bureaucracy, elements in the Yugoslav army, and Serbian nationalist intellectuals to invoke the massacre of hundreds of thousands of Serbs by the Croatian Ustaša leadership during World War II and to blame the reforms for undermining socialism and endangering Croatia's Serbs. Conservatives in the security forces and in the army, in particular, convinced Tito to act against the Croatian reformists.[30] The Croatian reformists were purged and tanks were sent to the outskirts of Zagreb. The following year the Serbian reformists were also purged, despite very strong resistance from the republic's central committee; similar purges in the other republics and provinces followed. As a result, the local-level reforms were effectively reversed, and a renewed ideologization took place.[31]

EFFECT OF THE RESPONSE. By casting the threat posed by reform in terms of ethnic nationalism, the conservatives shifted the focus of political debate away from the cross-republic reformist project, and toward the alleged threats from Croatian nationalism; this allowed them to argue that radical reform had in fact brought the emergence of nationalism and thus of counterrevolution.[32] By using the threat of external and internal enemies of socialism defined in ethnic national terms, they managed to divide the country's popular reformists. This enabled the conservatives to prevent the decentralization of the party and to reverse the essence of the reforms (although decentralization of the federation itself remained and was enshrined in the 1974 constitution).[33] In addition, the Yugoslav army now became a key political player, with the official role of

---

30. On the army's role in mobilizing war veterans against reformists in Croatia and in other republics, see A. Ross Johnson, *The Role of the Military in Communist Yugoslavia: An Historical Sketch*, No. P-6070 (Santa Monica, Calif.: Rand Corporation, January 1978), pp. 31–33; on the army's role in convincing Tito of the dangers of Croatian nationalism, see Robin Remington, "Armed Forces and Society in Yugoslavia," in Catherine McArdle Kelleher, ed., *Political-Military Systems: Comparative Perspectives* (Beverly Hills: Sage, 1974), p. 188; and Gow, *Legitimacy and the Military*, p. 58. On the role of the security forces in supplying Tito with detailed information, see Zdravko Vuković, *Od deformacija SDP do Maspoka i Liberalizma* (Belgrade: Narodna Knjiga, 1989), p. 586.
31. Stephen Burg, *Conflict and Cohesion in Socialist Yugoslavia* (Princeton, N.J.: Princeton University Press, 1983), pp. 181–183, 229. While confederalization remained in place, the economic mechanisms which were meant to integrate the country were removed, resulting in eight statist and autarkic units.
32. The fact that they argued against the reforms, which were reversed, while the confederalization of the country remained even after the purge of liberals, indicates that the main threat was the reforms.
33. Conservatives in Serbia also set the groundwork for a longer-term strategy, for example by allowing Dobrica Ćosić, who had been purged for denouncing reform as anti-Serbian in 1968, to continue to publish his nationalistically-oriented works. Thus throughout the 1970s he constructed a very specific version of Serbian nationalism, whose theme was that Serbs were the greatest

ensuring the domestic order against external and internal enemies; this made the army the natural ally of conservatives in the party. By 1974, 12 percent of the federal central committee were army officers, up from 2 percent in 1969.[34]

1980–87: THREATS TO CONSERVATIVES

When Tito died in May 1980, the debate over reform, which had been muffled, broke out into the open. The economic crisis triggered by the global recession of the late 1970s, the oil shock, and Yugoslavia's huge foreign debt burden ($20 billion by the early 1980s), as well as the negative results brought by ending reform in the early 1970s, all compelled radical systemic change. The reformists' proposals were indeed much more radical than in the early 1960s and their audience—managerial elites, democratically-oriented intellectuals, and party rank-and-file—were much more receptive. The proposals were therefore even more threatening to the conservatives than they had been in the 1960s, especially without Tito to moderate conflicts; the political conflict had become winner-take-all.

Serbian reformists were in the forefront of this struggle, and in the early 1980s the Serbian party was among the most liberal in the country. Members of the Serbian party leadership called for totally removing party influence at the local levels of the economy; for greater reliance on private enterprise and individual initiative; multiple candidates in state and party elections; free, secret elections in the party; and recognition and adoption of "all the positive achievements of bourgeois civilization," i.e., liberal democracy.[35] From within

---

victims of Yugoslavia, portraying them as a "tragic people." See for example his popular four-part series of historical fiction, *Vreme Smrti*, published in Belgrade between 1972 and 1979, which chronicles the tragedies of Serbia during World War I (during which it lost 25 percent of its population and 40 percent of its army), and which portrays Serbia as the innocent victim of its neighbors, its supposed allies and other Yugoslav ethnic nations. In English, published as Dobrica Ćosić, *Into the Battle* (part 1) (San Diego: Harcourt Brace, 1983); *Time of Death* (part 2) (New York: Harcourt Brace Jovanovich, 1977); *Reach to Eternity* (part 3) and *South to Destiny* (part 4) (San Diego: Harcourt Brace, 1983). See also the series of interviews in Slavoljub Dukić, *Čovek u svom vremenu: Razgovori sa Dobricom Ćosićem* (Belgrade: Filip Višnjić, 1989).

34. Robert Dean, "Civil-Military Relations in Yugoslavia, 1971–1975," *Armed Forces and Society*, Vol. 3, No. 1 (November 1976), p. 46.

35. These liberal positions especially linked the need for radical economic reform and a market system with an equally radical reform of the political system. See article by Serbian party leadership member Najdan Pašić, in *Danas*, October 12, 1982. Another Serbian leader, Mijalko Todorović, argued that the only solution to the economic crisis was "democratization of all political institutions." Similar views were expressed also by Pašić and Drača Marković, head of the Serbian party, indicating that this was the official position of the party. (Cited in *RFE Situation Report* No. 256, November 7, 1983). See also Pašić letter to the central committee on the political situation, November 1982, cited in *RFE Situation Report* No. 125, June 1, 1983; and his calls to purge the party of conservatives who blocked reform, *Politika*, September 10, 1984.

the party were also heard calls for private enterprise to become the "pillar of the economy," and even calls for a multi-party system. Reformists were also very critical of the Army's privileged political and budgetary position, and called very early on for cutting that influence.[36] Once again reformists were seeking to mobilize broader popular sentiment against conservative positions among party rank-and-file as well as the wider population, at a time when the economic crisis had discredited the conservatives' ideological stance.[37]

Due to the consensus nature of federal decision-making, the conservatives were at first able to hinder an outright reformist victory, but the terms of the debate nevertheless shifted in the favor of the reformists. By the mid-1980s secret multi-candidate elections were being held for party officers, and even some state posts were chosen in multi-candidate popular votes.[38]

RESPONSE TO THE THREATS. Conservatives in Serbia responded with a three-pronged strategy. The first was to re-emphasize orthodox Marxist themes, in an attempt to delegitimate liberal trends at the lower levels of the party. Although the conservatives were not very successful in the political debates over reform at the leadership level, at the local level in Serbia they imposed an orthodox ideological line, while at the same time raising the issue of Serbian nationalism. Most notable was the Belgrade party organization which, beginning in 1984, was headed by Slobodan Milošević. Soon after coming to power, Milošević began a campaign stressing ideological orthodoxy,[39] and sent out warnings to all Belgrade party units urging vigilance against "the dangerous

---

36. For example, in December 1982 the army budget was openly criticized in the Federal Assembly for having been increased by over 24 percent without the Assembly's approval. *Politika*, December 15, 1982. In 1984 the Young Slovene Communist Party organization even called for the abolition of the Yugoslav army (A. Tijanić, *Intervju*, March 30, 1984). Army officers enjoyed pay levels much higher than average Yugoslavs as well as housing privileges in a country where housing was in acute shortage. The budget was also quite high (around 4 percent of gross domestic product in the early 1980s at a time of sharp economic decline).

37. The degree of threat that the reforms posed varied, in part by region of the country. In the early 1980s, those party officials and managers from more economically developed regions— Slovenia and Vojvodina—tended to be reformist, while those from underdeveloped Montenegro, Macedonia, Kosovo, and Bosnia tended to oppose them. The Serbian economy was split between the underdeveloped regions in the south and the more developed regions in the north, around Belgrade, and around the other major cities in central Serbia. The Serbian party leadership was very liberal, although there was a constituency of conservatives who were threatened by reform. Croatia, although more developed, was dominated by conservatives mainly because of the 1971 purges. For characterizations of the republic leaderships, see Pedro Ramet, "The Limits to Political Change in a Communist Country: The Yugoslav Debate, 1980–1986," *Crossroads*, No. 23, pp. 67–79.

38. For example, Croatia and Slovenia had multi-candidate party elections by 1986; Bosnia-Hercegovina held multi-candidate popular elections for state presidency representative.

39. Slavoljub Dukić, "Trka za recenzentom," *Borba*, August 12, 1991, p. 11.

increase in anti-Yugoslav propaganda" from internal and external enemies, a warning that also dominated Yugoslav army leadership pronouncements.[40]

The second part of the conservatives' strategy was to shift attention toward ethnic issues. Thus, Milošević's tenure as party chief in Belgrade also saw the start of a nationalist campaign among Belgrade party members and "leftist" intellectuals, including Milošević's sociologist wife Mirjana Marković, which sought to defend "the national dignity of Serbia" and to protect its interest in Yugoslavia.[41] Belgrade also saw growing numbers of protests by Serbs from the province of Kosovo, claiming to be the victims of ethnic Albanian "genocide."[42] The fact that the demonstrations took place without police interference was a sign that they were at least tolerated by the Belgrade party.

In January 1986, despite very strong opposition from within the party leadership, Milošević was elected head of the Serbian party's central committee.[43] This period saw increased attention to the issue of Kosovo by a Belgrade-centered coalition of conservative party members, orthodox Marxist intellectuals, and nationalist-oriented intellectuals who repeated the charges of "genocide" against Serbs in Kosovo.[44] Journalists who were allied with Milošević, especially at the daily newspaper *Politika*, undertook a media campaign to

---

40. Dukić, "Strogo pov. optuznica," *Borba*, August 13, 1991, p. 11. See also the speech of General Jovičić, head of the army's communist party organization, in *Politika*, December 15, 1984.
41. Mira Marković, *Odgovor* (Belgrade, 1994), and *Duga*, December 1993, cited in *Vreme*, February 7, 1994.
42. Kosovo had been the heart of the medieval Serbian kingdom. But by 1981 it was 75 percent ethnic Albanian, and had received a high degree of autonomy in 1974. In the late 1970s Serbian conservatives had used the issue of Kosovo's autonomy as a way of attacking reformist positions. In this they were supported by conservative Serbs from Kosovo, who were being replaced by ethnic Albanians in party and government posts. In 1981, massive demonstrations by ethnic Albanians erupted throughout the province, which the Serbian conservatives cited as evidence of pervasive "Albanian nationalism." For background on Kosovo, see Branka Magaš, *The Destruction of Yugoslavia* (London: Verso, 1993); Banac, *National Question in Yugoslavia*; Elez Biberaj, "The Conflict in Kosovo," *Survey*, Vol. 28, No. 3 (Autumn 1984); Ramet, *Nationalism and Federalism*, pp. 156–171; essays in Arshi Pipa and Sami Repishti, eds., *Studies on Kosovo* (Boulder, Colo.: East European Monographs, 1984); for a Kosovan Albanian view, see *The Truth of Kosovo* (Tirana: Encyclopedia Publishing House, 1993); for a Serbian view, see Miloš Mišović, *Ko je tražio republiku, Kosovo 1945–1985* (Belgrade: Narodna Knjiga, 1987).
43. For how Milošević and his allies overcame strong opposition, see Slavoljub Dukić, "Kroz iglene uši," *Borba*, August 15, 1991, p. 11; "Pod okriljem Stambolića," *Borba*, August 16, 1991, p. 11.
44. Their main charge was that Serbs were the victims of genocide by the majority Albanian population, which they accused of attempting to create an ethnically pure state though rapes of women, children and nuns, destruction of Serbian cultural monuments, and other types of harassment which had resulted, they claimed, in a massive exodus of Serbs and Montenegrins from the province. For details of the charges as well as a rebuttal of them by an independent commission, see Srdja Popović, Dejan Janća, and Tanja Petovar, *Kosovski čvor: drešiti ili seći?* (Belgrade: Chronos, 1990). See also Magaš, *Destruction of Yugoslavia*, pp. 61–73.

demonize ethnic Albanians and to "confirm" the allegations of genocide.[45] Indeed, the issue of Kosovo now became the conservatives' main weapon against reformist forces within Serbia and in the wider federation, as Serbian conservatives insisted that the issue be the priority not only of the local Serbian party but also at the federal level as well.[46]

However, it soon became clear that this coalition's goals were not limited to Kosovo and Serbia. The third part of the conservatives' strategy was to portray Serbia as the victim of Yugoslavia, setting the stage for attacks on the other republics' autonomy. An ideological manifesto written by some members of the Serbian Academy of Sciences and Arts in 1985, although claiming to call for democracy, actually advocated the restoration of the repressive, centralized socialist system that existed before the 1965 reforms. It sharply attacked the 1965 reforms as the root of all evil in Yugoslavia and as being aimed against Serbs; declared Serbs in Kosovo and Croatia to be endangered; and denounced the "anti-Serbian coalition" within Yugoslavia.[47] Indeed, given the nature of decision-making in Yugoslavia, to prevent radical reform in Serbia the conservatives would have to ensure that it did not take hold in the other republics and at the federal level.

EFFECT OF THE RESPONSE. The result of the Serbian strategy was that questions of radical reform were shunted aside in order to deal with the pressing issue of "genocide" in Kosovo. Through a combination of press manipulation, mass rallies, and political manipulation, and a stress on Stalinist notions of "democratic centralism," by September 1987 Milošević managed to consolidate conservative control over the Serbian republic's party organization.[48] Those parts of the Serbian media that had been relatively independent were taken over by conservative editors allied with Milošević.

---

45. For example, see Magaš, *Destruction of Yugoslavia*, p. 109.
46. For example, in January 1986, 200 Serbian intellectuals, including some who had previously been identified as socialist humanists, signed a petition accusing the (reformist) Serbian and federal party leaderships of complicity in what they described as "the destructive genocide" against Serbs in Kosovo. See text in Magaš, *Destruction of Yugoslavia*, pp. 48–52.
47. For text, see "Memorandum SANU," *Naše Teme*, Vol. 33, No. 1–2 (1989), pp. 128–163. On Milošević's quiet support for the Memorandum, see Slavoljub Dukić, "Čudno Miloševićevo ponašanje," *Borba*, August 21, 1991, p. 13.
48. Reformists were purged from being "soft" on Albanians (because they wanted to negotiate a solution with the Albanians rather than impose one); for being openly critical of the media's inflaming of the Kosovo issue; for warning against the demonization of all ethnic Albanians; and for criticizing the chauvinistic version of Serbian nationalism being used by conservatives. Dragiša Pavlović, "Potcenjuje se srpski nacionalizam," *Borba*, September 25, 1987, p. 3; *Borba*, September 11, 1987. See also Slavoljub Dukić, *Borba*, August 26, 1991, p. 11; *Borba*, August 27, p. 11; *Borba*, August 28, p. 13; *Borba*, August 29, p. 11.

1988–90: THREATS TO THE STATUS QUO

The conservative coalition, although it had consolidated control over the Serbian party organization, still faced threats from reformist forces in other Yugoslav republic and provincial organizations (Serbia was only one of eight), as well as in the federal government, especially as the economic situation continued to deteriorate. Slovenia, with strong liberal and democratic currents, was in the vanguard of increasingly vocal calls for an end to the one-party system and for Yugoslavia to move closer to the west, as well as very sharp criticisms of the Yugoslav army.[49] Also threatening were the successes of Federal Prime Minister Ante Marković, a strong reformer who, despite Serbian opposition, managed to get Federal Assembly approval for radical transformation of the Yugoslav economy.[50]

RESPONSES TO THE THREATS. Over the course of 1988 and 1989, Milošević and his allies attempted to subvert the party leadership in other Yugoslav republics and to weaken the federal government through a strategy of appealing to an aggressive version of Serbian nationalism. This strategy was viable despite the Serbs' minority status in Yugoslavia, because Serbs were overrepresented among politically relevant actors including communist party officials and members in other republics, and within the federal bureaucracies.[51] As long as this remained the case, Serbian conservatives could "legiti-

---

49. Tomaž Mastnak, "Civil Society in Slovenia," in Jim Seroka and Vukašin Pavlović, eds., *The Tragedy of Yugoslavia: The Failure of Democratic Transformation* (Armonk: M.E. Sharpe, 1992), pp. 49–66; Gow, *Legitimacy and the Military*, pp. 78–88.

50. Marković, who became federal prime minister in March 1989, pushed the Federal Assembly to pass constitutional amendments setting the foundation for a market economy and for private enterprise to play a large role in the economy. He circumvented unanimity requirements (and thus the Serbian veto) by declaring further reforms as "urgent measures," which required only two-thirds support in the Assembly, and called for an end to subsidies for unprofitable enterprises. By the end of 1989, Marković had the strong support of the federal communist party apparatus, much of the Federal Assembly, the Croatian party and government, and foreign governments and financial institutions. Cohen, *Broken Bonds*, pp. 66–71.

51. This condition was clearly present within the "inner" Serbia (85 percent Serb), Vojvodina (56 percent Serb), and Montenegro (70 percent Montenegrin and Serb). By the early 1980s Serbs made up 60–70 percent of the army's officer corps and 47 percent of all communist party members in the country; they dominated key parts of the federal bureaucracy, and made up disproportionately large parts of the party membership in Croatia (around 35 percent) and Bosnia-Hercegovina (47 percent). Although at the upper levels of the federal bureaucracy an official policy of quotas existed, these were determined not by nationality but by republic. Thus Serbs from Croatia and Bosnia held positions based on their republic status rather than on their nationality. Within the bureaucracy itself Serbs also tended to dominate; for example, 50 percent of the foreign ministry and diplomatic service came from "inner" Serbia alone (without Kosovo or Vojvodina), which held only 25 percent of the country's population. *Vreme* (Belgrade), September 30, 1991, p. 33. See also Ramet, *Nationalism and Federalism*.

mately" gain power in all of Yugoslavia (and thereby legally recentralize the country) if they could dominate the federal party and state collective leaderships by controlling at least five of the eight votes.

To this end Serbian conservatives continued to focus on the image of threatened Serbs in Kosovo. They staged mass rallies of tens of thousands in every major town in Serbia as well as in other republics and in front of party headquarters and during party meetings; these rallies, decrying the "atrocities" in Kosovo, called for party leaders to step down.[52] The result was that the party leaderships in Vojvodina and Montenegro were ousted in October 1988 and January 1989.[53] The Kosovo party leadership, which had been hand-picked by the conservatives in Belgrade, was also pressured to acquiesce in the abolition of Kosovo's autonomy and the recentralization of Serbia. Although these moves provoked massive demonstrations and strikes among the province's Albanian population to protest the threat to its autonomy, in March 1989 the Kosovo assembly, subjected to fraud and manipulation by Belgrade, voted to end the province's autonomy.[54]

Similar pressure was also put on the Croatian government. Massive rallies organized from Belgrade were held in the rural Serb-majority region around Knin, with the intention of eventually moving on to Zagreb to overthrow the Croatian party leadership.[55] Likewise the ruling party in Bosnia-Hercegovina

---

52. These rallies drew on social dissatisfaction caused by the increasingly poor economic situation as well as images of persecution of Kosovo Serbs. They denounced the existing party leaderships at the federal level and in other republics of betraying the interest of Serbs. They were portrayed by the Serbian regime as an "anti-bureaucratic revolution," although, as one commentator points out, they never criticized the Serbian bureaucracy. Magaš, *Destruction of Yugoslavia*, pp. 206–207. One notable feature of these massive rallies was the presence of many posters and slogans praising Milošević personally (*RFE Situation Report* No. 8/88, September 23, 1988). See also the interview with former Serbian party leader, Dragoslav Marković, "Naš mir je, ipak, bio bolje," *Borba*, August 17–18, 1991, pp. 10–11. The direct link between this anti-reformist movement and extremist Serbian nationalists is seen in the fact that Mirko Jović, an organizer of the 1988 rallies, is also the founder of the Serbian guerrilla group "Beli orlovi," accused by Helsinki Watch of numerous atrocities against civilians in Croatia and Bosnia. Helsinki Watch has requested that Jović himself be investigated for war crimes. Helsinki Watch, *War Crimes in Bosnia Hercegovina* (New York: Human Rights Watch, 1992), p. 6; *Globus* (Zagreb), August 28, 1992, pp. 11–12, citing *Duga* (Belgrade).

53. For details, see Magaš, *Destruction of Yugoslavia*, pp. 170–172, 208; and *RFE Situation Reports*, Yugoslavia, Nos. 8 and 9, September 23 and October 11, 1988. One Montenegrin party official in October 1988 noted that "the protests about the terrorizing of the Serbian and Montenegrin minorities in Kosovo by the Albanian majority" was the work of Serbian "extremists." Reuters, October 13, 1988.

54. *Yugoslavia: Crisis in Kosovo* (New York: Helsinki Watch, 1990); Michael W. Galligan, et al., "The Kosovo Crisis and Human Rights in Yugoslavia," *Record of the Association of the Bar of the City of New York*, Vol. 46, No. 3 (April 1991), pp. 227–231; Magaš, *Destruction of Yugoslavia*, pp. 179–190.

55. Cohen, *Broken Bonds*, p. 130; the Serb-majority region's population was 65 percent Serb, and it included about 25 percent of Croatia's Serbian population; the rest lived in ethnically-mixed regions where they were not a majority.

discovered that Serbia's secret police were active in the republic.[56] In Slovenia the plan was cruder—hundreds of intellectuals and dissidents were to be arrested and the army was to be used to put down protests.[57]

The conservatives' strategy of consolidating control over the other republics through the use of aggressive Serbian nationalism was accompanied by increasingly vehement media demonization not only of Albanians, but also of Croats,[58] as well as an active campaign to portray Tito's Yugoslavia as specifically anti-Serbian.[59] It claimed that an authoritarian, Serb-dominated and centralized Yugoslavia was the only way to ensure the security and interests of all Serbs: such a Yugoslavia also, not coincidentally, would ensure the power interests of the conservative Serbian elites. In the face of the deteriorating economy, Milošević blamed Marković's reforms, and put forward his own program that rejected even the most modest of the reformists' proposals for economic and political change.[60]

Meanwhile the army, under Defense Minister Branko Mamula, openly sided with conservative positions and harshly attacked the political opposition. In the military itself, conservative Marxist-Leninist indoctrination was stepped up.[61] The army also endorsed Milošević's neo-socialist economic and political program, stressing in particular continued monopoly of the communist party and recentralization of the state.[62] In cooperation with Serbian conservatives,

---

56. Milan Andrejevich, "Serbia Accused of Interfering in Bosnian Affairs," *RFE*, October 23, 1989, cited in Gow, *Legitimacy and the Military*, p. 128.

57. *Mladina* (Ljubljana), May 20, 1988.

58. Images were stressed which evoked the specter of the wartime Croatian fascists, including prime-time television broadcasts of previously unshown graphic films from the Ustaša concentration camps. The implication—and at times explicit conclusions—of these and other such images was that Croats as a people were "genocidal." On the television images, see Biljana Bakić, "The Role of the Media in the Yugoslav Wars," draft master's thesis, University of Pittsburgh, Spring 1992; see also Ivo Banac, "The Fearful Asymmetry of War: The Causes and Consequences of Yugoslavia's Demise," *Daedalus*, Spring 1992, pp. 141–174.

59. For example, see Robert M. Hayden, "Recounting the Dead: The Discovery and Redefinition of Wartime Massacres in Late- and Post-Yugoslavia," in Rubie S. Watson, ed., *Memory and Opposition under State Socialism* (Santa Fe, N.M.: School of American Research Press, 1993), citing Ljubomir Tadić, "Kominterna i Nacionalno Pitanje Jugoslavije," *Književne novine*, September 15, 1988.

60. Milošević called for more efficient use of existing resources rather than any structural changes, emphasized "social ownership" rather than private property, stressed the priority of reforming (that is, strengthening) the federal organs, and rejected even the possibility of nonsocialist political parties, Cohen, *Broken Bonds*, pp. 55–58. On the multiparty system, see Milošević, in *NIN*, July 3, 1988, p. 14–15; Slobodan Vučetić, "Pravna država slobodnih ljudi," in *NIN*, July 30, 1989, pp. 10–15, cited in Cohen, *Broken Bonds*, p. 58.

61. Anton Bebler, "Political Pluralism and the Yugoslav Professional Military," in Seroka, *Tragedy*, pp. 126–127, 129.

62. Indeed, this platform, laid out in July 1989 by Defense Secretary Kadijević at the Conference of the Yugoslav Army's party organization, was "the most conservative of all the explicitly articulated platforms in Yugoslavia and the most dogmatic as far as political pluralism was concerned." Bebler, "Political Pluralism," pp. 129–131.

the military openly attacked reformists' calls to democratize the country, to reduce the military's political role, and to reform the military-industrial complex. Moreover, statements by top army officers "made it clear that they viewed the Army's internal mission in orthodox ideological terms."[63]

EFFECT OF THE RESPONSE.   Although this strategy gained Serbia control over four of the eight federal republics and provinces, and placed the purported threats to Serbdom at the center of political discourse, it also provoked backlashes in the other republics. In Slovenia, publication of the army's plans to crush dissent radicalized the party and wider population in Slovenia, where by mid-1988 an unofficial referendum on independence was held and the party began advocating introduction of a multi-party system. In Croatia, a bastion of conservatism since 1971, the Serbian moves provoked the reformist minority, so that by October 1988 the Croatian party proposed dismantling the communist party's leading role and encouraging private property.[64] Even conservative Serbs within the Croatian leadership criticized Milošević's strategy.[65] Likewise in Bosnia, which had previously been supportive of Milošević, the aggressive nationalist strategy and the threat to the Bosnian party leadership led it to distance itself from Serbia's positions.[66]

By the end of 1989, reformist forces had taken over the Croatian party, and both the Slovene and Croatian parties had scheduled multi-party elections for the spring of 1990 (despite attempts by conservative Serb allies of Milošević to prevent this in Croatia).[67] An attempt by Milošević to recentralize the federal party at an extraordinary League of Communists of Yugoslavia (LCY) Congress in January 1990 failed as the Slovene party walked out when its proposal for *de jure* party independence was rejected, and the Croatian, Bosnian and Macedonian parties refused to continue the meeting.

1990: THREATS TO THE STATUS QUO

In 1990, the greatest threat yet to the conservative Serbian coalition and its allies arose—the emergence of a political system in which the general population

---

63. Ibid., pp. 130–131.
64. Stipe Šuvar (one of the most orthodox of the Croatian leadership), October 17–19, 1988, in RFE Situation Report, Yugoslavia, No. 10/88, November 11, 1988.
65. For example, Dušan Dragosavac, a Serb and conservative leader in the Croatian party, denounced Milošević for creating national hatreds. *Danas,* December 13, 1988, cited in Magaš, *Destruction of Yugoslavia,* p. 216.
66. Gow, *Legitimacy and the Military,* p. 128.
67. See Josip Jović, "Centar bez srpskog krila," *Nedeljna Dalmacija,* February 11, 1990, pp. 10–11.

would choose political leaderships. The strategy of recentralizing Yugoslavia by use of mob rallies and aggressive Serbian nationalism to pressure communist party leaderships was clearly no longer feasible; likewise, there was little chance of winning an election in a country where only 39 percent of the population was Serb, especially since Milošević's strategy had alienated most non-Serbs.

The specific threats were now coming from three directions. The first was the fact that in the spring 1990 elections in Slovenia and Croatia, openly anti-socialist parties committed to a loosening rather than tightening of political ties had taken power, due in large part to a backlash against Milošević.[68] Federal decision-making bodies thus now included representatives from these two republics, marking the introduction of an irreconcilable ideological difference in terms of economic and political viewpoints. Indeed, the Slovenian and Croatian governments soon put forward formal proposals for confederalizing the country, utterly rejecting Serbia's calls for recentralization. Given the pressure for multi-party elections in the other Yugoslav republics, and the fall of communist parties throughout the rest of Eastern Europe, it seemed likely that other republics would join these calls.[69]

The second set of threats came from the policies of federal Prime Minister Marković. By early 1990 these policies were quite successful in lowering inflation and improving the country's economic situation, and he was very popular, especially within Serbia.[70] Taking advantage of these successes, and looking ahead to multi-party elections, he pushed bills through the Federal Assembly legalizing a multi-party system in the entire country, and in July 1990 formed a political party to support his reforms.

The biggest challenge, however, came from within Serbia itself. Encouraged by the fall of communist regimes in the rest of Eastern Europe and the victory of noncommunists in Croatia and Slovenia, opposition forces in Serbia began

---

68. On the Slovenian election, see Cohen, *Broken Bonds*, pp. 89–94; Milan Andrejevich, "On the Eve of the Slovenian Election," *Report on Eastern Europe*, Vol. 1, No. 16 (April 20, 1990), pp. 32–38; on Croatia, see Milan Andrejevich, "Croatia Goes to the Polls," *Report on Eastern Europe*, Vol. 1, No. 18 (May 4, 1990), pp. 33–37; and Cohen, *Broken Bonds*, pp. 94–102. On Milošević's role in the victory of the nationalist CDU in Croatia, see interview with former Croatian party head Stipe Šuvar, in "Jugoslavija nije razbijena i neće biti," *Nedeljna Borba*, May 5–6, 1990, p. 12.
69. Even the Bosnian communist party, formerly quite conservative, denounced Serbian presidency member Jović's statement that democratization was endangering the constitutional order of Yugoslavia. Enver Demirović, "I vanredni kongres obnove," *Borba*, May 18, 1990, p. 3.
70. In May 1990 Marković's popularity in Serbia surpassed that of Milošević; while the Serbian leader received a 50 percent approval rating, the federal prime minister's positive rating in Serbia was 61 percent. *Borba*, May 21, 1990.

organizing and pressuring the regime for multi-party elections, holding massive protest rallies in May. Although Milošević argued that elections could not be held until the Kosovo issue was resolved, by June the Serbian regime recognized that elections were unavoidable.[71]

RESPONSE TO THE THREATS. Within Serbia, the regime again resorted to the issue of Kosovo, working assiduously to provoke violent resistance from the Albanian population.[72] Despite these actions and the fact that the new Serbian constitution, adopted in September, effectively stripped Kosovo of its autonomy, the Albanian response was peaceful resistance.

While turning up the heat on Kosovo, the Serbian party also had to deal with opposition parties at home, including nationalist ones from the right (most notably the Serbian Renewal Movement, SRM, headed by writer Vuk Drašković), as well as from civically-oriented democratic parties. In the face of anti-communist nationalist party opposition, and in order to win the necessary two-thirds of the Serbian vote (since the party had alienated the non-Serbian 33 percent of the republic's population), the Serbian conservatives first undertook a strategy of averting a split of the communist party into a large pro-reform social democratic party that would more credibly appeal to the population's economic interest, and a small hard-line party (as happened in the rest of Eastern Europe). The Serbian party was renamed the Socialist Party of Serbia (SPS). The regime continued its control over the mass media, and greatly limited access of opposition parties to television. Economic problems were blamed on the "anti-Serbian" policies of Yugoslav federal Prime Minister Marković. The government also printed $2 billion (U.S.) in dinars for overdue worker salaries just before the December elections, with funds taken illegally from the federal treasury.

On issues of nationalism, the party had already very much distanced itself from the policies of Tito, especially those which forbade public expression of national sentiment. This fact, plus the fact that Yugoslav agriculture had remained in private hands, ensured the SPS most of the vote of peasants and those one generation off the land (a majority of the voters), and thus dampened anticommunist sentiment against it.[73] The SPS, linking the nationalist SRM to

---

71. Dušan Radulović and Nebojša Spaić, *U Potrazi za Demokratijom* (Belgrade: Dosije, 1991).
72. In July, Serbia dissolved the Kosovo Assembly and took over all institutions of the province; all Albanian language media were closed down; all Albanians were fired from positions of responsibility and replaced with Serbs, many fanatically anti-Albanian; Albanian workers were fired without cause; and there was a general harassment of the Albanian population. Galligan, "The Kosovo Crisis," pp. 231–234 and 239–258; Magaš, *Destruction of Yugoslavia*, pp. 262–263.
73. "Sto dana višestranačke Srbije," *NIN*, March 29, 1991, pp. 77–79.

Serbian extremists during World War II, portrayed the SRM as wanting to drag Serbia into war, and painted itself as a moderating and progressive force.[74] The SPS managed to win an overwhelming majority of parliamentary seats with the support of 47 percent of the electorate (72 percent of Serbia's Serbs).[75]

But the challenge to the conservatives continued from outside of Serbia, in the context of the Yugoslav federation. The Serbian conservatives' response was to continue to demonize other ethnic nationalities, and also to begin provoking confrontations and violent conflicts along ethnic lines and to discredit the very idea of a federal Yugoslavia, calling it the creation of a Vatican-Comintern conspiracy.[76]

Even before the 1990 elections the Belgrade media had stepped up its campaign against Croatia, and after the elections it accused the new Croatian ruling party, the Croatian Democratic Union (CDU) of planning to massacre Croatia's Serbian residents.[77] Nevertheless, in the May 1990 elections only a small minority of Croatia's Serbs had supported the Serbian nationalist party, the Serbian Democratic Party (SDP).[78] Following the elections, throughout the summer of 1990 the Serbian media also ran stories detailing the anti-Serb massacres of the World War II Croatian Ustaša regime, furthering the implicit link with the CDU,[79] and Belgrade and its allies began to provoke violent conflict in the Serbian-populated areas of Croatia. Between July 1990 and March 1991, Belgrade's allies took over the SDP, replacing moderate leaders with hard-liners. It portrayed the CDU as genocidal Ustaša; rejected all compromises with Zagreb; held mass rallies and erected barricades; threatened moderate Serbs and non-SDP members who refused to go along with the confrontational strategy; provoked armed incidents with the Croatian police, and stormed villages adjacent to the regions already controlled by Serbian forces and an-

74. Forty-nine percent of SPS voters stressed the importance of good inter-ethnic relations. *Vreme*, January 6, 1992.
75. For a detailed description of how the SPS managed to subvert the elections and cripple the opposition, see Radulović and Spaić, *U Potrazi za Demokratijom*.
76. Magaš, *Destruction of Yugoslavia*, pp. 263–264.
77. Ibid., p. 262.
78. In the 1990 elections, most of Croatia's Serbs, especially those who lived in ethnically-mixed and more economically-developed parts of the republic, had rejected the overt nationalism of the Serbian Democratic Party (SDP), and had voted instead for multi-ethnic parties. While 23 percent of Croatia's Serbs preferred the SDP, 46 percent preferred the reform communists and 16 percent the Coalition of National Reconciliation, both of which advocated harmonious inter-ethnic relations and improved material well-being, and rejected Milošević's strategy of recentralizing the country. Ivan Šiber, "The Impact of Nationalism, Values, and Ideological Orientations on Multi-Party Elections in Croatia," in Seroka, *Tragedy of Yugoslavia*, p. 143.
79. Hayden, "Recounting the Dead," p. 13.

nexed them to their territory.[80] Throughout this period, conciliatory moves by the Croatian regime were rejected, and moderate Serbs who disagreed with Belgrade's conflictual strategy were branded as traitors.[81] Although the campaign rhetoric and the actions of hard-liners in the CDU did give Croatia's Serbs cause for concern, rather than fostering negotiation and compromise with Zagreb, Belgrade exacerbated the Croatian Serbs' concerns.

Following Milošević's December 1990 victory in the Serbian elections, the situation in Croatia became even more confrontational as a hard-line group within SDP, working closely with Belgrade and armed by the Yugoslav Army, began to provoke armed conflicts with Croatian police in areas where Serbs were not in the majority.[82] Croatian Serbs were increasingly pressured to toe the SDP line, and Croats in the Serb-held "Krajina" region were besieged by Serbian armed forces and pressured to leave.[83] These purposely provoked conflicts were publicly characterized by Belgrade as "ethnic conflicts," the result of ancient hatreds, and the Yugoslav army was called in to separate the groups. At the end of February, Krajina proclaimed its autonomy from Croatia.

---

80. Cohen, *Broken Bonds,* pp. 131 and 134; Miloš Vasić, "Labudova pesma dr Milana Babića," *Vreme,* February 10, 1992, pp. 13–15.
81. For example, in June 1990 the CDU offered SDP leader Jovan Rašković a position as vice-president of the parliament; Belgrade's pressure on Rašković and other SDP members led him to reject the offer and walk out of the assembly, and to end negotiations with Zagreb on the Serbs' status in Croatia; Cohen, *Broken Bonds,* p. 86. During the referendum on sovereignty in August, though Zagreb condemned the voting, it made no move to stop it, or to remove the barricades that Serbian forces had thrown up around the territory. Ibid., p. 134. Indeed, outside observers note that despite Serbian accusations of a genocidal regime, Zagreb continued to moderate its rhetoric and act with "restraint." Helsinki Watch, "Human Rights in a Dissolving Yugoslavia," January 9, 1991, p. 7. In October, moderate SDP representatives from areas outside of Krajina (Slavonia, Baranja, Kordun, Istria), in negotiations with Zagreb, received official recognition of the SDP as the legitimate representative of Croatia's Serbian population and the promise (later confirmed) that the draft Croatian constitution would not include the description of the republic as the "national state of the Croatian people," one of the Serbs' main grievances. The CDU delegation also promised to resolve all other disputed questions quickly. SDP hard liners from Knin, however, denounced the moderate Serbs as traitors. Vasić, "Labudova pesma."
82. Jovan Rašković, one of the founders of the SDP, notes that at a February 26 meeting of the SDP leadership, 38 out of 42 members supported his call for moderation against extremist Milan Babić, who advocated a hard-line confrontational and military approach and who was in direct contact with Belgrade. The next day Babić proceeded to found his own party, the SDS Krajina; Rašković stated that at this time "for the first time I warned that this radical group which wanted to take over the SDP is a danger for us and that war will definitely result if they exacerbate things." See interview with Rašković, *Globus,* February 14, 1992, pp. 14–15. Shortly after this, armed clashes with Croatian police broke out in Pakrac, in western Slavonia, and at the Plitvice Lakes national park on the edge of Krajina.
83. The Croat-majority village of Kijevu outside Knin was besieged for eight months. Srdan Španović, "Čudo u Kirjevu," *Danas,* March 12, 1991, pp. 18–20.

These Serbian moves provoked Croat hard-liners to take repressive actions against Serbs in areas where the ruling party controlled the local government: these actions were pointed to by Belgrade's allies as proof of the threat to Serbs.[84] Despite calls by Croatian hard-liners to use military force, Zagreb lacked significant stocks of weapons (although it was seeking sources), and Croatian president Franjo Tudjman clearly feared providing the Yugoslav army with an excuse to crush the Croatian government. He was thus forced to accept the army's gradually expanding occupation of the areas where the SDP's authoritarian rule prevailed. This period saw the groundwork for a similar strategy being laid in Bosnia by Belgrade's ally there, Radovan Karadžić, head of that republic's SDS.[85]

As conflict heated up in Croatia, in negotiations over the future of Yugoslavia, Milošević and his allies refused to budge from his call for a more tightly centralized federation. He declared that if his demand was rejected, then the borders of Serbia would be redrawn so that all Serbs would live in one state.[86]

EFFECT OF THE RESPONSE. The result of this strategy of conflict was to further the destruction of Yugoslavia. The provocations and repression of even moderate Serbs in Croatia increased the territory under the Yugoslav army's control, and provoked reactions on the part of extremist Croats.

1991: THREATS TO THE STATUS QUO

This apparently successful strategy was suddenly interrupted when Serbia's political opposition held massive protest rallies in Belgrade on March 9 and 10.[87] Appealing to the wider population, the opposition, led by SRM chief Vuk Drašković, threatened to oust the regime by force of street rallies. Initially called to denounce the regime's tight control and manipulation of the media, the rallies also condemned Milošević's disastrous economic policies and his policy

---

84. For example, in western Slavonia, some hard-line CDU members from Hercegovina, "formerly petty criminals," were put into the police force and began harassing Serbs, and even local Croats were frightened. The result was that the SDP, which had little support in the region before, began to attract many Serbs. Zoran Daskalović, "Skupljenje povjerenja," *Danas*, March 12, 1991, pp. 13–14; Milan Bečejić, "Forsiranje straha," *Danas*, March 12, 1991, pp. 16–17.

85. Karadžić openly declared the goal of drawing ethnic borders, citing the Krajina experience, but ignoring the Muslims as a factor. Yet Bosnia's population was so ethnically intermixed that there really were no ethnic borders. See Golubović, Campbell and Golubović, "How not to Divide," in *Why Bosnia*. Karadžić also declared that "we have given Milošević a mandate to represent Serbs in Bosnia-Hercegovina if Yugoslavia disintegrates." *Borba*, February 26, 1991, p.7.

86. *Vreme*, March 4, 1991.

87. See Helsinki Watch, "Yugoslavia: The March 1991 Demonstrations in Belgrade," May 1, 1991; Zoran Miljatović, "9. mart, zvanična verzija," *NIN*, March 29, 1991, pp. 11–13.

of provoking conflict with other republics.[88] They called for the SPS to step down from power as other East European communists had done. Although Milošević's immediate reaction was to call the army to put down the demonstrations (since the republic's police forces were all in Kosovo), the military refused to use massive force.[89] This marked the start of the democratic opposition's rapid rise in popularity, and the beginning of an open split within the ruling SPS by democratic, pro-reform forces. Shortly thereafter massive strikes (including one of 700,000 workers) aimed specifically against Milošević's regime shook Serbia.

RESPONSE TO THE THREATS. Given the refusal of the army to use force, Milošević was forced to negotiate with his opponents. He accepted limited economic reform, printed more money to pay workers, and discussed the formation of a multi-party Serbian national council. At the end of March he secretly met with Croatian President Tudjman to agree on a division of Bosnia-Hercegovina, thus removing the possibility of Tudjman taking advantage of Milošević's then weak position. In April Milošević finally accepted the principle of confederation, and in early June, during talks over the future of Yugoslavia, he agreed to the principles on which such a confederation would be based.[90] Belgrade also pressured its Serbian allies in Croatia to negotiate with Zagreb, although the Serbs refused to reach an agreement.[91]

Yet at the same time, the strategy of provoking conflict along ethnic lines was also stepped up. Milošević himself labeled the protesters "enemies of Serbia" who were working with Albanians, Croats, and Slovenes to try to destroy Serbia, and ominously stressed the "great foreign pressures and threats" being exerted on Serbia and which gave "support to the forces of disintegration of Yugoslavia."[92] The media stepped up its portrayals of Croatia as a fascist Ustaša state, and in April graphically reported on the opening of caves in Bosnia-Hercegovina filled with the bones of thousands of Serb victims of the Ustaša; in August it broadcast the mass interment of the remains.[93]

---

88. For a list of initial demands, see Milan Bečejić, "Rafali u demokraciju," *Danas*, March 12, 1991, pp. 29–31; see also "Objava mira umesto rata," *Politika*, May 8, 1991, p. 8.
89. On use of force, see Helsinki Watch, "Yugoslavia," May 1991.
90. See "Kompromis i ustupci korak ka rešenju," *Borba*, June 7, 1991, pp. 1 and 3; and interview with Bosnian president Izetbegović, co-author (along with Macedonian president Gligorov) of the compromise plan, "Država na ljudskim pravima," *Vreme*, June 17, 1991, pp. 12–14.
91. Tanjug, April 15 and 16, 1991. This occasion was used, however, to further purge the SDP of moderates with the accusation of being "traitors" for having talked with Tudjman. This period saw further marginalization of other moderates, including Rašković, who was sent to Belgrade. Vasić, "Labudova Pesma," p. 14.
92. Milošević speech to Serbian parliament, *Politika*, May 31, 1991, pp. 1–2.
93. The funeral, presided over by the Serbian Orthodox patriarch, included a procession of coffins that stretched for one and one-half kilometers. Hayden, "Recounting the Dead," p. 13.

This period was also one of close cooperation between the Yugoslav army, the Belgrade regime, and the Bosnian SDP, as the three sides implemented "Project RAM," a plan to use military force to expand Serbia's borders westward and create a new Serbian Yugoslavia.[94] Thus in Bosnia in the spring of 1991, the SDP set up "Serbian Autonomous Regions" which were declared no longer under the authority of the republic government, a repetition of the Krajina strategy.[95]

The SPS at this time also began an open alliance with the neo-fascist Serbian Radical Party led by Vojislav Šešelj, ensuring Šešelj's election to the Serbian parliament in a by-election.[96] Šešelj's guerrilla groups were active in the ensuing escalation of conflict in Croatia. In this period, Belgrade also exerted growing pressure on moderate Serb leaders in Croatia's ethnically-mixed Slavonia region (where Serbs were not in the majority) to accept its confrontational strategy; in May, Krajina held a referendum to join with Serbia, and Belgrade-supported guerrillas, including Šešelj's "Četniks," flowed into Croatia, terrorizing both Serb and non-Serb populations in the more developed regions of Eastern and Western Slavonia (neither of which had Serb majorities).[97] These forces attacked Croatian police, in at least one case massacring and mutilating them, and began a policy of forcible ethnic expulsions in areas coming under their control. Moderate SDP leaders denounced Belgrade for provoking and orchestrating this confrontational strategy.[98]

---

94. On SDP cooperation with the Yugoslav army, see "Skica pakla," *Vreme*, March 9, 1992, p. 25. On project RAM, see *Vreme*, September 30, 1991; and the stenographic notes of the federal cabinet meeting at which this plan was discussed, in *Vreme*, September 23, 1991, pp. 5–12. Related to RAM, just after the street protests, Yugoslav Defense Minister Kadijević held secret talks in Moscow with Soviet Defense Minister Yazov (who would several months later lead the coup attempt against Gorbachev), and without the knowledge of civilian officials arranged for a large quantity of weapons, including planes, rocket systems, and helicopters, to be delivered to the Yugoslav army (ibid., p. 7).
95. Momčilo Petrović, "Odlučivaće sila?" *NIN*, April 19, 1991, p. 11.
96. Miloš Vasić, "Falsifikat originala," *Vreme*, June 17, 1991, pp. 8–9. Šešelj appealed to a virulent Serbian nationalism that demonized other nationalities, especially Albanians and Croats, called for building a Greater Serbia including all of Croatia "except what can be seen from the top of Zagreb's cathedral," and advocated expulsion of non-Serbs from Serbia. See the program of his "Chetnik movement" in *Velika Srbija*, July 1990, pp. 2–3.
97. Other Belgrade-supported paramilitary groups include those of Arkan ("Tigers"), and of Mirko Jović ("White Eagles"). On Belgrade's support of these groups and the local Serbian forces, see "Helsinki Watch Letter to Slobodan Milošević and General Blagoje Adžić," January 21, 1992, in *War Crimes in Bosnia-Hercegovina* (New York: Human Rights Watch, August 1992), p. 275. On the referendum, see *Politika*, May 13, 1991, pp. 1 and 5.
98. Vojislav Vukčević, head of the SDP organization in the Baranja region of Croatia, bordering on Serbia, in *NIN*, April 19, 1991, p. 14. Former SDP leader Rašković also denounced the hard-liners who had taken over the party, as well as Belgrade's strategy of conflict. *NIN*, May 3, 1991, p. 15.

In the face of this pressure, and in preparation for the new confederal agreement, in late June the Croatian government declared the start of a process of disassociation from Yugoslavia, specifically stating that it was not an act of unilateral secession and that Zagreb continued to recognize the authority of federal organs, including the army.[99] When the Serb-controlled army attacked Slovenia following its own declaration of sovereignty, Croatia refrained from helping the Slovenes, in order to avoid giving the army an excuse to attack Croatia.[100]

Nevertheless, the Yugoslav army, despite its public promises not to attack Croatia,[101] escalated the conflict in Croatia, and Serbian forces continued their strategy of provoking conflicts in Slavonia and on the borders of Krajina, terrorizing civilian populations, destroying Croatian villages and Croat parts of towns, bombing cities to drive out the population, and forcing Serbs on threat of death to join them and point out Croat-owned houses.[102] Serbs who openly disagreed with these policies were terrorized and silenced.[103] The human rights group Helsinki Watch noted that in the period through August 1991 (when the Croats finally went on the offensive and Croat extremists themselves undertook atrocities against civilians), by far the most egregious human rights abuses were committed by the Serbian guerrillas and the Yugoslav army, including indiscriminate use of violence to achieve their goals of terrorizing the Serb population into submission and driving out the non-Serb population.[104] This policy, by provoking extremists in Croatia into action, in effect

---

99. See the report by Chuck Sudetic, "2 Yugoslav States Vote Independence to Press Demands," *New York Times*, June 26, 1991, pp. A1 and A6.

100. These Yugoslav army attacks seemed in part to be in response to U.S. Secretary of State Baker's declaration in Belgrade that the most important U.S. priority continued to be a united Yugoslavia, which was apparently crucial in assuring the army that the international costs of military action would not be unbearable. For Baker's statement, see Thomas Friedman, "Baker Urges End to Yugoslav Rift," *New York Times*, June 22, 1991, pp. 1 and 4. Indeed, the usually reliable independent Belgrade weekly *Vreme* reported that just before Baker's visit the United States had sent special emissaries to offer the Yugoslavs the help of the 82nd Airborne Division if necessary; and a few days before the visit, Assistant Secretary of State Lawrence Eagleburger mentioned the possibility of NATO or CSCE aid to Yugoslavia. Roksanda Ninčić, "Kraj druge Jugoslavije," *Vreme*, July 1, 1991, p. 6.

101. Cited in *Danas*, July 23, 1991, p. 7.

102. See "Helsinki Watch Report on Human Rights Abuses in the Croatian Conflict," September 1991, in *War Crimes*, pp. 230–272; and "Helsinki Watch Letter to Milošević and Adžić," pp. 276–302.

103. See *NIN*, November 8, 1991, p. 15; *Vreme*, November 4, 1991, pp. 12–15l; and interview with moderate Zagreb-based Serbian Democratic Forum leader Milorad Pupovac in *Vreme*, October 21, 1991, pp. 12–14.

104. Helsinki Watch noted that "the majority" of human rights abuses by Croats "involved discrimination against Serbs," where individual managers demanded that Serb workers sign loyalty oaths to Croatia or be fired, as well as some police beatings; whereas abuses by the Serbian forces involved "physical maltreatment" and "egregious abuses against civilians and medical

became a self-fulfilling prophecy as the Serbian regime pointed to those atrocities as proof of its original charges.[105]

This war policy also destroyed the chances for Marković's reforms to succeed. Slovenia and Croatia, along with Serbia, had already been trying to block implementation of many aspects of his reform, but the Yugoslav army and Serbian guerrilla attacks killed any support in Slovenia and Croatia for a continued Yugoslavia, even among those who had advocated it; meanwhile, Milošević's moves to take over the federal presidency and marginalize the federal government by September 1991 led Marković to the conclusion that he had no choice but to resign. By summer, the army was also draining the federal hard currency reserves and taking up a vast proportion of the federal budget, which had been carefully managed by Marković.

The war also helped Milošević in his domestic crisis. In April 1991 the democratic opposition had been at a high point, predicting the imminent fall of the SPS. But the SPS used charges of genocide and the subsequent war in Croatia to suppress internal party dissent and to marginalize the democratic opposition by drowning out concerns about economic and political reform, and by accusing those who questioned the war of treason. The regime also used the war to try to destroy the opposition physically: it first sent to the front reservists from counties that had voted for opposition parties. Opposition leaders and outspoken anti-war activists were also sent to the front. Any criticism was met with physical threats and violence from neo-fascist gangs.[106] The regime also targeted the Hungarian minority in Vojvodina (an absolute majority in seven counties); although they were only three percent of Serbia's population, they represented seven to eight percent of reservists at the front and twenty percent of casualties.[107]

---

personnel," including the use of civilians as "human shields" in battle. It also accused the Yugoslav army of committing "serious human rights violations by attacking civilian targets with Serbian forces," including the mortar bombing of such cities as Vukovar and Osijek. Helsinki Watch ("Yugoslavia: Human Rights Abuses in the Croatian Conflict," September 1991). See also Blaine Harden, "Observers Accuse Yugoslav Army," on EC observers' similar charges, *Washington Post,* January 17, 1992, p. A23. The head of the main democratic nationalist party in Serbia, Vuk Drašković, has publicly stated that "there was no particular need for war in Slavonia." *Danas,* February 18, 1992. See also his denunciation of the war in *Vreme,* November 4, 1991, pp. 9–11.

105. For details of atrocities and abuses by Croatian forces, see Helsinki Watch, "Yugoslavia: Human Rights Abuses in the Croatian Conflict, September 1991"; and "Helsinki Watch Letter to Franjo Tudjman," February 13, 1992, in *War Crimes,* pp. 310–359.

106. Milan Milošević, "Srbi protiv Srba," *Vreme,* October 21, 1991, pp. 8–11; Helsinki Watch, Letter to Milošević and Adžić, *War Crimes,* pp. 302 and 304; Milan Milošević, "Panonska pobuna," *Vreme,* November 18, 1991, pp. 12–15.

107. In addition, 25,000 Hungarians fled Serbia. The leader of Serbia's Hungarian community described this policy as "violent changing of the ethnic structure" of Vojvodina. "Bekstvo od rata," *Vreme,* January 20, 1992, p. 31.

By September 1991 the army was attacking Dubrovnik, and thousands of Serbian and Montenegrin reservists were ranging around Bosnia-Hercegovina, terrorizing the Slavic Muslim population.[108] But at the same time there was growing discontent in Serbia about the war.[109] Thousands of young men hid or left the country to avoid being drafted, and whole units of reservists deserted from the front.[110] It was also clear that the SPS's hard-line allies in Moscow had failed in their attempts to seize power.[111] By November 1991, when the European Community threatened economic sanctions against Serbia, and Croat forces began taking back territory, Serbia accepted the principle of UN peacekeeping forces in the areas it controlled in Croatia.

By this time, the opposition in Serbia was again gaining momentum, drawing on the anti-war sentiment and discontent over continued economic decline. Condemning the SPS's economic policy, its war in Croatia, and even its conflictual policy in Kosovo, the opposition by February 1992 was gathering hundreds of thousands of signatures calling for Milošević's resignation and the convening of a constitutional assembly.[112] Once again, the regime pulled back, and it finally allowed UN troops to move into Krajina, put pressure on hardliners in Krajina, allowed moderate Serbs to negotiate with Zagreb,[113] set up meetings with the remaining four Yugoslav republics to negotiate a future Yugoslavia, and called for talks with Croatia.[114]

But at the same time, Serbia also stepped up the pressure on Bosnia, instituting an economic blockade of the areas not controlled by its SDP allies.[115] It now portrayed as the ethnic enemy the allegedly fundamentalist-Muslim

---

108. On reservists, see Mladen Klemenčić, "Srpska kama u trbuhu Bosne," *Globus*, September 27, 1991, p. 9.

109. For polling data, see Milan Milošević, *Vreme*, September 23, 1991, pp. 29–33.

110. See Dragan Todorović, "To nije njihova kolubarska bitka," *Vreme*, October 7, 1991, pp. 24–26; Milan Milošević, "Marš preko Drine," *Vreme*, October 7, 1991, pp. 20–22; Torov, *Danas*, October 1, 1991, p. 32.

111. In fact, the SPS was the only ruling party in Europe to have openly supported the attempted coup, declaring the beneficial effects of its success for the Serbian regime. See Strojan Cerović, "Staljinizam bez Kremlja," *Vreme*, August 26, 1991, pp. 16–17. For specific comments by SPS officials supporting the coup, see Hari Štajner, "Jeltsin preuzeo Gorbačova," *Vreme*, August 26, 1991, pp. 4–6; in *Vreme*, September 2, 1991; and in "Točak istorije ne može nazad," *Borba*, August 21, 1991, p. 4.

112. Milan Milošević, "Dogadjanje potpisa," *Vreme*, February 17, 1992, pp. 9–14; Mirjana Prošić-Dvornić, "Enough! Student Protest '92: The Youth of Belgrade in Quest of 'Another Serbia'," *The Anthropology of East Europe Review*, Vol. 11, Nos. 1–2 (Spring-Fall 1993), pp. 127–137.

113. See interview with chairman of CDU executive council Stipe Mesić, in *Globus*, February 7, 1992, pp. 6–7.

114. "Četiri republike za zajedničku državu," *Politika*, January 22, 1992, p. 1.

115. Helsinki Watch, *War Crimes*, p. 26.

population of Bosnia, who were said to be seeking to impose an Islamic state and to perpetrate genocide against the Bosnian Serbs.[116] Indeed, the same scenario was beginning in Bosnia. In December the SDP declared that it would form a republic, and in January 1992 the independent "Serbian Republic" was declared in the 66 percent of Bosnian territory that the SDP controlled, the "Serbian Autonomous Regions" that had been formed in 1991. SDP leader Radovan Karadžić declared at this time that Bosnia would never again be undivided.[117] Objecting to a referendum to be held in those parts of the republic not under SDP control, Serbian guerrilla forces began armed attacks on Croat and Muslim civilians in early March.[118] Despite this, the referendum, seeking approval for Bosnia-Hercegovina's independence, was approved by 63 percent of the republic's population (99 percent of those voting), including a large proportion of those Serbs who lived outside of SDP-controlled territory.[119] (Indeed, the Bosnian presidency continues to include Serbian members, as does the Bosnian army, whose deputy commander is a Serb; all have been branded traitors by the SDP.)

Within the next two months Serbian guerrilla groups had committed widespread atrocities, expelling and murdering non-Serbs, mostly in areas already controlled by the SDP.[120] By September 1992, Belgrade's Bosnian Serb allies had increased their territorial holdings by less than ten percent, to about seventy

116. One example of this propaganda came in March 1992, at the end of the Muslim holiday of Ramadan, when the SDP's press agency cited a made-up Koran verse in which, they claimed, Muslims were called on to kill Christians at the end of Ramadan. Ejub Štitkovac, "Kur'an po 'SRNI'," *Vreme*, April 27, 1992, p. 33. The Slavic Muslims of Bosnia are generally very secular. See Ivo Banac, "Bosnian Muslims: From Religious Community to Socialist Nationhood and Postcommunist Statehood, 1918–1992," in Mark Pinson, ed., *The Muslims of Bosnia-Hercegovina* (Cambridge: Harvard University Press, 1994), pp. 129–153.
117. The "Republic of the Serbian People of Bosnia-Hercegovina" was declared to include areas where Serbs were in a majority as well as in "those areas where the Serbian people is in a minority because of the genocide against it during the Second World War." Zehrudin Isaković, "Spor oko 'ako'," *Vreme*, January 13, 1992, pp. 17–18.
118. See Helsinki Watch, *War Crimes*, pp. 27–29; "Drugi Sarajevski atentat," *Globus*, March 6, 1992, pp. 3–6.
119. The SDP prevented the referendum from being carried out in the areas under its control, which included large numbers of non-Serbs. Although the SDP called for a total boycott by Serbs, 2 million people (63.4 percent of eligible voters) participated in the referendum. See *Referendum on Independence in Bosnia-Herzegovina: February 29–March 1, 1992*, cited in *War Crimes*.
120. For details of the atrocities and war, see *War Crimes*; *War Crimes in Bosnia-Hercegovina*, Vol. 2 (New York: Helsinki Watch, April 1993); Roy Gutman, *A Witness to Genocide: The 1993 Pulitzer-Prize Winning Dispatches on the "Ethnic Cleansing" of Bosnia* (New York: Macmillan, 1993). Alexandra Stiglmayer, ed., *Mass Rape: The War Against Women in Bosnia-Herzegovina* (Lincoln: University of Nebraska Press, 1994); Zehrudin Isaković, "Pocrveneli ljiljani," *Vreme*, April 6, 1992, pp. 6–7.

percent. As in Krajina, almost the entire non-Serbian population were killed or driven out, and Serbian dissenters were silenced and repressed.[121]

EFFECT OF THE RESPONSE.   The Serbian conservatives' strategy had a short-term goal of insuring their survival in power and preserving the structure of economic and political power in Serbia. In the long term, their strategy initially had the goal of creating a centralized, authoritarian Yugoslavia where the conservatives would crush all attempts at radical change and enforce their own orthodoxy. But when in 1990 the bases of political power shifted to the wider population, the conservatives were forced to change this strategy. Having discredited themselves in the eyes of the 61 percent of Yugoslavia's population that was non-Serb, the conservative coalition resorted to destroying the old multi-ethnic Yugoslavia, and creating on its ruins a new enlarged Serbian state with a large majority of Serbs in which they could use appeals to Serbian nationalism as a means of defining political interests, and thereby preserve the existing power structure. The violence itself and the retaliatory violence against innocent Serb civilians in Bosnia and Croatia have created a situation in which grievances defined in ethnic terms are sure to continue to play an important role in Serbian politics. Meanwhile, the regime has restructured and taken firmer control of the economy, and has blamed the accompanying economic hardships on the international sanctions.

Conclusion: Ethnic Conflict as a Political Strategy

Violent conflict described and justified in terms of ethnic solidarity is not an automatic outgrowth of ethnic identity, or even of ethnic mobilization. Violence on a scale large enough to affect international security is the result of purposeful and strategic policies rather than irrational acts of the masses. Indeed, in the case of the former Yugoslavia there is much evidence that the "masses," especially in ethnically-mixed regions, did not want war and that violence was imposed by forces from outside. The current major conflicts taking place along ethnic lines throughout the world have as their main causes not ancient hatreds, but rather the purposeful actions of political actors who actively create violent conflict, selectively drawing on history in order to portray it as historically inevitable.[122]

---

121. See, for example, Blaine Harden, "In Bosnia 'Disloyal Serbs' Share Plight of Opposition," *Washington Post*, August 24, 1992, pp. 1 and 14.
122. On Azerbaijan, see Dmitrii Furman, "Vozvrashchenie v tretii mir," *Svobodnaia mysl'*, No. 11 (1993), pp. 16–28; on various cases in the Caucasus and Central Asia, Georgii Derluguian, "'Ethnic' violence in the post-communist periphery," *Studies in Political Economy*, No. 41 (Summer 1993),

If such conflict is driven by domestic concerns, outside actors can try to prevent or moderate it by making the external costs of such conflict so high that the conflict itself would endanger the domestic power structure. The most obvious way is the use of military force. But to prevent such conflicts, the threat of force must be made early, and it must be credible. In the Yugoslav case the international community has not fulfilled either condition.

Such conflict might also be prevented or moderated by international attempts to influence the situation from within, striking at the root cause of conflictual behavior. While assuring minorities of their rights may be important, that alone does not address the roots of the conflict in cases such as this one. Rather, the target must be the real causes of conflictual policy: the provocation of violence by threatened elites, and the reasons for their conflictual behavior. Such a preventative policy must come early, but it is much less costly than a military solution. The international community can undertake policies such as ensuring multiple sources of mass information and active and early support for democratic forces. But in cases where domestic structural changes are being fostered by international actors, those actors must also be very attentive to the domestic political context into which they are intervening, and in particular should take into account the concerns of those who are most negatively affected by domestic changes. An example is to ensure those elites most affected by change of fall-back positions.

If violence along ethnic lines is caused by internal conflict, then negotiations over interests outside the domestic arena will be without effect, since the goal of the conflict is not in the international environment, *vis-à-vis* another state, but rather at home. To be truly effective, these internal factors must also be brought into negotiations.

What are the implications of this approach for understanding the link between nationalism and violent conflict in other parts of the world? If domestic conflict drives external conflict, and if the potential costs in the outside world are a key part of the domestic calculus, then we would expect such types of external conflict to be less likely in a truly threatening international environment. If the risk is too high, threatened elites will have more motivation to seek

pp. 45–81; on Africa, Binaifer Nowrojee, *Divide and Rule: State Sponsored Ethnic Violence in Kenya* (New York: Africa Watch, 1993); *Somalia: A Government at War with its Own People* (New York: Africa Watch, 1990); Amnesty International, *Rwanda: Mass Murder by Government Supporters and Troops* (New York: Amnesty International, 1994); Catherine Watson, et al., *Transition in Burundi* (Washington, D.C.: American Council for Nationalities, 1993); on India, Susanne Hoeber Rudolph and Lloyd I. Rudolph, "Modern Hate," *The New Republic,* March 22, 1993, pp. 24–29; on Lebanon, Barry Preisler, "Lebanon: The Rationality of National Suicide," Ph.D. dissertation, University of California, Berkeley, 1988.

a compromise solution with challengers at home. On the other hand, in conditions where the external threat to security is minimal, threatened elites may be more tempted to use conflict in the external arena as one part of their domestic political strategy. The end of the Cold War may therefore have its primary effects on the international arena not directly, through its influence on the structure of the international system, but rather indirectly, in domestic spheres around the world.

What explains absence of ethnic conflict under conditions of change? In the Russian case, Gorbachev's evolutionary style of incremental reform, where he brought conservatives step-by-step toward radical change, was one factor preventing a feeling of sudden threat among conservatives. Since then economic change has taken place gradually in Russia, and often the new owners of privatized enterprises are the former managers and party bureaucrats. Although this gives them a stake in the new system, if these firms are unprofitable or poorly run, a rash of bankruptcies may have a drastic effect. In addition, in the Soviet Union and then in Russia, because reformists are in control of the central government, they also control the media, making it very difficult for hard-liners to create images via television.

Extreme Russian nationalist Vladimir Zhirinovsky, who made a surprisingly strong showing in Russia's 1994 elections and whose expansionist rhetoric alarms many in Russia's "near abroad," is an example of a threatened elite resorting to conflictual policies. Zhirinovsky's rhetoric serves the domestic political aims of threatened elites in the security forces, forcibly pensioned party workers, and others. It is thus no coincidence that, like Milošević, Zhirinovsky and other extreme nationalist Russians speak in terms of threats to Russians outside of Russia; any conflict will thus most likely be outside of Russian Federation's borders.

Methodologically, the case of Serbia shows the importance of recognizing that political rhetoric is itself political behavior, and that conflict described in ethnic terms and taking place along ethnic lines, while it may be about ethnic issues, may be caused by issues not related to ethnicity. The ability of violence to create specific political contexts means that those provoking violent conflict may have as their goal something quite outside the direct objects of conflict. It is thus important to realize that the rhetoric of ethnic nationalist purists is exactly that: rhetoric. Within every group the definition of group interest is contested, and in fact that definition is the key to power.

Spiraling to Ethnic War | *Stuart J. Kaufman*

Elites, Masses, and Moscow in Moldova's Civil War

The continuing spread of ethnic violence seems set to replace the spread of communism as the central security concern in western capitals. Ethnic wars in Bosnia, Rwanda, Chechnya, and elsewhere frequently dominate the attention of policymakers and publics worldwide, and when top American officials say that "instability" is the major worldwide threat to American national security, ethnic wars are largely what they have in mind. The impression created by such rhetoric is that ethnic war can happen anywhere, an impression reinforced by the wide range of places where such wars have recently occurred, from Chiapas to Croatia, Iraqi Kurdistan to Sri Lanka.

There have been numerous attempts to explain the causes of these ethnic wars. One approach focuses on the role of mass passions or "ancient hatred" in driving ethnic violence.[1] A second theory suggests that inter-ethnic security dilemmas may be the key cause of ethnic war.[2] A third approach blames ethnic wars on manipulation by belligerent leaders. However, by focusing on only one cause of conflict—whether hostile masses, belligerent leaders, or the security dilemma—many of these arguments create the false impression that where that one factor is present, ethnic war threatens. They therefore exaggerate the threat of ethnic war.

Stuart J. Kaufman is Assistant Professor of Political Science at the University of Kentucky.

The author would like to thank Leokadia Drobizheva, Airat Aklaev, Nicholas Dima, Stephen Bowers, and Vasile Nedelciuc for their help in organizing this research. This research was supported by funds from the University of Kentucky, and by grants from the International Research and Exchanges Board and the Kennan Institute for Advanced Russian Studies, with funds provided by the U.S. Department of State (Title VIII) and the National Endowment for the Humanities. Valuable suggestions and advice were provided by Jeff Chinn, Charles Davis, Pal Kolsto, Karen Mingst, and Stephen Saideman. None of these people or organizations is responsible for the views expressed.

1. See, e.g., Robert D. Kaplan, *Balkan Ghosts: A Journey Through History* (New York: St. Martin's, 1993). Some more sophisticated approaches including this argument are Donald L. Horowitz, *Ethnic Groups in Conflict* (Berkeley: University of California Press, 1985); Crawford Young, *The Politics of Cultural Pluralism* (Madison: University of Wisconsin Press, 1976); and Elizabeth Crighton and Martha Abele MacIver, "The Evolution of Protracted Ethnic Conflict: Group Dominance and Political Underdevelopment in Northern Ireland and Lebanon," *Comparative Politics*, Vol. 23, No. 2 (January 1991), pp. 127–142.
2. Among the first to publish this insight was Barry R. Posen in "The Security Dilemma and Ethnic Conflict," *Survival*, Vol. 35, No. 1 (Spring 1993), pp. 27–47.

International Security, Vol. 21, No. 2 (Fall 1996), pp. 108–138
© 1996 by the President and Fellows of Harvard College and the Massachusetts Institute of Technology.

This article argues that all three factors—hostile masses, belligerent leaders, and inter-ethnic security dilemmas—are necessary if ethnic war is to result. These factors cause ethnic war by reinforcing each other in a spiral of increasing conflict: belligerent leaders stoke mass hostility; hostile masses support belligerent leaders; and both together threaten other groups, creating a security dilemma which in turn encourages even more mass hostility and leadership belligerence.

Furthermore, these three factors only emerge if the necessary preconditions are present. The preconditions for mass hostility are a set of ethnically defined grievances, negative ethnic stereotypes, and disputes over emotional symbols. Hostility serious enough to motivate ethnic war also requires a fear (usually exaggerated) of ethnic extinction, based on threatening demographic trends and a history of domination by one group over the other.

A security dilemma requires that the fears of extinction be mutual—that actions taken by one side to avert extinction be seen by the other side as threatening extinction for themselves. A security dilemma also requires a *de facto* situation of anarchy and—if it is to lead to war—the military means to enable both sides to fight.

Belligerent elites contribute to ethnic conflict through a process of "outbidding," in which they compete with each other to promote increasingly extreme nationalist positions. For outbidding to be possible, elites require political space—i.e., the freedom to engage in outbidding. Successful outbidding also requires either the presence of mass hostility, or the preconditions for mass hostility, so the masses will have reason to respond to extremist appeals.

Because each of the three main proximate causes of ethnic war is to some degree a cause of the others, there is no single path to war which all ethnic conflicts follow; rather, two different patterns are possible. One is the *mass-led* pattern, which begins with mass hostility. In these cases, hostile masses choose belligerent leaders and engage in actions which provoke a security dilemma; the escalating spiral of hostility and insecurity eventually results in war. The other pattern is *elite-led*; it begins with belligerent leaders who come to power when mass hostility is low. The leaders use the power of government and their influence over the media to encourage the growth of mass hostility and provoke a security dilemma, eventually leading to war. In either case, whether the pattern of escalation is mass-led or elite-led, the necessary preconditions for all three causes—mass hostility, belligerent elites, and a security dilemma—must, theoretically, be present if war is to result.

Foreign patrons may also play an important role in the origins of ethnic wars. Their main effect comes, I argue, through providing the means for extremists to cause war. Specifically, patrons can provide belligerent elites with resources which help them capture the government or create a rival government, and then begin the process of elite-led violence. Patrons can also provide the military means which enable extremist groups—whether mass-led or elite-led—to fight.

An additional distinction—between conflicts initiated by the dominant group and those begun by a subordinate group—helps in clarifying both the crucial factor promoting war in each case, and the most promising alternative for third parties interested in preventing it. Mass-led conflicts initiated by subordinate groups are *mass insurgencies,* driven primarily by intense fears of extinction: efforts at reassurance are the best alternative for third parties trying to prevent such wars. Mass-led conflicts initiated by dominant groups are cases of *popular chauvinism,* driven primarily by mass hostility; deterrence is the best third-party strategy in such cases. Elite-led conflicts initiated by dominant elites, cases of *government jingoism,* are driven by elite outbidding, so the best option for third parties is to offer inducements to the leaders to change their policy. Finally, elite-led conflicts initiated by subordinate groups are cases of *elite conspiracy,* and while also driven by elite outbidding, they are usually dependent on aid from foreign patrons, so they are uniquely vulnerable to strategies aimed at isolating them from outside sources of support.

Moldova's 1991–92 ethnic civil war illustrates the value of this approach for explaining the outbreak of ethnic war, providing examples of mass insurgency, popular chauvinism, and elite conspiracy. On the Moldovan side, the conflict began as a mass insurgency, but it became a case of popular chauvinism after Moldovan nationalists came to power in Moldova. On the side of the Russian-speaking secessionists in the Dniestr region, in contrast, the violence was a case of elite conspiracy, with support from Moscow playing a crucial role. The war in Moldova happened as it did because Moscow deterred mass-led violence on the Moldovan side, but later determined that its strategic interests were best served by supporting instead of preventing the Dniestrian elites' secessionism. Moscow therefore helped the Dniestrian elites to start the war, and then win it.

My argument begins, in the next section of this article, with a more detailed discussion of the causes of ethnic war, showing how the same three factors can cause either mass-led or elite-led violence. The following section examines the Moldovan case, outlining the preconditions that made war possible, and showing how the violence was mass-led on the ethnic Moldovan side, but elite-led on the Dniestrian side, with Moscow playing a crucial role in supporting the Dniestrian side. The concluding section shows how third parties can sometimes help avert ethnic wars, and why they sometimes cannot.

Spiraling to Ethnic War

Ethnic wars, which combine processes from both international relations and comparative politics, can be better understood if ideas from both theoretical traditions are combined. Four theoretical approaches are particularly relevant: the mobilization school of thought about internal violence, the competing "fear of extinction" theory of ethnic violence, the diversionary theory of war, and the "spiral model" of international conflict.[3] Combined, these approaches yield the argument that ethnic wars are driven by three mutually reinforcing factors: mass ethnic hostility, outbidding by belligerent elites, and a security dilemma between groups.

The basic logic is as follows: People do not engage in ethnic violence unless they are hostile, that is, unless they actively want to harm each other, and they cannot engage in large-scale organized violence—i.e., war—unless extremist elites mobilize the group for the fight. Elites mobilize their followers for violence by engaging in outbidding, competing with each other to formulate more and more extreme demands against other ethnic groups.[4] If outbidding goes far enough, its result is to make the policy goal of each group approximate the worst fears of the other.

Each group's fear of extinction may then become justified, because its existence as a community may really be threatened by the goals of the other. If this point is reached, each group is driven to increasingly extreme measures— especially the creation and use of armed forces—to protect itself and coerce other groups. The result is a security dilemma, a situation in which efforts by one side to make itself more secure have the effect of making the other side less secure.[5] It is the interaction of the three processes—ethnic outbidding

---

3. The most sophisticated mobilization theory of political violence is Charles Tilly, *From Mobilization to Revolution* (Reading, Mass.: Addison-Wesley, 1978). The competing theory is from Horowitz, *Ethnic Groups in Conflict*. On diversionary theories of war, see Jack S. Levy, "The Diversionary Theory of War: A Critique," in Manus I. Midlarsky, ed., *Handbook of War Studies* (Boston: Unwin Hyman, 1989). The classic exposition of the spiral model is Robert Jervis, *Perception and Misperception in International Politics* (New York: Columbia University Press, 1976).
4. This process is described and defined in Alvin Rabushka and Kenneth Shepsle, *Politics in Plural Societies* (Columbus, Ohio: Charles E. Merrill, 1972).
5. Posen, "The Security Dilemma and Ethnic Conflict."

leading to a security dilemma, the security dilemma encouraging ethnic out-bidding, and both dynamics promoting and promoted by ethnic hostility and fear—that drive ethnonationalist movements to war.

Ethnic hostility intense enough to cause violence requires both a grievance—a calculated judgment of injustice—*and* the emotional heat from hate and fear which provides the impulse for action and overrides countervailing considerations.[6] Contrary to the claims of rational choice theorists, rational grievances alone, while necessary, are not sufficient to motivate ethnic war. Indeed, at least as far back as Clausewitz, theorists of war have understood that hostile feelings are essential ingredients in motivating war among nations.[7] For ethnic civil wars, Donald Horowitz has shown that the emotional heat comes from a fear of group extinction, which is usually "anxiety-laden," or exaggerated by emotion.[8] This fear turns stereotypes into antipathies, making people feel hostile enough to risk their skins in battle, wreck their economic infrastructure, and put aside basic humanitarian values, all in the name of "self-defense."

The security dilemma in ethnic conflict differs from that in international relations theory: in Jack Snyder's terminology, it is closer to a "perceptual security dilemma" than to a "structural security dilemma."[9] It can be defined as a situation in which each side construes its security needs in a way which makes the other group fear that it is threatened with extinction. Structural conditions do matter in creating an ethnic security dilemma: there must, among other things, be a *de facto* situation of anarchy. But the neorealist concept of a security dilemma cannot be mechanically applied to ethnic conflict: anarchy and the *possibility* of a security threat are not enough to create a security dilemma between communities which may have been at peace for decades. An ethnic security dilemma requires reciprocal fears of group extinction, and such fears do not arise unless hostile masses define their security in extreme ways, or unless outbidding elites emerge to make the pursuit of such goals into policy.

NECESSARY PRECONDITIONS FOR ETHNIC WAR

Mass hostility, outbidding by belligerent elites, and a security dilemma are the main causes of ethnic war. But in theory they only arise when all of the

---

6. Carol Tavris, *Anger: The Misunderstood Emotion*, rev. ed. (New York: Simon and Schuster, 1989), p. 91.
7. Carl von Clausewitz, *On War*, ed. and trans. by Michael Howard and Peter Paret (Princeton, N.J.: Princeton University Press, 1976 [1832]), pp. 137–138 and *passim*.
8. Horowitz, *Ethnic Groups in Conflict*.
9. Jack L. Snyder, "Perceptions of the Security Dilemma in 1914," in Robert Jervis, Richard Ned Lebow, and Janice Gross Stein, eds. *Psychology and Deterrence* (Baltimore, Md.: Johns Hopkins University Press, 1985).

necessary preconditions—ethnically defined grievances, demographic threats, negative ethnic stereotypes, a history of ethnic domination, ethnic symbols, a reciprocal fear of group extinction, a *de facto* situation of anarchy, the military means to fight, and the political space for ethnic outbidding—are present.

NECESSARY PRECONDITIONS FOR MASS HOSTILITY. Mass hostility requires reasons for both rational dissatisfaction and emotional heat. The rational grievances always include some degree of economic pain: people who are economically satisfied are hard to mobilize politically, especially for movements which may harm the economy. If the grievances are to contribute to ethnic conflict, they must also be ethnically defined—that is, they must be grievances against another ethnic group.

The emotional charge that drives ethnic hostility comes from a fear of ethnic extinction. The necessary conditions for such fear are negative group stereotypes, threatened ethnic symbols, a threatening demographic situation, and a history of ethnic domination. The stereotypes are necessary to incline the people to be hostile to the stereotyped group. Symbols, such as flags, are needed because they provide an emotional connection between immediate issues and the fundamental questions of survival that motivate ethnic conflict.[10] Threatening demographic trends, such as minority status or a decline in population share, are necessary to provide the tangible evidence that a group may be headed toward extinction.

A history of ethnic domination, finally, makes the hypothetical threat of extinction both plausible and frightening, and it identifies a specific other group as the source of the threat.[11] The more a group's historians and journalists emphasize the group's past victimization, the more credible are the emotional charges of genocide which arouse gut-level fears, and the more appealing are hate-filled cries for vengeance.[12] If one side was dominator but not dominated, the history can be used to justify a fear of revenge by the other group.

NECESSARY PRECONDITIONS FOR A SECURITY DILEMMA. An ethnic security dilemma can only arise in a situation of *de facto* anarchy, in which the state is either unwilling or unable to protect all major groups, forcing groups to resort to self-help.

---

10. Donald Horowitz, "Making Moderation Pay: The Comparative Politics of Ethnic Conflict Management," in Joseph V. Montville, ed., *Conflict and Peacemaking in Multiethnic Societies* (Lexington, Mass.: Lexington Books, 1990).

11. Horowitz, "Making Moderation Pay."

12. Stephen Van Evera, "Hypotheses on Nationalism and War," *International Security,* Vol. 18, No. 4 (Spring 1994), pp. 5–39.

An ethnic security dilemma further requires that each side perceive the other side's efforts to avert extinction as threatening it with extinction. This requires that both sides see demographic conditions as potentially threatening. Most commonly—though not in all cases—such perceptions result from an "ethnic affinity problem," a situation in which the minority in some area is the majority in the broader region.[13] For example, Jews are a majority in Israel but a threatened minority in the broader Middle East region, while Palestinians are a threatened minority in Israel. The effect of such a situation is that both groups, by viewing borders differently, can think of themselves as potential minorities in danger of ethnic extinction. Both sides are then likely to see extreme measures—highly threatening to the other group—as necessary for their own survival.

A final requirement for an ethnic security dilemma, obvious but crucial, is the availability on both sides of the means to mobilize and fight. This requires arms, the resources to build an organization, and a territorial base. If a group lacks a territorial base, it cannot build a military organization and threaten the other group, so a security dilemma spiral cannot take off.

NECESSARY PRECONDITIONS FOR OUTBIDDING BY BELLIGERENT ELITES. Ethnic outbidding by elites is possible only if groups have enough political space to mobilize around ethnic issues: severe repression can prevent mobilization. To be effective, extremist appeals must also fall on willing ears, so outbidding can only work when the preconditions for mass hostility also exist.

These, then, are the necessary preconditions for ethnic war: ethnically defined grievances, negative stereotypes, demographic threats, histories of ethnic domination, emotion-laden ethnic symbols, reciprocal fears of group extinction, *de facto* political anarchy, and the political space and military means to act. Horowitz argues that the first six are present in every case of severe ethnic violence.[14] All of these factors appeared in recent cases of ethnic war, including Rwanda, the former Yugoslavia, Sri Lanka, Georgia, Azerbaijan, and Moldova.[15]

---

13. Horowitz, "Making Moderation Pay."
14. Horowitz, "Making Moderation Pay."
15. I show the presence of these factors in Yugoslavia and Azerbaijan in Stuart J. Kaufman, "An 'International' Theory of Interethnic War," *Review of International Studies*, Vol. 22, No. 2 (April 1996), pp. 149–171. On Georgia, see Stephen S. Jones, "Populism in Georgia: the Gamsakhurdia Phenomenon," in Donald Schwartz and Razmik Panossian, eds., *Nationalism and History: The Politics of Nation Building in Post-Soviet Armenia, Azerbaijan and Georgia* (Toronto: University of Toronto Press, 1994), pp. 127–149. On Sri Lanka, see K.M. de Silva, *Managing Ethnic Tensions in Multi-Ethnic Societies: Sri Lanka 1880–1985* (Lanham, Md.: University Press of America, 1986).

While these preconditions are all necessary for the outbreak of ethnic war, they are not sufficient. They lead to ethnic war only if there is some degree of mass hostility, or if elites begin engaging in outbidding. If the preconditions for hostility are merely dormant categories—if few people are actively concerned about demographic trends, and stereotypes do not lead to political blame, and so on—then war can be averted if elites cooperate to create new institutions, ending the situation of anarchy. If mass hostility is present, however, the result is *mass-led violence*; if it is not but elites choose to engage in outbidding, the result is *elite-led violence.*

THE MASS-LED VIOLENCE PATTERN

The mass-led pattern of ethnic war can only occur when mass hostility and all of its preconditions are present from the start, to the degree that at least one side feels a fear of ethnic extinction. In these conditions, only the coercive force of the state keeps ethnic conflict under control. When that force is removed, creating the political space for ethnic groups to mobilize, the conflict begins to escalate as people begin articulating their hostility and grievances. Mass ethnonationalist movements can spring into being almost overnight in such conditions. Intra-ethnic politics becomes a competition in ethnic outbidding, with elites forced to establish their ethnic *bona fides* and elicit support by promoting increasingly extreme goals,[16] most commonly, the subordination of other ethnic groups to their own.

These policies of ethnic domination are of course threatening to other groups, who may turn to their own extremist leaders in self-defense. The result, if the hostility is intense enough, is a spiral of ethnic extremism leading to war. The exact path to war varies, depending on whether the group initiating the violence is the dominant or the subordinate group. Combining this distinction with the mass-led/elite-led distinction results in a four-way typology which helps in defining which of the three causes of ethnic war is most important in each case (and, as will be shown below, the most promising policy alternatives for third parties who might want to act to prevent war). The typology, summarized in Table 1, identifies the following paths to war.

MASS INSURGENCY. If the initiator of mass-led violence is a subordinate group, the process is one of *mass insurgency*. In such cases the security dilemma, and the fears of ethnic extinction driving it, are particularly severe. The

---

16. This process is noted in Horowitz, "Making Moderation Pay"; and Rabushka and Shepsle, *Politics in Plural Societies,* among others.

Table 1. Paths to Ethnic War.

		Initiated by Dominants	Initiated by Subordinates
Mass-led	Process:	Popular Chauvinism	Mass Insurgency
pattern	Example:	Georgia	Nagorno-Karabakh
	Driving Force:	Mass Hostility	Insecurity
	Policy to Avert War:	Deterrence	Reassurance
Elite-led	Process:	Government Jingoism	Elite Conspiracy
Pattern	Example:	Serbia	Croatian Krajina
	Driving Force:	Elite Outbidding	External Aid
	Policy to Avert War:	Inducement	Isolation

Nagorno-Karabakh conflict illustrates this point: the Armenians of Karabakh remembered the 1915 genocide against them and feared extinction, so as soon as Gorbachev's policy of *glasnost* opened up the necessary political space in 1987, they began agitating for annexation of their region by Armenia. The Azerbaijanis, fearful of an Armenian-Russian combination aimed at dismembering their republic, resisted. The result was an explosion of mass-led violence that propelled nationalists to power on both sides.[17]

POPULAR CHAUVINISM. Where the dominant majority is the initiator of mass-led violence, I label the process *popular chauvinism*. In these cases, the main impulse for mobilization comes from mass hostility, necessarily aimed—since the group is already in charge—at repression of subordinate minorities. Fear plays a role—the repression is typically defended as necessary for group self-defense—but the real problem is that group interests are defined as requiring domination of others. An example is Soviet Georgia, which rewarded outbidding by Zviad Gamsakhurdia by electing him president in 1990 on a national chauvinist platform. Gamsakhurdia revoked the cultural and political autonomy of the minority Abkhaz, exacerbating their fears of ethnic extinction and causing a security dilemma spiral which led to all-out war in Abkazia in 1992.[18]

THE ELITE-LED VIOLENCE PATTERN
In cases of elite-led violence, extremist elites come to power when ethnic tensions are low, then turn the preconditions for mass hostility into active

17. For more detail, see Kaufman, "An 'International' Theory of Interethnic War."
18. Jones, "Populism in Georgia."

hostility. For example, using the propaganda resources of modern political organizations and mass media, leaders can amplify weakly held stereotypes and redefine unremarkable demographic trends as mortal threats to group survival. They can also use their power to control negotiations to provoke new conflicts with historic adversaries, and then block any potential compromise. Blaming the stalemate on the other group allows them to discredit alternative elites who promote moderate programs. Eventually, the extremists organize militias or armies to launch violent provocations. If the other side responds in kind, a security dilemma spiral takes off, continuously fed by violent propaganda.

One common motive for such elite behavior is ideology: certain elites may simply be zealots for their ethno-nationalist cause, and believe that pursuing extreme goals is justifiable regardless of risks and costs. Another motive is pursuit of personal power: promoting conflict with another group can simultaneously justify an extremist program which is predicated on a threat from rival groups, and create a "rally 'round the flag" effect which justifies the centralization of power in the hands of the extremist leadership in the name of the emergency of conflict.[19]

Elite-led conflicts, like mass-led ones, can be distinguished by whether they are initiated by the dominant group or the subordinate group.

GOVERNMENT JINGOISM. When the leaders who provoke violence are from the dominant group, I label the process of conflict escalation *government jingoism*. In these cases, elite outbidding is the major cause of war: the leaders create ethnic hostility and a security dilemma. Serbian leader Slobodan Milošević's political offensive against Serbia's Albanian minority is a recent example of a leader following such a policy. Milošević reawakened and stoked Serbs' ethnic hostility with deft demagoguery, media control, and political organization, creating the security dilemma spiral which later consumed much of Yugoslavia. Typical for such cases, Milošević's motivation was to forestall threats to his leadership position.[20]

ELITE CONSPIRACY. Where elite-led violence is provoked by leaders of a subordinate group, the process is one of *elite conspiracy*. In these cases, subordinate-group leaders create rival governments aimed at seceding from or taking

19. See Michael E. Brown, "The Causes and Regional Dimensions of Internal Conflict," in Michael E. Brown, ed., *The International Dimensions of Internal Conflict* (Cambridge, Mass.: MIT Press, 1996), p. 586.
20. See V.P. Gagnon, "Ethnic Nationalism and International Conflict: The Case of Serbia," *International Security*, Vol. 19, No. 3 (Winter 1994/95), pp. 130–166.

over the state. They use chauvinist propaganda to increase ethnic hostility, pursue extremist goals which provoke hostility from the other side, and provoke or organize violence in order to create a security dilemma. In these cases, too, ethnic hostility and the security dilemma are the result of elite policy, rather than the cause of it. The Serbian secessionist leaders in Croatia's Krajina region, organized and armed by Serbia, and successful in starting a war in spite of their early unpopularity, are examples of elite conspirators.[21]

FOREIGN PATRONS AS ENABLERS

The parties to ethnic civil wars are, by definition, groups within a state. Examination of the actions of those groups must therefore take center stage in a consideration of the causes of ethnic war. Nevertheless, foreign patrons frequently intervene in ethnic wars, and in some cases play a crucial role in causing the outbreak of war by providing the means to enable ethnic groups to fight. Patrons are most important in cases of elite conspiracy, in which a small group of elites from a subordinate ethnic group triggers violence. Since elite conspirators do not, by definition, begin with strong support from their own group (if they did, they would be leaders of a mass insurgency), foreign help is likely to be crucial in enabling them to provoke the conflict they desire.

Foreign patrons can be almost equally important in spurring conflicts along the other paths to ethnic war. Mass insurgencies may be able to mobilize people, but without military aid from abroad they are likely to be crushed militarily should they try to begin a war. In cases of popular chauvinism, foreign support might encourage governments to initiate a crackdown on minorities which they would otherwise have avoided. For government jingoists, finally, external patronage may be critical in helping them come to power. The rise to power of Croatia's jingoists under Franjo Tudjman, for example, was fueled not only by a backlash against Serbia, but by emigré Croats who gave Tudjman's party large sums of money, buying for him an enormous public relations advantage which helped him win Croatia's 1990 election.[22]

In all of these cases, the key role of foreign patrons is to help those groups who are inclined to fight get the means to do so. If the internal conditions for ethnic war are not present, foreign patrons can do little harm.

---

21. Stuart J. Kaufman, "The Irresistible Force and the Imperceptible Object: The Yugoslav Breakup and Western Policy," *Security Studies*, Vol. 4, No. 2 (Winter 1994/95), pp. 281–329. In this case, there was also some popular chauvinism on the Croatian side.
22. Kaufman, "The Irresistible Force and the Imperceptible Object."

Moldova's Ethnic War Spiral

Moldova's path to civil war illustrates and supports many of the points made above. Moldova provides an example of mass-led ethnic mobilization by an emerging dominant majority (on the Moldovan side) leading to the brink of ethnic war, and a successful effort at deterrence (by the Soviet government) which helped prevent the outbreak of war. It also provides an example of elite-led mobilization by a subordinate minority (on the Dniestrian side), and shows how later external intervention (from Moscow) contributed to the outbreak of war. Both examples illustrate how mass hostility, elite outbidding, and the security dilemma reinforce each other in the buildup to war.

THE COMPETING GROUPS

The conflict between the former Soviet republic of Moldova and its separatists on the left bank of the Dniestr river is largely an ethnic conflict. The ethnic lines are not neatly drawn: most of Moldova's ethnic Russians live outside the separatist Dniestr region, while the Dniestr region's ethnic mix before the war was over 40 percent Moldovan, 28 percent Ukrainian, and only 25 percent Russian. But in the Dniestrian region, and only there, the dominant sector of the population was the group, including Russified Moldovans and Ukrainians as well as Russians, which considered Russian its language and the Soviet Union its country. When ethnic Moldovans began demanding linguistic and other policies favorable to themselves in the 1980s, these "Russophones" united in opposition. Those in the Dniestr region used their territorial base to pursue secessionism; those outside that base found they had to defend their interests in other ways.

The Dniestrian Russophones are not, then, an ethnic group; they are a coalition of ethnic interests united in opposition to certain ethnic Moldovan interests. But this does not mean that the conflict is not an ethnic conflict. As Crawford Young has shown, ethnic identity is frequently made and remade in the crucible of ethnic conflict, and different identities are salient at different times. Conflict may therefore result in the activation of identities which hardly mattered before, and the appearance of catchall "groups" opposing more cohesive groups is not uncommon.[23] In this case, even the Moldovan identity was in flux during the conflict: some Moldovans considered themselves Romanians, while others—most, as it turned out—considered themselves a distinct

---

23. Young, *The Politics of Cultural Pluralism.*

nationality. The fact that both sides' group identities were redefined in the course of the conflict makes Moldova not an exceptional, but a typical case.

PRECONDITIONS FOR ETHNIC WAR IN MOLDOVA

The contemporary Republic of Moldova consists of two main parts. The larger region, Bessarabia, is a predominantly Romanian-speaking[24] region which was annexed by Russia in 1812, united with Romania in 1918, and reannexed by Stalin in 1940. The smaller portion, the region across the Dniestr River from Bessarabia, was never part of Romania, except for a brief military occupation in 1941–44. From 1924 to 1940, this Dniestr region formed the core of an autonomous area in Ukraine called the "Moldavian Autonomous Soviet Socialist Republic."[25]

Stalin's decision to unite these two regions into modern Moldova was the source of an ethnic affinity problem for both the Moldovans and the Dniestrians. The Moldovans viewed themselves as the local majority in Moldova, but a minority in the Russian-dominated Soviet Union. Furthermore, their future as a people was threatened by Soviet policies of Russification. Once Moldova began moving toward independence in the late 1980s, on the other hand, the Russophones of the Dniestr region saw themselves—previously part of the Soviet Russian majority—as a potentially threatened minority, especially if, as was openly discussed at the time, Moldova were eventually to unite with Romania.

To make matters worse, each group had a history of domination by the other. Moldovans had been ruled by Russians for a century and a half, in 1812–1918, 1940–1941, and 1944–1991. The Russophones, for their part, remembered that in World War II, Romania, then influenced if not dominated by the fascist Iron Guard, had allied itself with Nazi Germany, and it had treated Russians— especially Communists—with great brutality in 1941–44 when its troops occupied Soviet Moldavia, including the Dniestr region. Thus the Moldovans' history justified fear of domination by imperialist Russians, while the Russians' view of history justified fear of national chauvinist Romanians.

Soviet policy toward Moldova after the 1940 annexation also created contentious ethnic symbols and grievances. In order to justify the annexation of

---

24. The "Romanian" and "Moldovan" languages are identical. The choice of one or the other term depends on one's political preferences rather than any linguistic criterion. See Charles King, "Moldovan Identity and the Politics of Pan-Romanianism," *Slavic Review*, Vol. 53, No. 2 (Summer 1994), pp. 345–368.
25. King, "Moldovan Identity and the Politics of Pan-Romanianism," pp. 347–348.

Bessarabia, Stalin had decreed that the Romanian-speaking peasants in Soviet Moldova were "Moldovans," linguistically and historically different from the Romanian peasants on the other side of the Prut River. The key alleged difference was that the Moldovan language was Slavicized, using the Cyrillic alphabet (which was duly imposed) and including a large number of Russian loan words (which were also imposed).[26] Expressions of Romanian culture were banned, and Moldova's history was rewritten to deny any legitimate connection to Romania and to exaggerate the region's ties to Russia. Over the succeeding decades, Moscow brought large numbers of Russian and Ukrainian administrators and industrial workers into Moldova to run the new factories and to ensure Soviet control in the region.[27]

This history set the stage for disputes over ethnic symbols. On the Moldovan side, the central issue was language, and culture more generally. The Cyrillic alphabet symbolized the imposition of Russian rule and cultural Russification. Worse, it was not possible to use the Moldovan language very much, even with the Cyrillic script: most public and official purposes required Russian. In addition, Soviet Moldova's flag was dominated by the Soviet hammer and sickle in a field of red, while Moldovans preferred the tricolor flown by Romania.

These problems were exacerbated by economic grievances: ethnic Moldovans were underrepresented in many of the more desirable professional, managerial, and industrial production jobs, while they dominated the poorer agricultural sector. This situation began improving by the 1970s, but the economic hardships of the 1980s slowed further progress for ethnic Moldovans. Thus economic facts gave the Moldovans simultaneously a symbolic grievance ("the Russians get all the good jobs"), a political grievance ("we don't have the power to run our own lives"), and an economic grievance ("my job prospects, and my children's, are not good").

The problem was that any attempt to address these grievances would seem threatening to Russophones: imposing the priority of the Moldovan language and the Romanian tricolor flag (which had been flown by Romania in World War II) seemed to foreshadow a renewal of the chauvinist policies of fascist Iron Guard Romania, and giving better jobs to Moldovans meant taking them

---

26. Nicholas Dima, *From Moldavia to Moldova* (New York: Columbia University Press, 1991), pp. 94–98.
27. William Crowther, "The Politics of Mobilization: Nationalism and Reform in Soviet Moldavia," *Russian Review*, Vol. 50, No. 2 (April 1991), pp. 186–187; and Jonathan Eyal, "Moldavians," in Graham Smith, ed., *The Nationalities Question in the Soviet Union* (New York: Longman, 1990), p. 127.

from Russophones. These symbolic and economic issues exacerbated powerful, emotionally charged group stereotypes held by both groups: Moldovans labelled Russians and Ukrainians as interlopers or Communists, while Russians saw echoes of 1940s-style fascism in every manifestation of pro-Romanian nationalism.

Thus by the mid-1980s, all of the preconditions for mass hostility—rational grievances, negative stereotypes, disputes over emotional symbols, demographic fears, and a history of domination—were present in Moldova.

The political space which allowed these accumulated disputes to be expressed was provided by Mikhail Gorbachev's policy of *glasnost*, beginning in 1987. Though it was intended to encourage popular support for Gorbachev's economic reform plans, *glasnost* did far more to create opportunities for democratization and nationalist mobilization: the economic reforms were not popular, while democracy and nationalism were. With the preconditions for mass hostility already in place in Moldova, it would take little for outbidding appeals to resonate.

The failure of Gorbachev's reforms eventually weakened the Soviet state so much that by 1990 it lost control over ethnic conflicts in non-Russian areas. This weakness created a *de facto* condition of anarchy, with Soviet troops acting more like third-party interventionists than like police. Once the disintegrating Soviet army gave nationalist groups access to weapons, all of the preconditions for ethnic security dilemmas were in place.

MASS-LED MOBILIZATION ON THE MOLDOVAN SIDE

The initial ethnic mobilization in Moldova was a classic example of mass insurgency—it was a bottom-up movement, not one manufactured by government leaders, and it involved a subordinate group, the Soviet Union's Moldovan minority. It began in 1987 and 1988, when Moldovan intellectuals taking advantage of *glasnost* formed informal nationalist discussion groups, which quickly mushroomed into a massive Moldovan Popular Front. Feeding this growth was the personal experience of linguistic discrimination felt by most Moldovans: Moldovan students, for example, often could get an education only in Russian; would-be managers found their career paths blocked by Russophones; and intellectuals found the Moldovan language "degraded."[28]

---

28. On the situation in education, see Kathleen Mihalisko, "*Komsomolskaia Pravda* Defends Special Historical Issue of Moldavian Student Newspaper," *Radio Liberty Research Bulletin*, RL 182/88 (April 27, 1988), pp. 1–3; on workers' complaints, see *Current Digest of the Soviet Press* (hereafter *CDSP*, Vol. 41, No. 16 (May 17, 1989), pp. 6–8; on the state of the language, see *CDSP*, Vol. 41, No. 27 (August 2, 1989), pp. 9–10.

Nationalist organizations, therefore, did not need massive propaganda efforts to gather support. Indeed, they could not mount any: until nationalist leaders came to power in late 1989, Moldova's Communist leadership and most of the official media outspokenly opposed the Moldovan nationalist movement.[29] The nationalists had access to only a few publications at first.

Nevertheless, by August of 1989 the Popular Front managed to mobilize a crowd of between 300,000 and 500,000 (about 10 percent of the population of Moldova) at a "National Assembly" to demand that Moldovan be made the state language of Moldova.[30] Already feeling the pressure of smaller rallies, the previously rubber-stamp Moldovan parliament had a month earlier elected as its chairman Mircea Snegur, a member of Moldova's Politburo newly reborn as a moderate Moldovan nationalist. In September 1989, the parliament passed a pair of laws establishing Moldovan as the state language and broadening its functions.

This bottom-up pressure, expressed in continuing rallies throughout the fall of 1989—including a bloody clash with police in November—forced Moldovan elites to engage in nationalist outbidding. First, the anti-nationalist Communist Party chief, Simeon Grossu, was replaced by a moderate nationalist, Petru Lucinschi. Then, in May of 1990, Snegur and Lucinschi were outflanked and forced to accept the appointment of the extreme nationalist Mircea Druc, a Popular Front leader, as premier. Changes in the nationalist agenda, and the initial episodes of violence, followed the same bottom-up pattern. Leaders of the nationalist movement were originally aiming for moderate reform, and their early rallies reflected that moderation. Later in 1989, however, while Popular Front leaders' rhetoric generally remained moderate, their followers were displaying banners telling the local Russians, "Suitcase—Train Station—Home."[31]

Moldova's mass-led nationalist hysteria reached a peak around April 1990, when Parliament voted to replace Moldova's Soviet-style flag. There were nationalist protesters outside the parliament building throughout the days of debate on the issue, and some members of Parliament were reportedly intimidated into supporting nationalist positions.[32] Some Russophone members who

29. See, e.g., the leadership's official call to "rebuff nationalists" in *Sovetskaia Moldavia* (Kishinev), July 16, 1989, p. 1. For the general attitude of the media, compare *CDSP*, Vol. 41, No. 7 (March 15, 1989), with *CDSP*, Vol. 41, No. 46 (December 13, 1989), pp. 21–22.
30. Vladimir Socor, "Politics of the Language Question Heating Up in Soviet Moldavia," *RFE/RL Report on the USSR*, Vol. 1, No. 46 (September 8, 1989), p. 35.
31. Crowther, "Politics of Mobilization," pp. 192–196.
32. Vladimir Rylyakov, former Member of Moldovan Parliament, March 1995 interview, Tiraspol.

resisted were beaten by the crowd. Caving in to the pressure, the parliament accepted the Popular Front's demand that the Romanian tricolor be adopted as Moldova's new state flag. Not until after the flag law was passed, and a Russian student was beaten to death in May of 1990, did Snegur enforce calm on the streets.[33]

The driving force of this violence was a perceived security dilemma driven by a fear of ethnic extinction. As one Popular Front leader put it early on, "either we return to the Latin script and get [Moldovan designated] the state language, or else we shall disappear as a language and a nationality."[34] This concern was explicitly noted in the text of the September 1989 language laws. What drove nationalist extremists to violence was the resistance, first by the conservative government, and later by Russophones, to those measures (especially the language law) the nationalists considered necessary for their group's survival.

By the spring of 1990, the Soviet Union was in an advanced state of decline—Moldova had achieved *de facto* sovereignty in many respects—and Moldovan nationalists were firmly in charge in Moldova's capital, Chisinau. It is therefore useful to think about the Moldovan nationalist movement at this stage as a case of popular chauvinism by a local majority. While Popular Front leaders were influential in harnessing popular passions, the dominant fact of Moldovan politics was that hundreds of thousands were willing to turn out for "national assemblies."

While feelings were running high, however, ethnic hostility was relatively low: nationalists were more interested in forwarding their own interests than in repressing Russians. Indeed, few in Moldova showed the kind of white-hot ethnic hatred which fuels ethnic war.[35] Leaders, therefore, had a chance to prevent war, if they could refrain from engaging in outbidding and find a way to manage the inter-ethnic security dilemma.

Moderate Moldovan leaders did try to manage the conflict, but their efforts were ineffectual. Compromises in the 1989 language law, for example, satisfied no one, and the benefits from a "round table" discussion among all political

33. *CDSP,* Vol. 42, No. 21 (June 27, 1990), pp. 14–16.
34. Socor, "The Moldavian Democratic Movement: Structure, Program, and Initial Impact," *RFE/RL Report on the USSR,* Vol. 1, No. 8, (February 24, 1989), pp. 31–32.
35. Some evidence of tolerance among Moldovans, as measured in mass opinion surveys, is in Stuart Kaufman, Leokadia Drobizheva, and Airat Aklaev, "Nationalist Mobilization in Estonia and Moldova," paper prepared for American Political Science Association meeting, New York, September 1994.

groups in the spring of 1990[36] were immediately squandered in the parliamentary debate on changing Moldova's flag, when deputies from the Dniestr region were excluded from the discussion and beaten by mobs.[37] Most damaging of all, Snegur refused to consider offering any political autonomy to the Dniestrians, relying instead on coercive threats to suppress their move toward autonomy—threats he lacked the capability to carry out.[38] The reason for this policy was apparently simple stubbornness or failure of vision: as Valeriu Muravschi, premier during the 1991–92 fighting, explained, "We were not ready, on the moral-psychological plane, to recognize some kind of administrative territory [in the Dniestr region]."[39] The effect was to make violence even more likely, foreclosing compromise and exacerbating the security dilemma.

Nevertheless, the violence in this period was primarily the responsibility of Popular Front extremists. In October 1990, as the Gagauz minority in southern Moldova were preparing (illegally) to vote on an autonomy referendum for their self-declared Gagauz region, Popular Front leaders called for volunteers to stop the vote. Premier Mircea Druc—himself a Popular Front radical—agreed under pressure to legalize the volunteer detachments. Blocked by Soviet armed forces, the volunteers turned north to the Dniestr region instead, fighting a brief battle against Dniestrian volunteers in Bendery on November 2. On the same day, Interior Ministry troops acting on the authority of Druc and Interior Minister Costas—another Popular Front radical—clashed with better-armed Dniestrian volunteers in Dubossary, leaving about six dead.[40] These decisions seem to have resulted from a combination of incompetence and malice: Costas was perceived even by his colleagues as "too anti-Russian," while aides viewed Druc as "inexperienced" and "emotional."[41]

ELITE-LED VIOLENCE IN THE DNIESTR REGION

On the Dniestrian as on the Moldovan side, the preconditions for mass hostility and elite outbidding were all present by 1989. On the Dniestrian side, however, mobilization followed the pattern of elite conspiracy. Instead of a security dilemma leading to ethnic outbidding by elites, as happened on the Moldovan

---

36. See *Sovetskaia Moldavia*, April 11, 1990, p. 1; and ibid., April 18, 1990, p. 2.
37. *Dnestrovskaia Pravda* (Tiraspol), May 4, 1990, p. 3.
38. *Sovetskaia Moldavia*, September 4, 1990, p. 1.
39. Valeriu Muravschi, March 1995 interview, Chisinau.
40. *Sovetskaia Moldavia*, November 4, 1990, p. 1.
41. Kostash was described by Nicolae Chirtoaca, former national security aid to President Snegur, and Druc by Viktor Grebenschikov, former aide to Druc, currently aide to President Snegur, March 1995 interviews with Chirtoaca and Grebenschikov, Chisinau.

side, incumbent Russophone leaders in the Dniestr region used ethnic outbidding to exacerbate mass hostility and the security dilemma in order to preserve and increase their own power.

The first major issue for the Russophones, as for the Moldovans, was the language law. Under that law, Moldovan was made the sole state language, raising its symbolic status above that of Russian.[42] Moldovan was also to be the main business language. Finally—and most significantly for future developments—all political leaders, economic managers, service workers, and some others would, within five years, have to be bilingual.

Significantly, however, there was a provision that local governments could, if they gained the approval of the Council of Ministers, make Russian the language of government and industry in their localities. The cities of the Dniestr region therefore had an alternative to confrontation: if city councils had requested the exemption, and Chisinau had agreed, Russophone workers would have been relieved of the most onerous burdens of the language law. Only officials and managers would have been required to know Moldovan. Of course, the symbolic subordination of the Russian language was galling, but such subordination did not lead to separatist violence anywhere else in the collapsing Soviet Union. It might not have done so in the Dniestr either.

Separatist violence occurred because Russophone elites had much to gain, especially increased power and career opportunities for themselves, by promoting it. They also had much to lose—their jobs, their influence, and their perquisites—if they submitted to the language law. Dniestrian elites therefore chose to challenge the authority of the Moldovan government: within weeks, city councils in the Dniestr region had voted to defy the language law, and Tiraspol, the future Dniestrian capital, formally invited the others to join it in moving toward secession.

While Dniestrian politicians were voting to defy the language law, strikes in protest of that law broke out in Russian-manned factories throughout Moldova. The strikers were mostly industrial workers in the Dniestr region, people who could most easily have escaped the burdens of the law by requesting exemption. That they struck instead was due less to their own interests than to elite pressure: the strike committees were dominated by the workers' *de facto* bosses, including factories' Communist Party heads and deputy factory directors.[43] In

---

42. *Dnestrovskaia Pravda*, September 7, 1989, p. 2.
43. *Sovetskaia Moldavia*, August 25, 1989, p. 3.

some places, presumably where workers did not take the hint, managers reportedly resorted to a lockout to initiate the "strike."[44]

As the conflict escalated, the Dniestrian elites used a number of tactics to build a separatist coalition. First, they used their control over the local media to stir up hostility and fear against Chisinau. The Tiraspol newspaper, for example, repeatedly alleged that the language law was only the first step in a grander chauvinist Moldovan scheme to reduce Russians to second-class citizenship and deprive them of human rights.[45] Second, Dniestrian elites claimed historical justification: if the rest of Moldova reverted to its pre-1940 status outside the Soviet Union, they argued, then the Dniestr region should have the right to revert to its own pre-1940 status, as an "autonomous republic" in the Soviet Union. Third, they continued orthodox Communist policies, attracting the support of Communist ideologues and industrial managers suspicious of Moldova's economic reformism. Thus the ethno-nationalist conflict in Moldova (Moldovan vs. Soviet or Russian nationalism) was reinforced by a coinciding historical difference (past association with Romania vs. Russia) and an ideological divide (pro-communists vs. anti-communists).

The Dniestrian leadership's main approach to justifying itself, however, was not ideological or historical but military: it stoked violent conflict by provoking a security dilemma between Moldova and Dniestrian Russophones, then cast itself as the Russophones' defender. By openly defying the language law, and quickly thereafter moving toward self-proclaimed autonomy, Dniestrian leaders symbolically threw down the gauntlet in a way calculated to exacerbate the greatest fears of the Moldovan nationalists, that they would not be able to escape from Moscow-backed policies of Russification.

The Dniestrians also invited violence. For example, Dniestrian leaders mobilized volunteer detachments who blocked roads and bridges, provoking fights against Moldovan police forces such as the conflicts in Bendery and Dubosssary on November 2, 1990. The victims of the November violence, in turn, were treated as martyrs in the Tiraspol press to promote even more fear among Dniestrian Russophones and to justify further moves toward violent confrontation in self-defense.[46] The growth of these Dniestrian armed groups, combined with the growing threat of Dniestrian separatism, caused increased feelings of threat on the Moldovan side as well. The result was an escalating

---

44. Socor, "Politics of the Language Question," pp. 33–34; cf. Crowther, "Politics of Mobilization."
45. *Dnestrovskaia Pravda*, September 2, 1989, p. 1; ibid., September 5, 1989, p. 3; ibid., September 23, 1989, p. 3.
46. See, e.g., *Dnestrovskaia Pravda*, September 6, 1991, p. 1.

security dilemma which pushed the Dniestr region to the edge of large-scale violence, and which the Russophone elites used to justify the expansion of their own power.

After the August 1991 coup attempt in Moscow, Dniestrian leader Igor Smirnov turned to another tactic for promoting elite-led violence: he organized a December 1991 presidential election and referendum, proposing an "independent" Dniestr as a part of the Soviet Union but separate from Moldova. The terms of the referendum show that its purpose was not to consult local opinion on the future status of the region, but rather to bolster the Dniestrian leaders' bargaining position. The proposed end state for the Dniestr, "independence" within the Soviet Union, was not only contradictory; it was a mirage unless the major Soviet republics signed a union treaty, which was by then impossible. Promising such a chimera did, however, have the virtue for Dniestrian leaders of creating an appearance of popular "insistence" on independence from Moldova which would obstruct any future compromise with Chisinau.

The announced result of the vote was for Dniestrian "independence" and for Smirnov as president,[47] but it was not a reliable indication of support for Smirnov's war policy. The tally was suspect: the Dniestrian government was already resorting to intimidation and murder to suppress pro-Chisinau activity,[48] and officials recorded how each voter voted.[49] It is likely, therefore, that some voters were intimidated, and that the tally was falsified. These doubts are reinforced if one considers the region's demography: most ethnic Moldovans—comprising over 40 percent of residents in the region—probably favored Chisinau, and many of the 28 percent who were Ukrainians did not support the Dniestrian leadership's policies either.[50] Even those who voluntarily voted for "independence" were influenced by media manipulation: the Tiraspol press was telling voters that the alternative to independence was to submit to a "new inquisition" by Moldovan authorities, and eventually to be swallowed up in an extremely nationalist Romania.[51]

---

47. *CDSP,* Vol. 43, No. 46 (December 18, 1991), p. 12; and *CDSP,* Vol. 43, No. 50 (January 15, 1992), p. 29.
48. Stefan Uratu, Chairman, Tiraspol Heisinki Watch Committee, March 1995 interview, Chisinau.
49. Pal Kolsto and Andrei Edemsky with Natalya Kalashnikova, "The Dniestr Conflict: Between Irredentism and Separatism," *Europe-Asia Studies,* Vol. 45, No. 6 (1993), pp. 985–986.
50. *Foreign Broadcast Information Service Daily Report: USSR* (hereafter *FBIS*), March 18, 1992, p. 55.
51. *Dnestrovskaia Pravda,* September 27, 1991, p. 1; ibid., September 6, 1991, p. 1.

Nevertheless, with his position secured by the vote, Smirnov proceeded in earnest with the pursuit of the Dniestr "republic's" independence. From his standpoint, the "republic" faced a security dilemma: police units loyal to Chisinau controlled some parts of the region, providing bases for the oft-threatened Moldovan attempt to suppress the "republic" by force.[52] In early 1992, therefore, Smirnov launched a campaign of harassment to force out those pro-Chisinau policemen. By April, the fighting had escalated into positional warfare, with Chisinau's forces defending entire villages where they still had a presence, and the Dniestrian forces trying to drive them out. The bloodiest fighting seems to have occurred when Moldovan forces launched counterattacks in Bendery, a Russophone-dominated city just across from Tiraspol on Chisinau's side of the Dniestr River.[53] Elements of the 14th Army, the local Soviet military unit, quietly aided the Dniestrians, helping them win a succession of victories that spring. In a climactic battle for Bendery in June, the 14th Army openly intervened, driving the Moldovan troops out of the city and inflicting heavy losses.[54]

At this point, the Dniestrians had gained most of the territory they wanted— virtually all of their bank of the Dniestr, plus the Bendery area on the other side—and Chisinau saw the futility of further counterattacks against the 14th Army. Both sides therefore agreed to a cease-fire. The estimated casualty totals for the war range around one thousand dead on both sides.[55] After the war, the Dniestrians declared independence, a status recognized by no government but maintained *de facto* with continuing Russian aid.

MOSCOW'S ROLE AS PATRON FOR THE DNIESTR REGION

The Dniestr region had sympathizers in official Moscow from the very start of its conflict with Chisinau. Until the summer of 1990, that sympathy was expressed primarily as a modest pro-Dniestrian bias in Gorbachev's efforts at conflict management in Moldova. But by fall of that year, the interests of the Soviet government, and later of its Russian successor, had shifted toward support for Tiraspol as a way of defending Moscow's own political influence

52. Vladimir Solonari, Member of the Moldovan Parliament, March 1995 interview, Chisinau.
53. Socor, "Moldova's 'Dniester' Ulcer," *RFE/RL Research Report*, Vol. 2, No. 1 (January 1, 1993), p. 14. Cf. Neil V. Lamont, "Territorial Dimensions of Ethnic Conflict: The Moldovan Case, 1991– March 1993," *Journal of Slavic Military Studies*, Vol. 6, No. 4 (December 1993), pp. 576–612.
54. Charles King, "Eurasia Letter: Moldova with a Russian Face," *Foreign Policy*, No. 97 (Winter 1994), p. 111.
55. Charles King, "Moldova and the New Bessarabian Questions," *World Today*, Vol. 49, No. 7 (July 1993), p. 137.

and military bases in the region. As early as the fall of 1990, therefore, every major escalatory action the Dniestrians took was preceded by a clear show of support from Moscow. In many cases, aid from Moscow was what made the Dniestrians' strides toward independence possible.

Moscow's first effective support for the Dniestrians came in September of 1990, when Soviet Interior Ministry troops were dispatched to Tiraspol to protect the "Congress" of Russophone elites that declared the "Dniestr Republic" independent of Moldova within the Soviet Union.[56] The troops' intervention was largely aimed at conflict management—in this case, deterring Chisinau from suppressing the gathering by force, as it had threatened to do. It also had a second goal, however: to pressure Moldova to abandon its bid for independence or else face dismemberment.[57]

Now useful to the Kremlin as a tool, the Dniestrians soon began receiving more substantial help. Probably as early as 1990, the Soviet civil defense organization and DOSAAF, the official Soviet paramilitary organization, started supplying the Dniestrian volunteers with weapons.[58] Meanwhile, the Dniestrians had also secured the sympathy of the 14th Army by resisting Chisinau's anti-military legislation. The 14th Army troops—many of them natives of the Dniestr region—were further encouraged by the Defense Ministry's open tilt toward Tiraspol.[59] Thus by the time the first Moldovan-Dniestrian armed confrontation took place outside Dubossary in November 1990, the Dniestrian Russophones had not only their own armed volunteer formations, but also the expectation of support from Soviet troops.

Unfortunately for all concerned, Gorbachev misplayed his hand at this point. After the Dubossary incident, both Snegur and the Moldovan parliament signalled a willingness to accept Gorbachev's terms: they would consider a Union Treaty if Gorbachev would help end the Dniestrian separatist bid. But unwilling to abandon the Dniestrians, Gorbachev refused.[60] Snegur, in disgust, called for the December 1990 "National Assembly," at which between 500,000 and 800,000 Moldovans demanded independence from the Soviet Union and

---

56. *CDSP*, Vol. 42, No. 35 (October 3, 1990), pp. 27–28; *CDSP*, Vol. 42, No. 43 (November 28, 1990), pp. 5–6.

57. Valeriu Motei, March 1995 interview, Chisinau. Motei was a member of a Moldovan delegation which met with Gorbachev on the issue.

58. Stefan Uratu, March 1995 interview, Chisinau.

59. See *Krasnaia zvezda*, September 8, 1990, p. 5, trans. in *FBIS*, September 12, 1990, p. 98; and *Krasnaia zvezda*, April 5, 1990, trans. in *FBIS*, April 23, 1990, p. 135.

60. *Izvestia*, November 5, 1990, trans. in *CDSP*, Vol. 42, No. 43 (November 28, 1990), p. 7; and *Izvestia*, November 15, 1990, trans. in *CDSP*, Vol. 42, No. 46 (December 19, 1990), p. 24.

rejection of any union treaty. Thereafter, the Moldovan government was committed to that course.

After the December debacle, the Soviet government increased its aid to the Dniestr republic. The Soviet Agro-Industrial Bank helped the Dniestrians to set up their own national bank, enabling Tiraspol to break the Moldovan budget by withholding payments due to Chisinau.[61] Soviet KGB and interior ministry units were ordered to work with their (technically illegal) Dniestrian counterparts,[62] and Moscow turned a blind eye as the extra-legal Cossack movement dispatched paramilitary volunteers to Tiraspol.[63]

After the failed August 1991 coup in Moscow and Moldova's declaration of independence, Russian support became even more overt. Some 14th Army officers began threatening to defend the Dniestrian authorities,[64] while their commander, Major General Gennadii Yakovlev, was apparently taking bribes in exchange for turning over arms to the Dniestr's "Republic Guard."[65] Yakovlev even accepted, briefly, the post of Dniestrian defense minister.[66] Since most of these shows of support occurred before Smirnov's election as Dniestrian president in December 1991, it is probable that they played a role in reassuring Dniestrian voters that Smirnov's confrontational course was safe: they were, after all, under the protection of the 14th Army.

As the Dniestr war heated up in early 1992, the Yeltsin government, earlier divided and indecisive, began openly supporting Tiraspol. Russia quietly renewed its financial aid to Tiraspol by March,[67] and a series of supportive visits by Vice-President Alexander Rutskoi and other top Russian officials hinted at further aid to come.[68] Indeed, while the new 14th Army commander, Major General Netkachev, tried to keep his army neutral, he was supported neither by his superiors nor by his men, so he failed. By April, 14th Army troops were not only arming the Dniestrians but were increasingly fighting on their side, enabling them to win battle after battle.[69]

---

61. TASS, April 26, 1991, reprinted in *FBIS*, April 29, 1991, p. 55.
62. *Izvestia*, June 12, 1992, trans. in *CDSP*, Vol. 44, No. 24 (July 15, 1992), p. 13.
63. See *Izvestia*, March 6, 1992, trans. in *FBIS*, March 11, 1992, p. 55; and *Izvestia*, March 11, 1992, trans. in *FBIS*, March 12, 1992, p. 29.
64. TASS, September 23, 1991, trans. in *FBIS*, September 24, 1991, p. 77.
65. The fact that the 14th Army provided the Dnestrians with weapons was confirmed by Colonel Mikhail Bergman, Tiraspol garrison commandant, 14th Russian Army, March 1995 interview, Tiraspol. Cf. Interfax March 18, 1992, reprinted in *FBIS*, March 19, 1992, p. 72.
66. TASS, September 23, 1991, trans. in *FBIS*, September 24, 1991, p. 77.
67. Radio Odin, March 26, 1992, trans. in *FBIS*, March 26, 1992, p. 66.
68. King, "Moldova with a Russian Face," p. 112.
69. Socor, "Moldova's 'Dniestr' Ulcer"; cf. *CDSP*, Vol. 43, No. 50 (January 15, 1992), pp. 28–30.

The climax came in June, when Russia sent Major General Alexander Lebed to relieve the ineffective Netkachev and reassert Russian control over the 14th Army. Lebed's first major act was to order the 14th Army to intervene in the Bendery battle, sealing Tiraspol's victory in the war. Yeltsin then sent his vice-president, the pro-Tiraspol Rutskoi, to mediate a cease-fire freezing the Dniestrians' gains in place. The cease-fire was to be monitored by multilateral "peacekeeping" forces, mostly Russian troops partial to the Dniestrian side.[70] Contrary to promises that the 14th Army would be gradually withdrawn, Lebed was later allowed to increase 14th Army manpower by mobilizing local reservists.[71]

By helping Tiraspol gain autonomy, Russia ensured its access to the 14th Army's bases in the Dniestr region, and opened the door for a future attempt to annex the region, a course publicly urged by Lebed, among others.[72] The division of Moldova and the presence of Russian troops also provided Moscow with leverage to force Chisinau to join the Commonwealth of Independent States (CIS). Moscow's larger ambitions are perhaps suggested by Lebed's comment that the Dniestr region is "the key to the Balkans."[73] Indeed, Russia's Moldova policy is not an exception: Russia has promoted ethnic wars for its own strategic gain in the Transcaucasus and Tajikistan as well.[74]

CAUSES OF MOLDOVA'S ETHNIC WAR SPIRAL

Moldova's ethnic conflict began as a mass-led ethnic mobilization by the Soviet Union's Moldovan minority. By 1989, the insurgents had succeeded in bringing Moldovan nationalists peacefully to power in Chisinau, changing the process into one of popular chauvinism. Violence remained minimal, however, because Moldovans' feelings of hostility toward Russians remained fairly weak, and because Soviet troops deterred some of the aggressive impulses of Moldovan extremists. However, attempts to find a compromise acceptable to Tiraspol, Chisinau, and Moscow were thwarted by inflexibility in all three capitals.

---

70. *CDSP,* Vol. 44, No. 28 (August 12, 1992), p. 19.
71. *CDSP,* Vol. 44, No. 29 (August 19, 1992), pp. 20–21; *CDSP,* Vol. 44, No. 32 (September 9, 1992), p. 21.
72. *CDSP,* Vol. 42, No. 27 (August 5, 1992), p. 13; *CDSP,* Vol. 42, No. 30 (August 26, 1992), p. 20.
73. Vladimir Socor, "Isolated Moldova Being Pulled into Russian Orbit," *RFE/RL Research Report,* Vol. 2, No. 50 (December 17, 1993), pp. 9–15.
74. See Thomas Goltz, "Letter from Eurasia: The Hidden Russian Hand," *Foreign Policy,* No. 92 (Fall 1993), pp. 92–116, on the Transcausasus; and Keith Martin, "Tajikistan: Civil War Without End?" *RFE/RL Research Report,* Vol. 2, No. 33 (August 20, 1993), pp. 18–29, on Tajikistan.

The more violent phase of the conflict, in 1990–92, was driven by elite conspiracy—the demands of the elite-led minority separatist movement in the Dniestr region. War came in part because of Chisinau's inflexibility, but mostly due to Dniestrian intransigence and Moscow's encouragement of it. Dniestrian elites turned to separatism in pursuit of their personal self-interest, and aid from Moscow enabled them to provoke a security dilemma, which led to increasing violence but justified their hold on power. In the end, Moscow aided Tiraspol in fighting an aggressive war because doing so served Moscow's own interest, not least in keeping its own military forces in the region.

Policy Alternatives for Third-party Conflict Management

Unfortunately for third parties interested in preventing ethnic wars, the preconditions for ethnic war are generally difficult or impossible for outsiders to influence. Third parties cannot change ethnically defined grievances, negative stereotypes, symbolic disputes, threatening demographic trends, or histories of ethnic domination in foreign countries; and they cannot eliminate the fears of extinction which may result. In the long term, some of these problems can be ameliorated: third parties can promote economic policies that would reduce grievances, for example, or encourage the writing of fair-minded history to moderate perceptions of historical repression.[75] But third parties typically have little leverage in such areas, and their efforts are of little help in crises, when they are most likely to act. Another option, reducing the political space available to repressed groups, might help avert violence, but it requires an authoritarian crackdown which democratic third parties may not want to encourage.

The one precondition which is alterable by outside effort is military means, which suggests two possible strategies for averting war. First is isolation: denying the would-be initiator the means to start an ethnic war. Second is deterrence: military capability is a relative thing, so initiators might be deterred if they have to face an adversary much more powerful than they.

The main proximate causes of ethnic war—mass hostility, belligerent elites, and security dilemma spirals—can also be influenced from outside. While mass hostility is hard to change, people can sometimes be deterred from taking hostile action. Belligerent elites, often motivated by self-interest, may be dis-

---

75. Stephen Van Evera suggests promoting fair-minded history in Van Evera, "Hypotheses on Nationalism and War." Michael Brown notes the potential of wise economic policies, in Michael E. Brown, "Internal Conflict and International Action," in Brown, *International Dimensions of Internal Conflict.*

suaded from violence if they are offered inducements, such as aid in implementing a policy that can keep them in power without resort to outbidding. Security dilemmas can be ameliorated by policies of reassurance, such as mediation or peacekeeping.[76]

This, then, is the arsenal of policy options available to third parties interested in conflict management: reassurance, deterrence, inducement, and isolation. The choice of which to use depends on the situation. For example, inducements for elites are not likely to be helpful in cases of mass-led violence: since outbidding in such cases is driven by mass hostility, there is no point in trying to bribe leaders to be moderate; leaders who accepted the inducements would simply be replaced as a result of pressure from below. Similarly, isolation is of limited value when the initiator of conflict is the dominant group: dominant groups by definition control the apparatus of the state, including the army, so they already have military means. The choice of appropriate policies for averting war, then, can be guided by the typology based on these two factors—whether the conflict is mass-led or elite-led, and whether the initiating group is the dominant or subordinate group. (The logic is summarized in Table 1.)

REASSURING MASS INSURGENTS
In cases of mass-led conflicts initiated by subordinate groups, the most important cause of violence is insecurity, specifically the subordinates' fear of ethnic extinction. It is this fear that fans mass hostility, motivates support for outbidding elites, and leads to violence in self-defense. Conflict prevention policy must therefore focus on reassurance: assuaging the fear of group extinction which motivates violence.

The attitude of the state involved is crucial in making reassurance work. In most cases, the state's policies are the source of the subordinate group's existential fears, so any hope of reassuring the subordinate group depends on the state's willingness to attempt reassurance. The most constructive approach third parties can take is to encourage the state to reassure the subordinate group, perhaps offering economic aid conditioned on peaceful management of the ethnic dispute. The third parties can also aid in the conflict management process itself, by supplying mediators to assist negotiations or peacekeeping troops to dampen fears of violence on both sides, or by funding efforts at

---

76. A discussion of reassurance policies is in Janice Gross Stein, "Deterrence and Reassurance," in Philip E. Tetlock et al., eds., *Behavior, Society, and Nuclear War*, Vol. 2 (New York: Oxford University Press, 1991), pp. 8–72.

economic redistribution. If the state is determined to crack down on the insurgents, however, there is little third parties can do to prevent violence: threats of economic sanctions are likely to be ignored, and the more extreme recourse of arming the rebels is likely only to exacerbate violence.

If reassurance is to work, in fact, both sides must be willing to moderate their demands. In Macedonia, for example, the government has worked hard to reassure the minority Albanian community, making concessions on cultural issues and including Albanians as ministers in the government. United Nations peacekeeping troops were even introduced, largely (though not officially) to help avert Albanian-Macedonian ethnic violence by reassuring the minority Albanian community.[77] As a result, Macedonia has avoided the violence that plagued other parts of the former Yugoslavia in the early 1990s. In the Nagorno-Karabakh conflict, in contrast, even the efforts of a sovereign state—the Soviet Union before its collapse—were not enough to avert war, because both sides insisted on extreme goals: the Karabakh Armenians, especially, would settle for nothing less than annexation of their region by Armenia.

DETERRING POPULAR CHAUVINISTS
The violence in cases of popular chauvinism is driven primarily by mass hostility of the dominant group. The cause of conflict is that group's insistence on complete dominance over other groups. While the demand is justified as self-defense, the perceived insecurity is typically the result of exaggerated security demands: anything less than political dominance is considered threatening to group survival. This attitude can make third-party efforts at preventing war difficult, since it is not easy to reduce such hostility in the short term. The best that can be attempted is deterrence: third parties can, for example, threaten to back the subordinates against the dominants in case the dominants initiate violence. Reassurance efforts—primarily promoting moderation on both sides, and possibly the insertion of neutral peacekeepers—may also help by reducing threat perceptions.

The case of Moldova shows that such mass-led violence can be deterred. When Soviet troops interposed themselves in looming confrontations—guarding the Dniestrian "congress" in September of 1990, and blocking the Moldovan volunteers' march to the Gagauz region that November—they were successful at deterring violence. Deterrence worked because the crowd was

---

77. Stuart J. Kaufman, "Preventive Peacekeeping, Ethnic Violence, and Macedonia," *Studies in Conflict and Terrorism*, Vol. 19, No. 3 (July–September 1996), pp. 229–246.

directly confronted by the threatened deterrent—Soviet troops—not merely warned. It was where Soviet troops were not immediately present, as in the November 1990 Bendery and Dubossary incidents, that most instances of violence occurred.

Deterrence policies do not always work, however: if mass hostility is strong enough, or if elites also prefer confrontation, violence is not deterrable. And since extremists are likely to see the territorial integrity of the state—which would be infringed even by the introduction of peacekeepers—as being at stake, they are likely to refuse to allow peacekeepers in.[78] Such refusal may not be mere empty pride: in the Georgian case, the potential third party in 1990–91 was the Soviet Union, which by cracking down violently on Georgian nationalists in 1989 had forfeited any claim to impartiality. Third parties in such conditions are forced to choose between accepting the outbreak of war or providing aid to one side in it.

INDUCEMENTS FOR GOVERNMENT JINGOISTS

In cases of government jingoism, the threat of violence comes from belligerent leaders of the dominant group who use their control over government institutions to fan mass hostility and provoke a security dilemma. Third-party efforts in such cases must aim at finding a way to restrain the belligerent elites, most likely through some combination of inducement and deterrence. If the elites' resort to ethnic outbidding is motivated by opportunism—a simple effort to gain or hold power—the inducement might be a package of political and economic concessions which would enable them to maintain their power without having to resort to ethnic outbidding.[79] Slobodan Milošević, for example, resorted to ethnic outbidding in order to divert attention from demands for democratizing political reforms and market-oriented economic reforms which would have threatened his grip on power. Therefore, the only inducement that might have appealed to him would have been a Western policy of tolerating a socialist and authoritarian Serbia, probably inside a highly decentralized Yugoslavia. This inducement would have had to be supplemented by a deterrence policy involving threats to support secessionist minorities (e.g., Croats and Bosnians) in case Milošević chose violence.

As the farfetched nature of the example illustrates, these conflicts are particularly difficult to prevent. It may not have been possible to find a stable

---

78. Kaufman, "Preventive Peacekeeping, Ethnic Violence, and Macedonia."
79. I am indebted to Yao Aziabu for suggesting this inducement strategy.

compromise which would have enabled Milošević to stay in power without resort to national chauvinism. Furthermore, third-party leverage may be too weak to matter in such cases. Alternatively, elites might already have stirred up enough mass hostility to make retreat impossible, and third parties might be reluctant to reward unsavory ethnic extremists. In the case of Milošević, all of these considerations were significant barriers to war prevention.[80] In other cases, where the belligerent leaders are motivated by ideology rather than self-interest, inducement is even less likely to work. Unfortunately the best alternative, relying on deterrent threats (e.g., threatening to arm secessionist minorities) is, absent positive inducements, likely to escalate war rather than prevent it.

ISOLATING ELITE CONSPIRATORS

In cases of elite conspiracy, violence is caused by subordinate-group elites who promote mass hostility and provoke a security dilemma. One alternative for the threatened state in dealing with such elites is inducement: the state can try to co-opt the elite conspirators, offering them local power in exchange for loyalty. If the elites are motivated by ambition, such a policy can be very effective: co-optation was one of the reasons the Soviet Union survived as long as it did, for example. Indeed, the outbreak of the Dniestr war can be blamed partly on Chisinau's failure to co-opt the Dniestrian elites in time. Until the spring of 1992, Tiraspol's demand was for autonomy in a federal Moldova within the Commonwealth of Independent States, a position Moldovan President Snegur was willing to accept by 1994. If he had accepted it in early 1992, the war might have been avoided.

For elite conspirators who are not co-opted, their biggest hurdle is finding the resources to promote conflict. While government jingoists have the resources of the state, and leaders of mass insurgencies have mobilized mass movements behind them, elite conspirators have neither. They are therefore particularly vulnerable to isolation: if they lack the propaganda apparatus to promote their message, and the armed forces to provoke violence, they can do little harm. If third parties can cut off extremists' access to these resources by deterring foreign patrons, conflicts can be stopped before they begin.

The trouble with isolation strategies, as the Moldova case illustrates, is that foreign patrons are often difficult to deter. Indeed, given Moscow's view that

---

80. I make this argument in Kaufman, "The Irresistible Force and the Imperceptible Object."

the former Soviet states are its exclusive sphere of influence, its intervention may not have been deterrable at all.

Moscow's role in the Dniestr conflict shows, instead, what third parties can do if they invert the logic of conflict management. Instead of deterring Dniestrian aggression, the Russian army provided Tiraspol with the weapons to launch its offensive. Instead of reassuring the Dniestrians that a compromise with Chisinau could be had, Russian officials visiting Tiraspol confirmed their sense of grievance. Instead of providing the Dniestrian elites with inducements to compromise, Russia subsidized their intransigence. Finally, Russia's climactic intervention in the Bendery battle served not only to stop the war—though it did that—but also to ensure the Dniestrian victory. Without Russian support, the Dniestrians probably could not have launched their secessionist war, let alone have won it.

THE MODEST REQUIREMENTS FOR PEACE

The list of necessary preconditions for ethnic war is long, and war typically happens only if all are present, and if mass hostility or elite outbidding is strong enough to begin the spiral of conflict. Ethnic wars should be preventable, therefore, if any of these elements can be removed. This logic helps to explain why most of the post-Soviet states, in spite of their ethnic diversity and weak legitimacy, have remained so remarkably peaceful.

The examples of the Russian minorities in Estonia and Kazakhstan illustrate the point. Most of the preconditions for ethnic violence are or were present in both countries: grievances, stereotypes, threatened symbols, demographic threats on both sides, histories of domination, *de facto* anarchy, and political space; fears of community extinction and ethnic outbidding have resulted. The means to fight could probably be found. But because ethnic hostility is moderate, a security dilemma has not arisen: most of the Estonians' and Kazakhs' fears were addressed soon after they gained governing power, and a few modest concessions to the Russians have sufficed to moderate their fears and prevent a violent backlash. In Estonia, Western pressure helped avert more serious ethnic conflict, both by encouraging reassurance policies on the Estonian side, and by deterring intervention by Russia. Estonia's relative prosperity also helped. But in Kazakhstan, little more was needed than a bit of restraint by Kazakhs, local Russians, and Moscow. Moldova's tragedy notwithstanding, then, it may be easier to maintain inter-ethnic peace than many believe.

Explaining the Kashmir Insurgency

Šumit Ganguly

Political Mobilization and Institutional Decay

On December 8, 1989, members of the Jammu and Kashmir Liberation Front kidnapped Dr. Rubiya Sayeed, the daughter of the Indian Minister of Home Affairs, as she left a government hospital in Srinagar. The kidnappers refused to release her until several incarcerated members of their outlawed group were released. Following hasty negotiations over the next several days, the government in New Delhi agreed to meet the abductors' demands. In the weeks and months that followed, dozens of insurgent groups emerged and wreaked havoc throughout the Kashmir Valley, killing government officials, security personnel, and innocent bystanders. Although they were of varying ideological orientations, all the insurgent groups professed opposition to Indian rule in Jammu and Kashmir, and the authority of the Indian state virtually collapsed there.

Since December 1989, the strength of the insurgency in Jammu and Kashmir has fluctuated.[1] Faced with the wrath of many of the Islamic militant groups, more than 200,000 Hindus (known as *Pandits*) have fled the Kashmir Valley. Currently, nearly 400,000 Indian Army and paramilitary troops are deployed in the state. The security forces are battling at least a dozen major insurgent groups of varying size and ideological orientation, as well as dozens more minor operations. The more prominent of the insurgent groups include the nominally secular, pro-independence Jammu and Kashmir Liberation Front (JKLF) and the radical Islamic and pro-Pakistani groups Hizb-ul-Mujahideen (HUM), Hizbollah, Harkat-ul-Ansar, and Ikhwanul Muslimeen. At least 15,000

Šumit Ganguly is Professor of Political Science at Hunter College and at the Graduate Center, City University of New York. He is author of Between War and Peace: The Crisis in Kashmir *(forthcoming from Cambridge University Press and the Woodrow Wilson Center Press).*

This article is drawn from my forthcoming book. I wish to thank Kanti Bajpai, Traci Nagle, and Jack Snyder for their substantial comments and assistance.

---

1. See Šumit Ganguly, *Between War and Peace: The Crisis in Kashmir* (Cambridge, U.K., and Washington, D.C.: Cambridge University Press and Woodrow Wilson Center Press, forthcoming); Vernon Marston Hewitt, *Reclaiming the Past: The Search for Political and Cultural Unity in Contemporary Kashmir* (London: Portland Books, 1995). See also Jyoti Bhusan Das Gupta, *Jammu and Kashmir* (The Hague: Martinus Nijhoff, 1968), which provides an excellent historical account of the origins of the Kashmir problem in the context of Indo-Pakistani relations.

International Security, Vol. 21, No. 2 (Fall 1996), pp. 76–107
© 1996 by the President and Fellows of Harvard College and the Massachusetts Institute of Technology.

to 20,000 insurgents, police, paramilitary personnel, and civilians have lost their lives since the onset of the insurgency.[2] India's continuing accusations of Pakistani support for some of these insurgent groups have eroded relations between India and Pakistan.

As of mid-1996, the insurgency appears to have reached a stalemate. Despite substantial Pakistani assistance and the involvement of several thousand Afghan *mujahideen*, the insurgents cannot prevail on the battlefield. Nor have the Indian security forces been able to crush the insurgents militarily. The present government strategy appears to be three-pronged: to apply substantial military pressure on the insurgents, to sow discord in their ranks with offers of negotiation, and to revive the political process in the state. This strategy has evolved from the government's experience of defeating insurgent movements in the neighboring state of Punjab and in India's northeastern states.[3]

The insurgency is fraught with considerable theoretical and policy significance. At a theoretical level it demonstrates the dangers states face when political mobilization occurs against a backdrop of institutional decay. The failure of governments to accommodate rising political demands within an institutional context can culminate in political violence. Such dangers are especially acute in poly-ethnic societies when politicized and discontented ethnic minorities encounter few institutional channels for expressing political dissent.

The policy significance of this theoretical point is that as economic modernization proceeds, growing levels of literacy, higher education, and media exposure will contribute to increased political mobilization. This heightened political awareness will inevitably contribute to greater political demands. As Samuel Huntington cogently argued, the processes of economic modernization generate increasing demands for political participation by opening up new opportunities for physical, social, and economic mobility.[4] Furthermore, as

---

2. Michael E. Brown, ed., *The International Dimensions of Internal Conflict* (Cambridge, Mass.: MIT Press, 1996), Table 1, p. 5.

3. This strategy may be inapplicable to Kashmir for several reasons. First, neither the Punjab nor the northeastern states were the subjects of international territorial disputes. Because Kashmir is claimed by Pakistan, far greater international attention and scrutiny has been focused on the crisis there. Second, unlike the Punjab, the vast majority of Kashmir's population is alienated from the Indian state. Third, Kashmir's location makes foreign infiltration into the state and support for the insurgency far easier. India was able to seal the Indo-Pakistani border in the Punjab. Fourth, the insurgents in Kashmir have access to a vast arms bazaar that extends from Pakistan to Afghanistan. On this point see Jasjit Singh, *Light Weapons and International Security* (New Delhi: Indian Pugwash Society and British-American Information Council, 1995).

4. Samuel Huntington, *Political Order in Changing Societies* (New Haven, Conn.: Yale University Press, 1968).

Myron Weiner has demonstrated, accelerating mobility in the context of scarce resources in a poly-ethnic society can lead to mobilization along ethnic lines and result in inter-ethnic tensions.[5] Faced with such increased demands and other ethnic tensions, states can resort to coercive strategies, which are, inevitably, short-term palliatives. Over the longer haul, states, especially poly-ethnic states, have little choice but to develop institutional capacities for accommodating rising demands for political participation.

What explains the abrupt rise of violent ethno-religious fervor in 1989 in India's only Muslim-majority state? Apologists for the Indian position have contended that the insurgency is the result of Pakistani propaganda and logistical support and training for the insurgents.[6] Pakistani apologists, in turn, argue that the insurgency represents the spontaneous rise of ethno-religious sentiment amongst the oppressed Muslim community of Jammu and Kashmir.[7]

More scholarly explanations have sought to locate the origins of the insurgency in the clash of competing nationalist visions, rampant electoral malfeasances, the rise of a frustrated middle class, or the breakdown of a composite Kashmiri cultural identity.[8] These explanations, though not without merit, are at best partial. Some do provide useful insights into the origins of the insurgency. Others offer explanations for the timing of the insurgency. None of them, however, adequately explains both components.

This article provides a detailed account of the historical origins of the insurgency, placing it within the context of Indo-Pakistani relations and regional security. I then examine a number of general explanations of ethnic conflict as well as the particular arguments that have been put forth to explain the Kashmir insurgency, and suggest a new explanation which challenges this existing body of work. My theoretically grounded argument attempts to explain both the reasons for the outbreak of the insurgency and its particular timing, contending that two interlinked forces—political mobilization and institutional decay—best explain the origins of the insurgency in Kashmir. I

---

5. Myron Weiner, *Sons of the Soil: Migration and Ethnic Conflict in India* (Princeton, N.J.: Princeton University Press, 1978).
6. For a forceful statement of the Indian position, see K. Subrahmanyam, "Kashmir," *Strategic Analysis*, Vol. 23, No. 11 (May 1990), pp. 111–198.
7. One of the best statements of the official Pakistan position is Shaheen Akhtar, *Uprising in Indian-Held Kashmir* (Islamabad: Institute of Regional Studies, 1991).
8. For a variety of explanations for the origins of the Kashmir crisis, see Raju G.C. Thomas, ed., *Perspectives on Kashmir: The Roots of Conflict in South Asia* (Boulder, Colo.: Westview, 1992). Also see Asghar Ali Engineer, ed., *Kashmir: Secular Crown in Fire* (New Delhi: Ajanta Publications, 1992).

conclude with a discussion of the larger theoretical significance of the Kashmir case as well as possible policy prescriptions that flow from my analysis.

The Roots of Conflict: Tracing the Origins of the Insurgency

The first important facet of the Kashmir crisis involves Indo-Pakistani relations. Two of the three wars between India and Pakistan have been fought over the status of Kashmir. Pakistan's irredentist claim on Kashmir, based on the state's Muslim-majority population and its geographic contiguity, has twice prompted it to try militarily to seize the state. The first attempt took place shortly after the emergence of India and Pakistan from the detritus of the British Indian empire in 1947.[9] Pakistan made a second attempt to wrest control of Kashmir from India in 1965.

India, which is currently attempting to suppress the insurgency in the state, has held on to Kashmir with a tenacity equal to that demonstrated by Pakistan. Kashmir, with its Muslim-majority population, has long been an emblem of India's secular status; its very existence demonstrated that Muslims could thrive under the aegis of India's secular policy. Today, as India's secular fabric has raveled, the country's leaders seek to maintain their hold on Kashmir because they fear that Kashmir's exit from the Indian Union would set off powerful centrifugal forces in other parts of the country. Thus, the stakes for

---

9. At the time of independence and partition, two classes of states existed in the Indian Union: those of British India, ruled directly by the Crown, and the "princely states," nominally independent as long as they recognized the "paramountcy" of the Crown. Upon British withdrawal from the subcontinent, the doctrine of paramountcy was to lapse, and the rulers of the princely states had to choose to join either India or Pakistan, basing their decisions on geographic propinquity and demographic composition. Kashmir posed a peculiar problem: its monarch, Maharaja Hari Singh, was Hindu, his subjects were predominantly Muslim, and the state abutted both India and Pakistan. As Hari Singh vacillated on the question of accession, Pakistani troops disguised as local tribesmen attacked the western reaches of his state. Hari Singh appealed to New Delhi for military assistance. Prime Minister Nehru agreed to provide assistance only after two conditions were met: the maharaja had to sign the Instrument of Accession and join India, and Sheikh Mohammed Abdullah, the leader of the largest and most popular organization within the state, had to give his imprimatur to the accession. These conditions were met, and in late October 1947 Indian troops were airlifted into the Valley. They halted the advancing invaders but not before a third of the Valley had fallen into Pakistani hands. In January 1948 India referred the case to the United Nations. Between 1949 and 1960 the UN made a number of attempts to resolve the dispute, but none of its proposals proved acceptable to both sides. See Jyoti Bhusan Das Gupta, *Jammu and Kashmir;* Šumit Ganguly, *The Origins of War in South Asia,* 2nd ed. (Boulder, Colo.: Westview, 1995); Alistair Lamb, *Kashmir: A Disputed Legacy, 1846–1990* (Hertingfordbury, U.K.: Roxford Books, 1991); Prem Shankar Jha, *Kashmir, 1947: Rival Versions of History* (Delhi: Oxford University Press, 1996); H.V. Hodson, *The Great Divide: Britain-India-Pakistan* (Oxford, U.K.: Oxford University Press, 1969); and Major-General Akbar Khan, *Raiders in Kashmir* (Karachi: Pak Publishers, 1990).

both states involve far more than territorial claims: the question of control of Kashmir goes to the very basis of the state-building enterprise in South Asia.

The second dimension of the Kashmir crisis—namely, the rise of an ethno-religious insurgent movement—is the central concern of the present analysis. Why, after forty-two years of Indian rule, did an insurgency abruptly break out in 1989?

The explanations that have been proffered to date do not adequately answer this crucial question. The matter of timing is an important one: we must ask not only why the insurgency occurred at all, but also why it did *not* occur at any earlier time, particularly during 1965 when a war was fought in Kashmir between India and Pakistan. During that conflict, the Muslims in the Kashmir Valley would have had ready allies had they chosen to challenge the authority of the Indian state.

I contend that two interlinked forces of political mobilization and institutional decay best explain the origins of the insurgency in Kashmir. On the one hand, the developmental activities of the Indian government gave rise to accelerated political mobilization in Kashmir, making a younger generation of Kashmiris more conscious of their political rights. Simultaneously, on the other hand, the government was also responsible for the deinstitutionalization of politics in the state,[10] which drove the expression of political discontent into extra-institutional contexts. Eventually, with the last institutional avenues for the expression of dissent blocked, pent-up discontent culminated in violence.

1965: THE DOG THAT DID NOT BARK

Some historical perspective on the origins of the crisis demonstrates the key precipitating roles played by political mobilization and institutional decay. In 1965, the Pakistani military dictator Ayub Khan carefully orchestrated a strategy for fomenting a rebellion in Kashmir. The ultimate goal of this strategy, code-named "Operation Gibraltar," was to take advantage of the disturbed conditions within the state and seize Kashmir in a sharp, short war.[11] Despite this well-organized effort, no insurgency ensued. I argue that this was because conditions in the Kashmir Valley were not conducive to fomenting a rebellion.

---

10. The classic statement of this problem of political mobilization and institutional decay is Huntington, *Political Order in Changing Societies.*
11. The most dispassionate account of "Operation Gibraltar" and its aftermath is Russell Brines, *The Indo-Pakistani Conflict* (New York: Pall Mall, 1968). For a first-person account see Mohammed Musa, *My Version: India-Pakistan War 1965* (Lahore: Wajidalis, 1983).

Political developments in the subcontinent had led Ayub Khan to embark on this mistaken strategy. In 1962, India had been routed in a disastrous border war with China and had been humiliated by China's unilateral cease-fire after it had seized some 14,000 square miles of territory claimed by India.[12] In the aftermath of this crisis, India had turned to the United States and the United Kingdom to obtain military assistance, which, though forthcoming, was limited.[13] Nevertheless, the flow of Western arms and equipment into India[14] ignited a fear in Pakistani military circles that the window of opportunity for seizing Kashmir through the use of force might be about to close. Accordingly, a number of Ayub's advisers suggested to him that Pakistan needed to act soon if the Kashmir issue were to be resolved in Pakistan's favor.

A series of events in India reinforced Pakistani elite perceptions that the moment was propitious for attempting to wrest Kashmir away from India. First, in December 1963, riots that had a strong anti-Indian tenor had broken out in the Kashmir Valley following the theft of a holy relic, believed to be a hair of the Prophet Mohammed, from the Hazratbal mosque in Srinagar, the capital city of Jammu and Kashmir. The Pakistani leadership immediately construed these demonstrations as signs of pro-Pakistani sentiment. Second, in the wake of the death of Prime Minister Jawaharlal Nehru in 1964, Pakistani decision-makers inferred that India's unity was in peril without Nehru's towering influence. It was expected that various centrifugal forces, including caste, class, and ethnic cleavages would tear India apart.[15] Finally, a "limited probe" that the Pakistani military leadership conducted in April 1965 in an area known as the Rann of Kutch in the western Indian state of Gujarat failed to produce a vigorous response from the Indian military; the seemingly pusillanimous Indian response led the Pakistanis to believe that the Indians lacked stomach for battle.[16] Pakistani leaders reinforced these beliefs by falling back on racial and ethnic imagery, conjured up by British administrators for the purposes

---

12. Steven Hoffman, *India and the China Crisis* (Berkeley: University of California Press, 1990).
13. Raju G.C. Thomas, *Indian Security Policy* (Princeton, N.J.: Princeton University Press, 1989).
14. See, for example, "Survival or Extinction?" *Dawn* (Pakistan), November 28–December 2, 1964.
15. Many American social scientists and journalists made this prediction. The most influential, if alarmist, statement of this position can be found in Selig Harrison, *India: The Most Dangerous Decades* (Princeton, N.J.: Princeton University Press, 1958).
16. The Indo-Pakistani border in the area of the Rann of Kutch, which is mostly a trackless waste, was poorly demarcated during the time of partition. The Indian response was less than vigorous because Indian military analysts and politicians attached little significance to this tract. Indian troops engaged the Pakistani troops, but executed only a holding action—they did not expand the scope of the conflict. Following British mediation, India agreed to refer the dispute to the International Court of Justice.

of colonial administrative convenience, to explain India's lack of military prowess.[17]

Based on this series of dubious assumptions, Pakistan began to infiltrate regular soldiers disguised as local tribesmen into the Kashmir Valley in the summer of 1965. Much to the dismay of the Pakistanis, however, the Kashmiris in the Valley did not rise up in revolt and make common cause with the infiltrators. Yet this cannot be attributed to a lack of anti-Indian sentiment on the part of the Kashmiris. As the demonstrations in the wake of the Hazaratbal theft had demonstrated, such sentiments were widespread within the Valley. However, these sentiments did not automatically translate into support for Pakistan and a willingness to resort to large-scale violence to express their discontent with Indian rule.

If the Kashmiris were indeed a "captive" ethno-national group as Pakistani apologists assert (and had asserted since 1947), what explains their failure to revolt when presented with this opportunity? Conditions were propitious: within India, a new and untested prime minister was in office. Riots had recently broken out in southern India over the imposition of Hindi as the national language, and the Indian army was just recovering from the humiliating military debacle with China. Within Kashmir, substantial assistance and armaments were available from the several thousand infiltrators who had percolated into the Valley between June and August.

The answer lies in the fact that this generation of Kashmiris was politically quiescent. The Jammu and Kashmir National Conference, which in pre-independence days had played a vital role in challenging Kashmir's ruler, Maharaja Hari Singh, had dominated the politics of the state since independence. As long as the leadership of the National Conference did not raise the prospect of secession, the national government in New Delhi permitted the party wide latitude.[18] Consequently, the National Conference was free to engage in various forms of electoral malfeasance and skullduggery. The inhabitants of the Kashmir Valley tolerated the political chicanery of the National Conference partly out of loyalty to Sheikh Abdullah, the party's symbolic leader, and partly out of their lack of political sophistication, due to their low levels of literacy, education, and exposure to mass media. Consequently, the vast majority of Kashmiris, although they were discontented with elements of the prevailing

---

17. On this point see Šumit Ganguly, "Deterrence Failure Revisited: The Indo-Pakistani War of 1965," *Journal of Strategic Studies*, Vol. 13, No. 4 (December 1990), pp. 77–93.
18. Nehru, on the advice of Indian intelligence agencies, had Sheikh Abdullah removed from office 1952 on rather tenuous grounds. In fact, it was feared that Abdullah was on the verge of declaring Kashmir's independence.

political dispensation, lacked awareness of their political plight and the requisite organizational impetus, and therefore did not vigorously challenge the existing order.

Over the next twenty years, however, significant political changes within India at large and within Kashmir itself transformed the politically quiescent Kashmiris into a highly mobilized population. Kashmiris, routinely denied their voting rights in deeply flawed elections, witnessed the increasingly free exercise of franchise in other parts of India. Realization of this distinction grew with the expansion of education and mass media in Kashmir and contributed to a growing sense of resentment against the malfeasances of the Indian state.

THE TRANSFORMATION OF THE POLITICAL ORDER

Political mobilization in India, unlike many post-colonial states, took place early, and it defied the conventional pathways. During the nationalist struggle for independence, large numbers of India's adult populace entered the political arena. Under the extraordinary political leadership of Mohandas Gandhi, the Indian National Congress was transformed from an upper-middle-class, Anglicized organization into a broad-based mass political party. Gandhi's mass campaigns of civil disobedience promoted the notions of political accountability and universal franchise, and successfully mobilized India's indigent and still-illiterate peasantry.

After independence, several factors strengthened and expanded on Gandhi's legacy. For example, India started its independent history with at least notional universal adult franchise. Through the experience of elections at municipal, state, and national levels, increasing numbers of Indians became aware of the relationship between voting and public policy. Growing educational opportunities and concomitant increases in literacy and media exposure fed the momentum of political mobilization in India.

Such mobilization often contributed to class-based and ethnic agitations for autonomy and even secession.[19] The institutional capacities of the Indian state proved capable of dealing with these demands through a judicious mixture of negotiation, compromise, and coercion. For example, through the States Reorganization Act of 1956 and the development and implementation of the tri-language formula, India effectively dealt with the perils of linguistic agitation.[20] But although the country coped admirably with most demands for autonomy,

---

19. For further exploration of this issue, see Harrison, *India.*
20. Jyotirindra Das Gupta, *Language Conflict and National Development: Group Politics and Language Policy in India* (Berkeley: University of California Press, 1970).

its failure was quite striking in Kashmir. The Indian elite, including, albeit reluctantly, Prime Minister Nehru, were prepared to countenance various forms of political malfeasance in Kashmir because of the state's symbolic and strategic significance.

Nehru's successors Indira Gandhi and Rajiv Gandhi, faced with the extraordinary task of governing a poly-ethnic state ridden with every conceivable social cleavage, increasingly deinstitutionalized Indian politics.[21] Indira Gandhi, in particular, expanded central authority and demonstrated a proclivity for personalized rule. Furthermore, the imperatives of political survival drove Indira Gandhi and her son and successor steadily toward plebiscitary politics. The Gandhis not only concentrated power in New Delhi but also increasingly resorted to coercive strategies to deal with any challenges to the central government's authority. All too often, these autonomist demands were characterized as threats to India's unity. The coercive strategies that were used to deal with the perceived threats only magnified them. In turn, the Indian state responded with greater force, exacerbating the initial problem in a spiral of coercion.[22]

The post-Nehru political generation's record with institution-building is far from exemplary. However, even the post-Nehru phase of Indian politics has seen some remarkable success, particularly in the political mobilization of vast segments of India's electorate. Nearly five decades of electoral participation played a formidable role in furthering the mobilization of the electorate. The remarkable growth of literacy and mass media has also served to expand demands for political participation.

This combination of institutional decline and political mobilization can contribute to political instability. Much of the violent political turmoil that exists throughout India is attributable to these processes.[23] The crisis in Kashmir is the manifestation of an extreme version of political deinstitutionalization and accelerating political mobilization. The early decay of political institutions in

---

21. India's three other prime ministers between Nehru and Rajiv Gandhi served such short terms in office that they had limited impact, if any, on institution-building. Lal Bahadur Shastri, who succeeded Nehru, was in office for a little more than a year. Morarji Desai became the head of a coalition government, lasting less than two years, after Indira Gandhi's electoral defeat in 1977. Chaudhuri Charan Singh served as the interim prime minister for a month, until 1980, when Indira Gandhi returned to power.

22. See Kuldeep Mathur, "The State and the Use of Coercive Power in India," *Asian Survey*, Vol. 32, No. 4 (April 1992), pp. 337–349.

23. For a discussion of violent political agitation in India and its consequences for Indian democracy, see Raju G.C. Thomas, *Democracy, Security, and Development in India* (New York: St. Martin's Press, 1996).

Kashmir, which the government in New Delhi did little to stem (and in some cases encouraged), and the dramatic pace of political mobilization proved to be a combustible mix.

Alternative Explanations for Ethnic Conflict

Explanations for protracted ethnic conflict abound.[24] An all-too-common, journalistic explanation dwells on putative "ancient hatreds" that erupt with unerring frequency.[25] Other more scholarly explanations focus on the role of ethnic stereotyping in arousing inter-ethnic friction that leads to violence, or on the collapse of state authority and the ensuing intra-group solidarity that exacerbates the spiral of misgiving between ethnic groups. Still other explanations point to the repressive policies of dominant ethnic groups as the provocation for minority uprising.[26] These theories have varying degrees of explanatory power. None, however, provides a cogent explanation for the origins or the timing of the intractable ethnic insurgency currently raging in Kashmir.

ANCIENT HATREDS

The "ancient hatreds" theory of ethnic conflict has acquired considerable currency in popular and journalistic usage. It has frequently been invoked to explain both internal and inter-state conflict in South Asia.[27] A short examination of the historical record, however, reveals the limitations of this theory in

---

24. See Elizabeth Crighton and Martha Abele Mac Iver, "The Evolution of Protracted Ethnic Conflict: Group Dominance and Political Underdevelopment in Northern Ireland and Lebanon," *Comparative Politics*, Vol. 23, No. 2 (January 1991), pp. 127–142.
25. For a thoughtful critique of the "ancient hatreds" argument, see Lloyd and Susanne Rudolph, "Modern Hate," *New Republic*, March 22, 1993, pp. 24–29.
26. Literature on ethnic conflict includes Michael E. Brown, ed., *Ethnic Conflict and International Security* (Princeton, N.J.: Princeton University Press, 1993); Robert Gurr and Barbara Harff, *Ethnic Conflict in World Politics* (Boulder, Colo.: Westview Press, 1994); Donald Horowitz, *Ethnic Groups in Conflict* (Berkeley: University of California Press, 1985); Manus I. Midlarsky, ed., *The Internationalization of Communal Strife* (London: Routledge, 1992); and Joseph V. Montville, *Conflict and Peacemaking in Multiethnic Societies* (New York: Lexington Books, 1991). For a review and assessment of the literature on ethnic conflict, see Saul Newman, "Does Modernization Breed Ethnic Conflict?" *World Politics*, Vol. 43, No. 3 (April 1991), pp. 451–478.
27. On the invocation of this theory to explain inter-state conflict in South Asia, see S.M. Burke, *The Mainsprings of Indian and Pakistani Foreign Policies* (Minneapolis: University of Minnesota Press, 1974). For a challenge to the impression of unyielding conflict between India and Pakistan, see Šumit Ganguly, "Discord and Collaboration in Indo-Pakistani Relations," in Kanti P. Bajpai and H.C. Shukul, eds., *India, Pakistan, and International Society: Essays for A.P. Rana* (New Delhi: Sage Publications, 1995).

the South Asian context. It is undeniable that Islam came to South Asia as a conquering force. Furthermore, certain Muslim rulers, most notably Aurangzeb Alamgir in the eighteenth century, were hardly paragons of religious tolerance.[28] Yet the record of Hindu-Muslim relations during the period of Muslim rule in South Asia is not one of unrelieved discord and ethnic hatred. The interaction of various Hindu and Muslim communities for several centuries throughout South Asia produced significant syncretistic developments in art, literature, and architecture. Hindus and Muslims on occasion made common cause during the nationalist struggle against British rule. Perhaps the jingoistic rhetoric used by many modern-day politicians in India and Pakistan to distort the historical record to achieve short-term political ends invites the application of the "ancient hatreds" theory, but a dispassionate examination of the historical record suggests that the theory, like the rhetoric, is wrong.

More specifically, Islam did not come to Kashmir as a conquering faith, but through the influence of itinerant Sufi mendicants. Hindus converted to Islam not at the point of a sword, but through proselytization. Indeed, a number of Muslim saints were long revered by Hindus and Muslims alike. Furthermore, despite significant economic disparities between Hindu and Muslim communities that have widened over the last two hundred years, widespread ethnic violence did not erupt in Kashmir at any time until recently.[29]

ETHNIC STEREOTYPING

Ethnic stereotyping involves attributing particular traits of personality, character, and intelligence to members of other ethnic groups.[30] The features that are attributed to other groups may be positive or negative.[31] Even apparently positive stereotypes of other ethnic communities can have adverse conse-

---

28. See John Richards, *The Mughal Empire* (Cambridge, U.K.: Cambridge University Press, 1992).
29. Ian Copland, "Islam and Political Mobilization in Kashmir, 1931–34," *Pacific Affairs*, Vol. 54, No. 2 (Summer 1981), pp. 228–259.
30. For a discussion of the concept of "ethnic stereotyping," see Horowitz, *Ethnic Groups in Conflict*, esp. pp. 116–171. Also see the introduction in Brown, ed., *The International Dimensions of Internal Conflict*, pp. 21–22.
31. Some of the roots of ethnic stereotypes can be traced to the European colonial period. Colonial authorities often manufactured ethnic stereotypes for the purposes of imperial administrative convenience. One enduring ethnic stereotype that was promoted by the British was that of the "martial race," which was attributed to climate and geography: "In the hot, flat regions [southern India] . . . are found races, timid both by religion and habit, servile to their superiors, but tyrannical to their inferiors, and quite unwarlike. In other parts . . . where the winter is cold [northern India and what became Pakistan], the warlike minority is to be found." O'Moore Creagh, *Indian Studies*, as quoted in Hasan-Askari Rizvi, *The Military and Politics in Pakistan* (New Delhi: Konark, 1988), p. 138. See also Stephen P. Cohen, *The Indian Army* (Berkeley: University of California Press, 1971).

quences for inter-group relations, by fostering resentment among the "non-endowed."

Ethnic stereotyping does explain a great deal of the conflict and violence that has wracked South Asia. In Sri Lanka, for example, ethnic stereotypes of the Tamil minority were used by the Sinhalese majority to justify the former's systematic disenfranchisement. Ultimately, this polarized Sri Lankan politics and contributed to a pogrom against Tamils in the capital, Colombo, in 1983. Similarly, segments of the dominant Hindu community in India have generated ethnic stereotypes of Muslims. Such ethnic stereotyping, combined with the demagogic appeals emanating principally from the right-wing, jingoistic Bharatiya Janata Party (BJP) and its affiliated organizations, has contributed to widespread rioting and violence directed against various Muslim communities.[32] The fanning of such ethnic hatred reached its zenith in December 1992, when a well-orchestrated mob of BJP sympathizers stormed and destroyed a fourteenth-century mosque in Ayodhya in the north Indian state of Uttar Pradesh.[33] In the wake of the destruction of this mosque, riots swept India, during which several thousand Muslims were killed.

In the Kashmir case, the issue of ethnic stereotyping was largely irrelevant until the outbreak of the insurgency. Despite significant economic disparities between Hindus and Muslims, and Hindu dominance of most political and economic institutions, widespread communal hatred did not exist in Kashmir. Even if the two communities did not enjoy extensive social interaction, violent inter-ethnic conflict was not prevalent. Instead, a common bond of Kashmiri identity, popularly referred to as *Kashmiriyat*, prevailed.[34]

However, since the outbreak of the insurgency in 1989 and the flight of large numbers of Hindus from the Kashmir Valley, ethnic stereotypes are now coming to the fore. The displaced Hindus of the Kashmir Valley now tend to see their former Muslim neighbors as little better than marauders. The violence, the loss of life, and the destruction of property, as well as the entry of battle-hardened Afghan *mujahideen* into the fray, have contributed to the rise of ethnic stereotyping. The Muslim population of the Kashmir Valley, in turn, whose

---

32. See Veena Das, ed., *Mirrors of Violence: Communities, Riots, and Survivors in South Asia* (Delhi: Oxford University Press, 1990); and Asghar Ali Engineer, ed., *Communalism and Communal Violence in India* (Delhi: Ajanta, 1989).
33. For the controversy surrounding the Babri mosque, see S. Gopal, ed., *Anatomy of a Confrontation* (New Delhi: Viking/Penguin, 1991).
34. See T.N. Madan, "The Social Construction of Cultural Identities in Rural Kashmir," in T.N. Madan, ed., *Pathways: Approaches to the Study of Society in India* (New Delhi: Oxford University Press, 1995).

loyalties are widely questioned by the security forces, now distrust Hindus with equal vigor.

ETHNIC "SECURITY DILEMMA"

The concept of the ethnic "security dilemma" is derived from Neo-Realism.[35] In an anarchic international milieu lacking a paramount authority, states are the ultimate guarantors of their own security. Consequently, they must acquire the necessary military strength to protect their sovereignty and territorial integrity. The acquisition of such military capabilities, however, can be seen as threatening by other neighboring states. Neighbors unable to discern or trust the "defensive" quality of the state's weapons acquisitions also seek to arm themselves. Consequently, efforts undertaken to enhance one's own security end up undermining it; this is the "security dilemma."

Barry Posen has applied this theoretical construct to situations of state collapse in which domestic politics resembles the anarchic international order.[36] In the absence of state authority, a potential security dilemma resembling that faced by nation-states can emerge among discrete ethnic groups in a poly-ethnic state. When ethnic groups have to ensure their own security, their group identity can assume increased significance. Increased group identification, Posen argues, produces greater group cohesion and confers significant military advantages to infantry armies. Simultaneous increases in group cohesion among separate ethnic groups may lead each group to formulate a worst-case analysis of the others' intentions. Demagogic leaders all too frequently drive such analyses and selectively use the historical record to arouse ethnic passions. Under these conditions, groups with greater offensive capabilities may attack more vulnerable ethnic groups caught in geographic enclaves. Such actions can culminate in a vortex of action and reaction.

The ethnic security-dilemma theory provides a compelling explanation for ethnic violence in the Indian subcontinent at the time of British withdrawal in 1947, but not for the current spate of violence in Kashmir. At the time of the partition of British India and the creation of the independent states of India

---

35. The concept of the "security dilemma" is derived from John Herz, "Idealist Internationalism and the Security Dilemma," *World Politics*, Vol. 20, No. 2 (January 1950); and Robert Jervis, *Perception and Misperception in International Politics* (Princeton, N.J.: Princeton University Press, 1976). For the standard statement of the neo-realist position, see Kenneth Waltz, *Theory of International Politics* (Reading, Mass.: Addison-Wesley, 1979).

36. Barry Posen, "The Security Dilemma and Ethnic Conflict," in Brown, ed., *Ethnic Conflict and International Security*, pp. 103–124.

and Pakistan in August 1947, state authority collapsed for all practical purposes. As millions of Hindus and Muslims fled in opposite directions, anarchic conditions prevailed. Police and paramilitary forces were no longer neutral, and the departing British government lacked the necessary will and capacity to maintain order.[37] In this milieu, demagogic politicians from both communities exploited cultural myths and demonized political adversaries. These appeals both fostered group cohesion and provoked the anxieties of minority communities. As group cohesion and solidarity crystallized, both Hindus and Muslims, especially those trapped in geographic enclaves, feared significant power shifts. Accordingly, they targeted members of other communities to fend off a potentially dangerous future. Soon, competitive retaliation became the order of the day, and mass carnage spread across much of northern India.[38]

The ethnic security-dilemma theory has, however, little or no relevance in explaining the origins of the Kashmir crisis. The Hindu and Muslim populations in Kashmir had lived as neighbors for several hundred years, and had experienced three wars (between India and Pakistan, in 1947–48, 1965, and 1971) without significant inter-ethnic conflict. No existential threat confronted the Muslim community in the Valley in the years preceding the outbreak of the insurgency. While there is little question that, since the outbreak of the insurgency, intra-group cohesion and solidarity *has* dramatically increased within the Kashmir Valley, since 1990 the Valley has been virtually "cleansed" of its Hindu population. Consequently, the security dilemma explanation is more apposite to the aftermath of the outbreak of the insurgency. Today, as the authority of the Indian state is widely contested in Kashmir, the Hindu community does fear the wrath of the Muslim insurgents, and the members of the Muslim community not involved in the insurgency fear retaliation from the displaced Hindus.

ETHNIC DOMINANCE AND DISCRIMINATION

Finally, violence between communities sometimes results from widespread discrimination along ethnic lines. Ethnic discrimination refers simply to policies or actions that dominant ethnic groups pursue which result in inequalities in "ethnic group members' well-being or political access in comparison with

37. For a good introduction to the transfer of power and the conditions prevailing in South Asia in 1947, see Leonard Mosley, *The Last Days of the British Raj* (London: Weidenfield and Nicholson, 1961).
38. See Mary Doreen Wainwright and C.H. Phillips, ed., *The Partition of India: Policies and Perspectives* (London: Allen and Unwin, 1975).

other social groups."[39] A dominant ethnic community may be able to use an amalgam of coercion and rewards to ensure the quiescence of minority communities. In this context the Malaysian case is instructive. Repressive policies, coupled with the leavening effects of economic growth, have blunted the sharp edges of potential conflict in Malaysia. After riots in May 1969 threatened the political and social stability of the country, Malaysia embarked on an extensive strategy of social engineering. The policy sought explicitly to disassociate race from occupation. This policy of social restructuring, called *bumiputra* (literally, "son of the soil"), legalized discrimination in favor of ethnic Malays, the majority population. Yet despite this systematic and blatant discrimination, Malaysia has been able to maintain ethnic peace. The two principal ethnic minorities, the Chinese and the Indians, have remained politically quiescent. Although the Indian community in particular nurses many grievances, neither minority group has resorted to violence to redress its disadvantaged status. The reasons for Malaysia's ethnic peace are complex; briefly, it has been maintained through a deft mix of political coercion and economic growth. There is little question that ethnic Malays have been the principal beneficiaries of Malaysia's *bumiputra* policies. On the other hand, the two major ethnic minorities have also benefited to varying degrees from steady economic growth.[40]

This theory cannot explain the Kashmir case. The pre-independence Hindu ruler, Maharaja Hari Singh, did not pursue explicit policies designed to exclude Muslims from access to education or government employment. Nevertheless, the Muslim majority were subjected to widespread discrimination.[41] Yet only a handful of communally based challenges to his rule took place. In post-independence Kashmir, by contrast, the Muslims' legacy of past economic discrimination has, to some extent, been overcome. Disparities remain, but the grievances of the insurgents focus far more sharply on the shortcomings of the political process than on economic inequalities.

OTHER EXPLANATIONS FOR THE CRISIS

A number of more specific explanations for the crisis offer partial explanations for the origins of the crisis. For example, Ashutosh Varshney has traced the

---

39. Gurr and Harff, *Ethnic Conflict in World Politics*, p. 88.
40. S. Jayasankaran, "Balancing Act," *Far Eastern Economic Review,* Vol. 158, No. 51 (December 21, 1995), pp. 24–26; William Case, "Aspects and Audiences of Legitimacy," in Muthiah Alagappa, ed., *Political Legitimacy in Southeast Asia: The Quest for Moral Authority* (Stanford, Calif.: Stanford University Press, 1995).
41. Copland, "Islam and Political Mobilization in Kashmir."

origins of the crisis to the clash of three competing visions of nationalism: Kashmiri, secular, and Islamic.[42] At one level, his argument is apt: the Kashmir crisis does involve a clash of competing national visions. But this argument still fails to explain the specific timing of the insurgency. If the decline of secular nationalism is one of the factors behind the insurgency, then why did it not break out in the 1950s, when Sheikh Abdullah was dismissed under pressure from Hindu nationalist organizations in Jammu for his putative disloyalty to the Indian Union?[43]

Prem Shankar Jha, an Indian journalist, has argued that the revolt in Kashmir can be traced to middle-class frustrations. He contends that employment opportunities have not kept pace with the growth of an educated middle class in Kashmir. Consequently, the rebellion represents the expression of collective and growing frustration with the lack of economic opportunity. Furthermore, unlike Indians from other regions who seek employment in all parts of India, Kashmiris are unwilling to relocate.[44] Jha's argument is partially correct, but it fails to explain the depth of resentment against the Indian state, nor does it explain the ethno-religious dimensions of the insurgency. Finally, Jha's argument cannot account for why some of the insurgents argue for unification with Pakistan, given Pakistan's failure to develop the portion of Kashmir it has controlled since 1947.

Finally, Alistair Lamb, a British scholar, has written two narrative accounts of the historical factors that contributed to the insurgency.[45] His works are atheoretic and tendentious. Lamb selectively uses the historical record to highlight India's real and putative malfeasances in Kashmir. His work offers little explanation of the Kashmir conundrum.

Political Mobilization and Ethnic Conflict

I argue that the Kashmiri insurgency arose out of a process of political mobilization that was juxtaposed with steady institutional decay. The political mobilization of Kashmiris started later than in the rest of the Indian state, but it

---

42. Ashutosh Varshney, "Three Compromised Nationalisms: Why Kashmir Has Been a Problem," in Thomas, *Perspectives on Kashmir*, pp. 191–234.
43. See, for example, Ishtiaq Ahmed, *State, Nation, and Ethnicity in Contemporary South Asia* (London: Pinter, 1996), esp. pp. 145–146.
44. Prem Shankar Jha, "Frustrated Middle Class, Roots of Kashmir's Alienation," in Engineer, *Secular Crown on Fire*, pp. 34–37.
45. Lamb, *Kashmir: A Disputed Legacy*; and Lamb, *Birth of a Tragedy: Kashmir, 1947* (Hertingfordbury, U.K.: Roxford Books, 1994).

accelerated dramatically after the 1970s. Institutional decay in Kashmir began as early as the 1950s, much earlier than in the rest of India. These two trends intersected as a new generation of Kashmiris emerged on the political scene.

Political mobilization refers to the process by which individuals enter as actors into the political arena. It involves growing demands for political participation. Instead of remaining politically quiescent and accepting the existing political dispensation, mobilized populations actively seek to influence their political destinies. Political mobilization stems from increasing literacy, media exposure, access to higher education, and the concomitant growth of political knowledge.

Among minority populations in poly-ethnic societies, such increased political awareness usually leads to greater sensitivity to ethnic discrimination.[46] The growth of such sensitivity leads to greater demands for political involvement and participation. Under such conditions, ethnic groups may mobilize along ethno-political lines for collective action.[47] As demands for participation from an ethnic community grow, states can adopt two possible strategies of response. At one level, they can seek to repress the calls for increased participation. To this end, states can limit the free expression of ideas, incarcerate emergent political leaders, and place curbs on various forms of organized political activity. Such strategies of denial are, at best, short-term palliatives. In the longer term, if they wish to avoid widespread conflict and upheavals, states have little or no choice but to direct these demands into institutional arenas.

The possibility of these demands turning into violent conflict are especially great in poly-ethnic societies. As newly mobilized ethnic groups enter the political arena and face (or perceive) widespread and protracted discrimination, they will organize along ethnic lines to articulate and seek redress of their grievances. Such grievances may be accommodated and channeled through organizational and institutional channels, such as judicial, legislative, and other organizational entities that provide pathways for the articulation of grievances and representation for venting discontent. Frequently, states may lack adequate substantive resources to address all these demands. But even carefully crafted symbolic gestures and concessions can allay the strength of such demands.[48] Indeed, on a number of occasions, the Indian state has successfully provided this room for political maneuver and has fended off more intractable de-

---

46. See Weiner, *Sons of the Soil.*
47. Milton J. Esman, "Political and Psychological Factors in Ethnic Conflict," in Montville, *Conflict and Peacemaking in Multiethnic Societies*, pp. 53–64.
48. See Murray Edelman, *The Symbolic Uses of Politics* (Urbana: University of Illinois Press, 1972).

mands.[49] Such adroit responses were possible thanks to the existence of robust political institutions.

If, in contrast, states provide few institutional means for the expression of ethno-political grievances and fail to offer other rewards, newly mobilized ethnic minorities may resort to violence to express their demands. Faced with violent ethnic protest, states will tend to adopt largely coercive strategies. Such strategies are mostly counterproductive, however: repression alone does not beget political quiescence. On the contrary, it may have the effect of eliminating more moderate leaders and the radicalization of the movement.[50] Eventually, such strategies may culminate in a spiral of violence. Even if the violent political protest is suppressed, underlying grievances will remain and contribute to recrudescent violence.

The explanation offered here attempts to account for the rise of such ethno-political violence in four components or stages. First, it assumes the existence of a minority group in a poly-ethnic society that over time becomes aware of political and economic discrimination. Second, requisite institutional entities for the expression of such dissent are lacking. Third, faced with protracted discrimination and no available institutional means for expressing dissent, a segment of the community resorts to violence to alter the status quo. During this process, more moderate leaders who counsel restraint and compromise become increasingly marginalized. Fourth and finally, the state in question can either seek to make concessions and address the underlying grievances or resort to repressive tactics.[51]

The growth of political mobilization in Kashmir occurred at a slower pace than in the rest of India. The reasons lie in Kashmir's peculiar political history. In the closing days of the nationalist struggle in India, Kashmir was under the tutelage of Maharaja Hari Singh, not the most enlightened of princely rulers. Steady opposition to his reign gathered force as independence and partition approached. The principal opposition was organized behind the All Jammu and Kashmir National Conference. Its leader, Sheikh Mohammed Abdullah, had originally sought to mobilize Muslims in Jammu and Kashmir and to exact concessions from the maharaja. Accordingly, Abdullah's political party, which

---

49. See Subrata Kumar Mitra, "Room to Maneuver in the Middle: Local Elites, Political Action, and the State in India," *World Politics*, Vol. 43, No. 3 (April 1991), pp. 390–413.
50. Nikki R. Keddie, *Religion and Politics in Iran: Shi'ism from Quietism to Revolution* (New Haven, Conn.: Yale University Press, 1983).
51. On occasion, states may have to adopt a "talk and fight" strategy. Some ethno-national protesters may be well past the stage of concessions and compromises.

was founded in October 1932, was initially known as the All Jammu and Kashmir Muslim Conference. Under the influence of Jawaharlal Nehru, Abdullah broadened the party's political base; it renamed itself the Jammu and Kashmir National Conference after considerable vigorous debate. During World War II, the party moved closer to the principal nationalist organization, the Indian National Congress, and distanced itself from the Muslim League, led by Mohammed Ali Jinnah.[52] Within Kashmir, the National Conference spearheaded efforts to bring about political and economic reform. The platform announced by the National Conference in September 1944 proposed a new constitution that would lead to representative government based on universal adult franchise and that would guarantee civil and political rights to all Kashmiris. The platform also called for extensive state intervention in the economic arena to bring about equity and social justice.[53] Another organization, the Muslim Conference, founded in 1934, gravitated toward Jinnah and the Muslim League.

There is very little doubt that Abdullah's National Conference enjoyed widespread support within the state.[54] Yet Abdullah's strategy of political mobilization, although populist, was not democratic.[55] The organizational structure of the National Conference belied its socialist and democratic ideology.[56] As a political party, it was constructed largely around the person of Abdullah and his close advisers. Decision-making was highly centralized and concentrated in his hands. Little internal dissent was allowed. Abdullah's tight grasp of the reins of power contributed to tensions between him and some of his most trusted lieutenants, principally Mohiuddin Karra, Maulana Masoodi, and Mirza Afzal Beg.

Abdullah's successors, with the possible exception of G.M. Sadiq, perpetuated his authoritarian ways. As a result, no honest political opposition was ever

---

52. The Muslim League was the principal political party that promoted Muslim separatism in British India and was instrumental in the creation of Pakistan. Its support was found primarily among the landed gentry in the United Provinces of northern India. See Paul Brass, *Language, Religion and Politics in North India* (Cambridge, U.K.: Cambridge University Press, 1974); Prem Nath Bazaz, *The History of Struggle for Freedom in Kashmir* (Karachi: National Book Foundation, 1954), p. 179; and Das Gupta, *Jammu and Kashmir*.
53. Das Gupta, *Jammu and Kashmir*, pp. 66–67.
54. See Ian Copland, "The Abdullah Factor: Kashmiri Muslims and the Crisis of 1947," in D.A. Low, ed., *The Political Inheritance of Pakistan* (New York: St. Martin's, 1991).
55. For a detailed, if biased, account of Abdullah's strategies of mobilization and his rise to power, see Bazaz, *The History of Struggle for Freedom in Kashmir*.
56. This phenomenon was hardly unique to the Indian political context. For the classic statement of this discrepancy between ideology and organization, see Robert Michels, *Political Parties: A Sociological Study of the Oligarchical Tendencies of Modern Democracy* (New York: Dover, 1959).

allowed to develop in the state. An early analyst of the politics of Jammu and Kashmir wrote,

Time has now come to pass judgement on Abdullah's Government. Internally, it was hardly democratic. Opposition was suppressed, and civil liberties existed in name and for those who shared his views. His economic views were radical but he combined them with the working of the like-minded totalitarian Governments elsewhere. He enjoyed tremendous popularity, yet resorted to questionable means to gain an electoral majority.[57]

Abdullah's policies significantly limited the growth and development of political institutions within Jammu and Kashmir. Consequently, even though a Constituent Assembly was convened in October 1951 and the state adopted its own constitution, the mechanisms of political representation were stunted from the outset. Unlike elections in the rest of India, elections in Jammu and Kashmir were largely farcical. The National Conference and its operatives dominated the politics of the state.[58] Furthermore, the central government in New Delhi did little to stay the hand of the National Conference as long as it did not question the accession of Jammu and Kashmir into the Indian Union.

IMPROVING SOCIO-ECONOMIC CONDITIONS IN THE STATE

The National Conference did much, particularly in its initial years in power, to improve socio-economic conditions in the state. It provided the basis for the emergence of a new generation of Kashmiris better educated than their predecessors, more conscious of their political rights and prerogatives, and impatient with the earlier generation of political leaders. This generation would eventually come to challenge the National Conference.

Maharaja Hari Singh had done little to ameliorate the social and economic backwardness of his kingdom. During his reign, the principal source of income, land, was held largely by two classes of landlords. The *jagirdars* owned entire villages from which they extracted revenue. The monarch had granted them these *jagirs*, some in perpetuity. The *muafidars* were individuals such as *pandits* (Brahmins) or *faqirs* (Muslim mendicants) who paid no taxes on the lands assigned to them by the monarch. These two groups of landlords rented out most of the available cultivable land under exploitative conditions.[59]

57. Das Gupta, *Jammu and Kashmir*, p. 209.
58. The one important exception was the communal Praja Parishad Party, formed in November 1947 and led by Prem Nath Dogra and Balraj Madhok, which had a substantial following in the Hindu-dominated areas of Jammu.
59. Das Gupta, *Jammu and Kashmir*, p. 188.

Given its socialist proclivities, one of the first political initiatives that the National Conference undertook after winning office was to abolish this land-lordism. Two pieces of legislation were passed in 1950: the Abolition of Big Landed Estates Act and the Distressed Debtors Relief Act. The first confiscated all parcels of cultivable land greater than 23 acres and either distributed them to landless peasants or converted them into state property. The second created a board that instituted policies for the relief of debt. Although these initiatives alienated a significant segment of the Jammu-based Hindu landed gentry, they won Abdullah the powerful loyalty of lower- and middle-class Muslims and Hindus.[60] Long after Abdullah was dismissed as the prime minister[61] and incarcerated in 1953 for ostensibly conspiring to declare Kashmir's inde-pendence from the Indian Union, large segments of the Kashmiri peasantry remained loyal to him. And even though subsequent National Conference governments proved inept and corrupt, Abdullah's personal stature in Kashmir remained largely undiminished.

THE PROCESS OF POLITICAL MOBILIZATION

The socio-economic transformation of Kashmir, begun under Sheikh Abdullah and continued by his successors and increasingly by the national government in New Delhi, transformed the electorate from a politically passive to an increasingly politically alert and assertive population.[62] As Kashmiris acquired more and more education, were exposed to the mass media, and achieved greater social and physical mobility, they became aware that the free exercise of adult franchise existed in virtually all other parts of India. Only in Kashmir were elections routinely compromised. This discrepancy drove their discontent. After years of frustrated attempts at meaningful political participation, and in the absence of institutional means of expressing dissent, the resort to more violent means became all but inevitable.

One vital mechanism of political mobilization was the growth of educational institutions. Table 1 illustrates the dramatic growth in literacy rates during the 1970s and 1980s. In the ten years from 1971 to 1981, the overall literacy rate in

---

60. Das Gupta, *Jammu and Kashmir*, pp. 189–190.
61. The special circumstances of Jammu and Kashmir's accession to India permitted the chief minister of the state to be referred to as the prime minister.
62. For a sophisticated discussion of the economic transformation of Jammu and Kashmir, see M.L. Misri and M.S. Bhatt, *Poverty, Planning, and Economic Change in Jammu and Kashmir* (New Delhi: Vikas, 1994). Some economists argue that the increasing flow of money from the central govern-ment into Jammu and Kashmir created a dependent economy in the state. Interview with senior Jammu and Kashmir government economist, New Delhi, January 1994.

Table 1. Literacy Rates in Jammu and Kashmir, 1961–81.

	Male	Female	Total population	Increase
1961	16.97	4.26	11.03	
1971	26.75	9.28	18.58	68.45%
1981	36.29	15.88	26.67	43.54%

SOURCE: *Census of India 1981, Handbook of Population Statistics* (Delhi: Government of India, 1988), p. 60.

Jammu and Kashmir grew by more than 43 percent, the third fastest growth rate in the nation.[63] Table 2 shows a similarly dramatic increase in enrollments in educational institutions.

In addition to the growth of formal education, Kashmir saw a dramatic growth in *madrassa* (Islamic schools) education.[64] The growth of *madrassas* received a tremendous boost after 1983, with the emigration of a significant number of Bangladeshi *maulvis* (Muslim religious teachers) from the eastern Indian state of Assam to Kashmir after the massacre in the Assamese village of Nellie.

The growth in educational facilities at a variety of levels meant that increasing numbers of Kashmiris became literate. Literacy enables individuals to have a better comprehension of the social and political forces that affect their lives. Consequently, they gain an increased awareness of politics at local, national, and international levels.

The expansion of mass media also bolstered the process of political mobilization. As shown in Table 3, tremendous growth has taken place over the last four decades in the print media throughout India and in Kashmir in particular. In the span of approximately fifteen years, the number of newspapers published grew by some 500 percent.[65] In addition to the dramatic increase in the actual numbers of newspapers published, Kashmir also saw significant increases in newspaper circulation. Though the data are incomplete, they are nevertheless revealing. In 1982, total newspaper circulation in Kashmir was

63. For the ranking of literacy growth rates, see Afsir Karim and the Indian Defence Review Team, *Kashmir: The Troubled Frontiers* (New Delhi: Lancers, 1994), pp. 188 and 250.

64. Jagmohan, *My Frozen Turbulence in Kashmir* (New Delhi: Allied, 1993), pp. 179–180.

65. I am indebted to Professor Kanti Bajpai of the School of International Studies, Jawaharlal Nehru University, New Delhi, for these figures. They were compiled from *Mass Media in India* (New Delhi: Publications Division, Ministry of Information and Broadcasting, Government of India, various years). These volumes have been published more or less annually since 1978.

Table 2.   Educational Enrollments in Jammu and Kashmir, 1950–93.

	Primary	Middle	Secondary	General colleges	Universities	Specialized colleges
1950–51	78,000	20,000	5,600	2,779	—	—
1960–61	216,000	60,000	22,000	8,005	174	353
1968–69	362,000	105,000	51,000	16,718	1,285	2,208
1980–81	537,800	167,200	83,600	15,828	3,351	2,652
1985–86	663,700	232,700	132,800	20,089	4,139	4,206
1992–93	940,000	370,000	262,000	34,000	NA	NA

SOURCES: Government of Jammu and Kashmir, Department of Planning and Development, Directorate of Economics and Statistics, *Digest of Statistics, 1985–86;* Government of India, *Jammu and Kashmir: An Economic Profile* (New Delhi, 1995), p. 18.

estimated to be around 119,000. Two years later, the circulation had risen to 192,000. In another five years, the figure was 369,000. Interestingly, by 1990, newspaper circulation was down quite sharply—to only 280,000, perhaps due to militant threats against various newspapers, as well as to the flight of many Kashmiris from the Valley. In 1992 it stood at 297,000.[66]

Finally, Kashmir, along with other parts of India, has seen a significant growth in the electronic media, especially television and video and tape recorders. Kashmir was one of the earliest states in India to have access to television, because the Indian government wanted to ensure that the Kashmiris were not exposed only to Pakistani broadcasts. Thus Srinagar was the third "television center" to be commissioned in India after Delhi and Bombay in 1972. Access to television broadcasts is, of course, dependent on the availability of television sets. Making accurate estimates of the numbers of television sets in use is problematic, but the fact that licenses were required for the purchase of television sets before 1985 does provide some basis for an assessment. In 1981, for example, the Department of Posts and Telegraphs issued 3,262 licenses. By 1984, the number had increased sixfold to 20,896. It should be noted that the number of licenses issued, is at best, an imperfect indicator; by the mid-1980s fewer and fewer individuals bothered purchasing television licenses. The most recent estimate, made in 1992, suggests that Kashmir had 118,000 television sets, or 1 per 65 residents.[67]

66. Figures from *Mass Media in India*, various years.
67. Figures from *Mass Media in India*, various years.

Table 3. Newspapers Published in Jammu and Kashmir and in India, 1965–84.

	1965	1970	1975	1984
Jammu & Kashmir	46	102	135	203
All India	7,906	11,036	12,423	21,784

SOURCES: *Mass Media in India 1978* (New Delhi: Publications Division, Ministry of Information & Broadcasting, 1978); *Mass Media in India 1986* (New Delhi: Publications Division, Ministry of Information & Broadcasting, 1987).

The availability of videocassette recorders (VCRs) and videotapes has greatly expanded the reach of television coverage. Statistics on the availability of VCRs in Kashmir are hard to come by. In 1982, it is estimated, India overall had 180,000 VCRs, which accounted for 11.6 percent of those homes that had television sets. In 1983, the estimate of VCRs was 530,000, 34.2 percent of television-owning homes. In 1984, the figure had risen to 610,000. Although no Kashmir-specific data are currently available, Kashmir is probably not significantly different from other parts of India.

Given the dramatic expansion in literacy and media exposure, the current generation of Kashmiris is far more conscious of its political rights and privileges. This generation is also more aware of political developments well beyond the Valley of Kashmir and is far more politically sophisticated and knowledgeable than previous generations of Kashmiris who had been loyal to Sheikh Abdullah and his family.[68] This generation has proved unwilling to tolerate the political skullduggery that long characterized Kashmiri politics. The deinstitutionalization of Kashmiri politics would, however, prove very costly for the Indian state.

Explaining Political Decay

The literature of political development in the 1950s and 1960s assumed that, to use Robert Packenham's phrase, "all good things go together."[69] In other words, economic development would inevitably contribute to political devel-

---

68. The collapse of the Soviet empire in the late 1980s profoundly animated a younger generation of Kashmiris. Many reasoned that if the might of the Soviet empire could be challenged, so could the writ of the Indian state.
69. See Robert Packenham, *Liberal America and the Third World* (Princeton, N.J.: Princeton University Press, 1975).

opment.[70] Political development, for the most part, was assumed to mean the development of democratic institutions. Samuel Huntington in 1968 forthrightly questioned the premises of the first wave of the political development literature.[71] Far from contributing to democracy, Huntington argued, economic development might lead to widespread political instability, especially in the absence of robust political institutions. Such institutions, he contended, were critical for maintaining political order in societies undergoing rapid economic modernization. Modernization, in Huntington's view, opened up new possibilities of social and economic mobility, reduced the familiar ties of kith and community, and generated increasing demands for political participation. In the absence of well-developed political institutions that could mediate these demands, the quickening pace of economic modernization could give rise to political decay and eventually instability.[72] Huntington believed that among the vast majority of states in the post-colonial world, India had considerable promise because of the strength of its political institutions: a highly professional civil service, a well-developed electoral system, and a political party (the Indian National Congress) that encompassed a variety of interests.

THE PATH TO POLITICAL DECAY

The decline of those promising political institutions in India, especially since the days of Indira Gandhi, has been commented on at length elsewhere.[73] In Kashmir, the process of institutional decay started even before Indira Gandhi. The singular political tragedy of Kashmir's politics was the failure of the local and the national political leaderships to permit the development of an honest political opposition. From the time of independence to his dismissal from office in 1953, Sheikh Abdullah dominated the politics of Kashmir. Subsequent National Conference regimes used the prerogatives of office to prevent the growth of any meaningful opposition.

---

70. For an early critique of the these premises of political development and nation-building, see Walker Connor, "Nation-Building or Nation-Destroying?" *World Politics*, Vol. 24, No. 3 (April 1972), pp. 319–355.
71. Huntington, *Political Order in Changing Societies*.
72. For a thoughtful critique of Huntington, focusing on his emphasis on "political order" and his neglect of questions of the legitimacy of institutions, see Mark Kesselman, "Order or Movement? The Literature of Political Development as Ideology," *World Politics*, Vol. 26, No. 1 (October 1973), pp. 139–154.
73. See James Manor, "The Dynamics of Political Integration and Disintegration," in A. Jeyaratnam Wilson and Dennis Dalton, eds., *The States of South Asia: Problems of National Integration* (Honolulu: University Press of Hawaii, 1982).

New Delhi tolerated this because Kashmir, as India's only Muslim-majority state, was central to the nation-building enterprise in India.[74] Nehru and other national leaders contended that the existence of a Muslim-majority state in India demonstrated that all faiths could thrive under the aegis of a secular state. Pakistan's irredentist claim on Kashmir, along with the state's ambiguous international status, made India's national leadership especially concerned about Kashmir's position within the Indian Union. As a consequence, the national political leadership, from Jawaharlal Nehru onward, adopted a unified stand on the internal politics of Jammu and Kashmir: as long as the local political bosses avoided raising the secessionist bogey, the government in New Delhi overlooked the locals' political practices, corrupt or otherwise. Prime Minister Nehru, with characteristic candor, wrote to the Kashmiri journalist and activist Prem Nath Bazaz in 1962, "It is true that political liberty does not exist there in the same measure as in the rest of India. At the same time there is much more of it than there used to be."[75]

As a result of local chicanery and national laissez-faire, every election since the very first in March 1957, save those in 1977 and 1983, was marked by corruption and deceit.[76] Over the years, any opposition to the National Conference was steadily driven out of the institutional arena.

ETHNO-RELIGIOUS MOBILIZATION

Why did the mobilization in Kashmir take place along ethno-religious lines? Four factors are significant. First, the state is divided into districts that also produce a religious division. Srinagar and the surrounding Valley of Kashmir are predominantly Muslim. The districts of Leh and Kargil, which until 1979 formed the single district of Ladakh, have predominantly Buddhist and Muslim populations, respectively. Jammu is predominantly Hindu. The predominantly Muslim composition of the National Conference had little appeal among the Hindus of Jammu. Furthermore, acknowledging the difficulties of courting

---

74. See Ganguly, *The Origins of War in South Asia*.
75. Jawaharlal Nehru, as quoted in M.J. Akbar, *Kashmir: Behind the Vale* (New Delhi: Viking/ Penguin, 1991), p. 159.
76. These two elections were free of electoral malfeasances. In 1977, Abdullah had recently returned to power and was at the peak of his popularity. Consequently, he saw little reason to engage in electoral skullduggery. Furthermore, the newly formed Janata government was acutely conscious of its credentials for probity and fairness. In 1983, Farooq Abdullah, who had inherited his father's mantle, enjoyed considerable popularity. For a particularly harsh indictment of Sheikh Abdullah's rule in Kashmir, see Prem Nath Bazaz, *Democracy through Intimidation and Terror* (New Delhi: Heritage Publishers, 1978).

the Jammu Hindus, the National Conference all but wrote off Jammu for electoral purposes.[77] Buddhist-dominated Leh was also outside the ambit of National Conference politics.

Second, the geographic isolation of the Valley separated Kashmiri Islam from the larger currents of Muslim politics in India. Indian Muslims rarely made common cause with fellow Muslims in the Valley,[78] and the Muslims of the Valley never developed extensive ties with Muslim communities in the rest of India. As a consequence, they did not air their grievances as part of the national community but as a regional sub-community, with particular parochial concerns. Furthermore, divisions exist even among Kashmiri Muslims.

They were divided, first and foremost, by geography. Cut off from their co-religionists in Jammu by 15,000-feet mountain peaks, impassable in winter, the Muslims of Srinagar and its surrounding valley had evolved, over the centuries, a quite separate culture. While the people of Jammu spoke Dogri, a dialect akin to Punjabi, those of Srinagar spoke Kashmiri, which is closer to Persian; [the Muslims of Srinagar] built with brick and wood, rather than mud; and they dressed in a distinctive style typified, in the case of males, by the double pointed cap and the all-purpose cloak, the *farran*.[79]

Furthermore, Muslims face discrimination in the mainstream of Indian society, and there is no substantial Kashmiri Muslim expatriate community. Thus, the Muslims of the Valley were reluctant to venture into the rest of the country to seek their fortunes.

Third, as has been observed in other contexts, notably in Iran and Egypt, when secular politics fails to offer adequate channels for the expression of discontent, political mobilization tends to follow ethno-religious lines.[80] This avenue of protest had a long history in Kashmir. In the 1930s, Sheikh Abdullah's Muslim followers had battled those of Mirwaiz Yusuf Shah. Furthermore, even after independence a steady undercurrent of ethno-religious sentiment had swirled around the Jammat-i-Islami. On occasion, Sheikh Abdullah had even encouraged the followers of the Jammat to instill fear in New Delhi.

---

77. See Balraj Puri, *Simmering Volcano: Jammu's Relations with Kashmir* (New Delhi: Sterling, 1983).
78. One of those rare occasions was the theft of the *Moe-e-moqdas* (a hair of the prophet Mohammed) from the Hazaratbal Mosque in Srinagar in December 1963. News of this tragic incident set off rioting as far away as Calcutta.
79. Copland, "The Abdullah Factor," p. 224.
80. See William O. Beeman, "Images of the Great Satan: Representations of the United States in the Iranian Revolution," in Keddie, ed., *Religion and Politics in Iran;* and Fouad Ajami, "The Sorrows of Egypt," *Foreign Affairs,* Vol. 74, No. 5 (September/October 1995), pp. 72–88.

Abdullah threatened to unleash the forces of the Jammat unless New Delhi supported him unequivocally.[81]

A fourth and final factor was responsible for the ethno-religious direction of the movement: Pakistan, sensing an opportunity to weaken India's hold on Kashmir, funded, trained, and organized what had been a loose, unstructured movement into a coherent, organized enterprise directed toward challenging the writ of the Indian state in Kashmir.[82] The Soviet withdrawal from Afghanistan in 1990 and the subsequent collapse of the Soviet Union greatly facilitated Pakistan in arming and assisting the Kashmiri insurgents. Significant numbers of battle-hardened Afghan *mujahideen* could now be directed toward a new cause. These Afghans had more to offer than direct support; their experience of ousting the Soviets from Afghanistan provided a model of opposition and resistance to a powerful state and its well-organized military.

The success of the Palestinian *intifada* further reinforced both the violent aspect and the Islamic fundamentalist aspect of the insurgent movement in Kashmir. Owing to the Indian government's close links with the Palestine Liberation Organization, a sizeable number of Palestinian students had attended Kashmir University in Srinagar in the late 1970s and early 1980s. These Palestinian students became an important conduit for information about the success of the *intifada* against the Israeli forces on the Gaza and the West Bank. Their struggle animated many university students in Kashmir.[83]

In transforming the socio-economic landscape of Kashmir and producing a generation of politically aware Kashmiris, while also leaving the growth of political institutions in Kashmir stunted and corroded, the national and state-level governments left open few institutional channels for the expression of political discontent and dissent. Moreover, the national government construed demands for political autonomy as incipient secessionist moves. This set of policies inevitably drove the emergent generations of Kashmiris toward more extreme forms of political expression. As secular and institutional pathways of expressing political dissent were curbed, political mobilization and activism increasingly proceeded along an ethno-religious dimension.

---

81. See Ganguly, *Between War and Peace.*
82. See, for example, John Ward Anderson and Kamran Khan, "Pakistan Shelters Islamic Radicals," *Washington Post,* March 8, 1995, pp. A21–A22; and Edward W. Desmond, "Pakistan's Hidden Hand," *Time,* July 22, 1991, p. 23.
83. Interview with Mirwaiz Omar Farooq, Kashmiri Muslim religious leader and chairman of the All-Party Hurriyat Conference of Kashmir, New York, October 1995.

THE ROAD TO INSURGENCY

In the first two decades following the 1965 Indo-Pakistani war, Kashmir lay largely quiet. Even during the 1971 war, the majority of Kashmiris remained loyal to India. Furthermore, the breakup of Pakistan after the 1971 war dealt a significant blow to the Pakistani irredentist claim on Kashmir. Many Indian political commentators promptly questioned Pakistan's claim on the Muslims of Kashmir when it could not keep its two wings together on the basis of religious faith.

Between 1965 and 1989, however, the process of political mobilization and the undermining of political institutions throughout India, but particularly in Kashmir, accelerated. There was a brief respite in the mid-1970s, when the hopes of the politically aware Kashmiris were raised by the release and return of Sheikh Abdullah after years of house arrest. The government also agreed to review several pieces of central legislation that had been passed pertaining to Kashmir.[84] Abdullah's return to Kashmir was nothing short of triumphant. He promptly assumed the chief ministership and the leadership of the National Conference, and his party won a comfortable majority of seats in the next election in 1977, one of Kashmir's few openly conducted and fairly contested elections.

Yet this respite from Indira Gandhi's chicanery was brief. Sheikh Abdullah died in September 1982. He was succeeded first by his son, Farooq, a political neophyte who had none of the political survival skills required by the rough-and-tumble politics of the state and none of his father's charisma and political stature. In the 1983 state assembly elections, which were also reasonably fair (by Indian standards), Farooq rebuffed Indira Gandhi's efforts to forge an electoral alliance with the National Conference in Kashmir, and contested the elections alone. The National Conference again triumphed. But determined to install a Congress regime in Kashmir, Gandhi dismissed Farooq Abdullah on tenuous grounds in July 1984, replacing him with G.M. Shah, a disaffected member of the National Conference.

Shah's term in office was short and troubled. The abrupt dismissal of Abdullah had deeply offended a new generation of politically conscious Kashmiris. Shah, who commanded no wide following within the state, was seen as a central government stooge. During the next two years, a variety of political disturbances—strikes, demonstrations, and bombings—wracked the state.

---

84. Balraj Puri, *Towards Insurgency* (New Delhi: Orient Longman, 1993).

G.M. Shah proved singularly inept at curbing the rising tide of violence. In 1986, he too was dismissed on the grounds of corruption and failure to maintain public order in the state. In November of that same year, Rajiv Gandhi (who had become the prime minister following his mother's assassination in October 1984) signed an accord with Farooq Abdullah, under the terms of which Farooq was returned to the chief ministership of Jammu and Kashmir. This accord forms yet another critical turning point in precipitating the insurgency. Whatever sympathy and legitimacy that Farooq had had in the eyes of the emergent Kashmiri youth was now lost. The accord reduced him to the stature of a mere stalking horse for the Congress Party in Kashmir.

In the 1987 election, considered to be the most compromised in Kashmir's recent history, the Congress Party and the National Conference jointly contested the state assembly elections; they were opposed by the Muslim United Front (MUF), a conglomeration of political parties. In this election, voters were intimidated, ballot boxes tampered with, and candidates threatened. Whereas previous generations of Kashmiris, whose political consciousness was low, had long tolerated all manner of electoral irregularities, the generation that had emerged in Kashmir during the long years of Sheikh Abdullah's incarceration did not have the same regard for the Abdullah family, nor was it willing to tolerate such widespread electoral fraud. Indeed, it is rather telling that several key insurgent leaders, Shabir Shah, Yasin Malik, and Javed Mir, were polling agents for the Muslim United Front in the 1987 elections. These individuals, along with thousands of their peers, were well aware that most elections in India are largely free and fair. (Even when electoral fraud occurs elsewhere in the country, a free press and the watchdog role of the Election Commission lead to the countermanding of electoral returns). The extensive electoral malfeasances that they witnessed in 1987 convinced this younger generation of Kashmiris that the national government in New Delhi had scant regard for their political rights and reckless disregard for democratic procedures. With no other institutional recourse open for expressing their disenchantment with the flawed political process, they resorted to violence. The insurgency has taken the lives of tens of thousands, forced hundreds of thousands from their homes, and shows no sign of abating.

Conclusions

An examination of the origins of the insurgency in the Indian-controlled portion of Kashmir suggests a path along which ethno-religious movements may develop. The utility of this explanation may extend well beyond the subcontinent. Increasing political mobilization among minority communities is virtually inevitable across the globe. States may try to rely on coercive mechanisms to limit demands for political participation, but Kashmir is a striking reminder of the dangers. Attempts to fend off such demands through coercive means can only contribute to political deinstitutionalization in the long term. The costs of such institutional decay are, as the Kashmir insurgency demonstrates, extraordinarily high.

The growth of political assertiveness of minority communities in democratic states is virtually inevitable. As minorities acquire increased literacy and education, they will become more conscious of their political rights and will seek to assert them. Nondemocratic, poly-ethnic states can suppress minority demands for political participation through co-optation, coercion, or repression.

Democratic poly-ethnic states, however, cannot resort to such strategies with impunity. In the longer run, the adoption of such policies proves to be enormously corrosive of the very values that they uphold and espouse. The seven-year-old insurgency in Kashmir has already had pernicious effects on the Indian polity. To aid the armed forces in their efforts to contain the insurgency, the Indian government has passed draconian legislation that severely curbs personal freedoms and civil liberties in Kashmir. The legislation also enables members of the security forces to use force with virtual impunity.[85] These measures, once on the books, are difficult to reverse.

At another level, the failure of institutional mechanisms for resolving political problems leads to the adoption of coercive and military strategies, with adverse consequences. Continued reliance on the Indian army to quell civil unrest in Kashmir and other parts of India bodes ill for civil-military relations in India. Even the higher echelons of the Indian army have warned about the dangers of excessive reliance on the army to deal with civil violence.[86] The dangers of a military coup in India are hardly imminent. However, in any poly-ethnic state, the use of the army against particular ethnic groups poses the distinct danger of communalizing the armed forces. For example, a significant number of Sikh troops of the Indian army mutinied after the 1984 attack on the Golden Temple in the city of Amritsar in Punjab.

---

85. Asia Watch and Physicians for Human Rights, *Kashmir: A Pattern of Impunity* (New York: Asia Watch and Physicians for Human Rights, 1993).

86. Šumit Ganguly, "From the Defense of the Nation to Aid to the Civil: The Army in Contemporary India," in Charles H. Kennedy and David J. Louscher, eds., *Civil-Military Interaction in Asia and Africa* (Leiden: E.J. Brill, 1991), pp. 11–26.

Finally, the breakdown of political order in poly-ethnic states often provides ethnic compatriots in neighboring states with grounds to intervene.[87] Pakistan's irredentist claim to Kashmir has spurred its substantial involvement in this conflict. To date, India and Pakistan have successfully avoided another full-scale war. However, as the insurgency drags on, and border tensions persist, war may still ensue through a mix of misperception and inadvertence.

---

87. Michael E. Brown, "The Causes and Regional Dimensions of Internal Conflict," in Brown, *International Dimensions of Internal Conflict*, pp. 597–598.

Part II:
Options for International Action

Internal Conflict and International Action

Michael E. Brown

Chantal de Jonge Oudraat

An Overview

Internal conflict is widespread and often causes tremendous amounts of human suffering, posing serious threats to regional and international security along the way. The debate over international responses to the problems posed by internal conflict is framed by two main questions: first, what *can* the international community— broadly defined to include sovereign states, regional and international organizations, and nongovernmental organizations (NGOs)—do to prevent, manage, and resolve internal conflicts? Second, what *should* the international community do with respect to these problems?

The starting point for analyzing international efforts to deal with these problems is examining different policy instruments and different policy tasks. First, one needs to distinguish between ten different policy instruments available to international actors: humanitarian assistance; fact-finding; mediation; confidence-building measures; traditional peacekeeping operations; multifunctional peacekeeping operations; military and economic assistance; arms embargoes and economic sanctions; judicial enforcement measures; and military force. Second, one needs to distinguish between three main policy tasks: conflict prevention; conflict management; and conflict resolution.

In this chapter, we begin with an overview of the ten main policy instruments at the disposal of international actors.[1] We then turn to the special problems posed by conflict prevention, conflict management, and conflict resolution. Our aim is to identify the conditions under which different kinds of international actions are most likely to succeed. This provides a foundation for developing some policy recommendations.

We develop six main arguments along the way. First, the problems posed by internal conflict are formidable, but options for international action do exist. The track record of international efforts to deal with the problems posed by internal conflicts is mixed: some efforts have succeeded; others have failed. The challenge for scholars is to identify the conditions under which success is most likely. The challenge for policymakers is to act accordingly. Second, internal conflicts are complex, so actions taken to address these problems have to be multifaceted. There is no silver bullet for the internal conflict problem. Third,

---

1. This chapter is based on Chantal de Jonge Oudraat, "The United Nations and Internal Conflict," and Michael E. Brown, "Internal Conflict and International Action," both in Brown, ed., *The International Dimensions of Internal Conflict* (Cambridge, Mass.: MIT Press, 1996), pp. 489–535, 603–627.

internal conflicts have deep roots, so long-term efforts will be needed if prevention, management, and resolution efforts are to succeed. There are no quick fixes for these problems. Fourth, internal conflict is widespread and international resources are limited, so difficult choices will have to be made about when and where to act. This means, in effect, addressing some problems and ignoring others. Fifth, the international community should favor actions that have high probabilities of success and low costs. This would be a banal thing to say but for the fact that the international community often does precisely the opposite. The goal should be building a track record of success that lends credibility to international undertakings.

Sixth, internal conflicts fall into two basic categories as far as international actors are concerned: cases where local parties are willing to work for peace and give their consent to international involvement; and cases where they are not. There is a sharp line between cases where local authorities have given their consent to international intervention and cases where they have not. It is imperative for intervenors to know if they are engaged in cooperative or coercive exercises. Operations that have the approval of local authorities have higher probabilities of success and lower costs than their coercive counterparts, and should therefore be given a higher priority. This does not mean that coercive actions should never be undertaken: coercive actions are indeed warranted when important interests are engaged or when moral outrages, such as genocide, are being committed. Under these conditions, international action should be undertaken even if local parties have not given their consent to international involvement, and will have to be coerced to change their behavior. In cases such as these, there is still a lot that the international community can do to prevent or end violence, but the costs of action are higher and the probabilities of success are lower. Coercive actions should therefore be undertaken selectively, with great care, and with great determination.

The Instruments

International actors interested in preventing, managing, and resolving internal conflicts have ten main policy instruments at their disposal. Seven are cooperative measures that depend in important ways on the consent of local parties: humanitarian assistance; fact-finding; mediation; confidence-building measures; traditional peacekeeping operations; multifunctional peacekeeping operations; and military and economic technical assistance. Three instruments are fundamentally coercive: arms embargoes and economic sanctions; judicial enforcement measures; and military force. We discuss each instrument in turn, focusing on the problems associated with their use and the conditions under which they are most likely to be used successfully.

HUMANITARIAN ASSISTANCE

As we have seen in many parts of the world, internal conflicts often involve disruptions of food production and distribution channels, human rights abuses, and direct attacks on civilian populations, producing horrifying numbers of casualties and refugees.[2] Since the end of the Cold War, many humanitarian assistance efforts have been launched to deal with the problems created by internal conflicts and civil wars, and many of these operations have been carried out under battlefield conditions. In many cases, humanitarian relief supplies have been seized by warring factions and used as political weapons. In some, relief personnel have been attacked. Although humanitarian assistance efforts are generally seen as non-political by distant powers and international bureaucrats, they are often seen as deeply political by local belligerents because humanitarian efforts can affect the balance of power on the ground.

The right to receive humanitarian assistance in armed conflicts, including intra-state conflicts, was recognized in the 1949 Geneva humanitarian law conventions, as well as in the 1977 Protocols to the Geneva conventions. UN General Assembly resolutions in 1988 and 1991 gave new impetus to this principle, and widened its scope to include natural disasters and other emergency situations. These resolutions also called on all states to facilitate such assistance. The norm of humanitarian assistance based on the principles of impartiality and neutrality is hence well-established.

However, in places where government authority and civil society have broken down, respect for humanitarian law has often evaporated. These kinds of situations have posed formidable problems for humanitarian organizations.[3] They have been obligated to protect their personnel and relief supplies. In some

---

2. For more on humanitarian crises and humanitarian relief efforts, see Larry Minear and Thomas G. Weiss, *Mercy Under Fire: War and the Global Humanitarian Community* (Boulder, Colo.: Westview, 1995); John Borton, *NGOs and Relief Operations: Trends and Policy Implications* (London: Overseas Development Institute, 1994); Robert I. Rotberg and Thomas G. Weiss, eds., *From Massacres to Genocide: The Media, Public Policy, and Humanitarian Crises* (Washington, D.C.: The Brookings Institution, 1996).

3. Within the UN Secretariat, the key actors are the Department for Humanitarian Affairs (UNDHA) and the Emergency Relief Coordinator. The other main organizations within the UN system are: the UN High Commissioner for Refugees (UNHCR); the United Nations Children's Fund (UNICEF); the World Food Program (WFP); and the UN Development Program (UNDP). An Inter-Agency Standing Committee (IASC), composed of the heads of the humanitarian agencies, including the International Committee of the Red Cross (ICRC), addresses coordination issues. For an overview of the activities of NGOs, see Thomas G. Weiss, "Nongovernmental Organizations and Internal Conflict," in Brown, *International Dimensions of Internal Conflict*, pp. 435–459.

cases, relief organizations have tried to do this themselves, entering into negotiations with local leaders to obtain access to troubled areas and to obtain guarantees of safety for relief personnel. In many cases, the situation on the ground has been highly volatile, and humanitarian operations have consequently been suspended.

The UN Security Council has become involved in some humanitarian crises because it believed that humanitarian problems posed threats to international peace and security. In three instances in the early 1990s, the Council made the provision of humanitarian assistance the primary task of UN peacekeeping operations—in Somalia, Rwanda, and Bosnia. It even authorized its peacekeeping forces to protect humanitarian relief convoys and populations in need with "all necessary means," including the use of military force. However, as events unfolded in all three countries, the United Nations failed to protect vulnerable populations and fulfill its humanitarian promises: its leading members lacked the will to address the root causes of the conflicts and to use force decisively; they simply treated the humanitarian symptoms of strife, and did so in a half-hearted and half-serious manner. The UN's credibility consequently suffered. Equally significant, the Security Council's impotence and incompetence helped to undermine respect for the principles of humanitarian law. Its actions in these cases were not just ineffective, they were in important respects counterproductive.

FACT-FINDING

Launching a fact-finding mission is a first step that the United Nations and regional organizations (such as the Organization for Security and Cooperation in Europe) can and often do take to help prevent, manage, or resolve conflicts. The idea is to provide a detailed, impartial report on the issues in dispute.

Fact-finding missions come in many forms. Some come at the initiative of the state or states in question. Others come at the initiative of the UN Security Council, the General Assembly, the Secretary-General, or regional bodies. Any of these actors can conduct a fact-finding mission, but all fact-finding missions to the territory of a state require an invitation from or the consent of the state or states that are being examined. Some missions consist of a single person; others are larger undertakings.

The mandates of fact-finding missions also vary. Some try to determine the causes of a conflict, while others examine the role of neighboring powers in a conflict. Many investigate human rights abuses. Some fact-finding missions are launched before violence breaks out, and are therefore conflict prevention efforts. Others are launched during conflicts, and can be seen as conflict management or conflict resolution measures.

Fact-finding missions frequently lead to other initiatives, such as good offices and mediation efforts, peacekeeping operations of various kinds, and the employment of coercive instruments, including arms embargoes, economic sanctions, judicial actions, and the use of military force.

Fact-finding missions with respect to internal conflicts have become much more common since the end of the Cold War. Their mandates have ranged from general assessments of conflict situations (the UN mission to Uzbekistan and Tajikistan), to investigations of reports of ethnic cleansing (the UN mission in Georgia). The fact-finding mission to Uzbekistan and Tajikistan in September 1992 led to a number of diplomatic and humanitarian initiatives, culminating in December 1994 with the establishment of a traditional UN peacekeeping operation in the region. The mission to Georgia had a much more limited mandate, and was carried out while the United Nations had an observer mission in place.

Assessing the impact of fact-finding missions is very difficult. Many of these missions are carried out under conditions of confidentiality, and their findings are not always publicized. However, fact-finding missions carried out before violence breaks out have considerable potential as conflict prevention measures. The role of the UN Secretary-General in this context should not be underestimated. Similarly, fact-finding missions carried out after a conflict has broken out can be useful in gathering information for subsequent conflict management and conflict resolution efforts.

MEDIATION

When trouble is brewing and especially when violence breaks out, third parties, regional organizations, and the United Nations often offer to mediate disputes.[4] Although many policymakers see mediation as a panacea, the fact of the matter is that mediation efforts in intra-state disputes are successful only part of the time.

---

4. Our discussion of mediation is based on Stephen John Stedman, "Negotiation and Mediation in Internal Conflict," in Brown, *International Dimensions of Internal Conflict*, pp. 341–376. See also Roy Licklider, ed., *Stopping the Killing: How Civil Wars End* (New York: New York University Press, 1993); I. William Zartman, *Ripe for Resolution: Conflict and Intervention in Africa* (New York: Oxford University Press, 1989); Stephen John Stedman, *Peacemaking in Civil War: International Mediation in Zimbabwe, 1974–1980* (Boulder, Colo.: Lynne Rienner, 1991).

The chances of success are greatest, first of all, when mediators have a clear strategy with respect to the problems at hand. This means having a clear sense of what their political objectives are, a plan for attaining these goals, and an international consensus on this vision. This might seem obvious, but in many cases outside parties are motivated by the feeling that they need to "do something" to prevent or stop bloodshed, but they do not have a coherent plan of action. Most of the West's diplomatic efforts to end the war in Bosnia were crippled by an inability to identify preferred outcomes, to develop a coherent plan for bringing these outcomes about, and to maintain a consensus on this course of action. Second, mediation efforts must be timed to coincide with moments when at least one and preferably all of the parties to a conflict prefer talking to fighting. Again, this might seem obvious, but diplomats often fail to appreciate that there is little they can do when all of the disputants see combat as their best option. Third, mediators need to have leverage over the disputants—the more, the better. At a minimum, mediators have to be willing to walk away from the mediation table. They need to convince their interlocutors that they will be left to their own devices if they do not take negotiations seriously. The chances of success are greatest, however, when mediators are also in a position to offer inducements if a negotiated settlement is reached, and to threaten to take coercive action if one is not.

Reaching a negotiated settlement, however, is only the first step because many agreements fall apart in the implementation phase of the process. One implementation problem is that, in some cases, local parties enter into negotiations in bad faith. They are not interested in a negotiated settlement; rather, their aim is to buy time, strengthen their military positions, and press on with the fight in the hope of achieving a complete victory. Second, local parties often overestimate the benefits of signing a peace agreement. In particular, local leaders often overestimate their popularity and their chances in post-settlement elections. Since the losers in elections in war-torn states have uncertain futures, they often prefer a resumption of warfare to depending on the good will of their former adversaries. Third, local parties almost always cheat in one way or another when its comes to implementing peace agreements. Fighters are often kept out of cantonment areas and weapons are often withheld both to maintain political leverage in postwar politics and as a hedge against the possibility that war will resume. A final implementation problem is that the leaders of factions are unable to exert control over all of their supposed followers. Rogue forces and would-be warlords can pose serious problems for the implementation of settlements.

Since mediation efforts are not expensive undertakings, the international community naturally gravitates towards them. Policymakers can claim that they are "doing something" about troublespots, but they do not have to bear the costs of imposing economic sanctions or run the risks of taking military action. Mediation should not be thought of as a placebo, however. It is a policy instrument that should be used judiciously and under conditions that are likely to lead to success. This will strengthen its track record and the credibility of future mediation efforts.

CONFIDENCE-BUILDING MEASURES

Security concerns often lead to arms racing and the onset of violence; they can lead to escalations in violence, and they can make conflict resolution efforts difficult.[5] One way to reduce the uncertainties that drive arms races and undermine peace processes is to promote transparency. International actors can encourage local parties to make declarations about the size and deployment of their military forces, and about arms acquisitions and transfers. They can help to create buffer zones from which heavy weapons are excluded. They can help to form joint consultative committees, with representatives from all of the relevant local parties, to discuss and hopefully resolve these and other security problems. Promoting transparency will not help when groups have malign intentions towards one another, but it will dampen escalatory spirals when groups are driven to strengthen themselves by fears of the unknown.

International actors can play two main roles in this effort. First, they can help to devise transparency and confidence-building measures and, through mediation efforts, get local parties to agree to them. Obtaining the consent and cooperation of all of the relevant local parties is key. Second, international actors can help to implement agreements through the deployment of international monitors. Although transparency and confidence-building measures could, in theory, be used to help prevent and manage internal conflicts, these measures have been used most often in the post–Cold War era in conflict resolution efforts. These kinds of measures are frequently incorporated into the frameworks for traditional peacekeeping and multifunctional peacekeeping operations.

---

5. For more on confidence-building measures, see Joanna Spear, "Arms Limitations, Confidence-Building Measures, and Internal Conflicts," in Brown, *International Dimensions of Internal Conflict*, pp. 377–410.

TRADITIONAL PEACEKEEPING OPERATIONS

Peacekeeping operations were not included in the UN Charter. They were developed during the Cold War to control conflicts between states. The main concern was that regional conflicts might draw in the great powers and lead to a superpower confrontation.

A traditional peacekeeping force is a military force positioned between two or more disputants. It is deployed with the consent of the relevant local parties, and its main mission is to monitor an agreed-upon cease-fire. In such an operation, peacekeepers are authorized to use force in self-defense and to deter small-scale attacks, but they do not have any significant coercive capabilities or enforcement authority. Traditional peacekeeping operations are usually accompanied by diplomatic efforts to resolve the underlying political conflict, and they are usually authorized by the UN Security Council.

As far as internal conflicts are concerned, traditional peacekeeping operations can help bolster peace processes in a number of ways.[6] First, they can monitor the cantonment and separation of warring factions. The UN peacekeeping missions in Cyprus, Georgia, and the initial deployment of UNPROFOR in the former Yugoslavia are examples. Second, peacekeeping forces can monitor and verify the withdrawal of foreign troops from a conflict zone. Examples include the UN operations in the Congo, which oversaw the withdrawal of Belgian troops from the region; in Angola, which oversaw the withdrawal of Cuban troops; and in Afghanistan, which oversaw the withdrawal of Russian troops. Third, peacekeeping forces can monitor the cessation of aid to irregular forces and insurrectionist movements. Examples include the UN missions in Lebanon and Yemen. Fourth, peacekeeping forces can help ensure that the territory of one state is not used for attacks on others. Cases where UN forces sought to do this include Yemen, Lebanon, Central America, and Tajikistan. Fifth, peacekeeping forces can help discourage one state or party from attacking another. The preventive deployment of UN troops in Macedonia was designed with this in mind.

---

6. For more on traditional peacekeeping operations, see United Nations, *The Blue Helmets: A Review of United Nations Peace-keeping*, 2nd ed. (New York: United Nations, 1990); United Nations Institute for Disarmament Research (UNIDIR), "Peace-keeping, Peace-making, Peace Enforcement," *UNIDIR Newsletter*, No. 24 (December 1993); Mats R. Berdal, *Whither UN Peacekeeping?* Adelphi Paper No. 281 (London: Brassey's for the International Institute for Strategic Studies, 1993); Lori Fisler Damrosch, ed., *Enforcing Restraint: Collective Intervention in Internal Conflicts* (New York: Council on Foreign Relations Press, 1993); Donald C.F. Daniel and Bradd C. Hayes, eds., *Beyond Traditional Peacekeeping*, (New York: St. Martin's Press, 1995); William J. Durch, ed., *The Evolution of UN Peacekeeping: Case Studies and Comparative Analysis* (New York: St. Martin's Press, 1993).

During the Cold War, traditional peacekeeping operations were deployed in four internal conflict situations: in the Congo, Cyprus, Lebanon, and Yemen. These operations were successful from the standpoint of preventing a super-power confrontation from developing. However, they failed to keep hostilities from breaking out again locally. One could therefore say that these operations were fairly successful as conflict control measures, but not as conflict resolution efforts—which they were never intended to be.

Since the end of the Cold War, the need to avoid confrontations between Washington and Moscow has of course diminished. Yet, traditional peacekeeping operations remain useful instruments for the prevention, containment, and resolution of conflicts, including internal conflicts. They have the greatest promise in cases where the five permanent members of the UN Security Council (known in UN circles as the P-5) have interests (but not antagonistic interests) and in cases where the political conditions for resolving the conflict in question or deploying multifunctional peacekeeping personnel do not exist. Traditional peacekeeping forces have played useful roles in dampening the post–Cold War conflicts in Angola, Central America, and Tajikistan, for example.

One should keep in mind, however, that peacekeeping forces are deployed because two failures have already taken place. First, diplomatic efforts to keep the conflict from breaking out in the first place have failed. Second, the Security Council has failed to carry out its responsibilities effectively. Indeed, traditional peacekeeping forces have often been deployed in places where more powerful military forces with coercive, Chapter VII mandates were needed. UN deployments in the former Yugoslavia, for example, experienced many problems for this reason. Traditional peacekeeping forces, in short, are often deployed under challenging circumstances. This should be taken into account when one assesses their track record.

MULTIFUNCTIONAL PEACEKEEPING

Multifunctional peacekeeping operations were developed by the United Nations to address the complex problems posed by intra-state and regional conflicts and to take advantage of the political opportunities that emerged after the end of the Cold War.[7] With the end of the U.S.-Soviet competition for global influence, Washington and Moscow disengaged from regional conflicts in various parts of the world. Reduced levels of superpower patronage made peace

---

7. For more on multifunctional peacekeeping operations, see ibid.

settlements more likely in Central America, sub-Saharan Africa, and Southeast Asia, for example. Although peace settlements had become more likely, they still faced formidable obstacles. Years of civil war had made combatants deeply mistrustful of one another, and many countries needed to be completely reconstructed politically and economically. The United Nations was uniquely well-suited to play the role of impartial monitor and facilitator of reconstruction and rehabilitation efforts.

Traditional peacekeeping operations and multifunctional peacekeeping operations are similar in that they both depend on the full consent of the local parties, the use of force is basically limited to self-defense, and they have limited coercive or enforcement capabilities. However, they differ in three important respects.

First, traditional peacekeeping forces can be deployed once a cease-fire is reached, but multifunctional peacekeeping operations can only be launched after a comprehensive peace agreement has been reached. Multifunctional operations are strictly post-conflict undertakings.

Second, traditional peacekeeping operations concentrate mainly on military problems—monitoring cease-fires and keeping combatants separated, for example—whereas multifunctional peacekeeping operations seek to address a wide range of military, political, and economic problems. Multifunctional operations often include a traditional peacekeeping element, but they also help to demobilize armed forces and collect weapons; monitor the provisions of political settlements; design and supervise constitutional, judicial, and political reforms; organize and monitor elections; train local police; monitor potential human rights problems; and to help promote economic recovery and economic development.

Third, traditional peacekeeping operations are military undertakings that involve few civilians, whereas multifunctional peacekeeping operations involve a wide range of military and civilian personnel. In some multifunctional operations, separate organizational elements are set up for electoral, human rights, and humanitarian issues, for example. Most multifunctional operations have large numbers of people involved in the maintenance of law and order, and the training of local police forces.

Two main problems have plagued multifunctional peacekeeping operations. First, the scope and complexity of these operations have left ample room for organizational and administrative mishaps: inadequate planning; incompetent and poorly trained personnel; equipment shortages; ineffective communications between the field and UN headquarters; and insufficient financial resources. The lines of command between the UN Secretariat and specialized humanitarian and development agencies have not always been clear, and inter-agency coordination has often been flawed.

Second, in some cases, some of the local parties have not been serious about implementing political settlements and making peace: they have used peace agreements as tactical devices that enable them to rest, recuperate, reorganize, and then re-launch military offensives. Multifunctional peacekeeping operations work only when the local parties genuinely seek peace and enter into agreements in good faith. Under these circumstances, the United Nations can help the former combatants overcome their mutual mistrust, monitor the implementation of the agreement, and help reconstruct political and economic institutions. Its function is to serve as an impartial observer, facilitator, and tripwire. If non-compliant behavior is observed, the United Nations can blow the whistle, thereby alerting all concerned that violations of the agreement have taken place. However, except for unintentional and minor breaches of the peace that can be dealt with by the military or police elements of the peacekeeping force, multifunctional operations have limited coercive or enforcement capacities: they cannot force the parties to live up to the terms of the agreement. Multifunctional peacekeeping operations are not trusteeships.

It follows, therefore, that the United Nations needs to be extremely careful to ensure that local parties are acting in good faith and that they are serious about making peace before launching multifunctional operations. Otherwise, the United Nations might find itself drawn into open hostilities. Its authority, credibility, and effectiveness will be greatly undermined as a result. In short, anticipating implementation problems is one of the keys to successful multifunctional peacekeeping operations.

MILITARY AND ECONOMIC ASSISTANCE
The military and economic levers of power can be used either to persuade, through military, economic, and technical assistance, or to coerce, through the imposition of arms embargoes and economic sanctions. The extension of military assistance is usually the province of states, because regional and international organizations lack independent military resources of their own. Economic assistance, however, can be channelled through a wider range of international actors, including the United Nations and international financial organizations such as the International Monetary Fund (IMF) and the World Bank.

Extending military assistance as part of an effort to prevent, manage, or resolve a conflict is often a very tricky proposition. Building up one party to a conflict can aggravate the security concerns of others, who can in turn seek to acquire more arms for themselves. Arms races and escalatory spirals can ensue. These kinds of arms races and escalations were common during the Cold War because Washington, Moscow, and Beijing were eager to supply arms to competing factions in regional conflicts. Although the Cold War is now over, regional actors can still find alternative sources of arms if international powers provide military assistance to other local groups. Most arms producers are desperate for markets because they have excess production capacities and large stockpiles of weapons, and will therefore sell just about anything to just about anybody. The convention that arms would only be sold to governments, as opposed to insurgent groups, was undercut during the Cold War and has now broken down completely. In addition, the black market in arms has grown considerably. As a result, international actors have little control over the international arms market, and therefore they have a limited ability to fine-tune military balances in troubled regions.[8]

One of the developments on the economic front in recent years has been the emergence of what is known as "conditionality." This means attaching conditions or strings to economic grants or loans. The IMF and the World Bank, for example, often link economic packages to local commitments to pursue certain kinds of fiscal and political initiatives. In war-torn regions, economic assistance can be and often is linked explicitly to conflict resolution measures, which can have salutary effects on the prospects for peace processes.

ARMS EMBARGOES AND ECONOMIC SANCTIONS

The international community also has a range of coercive instruments at its disposal, starting with the imposition of arms embargoes and economic sanctions on troublemakers. Although embargoes and sanctions can be imposed by individual states or small groups of states, international actions are often coordinated through and authorized by regional organizations or the United Nations.

The adoption of mandatory arms embargoes and economic sanctions under Chapter VII of the UN Charter has increased dramatically since the end of the Cold War.[9] During the Cold War, the United Nations imposed mandatory sanctions only twice: against Rhodesia in 1966 and South Africa in 1977. Since

---

8. See Spear, "Arms Limitations, Confidence-Building Measures, and Internal Conflict."
9. For more on arms embargoes, see ibid. For more on economic sanctions, see Elizabeth Rogers, "Economic Sanctions and Internal Conflict," in Brown, *International Dimensions of Internal Conflict*, pp. 411–434.

1990, mandatory Chapter VII embargoes and sanctions have been imposed eight times, six in the context of internal conflicts: in the former Yugoslavia in 1991 and 1992; in Somalia in 1992; in Liberia in 1992; in Angola in 1993; in Haiti in 1993 and 1994; and in Rwanda in 1994.

The increased utilization of Chapter VII measures is a reflection of several broad developments: the end of Cold War antagonisms between Washington and Moscow; the revitalization of the UN Security Council; and the Security Council's willingness to address threats to international peace and security in a more resolute and forceful manner. However, it is also a reflection of the particular problems posed by internal conflicts. Many policymakers hope that arms embargoes will reduce weapon flows and the horrific levels of violence often found in civil wars. In addition, arms embargoes and economic sanctions are seen as vehicles for exerting influence over belligerents when one does not want to send one's own troops into the fray.

Arms embargoes and economic sanctions are most likely to be effective under two sets of circumstances. First, when a government has been taken over by a clearly illegitimate group, it will be comparatively easy to build an international consensus around the idea of imposing mandatory sanctions on the junta in question. This was the case, for example, in Haiti. Second, when a neighboring state is actively and openly meddling in the affairs of another and exacerbating a conflict, it will be comparatively easy to build an international coalition against the offending party (because it is violating the non-interference principle) and it will be comparatively easy to target the offending party (because it is a state, as opposed to a faction or some other poorly defined entity). This was the case, for example, with respect to Serbian intervention in Bosnia.

However, the use of these instruments is likely to be problematic with respect to internal conflicts for a number of reasons. First, arms embargoes will often have a limited effect on the level of violence in civil wars because these wars are usually fought with small arms and light weapons—mortars, machine guns, rifles, machetes, and the like. The international trade in light weapons such as these is extremely difficult to regulate, especially since much of this trade is conducted on the black market.

Second, economic sanctions can hurt innocent people or countries that have important trading relationships with the target state. This problem was foreseen by the drafters of the UN Charter: Article 50 gives states the right to consult with the Security Council if they will suffer unduly from sanctions imposed on another. The increase in Chapter VII sanctions makes this problem less of a theoretical one. Since most internal conflicts are taking place in the developing world and most sanctions are consequently being applied there, it follows that developing countries—countries that can ill-afford additional economic burdens—will often have to pay these collateral costs. The willingness of developing countries to comply with sanctions regimes will depend to a great degree on steps other powers and the United Nations might take to reduce these costs. Looking at it purely from a pragmatic standpoint, something needs to be done if the great powers want to use economic sanctions on a more regular basis: developing countries will be unable or unwilling to bear collateral costs if burdens are not redistributed. Sanctions regimes will be more likely to fall apart under these circumstances.

Third and more generally, ensuring compliance with embargoes and sanctions is difficult. Although the Security Council sets up sanctions committees to monitor the implementation of such measures and assess their effectiveness, it has to rely on reports from member states, which might not have the information needed and which might not be inclined to divulge all of their intelligence. The Security Council, moreover, has no real enforcement mechanism other than the use of military force, a blunt instrument that is likely to be used rarely, and only in the case of egregious violations.

JUDICIAL ENFORCEMENT MEASURES

The idea of creating an international criminal court has been discussed by the UN General Assembly and the UN International Law Commission at regular intervals ever since 1946. The possibility of establishing an international criminal court was also anticipated in the 1948 Genocide Convention. However, apart from the Nuremberg and Tokyo trials, no international body has been set up to try crimes under international law.

The failure to establish an international criminal tribunal may be attributed to both Cold War politics and to the profound aversion of states to allow another body to adjudicate with respect to acts committed on their territories, and to seeing their own nationals called before a jurisdiction other than their own. The end of the Cold War eliminated one of these obstacles, and the genocidal slaughters in the former Yugoslavia and Rwanda gave new impetus to the idea of establishing an international criminal court.

The Security Council's frustrations with respect to the former Yugoslavia and Rwanda led it to create an *ad hoc* international criminal tribunal for the former in 1993 and one for the latter in 1994. By establishing these tribunals on an *ad hoc* basis, the Security Council side-stepped the problems associated with creating a permanent international criminal court: it was able to move quickly. And, by establishing these tribunals under Chapter VII of the UN Charter—an unprecedented development—it side-stepped the problem of needing the consent of the relevant states and parties: Chapter VII resolutions are binding on all member states.

The tribunals have three main tasks: to prosecute persons responsible for serious violations of international humanitarian law; to deter further crimes; and to contribute to the restoration and maintenance of peace. The establishment of these tribunals has been met with a fair amount of skepticism. The capacities of the tribunals to bring to justice those who violated humanitarian law in the former Yugoslavia and Rwanda are limited. Although Chapter VII resolutions are legally binding on all member states of the United Nations, this does not necessarily mean that cooperation will be forthcoming. Indeed, much will depend on the extent to which authorities in the former Yugoslavia and Rwanda are willing to provide evidence to international investigators and hand over indicted persons. Another major problem is that the legal requirement to bring war criminals to justice is in conflict with the political requirement to bring conflict to an end: leaders in the former Yugoslavia and Rwanda will be unwilling to agree to peace settlements if legal indictments are sure to follow.

Although these tribunals clearly face problems, they may nonetheless play important roles in promoting reconciliation in war-torn countries. By attributing war crimes to specific individuals rather than blaming entire groups, they may make it easier for people to end hostilities and rebuild civil societies. The establishment of these tribunals, as imperfect as they may be in bringing to justice those responsible for war crimes, should also be hailed as important precedents in the defense of humanitarian law and human rights. They are small but important steps in the right direction.

THE USE OF MILITARY FORCE

The ultimate enforcement instrument at the disposal of states—acting unilaterally or multilaterally through regional organizations or the United Nations—is the use of military force.[10] In the first half of the 1990s, the UN Security

---

10. For more on the use of military force, see Anthony Clark Arend and Robert J. Beck, *International Law and the Use of Force* (London: Routledge, 1993); Laura W. Reed and Carl Kaysen, *Emerging Norms of Justified Intervention* (Cambridge, Mass.: American Academy of Arts and Sciences, 1993); Richard N. Haass, *Intervention: The Use of American Military Force in the Post–Cold War World* (Washington, D.C.: Carnegie Endowment for International Peace, 1994); Ivo H. Daalder, "The United States and Military Intervention in Internal Conflict," in Brown, *International Dimensions of Internal Conflict*, pp. 461–488; Damrosch, *Enforcing Restraint*.

Council authorized the use of force with respect to internal conflicts in Bosnia, Somalia, Rwanda, and Haiti.

Three conditions must be met if the Security Council is to use military force effectively under Chapter VII of the Charter. First, none of the five permanent members of the Council can oppose the use of force: any one of the five can veto a Security Council resolution authorizing military action. It is extremely important, moreover, for most of the P-5, particularly the United States, to support actively the military action in question. Unfortunately, this has rarely happened: China and Russia have been bystanders in Bosnia, Somalia, Rwanda, and Haiti; France, the United Kingdom, and the United States have lacked determination or consensus in Bosnia, Somalia, and Rwanda. Different interests and differences of opinion have not been washed away by the end of the Cold War. These differences have undercut and will continue to undercut the UN's ability to use force effectively. Developing a consensus among the P-5 is not a given, and will have to be done on a case-by-case basis.

Second, if military force is to be used effectively, the Security Council must identify and enunciate clear and consistent political objectives. This was done in Haiti; Operation Restore Democracy has consequently been a success. This was not done in Bosnia, Somalia, and Rwanda, where UN missions have been markedly less successful. The Security Council authorized Operation Turquoise in Rwanda, which was led by France, and Operation Restore Hope in Somalia, led by the United States. Although these operations were successful in terms of establishing a secure environment for the delivery of humanitarian relief, they did not address the political roots of the conflicts that created humanitarian crises. Nor did they provide a long-term presence. Chaos and slaughter returned when UN forces withdrew.

The third condition that has to be met if the United Nations is to use force effectively under Chapter VII of the Charter is that sufficient military forces have to be made available to the Security Council. The fact that the Council lacks military forces it can call upon, as provided for in Article 43 of the Charter, severely limits its ability to act. Although this does not preclude action, it makes UN operations totally dependent on the willingness of states, especially the P-5, to make troops available at a particular point in time. The United States is particularly key: it alone has the firepower, transport, command and control, communications, intelligence, logistics, and power projection capabilities needed for large-scale operations.

Decisions to contribute troops to UN operations will inevitably be based on idiosyncratic calculations about costs, benefits, and risks, and heavily influenced by domestic politics. An important consideration for many states will be the nature of the command and control arrangements for the operation in question. Many states will insist on retaining operational command over their own troops, especially whenever combat is likely. The United States stands out in this regard.

What many people think of as "UN enforcement actions" and "UN military operations" have been and will continue to be actions authorized by the UN Security Council but carried out by individual states or groups of states. Whether or not these kinds of operations will be launched, therefore, will depend to a significant degree on the extent to which state interests are engaged by particular problems. In many trouble spots, the interests of distant powers will not be engaged, and the prospects for UN-authorized military action will be extremely slim. One can argue, however, that because the P-5 have a special status within the United Nations and a special responsibility for maintaining international peace and security, they have a special obligation in this area.

The Tasks

International efforts to prevent, manage, and resolve internal conflicts face different problems and therefore merit individual attention.

THE IMPORTANCE OF CONFLICT PREVENTION

The idea of conflict prevention has a lot of intuitive appeal: conflict management and conflict resolution clearly have to contend with far more inflammatory situations. Conflict prevention, however, is far from simple.[11] Conflict is, after all, inherent in political, economic, and social life, even if violent conflict is not. Conflict, broadly defined, cannot be extinguished, only controlled. In addition, the forces that drive and trigger internal conflicts are many and powerful. Unfortunately, social scientists have not yet developed a full-fledged theory of the causes of internal conflict. As a result, there is no fully developed strategy for preventing such conflicts. That said, we can suggest three broad guidelines for international actors interested in preventing internal conflicts.

---

11. See Stephen John Stedman, "Alchemy for a New World Order: Overselling 'Conflict Prevention'," *Foreign Affairs*, Vol. 74, No. 3 (May–June 1995), pp. 14–20. For other views, see Michael S. Lund, "Underrating Preventive Diplomacy," *Foreign Affairs*, Vol. 74, No. 4 (July-August 1995), pp. 160–163; John Stremlau, "Antidote to Anarchy," *Washington Quarterly*, Vol. 18, No. 1 (Winter 1995), pp. 29–44.

ADOPT A TWO-TRACK STRATEGY FOR CONFLICT PREVENTION. First, if it is useful to distinguish between the permissive conditions and proximate causes of internal conflict, it follows that those interested in conflict prevention should have a two-track strategy.[12] One track should be a series of sustained, long-term efforts focused on the underlying problems that make violence likely. The other track should be a series of more aggressive efforts focused on the proximate causes of internal conflicts—the triggers that turn potentially violent situations into armed confrontations.

Both tracks need to be pursued. Long-term efforts to address the permissive conditions of internal conflicts are relatively low-risk undertakings, but they tend to be neglected by policymakers in national capitals and international organizations who are inevitably preoccupied with the crisis *du jour*. At the same time, the catalytic factors responsible for triggering violence—often in places where bloodshed could be avoided—merit careful attention and vigorous action.

PLACE MORE EMPHASIS ON UNDERLYING PROBLEMS AND LONG-TERM SOLUTIONS. Long-term efforts aimed at the underlying problems that make violence likely need to be given more emphasis and made more effective. This is easier said than done. If a simple formula existed for dealing with these problems, the world would be a more tranquil and happier place than it currently is.

Some factors are difficult or impossible to change, such as the military or economic value of a potentially secessionist region or the fear that secessionism in one region will lead to the unraveling of a multiethnic state. Ethnic geography and demographic patterns are other factors that are not particularly manipulable.

To the extent they change at all, the structural, political, economic, and cultural problems that predispose some places to violence change slowly.[13] This means that international efforts to influence events will have to be long-term undertakings. It also means that international efforts to address the root causes of internal conflict will have to be multifaceted in character. Efforts will have to be undertaken in several areas.

Security concerns and arms races contribute to instability and the potential for violence. As discussed earlier, one way to reduce the uncertainties that often drive arms races is to promote transparency and adopt confidence-building measures. In many cases, the challenge will be convincing governments that

---

12. See Michael E. Brown, "The Causes of Internal Conflict: An Overview," in this volume.
13. See ibid.

they face these kinds of instability problems and that they should agree to outside involvement in domestic security matters.

When people feel that existing political arrangements are unjust and incapable of being changed peacefully, the potential for violence increases dramatically. International actors can help promote peaceful political change by extending technical advice about constitutional and electoral reforms, for example. They can also exert considerable influence by linking financial assistance and the development of closer economic ties to political reforms—that is, by making financial aid and economic relationships conditional. They can also link membership in international economic, military, and political institutions to domestic political reforms. This has worked fairly well in East-Central Europe, where states are eager to join the European Union (EU) and the North Atlantic Treaty Organization (NATO) and willing to do whatever is necessary to improve their chances of being offered early admission to Western institutions.

A country's economic situation and economic prospects have tremendous implications for its potential for violence. If international actors are serious about preventing internal conflict and civil war, they have to do more than treat the military dimensions and military manifestations of the problem; they have to address the economic sources of conflict in troubled societies. International actors can help promote economic reforms the same way they can help promote political reforms: by extending technical assistance; by linking financial assistance and economic relationships to the implementation of reforms; and by linking membership in international organizations and institutions to reforms. States, international financial institutions, and other international organizations should work together to develop "mini-Marshall Plans" for countries in need of special economic attention. NGOs should devote more of their resources to these "silent emergencies," as opposed to *post hoc* responses to crises that have already exploded into violence and chaos.[14]

Finally, international actors need to address the cultural and perceptual factors that lead some countries towards violence. This means working to overturn patterns of cultural discrimination by safeguarding rights with respect to language, religion, and education. This also means working to revamp the distorted histories that groups often have of each other. Governments could be

---

14. As Thomas Weiss points out, this will be very hard for most NGOs to do because crisis-response efforts are the linchpins of their fund-raising campaigns. Weiss, "Nongovernmental Organizations and Internal Conflict."

asked to enter into international dialogues about group histories and to publish foreign criticisms of school curricula and textbooks.[15] Scholars and teachers should be brought into these dialogues. Pernicious group histories play important roles in galvanizing internal conflicts, and they need to be given much greater attention in conflict prevention circles.

NEUTRALIZE THE PROXIMATE CAUSES OF INTERNAL CONFLICT. Those interested in conflict prevention should pay more attention to the proximate causes of internal conflict. Internal conflicts can be triggered by any one of four clusters of proximate causes: internal, mass-level factors; external, mass-level factors; external, elite-level factors; and internal, elite-level factors.[16] However, many internal conflicts are triggered by domestic elites, and many of the conflicts that fall into this category are raw power struggles. It follows that international actors interested in conflict prevention should focus on this problem area.

Conflicts triggered by internal, mass-level factors—bad domestic problems—are often driven by ethnic strife. The key to negating pressures for ethnic violence is overturning perceived patterns of political, economic, and cultural discrimination. When tension is building, violence is looming, and distrust is mounting, international actors can help defuse potentially explosive situations by internationalizing the dialogue and injecting impartial observers and mediators into the equation. Fact-finding missions can be launched to help identify the origins of specific problems, human rights monitors can help ensure that injustices do not go unnoticed, and election monitors can help guard the integrity of political processes. The United Nations can be very helpful in this regard. Ethnic bashing and scapegoating in the media can be countered by international organizations and the international media, thereby helping to promote less emotionally charged debates.

Conflicts triggered by external, mass-level forces—bad neighborhoods—are sparked by waves of refugees or troops crashing across international borders, bringing turmoil and violence with them. Waves of refugees and motley gangs of renegade troops are hard to deter or control because they lack effective leadership. The international community can try to prevent refugee problems from becoming regional problems by setting up refugee camps and safe areas in the country where violence first started. To be effective, however, international actors will have to move quickly and convince refugees that safe areas

---

15. See Stephen Van Evera, "Hypotheses on Nationalism and War," in this volume.
16. See Brown, "Causes of Internal Conflict."

are genuinely safe. This will not be easy to do, given the international community's track record in Bosnia and Iraq. Preventive military deployments are another option.

Internal conflicts triggered by external, elite-level forces—bad neighbors—would seem to be easier to prevent. Specific actions can be proscribed, potentially troublesome governments can be identified, and a wide range of coercive actions can be threatened or taken with respect to renegade states. The preventive military deployment in Macedonia, for example, undoubtedly helped to discourage Serbia from causing trouble in that part of the Balkans. States are powerful actors, however, and they can therefore be difficult to dissuade, especially if leaders believe important national interests are at stake. Deterring bad neighbors from causing trouble in nearby states is particularly difficult when the neighbors in question are large and powerful. Russia, for example, clearly played a key role in triggering conflicts in Georgia and Moldova, but it was hard to influence because of its size, its position on the UN Security Council, and its firm conviction that Georgia and Moldova were part of its sphere of influence.

Finally, conflicts triggered by power struggles between opportunistic and desperate politicians are common, and should therefore receive special international attention. Since economic problems make escalation and violence more likely, emergency economic relief packages should be part of the equation when tensions rise and danger looms. Cynical campaigns to mobilize ethnic support, polarize ethnic differences, and blame other ethnic groups for whatever troubles a country may be experiencing are often responsible for inciting violence and leading countries into all-out civil wars. It follows that international actors interested in preventing these conflicts from becoming violent and escalating out of control should endeavor to neutralize hate-mongers and their propaganda. At a minimum, this means launching international information campaigns and anti-propaganda efforts to ensure that reasoned voices can be heard and alternative sources of information are available in political debates. In more extreme cases, when leaders call for the extermination of their adversaries or entire ethnic groups, as in Rwanda in 1994, more forceful measures will be called for. Taking coercive action is a big step, but some situations, such as calls to commit genocide or slaughter, should lead to forceful international action.

Many internal conflicts are triggered by self-obsessed leaders who will do anything to get and keep power. They often incite ethnic violence of the most horrific kind for their own political ends. If the international community is serious about preventing internal conflicts, it needs to think more carefully about the kinds of political behavior that should be proscribed and the kinds of actions it will be willing to take to steer or even seize control of domestic political debates. These are extremely difficult problems, both intellectually and politically, but they have to be confronted if international actors are to prevent the deadliest internal conflicts.

THE CHALLENGE OF CONFLICT MANAGEMENT

Once violence breaks out and fighting begins, escalation becomes much more difficult to control. Security concerns and arms races intensify, and attacks on civilians can spiral out of control. Compromise and settlement become more difficult. Conflict management is more challenging than conflict prevention, and should therefore be undertaken more selectively and with even more care. The costs and risks can be high. We would recommend the following three guidelines.

ACT EARLY TO KEEP VIOLENCE FROM ESCALATING. International actors worried about emerging internal conflicts should act sooner rather than later. Internal conflicts often begin with limited clashes that escalate only gradually. Put another way, a window of opportunity for crisis management exists even after violence breaks out. The longer international actors wait, the more intense conflicts become, and the more difficult conflict management becomes. International actors have a wide range of policy instruments at their disposal, including cooperative instruments such as mediation and the deployment of traditional peacekeeping forces, and coercive instruments such as arms embargoes, economic sanctions, and the use of military force.

Unfortunately, international motivations to take action are weakest in the early stages of internal conflicts, when levels of violence are low and windows of opportunity are open. Motivations to take action increase as levels of violence increase, but rising levels of violence also make conflict management efforts more difficult. In other words, international motivations to act are weakest when options are strongest, and motivations to act are strongest when options are weakest.

KEEP INTERNAL CONFLICTS FROM BECOMING REGIONAL CONFLICTS. International actors interested in conflict management should strive to keep internal conflicts from becoming regional conflicts. Internal conflicts usually become more difficult to control and resolve when neighboring states become involved. Additional sets of interests are injected into the equation, and additional resources are made available to combatants. Fighting often intensifies, and negotiations almost always become much more complicated.

This means addressing two problems. First, it means working to minimize the impact of internal conflicts on neighboring states, including refugee problems, economic problems, military problems, and instability problems. These kinds of problems often lead neighboring states to launch defensive or protective interventions. Second, international actors should work to discourage neighboring states from engaging in opportunistic acts of aggression, such as supporting rebel forces in order to influence the regional balance of power or launching opportunistic invasions.

There are reasons for being optimistic about the international community's ability to take effective action in this area. The problems that internal conflicts pose for neighboring states are easy to identify, even if they are not all easily solvable. The actions that neighboring states should be discouraged from taking are also easy to identify. Also, the UN Charter provides a legal foundation for taking action to maintain international peace and security. In addition, international actors are dealing with established governments in neighboring states, and governments can be engaged and influenced in ways that amorphous political movements and rebels groups cannot. If necessary, the full array of international policy instruments can be brought to bear on troublesome or potentially troublesome neighboring states, including threats to use economic sanctions and military force.

DISTINGUISH BETWEEN COOPERATIVE AND COERCIVE ACTIONS. It is essential for international actors contemplating intervention to distinguish between two fundamentally different kinds of problems: cases where the local parties are ready to stop fighting and are receptive to international involvement; and cases where they are not. The track record of international efforts to bring fighting to an end is good in the former, bad in the latter, and truly awful when the line about the terms of international engagement is blurred.

During the Cold War, peacekeeping operations were usually deployed to monitor cease-fires, and they were deployed with the consent of the relevant local parties. These operations consequently enjoyed a high rate of success. It was understood that there was a sharp line between these kinds of undertakings and the coercive operations launched under Chapter VII of the UN Charter.

This line began to get blurred in 1992, when UN Secretary-General Boutros-Ghali suggested that future peacekeeping operations might not depend on the consent of all local parties.[17] The UN-authorized missions to Somalia and the

---

17. See Boutros Boutros-Ghali, *An Agenda for Peace: Preventive Diplomacy, Peacemaking, and Peacekeeping* (New York: United Nations, June 1992), p. 11.

former Yugoslavia that followed were deeply troubled exercises, mainly because the line between consent and coercion was blurred. UN humanitarian operations in these two countries were presented as impartial efforts to relieve human suffering, but they were seen quite differently by local leaders who correctly understood that humanitarian relief had implications for the local balance of power. International efforts to put pressure on local leaders and open the way for humanitarian supplies failed, first, because international actors insisted on pretending that they were not engaged in coercion and, second, because they did not have sufficient forces on the ground to engage in effective coercion. In fact, the deployment of lightly armed units to escort humanitarian relief convoys was counterproductive: UN peacekeepers became prepositioned hostages, and completely undercut international efforts to bring the fighting to a quick end.

UN officials, to their credit, have learned from these mistakes, and by 1995 it was again an article of faith in UN circles that there was a sharp line between cooperative and coercive undertakings.[18] Some scholars and analysts continue to argue, however, that there is a gray area between cooperation and coercion, and that a "third option" or "middle option" exists.[19]

Our view is that the new thinking at the United Nations is correct: cooperative and coercive operations are fundamentally different kinds of undertakings, and it is essential for international actors to keep these two kinds of activities separate.[20] The UN-authorized missions to Somalia and Bosnia ran into trouble

---

18. See Boutros Boutros-Ghali, *Supplement to an Agenda for Peace: Position Paper of the Secretary-General on the Occasion of the Fiftieth Anniversary of the United Nations*, S/1995/1, January 1995, paragraphs 33–35; Shashi Tharoor, "United Nations Peacekeeping in Europe," *Survival*, Vol. 37, No. 2 (Summer 1995), pp. 121–134; Shashi Tharoor, "Should UN Peacekeeping Go 'Back to Basics'?" *Survival*, Vol. 37, No. 4 (Winter 1995–96), pp. 52–64. See also Charles Dobbie, "A Concept for Post–Cold War Peacekeeping," *Survival*, Vol. 36, No. 3 (Autumn 1994), pp. 121–148.

19. See Adam Roberts, "The Crisis in UN Peacekeeping," *Survival*, Vol. 36, No. 3 (Autumn 1994), pp. 93–120; Donald C.F. Daniel and Bradd C. Hayes, "Securing Observance of UN Mandates Through the Employment of Military Forces," unpublished manuscript, March 1995; Donald C.F. Daniel and Milton E. Miles, "Is There a Middle Option in Peace Support Operations? Implications for Crisis Containment and Disarmament," paper prepared for the UN Institute for Disarmament Research, November 1995; Adam Roberts, "From San Francisco to Sarajevo: The UN and the Use of Force," *Survival*, Vol. 37, No. 4 (Winter 1995–96), pp. 7–28.

20. It is certainly true that peacekeeping operations often engage in coercion at a tactical level (against renegade elements in the context of monitoring a cease-fire), in the course of policing activities (to stop looting), and in self-defense. However, this kind of coercion takes place with the consent of local leaders and usually within the framework of a cease-fire agreement. There is a big difference between this kind of "tactical" coercion and "strategic" coercion designed to secure an agreement from local leaders, change their political goals, or change the correlation of local military forces. Tactical coercion is normal and acceptable. Attempting to engage in strategic coercion with lightly armed peacekeepers deployed under misleading or obsolete pretenses is deeply problematic, as we have seen in the Horn of Africa and the Balkans.

because whatever consent had once been given began to evaporate when mission objectives expanded and international actors began to engage in more and more coercion.

This is not to say that international actors should eschew coercion, only that they need to distinguish between cooperative and coercive undertakings and be prepared to play hardball when they are engaged in the latter. Coercion *can* work, and the international community has many coercive policy instruments at its disposal. Individuals can be held accountable for their actions through the establishment of international criminal tribunals. Arms embargoes can be imposed on one party or another. Economic sanctions can be powerful sources of leverage, especially when one is dealing with central governments, neighboring states, and other easily identifiable and targetable actors. Military force can be threatened or used and, contrary to current thinking in the U.S. Department of Defense, it can be used in limited ways in support of limited objectives: safe areas can be established and protected; heavy-weapon exclusion zones can be established and enforced; and air power can be directed at specific targets such as arms depots, communications and transportation links, military bases, and forces in the field.[21]

Successful coercion depends on several things. First, international actors must recognize and admit that they are engaging in coercion: they should not delude themselves or try to delude their publics into thinking that threatening to use military force, for example, will be seen as a form of cooperative engagement. Coercion is not aimed at "conflict": it is aimed at governments, groups, and individuals who will see threats and coercive acts as forms of aggression. Second, international actors need to be clear about both their long-term political objectives and their short-term operational objectives. This is one of the reasons why coercion worked in Haiti and failed in Bosnia. UN mandates, which should be secured whenever possible, should be clear on these counts as well. Third, coercive actions need to be pursued with great political determination and with sufficient resources. When military forces are involved, this might mean deploying large numbers of heavily armed troops guided by clear and liberal rules of engagement. Lightly armed peacekeepers

---

21. We concur with Ivo Daalder, who argues that the Pentagon's all-or-nothing approach to the use of force limits U.S. military intervention to cases where vital interests are engaged. This puts the cart before the horse. National interests should define policy objectives, and policy objectives should determine how force is used. If interests and objectives are limited, one should be able to use force in a limited way. If one is unable to use force in a limited way for doctrinal reasons, then bureaucratic dogma is damaging national interests. See Daalder, "United States and Military Intervention in Internal Conflict."

should not be sent out to wage war, or into situations where they might reasonably be expected to engage in open combat. It is reckless and irresponsible to place peacekeepers and soldiers in such jeopardy.

Although coercion can work, the international community should emphasize cooperative conflict management actions over their coercive counterparts. Cooperative actions—such as sending mediators to help negotiate cease-fires and sending peacekeepers to help monitor cease-fires—are relatively low-cost, low-risk undertakings. They should be the mainstays of international efforts in this area. Coercion is more expensive and riskier, and should be employed only when important interests are at stake or when crimes against humanity, such as genocide or the deliberate slaughter of civilians, are being committed. The international community should engage in these kinds of high-cost, high-risk undertakings only when the stakes are high and only when it is determined to see a serious campaign through to the bitter end.

THE POTENTIAL FOR CONFLICT RESOLUTION

The end of the Cold War has led to the resolution of a number of conflicts—in El Salvador, Mozambique, Nicaragua—driven in large part by the geostrategic competition between Washington and Moscow. The international community, under the aegis of the United Nations, has played an active and important role in helping to bring these conflicts to an end. It has also helped to bring to an end the conflicts in Haiti, Namibia, and South Africa, which were not driven by Cold War dynamics, and it has helped to dampen tensions in Cambodia, Iraq, Tajikistan, and Western Sahara.

Conflict resolution is an enormously tricky proposition: it is hard for people to lay down their arms, rebuild ravaged political and economic systems, reconstruct civil societies, and reconcile when large amounts of blood have been spilled and vengeance has come to dominate political discourse. There are, however, reasons for being hopeful about the prospects for conflict resolution in some parts of the world, and about the ability of the international community, through the United Nations, to facilitate these conflict resolution processes.

HELP THOSE WHO WANT TO BE HELPED. The international community's resources are not unlimited, and difficult decisions will inevitably have to be made about where and when to try to lend a helping hand. The guiding principle should be to first help those who want to be helped.

When people are determined to keep fighting, there is little the international community can do to bring hostilities to an end unless it is willing and able to impose peace. This means employing coercive instruments with a heavy hand,

and in most cases this probably means unleashing a massive, crushing military blow followed by the long-term deployment of military forces and the imposition of an international trusteeship under the supervision of the United Nations. These are bound to be exceedingly expensive, open-ended operations. It is therefore highly unlikely that the international community will be inclined to go down this path. It did not do so in either Somalia or Rwanda, where humanitarian crises were intense and local military forces were comparatively weak.

Given that the international community has limited resources to devote to peace processes and a limited tolerance for pain, it makes sense for international efforts to be concentrated in places where combatants are tired of fighting, ready for peace, and looking for help. There is a lot that the international community can do to help resolve conflicts and make peace under these conditions, when it has the full consent and cooperation of the local parties. It can provide humanitarian assistance to refugees and others in need. It can launch fact-finding and mediation missions to help resolve outstanding political differences. Traditional peacekeeping forces can help keep former adversaries apart while cooperative disarmament efforts get under way. Multifunctional peacekeeping operations can help with political and economic reconstruction. The track record of international efforts in post-conflict settings such as these is good: again, there is a lot international actors can do to help people who genuinely want to make peace.

The key is making sure that one is dealing with people who genuinely want peace. Most people want peace, of course, but on their own terms. When they agree to peace settlements and elections, leaders of factions often assume that electoral triumph is in the offing. Problems can arise when elections turn out in unexpectedly unsatisfying ways: peace settlements that were attractive when high office appeared to be part of the package are much less attractive when it is not. When this happens, leaders can conclude that resuming the fight in the bush or the jungle is preferable to being a political non-entity. This is what happened in Angola after the September 1992 elections. The challenge for international actors is to make sure that local parties are acting in good faith, and that local leaders fully understand the potential ramifications of the peace process.

LAUNCH MULTIFACETED UNDERTAKINGS. Since the forces that drive internal conflicts are complex, conflict resolution efforts have to be multifaceted undertakings. The United Nations has launched a number of multifunctional peacekeeping operations since the end of the Cold War. The UN missions in

Cambodia, El Salvador, Haiti, Mozambique, Namibia, and Nicaragua are the most prominent examples. These wide-ranging, multifaceted operations have a fairly good track record, and offer some useful lessons for the future.

Ideally, international efforts to help resolve internal conflicts will address four sets of problems. The first order of business must be to bring military hostilities to an end and address attendant military and disarmament problems. Cease-fires have to be negotiated, implemented, and monitored. International mediators and peacekeeping forces can be tremendously helpful in this regard. Military adversaries then have to be persuaded to hand in their arms; buy-back schemes have been successful in El Salvador, Haiti, and Mozambique. Over time, rebel military forces and militia have to be demobilized, and national military forces, including appropriate representation from all relevant ethnic and political groups, have to be reconstituted. The key to continued progress is addressing the security concerns that former adversaries will inevitably have as disarmament and demobilization processes unfold. International actors can help to reassure local parties by monitoring these processes carefully and promoting transparency.

Second, international actors can help with political reconstruction. In the short term, this means helping to establish transitional governments, as well as fair and effective police forces and courts. In El Salvador, Nicaragua, South Africa, and elsewhere, the United Nations has helped to organize and supervise elections. The United Nations can also provide technical expertise with respect to constitutional reforms, the creation of federal system, the establishment of minority rights safeguards, and the like.

Third, international actors can help—indeed, they must help—with the long and difficult problem of economic reconstruction and the promotion of economic development. Many countries torn apart by internal conflict were in poor economic shape to begin with; years of war only made matters worse. As noted above, "mini-Marshall plans" involving the combined efforts of governments, international financial institutions, international development organizations, regional organizations, and multinational corporations will generally be needed.

Finally, international actors will have to help with the complex problem of rebuilding civil societies. This can involve activities ranging from the repatriation of refugees to the creation or re-creation of a free and fair press to the founding of schools. Getting groups to come to terms with the distorted and pernicious aspects of their histories and inculcating the values of compromise and tolerance in political and social discourse are among the most important problems war-torn countries face. In short, education is one the keys to long-term political stability. This is surely an area where the international community can make a difference.

MAKE LONG-TERM COMMITMENTS. One of the most depressing aspects of internal conflict is its recurring nature. In place after place, from Angola to India to Zaire, conflicts sputter to a halt, only to start up with renewed fury years or decades later. Internal conflict seems to go into a state of suspended animation from time to time, but it never seems to go away.

Conflict resolution is not easy, and it cannot be brought about in months or even a year or two. Conflict resolution is a long-term process, and if international actors are to contribute in useful ways to this process, they have to be willing, able, and prepared to make long-term efforts. Consider the magnitude of the problems most countries face in the aftermath of civil war: state structures have to be rebuilt; legal institutions and police forces have to be reconstituted; political institutions and electoral processes have to be re-established; industrial and agricultural activities have to be relaunched; communication and transportation systems have to be reconstructed; schools have to be reopened; and so on.

The goal should be to create a lasting peace that would allow international actors to walk away at some point: peace would be self-sustaining. This is not an impossible dream, but it most certainly is not a short-term proposition. Politicians in Western capitals who need immediate gratification and crave regular diplomatic triumphs need not apply. This is a job for serious international actors capable of making long-term commitments to deep-seated problems.

ENDURING DILEMMAS

What should the international community do about internal conflicts? The central dilemma confronting the international community is that peace, order, and stability are not the only values policymakers should seek to maximize. Political, economic, and social justice are equally important, and these two sets of values are not always in perfect harmony. Although policymakers should try to prevent conflicts as a general rule, they should not necessarily work to keep oppressed peoples from rising up against totalitarian leaders who will not accept peaceful political change. Although policymakers should try to keep armed conflicts from escalating as a general rule, they should not work to keep arms from people who have been attacked by others or who are being slaughtered in large numbers. And, although policymakers should try to resolve conflicts quickly, this becomes complicated when aggressors have the upper hand, which they often do. Under these conditions, bringing a war to a quick conclusion might not be compatible with bringing it to a just conclusion.

The challenge, of course, is to promote both sets of values—peace, order, and stability, on the one hand; political, economic, and social justice, on the other—at the same time. The best way to do this is for the international community to devote more effort to political and economic development and the broadening and deepening of civil societies. Internal conflict is not just a military problem: it is fundamentally a political, economic, and social problem. Addressing the military manifestations of internal conflict means dealing with the political, economic, and social roots of organized violence.

This leads to yet another policy dilemma. Although the international community's best bets for peace and justice are long-term conflict prevention efforts, the moral concerns and national interests of international actors are engaged most acutely when people are being killed or displaced in large numbers—that is, when an intense war is under way. In other words, the international community's motivations to act are strongest when the options for taking effective action are weakest.

This brings us to a final policy dilemma. When policymakers contemplate intervention in internal conflicts, the costs of international action are easy to measure and they have to be paid immediately: they include the financial costs of economic sanctions and military deployments; the risks to troops placed in harm's way; and the domestic political risks that policymakers might have to run. The costs of inaction are much harder to measure and are usually realized only in the long term: they include damage to core political values, international norms of behavior, international law and order, and regional and international stability. It is important to remember that almost all internal conflicts have regional dimensions, implications for regional security, and implications for international order. Internal conflicts are rarely self-contained pockets of turmoil. The costs of inaction are therefore real, as is the moral diminishment that attends inaction in the face of slaughter. Unfortunately but inevitably, the costs of action receive more attention than the costs of inaction in policymaking debates. Politicians invariably focus on the calculable, short-term costs that they will have to bear as political figures. Statesmen worry more about the long-term costs to national and international security that accumulate only with the passing of time—but true statesmen are few and far between.

Possible and Impossible Solutions to Ethnic Civil Wars

Chaim Kaufmann

$\mathbf{E}$thnic civil wars are burning in Bosnia, Croatia, Rwanda, Burundi, Angola, Sudan, Turkey, Azerbaijan, Georgia, Chechnya, Tajikistan, Kashmir, Myanmar, and Sri Lanka, and are threatening to break out in dozens of other places throughout the world.[1] Many of these conflicts are are so violent, with so much violence directed against unarmed civilians, and are apparently intractable, that they have provoked calls for military intervention to stop them. As yet, however, the international community has done little and achieved less.

Advocates of international action seek to redress the failures of local political institutions and elites by brokering political power-sharing arrangements, by international conservatorship to rebuild a functioning state, or by reconstruction of exclusive ethnic identities into wider, inclusive civic identities.[2] Pessimists doubt these remedies, arguing that ethnic wars express primordial hatreds which cannot be reduced by outside intervention because they have been ingrained by long histories of inter-communal conflict.[3]

Chaim Kaufmann is Assistant Professor of International Relations at Lehigh University.

The author's thanks are owed to many people. Robert Pape's extensive help made a decisive difference in the quality of the final product. Helpful criticism was provided by Henri Barkey, Richard Betts, Michael Desch, Matthew Evangelista, Charles Glaser, Emily Goldman, Robert Hayden, Ted Hopf, Stuart Kaufman, Rajan Menon, Bruce Moon, Roger Peterson, Jack Snyder, Stephen Van Evera, and the members of the PIPES Seminar at the University of Chicago.

---

1. Ted Robert Gurr, "Peoples Against States: Ethnopolitical Conflict and the Changing World System," *International Studies Quarterly*, Vol. 38, No. 3 (September 1994), pp. 347–377, lists fifty current ethnic conflicts of which thirteen had each caused more than 100,000 deaths to date.
2. Gerald B. Helman and Steven R. Ratner, "Saving Failed States," *Foreign Policy*, No. 89 (Winter 1992–93), pp. 3–20; William Pfaff, "Invitation to War," *Foreign Affairs*, Vol. 72, No. 3 (Summer 1993), pp. 97–109; John Chipman, "Managing the Politics of Parochialism," in Michael E. Brown, ed., *Ethnic Conflict and International Security* (Princeton, N.J.: Princeton University Press, 1993), pp. 237–263; Flora Lewis, "Reassembling Yugoslavia," *Foreign Policy*, No. 98 (Spring 1995), pp. 132–144; I. William Zartman, "Putting Things Back Together," in Zartman, ed., *Collapsed States: The Disintegration and Restoration of Legitimate Authority* (Boulder, Colo.: Lynne Rienner, 1995), pp. 267–273.
3. "Let no one think there is an easy or a simple solution to this tragedy," which results from "age-old animosities," said George Bush, "whatever pressure and means the international community brings to bear." Quoted in Andrew Rosenthal, "Bush Urges UN to Back Force to Get Aid to Bosnia," *New York Times*, August 7, 1992. For similar views see Colin L. Powell, "Why Generals Get Nervous," *New York Times*, October 8, 1992; Charles Krauthammer, "Bosnian Analogies; Pick Your History, Pick Your Policy," *Washington Post*, May 7, 1993; Conor Cruise O'Brien, "The Wrath of Ages: Nationalism's Primordial Roots," *Foreign Affairs*, Vol. 72, No. 5 (November/December 1993), pp. 142–149.

International Security, Vol. 20, No. 4 (Spring 1996), pp. 136–175

Both sides in the current debate are wrong, because solutions to ethnic wars do not depend on their causes.

This paper offers a theory of how ethnic wars end, and proposes an intervention strategy based on it.[4] The theory rests on two insights: First, in ethnic wars both hypernationalist mobilization rhetoric and real atrocities harden ethnic identities to the point that cross-ethnic political appeals are unlikely to be made and even less likely to be heard. Second, intermingled population settlement patterns create real security dilemmas that intensify violence, motivate ethnic "cleansing," and prevent de-escalation unless the groups are separated. As a result, restoring civil politics in multi-ethnic states shattered by war is impossible because the war itself destroys the possibilities for ethnic cooperation.

Stable resolutions of ethnic civil wars are possible, but only when the opposing groups are demographically separated into defensible enclaves. Separation reduces both incentives and opportunity for further combat, and largely eliminates both reasons and chances for ethnic cleansing of civilians. While ethnic fighting can be stopped by other means, such as peace enforcement by international forces or by a conquering empire, such peaces last only as long as the enforcers remain.

This means that to save lives threatened by genocide, the international community must abandon attempts to restore war-torn multi-ethnic states. Instead, it must facilitate and protect population movements to create true national homelands. Sovereignty is secondary: defensible ethnic enclaves reduce violence with or without independent sovereignty, while partition without separation does nothing to stop mass killing.[5] Once massacres have taken place, ethnic cleansing will occur. The alternative is to let the *interahamwe* and the Chetniks "cleanse" their enemies in their own way.

---

4. Ethnic wars involve organized large-scale violence, whether by regular forces (Turkish or Iraqi operations against the Kurds) or highly mobilized civilian populations (the *interahamwe* in Rwanda or the Palestinian *intifada*). A frequent aspect is "ethnic cleansing": efforts by members of one ethnic group to eliminate the population of another from a certain area by means such as discrimination, expropriation, terror, expulsion, and massacre. For proposals on managing ethnic rivalries involving lower levels of ethnic mobilization and violence, see Stephen Van Evera, "Managing the Eastern Crisis: Preventing War in the Former Soviet Empire," *Security Studies*, Vol. 1, No. 3 (Spring 1992), pp. 361–382; Ted Hopf, "Managing Soviet Disintegration: A Demand for Behavioral Regimes," *International Security*, Vol. 17, No. 1 (Summer 1992), pp. 44–75.

5. Although ethnic partitions have often been justified on grounds of self-determination, the argument for separation here is based purely on humanitarian grounds. The first to argue publicly for partition as a humanitarian solution was John J. Mearsheimer, "Shrink Bosnia to Save It," *New York Times*, March 31, 1993.

The remainder of this paper has three parts. The next part develops a theory of how ethnic wars end. Then, I present a strategy for international military intervention to stop ethnic wars and dampen future violence, and rebut possible objections to this strategy. The conclusion addresses the moral and political stakes in humanitarian intervention in ethnic conflicts.

How Ethnic Civil Wars End

Civil wars are not all alike.[6] Ethnic conflicts are disputes between communities which see themselves as having distinct heritages, over the power relationship between the communities, while ideological civil wars are contests between factions within the same community over how that community should be governed.[7] The key difference is the flexibility of individual loyalties, which are quite fluid in ideological conflicts, but almost completely rigid in ethnic wars.[8]

---

6. To avoid discounting fundamentally similar conflicts because of differences in international legal status, "civil" wars are defined here as those among "geographically contiguous people concerned about possibly having to live with one another in the same political unit after the conflict." Roy Licklider, "How Civil Wars End," in Licklider, ed., *Stopping the Killing* (New York: New York University Press, 1993), p. 9. Thus the Abkhazian rebellion in Georgia and the war between Armenia and Azerbaijan are both properly considered ethnic civil wars.

7. An ethnic group (or nation) is commonly defined as a body of individuals who purportedly share cultural or racial characteristics, especially common ancestry or territorial origin, which distinguish them from members of other groups. See Max Weber (Guenther Roth, and Claus Wittich, eds.), *Economy and Society: An Outline of Interpretive Sociology*, Vol. 1 (Berkeley, Calif.: University of California Press, 1968), pp. 389, 395; Anthony D. Smith, *National Identity* (Reno: University of Nevada Press, 1991), pp. 14, 21. Opposing communities in ethnic civil conflicts hold irreconcilable visions of the identity, borders, and citizenship of the state. They do not seek to control a state whose identity all sides accept, but rather to redefine or divide the state itself. By contrast, ideological conflicts may be defined as those in which all sides share a common vision of community membership, a common preference for political organization of the community as a single state, and a common sense of the legitimate boundaries of that state. The opposing sides seek control of the state, not its division or destruction. It follows that some religious conflicts —those between confessions which see themselves as separate communities, as between Catholics and Protestants in Northern Ireland—are best categorized with ethnic conflicts, while others—over interpretation of a shared religion, e.g., disputes over the social role of Islam in Iran, Algeria, and Egypt—should be considered ideological contests. On religious differences as ethnic divisions, see Arend Lijphart, "The Power-Sharing Approach," in Joseph V. Montville, ed., *Conflict and Peacemaking in Multiethnic Societies* (Lexington, Mass.: Lexington Books, 1990), pp. 491–509, at 491.

8. While the discussion below delineates ideal types, mixed cases occur. The key distinction is the extent to which mobilization appeals are based on race or confession (ethnic) rather than on political, economic, or social ideals (ideological). During the Cold War a number of Third World ethnic conflicts were misidentified by the superpowers as ideological struggles because local groups stressed ideology to gain outside support. In Angola the MPLA drew their support from the coastal Kimbundu tribe, the FNLA from the Bakongo in the north (and across the border in

The possible and impossible solutions to ethnic civil wars follow from this fact. War hardens ethnic identities to the point that cross-ethnic political appeals become futile, which means that victory can be assured only by physical control over the territory in dispute. Ethnic wars also generate intense security dilemmas, both because the escalation of each side's mobilization rhetoric presents a real threat to the other, and even more because intermingled population settlement patterns create defensive vulnerabilities and offensive opportunities.

Once this occurs, the war cannot end until the security dilemma is reduced by physical separation of the rival groups. Solutions that aim at restoring multi-ethnic civil politics and at avoiding population transfers—such as power-sharing, state re-building, or identity reconstruction—cannot work because they do nothing to dampen the security dilemma, and because ethnic fears and hatreds hardened by war are extremely resistant to change.

The result is that ethnic wars can end in only three ways: with complete victory of one side; by temporary suppression of the conflict by third party military occupation; or by self-governance of separate communities. The record of the ethnic wars of the last half century bears this out.

THE DYNAMICS OF ETHNIC WAR

It is useful to compare characteristics of ethnic conflicts with those of ideological conflicts. The latter are competitions between the government and the rebels for the loyalties of the people.[9] The critical features of these conflicts are that ideological loyalties are changeable and difficult to assess, and the same population serves as the shared mobilization base for both sides. As a result, winning the "hearts and minds" of the population is both possible and necessary for victory. The most important instruments are political, economic, and social reforms that redress popular grievances such as poverty, inequality, corruption, and physical insecurity. Control of access to population is also important, both

---

Zaire), and UNITA from Ovimbundu, Chokwe, and Ngangela in the interior and the south. The former were aided by the Soviets and the latter two, at various times, by both the United States and China. Daniel S. Papp, "The Angolan Civil War and Namibia," in David R. Smock, ed., *Making War and Waging Peace: Foreign Intervention in Africa* (Washington, D.C.: U.S. Institute of Peace, 1993), pp. 161–196, 162–164.

9. Landmarks on counterinsurgency include John Maynard Dow, *Nation Building in Southeast Asia*, rev. ed. (Boulder, Colo.: Pruett Press, 1966); Nathan Leites and Charles Wolf, Jr., *Rebellion and Authority: An Analytic Essay on Insurgent Conflicts* (Chicago: Markham, 1970); Douglas S. Blaufarb, *The Counterinsurgency Era: U.S. Doctrine and Performance, 1950 to the Present* (New York: Free Press, 1977); D. Michael Shafer, *Deadly Paradigms: The Failure of U.S. Counterinsurgency Policy* (Princeton, N.J.: Princeton University Press, 1988).

to allow recruitment and implementation of reform promises, and to block the enemy from these tasks.[10] Population control, however, cannot be guaranteed solely by physical control over territory, but depends on careful intelligence, persuasion, and coercion. Purely military successes are often indecisive as long as the enemy's base of political support is undamaged.[11]

Ethnic wars, however, have nearly the opposite properties. Individual loyalties are both rigid and transparent, while each side's mobilization base is limited to members of its own group in friendly-controlled territory. The result is that ethnic conflicts are primarily military struggles in which victory depends on physical control over the disputed territory, not on appeals to members of the other group.[12]

IDENTITY IN ETHNIC WARS. Competition to sway individual loyalties does not play an important role in ethnic civil wars, because ethnic identities are fixed by birth.[13] While not everyone may be mobilized as an active fighter for

---

10. "Guerrillas are like fish, and the people are the water they swim in." Mao Zedong, quoted in Shafer, *Deadly Paradigms*, p. 21.

11. "Winning a military war in Vietnam will be a hollow victory if the country remains politically and economically unstable, for it is under these conditions that a 'defeated' Viet Cong will be able to regroup and begin anew a 'war of national liberation'." Dow, *Nation Building*, p. viii.

12. A partial exception occurs under conditions of extreme power imbalance, when militants of the weaker ethnic group may have difficulty mobilizing co-ethnics, although this may be less because they do not desire ethnic autonomy or independence, than because they are not convinced that there is hope of successful resistance. The credibility of the PKK, for example, has been enhanced by military successes against Turkish forces. Henri Barkey, "Turkey's Kurdish Dilemma," *Survival*, Vol. 35, No. 4 (Winter 1993–94), pp. 51–70, 53.

13. Constructivist scholars of nationalism would not agree, as they argue that ethnic identities are flexible social constructions, which can be manipulated by political entrepreneurs and more or less freely adopted or ignored by individuals. Key works include Paul R. Brass, *Language, Religion, and Politics in North India* (Cambridge, England: Cambridge University Press, 1974); Benedict Anderson, *Imagined Communities: Reflections on the Origins and Spread of Nationalism* (London: Verso, 1983). Primordialists, by contrast, see ethnic identities as fixed by linguistic, racial, or religious background. Edward Shils, "Primordial, Personal, and Sacred Ties," *British Journal of Sociology*, Vol. 8 (1957), pp. 130–145; Clifford Geertz, "The Integrative Revolution: Primordial Sentiments and Civil Politics in the New States," in Geertz, ed., *Old Societies and New States* (New York: Free Press, 1963). For a recent defense, see Alexander J. Motyl, "Inventing Invention: The Limits of National Identity Formation," in Michael Kennedy and Ronald Gregor Suny, eds., *Intellectuals and the Articulation of the Nation*, book manuscript. A middle position, "perennialist," accepts that identities are social constructs but argues that their deep cultural and psychological roots make them extremely persistent, especially in literate cultures. See Walker Connor, *Ethnonationalism: The Quest for Understanding* (Princeton, N.J.: Princeton University Press, 1994). In this paper I do not take a position on the initial sources of ethnic identities or on their malleability under conditions of low conflict, but argue that massive ethnic violence creates conditions which solidify both ethnic boundaries and inter-ethnic hostility.

his or her own group, hardly anyone ever fights for the opposing ethnic group.[14]

Different identity categories imply their own membership rules. Ideological identity is relatively soft, as it is a matter of individual belief, or sometimes of political behavior. Religious identities are harder, because while they also depend on belief, change generally requires formal acceptance by the new faith, which may be denied. Ethnic identities are hardest, since they depend on language, culture, and religion, which are hard to change, as well as parentage, which no one can change.[15]

Ethnic identities are hardened further by intense conflict, so that leaders cannot broaden their appeals to include members of opposing groups.[16] As ethnic conflicts escalate, populations come increasingly to hold enemy images of the other group, either because of deliberate efforts by elites to create such images or because of increasing real threats. The intensification of the war in Southeastern Turkey, for example, has led the Turkish public more and more to identify all Kurds with the PKK guerrillas, while even assimilated Kurds increasingly see the war as a struggle for survival.[17] Following riots in Colombo in 1983 in which Sinhalese mobs killed 3,000 Tamils, even formerly liberal-minded Sinhalese came to view all Tamils as separatists: "They all say they are

---

14. Internal divisions may undermine the authority of group leaders or even lead to intra-group violence, but will not cause members of the community to defect to the enemy. The unpopularity of the Azeri regime in 1992 generated no support for concessions to Armenian territorial demands. Although there was a small-scale intra-Muslim war in the Bihać pocket in Northwest Bosnia from 1993 to August 1995, the anti-Sarajevo faction never surrendered any territory or Muslim civilians to the Serbs or Croats. Charles Lane, "The Real Story of Bihać," *The New Republic*, December 19, 1994, pp. 12–14; Roger Cohen, "Fratricide in Bosnia: Muslim vs. Muslim," *New York Times*, June 22, 1994.

15. High levels of intermarriage which produce children of mixed parentage could blur ethnic boundaries, but even levels of ethnic tension far short of war inhibit this. In Northern Ireland in the 1960s and 1970s, Catholic-Protestant intermarriages averaged 3–4 per cent. In Yugoslavia intermarriage rose in 1950s and 1960s, fell in 1966–69 during a period of ethnic tension, then rose again, and finally declined after 1981 as ethnic tensions increased. Especially in divided societies, ethnic identity rules often account for the identification of children of mixed marriages. In Northern Ireland nearly every wife converts to her husband's church. In Rwanda, Hutu or Tutsi identity is inherited from the father. John H. Whyte, "How is the Boundary Maintained between the Two Communities in Northern Ireland?" *Ethnic and Racial Studies*, Vol. 9, No. 2 (April 1986), pp. 219–233; Ruža Petrović, "The Ethnic Identity of Parents and Children," *Yugoslavia Survey*, Vol. 32, No. 2 (1991), pp. 63–76, 64; Alain Destexche, "The Third Genocide," *Foreign Policy*, No. 97 (Winter 1994–95), pp. 3–17, 6.

16. This does not occur in ideological civil wars, in which most people (except leaders whose commitments are widely known) can easily and quickly shift affiliations, although shifts may be the result of coercion as often as positive appeals.

17. Barkey, "Turkey's Kurdish Dilemma," pp. 57–58.

loyal to the government, but scratch a Tamil, any Tamil, and beneath the skin there is an Eelamist."[18] Non-ethnic identity categories, such as neighborhood and friendship, cannot compete: in 1994 much of the hierarchy of the Rwandan Catholic Church split on ethnic lines.[19]

Once the conflict reaches the level of large-scale violence, tales of atrocities—true or invented—perpetuated or planned against members of the group by the ethnic enemy provide hard-liners with an unanswerable argument. In March 1992 a Serb woman in Foča in Eastern Bosnia was convinced that "there were lists of Serbs who were marked for death. My two sons were down on the list to be slaughtered like pigs. I was listed under rape." The fact that neither she nor other townspeople had seen any such lists did not prevent them from believing such tales without question.[20] The Croatian Ustasha in World War II went further, terrorizing Serbs in order to provoke a backlash that could then be used to mobilize Croats for defense against Serb retaliation.[21]

In this environment, cross-ethnic appeals are not likely to attract members of the other group. The Yugoslav Partisans in World War II are often credited with transcending the ethnic conflict between the Croatian Ustasha and the Serbian Chetniks with an anti-German, pan-Yugoslav program. In fact it did not work. Tito was a Croat, but Partisan officers as well as the rank and file were virtually all Serbs and Montenegrins.[22] Only in 1944, when German withdrawal made Partisan victory certain, did Croats begin to join the Partisans in numbers, not because they preferred a multi-ethnic Yugoslavia to a Greater

---

18. Sinhalese businessman quoted in William McGowan, *Only Man is Vile: The Tragedy of Sri Lanka* (New York: Farrar, Strauss and Giroux, 1992), p. 102.

19. Donatella Lorch, "The Rock that Crumbled: The Church in Rwanda," *New York Times*, October 17, 1994.

20. Reported by Andrej Gustinčič of *Reuters*, cited in Misha Glenny, *The Fall of Yugoslavia* (New York: Penguin, 1992), p. 166. Another tactic used by extremists to radicalize co-ethnics is to accuse the other side of crimes similar to their own. In July 1992, amidst large-scale rape of Bosnian Muslim women by Serb forces, Bosnian Serbs accused Muslims of impregnating kidnapped Serb women in order to create a new race of Janissary soldiers. Roy Gutman, *A Witness to Genocide* (New York: Macmillan, 1993), p. x.

21. Aleksa Djilas, *The Contested Country* (Cambridge, Mass.: Harvard University Press, 1991), p. 122.

22. Partisan (as well as Chetnik) leaders were recruited mainly from among pre-war Army officers. Throughout most of 1942, the Partisans fielded two Montenegrin and four Serbian battalions, leavened with just a few fighters of other nationalities. A. Pavelić, "How Many Non-Serbian Generals in 1941?" *East European Quarterly*, Vol. 16, No. 4 (January 1983), pp. 447–452; Anton Bebler, "Political Pluralism and the Yugoslav Professional Military," in Jim Seroka and Vukašin Pavlović, eds., *The Tragedy of Yugoslavia: The Failure of Democratic Transformation* (Armonk, N.Y.: M.E. Sharpe, 1992), pp. 105–40, 106.

Croatia, but because they preferred a multi-ethnic Yugoslavia to a Yugoslavia cleansed of Croatians.

In both Laos and Thailand in the 1960s, the hill people (Hmong) fought the lowland people (Laos and Thais). The Hmong in Laos called themselves anti-communists, while Hmong on the other side of the Mekong River turned to the Communist Party of Thailand. The ideological affiliations, however, were purely tactical; most Hmong in Laos lived in areas dominated by the communist Pathet Lao and so turned to the United States for support, while most Hmong in Thailand were fighting a U.S.-allied government. Although in both countries both communists and anti-communists offered political reform and economic development, cross-ethnic recruitment bore little fruit, and the outcomes of the rebellions were determined mainly by strictly military operations.[23]

Ethnic war also shrinks scope for individual identity choice.[24] Even those who put little value on their ethnic identity are pressed towards ethnic mobilization for two reasons. First, extremists within each community are likely to impose sanctions on those who do not contribute to the cause. In 1992 the leader of the Croatian Democratic Union in Bosnia was dismissed on the ground that he "was too much Bosnian, too little Croat."[25] Conciliation is easy to denounce as dangerous to group security or as actually traitorous. Such arguments drove nationalist extremists to overthrow President Makarios of Cyprus in 1974, to assassinate Mahatma Gandhi in 1948, to massacre nearly the whole government of Rwanda in 1994, and to kill Yitzhak Rabin in 1995.[26]

---

23. Because of pre-existing clan rivalries, some Hmong in Laos fought on the Pathet Lao side. Blaufarb, *Counterinsurgency Era*, pp. 128–204; T.A. Marks, "The Meo Hill Tribe Problem in Northern Thailand," *Asian Survey*, October 1973; R. Sean Randolph and W. Scott Thompson, *Thai Insurgency: Contemporary Developments* (Beverly Hills, Calif.: Sage Publications, 1981), p. 17.

24. The proportion of Yugoslav residents identifying themselves not by nationality but as "Yugoslavs" rose from 1.7 percent in the 1961 census to 5.4 percent in 1981, but fell to 3.0 percent in 1991. Ruža Petrović, "The National Structure of the Yugoslav Population," *Yugoslavia Survey*, Vol. 14, No. 1 (1973), pp. 1–22, 12; Petrović, "The National Composition of the Population," *Yugoslavia Survey*, Vol. 24, No. 3 (1983), pp. 21–34, 22; Petrović, "The National Composition of Yugoslavia's Population," *Yugoslavia Survey*, Vol. 33, No. 1 (1992), pp. 3–24, 12.

25. *Balkan War Report*, February/March 1993, p. 14, quoted in Robert M. Hayden, "The Partition of Bosnia and Hercegovina, 1990–1993," *RFE/RL Research Reports*, Vol. 2, No. 22 (May 29, 1993), pp. 2–3. See also Blaine Harden, "In Bosnia 'Disloyal' Serbs Share Plight of Opposition," *Washington Post*, August 24, 1992. Hutu leaders in refugee camps in Zaire have murdered people suspected of wanting to return to Rwanda. "Telling Tales," *Economist*, August 13, 1994, p. 39.

26. See Fred C. Iklé, *Every War Must End* (New York: Columbia University Press, 1981), on the problems of soft-liners in international wars.

Second and more important, identity is often imposed by the opposing group, specifically by its most murderous members. Assimilation or political passivity did no good for German Jews, Rwandan Tutsis, or Azerbaijanis in Nagorno-Karabakh. A Bosnian Muslim schoolteacher recently lamented:

We never, until the war, thought of ourselves as Muslims. We were Yugoslavs. But when we began to be murdered, because we are Muslims, thing changed. The definition of who we are today has been determined by our killers.[27]

Choice contracts further the longer the conflict continues. Multi-ethnic towns as yet untouched by war are swamped by radicalized refugees, undermining moderate leaders who preach tolerance.[28] For example, while a portion of the pre-war Serb population remained in Bosnian government–controlled Sarajevo when the fighting started, their numbers have declined as the government has taken on a more narrowly Muslim religious character over years of war, and pressure on Serbs has increased. Where 80,000 remained in July 1993, only 30,000 were left in August 1995.[29] The Tutsi Rwandan Patriotic Front (RPF) showed remarkable restraint during the 1994 civil war, but since then the RPF has imprisoned tens of thousands of genocide suspects in appalling conditions, failed to prevent massacres of thousands of Hutu civilians in several incidents, and allowed Tutsi squatters to seize the property of many absent Hutus.[30]

What can finally eliminate identity choice altogether is fear of genocide. The hypernationalist rhetoric used for group mobilization often includes images of the enemy group as a threat to the physical existence of the nation, in turn justifying unlimited violence against the ethnic enemy; this threatening discourse can usually be observed by members of the target group. Even worse are actual massacres of civilians, especially when condoned by leaders of the perpetrating group, which are virtually certain to convince the members of the targeted group that group defense is their only option.

A Tamil justifying the massacre of Sinhalese in Trinco in Northern Sri Lanka in 1987 explained:

---

27. Mikica Babić, quoted in Chris Hedges, "War Turns Sarajevo Away from Europe," *New York Times*, July 28, 1995.
28. Susan L. Woodward, *Balkan Tragedy: Chaos and Dissolution after the Cold War* (Washington, D.C.: Brookings, 1995), p. 363.
29. Jonathan S. Landay, "Loyal Serbs and Croats in Sarajevo See Woe in Partition of Bosnia," *Christian Science Monitor*, July 30, 1993; Tracy Wilkinson, "Sarajevo's Serbs Face a Dual Hostility," *Los Angeles Times*, July 10, 1995; "Bosnia: The Coffee-cup State," *Economist*, August 26, 1995, p. 43.
30. *Rwanda Human Rights Practices, 1994* (Washington, D.C.: U.S. Department of State, March 1995); Donatella Lorch, "As Many as 2,000 are Reported Dead in Rwanda," *New York Times*, April 24, 1995.

This is a payback for [the massacres of] 1983 and all the years they attacked us, going back to 1956. Will it ever stop? I do not think it will. But at least with the Indians here now, we have some peace. If they were to leave, however, it would mean death to all Tamils. They will kill every one of us. If the Indian Army leaves, we will have to jump into the sea.[31]

IDENTIFYING LOYALTIES. A consequence of the hardness of ethnic identities is that in ethnic wars assessing individual loyalties is much easier than in ideological conflicts. Even if some members of both groups remain unmobilized, as long as virtually none actively support the other group, each side can treat all co-ethnics as friends without risk of coddling an enemy agent and can treat all members of the other group as enemies without risk of losing a recruit.

Although it often requires effort, each side can almost always identify members of its own and the other group in any territory it controls. Ethnicity can be identified by outward appearance, public or private records, and local social knowledge. In societies where ethnicity is important, it is often officially recorded in personal identity documents or in censuses. In 1994 Rwandan death squads used neighborhood target lists prepared in advance, as well as roadblocks that checked identity cards.[32] In 1983 riots in Sri Lanka, Sinhalese mobs went through mixed neighborhoods selecting Tamil dwellings for destruction with the help of Buddhist monks carrying electoral lists.[33] While it might not have been possible to predict the Yugoslav civil war thirty years in advance, one could have identified the members of each of the warring groups from the 1961 census, which identified the nationality of all but 1.8 percent of the population.[34]

Where public records are not adequate, private ones can be used instead. Pre–World War II Yugoslav censuses relied on church records.[35] Absent any records at all, reliable demographic intelligence can often be obtained from

31. McGowan, *Only Man is Vile*, p. 49. From 1987 to December 1989, the Indian Peacekeeping Force attempted to separate Sri Lankan and Tamil forces. The war continues.
32. Destexche, "Third Genocide," p. 8.
33. Lakshmanan Sabaratnam, "The Boundaries of the State and the State of Ethnic Boundaries: Sinhala-Tamil Relations in Sri Lankan History," *Ethnic and Racial Studies*, Vol. 10, No. 3 (July 1987), pp. 291–316, 294.
34. Petrović, "National Structure of the Yugoslav Population," p. 12. Yugoslav censuses include extremely detailed nationality information, including migration between regions by nationality, ethnicity of partners in mixed marriages, ethnic identity of children of such marriages, and the percentage of Serbs, Croats, and Muslims in each of the 106 municipalities in Bosnia. Petrović, "National Composition of Yugoslavia's Population" (1992); Petrović, "The Ethnic Identity of Parents and Children"; Dušan Breznik and Nada Raduški, "Demographic Characteristics of the Population of FR Yugoslavia by Nationality," *Yugoslavia Survey*, Vol. 34, No. 4 (1993), pp. 3–44.
35. Breznik and Raduški, "Demographic Characteristics," p. 3, n. 2.

local co-ethnics. In 1988 a Tutsi mob attacking the Catholic mission in Ntega, Burundi, brought with them a former employee who knew the hiding places where Hutu refugees could be found.[36] Muslim survivors report that throughout Bosnia in 1992 Serb militias used prepared lists to eliminate the wealthy, the educated, religious leaders, government officials, and members of the Bosnian Home Guard or of the (Muslim) Party of Democratic Action.[37]

Finally, in unprepared encounters ethnicity can often be gauged by outward appearance: Tutsis are generally tall and thin, while Hutus are relatively short and stocky; Russians are generally fairer than Kazakhs.[38] When physiognomy is ambiguous, other signs such as language or accent, surname, dress, posture, ritual mutilation, diet, habits, occupation, region or neighborhood within urban areas, or certain possessions may give clues. Residents of Zagreb, for example, are marked as Serbs by certain names, attendance at an Orthodox church, or possession of books printed in Cyrillic.[39]

Perhaps the strongest evidence of intelligence reliability in ethnic conflicts is that—in dramatic contrast to ideological insurgencies—history records almost no instances of mistaken "cleansing" of co-ethnics.

THE DECISIVENESS OF TERRITORY. Another consequence of the hardness of ethnic identities is that population control depends wholly on territorial control. Since each side can recruit only from its own community and only in friendly-controlled territory, incentives to seize areas populated by co-ethnics are strong, as is the pressure to cleanse friendly-controlled territory of enemy ethnics by relocation to *de facto* concentration camps, expulsion, or massacre.[40]

Because of the decisiveness of territorial control, military strategy in ethnic wars is very different than in ideological conflicts. Unlike ideological insurgents, who often evade rather than risk battle, or a counter-insurgent govern-

---

36. David Ress, *The Burundi Ethnic Massacres, 1988* (San Francisco: Mellen Research University Press, 1991), p. 103.
37. Gutman, *Witness to Genocide*, pp. 51, 94, 109–110, 139.
38. Despite claims that the Hutu-Tutsi ethnic division was invented by the Belgians, 1969 census data showed significant physical differences: Tutsi males averaged 5 feet 9 inches and 126 pounds, Hutus 5 feet 5 inches and 131 pounds. Richard F. Nyrop, et al., *Rwanda: A Country Study, 1985* (Washington, D.C.: Department of the Army, 1985), pp. 46–47, 63.
39. Kit Roane, "Serbs in Croatia Live in World of Hate, Fear," *San Diego Union-Tribune*, August 19, 1995.
40. Beginning in 1985, the Iraqi government destroyed all rural villages in Kurdistan, as well as animals and orchards, concentrating the Kurdish population in "victory cities" where they could be watched and kept dependent on the government for food. The Turkish government is currently doing the same, while the Burmese government has pursued this strategy against ethnic rebels at least since 1968. U.S. Senate Committee on Foreign Relations, *Civil War in Iraq* (Washington, D.C.: U.S. Government Printing Office [GPO], 1991), pp. 7–9; Michael Fredholm, *Burma: Ethnicity and Insurgency* (Westport, Conn.: Praeger, 1993), pp. 90–92.

ment, which might forbear to attack rather than risk bombarding civilians, ethnic combatants must fight for every piece of land. By contrast, combatants in ethnic wars are much less free to decline unfavorable battles because they cannot afford to abandon any settlement to an enemy who is likely to "cleanse" it by massacre, expulsion, destruction of homes, and possibly colonization. By the time a town can be retaken, its value will have been lost.[41]

In ethnic civil wars, military operations are decisive.[42] Attrition matters because the side's mobilization pools are separate and can be depleted. Most important, since each side's mobilization base is limited to members of its own community in friendly-controlled territory, conquering the enemy's population centers reduces its mobilization base, while loss of friendly settlements reduces one's own. Military control of the entire territory at issue is tantamount to total victory.

SECURITY DILEMMAS IN ETHNIC WARS

The second problem that must be overcome by any remedy for severe ethnic conflict is the security dilemma.[43] Regardless of the origins of ethnic strife, once violence (or abuse of state power by one group that controls it) reaches the point that ethnic communities cannot rely on the state to protect them, each community must mobilize to take responsibility for its own security.

Under conditions of anarchy, each group's mobilization constitutes a real threat to the security of others for two reasons. First, the nationalist rhetoric that accompanies mobilization often seems to and often does indicate offensive intent. Under these conditions, group identity itself can be seen by other groups as a threat to their safety.[44]

---

41. Serbs in Bosnia have destroyed and desecrated mosques, and raped tens of thousands of Muslim women, in part to eradicate the desire of any displaced Muslim to return to a former home. Gutman, *Witness to Genocide*, pp. 68, 70.

42. The political restraints on the use of firepower in ideological disputes do not apply in ethnic wars. Accidentally inflicting collateral damage on enemy civilians does little harm since there was never any chance of gaining their support. Even accidentally hitting friendly civilians, while awkward, will not cause them to defect.

43. While ideological wars may also produce intense security dilemmas for faction leaders who can expect to be treated as criminals if their side loses, most ordinary citizens do not face a severe security dilemma because the winning side will accept their allegiance.

44. Barry R. Posen, "The Security Dilemma and Ethnic Conflict," in Brown, *Ethnic Conflict and International Security*, pp. 103–124. Posen argues that nationalism and hypernationalism are driven primarily by the need to supply recruits for mass armies, and are thus likely to be more extreme in new states which lack the capacity to field more capital-intensive and less manpower-intensive forces (pp. 106–107). See also Posen, "Nationalism, the Mass Army, and Military Power," *International Security*, Vol. 18, No. 2 (Fall 1993), pp. 80–124.

Second, military capability acquired for defense can usually also be used for offense. Further, offense often has an advantage over defense in inter-community conflict, especially when settlement patterns are inter-mingled, because isolated pockets are harder to hold than to take.[45]

The reality of the mutual security threats means that solutions to ethnic conflicts must do more than undo the causes; until or unless the security dilemma can be reduced or eliminated, neither side can afford to demobilize.

DEMOGRAPHY AND SECURITY DILEMMAS. The severity of ethnic security dilemmas is greatest when demography is most intermixed, weakest when community settlements are most separate.[46] The more mixed the opposing groups, the stronger the offense in relation to the defense; the more separated they are, the stronger the defense in relation to offense.[47] When settlement patterns are extremely mixed, both sides are vulnerable to attack not only by organized military forces but also by local militias or gangs from adjacent towns or neighborhoods. Since well-defined fronts are impossible, there is no effective means of defense against such raids. Accordingly, each side has a strong incentive—at both national and local levels—to kill or drive out enemy populations before the enemy does the same to it, as well as to create homogeneous enclaves more practical to defend.[48]

Better, but still bad, are well-defined enclaves with islands of one or both sides' populations behind the other's front. Each side then has an incentive to attack to rescue its surrounded co-ethnics before they are destroyed by the enemy, as well as incentives to wipe out enemy islands behind its own lines, both to pre-empt rescue attempts and to eliminate possible bases for fifth columnists or guerrillas.[49]

---

45. The breakup of a multi-ethnic state often also creates windows of opportunity by leaving one group in possession of most of the state's military assets, while others are initially defenseless but working rapidly to mobilize their own military capabilities. Posen, "Security Dilemma and Ethnic Conflict," pp. 108–111.

46. Ibid., pp. 108–110.

47. Increased geographic intermixing of ethnic groups often intensifies conflict, particularly if the state is too weak or too biased to assure the security of all groups. Increasing numbers of Jewish settlers in the West Bank had this effect on Israeli-Palestinian relations. A major reason for the failure of the negotiations that preceded the Nigerian civil war was the inability of northern leaders to guarantee the safety of Ibo living in the northern region. Harold D. Nelson, ed., *Nigeria: A Country Study* (Washington, D.C.: U.S. GPO, 1982), p. 55.

48. Stephen Van Evera, "Hypotheses on Nationalism," *International Security*, Vol. 18, No. 4 (Spring 1994), pp. 5–39. Posen additionally points out that when populations are highly mixed it is easier for small bands of fanatics to initiate and escalate violence, while community leaders can deny responsibility for their actions, or may actually be unable to control them. Posen, "Security Dilemma and Ethnic Conflict," 109.

49. Although censuses from 1891 on show Greek and Turkish Cypriots gradually segregating themselves by village, violence between these still-intermingled settlements grew from 1955 onward. Tozun Bahcheli, *Greek-Turkish Relations since 1955* (Boulder, Colo.: Westview, 1990), p. 21.

The safest pattern is a well-defined demographic front that separates nearly homogeneous regions. Such a front can be defended by organized military forces, so populations are not at risk unless defenses are breached. At the same time the strongest motive for attack disappears, since there are few or no endangered co-ethnics behind enemy lines.

Further, offensive and defensive mobilization measures are more distinguishable when populations are separated than when they are mixed. Although hypernationalist political rhetoric, as well as conventional military forces, have both offensive and defensive uses regardless of population settlement patterns, some other forms of ethnic mobilization do not. Local militias and ethnically based local self-governing authorities have both offensive and defensive capabilities when populations are mixed: ethnic militias can become death squads, while local governments dominated by one group can disenfranchise minorities. When populations are separated, however, such local organizations have defensive value only.

WAR AND ETHNIC UNMIXING. Because of the security dilemma, ethnic war causes ethnic unmixing.[50] The war between Greece and Turkey, the partition of India, the 1948–49 Arab-Israeli war, and the recent war between Armenia and Azerbaijan were all followed by emigration or expulsion of most of the minority populations on each side. More than one million Ibo left northern Nigeria during the Nigerian Civil War. Following 1983 pogroms, three-fourths of the Tamil population of Colombo fled to the predominantly Tamil north and east of the island. By the end of 1994, only about 70,000 non-Serbs remained in Serb-controlled areas of Bosnia, with less than 40,000 Serbs still in Muslim- and Croat-controlled regions. Of 600,000 Serbs in pre-war Croatia, probably no more than 100,000 remain outside of Serb-controlled eastern Slavonia.[51]

Collapse of multi-ethnic states often causes some ethnic unmixing even without war.[52] The retreat of the Ottoman Empire from the Balkans sparked movement of Muslims southward and eastward as well as some unmixing of

---

50. Unmixing may be dampened when one side is so completely victorious that escape options of members of the losing group are limited. As Sri Lankan forces closed in on the Tamil stronghold of Jaffna in November 1995, some Tamil refugees fled to areas still controlled by Tamil forces, some out of the country, but some to areas behind government lines where relative peace may have offered the best immediate hope of safety. "Ghost Town," *Economist*, November 18, 1995, pp. 39–40.
51. *Fact Sheet: Azerbaijan* (Washington, D.C.: U.S. Department of State, May 2, 1994); Nelson, *Nigeria*, p. 54; Ravindran Casinader, "Sri Lanka: Minority Tamils Face an Uncertain Future," *Inter Press Service*, May 15, 1984; *Balkan War Report*, December 1994–January 1995, p. 5; *World Refugee Survey 1995* (Washington, D.C.: U.S. Committee for Refugees, pp. 128–130.
52. Robert M. Hayden argues that this result is inherent in the nation-state principle. Hayden, "Constitutional Nationalism and the Wars of Yugoslavia," paper prepared for the Conference on Post-Communism and Ethnic Mobilization, Ithaca, N.Y., April 1995, pp. 12–13.

different Christian peoples in the southern Balkans. Twelve million Germans left Eastern Europe after World War II, one and a half million between 1950 and 1987, and another one and a half million since 1989, essentially dissolving the German diaspora. Of 25 million Russians outside Russia in 1989, as many as three to four million had gone to Russia by the end of 1992. From 1990 to 1993, 200,000 Hungarians left Vojvodina, replaced by 400,000 Serb refugees from other parts of ex-Yugoslavia.[53]

ETHNIC SEPARATION AND PEACE. Once ethnic groups are mobilized for war, the war cannot end until the populations are separated into defensible, mostly homogeneous regions. Even if an international force or an imperial conqueror were to impose peace, the conflict would resume as soon as it left. Even if a national government were somehow re-created despite mutual suspicions, neither group could safely entrust its security to it. Continuing mutual threat also ensures perpetuation of hypernationalist propaganda, both for mobilization and because the plausibility of the threat posed by the enemy gives radical nationalists an unanswerable advantage over moderates in intra-group debates.

Ethnic separation does not guarantee peace, but it allows it. Once populations are separated, both cleansing and rescue imperatives disappear; war is no longer mandatory. At the same time, any attempt to seize more territory requires a major conventional military offensive. Thus the conflict changes from one of mutual pre-emptive ethnic cleansing to something approaching conventional interstate war in which normal deterrence dynamics apply. Mutual deterrence does not guarantee that there will be no further violence, but it reduces the probability of outbreaks, as well as the likely aims and intensity of those that do occur.[54]

There have been no wars among Bulgaria, Greece, and Turkey since their population exchanges of the 1920s. Ethnic violence on Cyprus, which reached crisis on several occasions between 1960 and 1974, has been zero since the partition and population exchange which followed Turkish invasion. The Armenian-Azeri ethnic conflict, sparked by independence demands of the mostly Armenian Nagorno-Karabakh Autonomous Oblast, escalated to full-

53. Rogers Brubaker, "Aftermaths of Empire and Unmixing of Peoples: Historical and Comparative Perspectives," *Ethnic and Racial Studies*, Vol. 18, No. 2 (April 1995), pp. 189–218; Sheila Marnie and Wendy Slater, "Russia's Refugees," *RFE/RL Research Report*, Vol. 2, No. 37 (September 17, 1993), pp. 46–53; Stan Markotich, "Vojvodina: A Potential Powder Keg," *RFE/RL Research Report*, Vol. 2, No. 46 (November 19, 1993), pp. 13–18.
54. Two additional factors that may enhance deterrence are balancing by third parties and the "aggressor's handicap": states are normally willing to fight harder to avoid losses than to seek gains.

scale war by 1992. Armenian conquest of all of Karabakh together with the land which formerly separated it from Armenia proper, along with displacement of nearly all members of each group from enemy-controlled territories, created a defensible separation with no minorities to fight over, leading to a cease-fire in April 1994.[55]

Theories of Ethnic Peace

Those considering humanitarian intervention to end ethnic civil wars should set as their goal lasting safety, rather than perfect peace. Given the persistence of ethnic rivalries, "safety" is best defined as freedom from threats of ethnic murder, expropriation, or expulsion for the overwhelming majority of civilians of all groups. Absence of formal peace, even occasional terrorism or border skirmishes, would not undermine this, provided that the great majority of civilians are not at risk. "Lasting" must mean that the situation remains stable indefinitely after the intervention forces leave. Truces of weeks, months, or even years do not qualify as lasting safety if ethnic cleansing eventually resumes with full force.

ALTERNATIVES TO SEPARATION

Besides demographic separation, the literature on possible solutions to ethnic conflicts contains four main alternatives: suppression, reconstruction of ethnic identities, power-sharing, and state-building.[56]

SUPPRESSION. Many ethnic civil wars lead to the complete victory of one side and the forcible suppression of the other. This may reduce violence in some cases, but will never be an aim of outsiders considering humanitarian intervention.[57] Further, remission of violence may be only temporary, as the defeated group usually rebels again at any opportunity.[58] Even the fact that

---

55. Russian mediation provided a fig leaf for Azerbaijani acceptance of defeat, but did not cause the outcome. Bill Frelick, *Faultlines of Nationality Conflict: Refugees and Displaced Persons from Armenia and Azerbaijan* (Washington, D.C.: U.S. Committee for Refugees, 1993); Hugh Pope, "Azeris Square Up to a Loser's Peace," *The Independent*, July 29, 1994.
56. Sammy Smooha and Theodore Harf, "The Diverse Modes of Conflict Resolution in Deeply Divided Societies," *International Journal of Comparative Sociology*, Vol. 33, Nos. 1–2 (January–April 1992), pp. 26–47, briefly surveys most alternatives. See also Charles William Maynes, "Containing Ethnic Conflict," *Foreign Policy*, No. 90 (Spring 1993), pp. 3–21.
57. On this solution, see Ian Lustick, "Stability in Deeply Divided Societies: Consociationalism versus Control," *World Politics*, Vol. 31, No. 3 (April 1979), pp. 325–344.
58. The Kurds in Iraq fought against the government in 1919, 1922–26, 1930, 1931, 1943, 1945–46, 1961–70, 1974–75, 1977, 1983, and 1985–88, and rebelled again when the central government was weakened by the Gulf War in 1991. Senate, *Civil War in Iraq*, pp. 24–26.

certain conquerors, such as the English in Scotland or the Dutch in Friesland, eventually permitted genuine political assimilation after decades of suppression, does not recommend this as a remedy for endangered peoples today.

RECONSTRUCTION OF ETHNIC IDENTITIES. The most ambitious program to end ethnic violence would be to reconstruct ethnic identities according to the "Constructivist Model" of nationalism.[59] Constructivists argue that individual and group identities are fluid, continually being made and re-made in social discourse. Further, these identities are manipulable by political entrepreneurs. Violent ethnic conflicts are the result of pernicious group identities created by hypernationalist myth-making; many inter-group conflicts are quite recent, as are the ethnic identities themselves.[60]

The key is elite rivalries within communities, in which aggressive leaders use hypernationalist propaganda to gain and hold power. History does not matter; whether past inter-community relations have in fact been peaceful or conflictual, leaders can redefine, reinterpret, and invent facts to suit their arguments, including alleged atrocities and exaggerated or imagined threats. This process can feed on itself, as nationalists use the self-fulfilling nature of their arguments both to escalate the conflict and to justify their own power, so that intra-community politics becomes a competition in hypernationalist extremism, and inter-community relations enter a descending spiral of violence.[61]

It follows that ethnic conflicts generated by the promotion of pernicious, exclusive identities should be reversible by encouraging individuals and groups to adopt more benign, inclusive identities. Leaders can choose to mobilize support on the basis of broader identities that transcend the ethnic division, such as ideology, class, or civic loyalty to the nation-state. If members

---

59. Pfaff, "Invitation to War"; Hopf, "Managing Soviet Disintegration"; Jack Snyder, "Nationalism and the Crisis of the Post-Soviet State," in Brown, *Ethnic Conflict and International Security*, pp. 79–102; Gidon Gottlieb, *Nation Against State* (New York: Council on Foreign Relations Press, 1993); Stephen Ryan, *Ethnic Conflict and International Relations*, 2d ed. (Aldershot, England: Dartmouth, 1995).

60. Malays and Assamese each assert local primacy by terming themselves in their own languages "sons of the soil," even though both are actually recent aggregations of sub-groups. Similarly, Sinhalese claim primacy in Sri Lanka in part based on a largely mythical claim of earlier migration than the Tamils. Donald L. Horowitz, *Ethnic Groups in Conflict* (Berkeley: University of California Press, 1985), p. 453; David Little, *Sri Lanka: The Invention of Enmity* (Washington, D.C.: U.S. Institute of Peace, 1994), pp. 26–36. Robert Donia and John Fine, *Bosnia and Hercegovina: A Tradition Betrayed* (London, Hurst and Co., 1994), argue that distinct ethnic identities did not exist there before 1875.

61. Brass, *Language, Religion, and Politics in North India*; Stanley J. Tambiah, *Buddhism Betrayed? Religion, Politics, and Violence in Sri Lanka* (Chicago: University of Chicago Press, 1992); V.P. Gagnon, Jr., "Ethnic Nationalism and International Conflict: The Case of Serbia," *International Security*, Vol. 19, No. 3 (Winter 1994/95), pp. 130–166; Woodward, *Balkan Tragedy*, pp. 225–236.

of the opposing groups can be persuaded to adopt a larger identity, ethnic antagonisms should fade away. In 1993 David Owen explained why reconciliation in Bosnia was still possible: "I think it's realistic because these people are of the same ethnic stock. . . . Many people there still see themselves as European and even now don't think of themselves as Muslim, Croat, or Serb."[62]

However, even if ethnic hostility can be "constructed," there are strong reasons to believe that violent conflicts cannot be "reconstructed" back to ethnic harmony. Identity reconstruction under conditions of intense conflict is probably impossible because once ethnic groups are mobilized for war, they will have already produced, and will continue reproducing, social institutions and discourses that reinforce their group identity and shut out or shout down competing identities.[63]

Replacement of ethnicity by some other basis for political identification requires that political parties have cross-ethnic appeal, but examples of this in the midst of ethnic violence are virtually impossible to find. In late 1992 Yugoslav Prime Minister Milan Panić attempted to reconstruct Serbian identity in a less nationalist direction. Running for the Serbian presidency against Milošević, Panić promised democratization, economic reform, and ends to the war in Bosnia as well as to UN sanctions. Milošević painted him as a tool of foreign interests, and Panić lost with 34 percent of the vote.[64]

In fact, even ethnic tension far short of war often undermines not just political appeals across ethnic lines but also appeals within a single group for cooperation with other groups. In Yugoslavia in the 1920s, Malaya in the 1940s,

---

62. "Interview with David Owen on the Balkans," *Foreign Affairs*, Vol. 72, No. 2 (Spring 1993), pp. 1–9, at 6–7.
63. War may actually create ethnic identities. "Where disaffected *ethnies* become alienated enough to terror and revolt . . . the movement itself can be the prototype and harbinger of a new society and culture. Its cells, schools, guerrilla units, welfare associations, [etc.] all presage and create the nucleus of the future ethnic nation and its political identity, even when secession is prevented and the community fails to obtain its own state." Smith, *National Identity*, p. 137. Bougainvilleans formerly identified themselves primarily by clan, but as a result of their unsuccessful effort to secede from Papua New Guinea, came to divide people primarily between "red skins" (the Papuan enemy) and "black skins" (themselves). Caroline Ifeka, "War and Identity in Melanesia and Africa," *Ethnic and Racial Studies*, Vol. 9, No. 2 (April 1986), pp. 131–149.
64. Parties aligned with Panić won 21 percent of the National Assembly seats compared to 40 percent for Milošević's party and 29 percent for an even more ultra-nationalist party. Milan Andrejevich, "The Radicalization of Serb Politics," *RFE/RL Research Reports*, Vol. 2, No. 13 (March 26, 1993), pp. 14–24. Similarly, when Fazlal Huq, a Muslim leader in Bengal, tried to promote a moderate line in the 1946 election campaign, he was denounced as a traitor by Muslim League leaders and his party wiped out at the polls. Leonard A. Gordon, "Divided Bengal: Problems of Nationalism and Identity in the 1947 Partition," in Mushirul Hasan, ed., *India's Partition: Strategy, Process, and Mobilization* (Delhi: Oxford University Press, 1993), pp. 274–317, at 295–301.

Ceylon in the 1950s, and in Nigeria in the 1950s and 1960s, parties that advocated cooperation across ethnic lines proved unable to compete with strictly nationalist parties.[65]

Even if constructivists are right that the ancient past does not matter, recent history does. Intense violence creates personal experiences of fear, misery, and loss which lock people into their group identity and their enemy relationship with the other group. Elite as well as mass opinions are affected; more than 5,000 deaths in the 1946 Calcutta riots convinced many previously optimistic Hindu and Muslim leaders that the groups could not live together.[66] The Tutsi-controlled government of Burundi, which had witnessed the partial genocide against Tutsis in Rwanda in 1962–63 and survived Hutu-led coup attempts in 1965 and 1969, regarded the 1972 rebellion as another attempt at genocide, and responded by murdering between 100,000 and 200,000 Hutus. Fresh rounds of violence in 1988 and 1993–94 have reinforced the apocalyptic fears of both sides.[67]

Finally, literacy preserves atrocity memories and enhances their use for political mobilization.[68] The result is that atrocity histories cannot be reconstructed; victims can sometimes be persuaded to accept exaggerated atrocity tales, but cannot be talked out of real ones.[69] The result is that the bounds of

---

65. Djilas, *Contested Country*, p. 86; Horowitz, *Ethnic Groups in Conflict*, pp. 336, 338–339, 635–638, 647. For a civic nationalism project under full peace, see Raymond Breton, "From Ethnic to Civic Nationalism: English Canada and Quebec," *Ethnic and Racial Studies*, Vol. 11, No. 1 (January 1988), pp. 85–102.

66. Although Brass, *Language, Religion, and Politics in North India*, argues that Muslim political identity was largely constructed in the 1920s and 1930s by political entrepreneurs painting exaggerated threats, by the mid-1940s the accelerating intercommunal violence was very real. Gordon, "Divided Bengal," pp. 303–304; T.G. Fraser, *Partition in Ireland, India, and Palestine: Theory and Practice* (New York: St. Martin's Press, 1984), pp. 112–114.

67. Thomas P. Melady, *Burundi: The Tragic Years* (Maryknoll, N.Y.: Orbis Books, 1974), pp. 12, 46–49; René Lemarchand, "Burundi in Comparative Perspective: Dimensions of Ethnic Strife," in John McGarry and Brendan O'Leary, eds., *The Politics of Ethnic Conflict Regulation: Case Studies of Protracted Conflicts* (New York: Routledge, 1993), pp. 151–171.

68. Ethnic combatants have noticed this. In World War II, the Croatian Ustasha refused to accept educated Serbs as converts because they were assumed to have a national consciousness independent of religion, whereas illiterate peasants were expected to forget their Serbian identity once converted. In 1992 Bosnian Serb ethnic cleansers annihilated the most educated Muslims. Gutman, *Witness to Genocide*, pp. 109–10; Djilas, *The Contested Country*, p. 211 n. 46. Tutsi massacres of Hutus in Burundi in 1972 concentrated on educated people who were seen as potential ethnic leaders, and afterwards the government restricted admission of Hutus to secondary schools. Melady, *Burundi: The Tragic Years*, pp. 46–49; Lemarchand, "Burundi in Comparative Perspective," pp. 161, 168.

69. Exposure of captured Iraqi government records of atrocities committed during the 1985–88 war helped Kurdish leaders mobilize people for the 1991 rebellion. Senate, *Civil War in Iraq*, p. 3; U.S. Senate Committee on Foreign Relations, *Kurdistan in the Time of Saddam Hussein* (Washington, D.C.: U.S. GPO, 1991), p. 2.

debate are permanently altered; the leaders who used World War II Croatian atrocities to whip up Serbian nationalism in the 1980s were making use of a resource which, since then, remains always available in Serbian political discourse.[70]

If direct action to transform exclusive ethnic identities into inclusive civic ones is infeasible, outside powers or international institutions could enforce peace temporarily in the hope that reduced security threats would permit moderate leaders within each group to promote the reconstruction of more benign identities. While persuading ethnic war survivors to adopt an overarching identity may be impossible, a sufficiently prolonged period of guaranteed safety might allow moderate leaders to temper some of the most extreme hypernationalism back towards more benign, albeit still separate nationalisms.[71] However, this still leaves both sides vulnerable to later revival of hypernationalism by radical political entrepreneurs, especially after the peace-keepers have left and security threats once again appear more realistic.

POWER-SHARING. The best-developed blueprint for civic peace in multi-ethnic states is power-sharing or "consociational democracy," proposed by Arend Lijphart. This approach assumes that ethnicity is somewhat manipulable, but not so freely as constructivists say.[72] Ethnic division, however, need not result in conflict; even if political mobilization is organized on ethnic lines, civil politics can be maintained if ethnic elites adhere to a power-sharing bargain that equitably protects all groups. The key components are: 1) joint exercise of governmental power; 2) proportional distribution of government funds and jobs; 3) autonomy on ethnic issues (which, if groups are concentrated territorially, may be achieved by regional federation); and 4) a minority veto on issues of vital importance to each group.[73] Even if power-sharing can avert potential ethnic conflicts or dampen mild ones, our concern here is whether it can bring peace under the conditions of intense violence and extreme ethnic mobilization that are likely to motivate intervention.[74]

---

70. Gagnon, "Ethnic Nationalism and International Conflict," p. 151.
71. Van Evera, "Managing the Eastern Crisis," proposes not to dissolve ethnic identities but to remove their xenophobic content by encouraging honest histories of inter-group relations.
72. Lijphart, "Consociational Democracy," *World Politics*, Vol. 21, No. 2 (January 1969). In fact, Lijphart argues that diffuse or fluid ethnic identities are undesirable, because design of a power-sharing agreement requires clear identification of the players. Lijphart, "Power Sharing Approach," pp. 499–500.
73. Lijphart cites Belgium as an archetypical example, as well as Malaysia, Canada, India, and Nigeria. "Power-Sharing Approach," pp. 492, 494–96.
74. Lijphart admits that power-sharing is more difficult under conditions of high conflict but prefers it anyway, arguing that pessimism in difficult cases would be self-fulfilling; power-sharing cannot work when it is not tried. Ibid., p. 497. On Yugoslavia, see Vucina Vasović, "A Plea for Consociational Pluralism," in Seroka and Pavlović, eds., *The Tragedy of Yugoslavia*, pp. 173–197.

The answer is no. The indispensable component of any power-sharing deal is a plausible minority veto, one which the strongest side will accept and which the weaker side believes that the stronger will respect. Traditions of stronger loyalties to the state than to parochial groups and histories of inter-ethnic compromise could provide reason for confidence, but in a civil war these will have been destroyed, if they were ever present, by the fighting itself and accompanying ethnic mobilization.[75]

Only a balance of power among the competing groups can provide a "hard" veto—one which the majority must respect. Regional concentration of populations could partially substitute for balanced power if the minority group can credibly threaten to secede if its veto is overridden. In any situation where humanitarian intervention might be considered, however, these conditions too are unlikely to be met. Interventions are likely to be aimed at saving a weak group that cannot defend itself; balanced sides do not need defense. Demographic separation is also unlikely, because if the populations were already separated, the ethnic cleansing and related atrocities which are most likely to provoke intervention would not be occurring.

The core reason why power-sharing cannot resolve ethnic civil wars is that it is inherently voluntaristic; it requires conscious decisions by elites to cooperate to avoid ethnic strife. Under conditions of hypernationalist mobilization and real security threats, group leaders are unlikely to be receptive to compromise, and even if they are, they cannot act without being discredited and replaced by harder-line rivals.

Could outside intervention make power-sharing work? One approach would be to adjust the balance of power between the warring sides to a "hurting stalemate" by arming the weaker side, blockading the stronger, or partially disarming the stronger by direct military intervention. When both sides realize that further fighting will bring them costs but no profit, they will negotiate an agreement.[76] This can balance power, although if populations are still intermingled it may actually worsen security dilemmas and increase violence—especially against civilians—as both sides eliminate the threats posed by pockets of the opposing group in their midst.

---

75. Indeed, Lijphart argues that the best way to avoid partition is not to resist it. If minorities, such as the Quebecois, know that they can secede if a satisfactory power-sharing agreement cannot be worked out, this exerts a moderating influence on bargaining. Lijphart, "Power Sharing Approach," p. 494. In short, partition is unnecessary when it is known to be feasible.
76. I. William Zartman, *Ripe for Resolution: Conflict and Intervention in Africa* (New Haven: Yale University Press, 1989).

Further, once there has been heavy fighting, the sides are likely to distrust each other far too much to entrust any authority to a central government that could potentially be used against them. The 1955–72 Sudanese Civil War was ended, under conditions of stalemate and limited outside pressure, by such an autonomy agreement, but the central government massively violated the agreement, leading to resumption of the war in 1983 and its continuation to the present.[77]

The final approach is international imposition of power-sharing, which requires occupying the country to coerce both sides into accepting the agreement and to prevent inter-ethnic violence until it can be implemented. The interveners, however, cannot bind the stronger side to uphold the agreement after the intervention forces leave. Lijphart argues that power-sharing could have prevented the troubles in Northern Ireland if the British had not guaranteed the Protestants that they would not be forced into union with Ireland, freeing them of the need to cooperate.[78] However, the union threat would have had to be maintained permanently; otherwise the Protestant majority could tear up the agreement later. The British did impose power-sharing as a condition for Cypriot independence, but it broke down almost immediately. The Greek Cypriots, incensed by what they saw as Turkish Cypriot abuse of their minority veto, simply overrode the veto and operated the government in violation of the constitution.[79] Similarly, while at independence in 1948 the Sri Lankan constitution banned religious or communal discrimination, the Sinhalese majority promptly disenfranchised half of the Tamils on the grounds that they were actually Indians, and increasingly discriminated against Tamils in education, government employment, and other areas.[80]

STATE-BUILDING. Gerald Helman and Steven Ratner argue that states in which government breakdown, economic failure, and internal violence imperil their own citizens and threaten neighboring states can be rescued by international "conservatorship" to administer critical government functions until the

---

77. The decisive acts were the division of the southern regional government specified in the agreement into three separate states, the imposition of Islamic law on non-Muslims, and—the trigger for violent resistance—an attempt to reduce regional self-defense capabilities by transferring Army units composed of southerners to the north. Ann Mosely Lesch, "External Involvement in the Sudanese Civil War," in Smock, ed., *Making War and Waging Peace*, pp. 79–106.
78. Lijphart, "Power-Sharing Approach," pp. 496–497.
79. Richard A. Patrick, *Political Geography and the Cyprus Conflict, 1963–1971* (Waterloo, Iowa: University of Waterloo, 1976).
80. Little, *Invention of Enmity*, pp. 55–56; Sabaratnam, "The Boundaries of the State."

country can govern itself following a free and fair election.[81] Ideally, the failed state would voluntarily delegate specified functions to an international executor, although in extreme cases involving massive violations of human rights or the prospect of large-scale warfare, the international community could act even without an invitation.[82]

As with imposing power-sharing, this requires occupying the country (and may require conquering it), coercing all sides to accept a democratic constitution, enforcing peace until elections can be held, and administering the economy and the elections. Conservatorship thus requires even more finesse than enforced power-sharing, and probably more military risks.

Helman and Ratner cite the UN intervention in Cambodia in 1992–93 to create a safe environment for free elections as conservatorship's best success.[83] However, this was an ideological war over the governance of Cambodia, not an ethnic conflict over disempowering minorities or dismembering the country. By contrast, the growth of the U.S.-UN mission in Somalia from famine relief to state-rebuilding was a failure, and no one has been so bold as to propose conservatorship for Bosnia or Rwanda.

Even if conservatorship could rapidly, effectively, and cheaply stop an ethnic civil war, rebuild institutions, and ensure free elections, nothing would be gained unless the electoral outcome protected all parties' interests and safety; that is, power-sharing would still be necessary. Thus, in serious ethnic conflicts, conservatorship would only be a more expensive way to reach the same impasse.

ETHNIC SEPARATION

Regardless of the causes of a particular conflict, once communities are mobilized for violence, the reality of mutual security threats prevents both demobi-

---

81. Helman and Ratner, "Saving Failed States." This proposal shares a number of assumptions with the 1960s nation-building literature; this literature argued that political order in modernizing societies requires strong political institutions which can attract loyalties previously given to traditional tribal, linguistic, cultural, religious, caste, or regional groupings. See Karl A. Deutsch and William J. Foltz, eds., *Nation-Building* (New York: Atherton, 1963); Reinhard Bendix, *Nation-building and Citizenship* (New York: John Wiley, 1964). As Walker Connor points out, this approach should be termed "state-building," because it centers on strengthening the *state* apparatus in what are often multi-ethnic states. Connor, *Ethnonationalism*, pp. 39–42.

82. Helman and Ratner, "Saving Failed States," p. 13. "If the forces in a country cannot agree upon the basic components of a political settlement—such as free and fair elections—and accept administration by an impartial outside authority pending elections, then the UN Charter should provide a mechanism for direct international trusteeship." Ibid., p. 16.

83. Ibid., pp. 14–17.

lization and de-escalation of hypernationalist discourse. Thus, lasting peace requires removal of the security dilemma. The most effective and in many cases the only way to do this is to separate the ethnic groups. The more intense the violence, the more likely it is that separation will be the only option.

The exact threshold remains an open question. The deductive logic of the problem suggests that the critical variable is fear for survival. Once a majority of either group comes to believe that the killing of noncombatants of their own group is not considered a crime by the other, they cannot accept any governing arrangement that could be captured by the enemy group and used against them.

The most persuasive source of such beliefs is the massacre of civilians, but it is not clear that there is a specific number of incidents or total deaths beyond which ethnic reconciliation becomes impossible. More important is the extent to which wide sections of the attacking group seem to condone the killings, and can be observed doing so by members of target group. In this situation the attacks are likely to be seen as reflecting not just the bloodthirstiness of a particular regime or terrorist faction, but the preference of the opposing group as a whole, which means that no promise of non-repetition can be believed.

Testing this proposition directly requires better data on the attitudes of threatened populations during and after ethnic wars than we now have. Next best is aggregate analysis of the patterns of ends of ethnic wars, supplemented by investigation of individual cases as deeply as the data permits. I make a start at such an analysis below.

HOW ETHNIC WARS HAVE ENDED

The most comprehensive data set of recent and current violent ethnic conflicts has been compiled by Ted Robert Gurr.[84] This data set includes 27 ethnic civil wars that have ended.[85] Of these, twelve were ended by complete victory of one side, five by *de jure* or *de facto* partition, and two have been suppressed by military occupation by a third party. Only eight ethnic civil wars have been ended by an agreement that did not partition the country. (See Table 1.)

---

84. The data set surveyed here combines two overlapping sets presented by Gurr in *Minorities at Risk: A Global View of Ethnopolitical Conflicts* (Washington, D.C.: U.S. Institute of Peace, 1993), pp. 296–297; and Gurr, "Peoples Against States," pp. 369–375.
85. The data set also includes 25 wars which have not ended; three in which cease-fire or settlement agreements were reached since 1994 but whose status is uncertain; four which represent episodes of ethnic rioting rather than wars over group rights, group autonomy, or territory; and three which were mainly or largely over ideology rather than ethnicity.

Table 1. Ethnic Civil Wars Resolved 1944–94.

Combatants	Dates	Deaths (000s)[1]	Outcome
Military victory (12):			
Karens vs. Myanmar	1945–	43[2]	Defeat imminent
Kurds vs. Iran	1945–80s	40	Suppressed
Tibetans vs. China	1959–89	100	Suppressed
Papuans vs. Indonesia	1964–86	19	Suppressed
Ibo vs. Nigeria	1967–70	2000[3]	Suppressed
Timorese vs. Indonesia	1974–80s	200	Suppressed
Aceh vs. Indonesia	1975–80s	15	Suppressed
Tigreans vs. Ethiopia	1975–91	350[4]	Rebels victorious
Uighurs etc. vs. China	1980	2	Suppressed
Bougainville vs. Papua	1988	1	Suppressed
Tutsis vs. Rwanda	1990–94	750[5]	Rebels victorious
Shiites vs. Iraq	1991	35	Suppressed
De facto or de jure partition (5):			
Ukrainians vs. USSR	1944–50s	150[6]	Suppressed, independent 1991
Lithuanians vs. USSR	1945–52	40[7]	Suppressed; independent 1991
Eritreans vs. Ethiopia	1961–91	350	Independent 1993
Armenians vs. Azerbaijan	1988–	15	De facto partition
Somali clans	1988–	350	De facto partition in N., ongoing in S.
Conflict suppressed by ongoing 3rd-party military occupation (2):			
Kurds vs. Iraq	1960–	215	De facto partition
Lebanese Civil War	1975–90	120[8]	Nominal power sharing, de facto partition
Settled by agreements other than partition (8):			
Nagas vs. India	1952–75	13[9]	Autonomy 1972
Basques vs. Spain	1959–80s	1	Autonomy 1980
Tripuras vs. India	1967–89	13	Autonomy 1972
Palestinians vs. Israel	1968–93	2	Autonomy 1993, partly implemented
Moros vs. Philippines	1972–87	50	Limited autonomy 1990
Chittagong hill peoples vs. Bangladesh	1975–89	24	Limited autonomy 1989
Miskitos vs. Nicaragua	1981–88	<1[10]	Autonomy 1990
Abkhazians vs. Georgia	1992–93	10	Autonomy 1993

NOTES:

[1] Figures are from Ted Robert Gurr, *Minorities at Risk: A Global View of Ethnopolitical Conflicts* (Washington, D.C.: U.S. Institute of Peace, 1993), and Gurr, "Peoples Against States: Ethnopolitical Conflict and the Changing World System," *International Studies Quarterly*, Vol. 38, No. 3 (September 1994), pp. 347–377.

[2] Gurr gives a combined total of 130,000 for three civil wars in Myanmar. Probably more than one-third of the total is attributable to the Karen.

[3] R. Ernest Dupuy and Trevor N. Dupuy, *Encyclopedia of Military History,* 4th ed. (New York: Harper and Row, 1993), p. 1447.

[4] 700,000 for Eritrean and Tigrean rebellions combined, including government forces and civilians, but not rebel combatants. Probably more than half the total attributable to Tigre. Alex de Waal, *Evil Days: Thirty Years of War and Famine in Ethiopia* (New York: Human Rights Watch, 1991), pp. 3, 5–6.

[5] Alex de Waal and Rakiya Omaar, "The Genocide in Rwanda and the International Response," *Current History,* Vol. 94, No. 591 (April 1995), pp. 156–161, at 156.

[6] Includes combatants on both sides, but not civilian losses. Thomas Remeikas, *Opposition to Soviet Rule in Lithuania, 1945–1980* (Chicago: Institute of Lithuanian Studies Press, 1980).

[7] Official Soviet estimate, not including losses by government forces. Heorhii Kasianov communication to author, November 27, 1995.

[8] Total for 1975–82. Richard A. Gabriel, *Operation Peace for Galilee: The Israeli-PLO War in Lebanon* (New York: Hill and Wang, 1984), pp. 45, 164–165.

[9] Gurr gives a combined total of 25,000 for the Naga and Tripura rebellions together.

[10] *The Reagan Administration's Record on Human Rights in 1986* (New York: The Watch Committees and Lawyers' Committee for Human Rights, 1987), pp. 93–94.

The data supports the argument that separation of groups is the key to ending ethnic civil wars. Every case in which the state was preserved by agreement involved a regionally concentrated minority, and in every case the solution reinforced the ethnic role in politics by allowing the regional minority group to control its own destiny through regional autonomy for the areas where it forms a majority of the population. There is not a single case where non-ethnic civil politics were created or restored by reconstruction of ethnic identities, power-sharing coalitions, or state-building.

Further, deaths in these cases average an order of magnitude lower than in the wars which ended either in suppression or partition: less than 13,000, compared about 250,000.[86] This lends support to the proposition that the more extreme the violence, the less the chances for any form of reconciliation. Finally, it should be noted that all eight of the cases resolved through autonomy involve groups that were largely demographically separated even at the beginning of the conflict, which may help explain why there were fewer deaths.

Intervention to Resolve Ethnic Civil Wars

International interventions that seek to ensure lasting safety for populations endangered by ethnic war—whether by the United Nations, by major powers with global reach, or by regional powers—must be guided by two principles. First, settlements must aim at physically separating the warring communities and establishing a balance of relative strength that makes it unprofitable for either side to attempt to revise the territorial settlement. Second, although economic or military assistance may suffice in some cases, direct military intervention will be necessary when aid to the weaker side would create a window of opportunity for the stronger, or when there is an immediate need to stop ongoing genocide.

DESIGNING SETTLEMENTS

Unless outsiders are willing to provide permanent security guarantees, stable resolution of an ethnic civil war requires separation of the groups into defensible regions.[87] The critical variable is demography, not sovereignty. Political

---

86. While it might seem more obvious to measure deaths in proportion to population, the logic of lessons drawn from observing enemy atrocities and the enemy group's reaction to their own atrocities implies that the absolute number of deaths may be a better predictor, although still imperfect.

87. Recent cooperation between the Irish and British governments to guarantee the rights of both groups has reduced the Catholic-Protestant security dilemma in Northern Ireland and allowed

partition without ethnic separation leaves incentives for ethnic cleansing unchanged; it actually increases them if it creates new minorities. Conversely, demographic separation dampens ethnic conflicts even without separate sovereignty, although the more intense the previous fighting, the smaller the prospects for preserving a single state, even if loosely federated.

Partition without ethnic separation increases conflict because, while boundaries of sovereign successor states may provide defensible fronts that reduce the vulnerability of the majority group in each state, stay-behind minorities are completely exposed. Significant irredenta are both a call to their ethnic homeland and a danger to their hosts. They create incentives to mount rescue or ethnic cleansing operations before the situation solidifies. Greece's 1920 invasion of Turkey was justified in this way, while the 1947 decision to partition Palestine generated a civil war in advance of implementation, and the inclusion of Muslim-majority Kashmir within India has helped cause three wars. International recognition of Croatian and Bosnian independence did more to cause than to stop Serbian invasion. The war between Armenia and Azerbaijan has the same source, as do concerns over the international security risks of the several Russian diasporas.[88]

Inter-ethnic security dilemmas can be nearly or wholly eliminated without partition if three conditions are met: First, there must be enough demographic separation that ethnic regions do not themselves contain militarily significant minorities. Second, there must be enough regional self-defense capability that abrogating the autonomy of any region would be more costly than any possible motive for doing so. Third, local autonomy must be so complete that minority groups can protect their key interests even lacking any influence at the national level.[89] Even after an ethnic war, a single state could offer some advantages, not least of which are the economic benefits of a common market. However, potential interveners should recognize that groups that control distinct territories can insist on the *de facto* partition, and often will.

---

some reduction of tension, but the permanence of peace may depend on the continuation of outside engagement. "Ireland's Premier Assures Protestants in North of Their Rights," *New York Times,* November 4, 1994.

88. Dmitri A. Fadeyev and Vladimir Razuvayev, "Russia and the Western Post-Soviet Republics," in Robert D. Blackwill and Sergei A. Karaganov, eds., *Damage Limitation or Crisis? Russia and the Outside World* (Washington, D.C.: Brassey's, 1994), pp. 107–123, at 116–117; Vitaly V. Naumkin, "Russia and the States of Central Asia and the Caucasus," in ibid., pp. 199–216, 207.

89. This was the preferred solution of Slovenes and Croats within Yugoslavia in 1989–90, and is the *de facto* position of the Herzegovinian Croats within the "Federation of Bosnia and Hercegovina" today. Hayden, "Constitutional Nationalism," p. 20.

While peace requires separation of groups into distinct regions, it does not require total ethnic purity. Rather, remaining minorities must be small enough that the host group does not fear them as either a potential military threat or a possible target for irredentist rescue operations. Before the Krajina offensive, for example, President Franjo Tudjman of Croatia is said to have thought that the 12 percent Serb minority in Croatia was too large, but that half as many would be tolerable.[90] The 173,000 Arabs remaining in Israel by 1951 were too few and too disorganized to be seen as a serious threat.[91]

Geographic distribution of minorities is also important; in particular, concentrations near disputed borders or astride strategic communications constitute both a military vulnerability and an irredentist opportunity, and so are likely to spark conflict.[92] It is not surprising that India's portion of Kashmir, with its Muslim majority, has been at the center of three interstate wars and an ongoing insurgency which continues today, while there has been no international conflict over the hundred million Muslims who live dispersed throughout most of the rest of India, and relatively little violence.[93]

Where possible, inter-group boundaries should be drawn along the best defensive terrain, such as rivers and mountain ranges. Lines should also be as short as possible, to allow the heaviest possible manning of defensive fronts.[94] (Croatian forces were able to overrun Krajina in part because its irregular crescent shape meant that 30,000 Krajina Serb forces had to cover a frontier of more than 725 miles.) Access to the sea or to a friendly neighbor is also important, both for trade and for possible military assistance. Successor state arsenals should be encouraged, by aid to the weaker or sanctions on the stronger, to focus on defensive armaments such as towed artillery and anti-aircraft missiles and rockets, while avoiding instruments that could make blitzkrieg attacks possible, such as tanks, fighter-bombers, and mobile artillery.

---

90. "The Flight of the Krajina Serbs," *Economist*, August 12, 1995, p. 42.

91. Dov Friedlander and Calvin Goldscheider, *The Population of Israel* (New York: Columbia University Press, 1979), p. 30.

92. Because the Arab towns of Lod (Lydda) and Ramle stood astride the main Tel Aviv–Jerusalem road, when Israeli forces drove out the Arab Legion garrisons in July 1948 they also expelled the inhabitants. Benny Morris, *1948 and After: Israel and the Palestinians* (Oxford: Clarendon Press, 1990), pp. 1–2. Glenny, *The Fall of Yugoslavia*, p. 185, says that in 1992 the most militant Serbs in Bosnia were those living in areas whose lines of communication to Serbia were most tenuous.

93. Hindu-Muslim violence has claimed approximately 25,000 lives in Kashmir since 1990, compared to about 3,000 in the rest of India. Gurr, "Peoples Against States," p. 371.

94. Military theorists believe that denser force-to-space ratios tend to shift the offense-defense balance toward defense. Stephen Biddle, "The Determinants of Offensiveness and Defensiveness in Conventional Land Warfare," Harvard University, Ph.D. dissertation, 1992, pp. 164–169.

These conditions would make subsequent offensives exceedingly expensive and likely to fail.

INTERVENTION STRATEGY

The level of international action required to resolve an ethnic war will depend on the military situation on the ground. If there is an existing stalemate along defensible lines, the international community should simply recognize and strengthen it, providing transportation, protection, and resettlement assistance for refugees. However, where one side has the capacity to go on the offensive against the other, intervention will be necessary.

Interventions should therefore almost always be on behalf of the weaker side; the stronger needs no defense. Moreover, unless the international community can agree on a clear aggressor and a clear victim, there is no moral or political case for intervention. If both sides have behaved so badly that there is little to choose between them, intervention should not and probably will not be undertaken.[95] Almost no one in the West, for instance, has advocated assisting either side in the Croatian-Serb conflict.[96] While the intervention itself could be carried out by any willing actors, UN sponsorship is highly desirable, most of all to head off possible external aid to the group identified as the aggressor.

The three available tools are sanctions, military aid, and direct military intervention. Economic sanctions have limited leverage against combatants in ethnic wars, who often see their territorial security requirements as absolute. Whereas hyperinflation and economic collapse have apparently reduced Serbian government support for the Bosnian Serb rebels and thus limited the latter's material capabilities, Armenians have already suffered five years of extreme privation rather than give up Nagorno-Karabakh.[97]

Whether military aid to the client can achieve an acceptable territorial outcome depends on the population balance between the sides, the local geography, and the organizational cohesion of the client group. Aid could not enable

---

95. This is why the strongest advocates of intervention in Bosnia have emphasized Serb crimes, while those opposed to intervention insist on the moral equivalence of the two sides. Anthony Lewis, "Crimes of War," *New York Times*, April 25, 1994; Charles G. Boyd, "Making Peace with the Guilty," *Foreign Affairs*, Vol. 74, No. 5 (September/October 1995), pp. 22–38.
96. Further, attempts at even-handed intervention rarely achieve their goals, leading either to nearly complete passivity, as in the case of UNPROFOR in Bosnia, or eventually to open combat against one or all sides. At worst, peace-keeping efforts may actually prolong fighting. See Richard K. Betts, "The Delusion of Impartial Intervention," *Foreign Affairs*, Vol. 73, No. 6 (November/December 1994), pp. 20–33.
97. Robert A. Pape, *Bombing to Win: Air Power and Coercion in War* (Ithaca, N.Y.: Cornell University Press, 1996), shows that even severe punishment rarely causes concessions on what states see as their homeland territory.

Chechen or Sikh secession, but has been decisive in Abkhazia, and leaks in the embargo have significantly helped Bosnia.[98] The more serious problem with "arm's length" aid is that it cannot prevent ethnic aggressors from killing members of the client group in territories from which they expect to have to retreat.[99] Aid also does not restrain possible atrocities by the client group if their military fortunes improve.[100]

If the client is too weak to achieve a viable separation with material aid alone, or if either or both sides cannot be trusted to abide by promises of non-retribution against enemy civilians, the international community must designate a separation line and deploy an intervention force to take physical control of the territory on the client's side of the line. We might call this approach "conquer and divide."

The separation campaign is waged as a conventional military operation. The larger the forces committed the better, both to minimize intervenors' casualties and to shorten the campaign by threatening the opponent with overwhelming defeat. Although some argue that any intervention force would become mired in a Vietnam-like quagmire,[101] the fundamentally different nature of ethnic conflict means that the main pitfalls to foreign military interventions in ideological insurgencies are either weaker or absent. Most important, the intervenors' intelligence problems are much simpler, since loyalty intelligence is both less important and easier: outsiders can safely assume that members of the allied group are friends and those of the other are enemies. Even if outsiders cannot tell the groups apart, locals can, and the loyalty of guides provided by the local ally can be counted on. As a result, the main intelligence task shifts from assessing loyalties to locating enemy forces, a task of which major power militaries are very capable.

On the ground, the intervenors would begin at one end of the target region and gradually advance to capture the entire target territory, maintaining a continuous front the entire time. It is not necessary to conquer the whole country; indeed, friendly ground forces need never cross the designated line.

---

98. For an argument that weapons aid and air threats would have been sufficient to end the war in Bosnia, see John J. Mearsheimer and Robert A. Pape, "The Answer: A Three-Way Partition Plan for Bosnia and How the U.S. Can Enforce It," *The New Republic*, June 14, 1993, pp. 22–28.
99. Bosnian Serb forces evidently killed several thousand Muslims before retreating from several towns in Northwest Bosnia in October 1995. Chris Hedges, "2 Officials Report New Mass Killings by Bosnian Serbs," *New York Times*, October 20, 1995.
100. Croatian forces attacked Serb refugees fleeing Krajina. Jane Perlez, "Thousands of Serbian Civilians are Caught in Soldiers' Crossfire," *New York Times*, August 9, 1995.
101. Henry Kissinger, "Bosnia Poses Another Vietnam-like Quagmire," *Houston Chronicle*, February 21, 1993; F. Charles Parker, "Vietnam, Bosnia, and the Historical Record," *In Depth*, Vol. 3, No. 2 (Spring 1993), p. 29.

After enemy forces are driven out of each locality, civilians of the enemy ethnic group who remain behind are interned, to be exchanged after the war. This removes the enemy's local support base, preventing counterinsurgency problems from arising. Enemy civilians should be protected by close supervision of client troops in action, as well as by foreign control of internees.

The final concern is possible massacres of civilians of the client group in territory not yet captured or beyond the planned separation line. Some of this must be expected, since ongoing atrocities are the most likely impetus for outside intervention; the question is whether intervention actually increases the risk of attacks on civilians.[102] A major advantage of a powerful ground presence is that opponent behavior can be coerced by threatening to advance the separation line in retaliation for any atrocities.[103]

Once the military campaign is complete and refugees have been resettled, further reconstruction and military aid may be needed to help the client achieve a viable economy and self-defense capability before the intervenors can depart. The ease of exit will depend on the regional geography and balance of power. Bosnia has sufficient population and skills to be made economically and militarily viable, provided that access to the outside world through Croatia is maintained. Although the weakness of the Turkish Republic of Northern Cyprus has required a permanent Turkish garrison, the almost equal weakness of the Greek Cypriots allows the garrison to be small, cheap, and inactive. U.S. Operation Provide Comfort helps secure the Kurdish enclave in northern Iraq by prohibiting Iraqi air operations as well as by threatening air strikes against an Iraqi ground invasion of the region. This intervention has no easy exit, however, since the Iraqi Kurds are landlocked and threatened by Turkey, which is waging a war against its own Kurdish minority. Real security for the Kurds might require partitioning Turkey as well as Iraq, a task no outside actor is willing to contemplate.

BOSNIA

Early intervention in Bosnia could have saved most of the lives that have been lost, and secured the Muslims a better territorial deal than they are going to get, but only if the international community had been willing to accept that by

---

102. Advance announcement of the partition line should reduce at least short-term incentives for ethnic cleansing, since there is no point to cleansing areas which the intervenors will seize anyway, and no need in areas which the intervenors do not propose to attack.
103. Pape, *Bombing to Win*, shows that credible threats to take territory by force do generate coercive leverage.

1992, restoration of civil politics in a multi-ethnic Bosnia had become impossible, and had been able to overcome its squeamishness about large-scale population transfers.

The Vance-Owen plan did not meet the minimum conditions for stable peace because it aimed at preservation of a multi-ethnic state, not ethnic separation. Each of the ten planned cantons would have contained large minorities, and some would have included enclaves totally surrounded by an opposing ethnic group.[104] The 1994 Contact Group proposal to divide Bosnia 51 percent–49 percent between a Muslim-Croat federation and the Bosnian Serbs would have been better, but incorporated serious instabilities such as the isolated Muslim enclaves of Žepa, Srebrenica, and Goražde, two of which were later overrun with great loss of life.

As the progress of the war has left fewer and fewer unmoved people still to move, more realistic proposals have gradually emerged. The agreement signed at Dayton in November 1995, despite lip service to a unitary Bosnia, ratifies and seeks to strengthen existing territorial divisions. This agreement gives grounds for qualified hope for a stable, relatively peaceful Bosnia.

Future peace in Bosnia depends on resolution of three issues. First and most important, while the military fronts have gradually settled along defensible lines in most areas of the country, serious demographic security dilemmas persist in two places—Serb-held suburbs of Sarajevo which both threaten the city's supply lines and are vulnerable themselves, and the surrounded Muslim enclave of Goražde in the Drina Valley.[105]

Accordingly, the Dayton agreement requires the withdrawal of all Bosnian Serb forces from these Sarajevo suburbs as well as from a corridor stretching from Sarajevo to Goražde, and assigns these areas to the Bosnian government. The Implementation Force (IFOR) is charged with ensuring compliance.[106] The widespread burning of homes by Serbs and others evacuating areas which will

---

104. The Vance-Owen plan did attempt to provide some regional self-defense by specifying that police would be cantonal while national defense would be supervised by an authority "designated by the International Conference on the Former Yugoslavia." "Annex: Proposed Constitutional Structure for Bosnia and Herzegovina," International Conference on the Former Yugoslavia, document STC/2/2, October 27, 1992. For a survey of several 1992–94 peace proposals, see Woodward, *Balkan Tragedy*, pp. 302–317.

105. Although the narrow "Posavina Corridor" that links the Eastern and Western parts of Bosnian Serb territory is vulnerable, the Muslims have no irredentist claims or security needs in this area, so fighting is unlikely to begin here although it is a likely site for Muslim retaliation for any Serb provocation elsewhere.

106. "General Framework Agreement for Peace in Bosnia and Herzegovina," Annex 1A (U.S. Department of State, November 21, 1995).

pass to control of another group is in a sense encouraging, as it suggests they do not expect to return. More worrisome is the fact that the corridor to Goražde will be only four kilometers wide, leaving the city once again vulnerable after the IFOR departs. A wider corridor here, perhaps in exchange for territory elsewhere, would have been better, even if it meant that more civilians would have to move now.[107]

The second issue is that the agreement, at least nominally, seeks to reconstruct some central government institutions with nationwide authority and a rotating presidency. It also requires all parties to permit the return of refugees.[108] These provisions are undesirable and unenforceable, and should be allowed to die quietly. The procedures provided for compensating refugees for lost property should be followed instead.

Third, while some have expressed concern that the Muslim-Croat federation could collapse, leading to a new war between Croats and Muslims, this worry is misplaced.[109] The future legal status of Herzegovina is unimportant; the Herzegovinian Croats have their own army, border posts where Croat and Muslim lines meet, and one-tenth of the seats in Croatia's Parliament. What is important is that, even though the Bihać pocket will remain cut off from other Muslim territory, neither side has an incentive to attack there or elsewhere. There are few co-ethnics for either to rescue from behind the other's lines, and neither can strengthen its strategic position by seizing territory from the other. Croatia needs no Muslim-held territory, and even a U.S.-armed Muslim army will not be strong enough to wage a successful offensive against the Croats.[110]

RWANDA AND BURUNDI

In general, the more intermingled the competing populations in an ethnic civil war, the greater the scale and ferocity of ethnic cleansing; thus, paradoxically, the greater the need to move people for ethnic separation, the more there are who need to be moved and the harder the task. Despite the urgency of

---

107. Sean Maguire, "Bosnian Serbs Avert Crisis Over Sarajevo Exodus," *Reuters World Service,* January 12, 1996. For IFOR doubts and Serb threats concerning the long-run safety of Goražde, see Chris Hedges, "Bosnia Enclave Looks Ahead Warily," *New York Times,* December 24, 1995.
108. "Framework Agreement," Annexes 3, 4, and 7.
109. John J. Mearsheimer and Stephen Van Evera, "When Peace Means War," *The New Republic,* December 18, 1995, pp. 16–18, 21. My analysis assumes that the Croats will not attempt to retain indefinitely their military control over three tiny enclaves in Central Bosnia which are completely surrounded by Muslim-controlled territory.
110. Any attempt to do so would also cost them all Western military aid and hence the ability to sustain heavy combat operations, as well as inviting a Croatian-Serb combination against them.

separating Rwandan Hutus and Tutsis in April 1994, their relatively even distribution throughout the country would have made it extremely difficult even if outsiders had been willing. Immediate intervention could have saved hundreds of thousands, but would have required the interveners to conquer the entire country, while encouraging Hutus to leave a designated Tutsi homeland as well as rescuing as many Tutsis as possible from the rest of the country.

Rwanda and Burundi today are occupied militarily by their respective Tutsi minorities; nominal power-sharing arrangements in both countries are shams. Hutu insurgencies continue in both countries, however, and in the long run the Tutsis' position in both countries is precarious.[111]

The international community is encouraging Hutu refugees to return to Rwanda and seeking to arrange genuine power-sharing both countries.[112] This is the worst thing to do. Instead, the Tutsis of both countries should be encouraged to relocate to a smaller, defensible, ethnically Tutsi state. This state should be supported by international patrons which would guarantee its security, especially by assuring that it would always be well-enough armed to fend off revanchist Hutu ambitions, as well as by persuading neighbors such as Uganda to grant trade access.[113] This would be an immense operation, involving the resettlement of probably more than one quarter of the 13 million combined population of both countries. The alternative, sooner or later, is another genocide.

Objections to Ethnic Separation and Partition

There are five important objections to ethnic separation as policy for resolving ethnic conflicts: that it encourages splintering of states, that population exchanges cause human suffering, that it simply transforms civil wars into inter-

---

111. Tutsis in Burundi have largely retreated to the major towns; while their position in Rwanda is currently stronger, insurgent activity is more likely to increase than decrease. James C. McKinley, Jr., "In the Grisly Shadow of Rwanda, Ethnic Violence Stalks Burundi," *New York Times*, January 14, 1996; Joyce Hackel, "A Genocide Later, Rwanda Again on Edge," *Christian Science Monitor*, November 28, 1995. The demographics are very uneven; Tutsis make up 14 percent of the population of Burundi, and were 9 percent in Rwanda before the 1994 genocide. See entries for "Rwanda" and "Burundi," *Academic American Encyclopedia* (New York: Grolier Electronic Publishing, 1995).
112. John Lancaster, "Carter, African Leaders Try to Solve Crisis in Rwanda," *Washington Post*, November 29, 1995.
113. The Rwandan Patriotic Front has enjoyed good relations with the Ugandan government. Raymond Bonner, "How Minority Tutsi Won the War," *New York Times*, September 6, 1994.

national ones, that rump states will not be viable, and that, in the end, it does nothing to resolve ethnic antagonisms.[114]

Among most international organizations, western leaders, and scholars, population exchanges and partition are anathema. They contradict cherished western values of social integration, trample on the international legal norm of state sovereignty, and suggest particular policies that have been condemned by most of the world (e.g., Turkey's unilateral partition of Cyprus). The integrity of states and their borders is usually seen as a paramount principle, while self-determination takes second place.[115] In ethnic wars, however, saving lives may require ignoring state-centered legal norms. The legal costs of ethnic separation must be compared to the human consequences, both immediate and long term, if the warring groups are not separated. To paraphrase Winston Churchill: separation is the worst solution, except for all the others.

PARTITION ENCOURAGES SPLINTERING OF STATES
If international interventions for ethnic separation encourage secession attempts elsewhere, they could increase rather than decrease global ethnic violence.[116] However, this is unlikely, because government use of force to suppress them makes almost all secession attempts extremely costly; only groups that see no viable alternative try. What intervention can do is reduce loss of life where states are breaking up anyway. An expectation that the international community will never intervene, however, encourages repression of minorities, as in Turkey or the Sudan, and wars of ethnic conquest, as by Serbia.

POPULATION TRANSFERS CAUSE SUFFERING
Separation of intermingled ethnic groups necessarily involves significant refugee flows, usually in both directions. Population transfers during ethnic conflicts have often led to much suffering, so an obvious question is whether

---

114. Robert Schaeffer, *Warpaths: The Politics of Partition* (New York: Hill and Wang, 1990), makes all these criticisms and several others.

115. The UN Declaration on the Granting of Independence to Colonial Countries and Peoples says that "all peoples have the right to self-determination" but also that "any attempt aimed at the partial or whole disruption of the national unity and territorial integrity of a country is incompatible with the purposes and principles of the United Nations." UN Resolution 1514(XV), 1960. For a recent defense of self-determination, see Michael Lind, "In Defense of Liberal Nationalism," *Foreign Affairs*, Vol. 73, No. 3 (May/June 1994), pp. 87–99.

116. Anthony Smith argues that the collapses of Czechoslovakia, Yugoslavia, the Soviet Union, and Ethiopia are having such a demonstration effect. Smith, "The Ethnic Sources of Nationalism," in Brown, *Ethnic Conflict and International Security*, pp. 27–41, 39.

foreign intervention to relocate populations would only increase suffering.[117] In fact, however, the biggest cause of suffering in population exchanges is spontaneous refugee movement. Planned population transfers are much safer. When ethnic conflicts turn violent, they generate spontaneous refugee movements as people flee from intense fighting or are kicked out by neighbors, marauding gangs, or a conquering army. Spontaneous refugees frequently suffer direct attack by hostile civilians or armed forces. They often leave precipitately, with inadequate money, transport, or food supplies, and before relief can be organized. They make vulnerable targets for banditry and plunder, and are often so needy as to be likely perpetrators also.[118] Planned population exchanges can address all of these risks by preparing refugee relief and security operations in advance.

In the 1947 India-Pakistan exchange, nearly the entire movement of between 12 and 16 million people took place in a few months. The British were surprised by the speed with which this movement took place, and were not ready to control, support, and protect the refugees. Estimates of deaths go as high one million. In the first stages of the population exchanges among Greece, Bulgaria, and Turkey in the 1920s, hundreds of thousands of refugees moved spontaneously and many died due to banditry and exposure. When after 1925 the League of Nations deployed capable relief services, the remaining transfers —one million, over 60 percent of the total—were carried out in an organized and planned way, with virtually no losses.[119]

A related criticism is that transfers require the intervenors to operate *de facto* concentration camps for civilians of the opposing ethnic groups until transfers can be carried out. However, this is safer than the alternatives of administration by the local ally or allowing the war to run its course. As with transfers, the risks to the internees depend on planning and resources.[120]

---

117. International institutions generally oppose transfers. The position of the UN High Commission for Refugees (UNHCR) is that it is better to bring "safety to people, rather than people to safety." UNHCR, Working Document for the Humanitarian Issues Working Group of the International Conference on the Former Yugoslavia (1992). As recently as August 1995, the UN proved reluctant to assist Serbs wishing to leave Krajina after its conquest by Croatia. Raymond Bonner, "Croats Celebrate Capturing Capital of Serbian Rebels," *New York Times*, August 8, 1995.
118. Frelick, *Faultlines of Nationality Conflict*, p. 11.
119. Schaeffer, *Warpaths*, 155–56; Michael R. Marrus, *The Unwanted* (New York: Oxford University Press, 1985); Richard Ned Lebow, *Divided Nations in a Divided World*.
120. Boer civilians interned by the British suffered grievously from insufficient provision of food and shelter, but ethnic Japanese relocated from the west coast in World War II suffered little or no increased incidence of death or illness. Of 120,313 internees, 1,862 died in custody, while there were

SEPARATION MERELY SUBSTITUTES INTERNATIONAL FOR CIVIL WARS

Post-separation wars are possible, motivated either by revanchism or by security fears if one side suspects the other of revisionist plans. The frequency and human cost of such wars, however, must be compared to the likely consequences of not separating. When the alternative is intercommunal slaughter, separation is the only defensible choice.

In fact the record of twentieth-century ethnic partitions is fairly good. The partition of Ireland has produced no interstate violence, although intercommunal violence continues in demographically mixed Northern Ireland. India and Pakistan have fought two wars since partition, one in 1965 over ethnically mixed Kashmir, while the second in 1971 resulted not from Indo-Pakistani state rivalry or Hindu-Muslim religious conflict but from ethnic conflict between (West) Pakistanis and Bengalis. Indian intervention resolved the conflict by enabling the independence of Bangladesh. These wars have been much less dangerous, especially to civilians, than the political and possible physical extinction that Muslims feared if the subcontinent were not divided.[121] The worst post-partition history is probably that of the Arab-Israeli conflict. Even here, civilian deaths would almost certainly have been higher without partition. It is difficult even to imagine any alternative; the British could not and would not stay, and neither side would share power or submit to rule by the other.

RUMP STATES WILL NOT BE VIABLE

Many analysts of ethnic conflict question the economic and military viability of partitioned states.[122] History, however, records no examples of ethnic partitions which failed for economic reasons.[123] In any case, intervenors have sub-

---

5,981 births to the same group. Two people were killed by military police during a demonstration in December 1942. U.S. Department of the Interior War Relocation Authority, *WRA: A Story of Human Conservation* (Washington, D.C.: U.S. GPO, no date), pp. 49, 146.

121. Aside from physical security concerns, Muslims also feared that a Congress-dominated India would discriminate against them in public service jobs, education, and land tenure. Lance Brennan, "The Illusion of Security: The Background to Muslim Separatism in the United Provinces," in Hasan, ed., *India's Partition*, pp. 318–355.

122. Schaeffer, *Warpaths*; Kamal S. Shehadi, *Ethnic Determination and the Break-up of States*, Adelphi Paper No. 283 (London: International Institute for Strategic Studies [IISS], 1993), p. 9. Amitai Etzioni, "The Evils of Self-Determination," *Foreign Policy*, No. 89 (Winter 1992–93), pp. 21–35, argues that secession states are likely to become both economic failures and undemocratic.

123. Despite considerable economic hardships, in part due to being blockaded by hostile neighbors, Macedonians do not appear ready to give up their independence nor Armenians their territorial claims in Nagorno-Karabakh. Lack of international recognition has depressed economic performance in the Turkish Republic of Northern Cyprus, but Turkish Cypriots are not interested in recreating the previous Cypriot state.

stantial influence over economic outcomes: they can determine partition lines, guarantee trade access and, if necessary, provide significant aid in relation to the economic sizes of likely candidates. Peace itself also enhances recovery prospects.

Thus the more important issue is military viability, particularly since interventions will most often be in favor of the weaker side. If the client has economic strength comparable to the opponent, it can provide for its own defense. If it does not, the intervenors will have to provide military aid and possibly a security guarantee.

Ensuring the client's security will be made easier by the opponent's scarcity of options for revision. First, any large-scale conventional attack is likely to fail because the intervenors will have drawn the borders for maximum defensibility and ensured that the client is better armed. If necessary, they can lend further assistance through air strikes. Breaking up conventional offensives is what high-technology air power does best.[124]

Second, infiltration of small guerrilla parties, if successful over a period of time, could cause boundaries to become "fuzzy," and eventually to break down. This has been a major concern of some observers of Bosnia, but it should not be. Infiltration can only work where at least some civilians will support, house, feed, and hide the guerrillas. After ethnic separation, however, any infiltrators would be entering a completely hostile region where no one will help them; instead, all will inform on them and cooperate fully with authorities against them. The worst case is probably Israel, where terrorist infiltration has cost lives, but never come close to threatening the state's territorial integrity. Retaliatory capabilities could also allow the client to dampen, even stop, such behavior.[125]

PARTITION DOES NOT RESOLVE ETHNIC HATREDS

It is not clear that it is in anyone's power to resolve ethnic hatreds once there has been large-scale violence, especially murders of civilians. In the long run, however, separation may help reduce inter-ethnic antagonism; once real security threats are reduced, the plausibility of hypernationalist appeals may even-

---

124. Because they can call on nationalist sentiments to strengthen defensive mobilization, ethnic rump states may be inherently more defensible than their multi-ethnic parents. Van Evera, "Hypotheses on Nationalism and War," p. 21 n. 30.
125. The record on this is mixed. The threat of Israeli retaliation did induce the Jordanian and Syrian governments to clamp down on terrorist attacks launched from their territory, but the much weaker (because ethnically fractured) Lebanese state could not.

tually decline.[126] Certainly ethnic hostility cannot be reduced without separation. As long as either side fears, even intermittently, that it will be attacked by the other, past atrocities and old hatreds can easily be aroused. If, however, it becomes and remains implausible that the other group could ever seriously endanger the nation, hypernationalist drum-beating may fall on deafer and deafer ears.

The only stronger measure would be to attempt a thorough re-engineering of the involved groups' political and social systems, comparable to the rehabilitation of Germany after World War II. The costs would be steep, since this would require conquering the country and occupying it for a long time, possibly for decades. The apparent benignification of Germany suggests that, if the international community is prepared to go this far, this approach could succeed.[127]

Conclusion

Humanitarian intervention to establish lasting safety for peoples endangered by ethnic civil wars is feasible, but only if the international community is prepared to recognize that some shattered states cannot be restored, and that population transfers are sometimes necessary.

Some observers attack separation and partition as immoral, suggesting that partitioning states like Bosnia would ratify the arguments of bloody-minded extremists such as Milošević and Tudjman that ethnic cleansing is necessitated by intractable ancient hatreds, when in fact they themselves whipped up hypernationalist fears for their own political ends. This argument is mistaken. The construction of ethnic hostility might have been contained by intervention in Yugoslav political discourses in the 1980s. It is too late now, but what the international community can still do is to provide surviving Muslims with physical security and a defensible homeland. The claims of justice demand that we go further, to the capture and trial of the aggressors, but that is beyond the

---

126. Mary E. McIntosh, et al., found that perception of threat—specifically a fear of impending attack from a country associated with the ethnic enemy—was a stronger predictor of ethnic intolerance than any other factor tested, including ethnic makeup of the community, rural versus urban origin, ideology, education, or economic status. McIntosh, "Minority Rights and Majority Rule: Ethnic Tolerance in Romania and Bulgaria," *Social Forces*, March 1995.
127. Elmer Pluschke, "Denazification in Germany," in Wolfe, ed., *Americans as Proconsuls: United States Military Governments in Germany and Japan, 1944–1952.* For a current proposal see Martin van Heuven, "Rehabilitating Serbia," *Foreign Policy*, No. 96 (Fall 1994), pp. 38–48.

scope of this article, the focus of which is the minimum requirements for protection of peoples endangered by ethnic war.[128]

Alternatively, one could argue that the Bosnia record demonstrates that the international community cannot muster the will even for much lesser enterprises, let alone the campaigns of conquest envisaged in this paper. Even if this is true, the analysis above has four values. First, it tells us what apparent cheap and easy solutions are *not* viable. Second, it identifies the types of solutions to aim at through lesser means—aid or sanctions—if those are the most that outsiders are willing to do. Third, even if we are not prepared to intervene in certain cases, it explains what we would like other, more interested, powers to do and not do. Fourth, if Western publics and elites understood that the costs of military intervention in ethnic wars are lower, the feasibility higher, and the alternatives fewer than they now believe, perhaps this option would become more politically viable.

Ultimately we have a responsibility to be honest with ourselves as well as with the victims of ethnic wars all over the world. The world's major powers must decide whether they will be willing to spend any of their own soldiers' lives to save strangers, or whether they will continue to offer false hopes to endangered peoples.

---

128. "Failure . . . to do something about mass murder and genocide corrodes the essence of a democratic society." Leslie Gelb, "Quelling the Teacup Wars," *Foreign Affairs*, Vol. 73, No. 6 (November/December 1994), pp. 2–6, at 6; Hodding Carter, "Punishing Serbia," *Foreign Policy*, No. 96 (Fall 1994), pp. 49–56.

Refugee Flows as Grounds for International Action

Alan Dowty and Gil Loescher

The end of the Cold War paralysis; a resurgence of primordial ethnic, communal, and religious clashes; the phenomenon of "failed states"; and reporting of humanitarian catastrophes as never before in world media have led many to claim a broader mandate for outside intervention in a state's internal conflicts. Traditional notions of security and sovereignty are being challenged, placing refugee issues much higher on the international agenda and creating new opportunities for international action. While international responses to humanitarian crises are still more often than not reactive and based on *ad hoc* initiatives, there is growing international awareness of the linkage between human rights abuses, forcible displacement of civilian populations, and local, regional, and international security.

The sobering experiences with interventions in protracted crises in Iraqi Kurdistan, Somalia, Bosnia, and Rwanda underscore the fact that humanitarian measures alone are seldom enough to deal with refugee problems. A wide range of actions, most of them far short of military action, can be taken to avert large-scale refugee crises. International humanitarian agencies, such as the United Nations High Commissioner for Refugees (UNHCR), currently promote the concept of "soft intervention"[1] to prevent situations from degenerating into violent conflicts. Sustained political and diplomatic initiatives, development assistance, human rights monitoring, and the strengthening of civil societies through the building of democratic institutions are all measures that would

Alan Dowty and Gil Loescher are Professors of International Relations at the University of Notre Dame and Fellows at the Kroc Institute for International Peace Studies. Dowty is the author of Closed Borders: The Contemporary Assault on Freedom of Movement *(Yale University Press, 1987) and Loescher is the author of* Beyond Charity: International Cooperation and the Global Refugee Crises *(Oxford University Press, 1993).*

The authors would like to thank Lori Fisler Damrosch, Luke Lee, Rosemary Foot, Allan Rosas and Jeff Crisp for their helpful comments and criticisms.

1. To many the concept "soft intervention" is incongruous, as the two words that make up the term seem mutually incompatible, particularly for a humanitarian agency such as UNHCR.

International Security, Vol. 21, No. 1 (Summer 1996), pp. 43–71

help prevent the outbreak of violence and the mass displacement of populations, if initiated early and given sufficient economic resources and political support. However, in internal situations where armed hostilities have already broken out and are accompanied by widespread violations of human rights, other more "hard" forms of intervention, including military action, may be necessary to bring such violations to a halt.

Acting early to avert refugee crises can be demanding, but it is considerably less expensive than dealing with the fallout of a full-blown and protracted crisis. The international community spent 1.4 billion dollars in humanitarian relief in the nine months immediately after the genocide in Rwanda[2] and will continue to pay for a long time in terms of protection of refugees and rehabilitation costs. Focusing more attention and putting up ten to twenty million dollars early on, for airlift and equipment for African peacekeepers, might have prevented much of the bloodletting, the physical devastation, and the mass exodus of some 2 million refugees from Rwanda. Brian Atwood, the director of the U.S. Agency for International Development (USAID), claims that in 1994–95, 28 complex crises (crises caused by the combination of civil and political conflicts and natural disasters) required the international community to spend $4 billion in humanitarian assistance and $5 billion in peacekeeping.[3] It doesn't make sense for the international community to continue to pour resources into emergency relief and post-crisis rehabilitation while it neglects basic causes that produce terrible upheavals and mass displacements.

Our thesis is that governments cannot afford to ignore the brutalities of civil and communal conflicts and human rights abuses that uproot entire communities. Such events engage the national security interests of states, particularly when internal conflicts result in wider regional wars and when the spillover of refugees destabilizes neighboring countries. A large-scale movement of people across national borders, under duress, internationalizes what might otherwise be purely domestic issues related to the causes of that movement. We argue that this is becoming a norm, in theory and in practice, that is increasingly accepted as grounds for international action, including armed intervention,

---

2. John Eriksson et al., *The International Response to Conflict and Genocide: Lessons from the Rwanda Experience, Synthesis Report* (Copenhagen: Dansk Kliche, Joint OECD/DAC Evaluation of Rwanda Operation, published by the Steering Committee of the Joint Evaluation of Emergency Assistance to Rwanda, 1996), p. 5.
3. Brian Atwood, Address to the National Association of State Universities and Land Grant Colleges annual conference, November 12, 1995.

against the state generating the refugee flow. This proposition is based, in turn, on three specific arguments that form the framework of this article:

First, we argue that deriving a right of international intervention from the imposition of a refugee burden on other states is a reasonable extension of customary law. The reason that customary law did not deal with the issue was not because principles of state responsibility were not applicable, but because "the refugee problem" was not a problem in inter-state relations before the twentieth century.

Second, we argue that, as a threat to peace and security, the imposition of refugees on other states falls under Chapter VII of the UN Charter and therefore legitimates enforcement action not subject to the limits of purely humanitarian intervention.

Third, we argue that whatever the theoretical debates, international intervention as a response to refugee flows is quietly becoming a *de facto* norm in state declaration and practice. Mass movements of people in northern Iraq, Liberia, and Haiti, to list but a few examples, have set precedents for international, regional, and unilateral intervention into the internal affairs of states. While this new norm may be emerging slowly and unevenly, intervention to prevent refugee flows is now a viable policy option in the international community.

In a sense, recent developments in the internationalization of refugee-creating situations represent an extension to inter-state relations of John Stuart Mill's basic principle of liberty among individuals: a state's freedom from external intervention is now understood to end when its domestic actions (or inactions) begin to impinge significantly on other states.

Before taking up these three arguments, however, we describe the burden that contemporary refugee flows typically impose on receiving states. We conclude our article by arguing that there is an emerging norm that intervention to prevent refugee flows may be justified on security grounds as well as humanitarian grounds. This link is logical, in that the flight of refugees serves as visible evidence of internal disorder and human rights violations that are of international concern. It also may provide the basis for criteria for outside intervention, which will become increasingly necessary as the global refugee problem acquires new international dimensions.

The Reality of the Burden

Perceptions of refugee issues in recent years have been changed by the quantum leap in numbers more than anything else. In 1951, when the UNHCR was established, there were some 1.5 million refugees by the strict international definition;[4] by 1980 there were 8.2 million; in 1996 there were about 14.5 million, plus another 23 million internally displaced persons fleeing mostly from intra-state conflicts.[5] Added to this is the advent of global satellite communications: television coverage of starving children in Somalia and butchery in Rwanda, of armed attacks on Kurds and Shi'ites in Iraq, or of concentration camps in Bosnia have made citizens of industrialized nations increasingly aware of human rights abuses leading to large-scale refugee movements. The very scale of the problem and the acceleration of demands overwhelm traditional refugee relief. Most refugee crises are protracted affairs, and the average humanitarian relief operation today lasts for 3 to 5 years.[6] Western publics become numbed by compassion fatigue, and Europe in particular faces a "dilemma of common aversion" in which any one state's efforts to reduce its own burden only increases the demands on others.[7] As a result, policies on international population movements need to be taken as seriously as trade policy or other foreign and security issues. Policymakers must factor the complications of mass refugee movements, both actual and potential, into their basic policy planning.

The reality of this burden has forced a growing recognition of the way refugee issues link the internal and external realms. As Stanley Hoffmann has said, "there is no way of isolating oneself from the effects of gross violations abroad: they breed refugees, exiles, and dissidents who come knocking at our doors—and we must choose between bolting the doors, thus increasing misery and violence outside, and opening them, at some cost to our own well being."[8] The impact of a refugee flow on countries of refuge can be measured in direct

---

4. According to the 1951 UN Convention Relating to the Status of Refugees, a refugee is one who, "owing to a well-founded fear of being persecuted for reasons of race, religion, nationality, membership of a particular social group or political opinion, is outside the country of his nationality and is unable, or owing to such fear is unwilling to avail himself of the protection of that country." This definition does not cover internal refugees who flee to a different region within their own country, nor those fleeing from pressures that are not persecution in the strict sense, such as economic deprivation, war or civil strife, or foreign occupation.
5. Statement by Sadako Ogata, UN High Commissioner for Refugees, on the occasion of the Inter-governmental Consultation on Asylum, Refugee and Migration Policies in Europe, North America, and Australia, Berlin, February 1, 1996.
6. Presentation by Peter Walker, "Challenges for an Operating Agency in the Next Five Years," at international conference, *Geneva and the Challenge of Humanitarian Action of the 1990s*, Geneva, February 16, 1996.
7. Rosemarie Rogers and Emily Copeland, *Forced Migration: Policy Issues in the Post–Cold War Period* (Medford, Mass.: Fletcher School of Law and Diplomacy, Tufts University, 1993), p. 116.
8. Stanley Hoffmann, *Duties Beyond Borders: On the Limits and Possibilities of Ethical International Politics* (Syracuse, N.Y.: Syracuse University Press, 1981), p. 111.

and indirect economic costs, in negative social and cultural consequences, in threats to security both internally and externally, and in its broader impact on the fabric of global stability.

The international community, through the international refugee regime, already bears a portion of the cost for refugee relief and assistance. But this is only part of the picture. For example, the total cost of processing asylum applications and offering social security to those awaiting decisions cost Western Europe about $11.6 billion in 1993, an amount roughly ten times the worldwide expenditure of the UNHCR for that year, and nearly one-seventh of total annual development aid made available to the Third World from the West.[9]

Yet most of the world's refugees are sheltered in the world's poorest states; the seventeen nations with the highest ratio of refugees to population have an annual average per capita income of about $920.[10] In Africa, for example, Guinea and the Ivory Coast have absorbed 750,000 Liberians, the Ivory Coast without establishing a single refugee camp. In less than two months in 1994, poor countries in Africa took in more than a quarter of Rwanda's population of about 8,000,000. Thus the cost falls disproportionately on nations least able to afford it, where the presence of large impoverished refugee populations further strains resources and perpetuates the poverty of the host nation.[11] Refugees need water, food, fuel, and land; the environmental impact in already-marginal areas may be devastating. When they compete for jobs, refugees drive wages down, and when they compete for scarce goods they create inflation.[12] They require social services beyond those provided by international agencies, putting further strain on domestic structures that may already have been inadequate.

---

9. International Centre for Migration Policy Development, *The Key to Europe: A Comparative Analysis of Entry and Asylum Policies in Western Countries* (Stockholm: Nortsedts Tryckeri AB, 1994), p. 82.

10. U.S. Committee for Refugees, *World Refugee Survey 1994* (Washington, D.C.: U.S. Committee for Refugees, 1994), p. 43.

11. Refugees are not always a burden on their local hosts; they may make a positive contribution to the economy in the areas where they settle. Refugees are survivors and often arrive in their new countries with skills, education, work practices, and personal resourcefulness that can have a highly positive impact on economic growth. For example, the arrival of 20,000 exiled Mozambicans in the sparsely populated Zambian area of Ukwimi in the late 1980s transformed the economic prospects for this region. Substantial international assistance was poured into the area, allowing roads, schools, health centers, and agricultural extension services to be established. All these facilities were available for use by both the Mozambicans and local Zambians. Unfortunately, these examples are often the exception rather than the norm, as current practice forces refugees to live in camps and to rely on the distribution of food and health supplies rather than encouraging them to contribute to their host's economies.

12. Rogers and Copeland, *Forced Migration*, p. 13.

As for the social and cultural impact, refugee movements often threaten inter-communal harmony and undermine major societal values by altering the ethnic, cultural, religious, and linguistic composition of host populations. In countries with racial, ethnic, religious, or other splits—that is, most existing countries—a refugee influx can place great strain on the system. Mass influxes can endanger social and economic stability, particularly in countries where ethnic rivalries may be virulent, where the central government is weak and consensus on the legitimacy of the political system is lacking, and where essential resources are limited. A large influx of refugees with ties to a particular domestic group can upset the internal balance and even threaten the existing system.

Refugees often become a political force in their host country, influencing its policies and particularly its relationship with the country of origin. In the United States, for example, refugee or immigrant communities have influenced U.S. policy toward Cuba, China, Cyprus, Haiti, Israel, Mexico, Nicaragua, Northern Ireland, Poland, Vietnam, and elsewhere. Refugee communities may align themselves with opposition parties and use this leverage as pressure on ruling governments to advance their own interests, as Afghan refugee groups in Pakistan backed fundamentalist groups in that country.

Universally, societies fear that uncontrolled migration may swamp their existing cultural identity. Refugees typically seek to preserve their own cultural heritage and national identity in line with their dream of an eventual return to their homeland, thus complicating their integration into the host society. In Europe, the gulf between the cultural background of contemporary refugee groups and that of Europeans causes special concern. There are serious reservations about the ability of these groups to assimilate and about the willingness of Western publics to tolerate aliens in their midst. These feelings, reinforced by racial and religious prejudices, pose difficult social and political problems for European governments. Xenophobic and racist attitudes are increasingly obvious among some segments of these populations, and racist attacks are increasing in every country hosting immigrant minorities. Anti-immigrant and anti-refugee feeling is being exploited by extreme right-wing parties throughout Europe, a development which distorts the politics of these nations and in some cases (such as the former East Germany) impedes the process of democratization.[13]

---

13. For elaboration of these arguments, see Gil Loescher, *Refugee Movements and International Security*, Adelphi Paper 268 (London: International Institute for Strategic Studies [IISS], 1992),

Security concerns for the host state begin with the question of whether it can physically control the refugee population, which frequently includes armed combatants. This is currently a critical problem with the Hutu refugees in Zaire, many of whom were perpetrators of the "machete genocide" in Rwanda. In the past, Afghan refugee leaders threatened to make their camps in Pakistan ungovernable if Pakistan made a deal with the government in Kabul. For over a decade, contending Cambodian exile groups maintained their headquarters in camps on Thai territory and posed serious problems for that government. In the Middle East, Arab political and military support for Palestinian refugees undermined some states' control of their own foreign and internal policies; in Lebanon, for example, the presence of a large Palestinian population was a key factor in the eruption of civil war, the collapse of central government, and eventual domination by Syria. Kuwait's fears regarding the loyalty of Palestinians led to their mass expulsion following the Gulf War.[14]

Since refugees often remain in or near border areas, control of cross-border terrorism or smuggling may be especially difficult. Raids and guerrilla activity across the border may drag the host state into an existing conflict, and in fact this may be the deliberate strategy of armed exile groups. The offer of sanctuary to refugees may in itself invite military retaliation; in response to real or perceived threats of "refugee warrior communities," refugee camps have increasingly become military targets (particularly in Africa and Central America). In some cases, host states have themselves helped to arm refugee fighting groups as a weapon against the country of origin, but then found themselves unable to control the consequences of having done so (particularly in the Middle East, the Horn of Africa, the Great Lakes Region of Africa, and Southeast Asia).

More often, mass expulsions are used by the sending country to deliberately destabilize or embarrass strategic or political adversaries. As Hoffmann notes, "states can easily export mischief, so to speak, by dumping refugees or economic migrants on neighbors."[15] Under such circumstances, expulsions are seriously destabilizing to receiving countries and in some cases are analogous

pp. 41–49; Leon Gordenker, *Refugees in International Politics* (New York: Columbia University Press, 1987), p. 207; Myron Weiner, "Introduction: Security, Stability, and International Migration," in Weiner, ed., *International Migration and Security* (Boulder, Colo.: Westview Press, 1993), pp. 11–19.

14. Ibid.

15. Stanley Hoffmann, "Sovereignty and the Ethics of Intervention," First Annual Theodore M. Hesburgh Lecture Series, Joan B. Kroc Institute for International Peace Studies, University of Notre Dame, January 24, 1995.

to military invasions. Arab states that forced out their Jewish communities after Israeli independence in 1948 expected the massive influx to overwhelm the newly established state (whose population doubled in three years). Officials of Southeast Asian states claimed during the late 1970s that the massive Vietnamese expulsion of ethnic Chinese was a veiled attempt to create racial and economic problems in their countries and to infiltrate enemy agents. Fidel Castro's expulsion of criminals and psychotics to the United States, as a part of the 1980 Mariel boatlift, was an even more obvious example of migration policy as a tool of foreign policy and was characterized by one White House official at the time as "bullets aimed at the United States." When refugees are being used as a weapon, the target state is within its rights in invoking the right of self-defense.[16]

The broader impact of refugee flows is in part a result of the fact that asylum-seekers are no longer limited to neighboring states. "Jet age" refugees now appear at the doorstep of distant nations; a larger proportion of them are finding their way to Western states in hope of better conditions. This comes on top of a steep rise in the number of illegal immigrants to the West from the Third World and Eastern Europe. The result is a refugee crisis that affects international relations more widely, over and above its impact within particular states. A U.S. attempt simply to erect new barriers against the South and the East would not make the problem go away, nor would it ensure a stable political base for international relations.

An angry, excluded world outside the West will almost inevitably create conditions in which extremist groups and governments will emerge and pose new security threats. The success of economic liberalism and political pluralism in the new democracies of Latin America, Eastern Europe, and the former Soviet Union is of decisive importance not only in averting future refugee and migrant flows, but also in the security realm. Failure to stem the tide of poverty, violence, persecution, and other refugee-inducing factors will be costly to the West in security terms. In countries where conditions are desperate, people will find ways to flee. Dealing effectively with refugees both at home and abroad is a matter of self-interest for industrialized states and coincides with their search for long-term global and strategic stability.

The previous focus on charity—that is, on relief and assistance after the fact—is not adequate. Charity alone often helps to perpetuate the injustice that

---

16. Loescher, *Refugee Movements and International Security*, pp. 32–33; see also Gordenker, *Refugees in International Politics*, pp. 188–189, and Weiner, "Introduction: Security, Stability, and International Migration," pp. 8–9.

caused the refugee flight, since it relieves the sending country of pressure to correct the injustice. For example, "Guatemala's well-meaning neighbors inadvertently are making it easier for Guatemala's regime to deny its people. . . . They are providing a mechanism through which Guatemala's rulers can remove people who might press for reform."[17] Worse, in Bosnia and elsewhere, until recently humanitarian assistance not only has been a substitute for more direct intervention by states and regional organizations, but has also been used by combatants to further their political objectives and to prolong the conflict. The emphasis internationally is therefore inevitably shifting "from humanitarian obligations to legal obligations of one state not to harm other states by imposing the burdens of unmanaged refugee flow."[18]

Part of the response to this heavier burden has been greater stress on the goal of repatriation. In the past, integration in place or resettlement in third countries—the other two traditional solutions—were more common, in part because they do not require a remedy to the original cause of flight. But given the jump in numbers and some favorable political developments (the end of the Cold War, moderation of other conflicts, and a wave of democratization), repatriation has become the preferred solution in theory and in practice. In Afghanistan, Burma, Cambodia, Ethiopia, Mozambique, Sri Lanka, Vietnam, and elsewhere, it has been implemented on a wide scale. According to the UNHCR, some 9 million refugees have returned home during the past 5 years.[19] A former Director of the U.S. State Department Bureau of Refugee Programs clearly identified "development of integration programs in the country of origin for returning refugees" as the priority in the U.S. approach to the issue.[20]

Since repatriation of refugees is impossible without addressing the reasons for their flight, attention has also turned to addressing these problems before the event rather than waiting to correct the situation afterwards. Hoffmann

---

17. Steven Luper-Foy, "Intervention and Guatemalan Refugees," *Public Affairs Quarterly,* Vol. 6, No. 1 (January 1992), p. 52.

18. Jack I. Garvey, "The New Asylum Seekers: Addressing Their Origin," in David Martin, ed., *The New Asylum Seekers: Refugee Law in the 1980s* (Dordrecht, Netherlands: Martinus Nijhoff, 1988), p. 187.

19. UNHCR, *The State of the World's Refugees: In Search of Solutions* (Oxford, U.K.: Oxford University Press, 1995).

20. Testimony by Warren Zimmermann, Director of the Bureau for Refugee Programs, before the Subcommittee on Foreign Operations of the Senate Appropriations Committee, June 30, 1993, in *Department of State Dispatch,* July 12, 1993 (Nexis). See also the discussion of "a new conception of the purposes and principles of the approach to the refugee problem" in Gervase Coles, "Approaching the Refugee Problem Today," in Gil Loescher and Laila Monahan, eds., *Refugees and International Relations* (Oxford, U.K.: Oxford University Press, 1989), pp. 390–391.

argues that "Red Cross ethics"—dealing only with the aftermath—may prolong the agony of a humanitarian disaster if adequate political and economic resources are not directed towards rehabilitation and reconciliation.[21] In any event, the problem cannot be resolved simply by staving off refugee flows and forcing people to remain in untenable conditions. Experts on refugee issues now urge that future efforts focus on the "root causes" of displacement *before* people are forced to flee, and that international action should be preventive more than ameliorative.[22]

This requires a closer look at the role of states themselves in causing mass exoduses. Certain kinds of government actions generate refugee flows, ranging from decrees and overt use of force, to more covert persecution, intimidation, discrimination, and inducements of unwanted groups to leave. Throughout history, states have used mass expulsion as a means of dealing with national minorities. A large proportion of the world's displacements also occur as a direct result of political and social revolutions. The overthrow of existing elites, violent internal conflicts to achieve dominance, the intolerance of dissent, and the drive for total consensus characterize most contemporary revolutions and have been the source of many of the world's major refugee movements. Non-state actors also bear responsibility for the recent explosion of refugee incidents around the world. In today's intra-state conflicts, civilian populations are both the target and the principal objective of states and their opponents. The practice of "ethnic cleansing" in its various guises by state and non-state actors contributes to widespread forcible displacement.

The great outpourings of the late 1970s triggered two important UN initiatives aimed at the *causes* of refugee flows. Under Canadian prodding, the UN Commission on Human Rights commissioned a study of "human rights and mass exoduses." The report was prepared by Sadruddin Aga Khan, the former High Commissioner for Refugees, and was presented at the end of 1981. It included a number of specific proposals for dealing with situations that

---

21. Hoffmann, "Sovereignty and the Ethics of Intervention."

22. For arguments along these lines, see Gil Loescher, *Beyond Charity: International Cooperation and the Global Refugee Crisis* (New York: Oxford University Press, 1993), pp. 180–205; Tom J. Farer, "An Inquiry into the Legitimacy of Humanitarian Intervention," in Lori Fisler Damrosch and David J. Scheffer, eds., *Law and Force in the New International Order* (Boulder, Colo.: Westview Press, 1991), p. 198; Jean-Pierre Hocké (a former UN High Commissioner for Refugees), "Beyond Humanitarianism: The Need for Political Will to Resolve Today's Refugee Problem," in Loescher and Monahan, *Refugees and International Relations*, p. 41; Alan Dowty, *Closed Borders: The Contemporary Assault on Freedom of Movement* (New Haven, Conn.: Yale University Press, 1987), pp. 251–255; Coles, "Approaching the Refugee Problem Today," p. 394; Zimmermann testimony.

threaten to produce refugees, including relating aid programs to the causes of mass exoduses, setting up an early-warning system to identify potential trouble spots, and appointing a special representative and observer corps who could intervene in such cases.[23]

In another move, led by the former West Germany, the General Assembly in 1982 established a Group of Governmental Experts on International Cooperation to Avert New Flows of Refugees (the "New Flows" group). Its mandate was to examine the causes of refugee flows and to suggest ways of handling them. The final report of this group, in 1986, recognized the "great political, economic and social burdens [of massive flows of refugees] upon the international community as a whole, with dire effects on developing countries, particularly those with limited resources of their own." Accordingly, it recommended intervention by the international community through the good offices of the Secretary-General, refugee-prevention actions by appropriate UN bodies (including the Security Council), and better use of aid programs to deter massive displacements.[24] The adoption of the final report by the General Assembly marked, in the words of one UNHCR official, an "emerging consensus on the legitimacy of taking action in the country of origin, so that people would not have to flee."[25] Efforts to carry out these intentions are discussed below.

The Applicability of Customary Law

Customary international law has nothing specific to say about refugees because the issue did not exist in the past. This is not because there were no refugees; numerous acts of persecution and expulsion accompanied the rise of the modern state in Europe and elsewhere. But the simultaneous development of the Westphalian concept of sovereignty created a presumption against interference by other states and—more importantly—there were almost always countries or colonial areas to which refugees could flee. Only in the twentieth century, when refugee flows exploded and came to be regarded as a threat, were legal

---

23. Aga Khan, *Study on Human Rights and Massive Exoduses*, United Nations, Economic and Social Council, Commission on Human Rights, December 31, 1981 (E/CN.4/1503).

24. UN Doc. A/41/324, May 13, 1986; see the analysis in Luke Lee, "Toward a World without Refugees: The United Nations Group of Governmental Experts on International Co-operation to Avert New Flows of Refugees," *British Year Book of International Law*, Vol. 57 (London: H. Frowde, 1986), pp. 317–336.

25. Luise Drüke, *Preventive Action for Refugee Producing Situations* (Frankfurt: Peter Lang, 1990), p. 209.

and institutional responses developed, and these responses understandably focused at first on helping already-existing refugees who were in need of protection and relief. Our first argument is that traditional doctrines do, however, provide a legal basis for action against a state that generates refugees. This was first pointed out in a little-noted article by R. Yewdall Jennings in 1939, a year marking the peak of an earlier "refugee crisis" of our century.[26] Jennings pointed out that "there is one aspect of the refugee problem to which the general and customary international law is relevant, and that is the consideration of the legality or illegality of the conduct of the state which creates a refugee population."[27]

Jennings took an approach, like that of this article, "which has regard not so much to the ethics of domestic policy as to the repercussions of that policy on the material interests of third states." Even in cases where a state may not be guilty of illegal acts, therefore, by flooding another state with refugees it creates grounds for the affected state to resort to measures of *retorsion*, defined in Oppenheim's classic treatise on international law as "retaliation for discourteous, or unkind, or unfair and inequitable acts by acts of the same or of a similar kind."[28] Such acts of retaliation or reciprocation are commonly used to force states to alter their treatment of aliens or their trade practices. For example, if a nation discriminates against aliens from another state, that state may retaliate against citizens of the first state within its borders. In the context of imposed refugee burdens, retorsion would clearly seem to justify at least economic sanctions designed to impose on the country of origin a cost equivalent to that forced upon the host nation.

Jennings goes further, however, arguing that "the wilful flooding of other states with refugees constitutes not merely an inequitable act, but an actual illegality, and *a fortiori* where the refugees are compelled to enter the country of refuge in a destitute condition."[29] He cites President Benjamin Harrison, who in 1891 based U.S. protests to Russia over its treatment of Jews on the argument that "a decree to leave one country is, in the nature of things, an order to enter another."[30]

---

26. R. Yewdall Jennings, "Some International Law Aspects of the Refugee Question," *British Year Book of International Law*, Vol. 20 (1939), pp. 98–114.
27. Ibid., p. 110.
28. Ibid., p. 111; L. Oppenheim, *International Law: A Treatise*, Vol. 2: *Disputes, War and Neutrality*, 7th ed., H. Lauterpacht, ed. (New York: David McKay, 1952), pp. 134–135.
29. Jennings, "Some International Law Aspects," p. 111.
30. President's Message to Congress, December 9, 1891, *British and Foreign State Papers*, Vol. 83, pp. 436–437, quoted by Jennings, "Some International Law Aspects," p. 112.

The illegality of this action, according to Jennings and subsequent commentators, derives from the generally accepted doctrine of the abuse of rights. In common law this is known as *sic utere tuo ut alienum non laedas* ("use your own property in such a manner as not to injure that of another"), a maxim that according to Oppenheim "is applicable to relations of States no less than to those of individuals" and is "one of those general principles of law recognised by civilised States which [the International Court of Justice] is bound to apply by virtue of Article 38 of its Statute."[31]

The doctrine of abuse of rights, then, establishes the legal responsibility of the state of origin even if this is not stated explicitly in refugee law: "there is ample authority for the proposition that a state is obligated to avoid the generation across its borders of damage to other states."[32] Numerous international treaties, declarations, and adjudications reflect this principle in various contexts. For example, in the Trail Smelter Arbitration (1941), the tribunal ruled that "no state has the right to use or permit the use of its territory in such a manner as to cause injury . . . in or to the territory of another or the properties or persons therein."[33] Similarly, in the Corfu Channel case (1949), the International Court of Justice held that a state from whose territory transboundary damages were generated is responsible if it had knowledge of the harm and the opportunity to act.[34] The 1972 Stockholm Declaration, from the first major UN conference on environmental cooperation, affirmed that "States have . . . the responsibility to ensure that activities within their area of jurisdiction or control do not cause damage to the environment of other States or of areas beyond the limits of territorial jurisdiction."[35]

Expulsion of a state's nationals to the territory of other states is in itself illegal in most cases. The legal right to remain in one's country, or to return to it, has acquired a strong standing. States no longer claim the right to expel citizens who have committed no crime; even exile, as a legal punishment of citizens convicted of a crime, has fallen into disuse. The illegality of expelling nationals is so commonly assumed that international documents, rather surprisingly, do

---

31. Jennings, "Some International Law Aspects," p. 112; Oppenheim, *International Law*, Vol. 1: *Peace*, 8th ed., H. Lauterpacht, ed. (London: Longmans, Green, 1955), pp. 346–347; see also Ian Brownlie, *Principles of Public International Law*, 3rd ed. (Oxford, U.K.: Oxford University Press, 1979), pp. 443–445; and Guy S. Goodwin-Gill, *The Refugee in International Law* (Oxford, U.K.: Oxford University Press, 1983), p. 228.
32. Garvey, "The New Asylum Seekers," p. 187.
33. The Trail Smelter Arbitration (U.S. vs. Canada), Trail Smelter Arbitral Tribunal, Case No. 315, *Annual Digest and Reports of Public International Law Cases, 1938–1940* (London: Butterworth and Company, 1941); see also Brownlie, *Principles of Public International Law*, pp. 285–286.
34. *International Court of Justice Reports* (The Hague: International Court of Justice, 1949).
35. UN Doc. A/CONF.48/14/Rev. 1 and Corr. 1, Principle 21.

not explicitly forbid it. It is, nevertheless, implicit in the body of conventions and agreements developed during and after World War II. The 1948 Universal Declaration of Human Rights, for example, provides in Article 13(2) that "everyone has the right to leave any country, including his own, and to return to his country." As Jennings had written several years earlier, it is "the undoubted duty of a state to receive back its own nationals."[36] If one has the right to return, then one certainly has the right not to leave in the first place.

Even exile as a legal punishment is conditional, moreover, on the willingness of another state to admit the expellee. This is a point often overlooked in discussions of *de facto* individual or mass expulsions: even where a state may have some justification for expelling one or more of its own citizens, no other state has an automatic obligation to admit them. If no state agrees to take them in, expulsion is not a legal option. There are no acceptable grounds for dumping expellees on the territory of a non-consenting state, including, for example, Israel's 1993 expulsion of Hamas activists from the West Bank and Gaza to an area of Lebanon over which the Lebanese government had no physical control.

The right of states to take away the citizenship of their own citizens—to denationalize them—is severely restricted, and even then a state cannot automatically expel those denationalized if no other state is prepared to receive them. Nor can a state denationalize citizens already out of the country simply in order to prevent their return, which amounts to the same thing. Furthermore, the failure to correct the conditions that led to a refugee outflow can be seen as evasion of a legal duty, since continuation of these conditions renders the right of return meaningless.[37]

To summarize, "established rules of international law . . . permit the conclusion that states are bound by a general principle not to create refugee outflows and to co-operate with other states in the resolution of such problems as may emerge."[38] This suggests an obligation to remedy the cause of the outflow as well as to provide for reparation to the affected parties. About the obligation of reparation there is little debate: violations of human rights that cause specific losses to the victims and to other states are grounds for claims of compensation or indemnity.[39] But can outside parties intervene to prevent tragedy in the first place?

---

36. Jennings, "Some International Law Aspects," p. 112.
37. Ibid., pp. 112–113; see also Paul Weis, *Nationality and Statelessness in International Law* (Westport, Conn.: Hyperion, 1956), pp. 123–129; Hurst Hannum, *The Right to Leave and Return in International Law and Practice* (Washington, D.C.: Procedural Aspects of International Law Institute, 1985), p. 79.
38. Goodwin-Gill, *The Refugee in International Law*, p. 228.
39. Brownlie, *Principles of Public International Law*, p. 520; Daniel H. Derby, "Deterring Refugee-Generating Conduct," in Ved P. Nanda, ed., *Refugee Law and Policy: International and U.S. Responses*

Recent international documents favor a broader definition of "state responsibility" that includes prevention of harm to others as well as reparation. The final report of the "New Flows" group of governmental experts, for example, declared that "averting massive flows of refugees is a matter of serious concern to the international community as a whole" and that such flows "carry adverse consequences for the economies of the countries of origin and entire regions, thus endangering international peace and security."[40] The link to "peace and security" is grounds for invoking Chapter VII of the UN Charter, which overrides claims of domestic jurisdiction. Similarly, the International Law Commission, in its "Draft Articles on State Responsibility," defined an international crime as "an internationally wrongful act which results from the breach by a State of an international obligation so essential for the protection of fundamental interests of the international community that its breach is recognized as a crime by that community as a whole." Included as examples of such crimes, justifying corrective action, are not only threats to peace and security but also "a serious breach on a widespread scale of an international obligation of essential importance for safeguarding the human being, such as those prohibiting slavery, genocide, *apartheid*."[41]

But how does this expansion of "state responsibility" relate to the traditional principles of non-intervention and domestic jurisdiction? The Permanent Court of International Justice recognized in a 1923 case that the definition of "domestic jurisdiction" is not fixed in perpetuity but changes as other conditions change.[42] In other words, "the sphere of 'domestic jurisdiction' is a relative one that contracts as the sphere of activity governed by international law and other sources of obligation grows."[43] Furthermore, it is a basic principle of international law that a state cannot rely on the provisions of its own laws in defense against a claimed breach of international obligations; international law takes precedence where the two conflict. It would follow, therefore, that as refugee

(Westport, Conn.: Greenwood Press, 1989), pp. 44–45, 53; Luke Lee, "The Right to Compensation: Refugees and Countries of Asylum," *American Journal of International Law*, Vol. 80 (1986), pp. 532–556.

40. UN Doc. A/41/324 (May 13, 1986), para. 63; Lee, "Toward a World without Refugees," p. 331.

41. International Law Commission, *Report on the Work of the Thirty-Third Session, 1981*, Ch. IV, in Ian Brownlie, *State Responsibility*, Part I (Oxford, U.K.: Oxford University Press, 1983), pp. 289–290.

42. Nationalities Decrees in Tunis and Morocco, Permanent Court of International Justice, Series B, No. 4, 24 (1923), quoted in Kelly Kate Pease and David Forsythe, "Human Rights, Humanitarian Intervention, and World Politics," *Human Rights Quarterly*, Vol. 15, No. 2 (May 1993), p. 293; see also Tim Schorn, *United Nations Intervention in Crises of Authority and Failed States: A New Basis in Theory and Practice*, unpublished Ph.D. Dissertation, University of Notre Dame, 1995.

43. Lori Fisler Damrosch, "Changing Conceptions of Intervention in International Law," in Laura W. Reed and Carl Kaysen, eds., *Emerging Norms of Justified Intervention* (Cambridge, Mass.: American Academy of Arts and Sciences, 1993), p. 95.

flows impose massively increased burdens on other states, domestic jurisdiction related to such issues would shrink and domestic provisions—even if "legal" by local standards—would come under increased challenge.

Customary law is thus hospitable to preventive action against refugee flows, even though the issue was not raised so long as refugee flows did not impose a significant burden on receiving states. With a few exceptions, forced migration prior to the middle of this century did not take place on a scale that caused noteworthy concern. The term "refugee" itself was invented only at the end of the seventeenth century, when French persecution of Protestants (following revocation of the Edict of Nantes in 1685) forced some 200,000–300,000 Huguenot *refugiés* into flight. But on the whole, such movements were not substantial enough to lead receiving states to protest.

Even when numbers were substantial, most pre-modern states did not feel inclined to protest. Throughout the long history of expulsion and flight, haven had usually been available because other states were willing, even eager, to admit the expelled population to their own territory. Population was usually viewed as wealth, both in economic terms and as the foundation of military power. The Jews who were expelled from various medieval European states as a foreign element, for example, were always able to find a haven with other rulers who welcomed their skills as artisans and merchants. The Ottoman Sultan Bajezet, in opening the door to Jews expelled from Spain in 1492, reputedly exclaimed: "Call ye this Ferdinand 'wise'—he who depopulates his own dominions in order to enrich mine?"[44] It is only in the twentieth century, with the closing of the open door in traditional lands of immigration (particularly the New World), and an explosion in the numbers of the "unwanted," that responsibility for the creation of refugees has become an issue of contention on the international agenda.

Refugee Flows as Threats to Peace under the UN Charter

Our second argument is that there is increasing recognition by the international community that massive refugee flows do in fact constitute a threat to international peace and security, and that they therefore justify use of the enforcement powers of the United Nations. We have already cited the 1986 report of the "New Flows" group, endorsed by the General Assembly, which explicitly defined such flows as a threat to peace and security, thus opening the door to

---

44. Cecil Roth, *History of the Jews* (New York: Schocken, 1961), p. 252.

action by the Security Council under Chapter VII several years later. Article 2(7), protecting the domestic jurisdiction of member states, specifically exempts from this protection enforcement actions taken under Chapter VII. A country that forces its people to flee or takes actions that compel them to leave in a manner that threatens regional peace and security has in effect internationalized its internal affairs, and provides a cogent justification for policymakers elsewhere to act directly upon the source of the threat.

This argument was made six decades ago by James G. McDonald, the League of Nations High Commissioner for Refugees, when he resigned in frustration at the lack of international action to halt the persecution in Germany causing refugee flows to neighboring countries. In his dramatic letter of resignation of December 27, 1935, MacDonald wrote that "it will not be enough to continue the activities on behalf of those who flee from the Reich. Efforts must be made to remove or mitigate the causes which create German refugees." Such efforts, declared McDonald, fell under the League's authority to deal with any matter affecting the peace of the world, since "the protection of the individual from racial or religious intolerance is a vital condition of international peace and security."[45] The argument is also made by contemporary analysts of refugee issues: "When there is aggression by a state against its own minority such that the domestic issue becomes an international one and is perceived to threaten peace and security because the minority begin a mass flight, then defensive military intervention is justified."[46] Others point out that if refugee flows constitute an "internationally wrongful act" or an "international crime" under the principles of state responsibility discussed above, this is also a violation of the Charter and therefore responses to it are not intervention in a state's domestic affairs.[47]

National and international bodies, and in particular neighboring states, also increasingly regard actions or policies that trigger mass expulsions or refugee movements as an international issue. From this perspective, grievous human rights abuses are not an internal matter when neighboring states must bear the cost of repression by having refugees forced on them. In recent years the Security Council itself has taken an increasingly inclusive view of "threats to peace" where actual hostilities remained limited largely to the territory of a

---

45. League of Nations document C.13, M.12, 1936, annex, quoted by Coles, "Approaching the Refugee Problem Today," pp. 409–410; see also Jennings, "Some International Law Aspects," p. 110.
46. Howard Adelman, "The Ethics of Humanitarian Intervention: The Case of the Kurdish Refugees," *Public Affairs Quarterly*, Vol. 6, No. 1 (January 1992), p. 75.
47. Lee, "Toward a World without Refugees," p. 332.

single state (discussed in more detail below).[48] The UN Security Council's Summit Declaration of 1992 identified "nonmilitary sources of instability in the economic, social, humanitarian and ecological fields" as threats to international peace and security, while specifying "election monitoring, human rights verification, and the repatriation of refugees" as "integral parts of the Security Council's efforts to maintain international peace and security."[49] As Rogers and Copeland note, "these expanded notions of what constitute threats to international or national security have important implications for the issue of forced migration: they make it easier to classify forced migration flows or the presence of forced migrants in a host country as security threats."[50]

This new thinking ties in with changing ideas of national sovereignty. While sovereignty is still regarded as a cornerstone of the international political and legal system, domestic matters previously shielded from outside interference are now targets of international action. Since an elementary justification for the state is its ability to provide reasonable security for its citizens, states that force these same citizens to flee call into question the very basis of their sovereignty.

Finally, there is the question of whether "sovereignty" is a consideration at all in the increasingly frequent case of "failed states" or "crises of authority" when there is no generally recognized government exercising effective authority over a state's territory. In such cases the absence of an invitation is hardly determinative; what we need are reasonable criteria for when a state ceases to be a state, conceding to the international community not only the right but also the duty to intervene. Clearly the sudden flight of large populations is itself one sign that a government is no longer functioning effectively.[51]

Intervening in refugee-producing situations on the basis of a threat to peace and security, rather than on a purely humanitarian basis, also changes some of the considerations and conditions in execution. "Proportionality" would remain a condition as in any sanctioned use of force, but the calculus would proceed on a different basis. Intervention would be aimed not just at the immediate relief of victims, but also at rectifying the conditions that comprise a continuing threat to the peace of other states. Obviously such an "enforcement" mission could require broader changes, including in the extreme case removal of the offending government. Accordingly the means employed may

---

48. Damrosch, "Changing Conceptions," pp. 100ff.
49. *Security Council Summit Declaration* (New York: United Nations, 1992).
50. Rogers and Copeland, *Forced Migration*, p. 12.
51. For a discussion of this issue see Schorn, *United Nations Interventions*.

move from milder forms of pressure—diplomacy or consent-based peacekeeping—to more coercive economic and military sanctions.

Secondly, the "disinterest" often specified for humanitarian interventions is not possible, since intervention to prevent refugee flows is justified precisely *because of* the impact on other states. The fact that this is a case of states acting in their own interest is one reason to hope that such actions will be more effective than such actions have often been in the past.[52] This leaves the issue of how interveners can be prevented from exploiting such situations for particular gains unrelated to the refugee flow that justified their action. The obvious answer would be to require multilateral legitimization and execution as much as possible; in a crude sense, "interest" would provide the motive power for such justified interventions, while multilateral mechanisms would provide the steering and control.

Intervention in Practice

Our third argument is that international intervention related to refugee flows has in fact become more frequent in state declaration and practice in the last two decades. Such intervention, in other words, is not only increasingly justifiable, but is actually happening. We begin with a discussion of unilateral military interventions, which are the most difficult to justify, and then proceed to the more easily accepted cases of UN-authorized unilateral and multilateral interventions, and finally to various forms of "soft" or non-military intervention.

Even during the Cold War, unilateral military interventions were carried out without the collective legitimization of the UN Security Council or other international bodies. In three such cases, "hideous repression within the target state, and consequent huge refugee flows" provided grounds for action.[53]

The first case was India's intervention in East Pakistan (Bangladesh) in 1971, after an estimated ten million refugees poured into India as a result of fighting sparked when Pakistan's government, dominated by West Pakistan, annulled

---

52. A recent study of four international interventions concluded that "cooperative governmental efforts to resolve problems of forced migration and other migration pressures will necessarily be based on states' interests, although informed by the same states' commitment to the protection of forced migrants." Rogers and Copeland, *Forced Migration*, p. 117. See also Adelman, "The Ethics of Humanitarian Intervention," p. 73.
53. Adam Roberts, "Humanitarian War: Military Intervention and Human Rights," *International Affairs*, Vol. 69, No. 3 (July 1993), p. 434.

an election won by a party based in East Pakistan. The burden on India's economy was enormous, and India suspected that the Pakistani government was trying to change the demographic balance between the two parts of Pakistan by forcing massive numbers of East Pakistanis into India. The second case was Vietnam's intervention into Cambodia in late 1978, to overthrow the notorious Pol Pot regime under which large numbers of Cambodians had fled to Vietnam. Also in 1979, Tanzania sent its forces into Uganda in support of Ugandan refugees based in Tanzania; the Tanzanian forces sought to overthrow the Idi Amin regime and to repel Ugandan incursions into Tanzania.

Humanitarian intervention was not the major thrust of any of these actions. While the burden of refugees in the Indian states of West Bengal, Tripura, and Assam was clearly an important factor, India's objectives also included the strengthening of its regional position *vis-à-vis* its traditional rival Pakistan. Similarly, Vietnam intervened in Cambodia for hegemonic reasons and not to put an end to Pol Pot's genocide. Tanzania intervened in self-defense, but its intervention was also influenced by the presence of active Ugandan exiles in Dar es Salaam.

In all three cases the targeted regime was toppled; Bangladesh became independent, Cambodia acquired a Vietnamese-sponsored government, and in Uganda a previous regime was restored. In all three cases, refugees (at least the original refugee group) were able to return home, relieving the burden on the intervening state. Though all three interventions were widely condemned as violations of national sovereignty, the official international condemnations were on the whole ritualistic and muted in light of the undeniable fact that the interveners had halted widespread massacres and flight. However, the interventions in Bangladesh and Cambodia did provoke strong counter-measures from global powers, who feared potential damage to their interests in these regions. For example, in order to deter India from attempting to extend its gains in the former East Pakistan by an attack on West Pakistan, the Nixon administration moved the U.S. 6th Fleet into the Bay of Bengal. In Cambodia, the Chinese government, furious over the loss of its close ally, the Khmer Rouge, to its historical archenemy, Vietnam, sought to give Hanoi a "bloody nose" by an attack on northern Vietnam in February 1979. Despite these events, it is significant that in all three cases, the international community made no moves to restore the previous regime or even to continue recognizing it (except that many states recognized the successors of the Khmer Rouge because they opposed Vietnam's puppet regime in Phnom Penh).

In dealing with Bangladesh, the General Assembly did not flatly condemn India, but discussed the situation in all its aspects including the return of refugees, and gave priority to condemnation of genocide over reaffirmation of the principle of sovereignty.[54] Subsequently the International Commission of Jurists, writing on the India-Pakistan case, set out four requirements for unilateral humanitarian intervention: 1) manifest guilt of the target government; 2) lack of practical peaceful means to correct the situation; 3) opportunity for the international community to act first; and 4) use of only necessary force, with accounting to the international community, and withdrawal as soon as practical. Both the Indian and Tanzanian interventions did arguably meet these conditions, though the Vietnamese ultimately did not because of their prolonged presence in Cambodia.[55]

There were other cases in which actual or potential refugee flows also played a role, as motivation or justification, in unilateral military interventions. Among these were India's intervention in Sri Lanka following a flow of Tamil refugees, and covert support of Afghan rebels by Pakistan and the United States during the 1980s.[56] Nor should it be forgotten that Palestinian Arab refugees were one of the justifications for the Arab states' war against Israel in 1948.

An easier case can be made for unilateral interventions authorized by the Security Council under Chapter VII. After invoking Chapter VII enforcement powers in only two cases (South Africa and Rhodesia) during its first forty-five years of existence, the Security Council has invoked them frequently since 1990. One such case was the authorization of U.S. intervention in Somalia in December 1992.[57] Although the U.S. intervention was basically motivated by humanitarian concerns, the presence of a refugee problem did play some part in UN consideration of the issue. For example, Security Council Resolution 814 (March 1993), took note of the large numbers of refugees displaced by the conflict and of "the difficulties caused to [neighboring countries] due to the presence of refugees in their territories," calling for their repatriation as part of the UN operation.[58]

The importance of Somalia as a precedent lies, however, primarily in two other aspects of the UN intervention. This was "the first time the organization

---

54. Fernando Teson, *Humanitarian Intervention: An Inquiry into Law and Morality* (Dobbs Ferry, N.Y.: Transnational Publishers), pp. 187–188; Weiner, "Introduction: Security, Stability, and International Migration," p. 24.
55. Schorn, *United Nations Interventions*, p. 50.
56. Weiner, "Introduction: Security, Stability, and International Migration," p. 24.
57. UN Doc S/RES/794, December 3, 1992.
58. UN Doc S/RES/814, March 26, 1993; see also Samuel M. Makinda, *Seeking Peace from Chaos: Humanitarian Intervention in Somalia* (Boulder, Colo.: Lynne Rienner, 1993), p. 67: "Somalia as a *state* did not pose a direct security threat to its neighbors, but its political instability and the high number of refugees emanating from it had destabilizing consequences in the region."

has intervened in the domestic affairs of a member state when that state has not presented a military threat to its neighbors."[59] Unlike Iraq in 1991 and Haiti in 1994, the Security Council did not invoke trans-border refugee flows to justify international action. Rather, Security Council Resolution 751 (April 24, 1993) stated that it was "the magnitude of the human suffering" in Somalia which constituted a threat to international peace and security. Second, intervention took place without the "consent" of the target state, on grounds that there was no effective government in Somalia to give or withhold such consent. Both of these conditions are likely to be applicable to refugee-generating crises in the future.

A second case of UN-authorized unilateral intervention, that of the United States in Haiti in September 1994, clearly involved refugees as a major factor. Two UN Resolutions noted the mass displacements of the Haitian population brought about by the behavior of the military regime, called attention to the burden this imposed on states in the area, and accordingly defined the situation as a threat to international peace and security calling for action under Chapter VII.[60] The U.S. government at this point was impelled to push for a quick resolution to the situation, in part because of the continuing embarrassment and political difficulties of dealing with Haitian refugees and would-be refugees. In his public address on the eve of intervention, President Clinton stressed the need "to secure our borders and preserve stability in our hemisphere," adding more specifically:

We have a particular interest in stopping brutality when it occurs so close to our shores. . . . As long as Cedras rules, Haitians will continue to seek sanctuary in our nation. This year, in less than two months, more than 21,000 Haitians were rescued at sea by our Coast Guard and Navy. Today more than 14,000 refugees are living at our naval base in Guantanamo. The American people have already spent $177 million to support them.[61]

A third recent case of UN-authorized unilateral intervention involved the French armed intervention in Rwanda in mid-1994 to secure a safe zone inside Rwanda for humanitarian purposes. While there was considerable skepticism about the true motivations of the proposed French intervention, particularly

---

59. Ibid., p. 61.
60. UN Doc. S/RES/841, June 16, 1993, imposed a mandatory trade embargo; S/RES/940, July 31, 1994, authorized U.S. intervention.
61. United States, The White House, Office of the Press Secretary, *Selected Remarks Prepared for Delivery by President William Jefferson Clinton on U.S. Policy toward Haiti*, September 15, 1994 (Internet).

since France had supported a regime in Kigali that had carried out massive human rights violations, no other major power had sufficient political or economic interest in this small central African country to act on its own. Thus the Security Council, in Resolution 929 (June 22, 1994), accepted the French offer to intervene on the grounds that "the magnitude of the humanitarian crisis in Rwanda constitutes a threat to security in the region." The mandate given to the French force was "to contribute to the security and protection of displaced persons, refugees and civilians at risk." The French force (Operation Turquoise) operated under Chapter VII and was authorized to use "all necessary means to achieve the humanitarian objectives."

A third category, armed interventions that are multilateral, should be less problematic than unilateral interventions. One such intervention began in late 1990, when the Economic Community of West African States (ECOWAS), with predominately Nigerian participation, undertook a limited intervention in Liberia to try to restore order in the midst of civil war. Continued fighting threatened security in the region, both through creation of a huge refugee outflow into neighboring countries ill-equipped to handle such influxes, and through the risk of a direct spillover of fighting. In late 1992, the UN Security Council imposed an embargo on arms sales to the contending Liberian forces and supported ECOWAS's efforts to enforce a ceasefire.[62] In 1996, four years later, the failure of ECOMOG troops to prevent renewed factional fighting and looting in Liberia's capital, Monrovia, caused international disillusionment with regional peacekeeping efforts to control inter-ethnic conflicts.

The most explicit and far-reaching precedent linking UN enforcement action under Chapter VII with prevention of a refugee crisis was Resolution 688 (April 5, 1991), on Iraqi Kurdistan. Following the end of the Gulf War, Iraqi suppression of widespread revolt in northern Kurdish areas created fears that the entire Kurdish population would be uprooted, a particularly grave prospect for neighboring Turkey, with its own Kurdish minority unrest. Accordingly, the Security Council noted that it was "gravely concerned by the repression of the Iraqi civilian population in many parts of Iraq, including most recently in Kurdish populated areas, which led to a massive flow of refugees towards and across international frontiers and to cross-border incursions, which threaten international peace and security."[63] International forces were deployed to Kurd-

---

62. David Wippman, "Enforcing the Peace: ECOWAS and the Liberian Civil War," in Lori Fisler Damrosch, ed., *Enforcing Restraint: Collective Intervention in Internal Conflicts* (New York: Council on Foreign Relations Press, 1993), pp. 157–203.
63. UN Doc. S/RES/688, April 5, 1991.

ish areas to protect the population; Iraqi forces were (under pressure) withdrawn from the same areas; and a *de facto* autonomous Kurdish area was established that allowed Kurdish refugees to return, at least, to safe havens in Iraqi Kurdish (not Turkish) territory.

It has been pointed out that this precedent was only possible in the aftermath of Iraq's military defeat; that the resolution attracted significant opposition (ten votes in favor, three opposed, and two abstentions including that of one permanent member, China); that there has been no international commitment to finding a political solution to the Kurds' plight; and that there has been unilateral Turkish intervention in Iraqi Kurdistan during the period of UN operations there.[64] Nevertheless, the fact remained that:

A precedent had been set . . . for military intervention in the domestic affairs of a state for the purposes of protecting a minority population from the repression of its own government. . . . A new option to the traditional three solutions for refugees . . . had been created, that is, preventing the refugees from crossing an international border in the first place by "humanitarian intervention," creating safe havens protected by foreign military forces within the national homeland of the refugees.[65]

Finally, there are various forms of non-military or "soft" intervention that are considered legitimate even without authorization under Chapter VII of the UN Charter. The fact that the UNHCR and other agencies now deal routinely both with countries that produce refugees and with situations involving internal displacement demonstrates an assumption that some forms of intervention are always permissible. Even in cases when Chapter VII could be invoked, it is usually preferable to proceed by less forcible methods if possible. For example, the United Nations Transitional Authority in Cambodia (UNTAC), while working under a peacekeeping mandate based in theory on the consent of all parties, exercised vast authority in implementing a peaceful settlement to that country's long civil war, including overseeing the successful repatriation of most of the refugees generated by that war and restoring their basic rights. The Security Council does not face an "all or nothing" choice between full-scale military intervention or doing nothing at all. Robert Pastor has suggested a decision-making calculus based on a table of "Threats, Injuries, and Options for the International Community." The table shows threats along one dimen-

64. Damrosch, "Changing Conceptions of Intervention," p. 103; Roberts, "Humanitarian War," pp. 438–439; N.D. White, *Keeping the Peace: The United Nations and the Maintenance of International Peace and Security* (Manchester, U.K.: Manchester University Press, 1992), pp. 46–47.
65. Adelman, "The Ethics of Humanitarian Intervention," p. 62.

sion, from "Aggression," through environmental degradation and refugee outflows, to "Economic Development and Social Justice" issues. The options range from collective intervention through peacekeeping, economic sanctions, and verbal condemnation to total inaction.[66]

Most UN activities related to refugees are soft interventions, and their scope is being expanded continually. The UN resolution establishing the Department of Humanitarian Affairs allows humanitarian aid to be provided with "the consent of the affected country," rather than at its request as was the case in the past.[67] In recent years, UNHCR has adopted a more active approach that has led to increased involvement in countries of origin, collaboration with a wide range of actors from the political and development arenas, and innovative practices intended to ease the shipment of humanitarian relief and shield civilians against military attacks. The objectives are to avert the onset of conditions that might force people to seek safety elsewhere, and to prepare for the repatriation and reintegration of previously uprooted populations. Recent innovations have included "cross-border, cross-mandate preventive zones" in which the UNHCR and other UN agencies divide the work along geographic lines, with one agency assisting all of the uprooted people in a given area, thus circumventing some of the issues and limitations raised by borders.

These measures have been complemented by a growing range of activities designed to strengthen the security of people within their homelands. Concepts such as "corridors of tranquility," "zones of peace," "humanitarian ceasefires," and "safe havens" have been developed within the context of traditional peacekeeping, often as a form of intervention on behalf of refugees. There is increased recognition of the importance of establishing an early international presence of UN and non-governmental organization (NGO) relief workers to permit international monitoring of the treatment of people, in-country protection, and confidence-building among warring factions. Positive results of early UNHCR presence have been achieved in places like Tajikistan. Often, however, the results of such efforts have been disappointing. For example, in the early stages of the UNHCR operation in former Yugoslavia, it was felt that by establishing a strong presence in the region, and by providing assistance to civilians caught in the crossfire of conflict, it would be possible to avert population displacements and limit the scale of the refugee problem. In reality,

---

66. Robert Pastor, "Forward to the Beginning: Widening the Scope for Global Collective Action," in Reed and Kaysen, *Emerging Norms*, pp. 139–141; see also Damrosch, "Changing Conceptions of Intervention," p. 91.
67. UN Doc. A/RES/46-182, December 19, 1991.

however, despite enormous investment,[68] the strategy of preventive protection was undermined by the intensity of the conflict and the ruthlessness with which the policy of ethnic cleansing was pursued.[69] Similarly, the expulsion of NGOs from Rwanda in late 1995 and the harassment of NGOs in Burundi in 1996 illustrate the vulnerability of humanitarian actors in civil war situations.

Most of these innovative measures were hastily formulated to respond to immediate and unanticipated needs, and have not been derived from any clearly defined strategy.[70] International action to prevent refugee problems continues to be hampered by the unwillingness of major governments to commit resources to engage in large-scale operations in the midst of internal conflicts, by the limited capacity of international organizations to undertake tasks they have been asked to assume, and by a lack of consensus regarding the protection of civilians in countries affected by armed conflict and the collapse of state authority.

Another indication of greater international attention and action regarding refugee movements has been the proliferation of regional conferences and meetings designed to stem refugee flows or promote the repatriation of refugees. In Europe over fifteen groups meet regularly to deal with migration issues, and in 1991 over 100 meetings took place on asylum issues alone.[71] The international conferences on the Comprehensive Plan of Action (CPA) on refugees from Vietnam, held under UN auspices in 1979 and 1989, and on the ending of the CPA in 1996, were important as precedents in pressuring the country of origin to cooperate in a solution to the problem, ultimately including repatriation with international verification of non-prosecution and fair treatment. Other regional conferences have been held on refugees in Southern Africa

---

68. At the height of the conflict in the former Yugoslavia, UNHCR had invested one-quarter of its staff and one-third of its budget in this operation.

69. UNHCR, *State of the World's Refugees: In Search of Solutions*, p. 50. However, according to one UNHCR official, in the later stages of the conflict in Bosnia-Herzegovina, an important deterrent to the most blatant forms of human rights abuses was the fear on the part of some people that such actions might make them liable to future indictment by the War Crimes Tribunal in the former Yugoslavia. Presentation by Karen Abu Zayed, "The Multiple Facets of Protecting and Assisting Refugees and Displaced Persons in Former Yugoslavia," at international conference, *Geneva and the Challenge of Humanitarian Action of the 1990s*, Geneva, February 15, 1996.

70. UNHCR emphasis on prevention and proactive measures has been criticized by human rights and refugee advocacy groups, who contend that such policies directly serve the interests of states, many of whom appear to have concluded that the easiest way of resolving the global refugee problem is simply to make sure that displaced populations are obliged to remain in their own country. Consequently, there is debate about the extent to which prevention is tantamount to "containment" and denial of asylum.

71. Rogers and Copeland, *Forced Migration*, pp. 109–111.

(SARRED, 1988), and Central America (CIREFCA, 1989).[72] More recent collaborative and multilateral endeavors include the 1996 Bosnian repatriation process and the May 1996 Conference on Displacement in the Commonwealth of Independent States (CIS), organized jointly by UNHCR, the International Organization for Migration (IOM), and the Organization for Security and Cooperation in Europe (OSCE). The objective of such efforts is to resolve refugee problems on a regional basis by strengthening the willingness and capacity of states to cooperate in managing population flows.

There have also been numerous unilateral initiatives by governments attempting to forestall threatened mass migrations. U.S. relations with Mexico and Cuba, as well as Haiti, have been dominated by such issues in recent years, and it has been a factor with other countries in the western hemisphere. Recently, the United States dispatched emergency food shipments to North Korea to avert famine, instability, and mass migration to South Korea. Germany has worked consistently to head off influxes from central and eastern Europe, often through infusions of aid and investment designed to reduce emigration pressures. Italy has offered incentives to Albania in order to prevent future waves of refugees on its doorstep. French fears of a mass outflow from Algeria has greatly affected in its relations with North Africa. Threats and pressures related to refugee outflows have dominated inter-state relations among several African governments as well as bilateral relations between India and Bangladesh, between Bangladesh and Myanmar (Burma), and between Nepal and Bhutan, to mention just a few cases.[73]

Conclusion

We have argued that refugee flows across national borders impose increasing burdens and threats on countries of refuge; that customary international law provides a basis for international action to prevent such flows; that as a threat to peace and security, refugee flows also legitimize UN enforcement action under Chapter VII of the Charter; and that intervention in military and non-military forms is becoming a norm, albeit haltingly, in state declaration and practice. The large-scale movement of people across national borders, under

---

72. Ibid., pp. 113–116; Drüke, *Preventive Action*, pp. 206–207, 218–219.
73. See Loescher, *Refugee Movements and International Security*, pp. 27, 46; Weiner, "Introduction: Security, Stability, and International Migration," pp. 22–24; Zimmerman testimony.

duress, internationalizes what might otherwise be purely domestic issues related to the causes of that movement.[74]

The international community is in the process of establishing the principle that policies of forced expulsion are unacceptable, and developing pressures and sanctions against such policies. Refugee movements are perhaps the clearest example of the claim that "once the consequences of a policy enacted for domestic purposes become external, the policy itself is open to international comment and action, with proclamations of 'sovereign rights' being no defence against outside interference."[75] As summarized in the words of Myron Weiner, "a country that forces its citizens to leave or creates conditions which induce them to leave has internationalized its internal actions. . . . If a people violate the boundaries of a neighboring country, then they and their government should expect others to intervene in their internal affairs."[76]

The case for intervention has been presented here without the general humanitarian arguments that have been widely debated elsewhere. In practice, of course, the issues are intertwined. For example, Stanley Hoffmann argues that "the norm of the formal equality of states . . . can legitimately be dented when a state seriously violates such principles as the right to self-determination, to democratic government, to life, etc., or behaves at home in a way that creates international disorder."[77] We have endeavored here to enlarge the dent based on the second part of this statement, that is, on grounds that the creation of refugees is most indisputably a creation of "international disorder." The combination of the two parts of Hoffmann's argument—the humanitarian concerns and the impact of disorder on others—synergistically produces a stronger case for intervention in any particular historical case.[78]

This connection is not simply an accidental one in which humanitarian intervention is fortuitously justified by the presence of refugees. The link is organic, in that "refugees are human rights violations made visible," in the words of a former U.S. Coordinator of Refugee Affairs.[79] Refugees serve as an

---

74. Similar conclusions are reached by Drüke, *Preventive Action;* see especially pp. 220–221.
75. John Chipman, "The Future of Strategic Studies: Beyond Even Grand Strategy," *Survival,* Vol. 34, No. 1 (Spring 1992), p. 112.
76. Weiner, "Introduction: Security, Stability, and International Migration," pp. 25, 26.
77. Hoffmann, "Sovereignty and the Ethics of Intervention."
78. See similar arguments in Adelman, "The Ethics of Humanitarian Intervention"; and Richard N. Haass, *Intervention: The Use of American Military Force in the Post–Cold War World* (Washington, D.C.: Carnegie Endowment for International Peace, 1994), p. 132.
79. Jonathan Moore, "Refugees and Foreign Policy: Immediate Needs and Durable Solutions," Lecture at John F. Kennedy School, Harvard University, April 6, 1987, quoted in Drüke, *Preventive Action,* p. 217.

index of internal disorder and as *prima facie* evidence of the violation of human rights and humanitarian standards. No other issue, perhaps, provides such a clear and unassailable link between humanitarian concerns and legitimate international security issues. While this link may in some cases provide justification for international action with positive humanitarian results where such justification might not otherwise exist, it may also work in the other direction to contain unwarranted interference that is argued for on supposed humanitarian grounds. Overextension can be avoided, as Howard Adelman argues, "if it is clear that such actions are only warranted when there is a threat to international peace and security as evidenced by the mass flight of inhabitants attempting to cross international borders."[80]

This suggests the necessity of establishing a framework of general principles to guide the international community in deciding when a domestic situation, because of its potential to involve other states, warrants action by the Security Council or by regional organizations. The flight of refugees is perhaps the most clear-cut expression of this potential, and is an increasingly critical global problem by any measure. Moreover, the global refugee problem is not going to disappear soon; in fact, it is assuming new dimensions that require new and different approaches. Charity is insufficient to deal with today's refugee crisis.

Refugee problems are essentially born out of political conflict, and they directly engage the interests of states all over the world. More active intervention by the international community is in the long-term interest of all governments; stability and growth depend generally on controlling disruptive forced migrations. The time is right for a new, comprehensive, and humane approach.

---

80. Adelman, "The Ethics of Humanitarian Intervention," p. 85.

Military Responses to Refugee Disasters

Barry R. Posen

$\mathbf{T}$he problem of refugees, both those who have crossed recognized international borders, and those "internally displaced" who have not, has recently achieved greater policy prominence in the developed world.[1] This new concern has also prompted a greater inclination to consider and apply military remedies to specific refugee problems. Policy makers, analysts, pundits, and activists now perceive vastly diminished constraints on the exercise of military power in the service of "good," compared to their views during the Cold War. The great preponderance of global power now enjoyed by the west due to the collapse of the Soviet Union, and the greatly increased capability of air power demonstrated in Operation Desert Storm, have both contributed to this tendency. This optimism is misplaced; I argue below that the application of military power to this set of problems will often prove politically and militarily difficult.

This essay first briefly reviews the political and military causes of refugee flows. (The essay is not concerned with economic sources of migration.) These are genocide/politicide, ethnic cleansing, harsh occupation or a repressive indigenous regime, the dangerous environment created by warfare, and the deterioration of local economies that often is caused by warfare. Then, the alternative military remedies to these causes are developed, and their general strengths and weaknesses are outlined. These remedies are aerial bombing, large safe zones, circumscribed safe havens, peace enforcement, and general war against the state or group deemed to be the principal cause of trouble.

Barry R. Posen is Professor of Political Science at MIT and a member of its Defense and Arms Control Studies Program. He is the author of Inadvertent Escalation *(Cornell University Press, 1991) and* The Sources of Military Doctrine *(Cornell University Press, 1984).*

A version of this essay will appear in *Migration and Refugees: U.S. and German Policies Toward Countries of Origin* (Berghahn Books, forthcoming in 1996). The Carnegie Corporation of New York provided support for this research. The MacArthur MIT/Harvard Joint Program on Transnational Security Issues sponsored a seminar presentation. William Durch, Taylor Seybolt, and Steve Van Evera offered critical comments, and Chikako Ueki was my research assistant. Thanks to all.

1. For a comprehensive introduction to the problem, see Myron Weiner, *The Global Migration Crisis: Challenge to States and to Human Rights* (New York: Harper Collins, 1995). See also United Nations High Commissioner for Refugees (UNHCR), *The State of the World's Refugees, In Search of Solutions* (Oxford: Oxford University Press, 1995); UNHCR, *The State of the World's Refugees, The Challenge of Protection* (New York: Penguin, 1993); Gil Loescher, *Refugee Movements and International Security*, Adelphi Paper 268 (London: International Institute for Strategic Studies [IISS], 1992).

International Security, Vol. 21, No. 1 (Summer 1996), pp. 72–111
© 1996 by the President and Fellows of Harvard College and the Massachusetts Institute of Technology.

The analysis is conducted at both a general deductive level and a specific operational level. The distinction between deterrent and coercive strategies is employed to illuminate the general difficulties of humanitarian military intervention. Broadly I conclude that these operations will more often take the form of compellence than deterrence. Because compellence is the more difficult political-military enterprise, advocates of these humanitarian operations should understand that success will require the commitment of substantial resources, perhaps for quite a long time. To coerce successfully, it is generally necessary to demonstrate the capability not merely to hurt, but to defeat the adversary.

The main discussion then assesses the practical applicability of the specific remedies to the specific causes. I discuss four of the five remedies in detail. I omit a detailed discussion of general war because plenty has been written on the subject. I examine each remedy in detail in terms of the specific political, geographical, and military factors that will affect the feasibility of its implementation. I briefly discuss how certain remedies may be combined. Finally I discuss whether and how each remedy might be applied to the causes of refugee flows I have identified. The complexity of the problem resists broad conclusions but most plausible remedies are serious military operations that require substantial, diverse capabilities. If "rescuers" cannot, in fact, muster such capabilities and the will to use them, it is improbable that scattered air attacks and diffuse threats will convince the assailant—the party whose actions precipitated the refugee flight—to cease its depredations.

The Causes of Mass Displacement

I identify five general political-military causes of mass displacement: genocide/politicide; ethnic cleansing; occupation; collateral damage; and primitive military logistics.

Genocide is employed here in the conventional sense of the word: a human community based on ethnic, national, or religious ties is singled out for extermination.[2] In modern times the Armenians and the Jews are the best-known victims. More recently the killings of the Tutsi people in Rwanda appear to be

---

2. Article 2 of the genocide treaty offers such a broad definition that virtually any political violence directed against a "national, ethnical, racial or religious group" qualifies as genocide. While the ethical intent is laudable, it is unlikely that most states will act according to such an expansive definition.

genocide. *Politicide* means the attempt to destroy a political idea, usually by destroying many if not all of those who hold that idea, or at least enough of them to terrorize others into abandoning it. The Khmer Rouge murdered hundreds of thousands to wipe out any positive attitudes towards a western style economy or society.

What starts as politicide often evolves into genocide. Saddam Hussein and the Iraqi Ba'ath party have attempted to wipe out the idea of Kurdish independence among Iraqi Kurds. In doing so they have tried to find and kill anybody who believes in this idea. Though it does not seem true that there was a policy to kill or eject all Iraqi Kurds, the task of "politicide" has been interpreted expansively by Iraqi security forces, producing consequences for the Kurdish population indistinguishable from deliberate genocide. This seems to be a common outcome where ethnic, national, or religious groups seek political autonomy or secession from governments determined to resist.

Ethnic cleansing is a term that has been propelled into political discourse by the wars of Yugoslavia's disintegration. I employ it for deliberate actions to induce populations to leave their homes. Several methods may be employed. Organized military or para-military forces or even mobs terrorize the target population, threatening it with harm or death, to induce out-migration. Considerable killing will occur, though the scale required to terrify people into departure may not be great.[3] Forcible deportation may be organized, in which people are escorted out of an area at gun point. Finally, deliberate starvation can be a tool of deportation. Food can be expropriated from a population, and farms burned, while the import of relief supplies is blocked. People leave in search of food. This has apparently been practiced in Africa.[4]

Yugoslavia is not the only place ethnic cleansing has occurred. Indian officials suspected Pakistan of ethnic cleansing when millions of Hindus fled East Pakistan (now Bangladesh) in 1971.[5] The "international community" has

---

3. As in the analysis of war, where one finds distinctions between light, medium, and heavy casualties, the analysis of political killing of unarmed civilians requires rough distinctions in the scale of death. Even in a world where civilian deaths have been measured in the hundreds of thousands, the killing of tens of thousands or even thousands may be sufficient to induce mass flight.

4. Loescher, *Refugee Movements and International Security*, pp. 52–53.

5. Richard Sisson and Leo E. Rose, *War and Secession: Pakistan, India and the Creation of Bangladesh* (Berkeley: University of California Press, 1990), pp. 147–148. The initial flow of refugees from the Pakistani crackdown consisted of Bengali Muslims, but the composition quickly shifted to 80 percent Hindu. See also Robert Jackson, *South Asian Crisis: India, Pakistan and Bangla Desh: A Political and Historical Analysis of the 1971 War* (New York: Praeger, 1975), pp. 75–76, who concurs with the suspicions of Indian officials. By June nearly seven million refugees had reached India.

even cooperated in the practice from time to time. Large-scale expulsions of Greeks from Turkey and Turks from Greece in 1923–26 were precipitated by the Greek-Turkish war.[6] Once the horrors of the initially unregulated population exchange became clear to the great powers, the League of Nations intervened to help manage the transfers. Similarly, there was a lot of ethnic cleansing in eastern Europe at the end of the First and Second World Wars. Many Germans were expelled from their homes; these expulsions were conducted in a quite inhumane fashion, until international agencies stepped in to manage them.[7] Those few Jews who survived the Nazi death camps were in some cases the object of violence by local populations.

Under some circumstances, warfare may involve competitive ethnic cleansing, which may deteriorate into competitive terrorism, murder, and even genocide. The parties to a war may be victims one day, and assailants the next; or victims in one place and assailants in another. In the wars of Yugoslavia's disintegration, Croats were victims of Serb cleansing and murder; they were assailants against and killers of Muslims; and they were finally assailants against Serbs. In the 1949 partition of India, Muslims and Hindus were both victims and agents of ethnic cleansing and of murder.

Fear of occupation is a third reason why populations leave their place of residence in large numbers. At worst, people may fear that the occupier will launch a genocide; why wait? Or people may fear that the occupier will try to drive them out, and that this will prove violent. Again, why wait? Even if genocide/politicide or violent expulsion are not the assailant's war aims, occupations are never pleasant. The native population has good reason to fear casual brutality, the arbitrariness of martial law, immediate expropriation of property, and systematic long-term economic exploitation. Presumably, the Hutu who recently fled Rwanda feared a "counter-genocide," and still do. Many of the Iraqi Kurds who fled to the Turkish border may simply have feared the likely brutality of Iraqi authorities. Many Afghan refugees who fled

---

6. Michael R. Marrus, *The Unwanted: European Refugees in the Twentieth Century* (New York: Oxford University Press, 1985), pp. 97–106.
7. See Alfred M. de Zayas, *Nemesis at Potsdam, The Anglo-Americans and the Expulsion of the Germans* (London: Routledge and Kegan Paul, 1977): "Transports into the Western zones in the summers of 1946 and 1947 were relatively organized and gave rise to considerably fewer casualties," p. 104. Elsewhere he notes that "if there had been no 'organized transfers' and if all the Germans had been expelled in the brutal manner that characterized the 1945 expulsions, the loss of life attributable to the flight and expulsion would not have been 2 million but perhaps 3 million or even more," p. 124. See also Alfred M. de Zayas, *A Terrible Revenge* (New York: St. Martin's, 1994), pp. 113–116.

to Pakistan following the Soviet invasion departed due to such fears. There are variants of this cause: Where the area is already occupied, and the occupation proves brutal, the local population may depart simply because it does not wish to be victimized. This occurred in Afghanistan. It is also possible for an indigenous regime to prove so repressive that many people feel that they must leave, particularly those identified with alternative political movements. The U.S. government judged that roughly a third of the people who fled Haiti on boats in 1994 could be political refugees.[8]

A dangerous environment is the fourth reason why populations leave their homes. People often simply flee the area of fighting, because the firepower employed does not easily discriminate between combatants and non-combatants. People seem to have moved back and forth in Lebanon depending on the location of the fighting. Documentary films from World War II and a host of subsequent wars illustrate the phenomenon. Most of the Chechen population that did not intend to fight left the city of Grozny before the Russians turned up. Whether or not these populations return depends upon a host of factors. If the territory is lost to an enemy, they are unlikely to go back. It is also unlikely that the former inhabitants will return to an area where the front has stabilized.[9]

The widespread employment of land mines adds a variant to this cause. Unlike battles, which are often short, or battle lines, which often move, land mines, once emplaced, stay roughly where they are. (Depending on soil type, they may move locally as a consequence of water and wind.) Because they are cheap, and in many ways, effective,[10] very large numbers have been deployed in places like Afghanistan, Angola, Cambodia, Iraq, and Laos.[11] Often, they were distributed deliberately to make it difficult for rural populations to earn a livelihood from the land. Thus, the mines were agents of "ethnic cleansing,"

---

8. Terry Atlas, "Haiti Tide May Force U.S. Hand," *Chicago Tribune,* July 4, 1994, p. 1.
9. The opposite can happen: apparently during Desert Storm civilians occasionally moved toward the sights and sounds of battle, because that was the best way to find the coalition troops, who might be prevailed upon for protection or sustenance.
10. In his memoir of service in Vietnam, Tobias Wolff writes, "You could never have too many mines. Fifty thousand wouldn't have been too many for me. Given the chance, I'd have lived smack in the middle of a minefield twenty miles wide." Tobias Wolff, *In Pharoah's Army: Memories of the Lost War* (New York: Vintage, 1994), p. 17.
11. Paul Davies and Nick Dunlop, *War of the Mines* (London: Pluto Press, 1994); see esp. Rae McGrath, "Landmines—The Global Problem," chapter 7, p. 126; and "The Reality of the Present Use of Mines by Military Forces," Appendix 3. "In some areas virtually all mountain grazing land was remotely mined and the whole agricultural infrastructure brought to a halt by the widespread mining," p. 156.

encouraging people to leave an area and, even after the fighting ceases, discouraging them from returning home.

The final cause of mass displacement might be termed *primitive logistics*. In many parts of the world, armed forces have little or no regular supply system. The acquisition of arms and munitions is the first priority for primitive armies. Food, medicine, and even vehicles may be expropriated by the troops in the field. As Machiavelli said, "iron will always find bread." During the Thirty Years War, Germany was devastated by logistics systems of this kind. It was said that one had to become a soldier to avoid starvation.

Primitive armies may steal so much food and livestock from an agricultural or pastoral population that these people cannot survive to plant and harvest a new crop, or they have no animals to manage. Alternatively, expropriation may so reduce the margin of subsistence that the arrival of a drought, on top of war, tips the entire population into an irremediable disaster. These people then move in search of food.

Of late, Africa seems to be the most common location of the primitive logistics problem. Somalia is probably the textbook case, featuring the extreme of clan gunmen first despoiling their countrymen, and then subsisting off the theft of international aid dispatched to ameliorate their suffering.

"Inadvertent excessive expropriation" may accompany deliberate scorched-earth policies designed to punish or evict specific populations, and it may be true that in most places it is deliberate policies that dominate. Nevertheless, the logistical problem should be viewed as analytically distinct.

Military Remedies

Five distinct potential military remedies to the causes of displacement are suggested by limited practical experience or deduction. All remedies are not appropriate for all causes, and some only have a chance of working under a very narrow range of circumstances.

Punishment of the assailant is very popular among those looking for cheap solutions. Rescuers seeking to help the victimized population should bomb the assailant's homeland to destroy what it values, such as its own population, its economic infrastructure, or its leaders. This punishment would continue until the refugee-producing behavior ceased.

The creation of a *"safe zone"* that protects the victim population where it normally lives is a second option. This is essentially the "Provide Comfort" model, employed with considerable success to protect Iraq's Kurds from the revenge of Saddam Hussein and the Ba'ath Party. The area where the prospective victims live is cordoned off from the assailant, who is denied access. In Iraq this was achieved through the threat to unleash coalition air power against any Iraqi forces, air or ground, that trespassed onto the declared safe zone.[12]

A third option is the creation of circumscribed *"safe havens"* where the displaced can seek protection and sustenance close to their homes, but not in them. Their normal life is essentially destroyed by the assailant. This was attempted most explicitly in Bosnia, where six towns were so designated. Informally this expedient was employed to some extent in the UN Congo operation (ONUC), UN operations in Lebanon (UNIFIL), and in the Restore Hope operation in Somalia.[13] Safe havens, called "Open Relief Centers," have been created without direct military protection in Sri Lanka, and reportedly have been respected by both sides in the Tamil secessionist war.[14] This seems to be the only instance of a successful undefended safe haven.

A fourth option is the imposition of some kind of *"enforced truce"* in the zone of conflict. Outsiders effectively seize some or all of the attributes of sovereignty. Minimally, they act as sheriff. The victimized population is protected from the assailant, but assailants are also protected from counter-attack by victims. The assailant/victim distinction may not be relevant as where, for example, there is mutually genocidal warfare. The enforced truce option was, to some extent, attempted in Somalia. Arguably, it was also what the UN really did in the Congo.[15]

The final military option is an *offensive war* to destroy the military power of the assailant, perhaps even to change the regime. Cold War politics made it inexpedient for observers to acknowledge that it was the Vietnamese invasion of Cambodia that ended the "killing fields." Vietnam undoubtedly invaded for its own reasons, but this was a decisive way to stop the killing. Similarly, the

---

12. A variant on this solution would be to arm the victims so extensively that they could repel the side whose actions had precipitated or were about to precipitate mass flight. The practical question is whether or not military assistance can be delivered quickly enough to affect the actions that produce refugees. Generally, the provision of weapons alone is unlikely to prove an expeditious solution to refugee problems, since the victims are probably in trouble because their military organization is weak or non-existent. Weapons alone do not an army make.

13. William J. Durch, ed., *The Evolution of UN Peacekeeping* (New York: St. Martin's Press for the Stimson Center, 1993), pp. 327, 333, on the first eleven months of the UN effort in the Congo. On Lebanon, see Mona Ghali, "United Nations Interim Force in Lebanon," ibid., pp. 199–200. See also United Nations, *The Blue Helmets*, 2d ed. (New York: United Nations, 1990); on ONUC see pp. 226–229 and on UNIFIL pp. 143–146.

14. *The State of the World's Refugees 1995* (Oxford: Oxford University Press, 1995), pp. 128–129.

15. William J. Durch, "The UN Operation in the Congo," in Durch, *Evolution of UN Peacekeeping*, pp. 315–352. Special Representative Dayal called it "massive intervention in the guise of non-intervention," p. 346.

defeat and expulsion of the Hutu-dominated Rwandan Army by the Rwandan Patriotic Front (RPF) decisively ended the killing of Tutsi. The Pakistani repression in East Pakistan (Bengal), which produced the flight of some ten million refugees to India, was ended by the December 1971 Indo-Pakistani War. Indeed, India's firm stand against Pakistan arose in part from its unwillingness to provide permanent homes for these ten million refugees, or to accept even more.[16] The bizarre record of Nazi Germany's energetic pursuit of the genocide against the Jews and the Gypsies, in the face of military defeats on every front and military problems that would have benefited at least somewhat from the resources diverted to the horror, suggests that only complete conquest could have ended the Nazi crime. Because this remedy is fairly straightforward, it will *not* be subjected to systematic analysis below. The examples noted above suggest the circumstances under which invasion will prove the only feasible solution.

The Strategic Context

Those contemplating the use of military force for humanitarian purposes should think of themselves as planning a major foreign policy initiative that will likely end in war. The threat or use of force for humanitarian purposes is as much an act of strategy as is the threat or use of force to achieve geostrategic goals. We should apply the same analytic tools. Advocates should be interested in estimating the political and military difficulties of the project they are about to undertake. Some political goals are easier to achieve with military power than others. Some military projects are easier than others. In subsequent sections I consider in detail the practical problem of applying specific military remedies to specific causes of refugee flows. Here I develop a framework to analyze the political context.

DETERRENCE OR COMPELLENCE

The most important question about any humanitarian intervention is whether it is fundamentally an act of deterrence or compellence. Each of the military

---

16. Sumit Ganguly, *The Origins of War in South Asia: Indo-Pakistani Conflicts Since 1947* (Boulder, Colo.: Westview, 1986), pp. 118–119, 122–123. See also Sisson and Rose, *War and Secession*, pp. 148; 177–178. The Indians, however, refused to cooperate with any UN initiatives to encourage voluntary repatriation of refugees to East Pakistan. The only solution to the refugee problem acceptable to India was the political restoration of the Awami League to power in East Pakistan, which would for all intents and purposes have split Pakistan in two, a great geopolitical victory for India. Thus, it would not be accurate to say that the refugee problem caused the 1971 war; it was rather the occasion for it. Sisson and Rose, pp. 188–191. See also Jackson, *South Asian Crisis*, pp. 66–69.

options discussed above has a passive and an active face. Clearly, rescuers would prefer to dissuade assailants from initiating actions that produce refugees. Most cases, however, involve an assailant that has already initiated its depredations; outsiders demand that the actions cease, and indeed that they be reversed. The first case corresponds roughly to the strategist's concept of deterrence, the second to compellence. Compellence is generally considered to be more difficult than deterrence. Humanitarian operations will more often partake of compellence than deterrence.[17] However, advocates of these operations often seem to imagine they are engaged in deterrence, and thus underestimate the difficulties. A second problem is that much of the thinking about deterrence and compellence arose from the problem of employing nuclear threats. The risk of nuclear escalation gives nuclear deterrence a special claim to effectiveness likely to be missing even from relatively unambiguous nonnuclear stand-offs between unitary nation states. Conventional "deterrence" among unitary nation-states has often failed. Refugee-producing crises are likely to be even more problematical than these classical conflicts.

Deterrence is judged less difficult than compellence for four main reasons. First, a dissuasive threat is usually leveled to protect an extant status quo. The willingness of the dissuader to suffer, fight, and die to protect that to which it has a long-standing claim should be clear to the challenger. The challenger should expect that the defender of the status quo cares more about the item in dispute than does the challenger. Second, the challenger has to turn a situation of peace into a situation of war, with all the risks and costs that entails. Given the presumption of a defender with a willingness to fight, the challenger must exchange the certainties of peace for the uncertainties of war. It is a big step. Even if the attacker doubts the "will" of the defender, the very act of starting the fighting often has the quality of triggering the deterrent actor's military threat. In the world of nuclear deterrence this is a very powerful force making for challenger inertia. This works to a lesser extent with conventional strategic relationships. Third, the defender of the status quo has massive credibility stakes; if it does not resist the challenge, this is an invitation to future predation, not only from the original challenger, but from others. Thus the challenger has reason to expect that while its own interest is only in the area in dispute, the defender has many other interests attached to the interest in question. Finally, it is easy to agree on the "stopping point," which is the starting point.

---

17. Thomas Schelling, *Arms and Influence* (New Haven, Conn.: Yale University Press, 1966), pp. 69–79.

Compellence (or coercion) is considered to be more difficult than deterrence (or dissuasion) for reasons that are the mirror image of those above. First, compellence generally tries to get the adversary to change some ongoing behavior in which it has developed some stake. Even the case of trying to get an aggressor to cease its aggression is often viewed by theorists as compellence, since once deterrence has failed, and the attacker has made the painful choice for war, launched an offensive, and had some success, it is now invested in the war. The balance of wills does not clearly favor the "coercer," even in a situation where the coercer is in fact trying to coerce an aggressor into ceasing its aggression. Second, the "peace-war" transition has already been made; fighting is underway. Third, the distribution of "credibility" stakes is more equal. In the case of deterrence, the side defending the status quo has a great deal more to lose than the side challenging it because to concede invites further challenges by the original aggressor *and* by others. The challenger loses its credibility as a bully by failing to carry through with the challenge, but does not necessarily invite predation, since its withdrawal says nothing about its inclination to protect its own core interests. Once war is underway, however, and some territory has changed hands, the object of compellence has its own interest in showing that the application of force, or the threat of escalation, cannot thwart its military power once it has decided to engage. Fourth, no obvious "stopping point" suggests itself. It is a matter for negotiation. The coercer says "stop"; the object asks "where?" The coercer says "here"; the object asks "why not there?"

Rescuers will more often find themselves in the active compellent mode than the deterrent mode, with all the difficulties that entails. The "causes" of mass population displacement, and the actual displacement, will likely be underway before rescuers decide to act. The propensity of any given political conflict to produce refugees is not well understood, because the conflicts themselves are not well understood, either generally, or specifically. Because these events usually do not occur in regions of traditional great power interest, even available information may not reach those who could act upon it. Interested international organizations, non-governmental organizations, journalists, and area-studies scholars may have some information that events are moving in a dangerous direction, but the evidence is often ambiguous. Their access to, or influence over, those who have the capability to act is likely to be limited. Because these crises seem to occur outside of the traditional arenas of great power conflict, the elements of great and middle power intelligence services and foreign offices that follow the areas in question are unlikely to enjoy high priority within their own bureaucracies, and their communications channels to higher authority are likely to be attenuated. Killing of the kind that occurred in Cambodia or Rwanda would not necessarily produce the kind of "signature" that high technology intelligence means would detect. It may take some time for disparate information to assemble into a recognizable pattern for outside observers. (In Rwanda, photos of streams and rivers full of corpses appeared only after many thousands had been killed. In totalitarian Cambodia, information on the politicide did not quickly reach the outside world.) The combination of inadequate understanding and attenuated internal communications channels is exacerbated by the unpredictable pace of these conflicts, and the refugee flows they produce. Violence can escalate very quickly, producing reasons for vast numbers of people suddenly to depart. People can move very quickly, and in large numbers, but it is not easy to know when they will start or how the pace might accelerate. These factors all contribute to the likelihood that rescuers will arrive late and find themselves undertaking compellence rather than deterrence.

It is quite likely that the will of the local party, the assailant, is stronger than that of the outside rescuers, because the stakes for the local party are so much greater. Indeed, outsiders are unlikely to have many classical "vital" interests at stake in these conflicts. Assailants often begin their depredations because of some deeply-held beliefs about the necessity of their actions. These often reflect extreme interpretations of old disputes among communities. Even when the helpless are being executed, the murderers have often convinced themselves that the helpless are a threat. In short, whether the refugees are fleeing because of deliberate murder, deliberate cleansing, or the unintended consequences of more traditional military action, the assailant is likely to care quite a lot about the outcome. It is extremely difficult for the rescuer to convince the assailant that it cares more, particularly when the source of the concern seems to be an erratic and capricious humanitarian impulse, which varies with the extent of international media coverage; the availability of other dramas in the global village; the skin color, culture, or religion of the victims; the question of whether the assailant happens to be a great nuclear power (Russia vs. Chechnya) or a weak local actor (Serbs vs. Bosnian Muslims).

The will of the assailant may vary with its political nature. A useful distinction is between a gangster regime and a mass mobilization polity. Some states are controlled by small bands of thugs who rule largely by terror. They may frighten large numbers of people into leaving the country. Their interest in power is mainly pecuniary, however. If challenged militarily from abroad, they will get no help from their own citizens. Having specialized in internal repression, they have little hope of standing against foreign militaries trained for war. The former governments of Haiti and Panama are good examples of such gangster regimes. Interestingly, even these governments were not easy to coerce, but they were easy to beat militarily.

Much tougher customers would be governments (or political movements) that preside over populations mobilized by religion, ideology, or national, ethnic, or tribal identity. These are also not easy to coerce, and neither are they likely to prove easy to fight. The Bosnian Serbs, the Iraqi Ba'ath (at least the Sunni Arabs), and the Somali clan warlords were not easy to push around. The Bosnian Serbs were only pushed to sign the Dayton accords by the combined military power of Croatia, the Bosnian Croats, the militarily rejuvenated Bosnian Muslims, large-scale NATO airstrikes, and a *diktat* by their patron, Slobodan Milosević. The Somali clans fought both U.S. and other UN troops ferociously, suffering hundreds if not thousands of casualties in the process. U.S. planners did not want to find out how well Iraqi Sunnis would fight for the Ba'ath regime if the coalition actually invaded Iraq. Iraqi Republican Guard units that had suffered intense aerial and ground attack by coalition units nevertheless fought ferociously to defend the regime against the Shi'a and Kurdish revolts.

The political organization of the rescuers is also an important factor in a compellence strategy. A coalition is likely to be less effective than a single interested nation-state.[18] But because many of these events fall outside traditional geostrategic concerns, no single state will take responsibility for finding a solution, so a coalition will be required to undertake the mission. Unlike traditional military coalitions, which are usually held together by shared fear of a particular enemy, this one will need to be held together by altruism. Collective responses even to traditional threats are difficult to organize. This is why Napoleon Bonaparte averred that if he had to make war, he preferred to do so against coalitions. While coalitions may have access to more aggregate military power by virtue of their cooperation, they also need elaborate proce-

---

18. Coalitions do bring some benefits, depending on the circumstances. For example, even weakly committed members of a rescuer coalition are removed as potential alliance partners for the assailant. Thus the western powers tried to keep Russia associated with their effort to end the war in Bosnia, including Russian forces in the NATO-commanded International Force organized to police the military provisions of the Dayton Accords. Similarly, some coalitions are more useful for compellence than others by virtue of their "ready made" quality. NATO is the obvious example. Members already have practiced for coalition warfare. NATO cohesion seems to be a value in itself for its members, which adds an element of traditional security interest to any altruistic enterprise.

dures for deciding on goals, strategies, and the allocation of contributions. The members of any coalition will vary in the extent of their commitment, and this is especially true of coalitions based on altruism.[19] Assailants may retard the performance of the coalition by diplomatic approaches to, or military attacks on, its weakest link, which might simply be the least committed member.[20]

The assailant has greater credibility stakes in the fight than does the "rescuer." The rescuer's national security is usually not at risk in the event of failure. The fact that the United States quickly departed Somalia after a few dozen casualties says little about how it might behave in the event of a challenge to a more traditional security interest. U.S. pusillanimity in Somalia may invite challenges from other bandit leaders to U.S. meddling in their affairs, but it says little about how the United States might act if Iran attacked Saudi Arabia. The local assailant is in a far different situation. If it bows to threats by rescuers, this would invite challenges by local adversaries. This would also provide incentives to its local adversaries to go find an external patron to back up these challenges. Serbs have to worry that backing down in Bosnia will produce challenges by Albanians in Kosovo.

Will is only one part of the coercer's strategy. Capabilities are the other critical factor. The first essential truth is that without the capability to conduct these military operations, the threat to conduct them will have little weight with assailants. The second essential but less obvious truth is that it is not necessarily easy to convince the assailant that the rescuer will bring to bear all the necessary capabilities even if the rescuer possesses them.[21] The precise capabilities that the rescuer will actually muster may turn out to be rather

---

19. The domestic constitutions of the rescuers will also affect the odds of success. Democracies may be easily motivated to consider or even initiate intervention due to their openness to information about terrible events, and their commitment to political principle and humanitarianism. Modern democracies, however, have also schooled their citizens to the basic paradigm of cost and benefit. The statesman's criterion of "vital interest" comes rather easily to the citizenry. The employment of modern military power costs a lot of money, inconveniences many people, and usually costs some lives.

20. The UN is often the vehicle of choice for these projects, which creates additional difficulties. It is often already preoccupied with several analogous problems. The UN decision-making system permits states with little, no, or contradictory interests in a given problem to have a say. The UN peace-keeping system relies on the voluntary contributions of troops, equipment, and money from its members as each contingency arises. Thus, though the UN may be the most politically attractive structure for a humanitarian coalition, it is a slow and unwieldy instrument.

21. Jonathan Shimshoni, *Israel and Conventional Deterrence: Border Warfare from 1953 to 1970* (Ithaca, N.Y.: Cornell University Press, 1988), pp. 5–33, for an analysis of the difference between nuclear and conventional deterrence. His observations are relevant to conventional compellence as well, and I have drawn on them liberally.

different than what it owns. (This problem is exacerbated when the rescuer is a coalition, the combat power of which depends on the sum total of individual contributions plus their ability to cooperate tactically and operationally.) If the Bosnian Serbs had genuinely believed they faced the force that defeated Iraq, they would likely have behaved rather differently than they did early in the Bosnian war. Assailants can gather information about the real extent of the capabilities they face through a series of probing actions. They can find out what the rescuers are willing to bring to the field; they can find out how good these capabilities are in the local tactical situation; and they can find out what kind of risks the rescuers are willing to take in the application of force. They can run all these experiments in comparative safety because they do not fear nuclear escalation. When the rescuers are altruistically motivated liberal democracies, assailants do not even have good reason to fear a sudden spasm of large-scale counter-value conventional bombing, because in most cases it would be politically complicated to explain to the public that the killing of civilians is necessary to prevent the killing of civilians.[22]

Finally, even active and successful demonstration of these capabilities by rescuers does not produce permanent results: repeated probing operations, low-level tests of will and capability, and local attack followed by tactical retreat are to be expected. Again, the missing threat of spasmodic escalation, the possibility of "more pressing business elsewhere" for the rescuer, and the ability of the assailant to innovate tactically during quiet periods, using the data about the rescuers' military capabilities gathered during the last flare-up of fighting, all create incentives for the assailant to try its luck later, particularly if the assailant remains unpersuaded of the rescuer's genuine will to protect the victims over the long haul.

Supporters of military intervention to eliminate the sources of refugee flows need to have some way of gauging the practicability of the projects they have in mind. In general, rescuers will find themselves practicing coercive diplomacy, that is, compellence. Coercive diplomacy is more difficult than deterrent diplomacy. Rescuers will first try to affect the behavior of the assailant with threats of military action. They hope to induce assailant compliance by the threat to punish, or the threat to establish and successfully defend a safe zone, or the threat to successfully defend a safe haven, or the threat to put in enough

---

22. Most military operations run some risk of creating events that may erode the support of the rescuer's own population. Even modern precision-guided munitions may kill civilians, either because targets have been mistakenly chosen or because weapons malfunction in flight. Counter-insurgency likewise invariably produces disturbing images.

good troops with sufficient authority to actually keep order, or the threat to destroy the assailant's armed forces. These threats are unlikely to work.

It is difficult to think of a case where coercive diplomacy accompanied by mere threats strongly affected the behavior of a producer of refugees. Invasion was necessary in the cases of East Pakistan (Bangladesh), Cambodia, and Rwanda. The intervention of substantial military forces and their engagement in some combat was required in Somalia and Bosnia-Herzegovina. Haiti was occupied without initial resistance, but the Cedras regime's capitulation was only assured when the assault force was literally warming its engines, and some combat did prove necessary after the occupation began. The only reason serious combat was not required in Operation Provide Comfort in Kurdish Iraq is that coercive diplomacy traded on the previous military action in Desert Storm, and on the threat mounted by strong residual forces close by.

Thus, intervention advocates should be under no illusions. Those who wish to help threatened peoples avoid becoming refugees will have to do much more than posture. They will need to muster the forces necessary to conduct the operations that have been identified as plausible solutions to the plight of the refugees. These forces will probably have to engage in actual combat, perhaps quite serious combat. Where decisive conquest of the assailant is impractical, it is likely that force will have to be used repeatedly, over a long time. For this reason, great care must be taken in the selection of military remedies, and in mustering sufficient military resources to execute these remedies.

Remedies and Realities

In this section, I discuss in detail the kinds of issues that arise in the selection of military remedies. Because the situation is more often one of compellence than deterrence, thorough military analysis is particularly essential.

PUNISHMENT BY STRATEGIC BOMBING

When trouble arises anywhere in the world, the first instinct of many is to bomb the miscreants, and through the infliction of pain, convince them to change their behavior.[23] In the course of the war in Bosnia, some commentators

---

23. Eliot A. Cohen, "The Mystique of U.S. Air Power," *Foreign Affairs*, Vol. 73, No. 1 (January–February 1994), pp. 109–124, reviews both the real and presumed lessons of air power from the Desert Storm experience. He wryly observes, "The lopsided struggle with Iraq has already affected the way Americans understand modern war, inducing the ornithological miracle of doves becoming hawks. More than one distinguished commentator who had reservations about aerial bom-

argued that Serbia proper should have been bombed.[24] But punitive conventional bombing—essentially strategic bombing—is a very problematical tool. Indeed, it has seldom, if ever, accomplished the purpose of changing the target's behavior.[25] Punishment bombing can be directed against any or all of four distinct classes of targets: the civilian population; the industrial infrastructure; the transportation, communications, and electricity generating capacity that knits a modern society together; or the political leadership. Each target set has a slightly different causal chain associated with it that is meant to lead to coercive success, but none of them have proven particularly effective. Many practical problems intervene.

TARGET SETS. Western political leaders and their air forces now abjure attacks on civilians. Desert Storm air operations explicitly, and for the most part successfully, avoided civilians. Given that the military operations discussed in this essay have a humanitarian objective, it seems unlikely that rescuers would choose this target set. Moreover, the bombing of populations did not produce capitulation during the Second World War. Bombing makes the targeted population angry and convinces them that the enemy actually is as terrible as their leaders' propaganda says. It also increases people's dependence on the state, and makes coordinated action to overthrow the regime very difficult, because individuals are simply worried about their personal survival.

Attacks on the economic infrastructure of a country are meant to destroy the sources of its war-making power. The concomitant erosion of the capability of its fielded military forces is meant to induce a realization that defeat is inevitable, and therefore surrender is warranted. This was the basic rationale for the

bardment in the Persian Gulf expressed a newfound belief in its utility as a tool of American foreign policy in the Balkans" (p. 110). He refers mainly to the *New York Times* columnist Anthony Lewis; ibid., fn. 2.

24. See the open letter presented to President Clinton on September 1, 1993, reprinted as "What the West Must Do In Bosnia," *Wall Street Journal*, September 2, 1993, p. A2, and signed by such notable figures as Margaret Thatcher, George Shultz, Zbigniew Brzezinski, and Albert Wohlstetter. It seems to call mainly for the destruction of military targets in Serbia. Anthony Lewis, "Speak for America," *New York Times*, April 26, 1993, p. A 17, suggests hitting "supply lines and other military targets, including some in Serbia itself." Richard Burt and Richard Perle, "The Next Act in Bosnia," *New York Times*, February 11, 1994, suggests hitting "strategic targets in Serbia itself."

25. Robert Pape, "Coercive Air Power in the Vietnam War," *International Security*, Vol. 15, No. 2 (Fall 1990), pp. 103–146. Pape notes that "the inadequacy of exploiting civilian vulnerability in the Vietnam case dovetails with the historical record of coercive air power. British civilians were harassed in World War I; British, German, and Japanese civilians were slaughtered in World War II; and Egyptian civilians were terrorized in the War of Attrition. Yet the exploitation of civilian vulnerability did not determine the outcome in any of these cases." See also Robert Pape, *Bombing to Win: Air Power and Coercion in War* (Ithaca, N.Y.: Cornell University Press, 1995). Pape's work has substantially influenced the discussion below.

bombing of Japan and Germany during the Second World War. Debate continues on many aspects of these campaigns, but it cannot be argued that conventional bombing produced surrender in either case. Since the Second World War, outside suppliers have provided most of the weaponry in regional conflicts, so industrial bombing could not easily affect the combat power of fielded forces.

A second rationale has thus emerged: the industrial base is a nation's wealth, an important value. The sacrifice of this value should usually seem disproportionate to the state's war aims, whatever they are. This variant of the theory has proven weak, however, because the industrial base of a given country does *not* necessarily matter more to its leaders or its people than its war aims. And this variant may not be useful for humanitarian intervention, simply because many countries do not have much of an industrial base to bomb.

The concept of bombing "critical nodes" or "centers of gravity" assumes that modern societies depend on a small number of potential targets to knit them together socially, politically, and economically. These would include power generation, telephone communications, radio and television, major bridges, perhaps the water supply to the cities. If these are destroyed, the control of the central government wanes; the good people of the society throw out the leaders whose policies engendered this chaos. Or, fearing this outcome, leaders desist from the offenses that precipitated the bombing. But urban industrial societies are probably not as fragile as the theory suggests.[26] When the bombing is successful, it may make conspiracy to overthrow the regime more difficult, since conspirators lose their ability to travel and communicate, and thus to concert action, it may also increase the dependence of the citizenry on the state for their survival.

This strategy has only been tried once, against Iraq in Operation Desert Storm. Much damage was done to Iraq's infrastructure but there is no evidence that Saddam's core Sunni Arab constituency was ever on the verge of rebellion. Iraqi technicians speedily repaired much of the damage after the war. On the other hand, this pattern of bombing, plus the more general destruction of Iraq's field forces, surely helped create the conditions that permitted rebellion in northern and southern Iraq by Kurdish and Shi'ite communities already predisposed to action. But the sequence of events suggests that neither rebellion would have occurred had it not been for the tactical defeat of the bulk of Iraq's ground forces. So, even with an already fissured society, air attacks on critical

---

26. Josef W. Konvitz, "Why Cities Don't Die," *Invention & Technology*, Vol. 5, No. 3 (Winter 1990) pp. 58–63.

nodes could not themselves precipitate a rebellion. This is thus, very nearly, a critical test of the "critical nodes" theory. If it did not work in Iraq, it is unlikely to work anywhere.

The United States as a matter of policy does not use political assassination as a tool of foreign policy. But the United States does not abjure military attacks on enemy leadership. U.S. war planes came very close to killing Libyan leader Moammar Khadafi; they certainly targeted every political and military command center in Iraq that they could find in the hopes of killing Ba'ath political and military leaders, particularly Saddam Hussein. The main problem with leadership attacks is that the elimination of a few individuals, or threats to their lives, may not produce decisions to change an important policy. Sometimes they will, but this ought not to be assumed. The near miss on Khadafi seems to have persuaded him to give up his dabbling in the support of overseas terrorism. Had Saddam been killed, it is quite plausible that a successor would have withdrawn from Kuwait. But it seems unlikely that the death of Radovan Karadzić would have much affected the policies of the Bosnian Serbs, or that the death of Pol Pot would have ended the killing fields of Cambodia. Finally, even when one or a few leaders are responsible for a given policy, they can prove surprisingly adept at hiding themselves.

PRACTICAL PROBLEMS WITH PUNITIVE BOMBING. There are many practical problems that must be overcome for a punitive bombing campaign to be a plausible remedy. First, are there appropriate targets for any of the four strategic bombing theories outlined above? In neither Rwanda nor Cambodia can one imagine a target set for punitive bombing strikes. Assailant and victim populations are often dispersed and intermingled. Moreover, in some civil wars the distinction between assailant and victim simply breaks down. War matériel is usually imported from abroad, and often consists of light weaponry that is cheap and easy to move, so industrial-base bombing would be pointless even if the targets existed. Many of the countries and regions that have produced large numbers of refugees do not have much of an industrial base to lose. The states or groups in conflict probably do not depend on "critical nodes" in any important way. Leaders are difficult to find and eliminate, and trouble may be caused by mass movements, in any case.

Second, even if there are appropriate targets, the rescuer may not be politically able to attack them. If the rescuers are operating under UN auspices, will the deliberate bombing of the assailant's civilian population be acceptable? Can liberal democracies acting independently of the UN simply start killing one group of people to convince them to stop oppressing, terrorizing, or killing another? Perhaps they can if the assailant's general population can be reliably identified with the crimes. But this seems the most likely situation for bombing to strengthen rather than weaken resistance, since such general ferocity is usually associated with an ideology that identifies the assailant population as the "defender."

Even if population bombing can be justified, the tight intermixing of killers and victims may make it difficult to attack only the guilty. Much of the killing is hand-to-hand. With the exception of Nazi Germany, one cannot argue that raids on the death camps will stop so much killing that some collateral damage to the victims is ethically acceptable.

Industrial facilities or "critical nodes" may seem a more ethically acceptable target set to rescuers, but a truly ruthless assailant may adopt the expedient of "staking out" members of the victim population all around them, since the targets can be easily deduced by the assailants' most junior intelligence officers. (Recall Sadaam Hussein's "guests.") This would produce an intense ethical dilemma for rescuer attack planners and airmen.

How about the assassination of leaders? Can the United Nations get into the business of trying miscreant leaders in absentia, and condemning them to execution by laser-guided bomb? Would a more traditional coalition of liberal democracies find it any easier to agree on such a policy? Perhaps a single nation, or a very narrow coalition, could decide that the execution of certain leaders was necessary and acceptable, but this seems likely to be a rare occurrence.

To summarize, some political entities do not offer suitable target sets for strategic bombing. Some strategic bombing target sets will not be acceptable to some rescuers. Some situations will mix the victims in with the assailants at the possible bombing targets, placing rescuers in a powerful ethical dilemma.

The third question is one of capabilities. Very few countries possess the capabilities to attack the full range of targets identified in the four strategic bombing theories. In particular, successful attacks on "critical nodes" or leadership require very sophisticated air forces. Attacks on industrial infrastructure require somewhat sophisticated airforces. Only attacks on population are "easy." While there are many combat aircraft in the world, few countries command the special capabilities demonstrated in Operation Desert Storm. In 1990, the U.S. Air Force had a total of slightly over 100 combat aircraft capable of accurately delivering laser-guided bombs at night.[27] Almost all were used

---

27. Since Desert Storm, the USAF figure has grown to roughly 450 such aircraft.

in the war, and they did the bulk of the precision-guided munitions (PGM) delivery for the entire coalition.[28] Since the Iraq war, more countries have acquired this capability, but it is still concentrated in liberal industrialized countries, and a few of their close allies.[29] Similar problems arise in the intelligence field; very few countries have the ability to gather the intelligence necessary to permit discriminate targeting. Thus, without the participation of the United States, it is not clear that particularly potent threats against "critical nodes" or leadership can be mounted.

"Access" to the theater of operations is also a crucial question. Fighter aircraft need bases from which to operate. Sustained operations at ranges greater than 600–700 km require substantial support from aerial tankers. The only country that owns tankers in large numbers is the United States. Beyond roughly 1500 km, sustained tactical air operations become difficult even with tankers, because it is just too hard for pilots and weapons operators to spend that much time in the cockpit.[30] Long-range operations also require complicated planning.

If reasonably close air bases cannot be obtained, the option does exist to employ long-range "strategic" bombers, such as the B-52, B-1b, or B-2. For the foreseeable future, these aircraft have at least one major limitation. There are few precision-guided munitions available for them, and those that do exist have rather limited capabilities.[31] These "dumb bombers" are, for now, mainly area-attack weapons. Except for the stealthy B-2, of which only 20 are currently planned, existing strategic bombers probably ought not to be dispatched over defended air space without fighter escort in any case, which re-surfaces the proximate basing issue.

In sum, there will be many political and military causes of mass population displacement for which strategic bombing is not even a practical answer. If practical, the record suggests that such bombing seldom independently pro-

---

28. The U.S. Navy may have owned a roughly equal number of such aircraft, perhaps half of which were deployed to the Gulf. They did not, however, deliver much precision-guided ordnance during the war. Britain employed an experimental system toward the end of the war; it is not clear if France then possessed aircraft with a night PGM-delivery capability.

29. The capability to deliver precision guided weapons in daylight is a bit more common, but this entails greater risk to the aircraft and crew.

30. These combat radii are my estimates based on diverse sources. Public information on this point has never been very good.

31. Air-launched conventional cruise missiles, though quite accurate by historical standards, are not sufficiently accurate for many of the most important strategic targets. The warheads are small and the missiles cost more than a million dollars each. The precision guided weapons currently employed by tactical aircraft are much more lethal and are useful against more diverse sets of targets. Several programs are underway to develop precision stand-off weaponry for heavy bombers.

duces positive political results. How many of the causes of population displacement could punitive bombing conceivably address?

MATCHING PUNITIVE BOMBING TO CAUSES. If genocide/politicide were the act of an organized government in a developed country, one or another variant of strategic bombing is at least a plausible remedy. In the the rare cases where a developed society has launched an explicit genocide against a discrete population, it may be that some combination of attacks on vital centers and leadership is the only option open to potential rescuers short of invasion. Given the heinousness of the situation, the mere possibility of success would justify an attempt at strategic bombing, though history gives us little reason for confidence in the outcome. One of the most important questions about strategic bombing will therefore be whether or not the situation is so horrible that it merits re-running an experiment that has so seldom worked. The genocide convention defines so many behaviors as genocide that it will be relatively easy for partisans of action to define the situation in this way. But given the low probability of success, and the possibility of making all but the most terrible policies of an assailant a great deal worse, it is my view that a narrow definition should be employed. For it to be "genocide" (or politicide), it would have to look a lot like the Nazi or Khmer Rouge crimes before this remedy should be considered seriously.

If ethnic cleansing were the source of displacement, and if the assailant state were developed and organized, punitive bombing might also be a plausible answer, though the rescuer runs a very real risk of so enraging the assailant that it turns from displacing the victims to murdering them.[32] The problem of refugees who flee because they fear occupation is more difficult. Here the "rescuer" is trying to force two sides fighting a traditional war to stop; more specifically the successful side is being told to stop. The rescuer is effectively entering an ongoing war on the side of the loser. What if the loser was the one who started it? The same problem may arise if refugees are merely fleeing the sound of the guns. In some cases they flee an internal war among approximate

---

32. This occurred on a small scale during the final Serb assault on the Srebenica "safe area" and a neighboring UN base in July 1995. UNPROFOR troops called for NATO close-air-support attacks against Serb tanks. "The NATO strikes stopped when Bosnian Serb commanders threatened to kill their Dutch hostages and to shell the Muslim refugees." John Pomfret, "Serbs Start Expelling Muslim Civilians From Seized U.N. Enclave," *Washington Post*, July 13, 1995, p. A 1; see also Chris Hedges, *New York Times* (News Service), July 13, 1995, "Wednesday, 1500 Bosnian Serb troops, backed by tanks, advanced at midday into Potocari. They overran the base with no resistance after they threatened to shell the refugees and kill the Dutch peacekeepers they are holding hostage if NATO warplanes intervened."

equals, so rescuers would have to bomb all the parties to the war. And of course, these wars often occur in places where there is not anything worth bombing. If occupation has already occurred, and refugees are fleeing its generalized brutality, the assailant has many hostages. The assailant can argue that if you bomb, it will kill them. Where refugees are simply fleeing the misery caused by primitive logistics systems, the nature of the problem suggests that the assailants do not have anything interesting to bomb.

SAFE ZONES

True "safe zones" have rarely been attempted. A threatened population remains settled in a distinct area that is effectively placed under the military protection of outsiders, who commit themselves to defend the zone, and to permit the inhabitants to live something like a normal life. There is little political or military precedent for operations of this kind. The protection of the Kurds in Northern Iraq following their unsuccessful rebellion catalyzed by Operation Desert Storm is the model and sole example.

A safe zone is a defensive or "denial" strategy. This is one of its attractions because at the most abstract level defense is easier than offense.[33] If one accepts the argument advanced above, that humanitarian intervention is basically an exercise in coercive diplomacy and hence the rescuer may actually be forced to fight, then rescuers should be interested in finding ways to lower the military cost of action. If defense is the stronger form of war, then setting up a situation where the assailant must attack is favorable to the rescuers and to the victims. A safe zone aims to provide physical protection to the threatened population. It convinces the assailant to stay away by developing a convincing ability to bar entry. Safe zones depend on real military power to defend them, and the willingness of rescuers to use it. Both the type and quantity of military power necessary to establish a safe zone are dependent on the specific situation. Some safe zones may be defended by high-quality air power; others might require ground power as well. Sometimes the threatened population might be able to supply the ground power if outsiders provide them with weaponry; sometimes outsiders must deploy ground forces. Demographic variables and more traditional military variables, such as distance, weather, topography, and vegetation,

---

33. Many will disagree with this statement. The defense enjoys well-known tactical advantages, sometimes including fortifications, obstacles, and mines. The defense usually knows the terrain better and can choose advantageous fighting positions. It usually has shorter lines of supply. Depending on the circumstances, the defense can trade space for time. In campaigns to protect one's own country, the defense also enjoys the support of the population.

will influence the size and quality of the necessary military force. Presuming that these variables are generally favorable to a safe zone, then the kinds of questions discussed earlier with regard to strategic bombing come into play. Are there bases nearby? Are there ports, roads, airstrips? Which countries are willing to act as rescuers? Can they bring the right kind of military power to bear?

Safe zones produce a *"de facto"* secession, which may be one of the strongest political obstacles to their employment. While there is currently a lively debate in the international law community on weakening the norm of non-intervention in the internal affairs of sovereign states, that norm still seems quite strong. In situations where the United Nations is involved, the relatively strong commitment of the smaller countries to the old norm will prove an obstacle to the organization of a safe zone. In actual practice, deviation from the sovereignty norm has followed a double standard: when the bad guys are weak, such as Iraq in Kurdistan, intervention pops to the top of the agenda; when they are strong, such as Russia in Chechnya, little is said.[34] Small countries thus are provided with regular evidence that the traditional norm is favorable to them. It is likely that the norm of non-intervention will continue to enjoy great legitimacy in many of the world's countries, simply because most are weak. There will be exceptions, but one should not assume that international approval for any given safe zone effort will be easy to mobilize.[35]

---

34. Even in the Kurdistan case, the secession issue arose. Diplomats spent some time developing the rhetorical formula of a "safe zone" in Iraq that would not carry the implication of political sovereignty for that zone. See the report and discussion on the Public Broadcast System television program "Newshour," April 10, 1991 (EBC and GWETA), particularly the remarks of Sir Brian Urquhart, former Under Secretary of the United Nations: "government's always concerned about anything which sets a precedent for eroding sovereignty. This discussion you just had . . . about an enclave or a safe haven is a perfect example of this. It seems to many persons looking on totally unworthy of the magnitude of the disaster, but nonetheless, it's a principle which governments find very important. Sovereignty is what defines government and their powers and authority, and if you make a precedent for denting it in one case, it tends to come back to you in another case which may concern you more closely. I think it's terrible, but that is where we are, and I hope we get further than that very soon."

35. See also Lori Fisler Damrosch, "Changing Conceptions of Intervention in International Law," in Laura Reed and Carl Kaysen, eds., *Emerging Norms of Justified Intervention* (Cambridge, Mass.: American Academy of Arts and Sciences, 1993), pp. 96–97; 100–106. Unilateral intervention, even against very murderous regimes, is still widely viewed as illegitimate. Though the UN has occasionally supported multilateral intervention for humanitarian purposes, the principle has not been clearly established. UN Resolutions authorizing humanitarian intervention in northern Iraq cited the international consequences of the refugee flows produced by Iraq's repression of the Kurds, but this is not quite a blanket authorization for humanitarian intervention. Even with this rationalization, however, the action authorized was limited; Chapter VII of the charter was not invoked because the People's Republic of China threatened a veto.

The "Provide Comfort" experience has prompted widespread interest in the safe zone concept. But the conditions for a successful safe zone are rarely as propitious as they were in northern Iraq. The Gulf War coalition had already badly damaged Iraqi military forces. They had done so with air power, and Iraqi leaders understood this very well. The coalition had complete command of the air and had a proven ability to destroy ground forces, day or night, in place or on the move. The coalition had plenty of aircraft in proximity to Iraq.[36] Iraqi ground forces had to traverse much open country to sustain attacks on the Kurds. They were very vulnerable to air attack. The Kurds themselves were doughty infantry fighters. If the Iraqis left their heavy equipment behind in order to get off the roads and to reduce their signature in order to elude detection by coalition intelligence and attack by coalition aircraft, Kurdish infantry would be able to fight them on approximately equal terms.

The credibility of the rescuers was unusually high because of the recent war with Iraq. President Bush had no interest in letting horrid television pictures of Kurdish misery destroy the glow of the Desert Storm victory. Turkey had made it clear that it was unwilling to take the Kurds in, but at the same time it did not want the ill-will of the United States and its European NATO allies, which it would have earned if it allowed the Kurds to die on the border in full view of television cameras. Turkey had also lent its bases to the coalition during the war for air strikes against Iraq, so there was little reason for Iraq to doubt Turkey's inclination to permit new air attacks on Iraqi forces. In short, the conditions were unusually favorable to the safe zone strategy, a state of affairs unlikely to be replicated.[37]

The conditions under which safe zones would make sense seem limited. They are most practical in internal conflicts where the existing pattern of settlement places the population at risk in one or two geographically limited areas. The threat could take the form of genocide/politicide, "cleansing," or even repression. This could arise from a civil war, in which the threatened

36. Operation Provide Comfort had a relatively good logistical infrastructure to support it. The large NATO air base at Incirlik, Turkey, may have been of particular importance to Iraqi calculations. During Desert Storm more than 150 U.S. aircraft were based there, in a task force dubbed "Proven Force" which flew nearly 4000 combat sorties. See U.S. Department of the Air Force, *Gulf War Air Power Survey*, Vol. V (Washington, D.C.: U.S. Government Printing Office [U.S. GPO], 1993), pp. 609–635. Incirlik is connected by oil pipeline to two logistical facilities on the coast. The base can thus be easily resupplied. See also Simon Duke, *United States Military Forces and Installations in Europe* (Oxford: Oxford University Press for Stockholm International Peace Research Institute [SIPRI], 1989), pp. 282–284; 288–291. More austere airstrips were situated closer to the Iraqi border.
37. Operations in Yugoslavia are supported by a very extensive NATO base structure in Italy. Duke, *United States Military Forces and Installations in Europe*, pp. 195–214.

group is too weak militarily to defend itself. Outsiders could sponsor a *de facto* secession. They might effectively increase the military power available to a secessionist movement to a level that permits success. If the threatened population had not initiated an armed secessionist rebellion, outsiders might do so on their behalf.

One can also imagine the organization of a safe zone in a more traditional inter-state war. Here, rescuers would simply intervene on behalf of the losing side, defending a piece of its territory. (Because refugees from elsewhere in the country might remain in the zone, it would also serve as a "safe haven.") They would snatch victory from the assailant, or at least limit its scope. Here the problem of intervention in the internal affairs of states will not arise, unless the threatened group is foolish enough to decline foreign assistance. But full-fledged entry into a war that has any number of causes that were previously uninteresting to outside powers, purely to prevent refugees, would seem unlikely. The side enjoying success in the war is likely to have very strong interests in the outcome. Outside intervention will be very unwelcome, and rescuers will surely have to count on a challenge to their intervention. On the other hand, unlike a situation of purely internal conflict, where an assailant views the rescuers as uninvited intruders into its own country, the assailant's presence in a country it has invaded is not inherently more legitimate than the rescuer's invited presence. The balance of wills does not so clearly favor the assailant.

Where the threatened population is relied upon to provide a substantial share of the military power to defend the safe zone, whether in a secessionist war, or in an international war, there is a very strong likelihood that its leadership will try to implicate the rescuers in much more than defense. They will try to get the rescuers to assist in reversing the gains of the assailant, perhaps even in a full scale offensive war to destroy the assailant's military power. Because of their presence on the ground, this will not simply be a matter of clear-cut rescuer decision. The military forces of the threatened population may conduct operations designed to produce situations that engage the rescuers' military power as directly as possible.

In situations of internal conflict, warfare may take a chaotic and primitive turn, becoming a war of all against all. Refugees may flee the sound of the guns, and fall victim to the primitive logistics. Here one can imagine a combination of the safe zone, the safe-haven, and the "enforced truce" methods. Outsiders would go into a place like Somalia or Rwanda, and choose one part of the country to dominate, permitting the residents to resume their lives, but also allowing displaced persons from other parts of the country to enter and find food, shelter, and protection from marauders. Marauders would either be kept out or intimidated into better behavior. There is ambiguity about French motives in the "Operation Turquoise" intervention, but arguably they attempted this in the last stages of their effort in the southwestern part of Rwanda.[38]

The credibility question will inevitably emerge in the implementation of safe zones. Will the assailant believe that the rescuers will actually fight if pressed? How many aircraft and pilots are the rescuers willing to sacrifice? Given the likely asymmetry of interests, and the categorical difficulties of conventional compellence, it is likely that the assailant will repeatedly challenge the rescuer. Neither mere declaration, nor the interposition of military force, will necessarily induce the assailant to back down. It will be wisest to count on some fighting.

Nevertheless, depending on the circumstances, the safe zone has certain advantages over other solutions. If the rescuers can get into a threatened area early enough, with sufficient combat power, the assailant has the onus of starting a war with one or more nation states, perhaps strong ones. In this narrow sense, the safe zone can harvest one of the advantages that deterrence holds over compellence. As discussed above, however, getting there early is difficult because rescuers are usually not motivated to act until after the trouble has started.

Finally, if the threatened area is reasonably homogeneous demographically, and is a well defined piece of territory, the rescuer can plausibly threaten that the more aggressive the assailant's challenge, the more likely they are to support the region's ultimate, internationally sanctioned, formal secession. The

---

38. The French-led "Operation Turquoise" was authorized by UN Security Council Resolution 929. The operation began on June 22, 1994, and by July 2 the French concluded that they could accomplish the most by declaring a safe zone in the southwestern fifth of Rwanda. Some 3000 troops were involved and 1.5–2 million people ended up in the zone. The French troops were already stationed in Africa, and organized a base of operations in neighboring Zaire. The Tutsi Rwanda Patriotic Front (RPF) military was dissuaded from entering the zone. There are two major questions. How much good did the French do for Tutsi inside the zone: how many were saved from Hutu murderers? Second, to what extent was the intervention a surreptitious way of protecting the remnants of the extremist-dominated Hutu government of Rwanda, which had been a French client for the preceding four years, from destruction by the RPF? See "Rwanda," *UN Monthly Chronicle* (December 1994), pp. 6–7; Alain Destexhe, "The Third Genocide," *Foreign Policy*, No. 97 (Winter 1994–95), pp. 11–12. Destexhe suggests that "several thousand Tutsis" were saved. Some observers believed that the French operation gave aid and refuge to the remnants of the Hutu government and army that had organized the Genocide in Rwanda. See "Rwanda," *Africa Research Bulletin*, Vol. 31, No. 6 (June 1–30, 1994), pp. 11482–11485; "Rwanda," *Africa Research Bulletin*, Vol. 31, No. 7 (July 1–31, 1994), pp. 11499–11501; "Rwanda," *Africa Research Bulletin*, Vol. 31, No. 8 (August 1–31, 1994), p. 11560.

assailant may still have something to gain by acting with restraint, although the rescuer will require very astute diplomacy to convince the assailant of this, because the assailant will also fear that the longer a safe zone lasts, the more likely it is for *de facto* secession to become *de jure* secession.

SAFE HAVENS

Sometimes rescuers will want to provide a sheltered refuge within an area of conflict where the displaced can go, but will not wish to cordon off large areas of a country to do it. In effect, rescuers are trying to arrange things so that victims can flee their homes without fleeing their country. The purpose may be as brutally pragmatic as forestalling a wholesale departure that would produce legitimate claims for refugee status in the interested countries. Or the purpose may be to help the refugees stay close to their original homes as part of a larger diplomatic strategy that aims to settle a conflict and permit them to return to their previous lives.

There are many reasons why a "safe haven" policy could prove expedient. Conflicts that produce refugees will often arise in places where groups—defined by religion, ethnicity, or nationality—are intermixed. A large safe zone of the type discussed above cannot be created unless the rescuers are themselves willing to engage in ethnic cleansing, throwing out the assailant group. Alternatively, the rescuers may not wish to be implicated in a strategy that looks like *de facto* secession. The rescuers may lack the military capability to pursue a safe zone policy due to their limited capabilities, or to the size of the theater of operations.

The type of warfare that is producing the trouble may also affect the choice of this military strategy. If the violence is conducted at an unsophisticated level, and consists of raids by small units or by local gangs, it may be impossible to find many targets for air attack. The smaller the signature of the assailant's military units, and greater the inherent intermixing of the two populations, the harder it will be to employ air power alone to protect the victims. Troops on the ground, interposed between the victim population and the assailants, may be the only sure way to keep the two apart. Yet rescuers may not wish to commit sufficient troops to keep order throughout the zone of conflict. Air power of the right kind can serve as an adjunct to ground forces in this situation, providing the heavy firepower that might dissuade the assailant's small units from challenging the rescuer's protection forces on the ground in the circumscribed save havens.

The practicability of the safe haven concept will also depend critically on whether or not the haven can be supplied with the necessities of life. Judging crudely from press figures on the airlift in Bosnia, delivery of a minimum of a pound of food per day seems essential for people to stay alive. Western troops in combat are assumed to require roughly five pounds of food per day. If there is cultivable land, seed and tools should be delivered to reduce future airlift requirements. Even if water is locally available, chemicals and machinery will be required to keep it pure. In all but tropical climates, blankets and shelter materials may be necessary. Some fuel may be necessary just to run basic humanitarian services; more could be necessary to provide warmth in the dead of winter. Rescuers' military units will require their own supplies, including fuel and munitions.

Though tremendous feats have been achieved by airlift since the outset of World War II, with the Berlin Airlift the best known "humanitarian" operation, overland transport by truck or rail is vastly more efficient.[39] Nevertheless, in the kind of conflict that would make a safe haven necessary, overland routes would often prove unreliable. It may simply be a fact that no safe haven policy has a chance in the absence of a substantial airlift capability in reserve. The possession of such a capability may even help discourage the assailant from interdicting ground convoys, since it knows the rescuer has an alternative pipeline.[40]

Conventional airlift is itself problematic. Airports can be closed to transport aircraft by heavy artillery and large surface-to-air missiles (SAMs), by relatively ubiquitous medium mortars (total weight 100 lbs. or less with ranges out to five km), by heavy automatic weapons, or by the threat of light-weight shoul-der-fired SAMs. So rescuer ground forces in the safe havens will need a capability to deal with many ground-based threats in order to help protect their own logistical support. It is also a good idea to have a parachute delivery capability in reserve, in the event that ground transport is interdicted and airfields are brought under fire.

The creation of safe havens is a difficult project, because they will often be surrounded by assailant territory. In this respect they partake of classical airborne operations, in which large forces are placed deep behind enemy lines. The economic infrastructure is unlikely to be able to support the large numbers

---

39. A port chosen as a safe haven would be the best possible situation from a supply point of view.

40. The payload of the aircraft will vary with both the distance the aircraft must travel, and the type of cargo. A good average payload for a C-130, the workhorse aircraft of humanitarian assistance, is about 13 or 14 short tons. U.S. Congressional Budget Office, *U.S. Airlift Forces*, April 1979, pp. 73, 76. Accurate parachute drops require considerable skill; currently only the United States has much real capability for accurate high-altitude drops, which are often preferred in order to avoid anti-aircraft artillery fire.

of refugees who arrive seeking help, so large quantities of supplies will need to be delivered. Key questions for rescuers are: how many safe havens should be organized, how large should they be, and where should they be located? What standard of safety should rescuers try to achieve? The answers will strongly influence how many ground troops will be required to protect them. The availability of tactical air power and its applicability under local conditions will also affect the size of the necessary ground force.

The number of people at risk and their distribution across the area of conflict will influence the number of havens required. Because good-sized towns have many assets useful to human survival, they would seem to be obvious candidates for havens. In addition, they often have airfields close by. Rescuers probably would not want to aggravate health problems and psychological distress, so it will be undesirable to crowd displaced persons together excessively. Moreover, if buildings are too crowded, assailant raids will produce many more deaths.

Once the size, location, and number of safe havens are settled, rescuers will then need to decide what density of troops, and of what type, they wish to have guarding the perimeter of the defended haven. This will depend partly on the size and capability of the assailant's forces, and partly on the level of protection desired. It will be more difficult to prevent casualties than to prevent conquest. Preventing an attacker from mounting a full-scale assault to take the safe area will often be achievable if the rescuers possess a large, competent, technologically sophisticated air force. Eliminating harassment by snipers and by erratic artillery and mortar fire probably requires substantial ground forces.

A safe haven policy is a reasonable antidote to several of the causes of refugee flight I have identified, but as usual the specific situation exerts a strong influence. A refuge for those fleeing genocide or politicide would certainly be one potential contribution. It is plausible, however, that the safe haven instrument is inherently too difficult to defend militarily against assailants whose political passions support genocide or politicide. Assailants will claw away at the safe havens even if they are defended; under some conditions, they will attempt siege warfare, particularly the interdiction of food supplies, water, and energy rather than direct attack. Because assailants are not leaving, they may settle on an attrition policy, and simply wait for the rescuers to tire of a difficult and dangerous mission.

Safe havens may work better against "ethnic cleansing." On the one hand, havens may help assailants, by providing an inviting refuge for people trying to decide whether to tough out the terrorist policies of the assailant, or to wait in a safe place in the hopes that this wave of trouble will pass. Thus, assailants may actually see some benefits to the havens. On the other hand, if the havens are close to the areas from which the refugees have been expelled, they leave open the possibility that the assailant's gains will be reversed at a later date. Assailants would clearly prefer the refugees to leave the area or country altogether. Hence, even in this case, the assailants will want to make life in the havens as unpleasant as possible, in the hopes that refugees will move on. They have other means to accomplish this, however. If they move their own people into the homes of those expelled, expropriating homes, land, and businesses, hopelessness about return may gradually spread in the refugee population, and they will try to exit the safe havens and go abroad. The defender of the safe haven, the rescuer, is gradually turned into a jailer, an uncomfortable position.

Safe havens will be difficult to employ against a harsh occupation, because the creation of a safe haven in the country in question would likely mean war with the occupier. This would only seem reasonable if the occupier is rather weak. And if the occupier is weak, a strategy of liberation, via invasion, would make more sense. It seems even more difficult to set up a safe haven inside the territory of a harsh and repressive regime. The objective of such a regime is likely to be the political control of its own people through intimidation and terror. It does not want people to leave; it wants them to behave. Moreover, to allow those who feel politically most in danger to reach such a safe haven would be tantamount to helping outsiders organize a rebel political party and army. The repressive regime simply will not want those on the run to reach a safe haven inside their country. Even if they are too weak to prevent an outside coalition from imposing such a haven, they are probably not too weak to detain or murder anyone foolish enough to try to reach it.

In an internal war, defended safe havens for those fleeing the sound of the guns may be practical, depending on the capabilities of the local combatants. There is a risk, however, that safe havens will become strategic assets or liabilities for the combatants as they did in Bosnia. Defense of safe havens by the UN could free Bosnian Muslim troops for offensive operations elsewhere. Safe havens may become rest and training areas for troops and logistical bases. Refugee aid may be diverted to military purposes.

Where people flee the sound of the guns in a full-scale international war, it seems unlikely that defended safe havens would work (although under some circumstances, depending on the motives of the actors, negotiated safe havens such as "open cities" are a possibility).

Safe havens are an excellent solution for the problem of starvation caused by primitive logistics. Here the rescuers are on a more traditional humanitarian mission. Armed protection is necessary precisely because the economy has broken down, and those with weapons are taking food from those without weapons. The rescuers simply provide military protection to traditional humanitarian assistance efforts. A delimited safe haven is chosen because it is militarily and administratively efficient. The local military actors are probably not especially strong relative to rescuer armies, otherwise they would not have resorted to pre-modern methods of requisition to feed themselves. They may, of course, find themselves in a difficult logistical situation once they no longer have a population to prey upon. But rescuers may also offer some inducements for their good behavior in the form of a share of the humanitarian aid.

The recent and perhaps historically singular effort to attempt a "safe haven" policy has been in Bosnia. Six towns and cities were designated as safe havens: Srebenica, Žepa, Tuzla, Goražde, Bihać, and Sarajevo.[41] The hope was that the residents could remain in relative safety. Displaced persons from the surrounding countryside who had previously taken refuge, or who were still looking for refuge, would find succor and protection there. These areas were provided with varying amounts of food and other resources, overland, by air lift, or by air drop. All had some UN military presence on the ground. The UN warned that if these areas were attacked, NATO air power might be called to defend them. Minor air attacks were in fact mounted around Sarajevo and Goražde. When Bihać was threatened in November of 1994, however, the UN declined to request NATO air strikes to defend the town, although some air attacks were mounted elsewhere. In the end the town held.[42] Srebenica and Žepa fell to the Serbs in 1995 with only limited NATO air action under the auspices of the UN to defend them.[43] When Goražde seemed threatened for the second time, NATO made its first explicit threat to employ air power on a substantial scale against the Bosnian Serb field army.[44] The Bosnian Serbs did not then take the town.

41. UN High Commissioner for Refugees, *The State of the World's Refugees: The Challenge of Protection* (New York: Penguin, 1993), "Protecting Assistance in Bosnia Herzegovina," pp. 79–82.
42. IISS, *Strategic Survey 1994/95* (London: IISS, 1995), pp. 94–98.
43. John Pomfret, "Witnesses Allege Abuses by Serbs," *Washington Post,* July 16, 1995, p. A1. "Srbenica fell on Tuesday [July 11] after Bosnian Serb forces, defying two largely cursory NATO airstrikes, rolled into the town with tanks and foot soldiers."
44. Craig R. Whitney, "UN Yields Air-Strike Control to Military," *International Herald Tribune (New York Times Service),* July 27, 1995, p. 1.

Other than the Bosnia experience, there are no clear real-world examples of an effort to establish safe havens against a competent, determined attacker. Even in Bosnia, there was no effort to create a genuinely safe "safe haven" until the NATO bombing campaign of August and September 1995, directed principally at the Serb siege of Sarajevo. Even that campaign did not face an adversary who seemed seriously intent on taking the city, but rather one trying to preserve its advantageous tactical positions. Given the limited ground forces assigned to the safe haven task in Bosnia, it is remarkable that four of six havens were never taken by the Serbs. When the project was first suggested, the UN Force Commander in Bosnia wanted roughly 32,000 additional troops to undertake it.[45] Only 7600 were authorized, and few of these were actually provided: for much of the war there were only about five thousand UN ground troops in and around Sarajevo, perhaps three thousand in and around Tuzla, and five hundred each in Goražde, in Bihać, and in Srebenica/Žepa.[46]

The complex record in Bosnia suggests that the overall resources of military capability and political will committed to the safe haven enterprise were somewhat inadequate, though a dispassionate analysis must acknowledge the success achieved. The civilian inhabitants of Sarajevo, Tuzla, Bihać, and Goražde suffered casualties from shelling and sniping. Interdiction of ground and air lines of communication meant short rations and a mean standard of living. These four largest safe havens did not fall to the Serbs, however. Goražde is a particularly important example of success, because it is close to Serbia, and seems an objective that the Bosnian Serbs clearly wanted, and nearly took. However, the combination of UN threats, peacekeeping troops, and Bosnian infantry was unable to prevent the fall of Srebenica and Žepa, or to prevent several intense combined-arms attacks on Bihać and Goražde. Thus, we have a crude measure of adequacy: some portion of the air combat and airlift resources of NATO, plus several thousand NATO troops acting as UN peacekeepers in the role of "alarm bell ringers," plus thousands of not-well-armed indigenous Bosnian Muslim infantry did successfully compel the Serbs

---

45. IISS, *Strategic Survey 1994/95* (Oxford: Oxford University Press for the IISS, 1995), pp. 95–96. Interestingly, the 32,000 additional troops requested by the UNPROFOR commander when the safe havens were first suggested, plus the 8000–9000 troops already present in the designated towns, divided by six, the number of safe havens, yields a troop strength of roughly 6000–7000 per safe haven, nearly identical to the troop strength at the U.S. Marine Corps defense of Khe Sanh during the Vietnam War, a roughly analogous military exercise. See fn. 47, below. I surmise that UN commanders employ a rough rule of thumb: do not attempt a serious defense of a town without at least 6000–7000 troops, a reinforced brigade.
46. Troop strengths from IISS, *The Military Balance 1994–95* (London: Brassey's, 1994), pp. 275–276.

to restrain their assaults on three–four of six safe havens.[47] Even Srebenica and Žepa, which fell to Serb attacks in the summer of 1995, remained untaken for a remarkably long time given their inherent military weakness. At the same time, however, repeated and sometimes successful challenges to this formidable (if rather poorly organized) aggregation of capabilities did occur.

As of spring 1996, the Bosnian Serbs seem to be cooperating with the Dayton Peace Accord. The circumstances that produced this cooperation tend to support the general proposition that compellence is difficult. In late August 1995, after a deadly mortar attack on Sarajevo, NATO opened an air and artillery campaign against the Bosnian Serbs. Ground offensives in western Bosnia by the Bosnian Muslims, Bosnian Croats, and units of the regular Croatian Army occurred more or less simultaneously and enjoyed considerable success.[48] These military successes provided the underpinnings of the U.S.-led effort that produced the Dayton accords, a complicated agreement that consigned 49 percent of the land in Bosnia to Serb control and which left the Bosnian Serb army intact. It took multiple military reverses, plus the offer of what appears to be a major proportion of Bosnian Serb war aims, plus considerable pressure from Serbia itself to produce Bosnian Serb acquiescence to the Dayton deal.

---

47. Another way of gauging the requirements for defending a truly threatened safe haven would be to examine the record of military operations that have placed large forces deep in enemy territory, and then attempted to resupply them by air and augment their firepower with tactical air attacks. One can think of some notable disasters, such as Stalingrad, Arnhem, and Dienbienphu. The most striking success, however, is Khe Sanh. John Prados and Ray W. Stubbe, *Valley of Decision: The Siege of Khe Sanh* (New York: Dell, 1991), pp. 303–307. From January 21 to April 14, 1968, roughly 6500 U.S. Marines and South Vietnamese troops were surrounded by 22,000 North Vietnamese and Viet Cong soldiers with nearly 150 heavy guns, mortars, and rocket launchers. The garrison was resupplied by parachute and helicopter, with about 15 transport aircraft and 50 helicopter sorties per day. Roughly 25,000 fighter-bomber and B-52 strategic bomber sorties dropped nearly 100,000 tons of bombs around Khe Sanh (p. 337). Thirty Marine howitzers and heavy mortars at Khe Sanh fired 159,000 rounds. During the roughly three months of the siege, three transport aircraft were lost and 26 heavily damaged; 33 helicopters were lost or damaged (pp. 432–438). At least 200 Marines were killed and 816 seriously wounded; it can be argued that 650 dead and 2598 wounded is a more reasonable estimate (Prados, p. 515). Had the Serbs been highly motivated, they could have created a similar kind of threat to Gorazde, because they had the necessary troop strength and weaponry. NATO airforces would have had to make a "Khe Sanh–sized" effort to defend the place. They could have succeeded, but the effort required would have been substantial.

48. The process by which both the regular Croatian Army and the Bosnian Muslim Army acquired sufficient arms and organization to fight the Serbs successfully is still an untold story. Anyone with a knowledge of weaponry who watched news footage of this war from its inception could not fail to notice the wholesale improvement in the armaments, uniforms, and even demeanor of both forces. These improvements were central to creating the military pressure that induced the Serbs to cooperate at Dayton. It would be a mistake to place too much emphasis on the role played by NATO airpower in this process. It was important, but I doubt that it would have been sufficient in the absence of expanded and improved Croatian and Muslim ground forces.

THE "ENFORCED TRUCE"

Certain patterns of violence that produce refugees may only be affected by outside intervention that attempts to establish a new source of "law and order." This model, however, is based on the assumption that rescuers can muster sufficient political or economic leverage, or are so intimidating militarily, that they may not need to shoot their way into the country. The target area is not so much invaded as occupied. So-called "failed states," where many armed factions vie for control, could conform to this model. Somalia is the best recent example; one could also argue that the UN operation in the Congo took this form. Because the local factions are too weak to keep rescuers from coming into the country, rescuers can calculate that it is theoretically possible to impose a peace, at least for a time. The purpose is to place enough military force into the area where fighting and killing are underway that little violence can occur out of sight of the rescuers. The rescuers bring enough military power that they can quickly do serious harm to any group breaking the peace. Indeed it is preferable to have sufficient presence that any incident that would break the peace is nipped in the bud.

The implementation of the "enforced truce" will depend on several practical constraints. The size and shape of the country, the number and size of the groups that need protection, and their arrangement will all bear on the size of force necessary to make the "peace" work. So will the scale of armament and military competence of the local fighters. Military analysts typically analogize from "similar" situations that have already occurred.[49] Thus the "soldier+ police-to-population" ratios in places like Northern Ireland or the West Bank are taken as good indicators of the minimum size of force that could be necessary. In Northern Ireland this ratio was roughly 20:1000 in a situation where there were probably never more than 1500 hardened shooters and bombers on all sides. Where local military forces are stronger and more capable than those in Northern Ireland, the 20:1000 ratio would probably be insufficient. "Soldier-to-terrorist" (20:1 in Northern Ireland) and "soldier-to-space" ratios are also relevant. Nevertheless, the Northern Ireland ratio of 20:1000 would suggest a minimum peacekeeping force of 90,000 to police the Vance-Owen plan in Bosnia.[50] It also suggests that NATO forces in Bosnia today

---

49. See, for example, James T. Quinlivan, "Force Requirements in Stability Operations," *Parameters: U.S. Army War College Quarterly,* Vol. XXV, No. 4 (Winter 1995–96), pp. 59–69.

50. See Barry R. Posen, "A Balkan Vietnam Awaits 'Peacekeepers'," *Los Angeles Times,* February 4, 1993. During and after the Tet offensive, when U.S. and South Vietnamese forces fought their foe to a bloody stalemate in a year of hard fighting, they probably outnumbered their enemy by 4:1.

are too weak to enforce the political provisions of the Dayton accords, particularly the return of refugees to their former homes, if the warring parties do not implement them voluntarily.

If a rescuer actually wants to protect all from all, the requirements can be very great. If, on the other hand, a rescuer only wishes to suppress local fighting and distribute food, then some economies may be possible. A small local presence backed up by highly mobile combat power may cow the local combatants into relative inactivity, though it will not provide a long-term solution, nor prevent all violence. This expedient will prove more effective if the locals are badly armed. These kinds of tricks worked well in the initial humanitarian intervention in Somalia, permitting a "soldier+police-to-population" ratio of 5–10 per thousand.[51] If a long-term solution is sought, and particularly if locals are to be induced to surrender their arms, then a very high level of local military presence may prove necessary to convince most people that they are safe from one another. And if the local armed forces are competent and committed, the price will be even higher.

Once the necessary force size is estimated, the question is whether it can be assembled, and if assembled, whether it can be transported to the area in question and re-supplied within a time-frame that is relevant to the political tempo of the crisis. While not widely discussed, this latter question was perhaps the first one on the lips of U.S. military planners when the genocide in Rwanda began to unfold and the UN Secretary General started to discuss military intervention.

If the problem is largely one of starvation caused by "primitive logistics," then the initial task of the rescuers may be relatively simple. They need only suppress the local fighting to a level where collateral damage is low, and defend the distribution of aid coming from outside the country. The same is true if short-term relief for people fleeing collateral damage is the objective. The actual destruction of the various armed factions is unnecessary. In terms of the logic of compellence, the rescuer is not asking much of the local combatants. None

---

If the Bosnian Serbs were credited with 50,000 fighters, and they were optimistically considered to be the only opponents to the plan, then perhaps 200,000 troops would have been necessary to police Vance-Owen.

51. Roughly 37,000 U.S. and allied troops in UNITAF proved sufficient to bring enough order to Somalia to permit aid to move unhindered, for a soldier+police-to-population ratio of roughly 5.5:1000. This ratio is probably misleading, because the U.S.-led operation covered only 40 per cent of the country. 10:1000 might thus provide a better benchmark. Approximately 24,000 UN troops in UNISOM II, backed by 14,000 U.S. troops under national command, proved insufficient in the subsequent operation for the more ambitious objective of "rebuilding" the Somali state. See *United Nations Peace-Keeping*, "Information Notes Update," (New York: United Nations, May 1994), pp. 104, 122.

are required to give up their war aims or surrender their military power to achieve those aims. Rather, the outsiders are simply demanding a "time-out." But the rescuer will have a difficult time deciding when and how to leave. Thus the temptation will be to expand the mission to make a successful state out of the failed state. This will mean entering the war on one side or another, or at least against one side or another. Alternatively, rescuers may try to create an entirely new political force in the country. Depending on local military skills and motivation, this can raise the cost to the rescuer substantially. Somalia is the obvious example of such a "mission creep."

An alternative would be to set limits on the intervention from the outset and make them clear to the local combatants. Order would be maintained until a new crop is planted and harvested and a second crop is in the ground, then the rescuers would depart, taking the international aid organizations with them. It would then be up to the local factions to decide if they wish to re-impoverish their countrymen, and themselves. They would get one chance. The problem would be making the threat credible, since international aid organizations do pretty much as they please.

The enforced truce may be a viable instrument in some peculiar cases of genocide, politicide, or ethnic cleansing. A locally strong majority often embarks on a campaign of violence against a minority. That majority is, however, too weak to prevent outsiders from coming in, but it is so strong that it can brutalize the minority with little opposition. The country itself is likely to be too underdeveloped for rescuers to find any targets worth bombing. And the populations are too intermixed for safe zones or safe havens to be a reasonable solution. The model here would have been Rwanda had the UN actually chosen to intervene. The limited French intervention did not have much trouble getting into the country with a small force; it seems plausible that the UN could likewise have gotten forces into the country without much initial opposition. In contrast, even if there had been widespread international understanding of the "killing fields" in Cambodia, it is likely that proposals for outside military intervention would have been rebuffed out of fear of ferocious Khmer Rouge resistance. The Vance-Owen plan would have negotiated the entry of tens of thousands of UN peace keepers who would have had the job of keeping Muslim, Serb, and Croatian gunmen apart from one another and from unarmed civilians. But without agreement among the three parties, neither the UN nor NATO had any intention of trying to force their way into the parts of Bosnia in dispute to impose a local peace.

Outside intervention to impose a permanent political solution to end an internal conflict is more difficult than intervention to elicit a pause in the fighting in order to ease the plight of refugees. The people to be protected are often the military and political objective of the assailants; indeed, in these situations each faction's non-combatants may be the targets of the other's combatants. However perverse this may seem from outside, the groups are committed to the killing. The rescuer is thus engaged in a war that resembles that most complicated political-military enterprise, counter-insurgency. Moreover, it is difficult to see how the mere enforcement of a pause in the killing is particularly constructive in situations of intense factional or intergroup violence. If political passions have produced an outbreak of mass killing, it is going to be difficult to stop. If the killing is stopped due to the intimidating local power deployed by the rescuers, and not due to the destruction of the multiple assailants' "combat capability" (whatever that means in this context), the rescuers will have to stay for a very long time. It may be difficult for the rescuers to convince the assailants that they care more about the safety of non-combatant victims than the assailants care about their destruction. Assailants might try to attack rescuers in order to raise the costs of humanitarian intervention. Alternatively, they may just wait until the rescuers depart.

Conclusion

This survey of the issues surrounding military intervention designed to affect the "production" of refugees constitutes a conceptual map of the issue. I have categorized the causes of refugee flows: genocide/politicide, ethnic cleansing, repressive conquerors or repressive regimes, the dangerous environment of war, and the impoverishment caused by primitive armies that live off the land. I have also developed some archetypal military remedies for refugee problems: strategic bombing, safe zones, safe havens, enforced peace, and a full-scale war against assailant groups or states. All except full-scale war are temporary expedients. They reduce hardship and save lives but they do not solve the original political problems that produced the violence that produced the refugees. It is probably true that a full-scale war is the best military answer to refugees produced by cruel occupations or highly repressive indigenous regimes.

Relying on the theory of military compellence, I have outlined some of the difficulties that will arise in trying to affect the political circumstances that produce refugees. Because I view the problem as one of conventional compellence, I deduce that the military requirements for success in any of these endeavors are substantial. Though any military strategist would echo Clausewitz's admonition that it is best to be very strong, particularly at the decisive point, this is particularly true for conventional compellence. Moreover, it will probably be necessary to use this force, not just threaten to do so, and to use it repeatedly. Therefore, I have reviewed the four military remedies in terms of their military logic and their tactical and logistical requirements.

Definitive conclusions are difficult without a more systematic effort to study the universe of cases of interventions that sought humanitarian goals in whole or in part. And given the wide diversity of circumstances, such lessons would need to be used with great care in any case. However, I offer some preliminary judgments.

SPECIFIC REMEDIES FOR SPECIFIC CAUSES

The most heinous of problems—genocide/politicide—may be the toughest to address with military power. In rare cases, a coercive bombing strategy may have some hope of working. Safe zones and safe havens may be employed when the pattern of settlement of the victims either concentrates them in a specific region, or makes it easy for them to concentrate themselves. Rescuers must consider, however, that the political passions that produce large-scale murder may prove very difficult to influence. Assailants may be strongly motivated to challenge rescuer safe zones and havens. In many cases, only complete invasion and occupation is likely to stop the crime; much killing of innocents can occur during such a campaign.

Where ethnic cleansing is an assailant's objective, it will often be the case that people are settled in particular regions, and thus safe zones or safe havens will prove pragmatic approaches. Safe zones and safe havens may also be reasonable remedies for people fleeing the sound of the guns, or the impoverishment caused by primitive logistics. When demographic, ecological, and geopolitical factors are favorable, the safe zone in particular is inherently an appealing remedy. Alone among the mechanisms described, it aims to permit large numbers of people to live nearly normal lives. A clear demarcation line between assailants and their putative victims tells the assailant when to stop. If the safe zone is large, rescuer air power may be able to prevent large assailant units from getting deep enough into the safe zone to do serious harm. The threatened population may be organized into lightly armed ground forces that can force the assailant into attack postures that facilitate air attack. If rescuers are both lucky and skillful, they may be able to transform the local situation into one of deterrence.

The one drawback to safe zones is their special political problem: the still powerful respect for sovereignty in international politics. Safe zones will often amount to *de facto* secession implemented by outside powers. This creates short-term obstacles to implementation, in that many smaller countries may not wish to legitimate such intervention. A longer-term problem is also created: what circumstances would encourage outside powers to withdraw their protection and permit the reintegration of the zone in question into the assailant state's system of government? This problem remains to be faced in Kurdistan.

Safe havens should be viewed as analytically distinct from safe zones. They are primarily refuges, not places of normal existence. They are an expedient to be adopted only in the most dire circumstances. They are very demanding of every aspect of military power, ground and air, and logistics. It is as if the Berlin Airlift and the Siege of Khe Sanh were combined into one operation.

Primitive wars of all against all cause refugees to flee the dangerous environment of combat and the depredations of uncontrolled requisitions. The enforced truce is the obvious response, perhaps combined with the safe zone and safe haven, but it is also particularly demanding of military power. A rough local peace among warring parties may not require a lot of firepower, nor incur many casualties, but substantial numbers of high-quality motorized, mechanized, and helicopter-borne infantry, and a great deal of patience and local knowledge, will be necessary. They may buy time for negotiators to try to effect a local political solution. Failing a local accord, rescuers will find themselves in a dilemma. They can attempt to impose a political solution by force, in effect joining the local war, or they can leave, with the risk that the situation will quickly deteriorate to the conditions that prompted the original intervention. The former will mean casualties, the latter human tragedy and political embarrassment.

THE FUTURE

When trouble of any kind arises, interested parties look to the United States for help because of its great power and influence. To cite only one example, the United States possesses by far the most capable and diverse air combat and airlift capabilities in the world. Air power, though not a decisive all-purpose tool, is an extremely useful one. The more exercises of this kind the United States does, the more the awareness of its array of special capabilities will spread, and the more frequently other countries, non-governmental organizations, and international organizations will look to the United States for help. Citizens of the United States should accustom themselves to these appeals, and learn how to analyze the odds of success.

While the problem of politically-induced refugee flows is not new, the magnitude of the problem seems to be growing. More importantly, as a result of the diffusion of liberal values in the polities of the most powerful states, the intensification of global communications precipitated by technological and economic change, the weakening of the intensity of great power rivalries, and the consciousness of the developed world's remarkable reservoir of Cold War–generated military power, arguments are now frequently offered that "we" should do something, even though traditional geopolitical interests may be absent. These altruistic impulses, and enabling conditions, ought not to obscure one important fact: in most of these cases, what good-hearted people are proposing is war. And war remains the realm of strategy, operations, and tactics; of forces and logistics; of destruction and death. "Humanitarian intervention" will often prove less gentle than it sounds.

Responding to State Failure in Africa

Jeffrey Herbst

$\mathbf{F}$ailed states in Liberia and Somalia have already caused millions of people to suffer grievously, and there is every indication that the central government apparatus is collapsing in other African countries. The international response to these failed states has focused mainly on how to resurrect them, while limiting the number of people harmed. However, the human tragedies caused by the failure of central institutions and the opportunities provided by profound economic and political changes now occurring throughout the global system compel investigation of other responses to state failure in Africa. The article suggests some alternative strategies to deal with failure in Africa, and elsewhere, that would involve significant changes in international legal and diplomatic practices. The goal is to develop a set of responses to state failure that would be more appropriate to the circumstances of a particular state's demise, and thereby move away from the current fixation on maintaining existing units.

The Paradox of Decolonization

In precolonial Africa, a wide variety of political organizations—villages, city-states, nation-states, empires—rose and fell. However, the formal colonization of Africa and the demarcation of the continent into national states between 1885 and 1902 replaced that diversity of forms with the European model of the national state.[1] After independence, Africa's heterogeneous political heritage was brushed aside in the rush by nationalists to seize the reins of power of the nation-states as defined politically and geographically by their European colonizers. Ironically, even as Kwame Nkrumah, Julius Nyerere, and Sekou Touré were proclaiming a break with Europe and the West, they uniformly seized upon that most western of political organizations—the nation-state—to rule.

Jeffrey Herbst is Associate Professor of Politics and International Affairs at the Woodrow Wilson School, Princeton University.

This research was part of a project on "Sovereignty and Self-Determination in the Post–Cold War World" based at Princeton's Center of International Studies and funded by the Sasakawa Peace Foundation. I am grateful to Henry Bienen, Walter Clarke, Robert Gosende, Steve Stedman, John Thomson, and two referees for helpful comments.

1. See I.M. Lewis, "Pre- and Post-Colonial Forms of Polity in Africa," in I.M. Lewis, ed., *Nationalism and Self Determination in the Horn of Africa* (London: Ithaca Press, 1983), p. 74.

International Security, Vol. 21, No. 3 (Winter 1996/97), pp. 120–144
© 1996 by the President and Fellows of Harvard College and the Massachusetts Institute of Technology.

The African embrace of the nation-state as theorized, designed, and demarcated by Europeans was propelled by several forces. First, many Africans were glad to be rid of the confused mixture of political institutions that characterized the precolonial period. Even as trenchant a critic of colonialism as Professor A. Adu Boahen noted that one of the positive aspects of European rule was the creation of new states with clearly defined (albeit inappropriate) boundaries in place of "the existing innumerable lineage and clan groups, city-states, kingdoms, and empires without any fixed boundaries."[2] Even as they borrowed the names of great states from Africa's past such as Benin, Ghana, and Mali, "the educated elites in West Africa—for a long time, it would be much the same in South Africa—saw Africa's own history as irrelevant and useless. . . . when it came down to brass tacks, to the question of who should take over from the British when the British withdrew, they demanded a more or less complete flattening of the ethnic landscape."[3] Of course, the leaders themselves had a profound interest in maintaining the nation-states they inherited from the Europeans because there was no guarantee, if they began to experiment with different types of political organization, that they would continue to be in power.

Immediately upon decolonization, the United Nations General Assembly—the gatekeeper to statehood—immediately declared the new countries to be sovereign and ratified their borders. The General Assembly was encouraged to do so by the new states who soon constituted a large percentage of that body, by the excitement generated worldwide as so many states gained their freedom largely through non-violent means and the determination to support those new experiments, and by the considerable anxiety worldwide to avoid the kind of violence that accompanied the division of the Indian subcontinent in the late 1940s. However, the UN grant of sovereignty by administrative fiat, simply because a country had achieved independence, was a revolutionary departure from traditional practices whereby sovereignty had to be earned.[4] Indeed, the central paradox of the international treatment of African states is that although sovereignty was granted simply as a result of decolonization, it was immediately assumed that the new states would take on features that had previously characterized sovereignty, most notably unquestioned physical control over the

---

2. A. Adu Boahen, *African Perspectives on Colonialism* (Baltimore, Md.: Johns Hopkins University Press, 1987), p. 95.
3. Basil Davidson, *The Black Man's Burden: Africa and the Curse of the Nation-State* (New York: Times Books, 1992), pp. 102–103.
4. Robert H. Jackson, *Quasi-States: Sovereignty, International Relations and the Third World* (Cambridge, U.K.: Cambridge University Press, 1990).

defined territory, but also an administrative presence throughout the country and the allegiance of the population to the idea of the state. Implicitly, the granting of sovereignty to the new nations also suggested that every country that gained freedom from colonization would be politically and economically viable, despite the fact that most colonies in Africa had been demarcated with the assumption that they would not become separate, independent states. Indeed, the principal criteria for state recognition today are a permanent population, a defined territory, and the ability to enter into relations with other states.[5] The ability to control and administer the territory assigned are irrelevant to the modern conception of sovereignty; the ability to develop ties to the population even more so.

The notion that Africa was ever composed of sovereign states classically defined as having a monopoly on force in the territory within their boundaries is false. Most colonial states did not make any effort to extend the administrative apparatus of government much beyond the capital city. "In most cases," the colonial governments "were little more than elementary bureaucracies with limited personnel and finances and were more comparable to rural country governments in Europe than to modern independent States."[6] After independence, African countries did try to extend the administrative reach of the state, but were always more focused on the urban populations.

Although sovereignty was for some countries little more than a legal fiction, it was relatively easy to maintain appearances in the 1960s and 1970s. Most African economies were growing, buoyed by global economic growth and relatively high prices for basic commodities, export of which formed the basis of most of the formal economies. The global strategic competition between the United States and Soviet Union also discouraged threats to the design of states in Africa or elsewhere. One of the implicit rules of the Cold War was that supporting efforts to change boundaries was not part of the game. In fact, where the great powers intervened, it was usually to protect the integrity of existing states (as in Zaire, Chad, and Ethiopia).[7]

Finally, no intellectual challenge was made to the immediate assumption of sovereignty by African states. Decolonization happened so quickly and Afri-

---

5. John Dugard, *Recognition and the United Nations* (Cambridge, U.K.: Grotius Publications, 1987), p. 7.
6. Robert H. Jackson, "Sub-Saharan Africa," in Robert H. Jackson and Alan James, eds., *States in a Changing World: A Contemporary Analysis* (Oxford, U.K.: Clarendon Press, 1993), p. 139.
7. I have developed this argument in Jeffrey Herbst, "The Challenges to Africa's Boundaries," *Journal of International Affairs*, Vol. 46, No. 1 (Summer 1992), pp. 17–31.

cans were so intent on seizing power that there was neither the time nor the motivation to develop new concepts of national political organization. Then, once the dozens of newly independent states were created, leaders found that the window of opportunity when they could have instituted revolutionary change in political structures was closing.[8]

The Facade of Sovereignty Overturned

The actual nature of some African countries' sovereignty is now being exposed. The long economic crisis that many African countries have experienced has caused a profound erosion of many governments' revenue bases. Even the most basic agents of the state—agricultural extension agents, tax collectors, census takers—are no longer to be found in many rural areas. As a result, some states are increasingly unable to exercise physical control over their territories. William C. Thom, the U.S. Defense Intelligence Officer for Africa, has written:

Most African state armies are in decline, beset by a combination of shrinking budgets, international pressures to downsize and demobilize, and the lack of the freely accessible military assistance that characterized the Cold War period. With few exceptions, heavy weapons lie dormant, equipment is in disrepair, and training is almost nonexistent. . . . The principal forces of order are in disorder in many countries at a time when the legitimacy of central governments (and indeed sometimes the state) is in doubt.[9]

Low or negative per capita growth in many African countries suggests that this sort of gradual dissolution will become more common in the future.[10]

The extremely limited revenue base of many African countries is also partially responsible for one of the most notable developments on the continent over the last thirty years: the change in the military balance between state and society. Whatever their other problems, African states at independence usually had control over the few weapons in their country. However, as states have atrophied, those who wish to challenge a government have been able to arm, helped by the weapons spillover from conflicts throughout the continent and

---

8. This point is made well by Julius K. Nyerere, *Uhuru na Ujamaa* (Oxford, U.K.: Oxford University Press, 1968), pp. 28 and 209.
9. William C. Thom, "An Assessment of Prospects for Ending Domestic Military Conflict in Sub-Saharan Africa," *CSIS Africa Notes*, No. 177 (October 1995), p. 3.
10. Across Sub-Saharan Africa, Gross National Product declined at an average rate of 0.8 percent from 1980 to 1993. World Bank, *World Development Report 1995* (Washington, D.C.: World Bank, 1995), p. 163.

the cheap price of armaments after the Cold War. Thus, armies, as in Rwanda, Ethiopia, and Chad, have challenged African governments; private security outfits such as the South African–based "Executive Outcomes" help governments such as Angola and Sierra Leone control their territory.

At the same time, international assistance to many African states is stagnant or declining. As donors redirect their aid from Cold War proxies to countries that are achieving some economic and political reform, countries that are failing spiral further downward. Somalia began to decline more sharply when it could no longer play the United States off against the Soviet Union in order to receive more aid. The decline in aid represents a fundamental break with the practice of the last one hundred years, which saw international actors offer support to the African state system, first through the creation of colonies, then by the enshrinement of sovereignty, and finally by the provision of financial resources without regard to domestic economic or political performance.[11] It is thus hardly surprising that so many African states have failed since the Berlin Wall fell, nor that those that collapsed include a notable number of states that had been richly rewarded by international patrons because of their strategic position during the Cold War but were subsequently cut off when aid donors became more concerned with economic and political performance (e.g., Ethiopia, Liberia, Somalia, Zaire).

As a result of this combination of forces, the centers of some states, notably Liberia and Somalia, collapsed when the contending parties were unable to break a military stalemate. More common are the states that are simply contracting because, while the centers still exist, they cannot extend their power very far over the territory they formally control. Zaire is perhaps the worst case: Mobutu seems intent on controlling whatever remains of the country he has bled dry, and the government has extremely limited control over territory outside the capital, to the point that some provinces no longer accept the national currency as legal scrip.[12] In a number of countries, the state is slowly being merged into a web of informal business associations instituted by rulers who have little interest in carrying out the traditional functions of the state and

---

11. For instance, from 1962 to 1988, six countries—Ethiopia, Kenya, Liberia, Somalia, Sudan, and Zaire—accounted for most U.S. foreign aid to Africa, despite their exceptionally poor economic and political performances. Indeed, all but Kenya can now be considered failed states despite American largesse. Michael Clough, *Free at Last: U.S. Policy toward Africa and the End of the Cold War* (New York: Council on Foreign Relations, 1992), p. 77.
12. Steven Metz, *Reform, Conflict, and Security in Zaire* (Carlisle, Penn.: U.S. Army War College, 1996), pp. 25, 35.

who do not recognize or respect boundaries while enriching themselves through trade.[13] However, it would be incorrect to suggest that all states in Africa are collapsing. Benin, Ghana, Tanzania, Uganda, and others are significantly increasing their states' capabilities due to the implementation of reform programs. A significant number of other countries are not enhancing state capabilities but are not in obvious decline at the moment. Africa thus presents a picture of heterogeneous state formation.

Unfortunately, the international community, in its response to state failure in Africa, has refused to acknowledge the structural factors at work, despite mounting evidence that the loss of sovereign control is becoming a pattern in at least parts of Africa. Rather, each state failure is taken as a unique event. No doubt, the confluence of factors supporting African sovereignty in the past was so strong that considerable inertia within international organizations now supports the assumption that there is no alternative to the current nation-states. Moreover, African diplomats, who are among the chief beneficiaries of current attitudes towards sovereignty, work hard to suppress any change in international diplomatic practices. For instance, even though it was obvious that Somalia had collapsed by December 1992, when the U.S.-UN intervention force was being planned, no one seriously considered trusteeship or any other legal concept other than continuing the fiction that Somalia was still a sovereign nation-state. Thus, the resolution on intervention to the Security Council was actually proposed by a former Somali prime minister, so that the UN could pretend that the Somali state was asking for the foreign troops.

Numerous critiques of the performance of African states also assume that there is no alternative to the status quo. For instance, the North-South Roundtable recognized that "institutional decay is currently of endemic proportion in Africa. In all sectors of the polity, the great institutions of the State have failed woefully. Evidence of institutional crisis abounds: in the political system, in the public service, in the management of the economy and even in the military."[14] Even so, the Roundtable restricted itself to asking how the existing states could be reinvigorated despite the long-term record of failure associated with Africa's extant political institutions. No energy was devoted to exploring alternatives.

---

13. William Reno, "War, Markets and the Reconfiguration of West Africa's Weak States," unpublished paper, Florida International University, September 1995, p. 1.
14. North-South Roundtable, *Revitalizing Africa for the 21st Century: An Agenda for Renewal* (Rome: Society for International Development, 1995), p. 15.

The now-burgeoning literature on failed states also focuses largely on preventing crises, so that states with poor track records can continue to exist, or on discovering methods to put the failed states back together. For instance, I. William Zartman, while admitting that a case can potentially be made for changes in the nature of the nation-state, still argues:

It is better to reaffirm the validity of the existing unit and make it work, using it as a framework for adequate attention to the concerns of citizens and the responsibilities of sovereignty, rather than experimenting with smaller units, possibly more homogeneous but less broadly based and stable. . . . In general, restoration of stateness is dependent on reaffirmation of the precollapse state.[15]

Thus, there has been little discussion of alternatives even to post-genocide Rwanda, despite its obvious structural problems and despite the fact that its current government, whose only constituency is the minority Tutsi, is obviously not viable.

Some suggest that alternatives to the nation-state will not develop because the international community has been so conservative in recognizing the viability of alternatives. Thus, Robert Jackson argues, "there is little evidence to suggest that the rules of this sovereignty game will not continue to be generally observed in the future as they have in the past."[16] However, as Hendrik Spruyt has argued, change in the nature of the constitutive units of the international system has not always taken place in a slow, incremental manner. Rather, there are long periods of stability followed by periods of sudden, chaotic institutional innovation. In such a manner did the sovereign state become the dominant institution in Europe.[17]

Now that so many of the props which supported the state system in Africa have been eliminated, the stage for revolutionary change has been set. Indeed, the norms of the international community are in tumult. UN Secretary-General Boutros Boutros-Ghali has written that "the time of absolute and exclusive sovereignty . . . has passed; its theory was never matched by reality."[18] More generally, the flux induced by the end of the Cold War opens up the possibility for new organizational forms. Already, "Kurdistan" in northern Iraq, the political organization that is now forming in the West Bank and Gaza, and the

---

15. I. William Zartman, "Putting Things Back Together," in I. William Zartman, ed., *Collapsed States: The Disintegration and Restoration of Legitimate Authority* (Boulder, Colo.: Lynne Rienner, 1995), p. 268.
16. Jackson, "Sub-Saharan Africa," p. 154.
17. Henrik Spruyt, *The Sovereign State and Its Competitors: An Analysis of Systems Change* (Princeton, N.J.: Princeton University Press, 1994), p. 186.
18. Boutros Boutros-Ghali, *An Agenda for Peace 1995* (New York: United Nations, 1995), p. 44.

"one country, two entity" creation in Bosnia are challenging the complete monopoly of the nation-state. That these creations were largely brokered by the great powers, previously among the most conservative forces in the international community, suggests that the scope for alternatives is increasing.

Finally, the dramatic failures of some states and the poor performance of many others has diminished the attachment that many in Africa automatically felt towards the new nation-states in the 1960s. Two entire generations have now lived under states that have failed to deliver the goods in terms of economic well-being, political order, or freedom. A new window of opportunity has therefore opened as many Africans begin to question the enshrinement of sovereignty for the nation-states designed by the Europeans. For instance, Dr. Christopher Bakwesegha, head of the Organization of African Unity's Division of Conflict Prevention, Management, and Resolution, has noted that although the OAU charter "still has this principle of non-interference, in reality it is being ignored."[19] While this may be an overstatement, given the attachment that many leaders feel to sovereignty, there may be increasing attention to alternatives.

Old and New Conceptions of African Sovereignty

Understanding what was lost when the Europeans imposed the territorial nation-state is a first step toward investigating what might be appropriate for Africa today. This is not to engage in misty-eyed nostalgia that somehow political formations developed hundreds of years ago can be replicated today. As Davidson notes, "the precolonial past is not recoverable."[20] However, understanding what the colonialists destroyed little more than a century ago should be helpful to the development of a more indigenous alternative to the nation-state as theorized, designed, and imposed by the Europeans.

Precolonial sovereignty had two features radically different from sovereignty exercised in modern Africa. First, in large parts of precolonial Africa, control tended to be exercised over people rather than land.[21] Land was plentiful and populations thin on the ground. Indeed, many precolonial polities were "surrounded by large tracts of land that were open politically or physically or

19. "As OAU Moves into Peace-Keeping, Non-Interference Concept is no Longer Sacrosanct," *Africa Recovery*, Vol. 9 (August 1995), p. 5.
20. Davidson, *The Black Man's Burden*, p. 315.
21. See Jack Goody, *Technology, Tradition and the State in Africa* (Cambridge, U.K.: Cambridge University Press, 1971), p. 30.

both."[22] As land was not seen as the constraining resource, exercising political power primarily meant control over individuals. Precolonial African practices were thus not that different from feudal Europe, where hard territorial boundaries were a rather late development.[23] However, the precolonial practices were radically different from the later European and post-independence African view that "states are territorial entities."[24]

The second notable aspect of precolonial political practices was that sovereignty tended to be shared. It was not unusual for a community to have nominal obligations and allegiances to more than one political center. As power was not strictly defined spatially, there was much greater confusion over what it meant to control a particular community at any one time. At the same time, communications and technology were so poorly developed that few political centers could hope to wield unquestioned authority, even over the areas that they were thought to control. Ivor Wilks, in writing about the Ashanti theory of sovereignty, noted that "rights of sovereignty were regarded as distinguishable from the exercise of authority." Thus, it was not an uncommon practice in Ashanti law for the land to belong to one authority (e.g., the southern provinces to the Asantahene) but for the people to owe allegiance to another (in the case of the south, to the Fante or the British Governor).[25] Indeed, such were the limits of territorial authority that the central government was often not concerned about what outlying areas did as long as tribute was paid.[26]

In this respect, precolonial Africa was similar to medieval Europe, where shared sovereignty—e.g., between the Church and various political units—was not uncommon.[27] However, again, this differs markedly from the modern notion of statehood, where sovereign control over each piece of territory is unambiguous: "there is never any doubt about where one stands, and that one always stands on the domain of a single sovereign state."[28]

---

22. Igor Kopytoff, "The Internal African Frontier: The Making of African Political Culture," in Igor Kopytoff, ed., *The African Frontier: The Reproduction of Traditional African Societies* (Bloomington: Indiana University Press, 1987), p. 10.
23. John Gerald Ruggie, "Continuity and Transformation in the World Polity: Towards a Neorealist Synthesis," *World Politics*, Vol. 35, No. 2 (January 1983), p. 274.
24. James Crawford, *The Creation of States in International Law* (Oxford, U.K.: Clarendon Press, 1979), p. 36.
25. Ivor Wilks, *Asante in the Nineteenth Century: The Structure and Evolution of a Political Order* (Cambridge, U.K.: Cambridge University Press, 1975), pp. 191–192.
26. Jan Vansina, *Kingdoms of the Savannah* (Madison: University of Wisconsin Press, 1966), pp. 82.
27. F.H. Hinsley, *Sovereignty*, 2nd ed. (Cambridge, U.K.: Cambridge University Press, 1986), p. 60.
28. Alan James, *Sovereign Statehood: The Basis of International Society* (London: Allen & Unwin, 1986), p. 31.

As a result, many precolonial African states were far more dynamic than has been the case in the world since 1945. Political organizations were created, and they rose and fell naturally in response to opportunities and challenges.[29] Many outlying territories found that they could escape their rulers' authority relatively easily. For instance, in the Central African kingdoms, "provinces could break off from the kingdom whenever circumstances were favorable. This happened in Kongo, in the Kuba kingdom, and in the Luanda empire, where every ruler who was far enough away . . . became independent."[30] Indeed, war was a common feature of precolonial African politics.[31] Political control in precolonial Africa had to be acquired through the construction of loyalties, the use of coercion, and the creation of an infrastructure. Indeed, political control over outlying areas could never be taken for granted given that the environment made it so difficult to continually exert control over any significant distance. For instance, the Ashanti empire was able to extend control over relatively large distances and have some of the attributes of a modern nation-state because of an extensive series of roads that converged on the capital, Kumasi. Of places beyond the great roads, it was said that "no Asante is familiar with these places because the King's highways do not run there."[32]

The imposition of territorial states by colonial authorities was thus a severe disruption of African political practices. The conception of the nation-state as introduced by the Europeans required only that territory be clearly demarcated. Authority was not dependent on popular support or legitimacy. Thus, Lord Hailey could write of the African officials through whom the British governed: "Everywhere the supervision exercised over them must bring home the lesson that the sanction for their authority is no longer the goodwill of their own people, but the recognition accorded to them by the administration."[33] For instance, in Ghana, the disjuncture between how colonial power was exercised and the old precolonial infrastructure of control became greater and greater as formal political authority migrated from the traditional Ashanti capital of Kumasi to the colonial capital of Accra. In fact, British administrators in the territory would argue as late as 1870 that there was no reason to maintain the old road network that had been central to the exercise of precolonial power.[34]

29. Among the many studies making this point, see S.I.G. Mudenge, *A Political History of Munhumutapa, c. 1400–1902* (Harare: Zimbabwe Publishing House, 1988), p. 76.
30. Vansina, *Kingdoms of the Savannah*, p. 247.
31. Robert Smith, *Kingdoms of the Yoruba*, 3rd ed. (London: James Currey, 1988), p. 99.
32. See Wilks, *Asante in the Nineteenth Century*, pp. 1–2.
33. Lord Hailey, *An African Survey* (London: Oxford University Press, 1938), pp. 539–540.
34. Wilks, *Asante in the Nineteenth Century*, p. 12.

There was nothing exotic about the precolonial African state system. Where Europe and Africa diverge is in the speed in which they moved from one system to another. The European evolution from the old system of states where territory was not well defined and sovereignty was shared was very slow, taking centuries. While the slow transformation from one system to another made it difficult for states to deal with crises, there were advantages to a state in not being called upon to exercise all aspects of modern sovereignty at once: for instance, in many European countries, local notables were still responsible for arresting criminals and providing social services long after the modern state was created, because the state did not have the capacity to carry out these functions.[35] Thus, in Europe there was time for relatively viable states to develop.

In Africa, however, there was an abrupt discontinuity between the old political order and the new one that essentially began with the Berlin West African Conference in 1885. In the space of a few decades, the facade of the new state system was formed and then, shortly thereafter, the states were given independence. The hard-earned structures of political control and authority that allowed for the exercise of political power in the precolonial period were abruptly cast aside, and there were almost no efforts to resurrect them. Indeed, the demarcation of Africa into colonies differed even from imperial practices in other areas of the world in the speed at which it was done, due to the multitude of countries seeking to rule the same area, and the reliance on force to the exclusion of developing loyalties among the subject population.[36]

The Implications of the New Sovereignty

The profound changes in the nature of sovereignty both aggravated decline in Africa and institutionalized it. First, the natural bias of African leaders to serve the urban population, who could threaten to riot and physically challenge leaders,[37] was encouraged because the new theory of sovereignty provided few incentives for leaders to develop networks of support in the rural areas. The Organization of African Unity and the United Nations bestowed recognition

---

35. Joseph R. Strayer, *On the Medieval Origins of the Modern State* (Princeton, N.J.: Princeton University Press, 1970), pp. 105–106.
36. Crawford Young, *The African Colonial State in Comparative Perspective* (New Haven: Yale University Press, 1994), p. 278.
37. See generally Robert H. Bates, *Markets and States in Tropical Africa* (Berkeley: University of California Press, 1981), pp. 31–33.

on governments that controlled their capitals, irrespective of whether those states had much of a physical presence in the rural areas. When there were attempts at revolt in the rural areas, the international community both implicitly and explicitly gave its approval to the use of force to quash the revolts, demonstrating that a state's treatment of its rural population would have little bearing on its international position. Thus, the bias toward urban dwellers and the neglect of the majority of Africans in the rural areas can be traced, in part, to a state system that encouraged elites to cultivate their urban constituencies.

Second, part of the failure to accommodate ethnic diversity in some states comes from the international community's acquiescence in the freezing of boundaries. If secession had been a viable threat, as it had been during the precolonial period, African politicians would have had a profound incentive to reach accommodation with disaffected populations, especially those that were spatially defined, lest they threaten to leave the nation-state. However, the international community's view that the boundaries were inviolable and that, therefore, the use of force was justified against potential secessionists, removed incentives for ethnic accommodation. Indeed, the great powers often went beyond acquiescence to actively providing arms and expertise for the crushing of secessionist movements, so that even obviously dysfunctional states could maintain their territorial integrity.

Perhaps more important, the current static state system in Africa has institutionalized weakness and decline, irrespective of the sources of failure. The current complete disassociation between a country's economic and political performance and its sovereign status means that, no matter how poorly a country performs, the international community continues to give it legitimacy, pretends that it is a functioning state, and supports efforts to preserve its integrity. Thus, even a country as dysfunctional as Zaire is still viewed as a viable unit and a sovereign country despite the fact that the writ of President Mobutu does not extend much beyond Kinshasa. If states as weak as some in Africa had existed in the precolonial era, they would have fallen apart or been conquered, potentially opening the way for more viable state structures to be created. However, the price of boundary stability has been that even dysfunctional states have claims on the international system. There are thus repeated efforts by the United States, the UN, or African neighbors to put back together Somalia, Liberia, and other countries even though there is little evidence that they ever worked well.

It is thus hardly a surprise that the African development experience has been peculiarly bad. Patrick Conway and Joshua Greene concluded that for the period 1976–86, "the macroeconomic performance and policies of African countries differed significantly from those of non-African developing countries in many respects. . . . African countries had lower investment and inflation rates. In addition, they exhibited lower rates of real economic growth even after adjustment for external and developmental factors."[38] Unfortunately, the evidence of poor performance is taken either as the best that could be done under the circumstances by advocates of current policies, or as an indication that the current policies are incorrect by those who want some other set of policies adopted.[39] Few have asked the more important question of whether the policies, even if correctly designed, are not working because the nation-states themselves are profoundly flawed.

The following sections first examine alternatives to existing states that would still operate within the current state system, and then examine alternatives to the nation-state itself. I provide an outline of options for policymakers who must in the short term work within the realities of current diplomatic practice, but who can also change standard operating procedures over the long term. The presentation of alternatives is made in the optimistic spirit that even areas in Africa that have experienced grave political failures can develop viable political institutions. I therefore reject the defeatist attitude that either nothing will work in some parts of Africa or that the status quo is the best that can be hoped for.

Alternatives within the Current International State System

The current unvarying reliance on the states that Europe gave to Africa must give way to a world which at least recognizes the possibility of alternatives. The recognition that reform is possible should be guided by two propositions. First, proposed alternatives must, in the end, come from the Africans themselves. No alternative to the nation-state is going to be forced on Africa, especially given the history of colonialism that began with the Berlin Conference. Second, the aim of any alternative should be to increase the dynamism of state formation, so that stronger national units can emerge and dysfunctional ones do not necessarily have to continue indefinitely. Not only would such

---

38. Patrick Conway and Joshua Greene, "Is Africa Different?" *World Development*, Vol. 21, No. 12 (December 1993), p. 2025.
39. See the critique of the latest World Bank report on Africa by Paul Mosley, Turan Subasat, and John Weeks, "Assessing *Adjustment in Africa*," *World Development*, Vol. 23, No. 9 (September 1995), pp. 1459–1473.

dynamism have strong resonance with the African past, it would also be critical to setting the essential foundation for political and economic development. Of course, dynamism also means instability, and potentially conflict. The downside of dynamism must be acknowledged and efforts made to ameliorate the damage that could occur if states are to become more fluid creations.

BREAKING THE INTELLECTUAL LOG-JAM

The first step toward developing new alternatives would be to provide the intellectual space necessary for Africans to present alternatives; this could be accomplished by publicly declaring that the international community is not blindly wedded to the current state system. This would be a revolutionary act that might help to break the intellectual log-jam that devotion to the status quo has caused. Given the state of African universities, the international community might have to go further and provide resources for think tanks and individuals who might want to analyze alternatives to the nation-state. Western donors are already providing significant amounts of money for "governance" to aid Africa's new democracies in their political transition. Some of this money could be redirected to the bigger question of whether some countries are presently viable. Once it is clear that there is at least some fluidity in the state system, African alternatives will not be long in coming. For instance, some leading politicians in Sudan are demanding that the people of Southern Sudan be able to "exercise their fundamental rights of reviewing the experience of the single sovereign state."[40] Of course, some of those proposing changes in the state system, and, by obvious implication, in their own countries, may risk the wrath of their own leaders. Indeed, Ken Saro-Wiwa and his colleagues were executed by the Nigerian authorities in 1995 because they demanded greater self-determination for the Ogoni people. Advocates of change in national design should be provided with protection, much like that currently provided by the international community for democrats urging liberalization in their own countries.

To date, it is not surprising that few countries have engaged in bold experiments regarding national design, given the skeptical international environment. Perhaps the most intriguing possibility for re-engineering an existing African state, especially in regard to the rights of minority groups, is the new Ethiopian constitution which provides for the possibility of secession based on

---

40. Alfred Taban, "Letter on Self-Determination," *Reuters*, November 12, 1995. The quotation is from an open letter sent by five leading politicians, including former Vice President Abel Alier, to the government of Sudan.

a two-thirds majority vote. This constitution has been backed by a large number of Western countries despite the fact that it explicitly challenges many of the notions of post–World War II diplomacy, especially as it has evolved in Africa. The logic behind the Ethiopian constitution is much the same as the logic driving the liberalization of capital controls worldwide: if a country has made a credible commitment that groups (or in the case of capital controls, money) can leave the country if the minorities (or owners of capital) are unhappy, this demonstrates a government's confidence that it will adopt policies that will not lead to a ruinous exit. Potential secessionists, understanding that they have considerable leverage *vis-à-vis* the central government, may therefore no longer fear marginalization. The Ethiopian constitution does go some way toward restoring the old precolonial practice whereby outlying areas could leave the existing political unit with relatively little difficulty if they are unhappy with their political leaders. Unfortunately, there are apparently no other examples in Africa of significant constitutional innovation to create a fundamentally new type of state practice in response to disintegration; Ethiopia only adopted its current rules after it lost a long civil war that led to the independence of Eritrea, its former province.

To aid further development of alternatives to the current state system, the international community and African countries can also begin to study African problems on a regional basis without regard to country boundaries. Despite seemingly endless rhetoric about the regional nature of many African problems, most reports and analytic works still use the existing nation-states as their unit of analysis. Studies of Southern Africa, for instance, are organized around the member countries of the Southern Africa Development Community (SADC). The intellectual framework continues to be dogmatically based on the current maps because in many cases multilateral agencies such as the United Nations and the World Bank—constituted solely by sovereign states—are conducting or funding the analysis. These agencies find it hard to work on any set of assumptions other than that the current boundaries will continue indefinitely, because the UN system itself is the source of the sovereignty which African leaders jealously guard.

The relatively few studies not based on existing boundaries are important to note because they suggest the possibilities that are opened when the old framework is discarded. Arguably, the most innovative recent work on African development is the West Africa Long Term Perspective Study published by the Club du Sahel. The study seeks to analyze West Africa as a whole to understand region-wide dynamics, and places rather less emphasis on political boundaries.

Indeed, it is one of the few official publications, perhaps the only one, to question the future of the state system. In a text box entitled "Rethinking the Shape of the West African State" the report notes, "Sahelian states are too large, sparsely populated, and hard to manage; some coastal states are too small and do not have a critical mass of population."[41] This analysis implies that the adoption of particular economic and political policies may be fruitless because the overall design of the nation is a permanent barrier to development irrespective of policy choice.

Academics have also conducted most of their analysis according to the territorial grid. One exception is Hans-Werner Sinn, who argues that the best way to aid Sahelian countries may be to provide aid to coastal West African countries with the expectation that migration toward the littoral nations will continue. Sinn's argument is that direct aid to the Sahel region produces less of a rise in aggregate output than does aid to the richer coastal countries, and that the development prospects of the Sahel are so limited that future aid is problematic.[42] Whether Sinn is right or not, he has produced the kind of regionally based analysis that is critical to Africa's future.

Donors can accelerate the process of designing new alternatives by using some of their aid for regional integration to promote alternatives and projects which treat sections of Africa as regions, as opposed to groupings of countries. Under current practices, foreign aid further reifies practices of approaching regional problems by using existing countries as the unit of analysis. For instance, aid to Southern Africa currently helps support the Southern African state system because its member countries have frequently used the SADC as an aid platform to garner more funds from the international community than would have been possible if each country had to ask for assistance by itself. The fact that the United States has closed its aid missions in Lesotho and Swaziland (for budgetary reasons) and will instead allocate assistance to those countries from Pretoria could be incorporated into a message to these countries, especially Lesotho, that the nature of their states, especially in the post-apartheid era, will have to be rethought. So far the Lesotho government has refused to entertain the idea of incorporation inside South Africa despite the fact that it is surrounded by its neighbor and that, with only ten percent of its land arable, has little hope of being viable. Indeed, given Lesotho's extraordinary

---

41. Club du Sahel, *Preparing for the Future: A Vision of West Africa in the Year 2020* (Paris: Club du Sahel, 1995), p. 47.
42. Hans-Werner Sinn, "The Sahel Problem," *Kyklos*, Vol. 4, No. 2 (1988), pp. 209–210.

aid dependence (three times the African average in the 1990s),[43] that small country may be a particularly good test of the possibilities for redesigning African states. At present, however, the government in Maseru dreams of taking parts of "the lost lands" back from South Africa.[44] Projects with a true regional scope and which allocate funds to recipients irrespective of the country they are in would be a further useful step not only in promoting development but in establishing a new intellectual framework.

RECOGNIZING NEW NATION-STATES

After thirty years of assuming that the boundaries of even the most dysfunctional African state are inviolable, another important initiative for the international community would be to consider the possibility of allowing for the creation of new sovereign states. Opening the possibility for new states to be created would challenge the basic assumption held by African leaders and the international community that boundaries drawn haphazardly during the scramble for Africa a century ago with little regard to the social, political, economic, or ethnic realities on the ground should continue to be universally respected. At the same time, allowing for more dynamism in the creation of African states would help recapture the element of the precolonial perspective on sovereignty that insisted that political control had to be won, not instituted by administrative fiat.

A criterion for recognition appropriate to the particular circumstances of Africa's failing states could be: does the break-away area provide more political order on its own over a significant period of time (say, five years) than is provided by the central government? By order, I mean functioning military, police, and judicial systems, which are the fundamental prerequisites for political and economic progress. These public goods are precisely what Africa's failing states do not provide. Such a standard would rule out many attempts at secession that were not of the utmost seriousness, and also return, to a degree, to older understandings of sovereignty that are resonant with the African past. The long-term aim would be to provide international recognition to the governmental units that are actually providing order to their citizens as opposed to relying on the fictions of the past. It would also place emphasis on the need for recognized states to provide order, a clarity that is missing in

---

43. World Bank, *African Development Indicators 1996* (Washington, D.C.: World Bank, 1996), p. 315.
44. Violet Maraisane, "Lesotho: Southern African Nation Ponders its Future," Inter Press Service, December 14, 1995.

suggestions that recognition of new states requires numerous tests (e.g., presence of democracy, granting the right to dissent, signing the Nuclear Non-Proliferation Treaty) that, while highly desirable, are not appropriate given the particular crisis that some African states face in just trying to control their territory.[45]

The primary objection to recognizing new states in Africa has been the basis for selection. Given that there are very few "natural" boundaries in Africa which would allow for the rational demarcation of land on the basis of ethnic, geographic, or economic criteria, the worry is that recognizing new African states will lead to a splintering process that would promote the creation of ever-smaller units, with seemingly endless political chaos. Thus, Gidon Gottlieb argues against the creation of new states because he fears "anarchy and disorder on a planetary scale."[46] The very real cost of new nation-state construction, especially the almost inevitable mass movement of people with all the suffering that such movements usually entail, is another important consideration for those who argue that Africa's boundaries must be preserved at any cost.

The argument is that once new states are recognized, descent down the slippery slope of microstate creation is inevitable. This argument credits the international community and Africans with no ability to discern the specifics of situations on a case-by-case basis. To say that new states should be recognized does not mean that criteria for state recognition cannot exist. It simply suggests that the criteria have to be created and that the dogmatic devotion to the current boundaries be discarded. If one criterion is based on who is providing order over the long-term, this would be a very difficult test; it would not lead toward the creation of many small states because it is simply not the case that potential secessionists exercise such unambiguous control in many parts of Africa. It was not the case, for instance, that Africa experienced a sudden splintering of states after Eritrea achieved its independence, or after the Soviet Union and Yugoslavia dissolved.

At some point, the reality of disintegrating, dysfunctional African states stands in such contrast to the legal fiction of sovereign states that experimentation with regards to new states is in order. For instance, in Somaliland (the breakaway northern province of Somalia that has declared its independence),

---

45. These tests, and others, are proposed for recognition of a new state by Morton H. Halperin and David J. Scheffer with Patricia L. Small, *Self-Determination in the New World Order* (Washington, D.C.: Carnegie Endowment for International Peace, 1992), pp. 84–94.
46. Gidon Gottlieb, *Nation against State* (New York: Council on Foreign Relations, 1993), p. 26.

order is being provided. A central government has been created with military units from across the country, a police force is operating and, in some parts of the country, local civil administrative structures operate.[47] In contrast, in the rest of Somalia there is chaos, despite the fact that the South has received a tremendous amount of foreign assistance and Somaliland very little. This is not to underestimate the problems facing Somaliland, which are numerous and daunting. However, the United States, the major European powers, and its African neighbors should consider recognizing Somaliland, given the potentially positive developments there that contrast with the chaos of Mogadishu. Clearly, the current international practice of waiting for a signal from Mogadishu to recognize Somaliland, when there is no government in Mogadishu to send such a signal, is bankrupt.

The resistance to creation of new states should also be tempered by recognition of the positive developments in Eritrea since its independence from Ethiopia. The international community continued to support the territorial integrity of Ethiopia until the Eritreans and their allies won an outright military victory. The donors—after decades of trying to convince the Eritreans that they would be better off as part of Ethiopia and that they would not be viable as an independent unit—now single out Eritrea as a success because of its sensible policies and commitment to development. The great powers' implicit acknowledgment that they were wrong about the viability of Eritrea is an important reminder that the commitment to the old borders has blinded many to the potential advantages of new states that may be better able to harness the commitment and energies of their peoples.

The consequences of adopting new rules regarding secession will also depend on the competence the international community demonstrates in confronting failed states and in sending out the right signals. The European Union's response to the dissolution of Yugoslavia was not planned well; the situation may well have been aggravated by the EU's continually changing positions.[48] A more thoughtful response to failed states, and in particular the development of criteria for changing diplomatic practices based on who is actually providing order, would help ameliorate the damage from what would be profound changes in diplomatic practice by reducing uncertainty amongst the participants.

---

47. Matt Bryden, "Somaliland at the Cross-Roads," found at the NomadNet home page: http://www.users.interport.net/~mmaren/brysomland.html, April 1996, p. 3.
48. Susan L. Woodward, *Balkan Tragedy: Chaos and Dissolution after the Cold War* (Washington, D.C.: The Brookings Institution, 1995), p. 187.

This is not to say that granting the right to secession to at least some groups which were able to establish order within their own areas would be without its dangers. Clearly, any signal from the international community that its commitment to the territorial integrity of African states is being reduced could result in considerable instability and uncertainty, and would be met by vehement opposition on the part of many African states which have grown dependent on the post–World War II understanding of sovereignty.

However, the reality on the ground in some African countries is that sovereign control is not being exercised by the central state in outlying areas, and sub-national groups are already exerting authority in certain regions. By recognizing and legitimating those groups, the international community has the opportunity to ask that they respect international norms regarding human rights and also has a chance to bring them into the international economy. For instance, even during intervention in Somalia, initiated explicitly because the central government apparatus had collapsed in Mogadishu, the World Bank and the International Monetary Fund offered no assistance to Somaliland, although the breakaway government in Hargeisa was at least providing some services to its citizens.[49] A less dogmatic approach to sovereignty would have allowed the international community to begin to help a substantial number of people. If the new sub-national arrangements are ignored, they will continue to be more like institutionalized protection rackets than states that guard the rights of their citizens. Local rulers who are actually exercising elements of sovereign control will focus on informal trade, often involving drugs, guns, and poached animals, to survive, rather than beginning initiatives to promote economic development that would aid all of the people in their region. The international community thus faces the choice between ignoring successful secessionist movements and thereby forcing them to remain semi-criminal affairs, or trying to help create new state institutions. The fact that some African states will dissolve will be the reality no matter which policy stance is adopted.

Alternatives to the Sovereign State

A far more revolutionary approach would be for at least parts of Africa to be reordered around some organization other than the sovereign state. While such reforms would be a dramatic change for international society, their adoption would be an important acknowledgment of what is actually happening in parts

---

49. John Drysdale, *Whatever Happened to Somalia?* (London: HAAN Associates, 1994), p. 147.

of Africa where many states do not exercise sovereign authority over their territories. Indeed, in a world where capital knows no boundaries and where force projection over distance is increasingly easy, it is peculiar that political power continues to be firmly demarcated according to territory. Developing alternatives to the current understanding of sovereignty would be consistent with older African practices where sovereignty was sometimes shared and where there were many different arrangements regarding the exercise of political authority depending on local circumstances.

It will primarily be up to the Africans to come up with alternatives to the nation-state. However, the international community can play an important role in signaling that the atmosphere has changed and that there is at least the possibility that alternatives to the sovereign state could be accepted. Indeed, alternatives to the nation-state are being developed now. For instance, the anarchy of Somalia has prompted some scholars to, finally, discuss alternatives to the old, failed political order.[50]

MAKING INTERNATIONAL INSTITUTIONS MORE FLEXIBLE

An important area to explore would be experiments that account for the diminishing control that some African governments exercise over distance. In areas far from the capital, other actors, including traditional leaders and local warlords who have moved into the vacuum created by the collapse of the local branches of the state, may exercise substantial control, provide security, and collect taxes. In some of the failed or failing states in Africa, rural communities already face a complex situation where sovereign control is only exercised partially, if at all, by the central government. These situations differ from the criteria discussed above for recognizing new states because no obvious authority exercises clear control over a defined piece of territory. Unfortunately, this confused situation is probably much more likely in collapsing African states than the appearance of a new force that can actually exercise sovereign authority over a defined piece of territory.

In response to the confused situation in some African countries, the institutional framework governing international organizations could be loosened. It would be particularly useful to encourage the participation by subnational units, be they potential breakaway regions or simply units such as towns or

---

50. See the report by consultants from the London School of Economics and Political Science, *A Study of Decentralised Political Structures for Somalia: A Menu of Options* (London: London School of Economics and Political Science, 1995).

regions that have been largely abandoned by their own central government, in technical meetings, and later directly, in organizations such as the World Health Organization, UN International Children's Emergency Fund, and UN Development Program that provide resources directly for development.

Participation in technical and service delivery organizations by traditional leaders or "warlords," who currently exercise authority and may deliver services but are not sovereign, is appealing because international acceptance could be calibrated to the kind and conditions of power actually being exercised. Thus, if a region's schooling has become largely dependent on the leadership and funds provided by a traditional leader, he might develop some kind of formal relationship with the relevant UN agency. The agency would need to examine whether the new leaders are able to exercise their authority for a sustained period of time, and to make judgments about the degree of assistance based on human rights concerns, just as the international community does now for countries that seek aid. Such a stance might be more helpful to the people of a region than pretending the old political arrangements still work. If the government of a country objects to losing authority, it should be forced to prove that it can actually govern the region.

Making critical international institutions more flexible would be more important than having the General Assembly or other highly political organizations begin to recognize subnational ethnic groups.[51] Because it is the source of sovereignty, highly visible, and political, recognition by the General Assembly is probably the last step for a region or group of people breaking away from their old nation-state. In the indeterminate position that some regions of some African countries will occupy, focusing on service delivery is more important.

The diplomacy of integrating non-state actors into what were previously clubs of sovereign nations would, of course, be difficult. However, in a variety of circumstances, the international community has proved adept at adapting to diplomacy with something other than the traditional sovereign states. As William Reno demonstrates, foreign companies have not been reluctant to deal with informal authority in Liberia and Sierra Leone, willing to work with anyone who has real rather than theoretical control over a territory.[52] Similarly, while the international community does not, in general, recognize Taiwan as a

---

51. This is suggested by Gottlieb, *Nation against State,* p. 39.
52. See William Reno, *Corruption and State Politics in Sierra Leone* (Cambridge, U.K.: Cambridge University Press, 1995), pp. 128–182.

separate country, that has not stopped the vast majority of countries from having normal commercial relations with Taipei and, at times, what look suspiciously like diplomatic relations. Once the sovereignty issue has been addressed, it should not be that hard for technical agencies to begin relating to those units that are providing services. Indeed, such an approach would also be a logical, if still revolutionary, evolution from current practices that tacitly allow non-governmental organizations to cross borders during humanitarian crises without devoting much attention to the niceties of sovereignty.

DECERTIFYING FAILED STATES

A further step that the United States, and other countries, can take would be to formally recognize that some states are simply not exercising formal control over parts of their country and should no longer be considered sovereign. For instance, the U.S. government already decertifies countries, effectively reducing their eligibility for American aid, that are not attempting to stop the production and trans-shipment of narcotics. Indeed, the U.S. legislation goes further and demands that countries prevent and punish the laundering of drug-related profits and "bribery and other forms of public corruption which facilitate the production, processing or shipment" of drugs. Thus, Nigeria was decertified in part because it did not investigate any senior officials alleged by the United States to be involved with drugs.[53] The United States is effectively arguing that these countries are not executing their sovereign responsibilities in regard to the enforcement of their own laws. A similar decision could be reached if a state is not exercising other aspects of sovereign control, including the failure or inability to project authority in large parts of its territory over a long period of time. Using this criterion, the United States should finally recognize Zaire for what it is and decertify it as a sovereign nation. It should be no more difficult to ascertain that a state is not governing over parts of its own country than it is to determine that senior officials are involved in drug trafficking but are not being prosecuted.

Decertification would be a strong signal that something fundamental has gone wrong in an African country, and that parts of the international community are no longer willing to continue the myth that every state is always exercising sovereign authority. Concretely, decertification might trigger the

---

53. The relevant U.S. laws are cited in Committee on Foreign Affairs, *International Narcotics Control and United States Foreign Policy: A Compilation of Laws, Treaties, Executive Documents and Relevant Materials,* U.S. House of Representatives, December 1994, p. 31. The presidential message decertifying Nigeria can be found in ibid., p. 543.

initiation of new efforts by other countries, including major donors and neighbors, at finding other leaders who are exercising control in parts of the country. Decertification would remove other privileges of sovereignty, including appointments to the rotating positions on the Security Council. It is paradoxical that the United States strongly opposed Libya's attempt to gain a seat on the Security Council because of its support for international terrorism, but seemingly had no problems with Zaire being on the United Nations' most powerful body despite that country's obvious dysfunctional nature.

Whatever concrete measures are taken, decertification would provide some avenue out of the current impasse, where there is no status to accord a country other than sovereignty irrespective of domestic realities. Decertification should be a rare step that would be used only as a last resort. Indeed, making decertification relatively difficult would also make its signal that much more powerful when it was used. Decertification would also have the advantage of correctly stating that the United States and other important actors understand that some countries are not sovereign, even if it is not clear what they are. Decertification could thus be a "halfway house" for countries that are at some later point able to reconstitute their sovereign authority. As such, it might be viewed not as a punishment but as a simple acknowledgment of reality. Alternatively, decertification could be the first step in recognizing that a state has died, if it ever lived, and that something else has to take its place.

It is an irony that the countries the United States does not recognize now (including Cuba, Iraq, Libya, and North Korea) are, by any measure, states. Indeed, the problem with those countries, according to the United States, is that their states have far too much control over their societies. In turn, African states that have little control over their societies continue to be recognized as states. Decertification would provide a way to avoid immediately categorizing those countries that have weak states with pariah countries like Libya or North Korea.

Decertification would require what the United States and other great powers dislike doing: altering the rules by which diplomacy is conducted. Great powers are notoriously conservative when it comes to the structure of the international system: witness the U.S. opposition to the breakup of the Soviet Union. No doubt, many diplomats would raise practical objections to decertification, arguing that it is against current practices of state-to-state relations. That is precisely the point. The situation in parts of Africa, and perhaps elsewhere in the developing world, has now diverged so dramatically from the legal fiction that it would actually be in the long-term interest of the great powers to create a new category for states that really can no longer be considered sovereign. While decertification might apply to a very limited number of countries, those are precisely the countries that will inevitably occupy the time and attention of policymakers across the world who search for a solution to mass human suffering.

The idea that complex humanitarian disasters of the type experienced by Somalia and Liberia must, at some level, be the responsibility of the international community is a new phenomenon in international relations, and is at odds with the post–World War II notion of sovereignty for any territory that can achieve self-rule. Accordingly, new tools must be developed to deal with these problems, and the old practice of simply accepting that all countries must always be sovereign should be rejected. Decertification of some countries that have demonstrated an inability over a long period of time to rule their territories could be part of the new arsenal of techniques needed to address new problems the international community faces.

Conclusion

The international society has yet to acknowledge that some states simply do not work. Indeed, it will require significant effort simply to create an environment where the possibility of alternatives to the current nation-states is admitted. Ending the intellectual log-jam caused by the current insistence on retaining the old nation-states would allow Africans in particular to begin to develop, for the first time in over a century, indigenous plans for their nation-states. Given the extent of the problems in Africa's failing states, it would be incorrect to suggest that any innovation will be low-cost, or will be guaranteed to address the root causes of failure. However, the very magnitude of the problems affecting millions of people also suggests that the current emphasis on resuscitating states that have never demonstrated the capacity to be viable is a mistake.

Lessons of Liberia | *Herbert Howe*

ECOMOG and Regional Peacekeeping

Long-standing ethnic, geographical, and religious conflicts continue to ravage significant sections of the developing world. Wars in Cambodia, Liberia, El Salvador, Afghanistan, and Rwanda have inflicted massive human suffering and economic destruction. Other countries, including Iraq, Nigeria, Burundi, and several former Soviet republics may soon erupt into large-scale violence.[1]

States often lack adequate military and police forces to control many of these conflicts. Western nations, especially since the recent intervention in Somalia, hesitate to help police conflicts which do not threaten their own vital interests. The West and the United Nations have argued that subregional organizations and individual states should assume increasing security responsibilities. Yet when Boutros Boutros-Ghali, Secretary-General of the United Nations, recently called upon sixty non-African states to form a standby peacekeeping force for Burundi, only one state (Bangladesh) agreed.

If individual states lack the capability and if Western states lack the willingness to control third-world conflicts, what other options exist? This article examines the possible effectiveness of subregional military groupings by analyzing ECOMOG (Economic Community of West African States Cease-fire Monitoring Group), a combined West African force, in the Liberian conflict of 1989–96.

Advocates of subregional forces argue that these groupings, when compared to nonregional intervenors, have both political and military advantages.[2] Subregional forces understand the conflict better, enjoy greater political accep-

Herbert Howe is Research Professor of African Politics at Georgetown University's School of Foreign Service.

The author is grateful to those West Africans and Americans who offered valuable assistance. Among those were Ambassador Herman Cohen, General John Inienger, Kathleen List, Anthony Marley, Timothy Sisk, Stephen Stedman, Ambassador Andrew Steigman, Ambassador William Twaddell, and Jennifer Windsor. The author's parents, Professors Herbert and Evelyn Howe, once again strove to impart writing skills to their son.

1. Several writers predict that a combination of political, cultural, economic, and environmental reasons foretell a near-apocalyptic, or at least highy conflictual, future for much of Africa. See Samuel P. Huntington, "Clash Of Cultures," *Foreign Affairs,* Vol. 72, No. 3 (Summer 1993), pp. 4–34; and Robert Kaplan, "The Coming Anarchy," *Atlantic Monthly,* Vol. 273, No. 2 (February 1994). A rejoinder to Kaplan is Carol Lancaster, "The Coming Anarchy," *CSIS Africa Notes,* No. 163 (August 1994).
2. For a discussion of the possible advantages of subregional forces, see Gareth Evans, *Cooperating For Peace* (Canberra: Allen and Unwin, 1994).

International Security, Vol. 21, No. 3 (Winter 1996/97), pp. 145–176
© 1996 by the President and Fellows of Harvard College and the Massachusetts Institute of Technology.

tance by the combatants, will demonstrate a stronger and more lasting commitment, and can deploy relevant (and often cheaper) equipment and personnel. This article, by using ECOMOG's six-year Liberian involvement, disputes these claims and argues that an inadequate peacekeeping force may instead prolong a war and weaken regional stability. The lessons of ECOMOG, generally negative, are important for any future subregional force.

ECOMOG entered strife-torn Liberia in late August 1990. Initially composed of soldiers from five West African states, ECOMOG has lost about seven hundred men in combat while trying to establish a cease-fire. Its major opponent has been the National Patriotic Front of Liberia (NPFL) headed by Charles Taylor. A cease-fire agreement in August 1995, "the Abuja Agreement," brought together all major combatants into a transitional government. ECOMOG still remained in Liberia in mid-1996, but fighting between various factions prevented ECOMOG from having a cease-fire to monitor.

The Liberian conflict is symptomatic of a growing number of third-world conflicts in countries where state legitimacy has eroded or disappeared, where poorly disciplined insurgencies of dispossessed and alienated rural youth acquire cheap modern weaponry and, with the aid of foreign business interests, loot the nation and rob it of its chances for development. Liberia's struggle illustrates the need for, but also the difficulties facing, foreign intervention forces.

While the Liberian war reflects several common problems, ECOMOG's intervention established several important precedents. ECOMOG became the first subregional military force in the third world since the end of the Cold War, and the first subregional military force with whom the United Nations agreed to work as a secondary partner. Liberia was one of the first conflicts where both the United Nations and the major regional organization, the Organization of African Unity (OAU), redefined traditional ideas of sovereignty in order to permit external intervention.

This article presents the background to the Liberian struggle, and outlines the creation and participation of ECOMOG in the conflict. It then reviews ECOMOG's successes and failures to derive lessons for subregional peacekeeping or peace enforcement forces.

Background to the Liberian Struggle

When ECOMOG arrived in Liberia in August 1990, it entered a country with a challenging geography, exploitable natural resources, and strong ethnic and historical divisions. Liberia is about the size of Tennessee and has a low coastal plain that merges into forested hills and mountains. Much of the interior is impassable by automobile, especially during the rainy season. The country has seventeen ethnic groups, none of which comprises more than 20 percent of the population. Among these groups, besides the "Americo-Liberians" who ruled Liberia until 1980, are the Mano and Gio in the north, the Mandingo in the west, and the Krahn in the northeast. Liberia's pre-war population was slightly over two million. Considerable amounts of iron ore, timber, some gold and diamonds, and rubber constitute Liberia's major resources.

Scholars such as Gus Liebenow and Christopher Clapham have documented the historical roots of Liberia's present conflict.[3] The American Colonization Society, assisted by the U.S. Navy, resettled freed slaves on "Liberia's" shores in the 1820s. These "Americo-Liberians" never comprised more than five percent of Liberia's population but gained national political control. Liberia became independent in 1847 and the Americo-Liberians' "True Whig Party" soon began a continuous rule that lasted until 1980.

Political domination, economic exploitation, and the lack of widespread education prevented a common Liberian nationalism. Many observers believe that the Americo-Liberians soon displayed some of the worst traits of the antebellum U.S. south. Victims of American slavery became the victimizers of "the natives."[4] Economic exploitation of natural resources and labor without adequate compensation were common.

Future governments did begin political reform, but two trends in the 1970s sealed the True Whigs' fate: a major drop in the terms of trade (higher oil prices and lower commodity export prices), and the government's underbudgeting of the Armed Forces of Liberia (AFL).

On April 12, 1980, indigenous non-commissioned officers successfully toppled Americo-Liberian rule. The coup enjoyed widespread initial support. But Samuel Doe, who promoted himself from Master Sergeant to General, drove

---

3. J. Gus Liebenow, *Liberia: The Evolution Of Privilege* (Ithaca, N.Y.: Cornell University Press, 1969); and Liebenow, *Liberia: The Quest For Democracy* (Bloomington: Indiana University Press, 1987); Christopher Clapham, *Liberia and Sierra Leone: An Essay in Comparative Politics* (Cambridge: Cambridge University Press, 1976).

4. "In what came to be called the Americo-Liberian community, an early distinction was made by the settlers and others between themselves and the 'natives,' as they called the indigenous population." Harold Nelson, "Historical Setting," in Harold Nelson, ed., *Liberia: A Country Study* (Washington, D.C.: American University, 1984), p. 22. In 1931, the League of Nations reported that Liberia "represents the paradox of being a Republic of 12,000 citizens with 1,000,000 subjects." Nelson, *Liberia: A Country Study*, p. 45.

the country into deeper ethnic hostility and economic ruin and paved the way for Liberia's civil war.

The Doe government began its rule violently by publicly executing leading officials of the *ancien regime*. During the 1980s, Doe heavily politicized—"ethnicized"—the AFL, making it essentially a Krahn Presidential Guard. In 1985 the AFL killed as many as 3,000 Mano and Gio civilians following a coup attempt. Widespread corruption and the flight of Americo-Liberians brought economic chaos.

The United States and Nigeria supported the Doe government. Ever since World War II, the United States had viewed Liberia as having some strategic importance. Liberia allowed various U.S. strategic installations, e.g., radio transmission stations, and strongly supported the United States in most foreign policy debates.

During the 1980s, the Reagan administration poured about half a billion dollars of aid into this nation of 2.5 million people. The United States did press Doe to hold national elections in 1985 but, despite gross election irregularities, Washington continued to support the Doe regime.[5] Oil-rich Nigeria, by far the most powerful West African state, sought expanded political influence. It competed vigorously against continuing French influence in the subregion (as well as becoming black Africa's leading opponent against South Africa's apartheid regime). Nigeria used economic assistance to strengthen its ties with neighboring Anglophone states, and Doe's Liberia was one of the leading examples. Nigeria's President, Ibrahim Babangida, provided Liberia with debt relief and some road and educational financing. But several French-speaking nations, notably Cote d'Ivoire, intensely disliked the Liberian government for a variety of personal and political reasons.[6]

Having survived numerous coup attempts, Doe initially paid little attention to the small National Patriotic Front of Liberia (NPFL)—one hundred or fewer men—which entered Nimba county from neighboring Cote d'Ivoire on Christ-

5. An interesting article on this period is Reid Kramer, "Liberia: A Casualty of the Cold War's End?" *CSIS Africa Notes,* No. 174 (July 1995). Kramer argues that the U.S. supported Doe as part of its strategy to topple Libya's Muammar al-Qaddafi.

6. Traditional colonial rivalries and present Anglophone suspicion of continuing French influence played the major role. But personality also figured prominently. President Houphouet-Boigny, the octogenarian ruler of Cote d'Ivoire, disliked the youthful and semi-literate Samuel Doe, who violently seized power and then executed former Liberian officials. Doe condemned to death A.B. Tolbert (the brother of President William Tolbert). His widow, Daise Tolbert, was Houphouet-Boigny's god-daughter; she later married Blaise Campaore, president of Burkina Faso. Not coincidentally, both Houphouet-Boigny and Campaore helped Charles Taylor, Doe's major opponent.

mas Eve, 1989. Charles Taylor, a former Doe official and alleged embezzler of $900,000 from the government, led the largely Mano-Gio NPFL.[7] Libya had trained a core of his fighters, Burkina Faso had supplied them with Libyan weaponry, and Cote d'Ivoire had allowed them free transit across the border into Nimba county. Taylor's force espoused no ideology beyond "democracy" and opposition to Doe, but drew significant support from Liberians united in their opposition to the Krahn (and Mandingo) rule of Samuel Doe.

The threat by Charles Taylor's NPFL was real. Doe belatedly rushed a battalion of the AFL to Nimba county. The troops created more hostility against the already unpopular Doe by further brutal treatment of the Gio and Mano ethnic groups. Taylor took advantage of this anti-Doe backlash, and his NPFL force quickly spread through much of Liberia. By July 1990, it had reached Monrovia's outskirts. Although Taylor's forces numbered perhaps 10,000, they lacked substantial military training, and about 30 percent of its fighters were under the age of 17.

Taylor's onslaught, and its counter-reaction, created significant savagery. On July 2 Taylor began his attack against Monrovia. NPFL forces singled out Krahn and Mandingo civilians for terminal retribution; the AFL, ostensibly a more disciplined unit, committed such atrocities as a massacre in St. Peter's Lutheran Church on July 29.[8]

By August, Doe's government had clearly lost control of Liberia, as his shrinking regime hunkered down in government buildings. Mediation efforts by religious and other organizations (Liberian and non-Liberian) failed: Doe refused widespread demands—including one by Charles Taylor—that he resign.

A new faction, the INPFL (the Independent National Patriotic Front of Liberia), split off from Taylor's NPFL. The INPFL, led by Prince Yourmie Johnson, fought both the AFL and the NPFL. Combatants from all three groups were destroying Liberia's economic infrastructure. The fighting killed many more civilians than soldiers. Monrovia's refugee-swollen population feared

---

7. Charles Taylor had been Director-General of Liberia's General Services Agency shortly following the 1980 coup. After some two years, Taylor left Liberia for America and began criticizing the Doe government. The Liberian government subsequently accused him of embezzling $900,000 and requested extradition. Taylor was imprisoned, awaiting extradition hearings, but managed to escape and travel back to West Africa, where he created the NPFL.

8. AFL personnel killed about 250 civilians seeking sanctuary in St. Peter's, wounding several hundred others (the bodies rotted on church pews for three months). The AFL pursued survivors to a vacant USAID compound, where it killed several hundred more.

mass starvation and an incipient cholera epidemic. After July 2, relief ships dared not enter Monrovia, since Lloyds of London refused to issue insurance.

The member states of ECOWAS, the Economic Community of West African States, had been watching the nearby devastation with growing trepidation. ECOWAS, founded in 1976, was the only West African organization that included all sixteen of the region's states (nine Francophone states, five Anglophone, and two Portuguese-speaking).[9] Its mission was economic: to increase trade and self-reliance through trade liberalization and currency convertibility. It also called for the free movement by West Africans through the region. ECOWAS had never fielded a military force, although it had two defense protocols for mutual self-defense.

Some ECOWAS states feared that the war would increase refugee flows and political instability in their already impoverished states and further persuade already hesitant foreign investors not to invest in West Africa. Several ECOWAS states worried about significant numbers of their citizens trapped in Liberia.[10]

No major power had expressed a desire to intervene militarily. Although the United States had vastly more ties to Liberia than did any other African country, it limited its involvement. Washington assisted initial mediation efforts but never seriously considered military intervention to end the conflict.[11] The Soviet Union—a major reason for U.S. involvement in Africa after 1960—had ceased to exist. Iraq's invasion of Kuwait (and the possibility of U.S. intervention) was capturing U.S. attention by late summer 1990. Additionally, the American media—especially television—had not significantly covered Libe-

9. The major Anglophone countries involved in the Liberian war were Nigeria, Ghana, and Sierra Leone. The major Francophone states were Cote d'Ivoire and Burkina Faso, both of which supported the NPFL, and Guinea and Senegal, which contributed troops to ECOMOG. Most authorities agree that among the reasons for ECOWAS' failure was that states placed their own needs (and finite resources) above those of the region, and that national and regional instability also lessened ECOWAS' effectiveness. In 1990 Ruby Ofori wrote that its "15 year history has been rocked by border disputes, mass deportations, and mini wars, not to mention the personal animosities between rival heads of state and deep seated rifts in anglo-francophone relations." Ruby Ofori, "Dream of Unity," *West Africa*, May 28–June 3, 1990, p. 882.

10. Significant numbers of Guineans, Nigerians, and Ghanaians were living in Liberia. Guinea alone had perhaps 30,000. At one point Taylor held 3,000 Nigerians hostage within the Nigerian embassy's grounds. Nigerian individuals held significant investments in Liberia; specific figures, however, are lacking.

11. The United States staged three limited military interventions, in 1990, 1992, and 1996, to extricate American and other foreign nationals from the fighting. The United States supplied $500 million of relief to Liberians and gave about $75 million in military assistance, mostly to individual ECOMOG countries. The United States also supported, both financially and politically, several major peace conferences. Critics accuse the United States, especially after the 1993 Cotonou and 1995 Abuja agreements, of delaying delivery to Liberia of needed logistical equipment.

ria's conflict and the civilian suffering. The United States had no desire to save its former client Doe, and Washington disliked both Taylor and Johnson.

The Organization of African Unity (OAU) and the United Nations paid scant official attention to Liberia's suffering. The OAU, Africa's major continent-wide organization, has always opposed military interference without invitation in the internal affairs of a fellow African state. In July 1990, Liberia's UN ambassador tried but failed to have the Security Council consider the crisis. Not until January 1991—thirteen months after the war's start and five months after the establishment of ECOMOG—did the Security Council publicly comment upon the war.[12]

ECOMOG'S BIRTH

Anglophone Nigeria was the leading supporter of a West African force for Liberia. In April 1990, at the urging of Nigeria's President Ibrahim Babangida, a group of five ECOWAS members established a Standing Mediation Committee (SMC) to resolve Liberia's conflict peacefully.[13] For three weeks in July an all-inclusive grouping of Liberian movements attempted and failed to obtain a peace settlement leading to elections. By August, no peace settlement existed. Seeing no alternative, and believing that any further delay could result in a final bloodbath in Monrovia, the Committee on August 7 created the ECOWAS Ceasefire Monitoring Group, ECOMOG. Still hoping for a political resolution, it also called for a broadly-based interim government of Liberians to rule until elections occurred under international supervision.

ECOMOG received a broad mandate that encompassed both peacekeeping and peace enforcement.[14] ECOMOG was "to conduct military operations for

---

12. Several nations in 1990 opposed UN involvement. African supporters of Taylor, notably Cote d'Ivoire, argued against UN involvement, as did the two African members of the Security Council, Ethiopia and Zaire, who "evidently wished to avoid creating a precedent [of intervention] that might someday apply to them." David Wippman, "Enforcing the Peace: ECOWAS and the Liberian Civil War," in Lori Fisler Damrosch, ed., *Enforcing Restraint* (New York: Council on Foreign Relations, 1993), p. 165.

13. Three Anglophone states (Nigeria, Gambia, and Ghana) and two Francophone states (Mali and Togo) comprised the SMC. The three Anglophone states would become heavily involved in ECOMOG, whereas the two Francophone states did not.

14. *Peacekeeping* operations are conducted with the consent of the previously warring parties in order to promote security. A peacekeeping force is essentially neutral between the contenders. Its mandate does not extend beyond immediate self-defense. *Peace enforcement* operations, in contrast, act to restore peace between currently hostile parties, at least some of whom do not consent to the peacekeepers. A peace-enforcing unit goes beyond self-defense: it will pursue, and perhaps destroy, the violator of a commonly agreed-upon settlement. See A. LeRoy Bennett, *International Organizations: Principles & Issues* (Englewood Cliffs, N.J.: Prentice Hall, 1991), esp. pp. 140–160; Margaret A. Vogt, "The Problems and Challenges of Peace-Making: From Peacekeeping to Peace Enforce-

the purpose of monitoring the ceasefire, restoring law and order to create the necessary conditions for free and fair elections to be held in Liberia," and to aid the "release of all political prisoners and prisoners of war."[15]

Other more implicit and less Liberian-oriented goals helped prompt ECOMOG's creation. Chike Akabogu of Nigeria's *Concord* Newspapers wrote that a successful ECOMOG intervention would strengthen a largely moribund ECOWAS and create a precedent of regional cooperation that the rest of Africa could follow. Additionally, "it would signal to the rest of the world that African nations were also ready and capable of responding to the critical economic, political and security challenges of the new world order, without prompting from erstwhile colonial powers."[16]

ECOMOG faced immediate problems of political unity, military capabilities, and uncertain funding. ECOWAS itself was badly divided—mostly between English and French-speaking states—throughout ECOMOG's existence. France had continued close political and economic links with its former colonies, most of whom feared Nigerian dominance of the region. Nigeria's gross national product and population matched that of the combined fifteen other ECOWAS members. While Nigeria was the strongest Anglophone power in the region, Cote d'Ivoire was the leading proponent of Francophone Africa. During the Nigerian Civil War (1967–70), Cote d'Ivoire had actively assisted Biafra's secessionist attempt against Nigeria. The different colonial legacies, continuing disparities, and the domestic needs of the individual members continued to impede regional cooperation in the early 1990s.

Demonstrating ECOWAS's disunity was the fact that most of the ECOMOG contributors came from Anglophone states: Nigeria, Ghana, Sierra Leone, and Gambia (Guinea initially was the only Francophone state). Nigeria would supply about 70 percent of ECOMOG's men and matériel over the next five years. Although its name (ECOWAS Cease-fire Monitoring Group) suggested ECOWAS approval and sponsorship, only the Standing Mediation Committee

ment," in Margaret A. Vogt, ed., *The Liberian Crisis and ECOMOG: A Bold Attempt at Regional Peacekeeping* (Lagos, Nigeria: Gabumo Publishing Co., 1992); and A. Munro, "A New World Disorder? Crisis Management Post–Cold War, *RUSI Journal*, Vol. 140, No. 1 (1995).

15. "ECOWAS Standing Mediation Committee," Decision A/DEC, August 1, 1990, on the Cease-fire and Establishment of an ECOWAS Cease-fire Monitoring Group for Liberia, Banjul, Republic of the Gambia, August 7, 1990; cited in Mark Weller, ed., *Regional Peace-Keeping and International Enforcement: The Liberian Crisis*, Cambridge International Document Series, Vol. 6 (Cambridge: Cambridge University Press, 1994), p. 68.

16. Chike Akabogu, "ECOMOG Takes The Initiative," in Vogt, *The Liberian Crisis*, p. 86.

members had decided to create the force. By the time of ECOMOG's August embarkation, ECOWAS's supreme body had not officially sanctioned ECOMOG and its "Operation Liberty."[17] Several Francophone states in ECOWAS, notably Burkina Faso and Cote d'Ivoire, supported the insurgent Taylor. Blaise Campaore, President of Burkina Faso, warned of ECOMOG's hostile reception.[18]

ECOMOG also faced internal political divisions. Contributing members to ECOMOG disagreed about its goals and methods; e.g., should ECOMOG act only as a peacekeeper or, if necessary, also as a peace enforcer against Taylor's NPFL? Nigeria's dominance within ECOMOG was a continual concern, although this was rarely expressed publicly.

Partly to lessen tensions between contributors, ECOMOG diversified its command structure: despite Nigeria's status as the major supplier of men, matériel, and money, Ghana was to provide the Force Commander, Guinea the Deputy Commander, and Nigeria the Chief of Staff. All five countries received some command positions. Nigeria provided economic incentives such as concessionary oil for nations to join and remain in ECOMOG.[19]

ECOMOG could not call upon a strong history of regional military cooperation. It was an *ad hoc* creation. Previous joint military activities had been intermittent, low-level, and not notably successful.[20]

Funding was a problem. The SMC established the Special Emergency Fund, whose initial goal was for $50 million from African states and any other donors. But international passivity toward the conflict and the parlous financial state of most ECOMOG members resulted in incomplete funding for the new force.

---

17. ECOWAS did give formal approval in November, 1990.
18. In August, Campaore expressed "total disagreement" with ECOMOG's planned intervention, and warned prophetically of "an eventual expansion of the internal conflict, which could break out among member countries if an intervention force is sent to Liberia." Campaore, quoted in BBC Monitoring Report, "Report: Taylor To Visit Banjul; Burkinabe Leader Rejects ECOWAS Intervention," August 13, 1990, cited in Weller, *Regional Peace-Keeping*, p. 85. Charles Taylor threatened ECOMOG with a "very, very high price" for any Liberians killed and warned that "we'll fight to the last man. . . . I've given orders to open fire on any strangers setting foot on our territory." Taylor, quoted in BBC Monitoring Report, "Report: Banjul Talks Begin; ECOMOG Again Delayed; Taylor Warns He Will Fight," August 21, 1990, cited in Weller, *Regional Peace-Keeping*, p. 86.
19. Nigeria supplied concessionary, or possibly free, oil to President Jerry Rawlings of Ghana before Ghana's 1992 presidential elections.
20. Between November 1981 and June 1982, the OAU had sponsored a three-nation West African intervention force in Chad. But the force lacked a clear mandate and "suffered from severe financial and logistical handicaps." Herman Cohen, "African Capabilities," in David Smock and Chester Crocker, eds., *African Conflict Resolution* (Washington, D.C.: United States Institute of Peace, 1995), p. 80. Similar deficiencies would reappear with ECOMOG.

ECOMOG'S ENTRY INTO LIBERIA

In mid-August 1990, the ECOMOG force of about 2,700 men arrived in Sierra Leone; Liberia's western neighbor would serve as ECOMOG's forward staging base.

General Arnold Quainoo of Ghana, ECOMOG's Force Commander, believed that the NPFL would lay down its arms once ECOMOG made clear both its determination and its armed capability. General Quainoo was wrong. On August 25, ECOMOG landed on Monrovia's beaches amidst hostile fire.

The three factions split in their reaction. Prince Yourmie Johnson's INPFL eagerly offered cooperation, as did the AFL, while Charles Taylor's NPFL artillery quickly zeroed in on ECOMOG's forces. The INPFL and the AFL cooperated with ECOMOG for two self-serving reasons: each was too weak to challenge ECOMOG directly, but each could benefit from ECOMOG's protection and from any destruction ECOMOG inflicted upon Taylor. The INPFL's initial aid to ECOMOG gave it special privileges, which included unhindered armed access to ECOMOG headquarters.

ECOMOG's overall strategy was for its conventional military force to intimidate the three factions while an interim government tried to resolve political differences and prepare Liberia for peaceful elections. On August 27 the Standing Mediation Committee convened the "All Liberia Conference" of seventeen Liberian political groupings and parties. The Conference endorsed the SMC's peace plan and elected an interim president, Professor Amos Sawyer, and a legislature. ECOWAS hoped to limit its political responsibilities and thus avoid ECOMOG being perceived as "an army of occupation." The interim government of Liberians, rather than ECOWAS or ECOMOG, was to exercise sovereignty over Liberia.

Although ECOMOG established a beachhead, at first it moved slowly against the NPFL. ECOMOG's Force Commander,[21] General Quainoo, considered his role that of peacekeeper, rather than peace enforcer.

Problems mostly caused by ECOMOG's inexperience quickly arose. A surprise NPFL attack caught ECOMOG unawares and almost overran its headquarters. On September 9, INPFL forces murdered seventy Doe bodyguards—at ECOMOG's headquarters—and then murdered Doe himself nearby. The AFL suspected ECOMOG connivance, and AFL soldiers torched sections of Mon-

---

21. Quainoo, a three-star general, was ECOMOG's only Force Commander. Subsequent ECOMOG commanders, all of them two-star generals, have had the title of Field Commander.

rovia. Soon afterwards, the INPFL detained a platoon of Nigerians until ECO-MOG swapped two 105mm howitzers for them.

A close observer of these events says that "Quainoo was rattled; he simply wasn't capable."[22] Quainoo reportedly called a meeting where he called for ECOMOG withdrawal from Liberia. Nigerian Brigadier C.K. Iweze, Quainoo's second-in-command, acknowledges that "most of the soldiers welcomed the thought of the said withdrawal."[23]

Nigeria worried that ECOMOG, which Nigeria had largely created, might not survive. Nigeria asserted its dominance of ECOMOG by having Dawda Jawara, who was Chairman of ECOWAS's Authority of Heads of State and Government, replace Quainoo with the more aggressive Major-General Joshua Dogonyaro of Nigeria.[24]

Nigeria also persuaded ECOMOG to shift temporarily from peacekeeping to peace enforcing. Nigeria and Ghana supplied 3,000 additional men, more offensive weaponry and some offensive air capability. ECOMOG now took the offensive. By October, Dogonyaro was using Nigeria's 77th Airborne Battalion and the two Ghanaian battalions to outflank the now-retreating Taylor.

The military pressure forced Taylor to sign a cease-fire at Bamako, Mali, on November 28. ECOMOG member states had had little previous knowledge of Taylor and assumed (or hoped) that he signed the cease-fire in good faith. Between August and the end of November 1990, ECOMOG had moved from peacekeeper to peace enforcer; with the Bamako cease-fire, it moved back to peacekeeper. ECOMOG controlled Monrovia, whereas Taylor controlled what he termed "Greater Liberia"—practically all of the rest of Liberia.

ECOMOG's offensive certainly saved thousands of lives by preventing a factional battle for Monrovia and by restoring peace that allowed food and medical supplies to enter Monrovia. The offensive also provided breathing space for subsequent negotiations. The cease-fire, although increasingly shaky, lasted for two years. Joshua Iroha of Nigeria served as ECOWAS's Special Representative in trying to reach a lasting peace settlement.

However, the relative peace also allowed all sides to rebuild themselves militarily. Burkina Faso resupplied the Taylor insurgency's limited needs. Taylor also built his own resource base by extorting resources from several large

---

22. Telephone interview with a former U.S. government official who was stationed in Monrovia in 1990 and 1991, October 15, 1995.
23. C.K. Iweze, "Nigeria in Liberia: The Military Operations of ECOMOG," in Vogt, *The Liberian Crisis*, p. 233.
24. Sir Dawda Jawara was also president of The Gambia from 1966 until a 1994 military coup.

businesses and by selling gold, diamonds, and hardwoods to commercial middlemen.

The prolonging of the war also allowed new factions to form. Johnson's INPFL, having split from Taylor's NPFL, would fight until late 1992. Taylor spread the war beyond Liberia by creating and arming a spin-off faction, mostly composed of dissident Sierra Leoneans called the Revolutionary United Front (RUF). He hoped to tie down ECOMOG troops from Nigeria, Guinea, and Sierra Leone, and to pressure the Sierra Leonean government into withdrawing support of ECOMOG. RUF invaded Sierra Leone in March 1991.[25]

Many anti-Taylor refugees, mostly Krahn and Mandingo, had fled to Sierra Leone. These refugees, among whom were many former AFL soldiers, reacted to the RUF invasion by forming ULIMO (United Liberation Movement of Liberians For Democracy) around May 1991. Soon ULIMO was skirmishing with RUF and by February 1992 had crossed into Liberia. ULIMO later split into two forces: the mostly Mandingo ULIMO-K and later the mostly Krahn ULIMO-J. The AFL lost many of its soldiers, who joined ULIMO-J or another Krahn faction, George Boley's Liberian Peace Council (LPC), which operated in southeast Liberia.

The Krahns' armed power far exceeded their numerical strength. They comprised only 4 percent of Liberia's population and therefore feared for their survival, given their close identification with the repressive Doe regime. Not surprisingly, the Krahn had then equipped themselves heavily, from AFL armories or from covert ECOMOG deliveries.

Few, if any, of these groups took ideological positions; most voiced instead some ethnic defensiveness or personal dislike of an opposing faction leader. Self-enrichment was often a major goal; all of these factions helped support themselves by looting various resources which they then sold to international middlemen. Human Rights Watch/Africa said the factions' human rights records ranged "from suspect to abysmal."[26]

ECOMOG at times provided ULIMO-K, ULIMO-J, and the LPC with arms, ammunition, intelligence, transport, and free passage to help press the war against Taylor. For example, in 1990 it provided ammunition to the INPFL and to the AFL. Though documentation is sparse, ECOMOG at the unit level apparently provided troop transport and protection and transport for the

---

25. The Nigerian, Guinean, and Sierra Leonean troops did not fall under ECOMOG's command since they were stationed outside of Liberia.

26. Janet Fleischman and Lois Whitman, *Easy Prey: Child Soldiers In Liberia* (New York: Human Rights Watch/Africa, 1994), p. 9.

factions' loot. Such shipments raised capital for these groups. Guinea supported the mostly Mandingo ULIMO-K. Nigeria first supported ULIMO-K, but later switched its support to the breakaway ULIMO-J.

ECOMOG had first realized the usefulness of factions when it employed Prince Johnson's INPFL for combat and intelligence during ECOMOG's first several weeks in Monrovia, when the INPFL guided ECOMOG troops through the baffling swamps of Monrovia. Later, ECOMOG air-transported ULIMO into Monrovia, and ULIMO guided ECOMOG through the swamps.

Most ECOMOG and Nigerian contacts with the factions occurred for two reasons. Some ECOMOG officers had become frustrated with ECOMOG's political and military limitations—adherence to a peacekeeping mandate, fear of high body counts and escalating financial costs, and scant counterinsurgency capability—and saw the factions as an effective force to realize ECOMOG's military goals. The Liberian factions knew the countryside better, cost less to operate, and if killed did not cause political problems back home in ECOMOG countries. Basic greed was a second reason. Individual ECOMOG officers assisted the factions in their looting by providing armed protection and transport.[27]

Peace talks, notably those at Yamoussoukro, Cote d'Ivoire, between July and October 1991, vainly attempted to bring a more lasting peace. The Yamoussoukro accords provided for a cease-fire, disarmament, encampment, an interim government and various steps towards elections. To increase non-Nigerian presence in ECOMOG, Senegal, with U.S. financing, sent two battalions to ECOMOG in late 1991.

The Liberian conflict exacted wider political casualties. Sierra Leonean soldiers, mostly ECOMOG veterans, fought RUF in early 1992. The war was destroying the country's economy, and the ECOMOG soldiers suffered from missing paychecks, irregular supplies, and minimal logistics support. In April 1992, these soldiers overthrew Joseph Momoh, Sierra Leone's president.

The Yamoussoukro cease-fire between the NPFL and ECOMOG continued throughout much of 1992, despite the growing fighting between ULIMO and the NPFL. ECOMOG soldiers began dispersing throughout much of Liberia, as called for by the Yamoussoukro accords, in late April 1992.

Yet events on the battlefield were undermining conference agreements. Citing the spread of ULIMO—by August, 1992, it had captured much of north-

---

27. A 1995 example offered by diplomats in Liberia was that of a Nigerian colonel who traded timber rights in his command sector for a monthly payment of five hundred dollars.

western Liberia—Taylor refused to disarm and continued to fight ULIMO and also to mistreat some ECOMOG peacekeepers.[28]

On October 5, 1992, the NPFL irrevocably broke the cease-fire by mounting "Operation Octopus," a two-month siege of ECOMOG-held Monrovia. Burkina Faso soldiers may have led the NPFL's offensive.[29] ECOMOG's departing Field Commander, General Ishaya Bakut, reflected ECOMOG's, and especially Nigeria's, disenchantment with Taylor: "I now realize that I was wrong about Taylor's intention. It is quite clear that Taylor is not sincere about disarmament nor is he willing to let anything stand between him and the Executive Mansion."[30]

Taylor's aggression had again pushed ECOMOG into peace enforcement. ECOMOG began some five months of fighting, its first peace enforcement actions in almost two years. (Between ECOMOG's August 1990 landing and October 1992's Operation Octopus, the worst single day of casualties had occurred when twenty-seven ECOMOG officers died from drinking wood alcohol marketed as Scotch whiskey or gin). By late December, ECOMOG's General Adetunji Olourin had pushed the NPFL out beyond Monrovia's suburbs. By April, ECOMOG had taken the major towns of Harbel and Kakata and then the port of Buchanan, 90 miles from Monrovia.

By mid-1993, Taylor was retreating throughout much of Liberia and was losing his economic base. *Africa Confidential* observed that Taylor "is in the difficult position of leading a guerrilla force which has to hold vast swatches of territory on a sharply declining revenue base."[31] ECOMOG had captured major revenue sources such as the Firestone rubber plantation and the port of

---

28. In one case, the NPFL surrounded a Nigerian contingent that ECOMOG had ordered to withdraw to Monrovia. Following intervention by former U.S. President Jimmy Carter, the NPFL released the Nigerians, but only after stripping them of their uniforms, weapons, and personal effects. This and other Taylor humiliations, e.g., the NPFL killing of three Nigerian journalists, further embittered ECOMOG, and especially Nigerian officers, against the NPFL. Carter and the International Negotiations Network of the Carter Center (Emory University) worked for a Liberian cease-fire. Carter visited Liberia and met with Taylor in late 1991. Many Liberians felt that Carter was too accepting of Taylor, especially when Carter proposed that ECOMOG remove all of its offensive weaponry from Liberia during the cease-fire. See "Report: AFP Report On Jimmy Carter's Proposals at Yamoussoukro Summit," November 1, 1991, cited in Weller, *Regional Peace-keeping*, p. 217.

29. Interview, Margaret Vogt, International Peace Academy, February 18, 1996.

30. "Bakyut Says He Has 'No Confidence' in Taylor," Agence France Presse, October 10, 1992, quoted in Kevin George, *The Civil War In Liberia: A Study of the Legal and Policy Aspects of Humanitarian Intervention*, unpublished manuscript, Washington, D.C., 1993, p. 63.

31. "Liberia: The Battle For Gbarnga," *Africa Confidential*, May 23, 1993, p. 2.

Buchanan. Those French and Lebanese trading interests which had been aiding the NPFL fled.

ECOMOG's aggressive peace enforcement once again forced Taylor to negotiate. A July 1993 meeting in Cotonou, Benin, saw the combatants agree to another cease-fire, a coalition interim government, and free elections within seven months of the cease-fire. The Cotonou agreement attempted to assuage continuing worries about a biased, Nigerian-dominated ECOMOG by incorporating United Nations involvement and by sanctioning the inclusion of east African troops into ECOMOG.

Cotonou marked the first time that the UN had ever agreed to cooperate with a non-UN peacekeeping force. The UN dispatched UNOMIL, the United Nations Observer Mission in Liberia.[32] In early 1994, 368 UN observers arrived in Monrovia. About the same time, a battalion each of Tanzanian and Ugandan troops, under ECOMOG command and financed by the United States, also arrived in early 1994.[33]

The factions, however, began working against ECOMOG's aims. Just as ULIMO had helped scuttle the Yamoussoukro talks, so in late 1993 another ECOMOG-supported faction, the Liberian Peace Council (LPC), threatened Cotonou. The LPC quickly began fighting the NPFL. Supporters of ULIMO member Alhaji Kromah also began disregarding ECOMOG; in mid-December at Kakata they blocked food aid intended for NPFL areas. ECOMOG, and Nigeria in particular, grew increasingly angry at Kromah's independence and aided, if not incited, a split. In March 1994 ULIMO officially split into the two factions, with the original, mostly Mandingo, ULIMO becoming ULIMO-K and the Krahn group becoming ULIMO-J. Continued fighting forced the UN to reduce its observer mission drastically to about sixty in mid-1995.

Fighting continued in mid-1994, despite a Cotonou-decreed new government (the Council of State) and ECOMOG attempts at demobilizing the factions. In July, a Coalition of Forces, comprising the Krahn's AFL, LPC, and ULIMO-J,

---

32. UNOMIL had the following responsibilities: "to monitor the ceasefire, to monitor the UN and ECOWAS arms embargo, to assist in the disarmament and demobilization of combatants, to observe and verify the election process, to help with coordination of the humanitarian aid effort [and] to report on human rights violations." "UN Observer Mission In Liberia," full-page UNOMIL advertisement in *The Eye* (Monrovia), June 23, 1995, p. 6.

33. The United States provided $32 million, which paid for transport to and from Liberia, eleven five-ton trucks and 14 "Humvee" vehicles, tents, and battalion-level radio equipment for the two battalions. The United States had also discussed with Zimbabwean and Egyptian officials the possibility of financing troops from those two nations. Some U.S. officials claim that Zimbabwe initially wanted $100 million in cash and equipment from the United States before Zimbabwe would provide two battalions to ECOMOG.

captured Taylor's headquarters at Gbarnga with ECOMOG's blessing. Taylor recaptured Gbarnga in September.

The Liberian conflict claimed another political casualty. Gambian soldiers in ECOMOG (about 30 at any given time) had complained that they had not received their extra pay for serving in ECOMOG. On July 23, 1994, the Gambian military overthrew Sir Dawda Jawara.

Mid-year meetings in 1995 between Taylor and Sani Abacha, Nigeria's Head of State, in Abuja, Nigeria, paved the way for a peace settlement on August 19. By early 1996, a fragile peace floated above Liberia, and there was some hope that if ECOMOG controlled its former allies, the elections scheduled by the Abuja accord for August 1996 would occur. Charles Taylor might win national elections and thus come to power peacefully under the eyes of ECOMOG soldiers.

However, ECOMOG did not control the factions. In early January 1996, the two ULIMO factions fought at Tubmanberg and an attempt to quell the fighting resulted in about fifty dead ECOMOG soldiers. Then in April 1996 the NPFL, temporarily aligned with ULIMO-K, attacked the three Krahn groups (the LPC, ULIMO-J, and the AFL) in Monrovia. The fighting killed an unknown number of Monrovians and destroyed sections of Monrovia. This upsurge in violence prevented the August 1996 elections from taking place. Elections are now scheduled for late May 1997, with a new government to be installed by mid-June. Thus, by mid-1996 Liberia appeared as lacking in hope as it did almost six years earlier, when ECOMOG soldiers first landed in Liberia.

Analysis of ECOMOG

The world in 1990 welcomed ECOMOG, hoping that it could become a model for future subregional forces which might exhibit political and military advantages over Western military units. Such a force could enjoy greater political acceptance among the combatants, display more knowledge about the contested country's political issues and physical geography, and maintain a greater commitment to ending a nearby struggle whose suffering could affect neighboring states. Additionally, it could employ more suitable military capabilities. These four factors—acceptance, knowledge, commitment, and military suitability—could, it was hoped, quickly resolve regional conflicts. In this section I examine how well ECOMOG met these hopes.

POLITICAL ACCEPTANCE

Will Africans accept other African peacekeeping forces more willingly than those from outside the continent? The Liberian experience suggests that existing subregional (and bilateral) differences could pose several serious problems.

First, new subregional forces will reflect existing political tensions. For example, subregional cleavages—Francophone vs. Anglophone; Nigeria's status as West Africa's economic and military juggernaut—created difficulties for ECOMOG. Robert Mortimer notes that "the multilateral, but Nigerian-dominated, force is more a classic study of competing national interests in the West African subregion than . . . a case study in regional peacekeeping."[34]

Burkina Faso and Cote d'Ivoire supported Taylor, while Guinea and Senegal supported ECOMOG. Most other Francophone states favored ECOMOG as a peacekeeper rather than a peace enforcer and, at least by 1992, were seeking a stronger UN presence to lessen Nigeria's influence.

Serious Anglophone-Francophone divisions also occurred within ECOMOG. To the Guineans, "being asked to fight was a deliberate attempt by the Anglophones to eliminate the Francophones."[35] During Operation Octopus, as Nigeria and Sierra Leone pursued a major offensive against Taylor's NPFL, most of the Francophone participants in ECOMOG resisted, believing that a peaceful UN involvement would lessen antagonism between ECOMOG and the NPFL.[36] Nigeria's effective control over ECOMOG's operations frequently irritated numerous non-Nigerian officers: "Big Brother" was a term used frequently to refer to the Nigerian contingent.

Second, national aims of the contributing states may collide with those of the subregional force. The immediate result—increased tension within the multinational force and a corresponding drop in efficiency—could prompt a contingent to abandon the alliance.

Several examples of national desires aggravating ECOMOG tensions appeared in the war's first few months. For example, Nigeria had agreed that a Ghanaian should always command ECOMOG but, following General Quainoo's apparent incompetence, Nigeria pushed to have him removed; since late 1990 only Nigerians have commanded ECOMOG, a fact resented by non-Nigerian officers.

---

34. Robert Mortimer, "ECOMOG, Liberia, and Regional Security," in Ed Keller and Don Rotchild, eds. *Africa In The New International Order* (Boulder, Colo., Lynne Rienner, 1996), p. 162.
35. Iweze, "Nigeria," p. 226.
36. See Wippman, "Enforcing the Peace," p. 173.

ECOMOG had ordered in August 1990 that fighting vehicles should be the first to land on Monrovia's beaches but, Iweze recalls, "some countries decided [otherwise] and started bringing in their five and ten ton trucks loaded with fish and rice. . . . We were lucky that the opposing forces did not meet us with a higher degree of opposition. . . . We would have been sitting ducks." ECOMOG suffered from numerous other examples of independent decision-making.[37]

The political background of a subregional force's governments will affect the force's political legitimacy and probably also its acceptance. ECOMOG's mandate included "creat[ing] the necessary conditions for free and fair elections," a novel function for most of ECOMOG's forces.[38] Few of the governments contributing to ECOMOG had been democratically elected; most, indeed, had gained power through military force, like Taylor himself was attempting, and few of them tolerated much domestic dissent.

Existing political baggage may limit Western support. U.S. "decertification" of Nigeria for involvement in the international drug trade hurt ECOMOG's already serious financial plight. As a result, the United States provided bilateral assistance to all nations except Nigeria until late 1995. ECOMOG officials correctly claim that bilateral funding contributed to disparate military capabilities and jealousy among its members.

A regional force's conduct will, *ipso facto*, affect the force's acceptance. A major worry for an intervention force is that a prolonged presence may change public perception of the force from an army of liberation to an army of occupation. ECOMOG largely avoided this by wisely not assuming sovereignty for Liberia. ECOWAS' Standing Mediation Committee had encouraged a Liberian interim government and ECOMOG publicly cooperated with local authorities. Yet many Monrovians were of two minds about ECOMOG: a heartfelt—sometimes tearful—appreciation for its saving Monrovia in 1990 and 1992 was often balanced by anger about suspected widespread corruption and high-handedness.

---

37. Iweze, "Nigeria," p. 222. Soon after landing, the Guinean battalion was to capture territory around Spriggs-Payne airfield and wait for a linkup with the Ghanaian battalion. But, perhaps on orders from Conakry, the Guineans, without notifying ECOMOG headquarters, decided to leave the captured territory in order to liberate their embassy. The NPFL surrounded them and the Ghanaian battalion finally rescued them with losses of men and matériel. The Ghanaian battalion landed with a well-stocked mobile hospital, but disregarded a common pooling policy. Therefore, writes Iweze, "only Ghanaian soldiers were being given attention in terms of surgery." Iweze, "Nigeria," p. 237.
38. Weller, *Regional Peace-Keeping*, p. 68.

Alliances with local factions, while offering an outside force some military advantages, may lessen the intervenors' political standing. In particular, a subregional force's acceptance of, and by, some factions will lessen its acceptance by others. Torture, rape, pillage and even examples of cannibalism by ECOMOG-supported factions hurt ECOMOG's general political acceptance. A subregional force has less control over factions—and their misdeeds—than over its own troops.

ECOMOG's African composition, by itself, did nothing to gain Charles Taylor's acceptance. He distrusted ECOMOG before it landed, and ECOMOG's quick military cooperation with the AFL and INPFL cemented his anger. Taylor called for Liberian unity against purported Nigerian hegemony. The AFL and INPFL welcomed ECOMOG, not so much as fellow African peacekeepers, but as possible allies against the NPFL.[39] Taylor's NPFL and its regional backers, Burkina Faso and Cote d'Ivoire, opposed ECOMOG, in part, because of Nigeria's support of Doe, its dominance within ECOMOG, and its perceived regional intentions.

A respected external organization with no direct interest in the conflict, other than seeing it resolved, can bestow needed legitimacy and acceptance, but the subregional force may dislike and work against such an organization. UNOMIL could have acted as a watchdog for ECOMOG, yet UNOMIL had little independent authority. ECOMOG cooperated, grudgingly, at best, with UNOMIL. Several UNOMIL officials complained that ECOMOG did not want UNOMIL observing activities relating to arms flows, human rights abuses, and food shipments. The overall result was that ECOMOG lost a chance to restore some of its desired neutrality and public acceptance.[40]

GREATER KNOWLEDGE

The West's limited knowledge of the developing world can endanger military interventions, as the United States and the UN realized in the case of Somalia. Will countries from the same subregion necessarily have superior or even adequate knowledge? Not necessarily, according to ECOMOG's experience.

---

39. Surprisingly, ECOWAS may not have anticipated this challenge to its neutrality. Iweze writes that, at the creation of ECOMOG, "we asked the ECOWAS Secretariat for our anticipated reaction to the leaders of the warring factions should we meet them. Unfortunately, the leadership could not provide an answer." Iweze, "Nigeria," p. 219.
40. General John Inienger, ECOMOG's Field Commander in 1995, vigorously disputed allegations about corruption, human rights abuses, and aid to the factions. General Inienger also argued that the UN should "come to Liberia's aid by providing resources [to ECOMOG]. We can perform the job." Interview with General John Inienger, June 29, 1995.

Despite geographical proximity, neighboring states in Africa often have surprisingly limited knowledge about each other. Ignorance about Liberia hurt ECOMOG's military operations and the framing of a precise mandate.

West Africa has a wide range of ethnic, linguistic, and cultural groupings as well as a lack of regional transport and communication and political-economic cooperation. West African states knew Liberia better than did any other state (with the exception of the United States), but ECOMOG's initial understanding of Taylor and his motives proved negligible. It certainly misjudged Taylor's willingness and ability to resist the multinational force. ECOMOG officers note that ECOMOG lacked substantial understanding about Taylor's organization and the strength of his domestic support. These officers acknowledge that ECOMOG initially assumed that the superior firepower of their conventional, professional force would *a priori* intimidate the ragtag NPFL.[41] This fatal assumption encouraged the broadness of ECOMOG's mandate; the assumption was that it could quickly achieve the cease-fire it was to monitor. Furthermore, both ECOWAS and the United States underestimated the willingness of Burkina Faso, Cote d'Ivoire, and private businesses to assist the NPFL and thus prolong the conflict. Lack of intelligence hurt ECOMOG's tactical capabilities. Iweze writes that ECOMOG based its initial planning on a "tourist map of Monrovia."[42] ECOMOG lacked adequate topographic maps until the United States provided them.[43]

ECOMOG and ECOWAS compounded their initial ignorance about the conflict by not adequately supporting their political Special Representative. Ambassador Joshua Iroha, who later became Nigeria's ambassador to Liberia, did serve as ECOWAS Special Representative, but a lack of funding, disagreements over areas of responsibility, and personality differences led to his withdrawal after about two years.

Knowledge, along with military capabilities, is crucial for specifying whether the intervenors should pursue peacekeeping or peace enforcing. ECOMOG's ignorance encouraged the new force to seek numerous—and contradictory—goals. ECOMOG first assumed that it would be a peacekeeper, an interpositional force between armed but peaceful forces as in Cyprus. It believed that the NPFL would cease fighting when confronted by ECOMOG, and that ECO-

---

41. Interview with Ghanaian diplomat, June 16, 1995; discussions with ECOMOG/ECOWAS personnel.
42. Iweze, "Nigeria," p. 221.
43. The United States withheld some intelligence from ECOMOG but did furnish maps. No country, including the United States, had 1:50,000-scale maps of all of Liberia, which ECOMOG officers wanted even though, as one U.S. military analyst noted, "this was the part of Africa we knew best." Interview with a U.S. military analyst, October 15, 1995.

MOG's conventional strength would quickly defeat Taylor's forces if the NPFL did choose armed resistance. Until 1992's Operation Octopus, much of ECOWAS believed that Taylor would settle for a power-sharing agreement. Only after that did ECOWAS and ECOMOG fully realize Taylor's unqualified political ambition.

The uncertain mandate—interpreted differently by contributing nations—weakened ECOMOG's initial military capabilities. Iweze writes that "because the structure of the Force was not clear from the onset, many troops arrived without personal weapons . . . Some contingents comprised . . . para-military forces [having] essentially those [weapons] of customs and immigration duties."[44]

ECOMOG's mandate—"to keep the peace, restore law and order and ensure respect for the ceasefire"[45]—was, as one leading Western diplomat in Liberia concluded, "way too mushy."[46] It simultaneously attempted impartial peacekeeping (without a peace to keep) and biased peace enforcement. ECOMOG's title—"Ceasefire Monitoring Group"—suggests the former interpretation, but the active NPFL antagonism sometimes forced the latter.

COMMITMENT

A subregional force may exhibit greater resolve toward solving the conflict, but this commendable goal could produce unfortunate results which would prolong the hostilities. A war's prolongation can sap the will of the force's contributors. The ECOMOG states clearly did not expect the war to last very long: a top Ghanaian Foreign Ministry official thought of six months as the absolute maximum period.[47] Yet all of the original contributors remained, despite the financial costs. The reasons ranged from humanitarianism to a concern for regional stability to fear of losing political face. Nigeria has suffered perhaps six hundred killed in action and spent perhaps a billion dollars, above normal operating costs, on a conflict that did not directly affect its own security, at a

---

44. Iweze, "Nigeria," p. 220.
45. ECOWAS Authority of Heads of State and Government, "DEC.A/DEC 2/November 1990, Relating To the Adoption Of an ECOWAS Peace Plan For Liberia and the Entire West Africa Sub-Region," Bamako, Republic of Mali, November 28, 1990, cited in Weller, *Regional Peace-Keeping,* p. 112.
46. Interview with American diplomat, June 23, 1996. Ibrahim Gambari, Nigeria's ambassador to the UN, concurs that the mandate, "at least at first, was ambiguous. Neither the diplomats nor the soldiers charged with implementing it knew what to make of it. They did not know whether they were a peacekeeping or a peace-enforcing body. . . . Consequently, 'complications, dissensions and dissonance' were rife in their interpretation of the ECOMOG mandate." Ibrahim Gambari, "The Role of Foreign Intervention in African Reconstruction," in I.W. Zartman, ed., *Collapsed States* (Boulder, Colo.: Lynne Rienner, 1995), p. 231.
47. Interview with Ghanaian diplomat, June 16, 1996.

time when its 1995 foreign debt stood at $35 billion. No Western nation, especially following the Somalian intervention, could match such commitment. Yet while the original five ECOMOG contingents remained in Liberia, they did not actively attempt to end the war militarily.

Rather than acknowledge failed commitment by withdrawing from a prolonged conflict, the subregional force may alter its strategy; this, paradoxically, may further prolong the struggle. It might take on a more conservative strategy, with the use of surrogates and adoption of peacekeeping rather than peace enforcement.

ECOMOG states remained in Liberia only by lessening the force's involvement and aiding the factions which, in turn, prolonged the war and looting. By not carrying the war outside of Monrovia, except when attacked in late 1992, ECOMOG allowed Taylor to recover from his defeats in 1990 and 1992, and to loot much of the Liberian countryside.

ECOMOG increasingly supported the surrogates who demonstrated more commitment to fighting Taylor than did ECOMOG. Since these factions operated out of ECOMOG's sight and because their goal—containing Taylor—aided ECOMOG, they generally had *carte blanche* in their everyday operations. Abuse of human rights became the norm. Taylor increasingly could not engage ECOMOG because of multi-front pressure from ULIMO-K, ULIMO-J, and the LPC. But this led to the growth of quasi-independent factions, a loss of ECOMOG neutrality, and greater devastation of rural Liberia. ULIMO's fighting against the NPFL helped undermine the Yamoussoukro Accords; the LPC's attacks against the NPFL hurt implementation of the Cotonou agreements. When ECOWAS and ECOMOG finally gained a peace settlement with Taylor in 1995, the factions began to oppose ECOMOG.

Deciding upon, and then maintaining, a mandate is often difficult: regional, domestic, and local politics affect the process. Nigeria and Ghana strongly disagreed about Charles Taylor. For most, although not all, of ECOMOG's first three years, Nigerian officers considered Taylor the main impediment to peace and hoped to pursue him vigorously, sometimes with air strikes and assassination attempts. Ghana, however, felt that the powerful Taylor was essential to Liberia's peace, and that demonizing and actively pursuing him would only prolong the war.[48]

---

48. A top-ranking Ghanaian diplomat felt that "Guinea, Sierra Leone, and Nigeria saw the NPFL as the enemy. This preoccupation was not helpful—it drove the NPFL into a corner." Ibid.

Changing politics within contributing nations may alter the mandate. Nigeria's concerns about the political and economic costs of a possible Vietnam-like quagmire increasingly weakened that nation's peace enforcement strategy. Herman Cohen notes that "Nigeria worried about its participation in ECOMOG becoming a domestic issue . . . and worked to keep it from becoming one."[49] Field commander appointments fluctuated between aggressive leaders such as Dogonyaro and Olourin who pressed the war but caused more casualties, and the more passive generals such as Kupolati and Bakut, who only maintained the stalemate but incurred less cost and fewer casualties.

Local political realities will also affect the mandate. Taylor's popularity (and Doe's unpopularity) weakened ECOMOG's solidarity. The AFL had committed most of the atrocities by August 1990. At least until Doe's death, Taylor did not appear clearly as *the* enemy to some ECOMOG members. Taylor had started and led the crusade against the despotic Doe, he had a substantial following of Liberians and, at least until Doe's death, he claimed to abjure personal political gain.

SUITABILITY OF MILITARY CAPABILITIES
Does a third-world subregional grouping enjoy some military advantages over a Western force? It could field equipment and personnel well-suited for the terrain, an adequate intelligence capability, and a strong strategic sense at a reasonable cost.

ECOMOG, however, lacked much of the equipment, maintenance, manpower, administration, and intelligence required for counterinsurgency in Liberia. ECOMOG's Order of Battle was not suited for counterinsurgency.[50] Modern counterinsurgency warfare almost invariably requires significant use of helicopter and spotter aircraft; in mid-1995, however, ECOMOG's only helicopter was for the Field Commander's personal travel (previously one Nigerian helicopter was in Monrovia and two were in Sierra Leone). Other equipment was often costly and ill-suited for Liberia's heavily forested interior, e.g., main battle tanks.

Inadequate maintenance, often a serious problem in third world militaries, plagued ECOMOG. Several countries did have helicopters, yet much of the

---

49. Interview with Herman Cohen, October 1995. Ambassador Cohen served as Assistant Secretary of State for Africa under President Bush.
50. ECOMOG's potential Order of Battle (OB) was impressive at first glance. Nigeria alone had 257 tanks, 95 combat aircraft, an 80,000-man army, artillery, and a navy with several frigates, corvettes and missile craft. But Order of Battle is often deceiving about military capability.

equipment was not battle-ready, or else the countries preferred to hoard it for their own domestic defense. Defense analysts in late 1995 noted that most of Ghana's eight helicopters and Nigeria's fifteen armed helicopters had not flown for several years, owing to the expensive maintenance—generally, four hours of maintenance for every flying hour—that helicopters require.[51]

Communications posed a basic problem. For too long ECOMOG lacked lateral (within national contingents) and horizontal (between contingents) capability. ECOMOG's forward checkpoints in October 1992 lacked radios to inform ECOMOG headquarters of Taylor's start of "Operation Octopus."[52]

Incompatibility of equipment hampered ECOMOG, albeit decreasingly. National contingents arrived in 1990 with various mixtures of Western and Eastern bloc equipment.[53]

A possible selling point of ECOMOG was its low cost, relative to the more sophisticated first world forces. Pay scales and logistical support certainly are less expensive. Yet ECOMOG's matériel, which often was not especially suited to counterinsurgency, and its inadequate maintenance restricted ECOMOG's military capabilities.

ECOMOG's manpower—a maximum of about 12,500 but sometimes as low as 2,700—was too small for peace enforcement or even for effective peacekeeping. Several West African officials speculated that ECOMOG would need 20,000 men for peace enforcement, rather than the 6,000–10,000 it usually had. Some of ECOMOG's checkpoints were as much as twenty-two kilometers apart. ECOMOG's size (and amount of equipment) was large enough to prevent a final battle for Monrovia, but the force was not large enough to push the factions into successful peace talks. Prolongation of the war was the result.

Inclusion of non-regional forces may provide mixed results. The addition of Tanzanian and Ugandan soldiers in February 1994 provided more men and "de-Nigerianized" ECOMOG, a long-standing Taylor and Francophone de-

---

51. Apparently for the same reason, Nigeria used only two of its twenty-one Alpha ground attack fighters in Liberia (reportedly none flew there during 1995). Nigeria rarely committed any of its approximately twenty-two MiG-21 fighters; only two of its fifteen Jaguar reconnaissance fighters have seen even limited use.

52. ECOMOG's communications capability improved, but even in mid-1995 ECOMOG officers (including General Inienger) and Western observers quickly commented upon ECOMOG's lack of radios. Communications with the ECOWAS Secretariat in Lagos, Nigeria were, at least initially, problematic: quite early in the operation, an important ECOWAS decision did not reach ECOMOG headquarters for a month. Iweze, "Nigeria," p. 238.

53. During the 1990–92 cease-fire, Nigeria provided compatible radio equipment at the battalion level, but even then, companies in different contingents could not communicate with each other, often because of different frequencies.

mand.[54] What limited information is available on the Tanzanian and Ugandan ECOMOG experience, however, suggests that these two non–West African forces displayed even less commitment than did the West African contingents. The Tanzanians and Ugandans rarely saw combat, and when they did they sometimes performed inadequately. In a 1994 situation, the NPFL confronted several Tanzanian companies—a total of about 300 men—which decided not to fight but to surrender all their equipment, including U.S. radios as well as their personal weapons and kits. While the Tanzanians may have been stretched too thin, the episode lowered morale by angering other ECOMOG officers.[55]

A subregional force will require, beyond sheer numbers, an effective joint command (a major challenge for multinational forces), strong administrative and intelligence capabilities, and suitable training. ECOMOG generally lacked these capabilities and therefore relied increasingly upon anti-Taylor factions, with resulting problems.

Lack of administrative skills and of effective oversight of possible corruption are especially likely within an *ad hoc* multilateral force, and will lower morale. Initial problems may have been unavoidable, given the speed of ECOMOG's creation. For example, Iweze reveals that ECOMOG's logistical planning unit did not contain any logistics officers.[56]

The junior officers in the Nigerian and Sierra Leonean contingents often did not receive their pay for several months. Partly as a result, soldiers within these units resorted to the black market or theft from humanitarian relief shipments. Poor payroll administration within the Sierra Leone contingent apparently helped topple the Momoh government. Crime by ECOMOG soldiers (who certainly were not the only, and probably not the worst, plunderers of Liberia) drained or diverted material and manpower resources, while alienating many previously welcoming Liberians. Non-Nigerian forces sometimes privately complained that Nigerian dominance of ECOMOG resulted in the lack of prosecution of Nigerian officers for alleged improprieties.

An external force will often lack basic tactical intelligence. Despite their geographic closeness to Liberia, ECOMOG contributors lacked sufficient tacti-

---

54. The two contingents, a battalion from each country, had all their expenses paid by the United States (which also allowed them to retain U.S.-supplied equipment).
55. One high-ranking Nigerian intelligence officer bitterly complained that "the Tanzanians were here just to satisfy their country, not because of any commitment. The Ugandans were worse: they didn't want to work with anyone." Interview with Nigerian intelligence officer, July 1995.
56. Iweze, "Nigeria," p. 236.

cal intelligence.[57] (Language incompatibility was a relatively minor problem. Few ECOMOG officers knew Liberian languages, but this would have been a serious problem only if ECOMOG had conducted intensive peace enforcement).

Regional forces may not have experience even with nearby physical geography. African forces had not fought previously in terrain similar to Liberia's (their recent peacekeeping experiences had been in Chad and Lebanon). ECOMOG members had little counterinsurgency experience, and in 1990 only Ghana and Senegal had any jungle warfare training centers.[58]

Finally, few if any of ECOMOG's pilots had previously flown in combat situations. They did succeed in harassing supply lines and lowering troop morale within the NPFL when counterattacking during "Octopus." Yet too often, ECOMOG planes accidentally hit relief convoys and medical facilities. Ensuing protests, along with inadequate maintenance, led to curbs on ECOMOG's air power.

ECOMOG faced difficult problems inside Liberia beyond those of equipment or personnel. The traditional advantages of an indigenous irregular force against a conventionally-trained foreign force often reasserted themselves. Liberia's vegetation, its often mountainous terrain, and its long rainy season from July to December posed natural impediments to any major mechanized operations. "It's good ambush country, almost anywhere outside of Monrovia," notes a Western military analyst.[59] The lack of interior roads, coupled with the complete lack of transport helicopters, presented obvious logistical difficulties.

Distinguishing between combatants and noncombatants proved difficult, especially since the NPFL had no uniforms and often employed children as soldiers, as in Taylor's "Boys Own Unit."[60] ECOMOG's morale plummeted when its soldiers had to fire in self-defense upon child soldiers.

---

57. Iweze characterizes the ECOMOG operation as "a classical case of launching troops into a theatre of operation without any form of intelligence." Iweze, "Nigeria," p. 240. Major-General Rufus Kupolati acknowledged that "definitely we had problems at the start of the operation. You need good intelligence of where you are going to operate. That was definitely lacking. And to get good intelligence you need very good maps and [we] found these were just not available." Kupolati, quoted in Jimmi Adia, "ECOMOG Force Commanders," in Vogt, *The Liberian Crisis*, pp. 256–257.
58. Some ECOMOG countries, notably Nigeria, subsequently gave their Liberia-bound troops jungle warfare training.
59. Interview with Western military analyst, September 3, 1995.
60. Fleischman and Whitman, *Child Soldiers In Liberia*. Human Rights Watch/Africa estimates that ten percent of the some 60,000 fighters are under the age of fifteen.

Even by the time of Operation Octopus—two years after ECOMOG's arrival—Western observers noted glaring limitations within ECOMOG. U.S. State Department cables stated that "ECOMOG [since October 15] has not acquitted itself with distinction; with the notable exception of the Senegalese and Guineans, some elements have been worse than useless." The cables described Nigerians as "unmotivated and poorly-led" prior to the arrival of ECOMOG's new Field Commander, Adetunji Olourin.[61]

A multilateral force reflects the existing ethos of each of its contributors. The record of the ECOMOG forces has been mixed. Most observers give high marks to the Ghanaians while criticizing others, especially the Nigerians. The Strategic Studies Institute of the U.S. Army War College contends that "during the decades of military rule, the Nigerian armed forces have lost nearly all semblance of professionalism and become thoroughly corrupted. Senior officers all become immensely rich through theft, while junior officers and enlisted men live in poverty."[62] The high level of corruption drained significant resources from ECOMOG's military capabilities; pilfering within Liberia angered Liberians who previously had been grateful for ECOMOG.

A weak subregional organization can create only a weak military force. Faced by pressing domestic concerns and generally moribund economies, West African states had never supported ECOWAS sufficiently. ECOWAS's failure at achieving most of its economic goals between 1976 and 1990 further lessened subregional support. Limited institutional allegiance can cause unkept promises, financial shortfalls, and lack of effective enforcement for the military force, especially over a prolonged conflict.

The weak ECOWAS lacked an enforcement mechanism to assure effective agreement, even after November 1990, when all ECOWAS members—even Francophone Burkina Faso and Cote d'Ivoire—belatedly endorsed the SMC's peace plan. ECOWAS took no disciplinary action against these two states which, despite their endorsement, continued to aid the NPFL against ECOMOG.

Local allies could aid or diminish a regional force's military (and political) capabilities. Many of the same reasons suggested for a regional force's creation—greater knowledge and commitment, lower costs, and less political fall-

---

61. "Liberia: Listening In To Washington," *Africa Confidential*, November 20, 1992, p. 7. U.S. officials verify the accuracy of these leaked cables.
62. Kent Hughes Butts and Steven Metz, *Armies and Democracy in the New Africa: Lessons From Nigeria and South Africa* (Carlisle, Penn.: Strategic Studies Institute, U.S. Army War College, 1996), p. v.

out over casualties—explain why ECOMOG supported the anti-Taylor factions. Certainly the factions understood Liberia's topography, terrain, languages, and customs much better than the foreign ECOMOG force. They were, moreover, much cheaper, requiring only limited support; they often had much stronger reasons for fighting and their deaths did not place a political burden upon the foreign force. Moreover, individual ECOMOG officers had economic incentives: they benefited by acting as the conduit for looted goods via ECOMOG-controlled ports and airfields. While initially militarily useful, the irregulars increasingly threatened the peace process and, along with ECOMOG's unclear mandate, lack of acceptance within the region, and mediocre military capabilities, probably prolonged the conflict.

ECOMOG's cooperation with the factions weakened its desired neutrality. Furthermore, the factions constantly tried to use ECOMOG for their own purposes. For example, the INPFL ransomed Nigerian ECOMOG soldiers for weaponry, and the LPC wanted ECOMOG to garrison areas around Buchanan captured by the LPC so that the LPC could use as many of its troops as possible for forward operations. Factions sometimes attempted, through the use of false intelligence, to provoke ECOMOG attacks against other factions. "Every faction comes here to use us—we can't trust any of them," complained a highly placed Nigerian intelligence officer.[63]

By supporting the factions, ECOMOG risked creating Frankenstein monsters that could threaten any peace settlement. A diplomat in Liberia said that "the factions at various points [in time] have been uncontrollable."[64] Looting and smuggling have provided the factions with some independent financing, and in the summer of 1995 ECOMOG troops fought ULIMO-J, after ULIMO-J had secured and begun exploiting a diamond field. All the factions have skirmished with ECOMOG forces and several times have engaged them in significant firefights. Prolongation of the war risks devolution of faction power away from any central command and to smaller units.[65] Lack of clear command and control will allow faction "soldiers" to switch sides.

Factions lack a clear command-and-control system. Individual fighters do not receive standardized military training or the political indoctrination that helps mold *espirit de corps*. Individual, or perhaps small unit, gain may be the

---

63. Interview with Nigerian intelligence official, July 1995.
64. Interview with diplomat, July 5, 1995.
65. A UNOMIL representative worried that "regional commanders are becoming local heroes. . . . They make independent statements, [and] chang[e] sides. . . . Everyone wants to be president." Interview with UNOMIL official, June 15, 1995.

guiding *raison d'etre*, rather than sacrifice for a desired ideology. Without a centralizing ethos or control of communications, a faction's leader runs the risk of losing control to local commanders.

This diffusion of power will pose a policing problem to the subregional force. Lack of control may allow local human rights abuses which discredit the faction's political reputation. Lack of control may lead to localized actions which trigger international reaction. Another possible result of the decentralized, somewhat apolitical forces is a concerted rebellion against a political settlement that tries to close down their pillaging operations.

Factions may prolong their struggle by linking up with private businessmen. This external support not only aids the groups' military capabilities but may make them reluctant to settle for political negotiations which would end their pillaging.

ECOMOG planners had not realized how easily the rebel NPFL could sustain itself economically and militarily. The French government aided commercial ties in NPFL territory; it helped promote a major iron ore mining operation there. Such action worked against Nigerian commercial influence and supported the anti-ECOMOG stance of Burkina Faso and Cote d'Ivoire. In 1991, "Greater Liberia"—Taylor's term for the area he controlled—was "France's third largest supplier of tropical timber," according to William Reno.[66]

Prolongation of a conflict allows such networks to grow. Taylor developed a parallel economy in "Greater Liberia." Reno writes as late as 1995 that "Taylor's 'Greater Liberia' boasts a vigorous trade in timber, agricultural products and minerals, and hosts numerous foreign firms and regional trade networks."[67] Taylor sold timber concessions to foreign companies; indeed, he sometimes sold the same concessions several times over.

Lessons for Subregional Forces

The failures of ECOMOG, many of which ECOMOG was powerless to affect, are just as significant as ECOMOG's successes as lessons for future subregional peacekeeping or peace enforcement forces.

Intervenors should have a strong knowledge of regional affairs and should be able to judge whether their own political and military capabilities are equal

---

66. William Reno, "Global Commerce, 'Warlords,' and the Reinvention of African States," paper presented at the African Studies Association annual meeting, Orlando, Florida, November 1995, p. 14.
67. Reno, "Global Commerce," p. 12.

to the proposed task. The difficulties of ECOMOG's attempts at peace enforcement suggest strongly that states should not enter an ongoing conflict without a clearly adequate force. ECOMOG's experience demonstrates an obvious but important lesson: it is infinitely easier to enter than to leave a conflict. The hastily assembled ECOMOG lacked the acceptance, knowledge, and military capability to act as effective peacekeepers or as peace enforcers. Its six-year commitment has continued largely through the use of undisciplined surrogates.

Temporary coalitions, especially of relatively poor states, should limit their mandate to that of peacekeeping rather than peace enforcement. Any subregional force should hesitate about an emotional decision to intervene for strictly humanitarian reasons before assessing the possible military, political, and economic pitfalls.

ECOMOG could have avoided many of its pitfalls if it had been an experienced standing force. But various political and economic considerations rule out permanent forces throughout the third world. An alternative could be much greater cooperation, such as combined field exercises between national units so that an *ad hoc* force could begin operations more effectively.

Countries which expect to participate in any future temporary or permanent forces should work towards greater standardization of equipment and greater cooperation in subregional training. Defense expenditures should emphasize relatively low-cost counterinsurgency items such as spotter planes and radios rather than jet fighters and main battle tanks. (It is noteworthy that since late 1994, the Chiefs of Staff of the ECOMOG forces have been meeting with some regularity to discuss greater coordination of national units.)

Any subregional force would probably need to increase its support system, or "logistical tail." While several ECOMOG countries had aircraft, all too often a lack of maintenance grounded these planes and helicopters. Efficient administrative procedures, including fair payroll disbursal, are necessary. Administration within most individual ECOMOG militaries was mediocre at best: a hasty amalgamation of these systems only multiplied the problems.

A subregional military force should have a centralized structure whose authority would lessen the influence of a major contributor on ECOMOG's strategy and tactics. Several ECOMOG officers agreed that centralized funding and disbursement could lessen the dominance of a single contributor like Nigeria by financing greater participation by more countries.[68] It could also

---

68. Nigerians are divided about the wisdom of future regional forces. A permanent force under the ECOWAS Secretariat would, according to Iweze, "eliminate the possibility of mis-conceptual-

lessen the payroll fraud that plagued several of the national contingents. External aid on a regional, not bilateral, basis could increase the compatibility and the equality of equipment.

Perhaps a subregional peacekeeping force could be a "First Reactor" that could enter quickly upon agreement of the warring parties, and then step aside for, or operate alongside, a better-equipped UN peacekeeping force.[69] A major advantage that ECOMOG had over typical UN peacekeeping forces was its ability to form and begin operations quickly. Three major disadvantages—which a stronger UN force could have addressed—were ECOMOG's lack of suitable military capabilities, its loss of its initial neutrality, and apparent corruption by numerous personnel. Admittedly, the UN's present difficulty in fielding new forces makes this suggestion less likely to be carried out.

All of the above points are moot if a regional force lacks a high degree of professionalism, which includes the abstention of officers and enlisted men from profiteering. There is no easy solution to ending this corruption. As the major force within ECOMOG, the Nigerian contingent apparently operated with few constraints.

Prompt blessing of the force by the United States, or by outside organizations such as the OAU or the UN, could aid the subregional force's credibility. Several observers felt that the involvement of a neutral outside organization should start concurrent with the regional peacekeeping force and that the organization should have some independent power. UNOMIL entered Liberia several years after ECOMOG and had, at best, only monitoring powers, most of which ECOMOG effectively controlled (e.g., checkpoint control over night-time travel). A regional force must be willing to cooperate with the UN. ECOMOG's general disdain of the UN's capabilities elsewhere, resentment about the UN's late arrival—two years after ECOMOG's—in Liberia, and its looking-over-our-shoulder attitude strongly influenced ECOMOG's attitude towards UNOMIL.

Cooperating with local factions offers some short-run tactical advantages to a peacekeeping force but threatens its necessary neutrality and poses longer-run political problems.

---

izing the situation from a military angle." Iweze, "Nigeria," p. 239. When asked if Nigeria should participate in a future regional force, Ambassador Iroha replied, "I doubt it, if we have to pay for our own troops." Interview with Ambassador Iroha, July 2, 1995. The Nigerian government claims that ECOMOG has cost it over four billion dollars. Non-Nigerian forces dispute this figure but still place the sum at around one billion dollars.

69. For a general elaboration of a layered response, see Timothy Sisk, "Institutional Capacity-Building for African Conflict Management," in David Smock and Chester Crocker, eds., *African Conflict Resolution* (Washington, D.C.: United States Institute of Peace Press), 1995.

A subregional peacekeeping force should consider an overt political presence. An in-country political representative could assist negotiations between the warring parties, as well as the *ad hoc* negotiations that arise between the forces or with the relief agencies. "We had to do these talks, but that's not what we were trained in," mentions a high-ranking Nigerian officer. "We would have welcomed a professional negotiator."[70] A Special Representative could also oversee the regional force's adherence to human rights, which would strengthen the force's neutrality and acceptance. A future force should also consider a civic action program: well-publicized initiatives in basic health and education will offer a more benign image of the foreign intervention.

Conclusion

The nations of ECOMOG richly deserve credit for trying to end Liberia's carnage, and for creating ECOMOG so quickly while the rest of the world stood by. These African states allowed serious humanitarian concerns to erase their traditional hesitation to interfere in another state's internal affairs.

However, ECOMOG's efforts largely failed. It entered a contested situation with inadequate resources. It did not enjoy wide political support; it lacked detailed knowledge of Liberia and the conflict; its military capabilities and mandate were ineffective; and its commitment to remain had some destabilizing effects, notably the aiding of surrogate forces.

Furthermore, ECOMOG's participation appears to have prolonged the conflict. This encouraged a spillover into Sierra Leone, the toppling of the Gambian government, and an increase of refugees into several countries. Subregional stability was a goal of ECOMOG, but greater subregional instability was the result. As a result, the precedent and record of ECOMOG might not discourage future insurgencies, while ECOMOG's six years of sacrifice might discourage future subregional forces.

Poorly-policed third world conflicts can rapidly spin uncontrollably, toppling governments and mortgaging a nation's human and physical potential. Control of these conflicts is essential. ECOMOG's record is, at best, uneven, but both its successes and failures offer valuable lessons for future subregional military forces.

---

70. Interview with Nigerian intelligence officer, July 1995.

Suggestions for Further Reading

$\mathbf{T}$he scholarly litera-
ture on nationalism and ethnic conflict is truly massive, especially if one also
includes the countless articles and books written on international responses to
the problems posed by nationalist and ethnic conflicts. The following list,
therefore, is far from exhaustive. For further references, see the citations found
in the chapters in this volume.

Anderson, Benedict. *Imagined Communities: Reflections on the Origins and Spread of Nationalism.* London: Verso, 1983.

Andreopoulos, George J., ed. *Genocide: Conceptual and Historical Dimensions.* Philadelphia: University of Pennsylvania Press, 1994.

Berdal, Mats. *Whither UN Peacekeeping?* Adelphi Paper No. 281. London: International
Institute for Strategic Studies, 1993.

Betts, Richard K. "The Delusion of Impartial Intervention." *Foreign Affairs,* Vol. 73, No.
6 (November–December 1994), pp. 20–33.

Boutros-Ghali, Boutros. *An Agenda for Peace.* New York: United Nations, 1992.

Brass, Paul, ed. *Ethnic Groups and the State.* London: Croom Helm, 1985.

Brown, Michael E., ed. *Ethnic Conflict and International Security.* Princeton, N.J.: Princeton
University Press, 1993.

Brown, Michael E., ed. *The International Dimensions of Internal Conflict.* Cambridge, Mass.:
MIT Press, 1996.

Buchanan, Allen. *Secession: The Morality of Political Divorce from Fort Sumter to Lithuania
and Quebec.* Boulder, Colo.: Westview Press, 1991.

Buchheit, Lee C. *Secession: The Legitimacy of Self-Determination.* New Haven, Conn.: Yale
University Press, 1978.

Bull, Hedley. "Civil Violence and International Order." In *Civil Violence and the International System,* Adelphi Paper No. 83. London: International Institute for Strategic
Studies, 1971, pp. 27–36.

Chalk, Frank, and Kurt Jonassohn, eds., *The History and Sociology of Genocide: Analyses
and Case Studies.* New Haven, Conn.: Yale University Press, 1990.

Chatterjee, Partha. *The Nation and Its Fragments: Colonial and Postcolonial Histories.* Princeton, N.J.: Princeton University Press, 1993.

Chazan, Naomi, ed. *Irredentism and International Politics.* Boulder, Colo.: Lynne Rienner
Publishers, 1991.

Conner, Walker. *Ethnonationalism: The Quest for Understanding.* Princeton, N.J.: Princeton
University Press, 1994.

Damrosch, Lori Fisler, ed. *Enforcing Restraint: Collective Intervention in Internal Conflicts.*
New York: Council on Foreign Relations Press, 1993.

Daniel, Donald C.F., and Bradd C. Hayes, eds. *Beyond Traditional Peacekeeping.* London:
Macmillan, 1995.

De Silva, K.M., and R.J. May, eds. *Internationalization of Ethnic Conflict.* London: Pinter
Publishers, 1991.

Deutsch, Karl W. *Nationalism and Its Alternatives.* New York: Alfred A. Knopf, 1969.

Deutsch, Karl W. *Nationalism and Social Communication: An Inquiry Into the Foundations of Nationalism,* 2nd ed. Cambridge, Mass.: MIT Press, 1966.

Diehl, Paul. *International Peacekeeping.* Baltimore, Md.: Johns Hopkins University Press, 1993.

Durch, William J., ed. *The Evolution of UN Peacekeeping: Case Studies and Comparative Analysis.* New York: St. Martin's, 1993.

Eckstein, Harry, ed. *Internal War: Problems and Approaches.* Westport, Conn.: Greenwood Press, 1964.

Esman, Milton J. "Ethnic Actors in International Politics." *Nationalism and Ethnic Politics,* Vol. 1, No. 1 (Spring 1995), pp. 111–125.

Esman, Milton J., ed. *Ethnic Conflict in the Western World.* Ithaca, N.Y.: Cornell University Press, 1977.

Esman, Milton J. *Ethnic Politics.* Ithaca, N.Y.: Cornell University Press, 1994.

Esman, Milton J., and Shibley Telhami, eds. *International Organizations and Ethnic Conflict.* Ithaca, N.Y.: Cornell University Press, 1995.

Etzioni, Amitai. "The Evils of Self-Determination." *Foreign Policy,* No. 89 (Winter 1992–93), pp. 21–35.

Evans, Gareth. "Cooperative Security and Intra-State Conflict." *Foreign Policy,* No. 96 (Fall 1994), pp. 3–20.

Fein, Helen. "Explanations of Genocide." *Current Sociology,* Vol. 38, No. 1 (Spring 1990), pp. 32–50.

Fein, Helen, ed. *Genocide Watch.* New Haven, Conn.: Yale University Press, 1992.

Gellner, Ernest. *Encounters With Nationalism.* Oxford: Blackwell, 1994.

Gellner, Ernest. *Nations and Nationalism.* Oxford: Blackwell, 1983.

Glazer, Nathan, and Daniel Moynihan, eds. *Ethnicity: Theory and Experience.* Cambridge, Mass.: Harvard University Press, 1975.

Gottlieb, Gidon. *Nation Against State: A New Approach to Ethnic Conflicts and the Decline of Sovereignty.* New York: Council on Foreign Relations Press, 1993.

Greenfeld, Liah. *Nationalism: Five Roads to Modernity.* Cambridge, Mass.: Harvard University Press, 1992.

Gurr, Ted Robert. *Minorities at Risk: A Global View of Ethnopolitical Conflicts.* Washington, D.C.: U. S. Institute of Peace Press, 1993.

Gurr, Ted Robert. "Peoples Against States: Ethnopolitical Conflict and the Changing World System." *International Studies Quarterly,* Vol. 38, No. 3 (September 1994), pp. 347–377.

Gurr, Ted Robert. *Why Men Rebel.* Princeton, N.J.: Princeton University Press, 1970.

Gurr, Ted Robert, and Barbara Harff. *Ethnic Conflict and World Politics.* Boulder, Colo.: Westview Press, 1994.

Halperin, Morton H., and David J. Scheffer with Patricia L. Small. *Self-Determination in the New World Order.* Washington, D.C.: Carnegie Endowment for International Peace, 1992.

Hannum, Hurst. *Autonomy, Sovereignty, and Self-Determination: The Accommodation of Conflicting Rights.* Philadelphia: University of Pennsylvania Press, 1990.

Helman, Gerald, and Steven Ratner. "Saving Failed States." *Foreign Policy*, No. 89 (Winter 1992–93), pp. 3–20.

Heraclides, Alexis. "Secessionist Minorities and External Involvement." *International Organization*, Vol. 44, No. 3 (Summer 1990), pp. 341–378.

Heraclides, Alexis. *The Self-Determination of Minorities in International Politics.* London: Frank Cass, 1991.

Hobsbawm, Eric J. *Nations and Nationalism Since 1780: Programme, Myth, Reality.* Cambridge, U.K.: Cambridge University Press, 1990.

Horowitz, Donald L. *Ethnic Groups in Conflict.* Berkeley: University of California Press, 1985.

Human Rights Watch. *Slaughter Among Neighbors: The Political Origins of Communal Violence.* New Haven, Conn.: Yale University Press, 1995.

Huntington, Samuel P. "Civil Violence and the Process of Development." In *Civil Violence and the International System*, Adelphi Paper No. 83. London: International Institute for Strategic Studies, 1971.

Huntington, Samuel P. *Political Order in Changing Societies.* New Haven, Conn.: Yale University Press, 1968.

James, Alan. *Peacekeeping in International Politics.* New York: St. Martin's 1990.

Kedourie, Elie. *Nationalism*, 4th ed. Oxford: Blackwell, 1993.

Kellas, James G. *The Politics of Nationalism and Ethnicity.* London: Macmillan, 1991.

Kressel, Neil J. *Mass Hate: The Global Rise of Genocide and Terror.* New York: Plenum Press, 1996.

Kuper, Leo. *Genocide: Its Political Use in the Twentieth Century.* New Haven, Conn.: Yale University Press, 1981.

Little, Richard. *Intervention: External Involvement in Civil Wars.* Totowa, N.J.: Rowman and Littlefield, 1975.

Luard, Evan, ed. *The International Regulation of Civil Wars.* London: Thames and Hudson, 1972.

Mayall, James. *Nationalism and International Society.* Cambridge, U.K.: Cambridge University Press, 1990.

Maynes, Charles William. "Containing Ethnic Conflict," *Foreign Policy*, No. 90 (Spring 1993), pp. 3–21.

McNeill, William H. *Polyethnicity and National Unity in World History.* Toronto: University of Toronto Press, 1986.

Midlarsky, Manus I., ed. *The Internationalization of Communal Strife.* London: Routledge, 1992.

Minahan, James. *Nations Without States: A Historical Dictionary of Contemporary National Movements.* Westport, Conn.: Greenwood Press, 1996.

Montville, Joseph V., ed. *Conflict and Peacekeeping in Multiethnic Societies.* Lexington, Mass.: Lexington Books, 1990.

Newman, Saul. "Does Modernization Breed Ethnic Political Conflict?" *World Politics*, Vol. 43, No. 3 (April 1991), pp. 451–478.

Nordlinger, Eric A. *Conflict Regulation in Divided Societies.* Cambridge, Mass.: Harvard University Center for International Affairs, 1972.

Posen, Barry R. "The Security Dilemma and Ethnic Conflict," *Survival*, Vol. 35, No. 1 (Spring 1993), pp. 27–47.

Premdas, Ralph R., S.W.R. de A. Samarasinghe, and Alan B. Anderson, eds. *Secessionist Movements in Comparative Perspective*. London: Pinter Publishers, 1990.

Rosenau, James N., ed. *International Aspects of Civil Strife*. Princeton, N.J.: Princeton University Press, 1964.

Ross, Marc Howard. *The Culture of Conflict: Interpretations and Interests in Comparative Perspective*. New Haven, Conn.: Yale University Press, 1993.

Rothchild, Donald, and Alexander J. Groth. "Pathological Dimensions of Domestic and International Ethnicity." *Political Science Quarterly*, Vol. 110, No. 1 (Spring 1995), pp. 69–82.

Rothschild, Joseph. *Ethnopolitics: A Conceptual Framework*. New York: Columbia University Press, 1981.

Rule, James B. *Theories of Civil Violence*. Berkeley: University of California Press, 1988.

Samarasinghe, S.W.R. de A., and Reed Coughlin, eds. *Economic Dimensions of Ethnic Conflict*. London: Pinter Publishers, 1991.

Sisk, Timothy D. *Power Sharing and International Mediation in Ethnic Conflicts*. Washington, D.C.: U.S. Institute of Peace Press, 1996.

Smith, Anthony D. *The Ethnic Origins of Nations*. New York: Basil Blackwell, 1986.

Smith, Anthony D. *The Ethnic Revival in the Modern World*. New York: Cambridge University Press, 1981.

Smith, Anthony D. *National Identity*. London: Penguin, 1991.

Smith, Anthony D. *Nations and Nationalism in a Global Era*. Cambridge, Mass: Polity Press, 1995.

Smith, Anthony D. *Theories of Nationalism*. New York: Holmes and Meier, 1983.

Snyder, Jack. "Nationalism and the Crisis of the Post-Soviet State," *Survival*, Vol. 35, No. 1 (Spring 1993), pp. 5–26.

Staub, Ervin. *The Roots of Evil: The Origins of Genocide and Other Group Violence*. Cambridge, U.K.: Cambridge University Press, 1989.

Von Hippel, Karin. "The Resurgence of Nationalism and Its International Implications." *Washington Quarterly*, Vol. 14, No. 4 (Autumn 1994), pp. 185–200.

Waltz, Kenneth N. *Man, the State and War: A Theoretical Analysis*. New York: Columbia University Press, 1959.

Weiner, Myron. "Peoples and States in a New Ethnic Order?" *Third World Quarterly*, Vol. 13, No. 2 (1992), pp. 317–333.

Young, Crawford. *The Politics of Cultural Pluralism*. Madison: University of Wisconsin Press, 1976.

Zartman, I. William, ed. *Collapsed States: The Disintegration and Restoration of Legitimate Authority*. Boulder, Colo.: Lynne Rienner Publishers, 1995.

International Security

Center for Science and International Affairs
John F. Kennedy School of Government
Harvard University

Articles in this reader were previously published in **International Security**, a quarterly journal sponsored and edited by the Center for Science and International Affairs at the John F. Kennedy School of Government at Harvard University, and published by MIT Press Journals. To receive subscription information about the journal or find out more about other readers in our series, please contact MIT Press Journals at 55 Hayward Street, Cambridge, MA, 02142.